Defending possession proceedings

SIXTH EDITION

Nic Madge, Derek McConnell,
John Gallagher and Jan Luba QC

 Legal Action Group
2006

Sixth edition published in Great Britain 2006
by LAG Education and Service Trust Limited
242 Pentonville Road, London N1 9UN
www.lag.org.uk

First edition 1987
Second edition 1989
Third edition 1993
Fourth edition 1997
Fifth edition 2002

British Library Cataloguing in Publication Data
a CIP catalogue record for this book is available from the British Library.

Crown copyright material is produced with the permission of the
Controller of HMSO and the Queen's Printer for Scotland.

ISBN-10 1 903307 30 9
ISBN-13 978 1 903307 30 4

Typeset by Regent Typesetting, London
Printed in Great Britain by Hobbs the Printer, Totton, Hampshire

Defending possession proceedings

sixth edition

Nic Madge is a Circuit Judge. He was formerly a recorder and district judge and head of the Housing Department at Bindman and Partners, London. He is author of *Housing Law Casebook* (LAG, 4th edn, 2008), *Annotated Housing Statutes* (Sweet & Maxwell, 2005) and a member of the senior editorial board of *Civil Procedure* ('the White Book') (Sweet & Maxwell). He writes regularly on housing law and procedure, including contributions to *Law Society's Gazette, New Law Journal* and co-authors 'Recent developments in housing law' in *Legal Action*. He is a founder member of the Housing Law Practitioner's Association.

Derek McConnell is a solicitor at South West Law in Bristol. Since 1978 he worked in a number of law centres, and then in private practice, specialising in housing law. He writes the regular 'Owner-occupier' updates in *Legal Action* and tutors widely on housing law, specifically residential mortgage law.

John Gallagher is Principal Solicitor with Shelter, and has specialised in housing and homelessness law for 20 years. He previously worked at SHAC (the London Housing Aid Centre), at Nottingham Law Centre and in private practice in Liverpool. He is an Executive member of the Housing Law Practitioners' Association.

Jan Luba QC is a barrister in the housing team at Garden Court Chambers in London. He was called to the Bar in 1980 and was made Queen's Counsel in 2000. He is one of the leading authorities on housing law and practice. Jan is co-author of a number of housing law titles including *Repairs: tenant's rights* (LAG) and *Housing Allocations and Homelessness* (Jordans), and writes, with Nic Madge, the monthly series 'Recent developments in housing law' in *Legal Action*. He sits as a Recorder in the civil and criminal courts and as a judge of the Employment Appeal Tribunal.

The Legal Action Group is a national, independent charity which campaigns for equal access to justice for all members of society. Legal Action Group:
- provides support to the practice of lawyers and advisers
- inspires developments in that practice
- campaigns for improvements in the law and the administration of justice
- stimulates debate on how services should be delivered.

Developments since June 2006

Since this sixth edition of *Defending Possession Proceedings* was published, the following important legislative and case law developments have taken place. Please note that this is not a comprehensive list of statutory or other changes since 2006. Readers should consult the monthly articles '*Recent developments in housing law*' by Jan Luba QC and Nic Madge which appear in *Legal Action*. See also the housing section of Nic Madge's website: www.nicmadge.co.uk.

The references below denote the principal paragraphs in this book which should be read in the light of these changes.

1.26 See *Mansfield DC v Langridge* [2008] EWCA Civ 264, in which the defendant was held to have a secure licence of accommodation under section 79(3) of the Housing Act 1985, although the council had intended the accommodation to be temporary only.

3.94–3.100 In *Lewisham LBC v Malcolm and Disability Rights Commission (Intervener)* [2008] UKHL 43, the House of Lords by a majority held that the test of 'less favourable treatment' under the Disability Discrimination Act (DDA) 1995 was not that adopted in previous case law such as *Manchester City Council v Romano and Samari* (see para 3.98). The correct comparison is with any other secure tenant who has behaved in the same way as the disabled tenant. The House considered that DDA 1995 might provide a defence to possession proceedings, but only in circumstances where it could be shown that the possession claim amounted to unlawful discrimination, ie by comparison with how the landlord would have treated a non-disabled tenant who had behaved in a similar way.

3.175–3.184 In relation to ground 16, see *Manchester CC v Benjamin* [2008] EWCA Civ 189 (factors relevant to the court's discretion); *Wandsworth LBC v Randall* [2007] EWCA Civ 1126 (household requirements to be assessed at date of hearing); *Newport City Council v Charles* [2008] EWCA Civ 1541(failure to notify death of tenant); and *Bracknell Forest BC v Green and Green* [2009] EWCA Civ 238 (court's discretion: relevance of tenant's personal circumstances).

4.75–4.77 With effect from 20 May 2009, when Schedule 11 of the Housing and Regeneration Act 2008 came into force, the position of the tolerated trespasser has been addressed by statute. The effect of Part 1 of Schedule 11 is to amend the Housing Acts 1985 and 1988 to provide that secure and assured tenancies will not come to an end following a possession order until either the order has been executed or the tenant has vacated. (The House of Lords had already determined that this was the case under the previous law so far as assured tenancies were concerned: *Knowsley Housing Trust v White* [2008] UKHL 70.) For the benefit of existing tolerated trespassers, Part 2 of Schedule 11 creates new replacement tenancies of the same statutory nature as their former tenancies. Whether the landlord or tenant will become retrospectively liable for breaches of tenancy obligations (eg for the landlord's failure to repair) during the 'termination period' will be a matter for the discretion of the court (para 21, Sch 11).

The position where there has been a change of landlord during the termination period is governed by the Housing (Replacement of Terminated Tenancies) (Successor Landlords)(England) Order 2009 SI No 1262, and the Housing (Replacement of Terminated Tenancies)(Successor Landlords)(Wales) Order 2009 SI No 1260 (W.112), both of which also came into force on 20 May 2009. The principal effect of the Orders is that, where there has been a change of landlord during the termination period, the occupier will still have a replacement tenancy, and if the tenancy regime under the new landlord is different from that which governed the original tenancy, the new tenancy will be that which is closest to the original. Thus, in the most familiar situation, where there has been a stock transfer between a local authority and a housing association, those tolerated trespassers who were formerly secure council tenants will have received a full assured tenancy on the commencement date.

5.31–5.42 In *McCann v United Kingdom* (European Court of Human Rights, application no 19009/04, 13 May 2008), the ECtHR was asked to adjudicate on a local housing authority's use of summary possession proceedings against a former joint secure tenant where the other joint tenant had served notice to quit to terminate the tenancy. The Court held that the applicant had been dispossessed of his home without having the opportunity for the proportionality of the order to be determined by an independent tribunal; and that, by reason of the lack of procedural safeguards, there had been a violation of article 8 of the Convention.

The effect of *McCann* was considered by the House of Lords in *Doherty v Birmingham CC* [2008] UKHL 57. *Doherty* was applied by the Court of Appeal in *Doran v Liverpool CC and Secretary of State for Communities and Local Government (Intervener)* [2009] EWCA Civ 146 and in *McGlynn v Welwyn Hatfield DC* [2009] EWCA Civ 285.

In *Doherty*, the House of Lords affirmed its stance in *Kay v Lambeth LBC* [2006] UKHL 10 that there are only two possible 'gateways' whereby a successful defence may be raised to a claim for summary judgment where a public authority landlord is otherwise entitled to recover possession under domestic law: (a) a seriously arguable challenge under article 8 to the law itself under which the possession order is sought, but only where it is possible to adapt the domestic law to render it compliant with Convention rights; or (b) a seriously arguable challenge on conventional judicial review grounds to the public authority's decision to recover possession. The House considered that the basic law remained that set down in *Kay*, namely, that a public authority which is exercising its unqualified right to possession is not acting in violation of the occupier's article 8 rights. However, the formulation adopted in *Kay* needed to be modified to some extent. It was open to a defendant to argue under 'gateway' (b) that a possession order should not be made unless the court was satisfied that the decision to seek a possession order was not unreasonable (see Lord Hope at para 55).

There is a continuing tension between ECtHR decisions and those of the English and Welsh Courts. In *McCann*, the Court stated:

> The loss of one's home is a most extreme form of interference with the right to respect for the home. Any person at risk of an interference of this magnitude should in principle be able to have the proportionality of the measure determined by an independent tribunal in the light of the relevant principles under article 8 of the Convention, notwithstanding that, under domestic law, his right of occupation has come to an end.

Although it is probably still the case that article 8 cannot itself provide a defence to a possession claim, it is arguable that public law defences are no longer limited to *Wednesbury* unreasonableness. See Nic Madge, 'Article 8: La Lutta Continua?' [2009] JHL 43.

It is, however, well established that a defence on public law grounds to a summary claim for possession can and should be raised in the county court, and that factual issues can be resolved by evidence before the judge (see, for example, Lord Scott in *Doherty* at para 84).

6.32–6.34 In *R (on the application of Weaver) v London & Quadrant Housing Trust* [2009] EWCA Civ 587, the Court of Appeal held that the housing trust, as a hybrid public authority, did not engage in an act of a private nature for the purposes of section 6(5) of the Human Rights Act 1998 when it took steps to terminate a tenancy, and the decision to do so was subject to scrutiny on human rights principles, if necessary in judicial review proceedings.

8.95 A claim that the review procedure in respect of demoted tenancies was not compatible with article 6 of the Convention was rejected by the Court of Appeal in *R (on the application of Gilboy) v Liverpool City Council and Secretary of State for Communities and Local Government (Interested Party)* [2008] EWCA Civ 751.

9.6 See *Andrews and Andrews (Executors of W Hodges deceased) v Cunningham* [2007] EWCA Civ 762, in which it was held that the words 'Assured tenancy' on the cover of a rent book did not constitute a statement 'that the assured tenancy to which it relates is not to be an assured shorthold tenancy' within paragraph 1(2)(c) of Schedule 2A of the Housing Act 1988, with the result that the tenancy created was an assured shorthold tenancy.

9.22 Section 215 of the Housing Act 2004 (notice under Housing Act 1988 s21 invalid where the landlord has not complied with the requirements of a tenancy deposit scheme) came into force on 6 April 2007.

20.4 In *Richardson v Midland Heart Limited* (2008) 31 L & TR 530, it was held that an order for possession of a shared ownership property made under ground 8 of the assured tenancy grounds for possession was sufficient also to terminate the shared ownership tenant's long leasehold interest.

32.2 Housing benefit on private rented accommodation is now paid to new claimants by way of the Local Housing Allowance (LHA), introduced from 7 April 2008. The LHA is a flat-rate allowance based on the size of the property and the area in which a person lives. LHA rates are set by the Rent Service according to Broad Rental Market Areas.

34.1 In *Horsham Properties Group Ltd v (1) Clark (2) Beech (3) GMAC RFC Ltd (Third Party) (4) Secretary of State for Justice (Intervener)* [2008] EWHC 2327 (Ch), it was held that the exercise of the power of sale by receivers acting on behalf of a mortgagee under section 101 of the Law of Property Act 1925 – which enables a lender to sell the mortgaged property in certain circumstances without first seeking a court order for possession – did not amount to a deprivation of possessions contrary to article 1 of the First Protocol of the ECHR. In June 2009, the Government announced that it would legislate to reverse this decision.

35.8 Lenders bringing mortgage possession proceedings are expected to comply with the Mortgage Arrears Pre-action Protocol, which came into effect on 16 November 2008 (CPR 48th Update). The Protocol is to be found at www.justice.gov.uk/civil/procrules_fin/contents/protocols/prot_mha.htm.

John Gallagher
Nic Madge
Derek McConnell
Jan Luba QC

July 2009

Preface

The aim of *Defending Possession Proceedings* is to assist advice workers, solicitors, barristers and others called upon to help defendants or potential defendants to possession claims. *Defending Possession Proceedings* is not, and could not be, a treatise on all the relevant law of tenancies and mortgages. There are other weighty tomes, some comprising several volumes, which fulfil that function. *Defending Possession Proceedings* is essentially a practical book. We concentrate on matters of practice and procedure and relevant substantive law. We have aimed to write it in a user-friendly way, so that it contains information which is of use to the most experienced legal practitioners, yet is still understandable to the least experienced housing advisers.

The task of advisers and lawyers helping those facing possession proceedings has become increasingly difficult in the twenty years since we started writing the first edition. The number of possession claims is again rising – from 227,178 in 2003, to 232,257 in 2004 and 260,027 in 2005.[1] The availability of public funding (formerly legal aid) seems to become more and more restricted. The number of solicitors willing to provide assistance seems to decline. On the other hand, the law has become more and more complex – demonstrated by the fact that this sixth edition is more than three times longer than the first edition. Since publication of the first edition, the pace of change to housing law has become ever more rapid. Since the last edition the major statutory change has been the Anti-social Behaviour Act 2003, introducing the concept of demoted tenancies and adding specific factors which judges must take into account when considering reasonableness. Procedurally, CPR Part 55 has been amended to include claims against trespassers, interim possession orders and demotion claims. The Court of Appeal and House of Lords have been no less active – with perhaps half a dozen major cases appearing every month. For example, the landmark decisions of *Leeds CC v*

---

1   Table 4.1, Judicial Statistics Annual Report, 2005.

Price; Lambeth LBC v Kay [2006] UKHL 10; [2006] 2 WLR 570, *Harlow DC v Hall* [2006] EWCA Civ 156; (2006) *Times* March 15; and *Bristol CC v Hassan; Bristol CC v Glastonbury* [2006] EWCA Civ 656; (2006) *Times* 17 July, have all appeared after the manuscript of this edition was delivered to our publishers. Also, since delivery of the manuscript, the Head of Civil Justice has approved a Rent Arrears Pre-Action Protocol and a new form of Postponed Possession Order (Form N28A) – with associated new text for Practice Direction 55 – to take into account the Court of Appeal judgement in *Hassan*. We have attempted, through major revisions and rewriting at page proof stage, to update the text to take all of these into account

It is tempting to compare the current state of housing law with the Ottoman Empire in 1913 – the sick man of Europe. The empire has grown haphazardly over the centuries. Successive sultans and viziers have added piecemeal to the structure. Parts have been lost or discarded over the years. The outermost borders have lost touch with the centre. There are undoubtedly some efficient organisations and some architectural gems, but it is becoming increasingly difficult to find them. They are hidden among Byzantine procedures and the tortuous wording of statutes. Pessimists will say that the empire is about to collapse, to disintegrate prior to partition by the major powers at a housing law equivalent of the Treaty of Versailles. Whether or not that is right, there is a major need for reform. Over the last few months the Law Commission has published important proposals – *Renting Homes* (Law Com No. 297) and *Housing: proportionate dispute resolution; an issues paper* (March 2006). Not all housing advisers and lawyers will agree with all of these proposals, but they are the housing law equivalent of the radical reforms promulgated by Mustafa Kemal Ataturk, president of Turkey from 1920 to 1938, who dragged the former Ottoman Empire into the twentieth century and established a strong, although far from perfect, modern, secular state. Root and branch reform of housing law and procedure is long overdue. Urgent and careful consideration should be given to these proposals.

As ever, we are very grateful to those colleagues who have written to us with suggestions and comments on earlier editions. We have taken them into account where possible. Comments on this edition (addressed to us c/o the Legal Action Group) are warmly welcomed.

Many of the issues dealt with in this book are the subject of regular discussions at the meetings of the Housing Law Practitioners Association (see www.hlpa.org.uk). In addition, our material can be updated by reference to Nic Madge and Jan Luba's 'Recent Developments in Housing Law', a monthly column in *Legal Action*, and by

Derek McConnell's annual review 'Owner-occupiers: Recent Developments' which also appears in *Legal Action* in April.

That this edition has been produced at all is a tribute to the efficiency and helpful prompting of the LAG staff (with particular thanks to Esther Pilger who has shown the talent of a diva and the patience of a saint) and Lesley Exton at Regent Typesetting, who has worked like a stakhanovite, especially when dealing with the major re-writing which occurred at page proof stage. Their contribution has been first class. The remaining mistakes (if any) are ours.

The law in England and Wales is stated as at 1 June 2006, although where possible later developments have been incorporated.

Nic Madge
Derek McConnell
John Gallagher
Jan Luba QC

For reasons of space, it has been impossible to include a complete range of citations of cases in individual footnotes. However, citations in all major law reports are included in the table of cases. Any reader who does not have access to the law reports referred to in a footnote citation should therefore refer to the table of cases.

Contents

How to use this book

Defending Possession Proceedings has, since its first edition in January 1987, been designed as a reference book dealing with all aspects of law relating to possession proceedings against most occupiers of resi-dential property. It also, equally importantly, seeks to guide advisers in dealing with a possession claim as it goes through the process from the letter before action to the aftermath of the bailiff's eviction. The book deals with the three principal types of occupier, namely, the social housing tenant, the private tenant and the mortgage borrower.

The years since the Housing Act 1980 (which first introduced security of tenure for public sector tenants) have seen a blurring between social housing and private sector tenants, particularly as far as hous-ing association tenants are concerned. Where an adviser is clear as to the type of tenancy which an occupier has, then reference should be made to the relevant Part of the book. However, where it is unclear, the brief introduction to the types of tenancy, found at the beginning of each part, should be considered.

As the procedures and issues involved in possession proceedings differ somewhat between tenants and mortgage borrowers, these are dealt with separately. Part III of the book contains a discussion of pos-session procedure and related points as they affect residential tenants and other occupiers, and Part IV deals with the procedure and other issues as they affect mortgage borrowers.

The appendices contain a set of precedents which practitioners might find useful. An instructions checklist is also included as an aide-memoire. In particular those practitioners who are liable to file auditing by the Legal Services Commission as part of its franchise monitoring procedures might find the checklist helpful. This edition also includes the Protocol for possession claims based on rent arrears and CPR Part 55 and practice directions.

Table of cases

For reasons of space, it has been impossible to include a complete range of citations of cases in individual footnotes. However, citations in all major law reports are included in the table of cases. Any reader who does not have access to the law reports referred to in a footnote citation should therefore refer to the table of cases.

References in the right-hand column are to paragraph numbers.

Table of statutes

References in the right-hand column are to paragraph numbers.

Table of statutory instruments

References in the right-hand column are to paragraph numbers.

Table of European legislation

References in the right-hand column are to paragraph numbers.

Abbreviations

ASBO	Anti-social Behaviour Order
CA	Court of Appeal
CCR	County Court Rules
CPR	Civil Procedure Rules
DCLG	Department for Communities and Local Government
DoE	Department of the Environment
DWP	Department for Work and Pensions
ECHR	European Convention on Human Rights
ECtHR	European Court of Human Rights
FSA	Financial Services Authority
FSO	Financial Services Ombudsman
HA	Housing Act
HAT	Housing action trust
HB Regs	Housing Benefit Regulations 2006 SI No 213
HL	House of Lords
HMO	House in multiple occupation
IPO	Interim possession order
IS Regs	Income Support (General) Regulations 1987 SI No 1967
JSA Regs	Jobseeker's Allowance Regulations 1996 SI No 207
LBC	London Borough Council
LSVT	Large Scale Voluntary Transfer scheme
ODPM	Office of the Deputy Prime Minister
PCOL	Possession Claims Online
RA	Rent Act
RSC	Rules of the Supreme Court
RSL	Registered social landlord

Public sector occupiers

Introduction to Part I

I.1   Part I of this book is concerned with possession proceedings brought against occupiers living in 'public sector' housing. Its main focus is on tenants and licensees of local authorities and housing action trusts. However, until 1989 most other social landlords – housing associations, housing trusts and housing co-operatives – operated broadly the same tenancy regime as local authorities and issues arising under that regime for those landlords are dealt with here too. The term 'public sector' is therefore used to describe that part of the social housing sector which is regulated by the Housing Act 1985. In respect of the remainder of the social rented sector, in the wake of the changes wrought by the Housing Act 1988, possession proceedings against *assured* tenants of the associations, trusts and co-operatives are now dealt with in Part II.

I.2   Since 1980 most occupiers of public sector accommodation have enjoyed security of tenure as *secure* tenants or licensees. Their code of protection, set out in Housing Act 1985 Pt IV, prevents landlords from recovering possession except by establishing before a county court judge that grounds set out in the Act can be proved. In most cases, occupiers are further protected by a discretion the court exercises as to whether the particular circumstances justify the making of the order. On paper therefore, public sector occupiers have considerable protection against loss of their homes.

I.3   However, this statutory protection has not led to any perceptible decline in the number of possession actions commenced against secure occupiers. Over 126,000 public and social landlord actions were started in 2005.[1] Research has repeatedly shown that public sector possession cases receive insufficiently thorough attention in

---

1   *Judicial Statistics England and Wales for the Year 2005*, May 2006, Cm 6799, Table 4.5.

some county courts. Researchers claim that in some parts of the country the speed with which possession cases are heard indicates little regard for security of tenure and an emphasis on quick disposal. Possession orders are made in the majority of cases and thousands of occupiers are actually evicted each year as a result.[2] The most recent research has emphasised the need for more tenants to attend court and more consistent handling of housing possession cases.[3]

1.4 Most of these cases are in reality 'debt collecting' actions. The main thrust of the proceedings is to threaten repossession on the ground of rent arrears unless the occupier resumes regular and full payment of rent due and owing. This happens notwithstanding the government's repeated exhortations to public landlords to see possession proceedings only as the last resort in recovering arrears.[4] Landlords presumably regard possession proceedings as a 'bigger stick' to wield against defaulting tenants than other available recovery procedures. This practice, which might appear to some to verge on an abuse of the process of the court, received critical scrutiny from Lord Woolf's review of civil justice,[5] but appears not to have abated. The likely introduction of a new Rent Arrears Pre-Action Protocol (see para 3.34) will hopefully lead to a reduction in the overall number of possession proceedings and a sharper focus on the statutory criteria limiting the circumstances in which possession orders can be made.

1.5 Following a very effective lobbying campaign by public sector landlords, the Housing Act 1996 introduced a general reduction in the security of tenure of public sector tenants. From 12 February 1997 councils and housing action trusts have had power to put their new tenants 'on probation' for their first year by the grant of 'introductory tenancies' (considered in chapter 8). From the same date the grounds for possession against secure tenants were added to and existing grounds were broadened. The safeguard that there must usually be a 'notice seeking possession' before court proceedings are commenced was punctured by a new provision allowing such notice to be dispensed with (see para 2.10). With effect from 30 June 2004, following further amending legislation in the Anti-Social Behaviour Act 2003, social landlords have been able to apply to the court for a 'demotion

2   *Judicial Statistics England and Wales for the year 2005*, May 2006, Cm 6799, Table 4.20.
3   C Hunter et al, *The Exercise of Judicial Discretion in Rent Arrears Cases*, Department of Constitutional Affairs Research Series 6/05, 2005.
4   *The Use of Possession Actions and Evictions by Social Landlords*, ODPM, June 2005.
5   Woolf, *Access to Justice: Final Report*, HMSO, 1996, ch 16.

order', whereby the security of tenure of a secure or assured tenant is removed and the tenancy reduced to probationary status for a trial period of one year.

I.6 Much of Part I of the book is concerned with advising in the statistically most common case of a rent arrears possession action brought against a secure occupier. It is, of course, possible for secure occupiers to lose their secure status as a result of circumstances other than repossession and indeed some residents never acquire security at all. The situation of such occupiers is also considered (see para 5.26).

I.7 The first chapter provides a short summary of security in the public sector. Chapter 2 deals with the situations in which security is threatened or lost. The third chapter deals with the grounds for possession proceedings against secure occupiers and chapter 4 deals with preparation of defences. Chapter 5 covers a miscellany of other situations affecting public sector occupiers. Chapters 6 and 7 deal with the occupiers of housing association and housing action trust properties respectively. Chapter 8 deals with the framework of introductory tenancies and the different regimes governing demoted tenancies. Reference should also be made to Part III which deals with possession procedure.

I.8 Throughout Part I, statutory references are to the Housing Act 1985 unless otherwise stated.

The secure occupier

Introduction

1.1   The rights to security of tenure of those in the public sector operate as a supplement to the ordinary common law rules of landlord and tenant. Under those rules, the landlord needed only to bring the contractual arrangement to an end in accordance with its terms and the occupier's right to possession then ceased. Security of tenure in the public sector, first introduced by the Housing Act 1980, now derives from Housing Act 1985 Pt IV and operates by way of providing the contractual tenant with a 'cloak' of security. As will be seen, in an ordinary case, the landlord can only bring the tenancy to an end by making an application to a court.

Secure tenancies

1.2   The greatest security of tenure available in the public sector is accorded to those who are 'secure tenants'. Most council and other public sector tenants are secure tenants. However, it is always important to check that all the hallmarks of a secure tenancy, as set out below, are present in each case.

1.3   A secure tenancy exists at any time when all of the following conditions (extracted from Housing Act 1985 ss79–81) are satisfied:

- the property is a 'dwelling-house';
- the landlord is a prescribed public body;
- the tenant is an individual;
- the tenant occupies the property as his or her only or principal home;
- the property was let as a 'separate dwelling';
- the tenancy is not in an exempt category.

Each of these requirements is discussed in turn below.

The property is a 'dwelling-house'

1.4   The term 'dwelling-house' covers both houses and parts of houses[1] and extends to any land let together with the dwelling-house other than agricultural land exceeding two acres.[2] Neither of the words 'house' or 'dwelling-house' is further defined in Housing Act 1985 Pt

---

1   HA 1985 s112(1).
2   HA 1985 s112(2).

IV. The phrase 'part of a house' is sufficiently broad to include flats, rooms, apartments and bed-sitting rooms and possibly accommodation in some hostels.

1.5 It was previously thought that a single room let furnished, without cooking facilities and situated in a hostel was not a 'dwelling-house' for the purposes of the security of tenure provisions.[3] However, it is now clear that a 'dwelling-house' is simply a house or part of a house in which a person lives.[4]

The landlord is a prescribed public body

1.6 The landlord must be one of the authorities or bodies within the list set out in Housing Act 1985 s80(1) and (2), as amended. If there are joint landlords they must *all* be in the list.[5]

80 (1) The landlord condition is that the interest of the landlord belongs to one of the following authorities or bodies –
a local authority,
a new town corporation,
[a housing action trust]
an urban development corporation,
...
the [*Relevant Authority*]
a housing trust which is a charity, or
a housing association or housing co-operative to which this section applies.
(2) *This section applies to –*
(a) a [registered social landlord] other than a co-operative housing association, and
[(b) a co-operative housing association which is not a registered social landlord.
(3) If a co-operative housing association ceases to be [a registered social landlord], it shall, within the period of 21 days beginning with the date on which it ceases to be [a registered social landlord], notify each of its tenants who thereby becomes a secure tenant, in writing, that he has become a secure tenant.
[(4)This section applies to a housing co-operative within the meaning of section 27B (agreements under certain superseded provisions) where the dwelling-house is comprised in a housing co-operative agreement within the meaning of that section.]

3 *Central London YMCA Housing Association Ltd v Goodman* (1992) 24 HLR 109, CA.
4 *Uratemp Ventures Ltd v Collins* [2001] UKHL 43; [2002] 1 AC 301; (2001) 33 HLR 972, HL.
5 *R v Plymouth CC and Cornwall CC ex p Freeman* (1987) 19 HLR 328, CA.

1.7   The words in the first square brackets in s80(1) were added by Housing Act 1988 s83(2). The words in square brackets in s80(3) were
substituted by Housing Act 1996 (Consequential Provisions) Order
1996 SI No 2325 Sch 2 para 14(8). The words in square brackets in
s80(4) were substituted by Housing and Planning Act 1986 Sch 5
para 26. The words in italics were repealed by Housing Act 1988 s140
and Sch 18 but are reprinted here because they still apply for transitional purposes.[6]

1.8   The changes reflect the general policy intention (see para 1.1) that
most *new* lettings (ie, since 15 January 1989) by housing associations,
trusts and other registered social landlords should *not* come within
the secure tenancy regime. Secure tenancies granted by such landlords *before* that date will retain their secure status and such landlords may grant some new secure tenancies but only in very narrowly
defined circumstances.[7] Surprisingly, it is still possible for a non-
secure tenancy held from such a landlord automatically to 'become'
secure. This occurs when a registered social landlord acquires property with sitting Rent Act tenants[8] or if the transitional provisions in
Housing Act 1988 Sch 18 para 4 are activated by some change in the
landlord's status.[9]

1.9   Secure tenants are most commonly tenants of a 'local authority'. That term is widely defined by Housing Act 1985 s4(e) and now
includes combined fire authorities.[10] For discussion of the special
position of housing association, housing co-operative and housing
trust occupiers, see chapter 6. For the position of housing action trust
occupiers, see chapter 7.

1.10   If the interest of the landlord is transferred after the grant of the
tenancy to a non-prescribed body, for example, by the sale of council
property into the private sector or to a registered social landlord, any
sitting secure tenants lose secure status although they may become
'assured' tenants under provisions regulating private sector tenancies.[11] For the circumstances in which a public sector landlord may
seek to recover possession before such a sale, see para 3.150.

1.11   Since 1993, over 928,500 dwellings have been transferred out of

---

6   HA 1988 Sch 18 para 4.
7   HA 1988 s35(4).
8   HA 1988 s35(5).
9   *Bhai v Black Roof Community Housing Association* [2001] 2 All ER 865; (2001)
    33 HLR 607, CA.
10 Combined Fire Authorities (Secure Tenancies) Regulations 1998 SI Nos 2213
    (England) and 2214 (Wales).
11 See HA 1985 Pt II and HA 1988 s38.

council ownership under the Large Scale Voluntary Transfer (LSVT) scheme. There have been 207 approved LSVTs involving 158 local authorities.[12] All sitting tenants will have ceased to be secure at completion of the sale.

The tenant is an individual

1.12 The tenant must be an individual person[13] or a group of individuals holding as joint tenants. Therefore, a tenancy cannot be secure if the tenant is a company, a charity, a short-life housing association[14], a co-operative or a public authority. The sub-tenants of such bodies may of course themselves be secure or protected tenants as against their immediate landlords. If a tenancy is purportedly granted to a company but both parties understand that the true occupier with possession will be an individual, that individual holds as a secure tenant because the agreement is a 'sham'.[15]

The 'only or principal home' rule

1.13 The tenant must occupy the property as his or her only *or* principal home.[16] A secure tenant may, therefore, have more than one home but have a 'secure' tenancy only in relation to the principal one. Where there are joint tenants, at least one of them must occupy as his or her only or principal home.[17]

1.14 Temporary absences caused by holidays, stays in hospital, working abroad, etc, do not affect security, but a permanent absence will lead to loss of security. For the difficulties which arise from extended absences see the discussion at para 2.36.

1.15 If an absent tenant is married or has a registered civil partner and the home has been the shared home, his or her spouse or civil partner can preserve the security of the tenancy by continuing in occupation during the tenant's absence.[18] There is no equivalent automatic

---

12 Details available from DCLG website, www.dclg.gov.uk. See Housing Transfer Cases. (Statistics issued 15 February 2006.)

13 HA 1985 s81.

14 *Camden LBC v Shortlife Community Housing Ltd* (1993) 25 HLR 330; (1992) 90 LGR 358, HC, *Kay and others v Lambeth LBC* [2006] UKHL 10; [2006] 2 WLR 570, HL.

15 *City of London v Ukpoma* (1996) 1 L & T Rev D8; September 1996 *Legal Action* 11.

16 HA 1985 s81.

17 HA 1985 s81.

18 Family Law Act 1996 s30(4)(b), amended by Civil Partnership Act 2004 Sch 9 para 1, with effect from 5 December 2005.

provision for cohabitants or other family members to be deemed to be preserving the absent tenant's security of tenure, but if a cohabitant or former cohabitant successfully applies for an 'occupation order' under Family Law Act 1996 s36(1) he or she will be treated as satisfying the 'only or principal home' rule on behalf of the absentee tenant (see chapter 30).[19]

The 'let as a separate dwelling' requirement

1.16   This has three components: the letting must have been 'as' a separate dwelling; the premises let must be a 'dwelling' (in a 'dwelling-house', see para 1.4); and the dwelling must have been let as a 'separate' dwelling.[20]

1.17   The first of these components deals with the nature of the tenancy. Was it a letting of premises 'as' a separate dwelling? In *Webb v Barnet LBC*,[21] the council let a house, yard, workshop and associated buildings for use by a motor repair business. The tenant used it in this way until retirement and continued in occupation of the house once the business had closed. It was held that the tenancy was not secure. The original letting had been for commercial use, not for use 'as' a separate dwelling. In *Tomkins v Basildon DC*,[22] the tenant had a lease of a bungalow and kennels. The authorised use of the premises was for the training of greyhounds, and the letting was accordingly a business tenancy under Part II of the Landlord and Tenant Act 1954. Eventually, commercial activity ceased and the premises were used only as a residence. On the expiry of the lease, the tenant continued to live in the bungalow and claimed housing benefit in respect of the rent. However, the property had not been 'let as' a separate dwelling. The landlord had been content not to enforce the tenant's covenant for business use, but this was not sufficient to amount to an agreed variation of the letting condition.

1.18   It should be noted that the security of tenure provisions only cover 'a' separate dwelling, ie, one unit of accommodation. It may, however, be possible for two adjoining units let to the tenant to be combined to form a single dwelling for these purposes.[23]

---

19   Family Law Act 1996 s36(13) and see *Gay v Sheeran and Enfield LBC* (2000) 32 HLR 1126, CA.
20   HA 1985 s79(1).
21   (1988) 21 HLR 288.
22   [2002] EWCA Civ 876; [2003] L&TR 7.
23   *Jenkins v Renfrew DC* 1989 SLT (Lands Tr) 41, but cf *Kavanagh v Lyroudias* [1985] 1 All ER 560, CA.

1.19　　The second component deals with the subject of the letting. It must be a 'dwelling'. This is something more than simply a physical unit of four walls, a floor and a ceiling (as that test would be satisfied by a garage or storeroom), but it can be difficult to identify with precision. In *Uratemp Ventures Ltd v Collins*,[24] the subject of the letting was a single room in a hotel. The House of Lords decided that it was the place in which the tenant lived, or had his 'home'. It was no requirement of the concept of 'dwelling' that it should be a place where the tenant cooked or ate, although it would be the place where he usually slept.

1.20　　Third, the premises must have been let to the tenant as a 'separate' dwelling.[25] Usually this condition is satisfied because the tenant and his or her family are the only occupiers of the property concerned. If, however, parts of a building are shared with other tenants this does not affect security unless the sharing is of living accommodation (kitchen,[26] lounge, dining room or bedroom).[27] Such sharing means that the tenant has not been let a 'separate' dwelling. Thus, in the case of an ordinary residential house or flat, a tenant or licensee of a single bedroom in the property who shares the kitchen, living room, etc, with the occupiers of the other bedrooms, will not have a 'separate' dwelling for these purposes.[28]

1.21　　Obviously, secure status is not lost just because living accommodation is shared by the tenant with other members of the tenant's own household or with lodgers.

The tenancy is not in an excluded category

1.22　　Certain categories of tenancy are excluded from full security of tenure:

- Tenancies in one of the classes exempted from protection by Housing Act 1985 Sch 1, as amended by Housing Act 1996 Sch 16 para 2.[29] Detailed consideration of each of the classes is beyond the

---

24　[2001] UKHL 43; [2002] 1 AC 301; (2001) 33 HLR 972, HL.

25　HA 1985 s79(1).

26　Note the important distinction for these purposes between the shared occupation of a kitchen and the sharing of limited use of a kitchen (eg, to wash up or cook) described in *Uratemp Ventures Ltd v Collins* [2002] 1 AC 301; [2001] 3 WLR 806, HL at [58] of the judgment.

27　See *Kensington and Chelsea RBC v Haydon* (1984) 17 HLR 114, CA on the effect of sharing with a hostel worker, and generally *Thomson v Glasgow CC* 1986 SLT 6, noted at December 1986 *Legal Action* 165, Lands Tr.

28　*Parkins v Westminster CC* (1998) 30 HLR 894; [1998] 1 EGLR 22, CA and *Smith v Hackney LBC* August 1998 *Legal Action* 21, CA.

29　HA 1985 s79(2)(a).

scope of this work, but the categories may be summarised as:
- long tenancies (defined in Housing Act 1985 s115);
- introductory tenancies (see chapter 8);
- demoted tenancies (see chapter 8);
- premises occupied in connection with employment;[30]
- land acquired for development;[31]
- accommodation for homeless people (see para 5.16);
- temporary accommodation for people taking up employment;[32]
- 'private sector leasing' accommodation (see para 5.20);
- temporary accommodation during works;
- agricultural holdings;
- licensed premises;
- student lettings;
- Landlord and Tenant Act 1954 tenancies (business tenancies); and
- almshouses.
- accommodation provided to asylum seekers;[33]
- temporary accommodation for displaced persons.[34]

- Tenancies ceasing to be secure after the death of the secure tenant[35] (see para 2.32).
- Tenancies ceasing to be secure following assignment, parting with possession or full subletting (see HA 1985 s79(2)(c) and para 2.40 below).
- Tenancies at will.[36]

---

30 HA 1985 Sch 1 para 2; *Hughes v Greenwich LBC* [1994] 1 AC 170; [1993] 3 WLR 821, HL; *Elvidge v Coventry CC* [1994] QB 241; [1993] 3 WLR 976, CA; *South Glamorgan DC v Griffiths* (1992) 24 HLR 334; [1992] 2 EGLR 232, CA; *Surrey CC v Lamond* (1999) 31 HLR 1051, CA; *Brent LBC v Charles* (1997) 29 HLR 876, CA; and *Greenfield v Berkshire CC* (1996) 28 HLR 691, CA. For modern illustrations see *Lee v Neath & Port Talbot CC* June 1998 *Legal Action* 10 and *Coleman v Ipswich BC* [2001] EWCA 852, August 2001 *Legal Action* 23.

31 HA 1985 Sch 1 para 3; *Attley v Cherwell DC* (1989) 21 HLR 613, CA; *Harrison v Hyde Housing Association Ltd* (1991) 23 HLR 57; (1989) *Times* 17 July, CA; *London & Quadrant Housing Trust v Robertson* (1991) unreported, but noted at September 1991 *Legal Action* 15; and *Lillieshall Road Housing Co-operative v Brennan* (1992) 24 HLR 193; [1991] EGCS 132, CA.

32 HA 1985 Sch 1 para 5; *Campbell v Western Isles Island Council* 1989 SLT 602, CS, noted at December 1989 *Legal Action* 13.

33 HA 1985 Sch 1 para 4A, inserted by Immigration and Asylum Act 1999 Sch 14 para 81.

34 HA 1985 Sch 1 para 4B, inserted by the Displaced Persons (Temporary Protection) Regulations 2005 (SI No 1379).

35 HA 1985 s79(2)(b).

36 *Banjo v Brent LBC* [2005] EWCA Civ 287; [2005] 1 WLR 2520; [2005] HLR 33.

Tenancies in equity

1.23   Most secure tenancies are tenancies valid at law as between land-lord and tenant. There are, however, circumstances in which a land-lord purports to grant the tenant a tenancy valid in law but cannot in fact do so. For example, a tenant may die leaving no will and no successor. In such circumstances the legal tenancy devolves in the unadministered estate of the deceased to the Public Trustee. A land-lord, unaware that this has occurred, may 'relet' the empty property to someone else. This new tenant cannot be given the legal tenancy as that remains held by the Public Trustee. In such circumstances the 'new' tenant holds a tenancy taking effect in equity only.[37]

1.24   Likewise, a landlord may purport to grant a tenancy to a person under 18. That person cannot hold a legal tenancy but he or she has a right to occupy in equity.[38]

1.25   A tenancy in equity enjoys security of tenure just as much as a legal tenancy if all the hallmarks of secure status (described above) are in place.

Secure 'licensees'

1.26   Although it is not a common occurrence, a landlord authority may grant a licence rather than a tenancy to the occupier of council or other public sector property (for example, because the occupier is under 18 years of age and thus incapable at law of holding a tenancy). Whether or not the occupier pays 'rent' or a 'licence fee' or any other charge, such licence is secure if all the hallmarks outlined in relation to a secure tenancy apply.[39] Such licences can be granted quite casu-ally and almost inadvertently.[40]

1.27   This extension of security to public sector licensees renders sub-stantially less significant the distinction, still important in the private sector, between those with licences and those with tenancies.

1.28   It should be stressed that the licence agreement must have con-ferred the exclusive right to occupy a 'separate dwelling'. Thus, a resi-dent in a hostel with specialist support facilities under an agreement permitting the owners unrestricted access to the room and containing

---

37   *Epping Forest DC v Pomphrett* (1990) 22 HLR 475, CA.
38   *Kingston upon Thames RLBC v Prince* (1999) 31 HLR 794; [1999] 1 FLR 593, CA; *Newham LBC v Ria* [2004] EWCA Civ 41; (2004) 148 SJLB 113, CA.
39   HA 1985 s79(3).
40   See, eg, *Lambeth LBC v Stroud*, September 1991 *Legal Action* 14.

power to require the occupier to share (and/or require the occupier to move to another room), does not have a licence to occupy as a separate dwelling and does not therefore have security of tenure.[41] Similarly, a licence which is simply a subsidiary agreement associated with a secure tenancy of a dwelling (such as permission temporarily to use additional rooms during building work) does not itself amount to a licence to occupy premises as a 'separate dwelling'.[42]

1.29   Occupiers who initially enter the property as trespassers and are then given licence to remain as a temporary expedient do not benefit from security of tenure.[43] Thus, even squatters whom it is not proposed to evict for some time are outside the main protection of security (for their situation see chapter 25). It should be noted that if a licence is granted to the squatter other than as a temporary expedient, the licensee immediately benefits from security. Alternatively, the squatter could acquire security from being granted a tenancy of the property.

Going in and out of secure status

1.30   Housing Act 1985 s79(1) accords a contractual tenancy or a licence 'secure' status '... at any time when ...' all the hallmarks of security set out at para 1.3 above are satisfied. Thus a tenancy or licence may lose security for want of satisfaction of one of the conditions but later become secure again on its subsequent fulfilment. The section is thus aptly described as having 'ambulatory' effect.[44]

1.31   If a landlord seeks possession on the basis that the tenancy has lost protection and the contractual tenancy has been determined by notice to quit, it is thus crucial to consider whether the tenancy was in or out of the protection of the Act at the date of expiry of that notice.[45] If the tenancy was secure at the date of its expiry the notice to quit will have been of no effect.

1.32   If a check through this chapter has revealed that the occupier is *not* a secure tenant or licensee, go directly to para 5.26 (tenants) or para 5.29 (licensees).

---

41   *Westminster CC v Clarke* [1992] 2 AC 288; [1992] 2 WLR 229; (1992) 24 HLR 360, HL.

42   *Tyler v Kensington & Chelsea RLBC* (1991) 23 HLR 380, CA.

43   HA 1985 s79(4). See *R v Southwark LBC ex p Bannerman* (1989) 22 HLR 459, QBD.

44   *Basingstoke & Deane BC v Paice* (1995) 27 HLR 433; [1995] EGCS 54, CA and *Manchester CC v Finn* [2002] EWCA Civ 1998; [2003] HLR 41, CA at 32.

45   *Hussey v Camden LBC* (1995) 27 HLR 5, CA.

Security threatened

Introduction

2.1   This chapter considers the circumstances in which the landlord or the occupier can place the security of tenure in jeopardy. The initial focus is, of course, on the typical case of landlord-initiated action. Throughout this chapter the term 'secure tenancy' is used to refer to both secure tenancies and secure licences unless the contrary is expressed.

Landlord-initiated

Landlord threatens possession proceedings

2.2   A secure tenancy cannot legally be brought to an end by a landlord otherwise than by obtaining a court order for possession.[1] The landlord must therefore initiate court proceedings to recover possession unless the occupiers themselves have brought to an end the security of tenure, in one of the ways described below (paras 2.16 onwards), and even in those cases a landlord is likely to need a court order before recovering possession[2] unless the premises have been left vacant.

2.3   Usually, the landlord gives the tenant some informal notice by letter, interview or home visit, that possession proceedings may be taken unless the tenant remedies a specific default, for example, pays any outstanding rent, ceases to commit nuisances, etc. In rent arrears cases, these steps are required by the Rent Arrears Pre-Action Protocol (see para 3.34).

2.4   The first formal step the landlord must normally take if intending to press ahead to recover possession is service of a notice, commonly known as 'notice of seeking possession'. The purpose of the notice is, in summary, to inform the tenant of the matters the landlord will rely on, to identify for the tenant the legal ground on which possession will be sought and to set out the date after which possession proceedings may be started. This is not a 'notice to quit' and therefore does not attract the requirements for such a notice set out in the Protection from Eviction Act 1977 (described at para 12.8). Nor does the notice of seeking possession operate to end the tenancy on its expiry. Only a subsequent possession order can end the tenancy. If the tenant in receipt of a notice of seeking possession decides to leave, he or she must bring the tenancy to an end by service of a notice to quit or by agreeing a surrender of the tenancy with the landlord.

---

1   HA 1985 s82(1).
2   Protection from Eviction Act 1977 s3.

2.5 In order to be effective the notice must meet the requirements of Housing Act 1985 s83(2):

> (2) A notice under this section shall –
>> (a) be in a form prescribed by regulations made by the Secretary of State,
>> (b) specify the ground on which the court will be asked to make the order, and
>> (c) give particulars of that ground.

Each of the requirements of Housing Act 1985 s83(2) is considered in chapter 4 (see paras 4.11–4.31).

2.6 The Act also requires the notice to specify certain dates. If the notice sets out ground 2 (nuisance) as one of the grounds for possession then the notice must also state: (1) that possession proceedings may be begun immediately; and (2) the date sought by the landlord as the date on which the tenant is to give up possession.[3] In any other case the date to be specified should be the date after which possession proceedings may be begun.[4]

2.7 In respect of any notice, unless the exception relating to ground 2 applies, the 'specified date' is to be no earlier than the date on which the tenancy could, under common law or in contract, have been brought to an end by notice to quit served on the tenant that day. For a weekly periodic tenancy that will mean that the date specified cannot be less than four weeks from the date on which the notice is given.[5]

2.8 Where the tenancy is a periodic tenancy the notice ceases to be effective 12 months from the specified date.[6] This means that if the landlord wishes to proceed to recover possession on the basis of the notice, possession proceedings must be begun within 12 months of the specified date.[7] Note that this is a longer period than simply 12 months running from the date of service of the notice.

2.9 Special provision is made for notices given in respect of fixed-term secure tenancies.[8]

2.10 Failure to comply with any of these strict procedural requirements may give rise to a defence to any proceedings brought on the basis of that notice (see chapter 4). However, it is open to a landlord to commence possession proceedings without serving a notice and then

---

3 HA 1985 s83(3)(a).
4 HA 1985 s83(4).
5 Protection From Eviction Act 1977 s5.
6 HA 1985 s83(3)(b) and (4)(b).
7 HA 1985 s83A(1) and (2).
8 HA 1985 s83(6).

seek to rely on the court's discretionary power to dispense with the requirement for a notice.[9] The exercise of the same power may be sought by a landlord who serves a defective notice. The scope of this power is considered in chapter 4. Most landlords would prefer the assurance of serving a proper notice at the outset and it is likely to be only in the most urgent or unusual circumstances that the landlord starts proceedings without having served a notice of seeking possession at all.

2.11   The procedure to be followed by a landlord in seeking to recover possession through the courts is outlined in chapter 21. What the landlord needs to prove is discussed in chapter 3. The defences available to secure occupiers are reviewed in chapter 4.

2.12   Occasionally, even the landlords of secure tenants seek to recover possession unlawfully without first taking proceedings. The relevant law on securing remedies for unlawful eviction is reviewed in Arden and Partington's *Quiet Enjoyment*.[10] The 'penal' damages awarded under Housing Act 1988 s28 arising from the tort of statutory unlawful eviction are available as much against public and social landlords as private landlords.[11]

Landlord proposes to sell the property

2.13   A secure tenancy remains secure only for so long as the landlord condition remains satisfied, ie, the landlord is a prescribed public body.[12] Once the freehold or head lease is transferred to a body other than one of those prescribed in Housing Act 1985 s80(1) (set out at para 1.6 above), security of tenure under the Housing Act 1985 is lost, although the contractual tenancy itself continues and binds the new landlord. In recent years, many local housing authorities have transferred all or part of their housing stock to housing associations or other registered social landlords. In these circumstances, the sitting tenants usually obtain protection against the new owners as assured tenants under Housing Act 1988 Pt I.[13]

2.14   A proposal by the landlord to sell or transfer the whole or part of its housing stock thus threatens the 'secure' status of the tenants of

---

9   HA 1985 s83(1)(b).

10   6th edn by Arden, Partington, Carter and Dymond, LAG, 2002.

11   See *White v Lambeth LBC* September 1995 *Legal Action* 20 (£18,000) and *Osei-Bonsu v Wandsworth LBC* [1999] 1 WLR 1011; (1999) 31 HLR 515, CA (£30,000 reduced on appeal to £10,000).

12   HA 1985 s80(1) and see para 1.6.

13   HA 1988 s38.

dwellings to be disposed of. Once the proposal becomes a positive decision to sell to a particular buyer, the secure tenants must be consulted.[14] The procedure for disposal to non-public sector landlords is governed by the consultation requirements of Housing Act 1985 s106A and Sch 3A[15] which make more detailed provision than the general consultation arrangements made under Housing Act 1985 s105.[16] Where the landlord is a housing action trust, the Housing Act 1985 s105/106A procedure is replaced by arrangements specified in Housing Act 1988 s84 (see para 7.14).

2.15   The landlord may not wish to sell with 'sitting' tenants but would prefer to sell with vacant possession. Such a landlord may attempt to secure vacant possession by taking possession proceedings against those who will not vacate voluntarily. In such cases the procedures as to a notice seeking possession (see above) and grounds for possession (see chapter 3) must be satisfied. The Housing and Planning Act 1986 introduced ground 10A to Housing Act 1985 Sch 2 to allow landlords a limited opportunity to recover possession in such circumstances (see para 3.150). However, the Secretary of State's consent is required to such a proposed disposal and the landlord must undertake a consultation exercise with the tenants to be displaced before seeking such consent.[17]

Tenant-initiated

Tenant gives notice to quit or surrenders the tenancy

2.16   Nothing in the Housing Act 1985 restricts the ability of tenants to determine their own tenancies.

2.17   A secure tenant may seek to end his or her own fixed-term or periodic tenancy by *surrender*. Surrender is the termination of the tenancy by mutual agreement between landlord and tenant. Such agreement is best demonstrated by a deed of surrender. If there is no deed, surrender can be achieved by operation of the common law. Such a surrender arises where the tenant plainly acts so as to give the landlord possession (for example, by emptying the property and returning the keys and rent-book) and the landlord responds by

14   *Short v Tower Hamlets LBC* (1986) 18 HLR 171, CA.
15   Added by Housing and Planning Act 1986 s6.
16   See Department of the Environment Circ 6/88.
17   HA 1985 Sch 2 Pt V and DoE Circ 14/87.

accepting possession (for example, by acknowledging that the tenancy is over, and taking steps to relet). In *Brent LBC v Sharma and Vyas*[18] the tenant wrote to her landlord stating that she was no longer living in the property and would not be returning. The landlord responded by closing the rent account. This was held to amount to a concluded surrender by operation of law.

2.18   The concept of surrender by operation of law is more fully described in paras 12.36–12.43.

2.19   It may even be possible to imply a surrender from circumstances in which the tenant simply abandons the premises and the landlord, finding them empty, simply secures them (see para 2.52). A landlord relying on what seems to be such an implied offer of surrender by a secure tenant must, however, expect to exercise some caution given that a secure tenancy is a valuable asset not likely to be given up lightly by some informal act by the tenant. For example, in *Zionmor v Islington LBC*,[19] the tenant – in an attempt to gain relief from harassment by his neighbours – posted on a communal noticeboard a notice that he had ceased to reside in his flat. He then went away for a while leaving a friend in occupation. The council, upon finding the flat appearing to be empty, changed the locks. It was held that (1) the tenant's leaving a friend in possession was inconsistent with a suggestion that he wished to bring the tenancy to an end, and (2) changing the locks and boarding up were not unequivocally acts of acceptance of surrender – they might equally be explained by an intention to protect the council's stock during the tenant's temporary absence. On the facts, there had been no surrender.

2.20   In the case of a *fixed-term* secure tenancy, the tenant may bring the tenancy to an end by giving such notice as may be required by any *break clause* in the contract.

2.21   *Periodic* tenancies can be ended by serving on the landlord proper *notice to quit*. Such a notice operates unilaterally and brings to an end both security of tenure and the tenancy itself. To be effective any such notice must be in writing and meet contractual[20] and statutory requirements.[21]

2.22   In most cases, the tenant is genuinely surrendering or giving notice in order to quit the premises and is moving to accommoda-

---

18   (1993) 25 HLR 257, CA.
19   (1997) 30 HLR 822, CA.
20   *Community Housing Association v Hoy* December 1988 *Legal Action* 18.
21   The main statutory requirements are contained in Protection From Eviction Act 1977 s5, reproduced at para 12.8.

tion elsewhere. Disputes can arise, however, if the attempt to determine the tenancy arises in the context of the breakdown of a family or marital relationship.

2.23   A *sole* tenant is free to end his or her tenancy by notice to quit or surrender irrespective of the concerns or interests of other occupiers including family members. There may, however, be an exception if the property has been the matrimonial home, the non-tenant spouse or civil partner remains in occupation and the simple purpose of the termination is to render that person homeless. The courts have been reluctant to permit surrender[22] or uphold notices[23] which are used as devices to overcome 'home rights', that is, the rights of occupation of a spouse or civil partner (arising under the Family Law Act 1996 as amended by the Civil Partnership Act 2004[24]) in this way. If the sole tenant spouse or civil partner has purported to surrender, it may be argued by the non-tenant spouse or civil partner that there can have been no termination by operation of law as the tenant cannot give possession so long as he or she remains in residence (but for an example of where such a surrender has been recognised by the courts as effective to terminate the sole tenancy see *Sanctuary Housing Association v Campbell*[25]). If the sole tenant has given notice to quit, the non-tenant spouse or civil partner may be able to assert the invalidity of the notice if it can be shown that the notice failed to comply with the contractual or statutory requirements (see above) but as between sole tenant and landlord the landlord could waive a deficiency in the notice and thus restore its validity.[26] If the notice is in valid form or a surrender is prima facie effective, the non-tenant spouse or civil partner is not able to apply in family proceedings for the setting aside of a disposal of the home in this way.[27] The giving of a notice to quit is not a 'disposal' for these purposes.[28]

2.24   The position is different if there is a *joint tenancy*. While the joint tenancy subsists neither party is usually able permanently to exclude the other from the home. It is also not possible for one joint tenant,

---

22 See *Hoggett v Hoggett* (1980) 39 P & CR 121, CA.

23 See *Griffiths v Renfree* (1989) 21 HLR 338; [1989] FCR 551, CA.

24 Schedule 9 para 1 amending Family Law Act 1996 s30.

25 [1999] 1 WLR 1279; (2000) 32 HLR 100, CA.

26 *Hackney LBC v Snowden* (2001) 33 HLR 49; [2001] L & TR 60, CA and *Lewisham LBC v Lasisi-Agiri* [2003] EWHC 2392 (Ch); [2003] 45 EGCS 175.

27 Matrimonial Causes Act 1973 s37 and see, generally, chapter 30.

28 *Newlon Housing Trust v Al-Sulaimen* [1999] 1 AC 313; [1998] 3 WLR 451; (1998) 30 HLR 1132, HL.

acting alone, to surrender the tenancy or (subject to the express terms of the tenancy) give a 'break clause' notice to end a fixed-term tenancy. If, however, one party gives notice to quit a *periodic* tenancy to the landlord, the whole tenancy determines on its expiry even if the effect would be to leave the other tenant homeless.[29] Attempts to challenge the effect of such a notice, whether based on a claimed breach of trust or on the principles of article 8 of the European Convention on Human Rights (right to respect for private and family life, home and correspondence) have proved unsuccessful.[30] See paras 5.31 onwards. As a matter of law a joint tenant is free to give such a notice to quit even if he or she is the subject of an order of the court not to 'exclude' the other.[31] The remaining joint tenant may be able to demonstrate that the tenancy subsists if the notice was invalid due to failure to comply with contractual or statutory requirements: for example, the notice is ineffective if given in respect of a weekly tenancy for a shorter period than the four weeks prescribed by Protection From Eviction Act 1977 s5[32] or failing to expire at the end of a period of a periodic tenancy.[33] However, if the notice is valid the other joint tenant spouse or civil partner is not able to apply in matrimonial proceedings for the setting aside of disposal of the home in this way.[34] This is again because the giving of a notice is not a 'disposal' of family assets.[35]

2.25   The occupier who believes that a notice to quit may be given by his or her (former) partner, whether as joint or sole tenant, would be best advised to make a without notice application for an injunction to restrain the giving of such notice (see chapter 30). It has been suggested that such an injunction may be granted under the court's inherent jurisdiction in matrimonial matters or in proceedings

---

29 *Hammersmith & Fulham LBC v Monk* [1992] 1 AC 478; [1992] 3 WLR 1144; (1992) 24 HLR 207, HL approving *Greenwich LBC v McGrady* (1982) 6 HLR 36; 81 LGR 288, CA.

30 See *Crawley BC v Ure* [1996] QB 13; (1995) 27 HLR 524, CA, *Notting Hill Housing Trust v Brackley* [2001] EWCA Civ 601; [2002] HLR 10 CA. In respect of challenges to the procedure under the Human Rights Act 1998 and article 8 of the ECHR, see *Harrow LBC v Qazi* [2003] UKHL 43; [2004] 1 AC 983; (2003) HLR 75, *Bradney v Birmingham City Council, Birmingham City Council v McCann* [2003] EWCA Civ 1783; [2004] HLR 27 and *R (McCann) v Birmingham CC* [2004] EWHC (Admin) 2156. See also paras 5.31 onwards.

31 *Harrow LBC v Johnstone* [1997] 1 WLR 459; (1997) 29 HLR 475, HL

32 *Hounslow LBC v Pilling* [1993] 1 WLR.1242; [1994] 1 All ER 432, CA.

33 *Camden LBC v Lahouasnia* March 1998 *Legal Action* 12.

34 Matrimonial Causes Act 1973 s37.

35 *Newlon Housing Trust v Al-Sulaimen* [1999] 1 AC 313; [1998] 3 WLR 451; (1998) 30 HLR 1132, HL.

brought under Matrimonial Causes Act 1973 s37[36] or Children Act 1989 Sch 1 where there are children of the family.[37]

2.26   Once the notice to quit validly given by the sole or joint tenant has expired, the landlord can physically retake possession if the premises are empty. Otherwise, simple possession proceedings can be taken against anyone left in occupation (such as any former joint tenant). It is not open to that occupier to defend by impugning the motives of the landlord in recovering possession in such circumstances[38] unless exceptionally it may be argued that the landlord, as a public body, has acted unlawfully in bringing the proceedings: see paras 5.41–5.42.

Tenant dies [see also chapter 18: Death]

2.27   If one *joint tenant* dies, and the other remains in occupation, the tenancy devolves by survivorship and the last remaining joint tenant becomes a sole secure tenant by operation of law (albeit one treated as a 'successor' so that there can be no further succession on his or her own death).[39]

2.28   If a *sole tenant* (or the last remaining joint tenant) dies, neither the tenancy itself nor security of tenure automatically ends. If there is a person in occupation entitled to succeed the tenant – and the tenant was not him or herself a 'successor'[40] – the secure tenancy automatically vests in the successor: Housing Act 1985 s89(2).

2.29   In summary, those entitled to succeed are: (1) the spouse or civil partner[41] of the tenant; or (2) another member of the tenant's family. In both cases the successor must have been occupying the dwelling as his or her only or principal[42] home at the time of the tenant's death. In the case of family members other than spouses or civil partners, the potential successor must additionally have lived with the tenant throughout the 12-month period ending with the tenant's death.[43] The full 12 months need not have been spent in the property, succession

---

36 *Bater v Greenwich LBC* (2000) 32 HLR 127, CA.

37 *Re F (minors)* [1994] 1 WLR 370; (1993) 26 HLR 354, CA.

38 *Newham LBC v Hills* October 1998 *Legal Action* 22, CA.

39 HA 1985 s88(1)(b).

40 Defined in HA 1985 s88.

41 HA 1985 s87(a) as amended by Civil Partnership Act 2004 Sch 8 para 20.

42 *Peabody Donation Fund Governors v Grant* (1982) 6 HLR 41; (1982) 264 EG 925, CA.

43 HA 1985 s87(b); see *Camden LBC v Goldenberg* (1996) 28 HLR 727, CA and *Wandsworth LBC v Morgan* January 2000 *Legal Action* 25, CA.

to which is claimed.[44] The situation where there is more than one potential successor is dealt with by Housing Act 1985 s89(2).

2.30   The phrase 'member of the family' is defined by Housing Act 1985 s113 as amended by Civil Partnership Act 2004, Sch 8 para 27:

> 113(1) A person is a member of another's family within the meaning of this Part if –
>   (a) he is the spouse or civil partner of that person, or he and that person live together as husband and wife or as if they were civil partners, or
>   (b) he is that person's parent, grandparent, child, grandchild, brother, sister, uncle, aunt, nephew or niece.
> (2) For the purpose of subsection (1)(b) –
>   (a) a relationship by marriage or civil partnership shall be treated as a relationship by blood,
>   (b) a relationship of the half-blood shall be treated as a relationship of the whole blood,
>   (c) the stepchild of a person shall be treated as his child, and
>   (d) an illegitimate child shall be treated as the legitimate child of his mother and reputed father.

2.31   The list in s113 exhaustively defines the family members who may succeed.[45] It will be seen that Housing Act 1985 s113(1)(a) applies to a cohabitant of the deceased who has lived with the deceased in a cohabiting relationship, whether heterosexual or same sex, for at least 12 months.[46] Cousins[47] or foster children[48] are not in the prescribed list, but a minor who fulfils the statutory conditions can succeed to a tenancy in equity.[49]

2.32   Where there is no person entitled to succeed, security is lost[50] and the tenancy itself vests in the estate of the deceased. Thereafter it will be disposed of as a non-secure tenancy in the administration of the estate, usually by being surrendered to the landlord by the executors or administrator.[51] If the deceased tenant did not leave a will, the tenancy vests in the Public Trustee until such time as letters of administration are taken out by the next of kin: see chapter 18. However, special provision is made to deal with the situation which arises if a

44   *Waltham Forest LBC v Thomas* [1992] 2 AC 198; (1992) 24 HLR 622, HL.
45   *Michalak v Wandsworth LBC* [2002] EWCA Civ 282; [2003] 1 WLR 617.
46   *Westminster City Council v Peart* (1992) 24 HLR 389, CA.
47   *Brent LBC v Fofana* September 1999 *Legal Action* 28, CA,
48   *Sheffield CC v Wall* [2006] EWCA Civ 495; May 2006 *Legal Action* 31, CA.
49   *Kingston upon Thames RLBC v Prince* [1999] 1 FLR 593; (1999) 31 HLR 794, CA and *Newham LBC v Ria* [2004] EWCA Civ 41; and see para 1.24 above.
50   HA 1985 s89(3).
51   See M Lee, 'The periodic tenancy and death of a tenant' (1983) 80 LS Gaz 883.

court exercising family law jurisdiction has earlier directed what is to happen to the tenancy in the event of the tenant's death.[52]

2.33   Following the death of a tenant, disputes not infrequently arise between the landlord and occupiers who assert that they are entitled to succeed to the tenancy. In such cases, if the landlord is satisfied that there has been no statutory succession, it may determine the tenancy by notice to quit (by service of such notice on the executor or administrator or Public Trustee) and start ordinary possession proceedings against those left in occupation. (It would be unusual for the landlord to serve a notice seeking possession while asserting that the occupier has not become the secure tenant but each notice might be expressed to be served without prejudice to the other.) The occupier may then defend on the basis that he or she is a secure tenant having properly 'succeeded' the deceased tenant, in which case an adjournment of what appeared to be straightforward possession proceedings may be necessary.[53] Or, more unusually, occupiers may defend on the basis that since the death of the tenant they have been accepted as tenants in their own right, although the making and acceptance of payments while a disputed issue of succession is resolved are insufficient on their own to show an intention on the landlord's part to create a tenancy.[54] The burden of proof is on the occupier to establish the right to succeed, including the requirement that a family member has lived with the deceased tenant throughout the 12-month period before the latter's death.[55] The defendant claiming to have succeeded would be well advised to make arrangements to put aside sums equivalent to the rent or to make a claim for housing benefit because, if he or she is successful in establishing succession, he or she will be liable to pay the rent from the moment of death.

2.34   If the landlord admits that a succession has taken place but claims that the successor is under-occupying, see para 3.175.

2.35   If the landlord is asserting that the occupier is a trespasser (often described as an 'unauthorised occupier') it cannot simply rush into proceedings on the basis that it has a right to possession against the trespasser (see chapter 25). The occupier who is able to show, in such proceedings, that the deceased tenant's tenancy has not been properly

52 HA 1985 s89(3) as substituted by HA 1996 Sch 18 para 10 and as amended by the Civil Partnership Act 2004 Sch 8 and Sch 30.

53 *Camden LBC v Hall* March 1998 *Legal Action* 11, CA.

54 See *Hammersmith and Fulham LBC v Jastrebska* May 2001 *Legal Action* 22, ChD.

55 *Peabody Donation Fund Governors v Grant* (1982) 6 HLR 41; (1982) 264 EG 925, CA.

determined (for example, by service of notice on the executor/admin-istrator or the Public Trustee[56]) has a complete defence to the action.[57] Once the landlord has served an effective notice to quit on the person responsible for the deceased tenant's estate it may, if there is no occu-pier, simply take possession.

Absentee tenant

2.36   Absence from the property, however longstanding, does not of itself bring the *tenancy* to an end. However, the *security of tenure* of the secure tenant may be placed in jeopardy by long-term absences.

2.37   As already mentioned above (para 1.13) a secure tenancy remains secure only for so long as the tenant (or one of the joint tenants) 'occu-pies the dwelling-house as his only or principal home'.[58] A very pro-longed absence may indicate that the tenant no longer occupies the property as a home and thus the security may lapse. A landlord may seize the opportunity of such a lapse by serving a notice to quit to bring to an end the then insecure tenancy. For the requirements of a valid notice to quit, see paras 12.6–12.21.

2.38   There are several possible variations on the scenario of the absen-tee tenant.

The tenant has 'assigned' the tenancy to a new tenant and left

2.39   For discussion of this see para 2.64.

The tenant has sublet, or otherwise parted with possession of, the whole property to others

2.40   Here the security of tenure is brought to an end not only by the ten-ant's own failure to occupy but also by specific provision that sub-letting or parting with possession of the whole of the property let to the tenant causes loss of security.[59] This loss of security cannot be repaired by ousting the subtenants and returning to the property because Housing Act 1985 s93(2) provides that the tenancy cannot again become a secure tenancy.[60] Security may even be lost inadvert-

---

56   See the Public Trustee (Notices Affecting Land) (Title on Death) Regulations 1995 SI No 1330. As to service of such notice, see *Practice Direction (Probate: Notice to Quit)* [1995] 1 WLR 1120.

57   *Wirral BC v Smith and Cooper* (1982) 4 HLR 81, CA.

58   HA 1985 s81.

59   HA 1985 s93(2).

60   *Merton LBC v Salama* June 1989 *Legal Action* 25, CA.

ently by the unintentional creation of what is later held to be a true subtenancy.[61] Where there was evidence that all the rooms in a property were occupied by persons other than the tenant and her family, the court was entitled to conclude that there had been an unlawful subletting of the whole of the premises.[62]

2.41   If there has been a true subletting of the whole then security is plainly lost.[63] But it does not necessarily follow that, just because as a matter of fact the tenant is absent and others are in occupation, security has been lost by 'parting with possession'.[64] It may be that those in occupation are mere 'house-sitters' or other licensees simply taking care of the premises pending the return of the tenant and there has been no parting with possession at all.[65]

2.42   If the landlord considers there has been a parting with possession or subletting of the whole it may serve an ordinary notice to quit on the true tenant[66] and, once that has expired, start possession proceedings to recover possession against both the true tenant and the actual occupiers. If there is simply a suspicion that the tenant may have sublet, a letter before action seeking information about the true position may protect the landlord in costs if it is later unsuccessful in establishing full subletting.[67]

2.43   The position of any subtenants is considered at para 5.2.

The tenant is absent for a long period (but intends to return)

2.44   Most tenants are temporarily away from their homes from time to time – on holiday, receiving medical treatment, working away from home, and suchlike. Some tenants may be absent for long periods, perhaps many years, through working abroad, travelling, visiting relatives overseas, or otherwise. In such cases, furniture and other belongings are usually left in the property and in the case of prolonged absence a 'caretaker' (usually a friend or relative) may have been let into occupation to take care of the property and to ensure the rent is paid.

---

61 *Brent LBC v Cronin* (1998) 30 HLR 43, CA.

62 *Lambeth LBC v Vandra* February 2006 *Legal Action* 29.

63 *Muir Group Housing Association Ltd v Thornley* (1993) 25 HLR 89, CA.

64 *Hussey v Camden LBC* (1995) 27 HLR 5, CA.

65 *Basildon DC v Persson* September 1995 *Legal Action* 13 and *Islington LBC v LaMarque* September 1991 *Legal Action* 14.

66 Some landlords react to such situations by serving a notice seeking possession as well as ordinary notice to quit, each expressed to be without prejudice to the other.

67 *Brent LBC v Aniedobe* January 2000 *Legal Action* 25, CA.

2.45   However, long absences may give rise to the suggestion that security of tenure has been lost. The issue then is whether the tenant is still occupying the property in question as his or her principal home and thus satisfying the 'tenant condition' in Housing Act 1985 s81 (see para 1.13).

2.46   The true question is whether the absence is temporary, in the sense that the tenant intends to return, and whether that intention is manifest from the physical signs of readiness of the premises for reoccupation. The Court of Appeal has held that the correct approach in secure tenancy cases is to consider all the surrounding circumstances to determine whether those conditions are fulfilled. In *Crawley BC v Sawyer*,[68] a tenant was away from his home for over a year. The gas and electricity were disconnected. The tenant had moved in with his girlfriend and they intended to buy a property together. The council served notice to quit. The couple's relationship broke down and the tenant moved back to his home. The county court judge held that the council property had throughout remained his home and the tenant always intended to return. The Court of Appeal did not interfere with that finding.

2.47   In contrast, in *Jennings v Epping Forest DC*,[69] the tenants, an elderly couple in failing health, left their council home and took a flat near to their daughter's home. Once there, the husband's health deteriorated and he was admitted to a residential home. His wife stayed in the new flat to be near him. The trial judge (the point not being in issue in the appeal) had no difficulty in finding that security of tenure had been lost. There was no prospect of, or intention to, return to the original home.

2.48   The most common difficulties over long-term absence arise from: tenants going abroad for indeterminate periods to visit relatives or to travel; tenants serving terms of imprisonment; tenants receiving long-term hospital treatment;[70] and tenants moving into residential care homes.[71]

2.49   The case of the *prisoner* is relatively straightforward as he or she can be promptly located and usually asserts an intention to return even when serving a lengthy term.[72] The case of a very elderly or

---

68 (1988) 20 HLR 98, CA.

69 (1993) 25 HLR 241, CA.

70 See *McLoughlin's Curator Bonis v Motherwell* 1994 SLT (Lands Tr) 31.

71 *Hammersmith and Fulham LBC v Clarke* (2001) 33 HLR 77, CA.

72 See *Notting Hill Housing Trust v Etoria* April 1989 *Legal Action* 22, *Oldham MBC v Walker* January 1999 *Legal Action* 26 and *Amoah v Barking and Dagenham LBC* (2001) 81 P & CR D12; March 2001 *Legal Action* 28, ChD.

mentally ill tenant in a caring institution is more problematic, as it can be difficult to establish that he or she has both the intention and the prospect of returning to resume occupation (but see cases in the Rent Act context, discussed at para 14.9). There may well be difficulties with 'fleeting changes of mind' in such cases which makes a focus on the real or 'enduring' intention of the tenant all the more important.[73]

2.50   In the tenant's absence, the landlord may find either an apparently empty property or a 'caretaker' in occupation. A landlord wishing to recover possession may then serve an ordinary notice to quit on the absentee tenant (on the basis that security has lapsed) and physically recover possession – if there is no one in occupation – or start possession proceedings. (The landlord may face not inconsiderable difficulties in serving the true tenant with notice to quit – see para 2.62.) A tenant who can show that, notwithstanding prolonged 'temporary' absence, he or she continues to occupy the property as his or her principal home, retains security of tenure and may successfully defend the action or secure reinstatement.

2.51   For the position of a tenant clearly having two homes, see para 2.61.

The tenant has 'disappeared'

2.52   It is not unusual, particularly in serious rent arrears cases, for the landlord to find that the tenant has abandoned the premises leaving them vacant or with 'unauthorised' occupiers in possession. The landlord will want quickly to regularise the position and relet.

2.53   However, if the landlord commences proceedings to recover possession against the 'trespassers' (see chapter 25) too hastily, without first determining the tenancy at common law, the occupiers will have a complete defence to the action on the basis that the landlord does not have an immediate right to possession.[74]

2.54   In certain limited circumstances, it may be possible for the landlord to show that the tenant has, by his or her action, surrendered the tenancy, thus entitling the landlord to recover possession (see para 2.19). In order for this to be established the court must be satisfied that, at the very least, 'a tenant had left owing a very substantial sum of money and had been absent for a substantial time'.[75] The burden of proof is on the landlord.

---

73 *Hammersmith and Fulham LBC v Clarke* (2001) 33 HLR 77, CA.
74 *Preston BC v Fairclough* (1982) 8 HLR 72, CA.
75 Ibid, per Griffiths LJ at 73.

2.55   The courts have varied in their approach as to whether simple abandonment is sufficient, on the facts, to amount to an offer by the tenant to surrender, in the public sector. In *Preston BC v Fairclough*[76] the tenants had left another family in occupation but there was no evidence of the tenants' own date of departure or the amount of rent in arrears if any. The court held that surrender was not established. In *R v Croydon LBC ex p Toth*,[77] the premises had been left empty for several weeks, all furniture had been removed and £488 rent was outstanding. It was held that termination by surrender was made out when the landlord simply took possession of the empty flat.

2.56   If the landlord deals with a case of 'abandonment' by serving proper notice to quit, it may recover possession of the vacant property on expiry or commence summary proceedings for possession against any occupiers. The difficulties of serving notice on the absentee tenant are discussed at para 2.62.

The tenant has left a non-tenant spouse/civil partner/cohabitant in occupation

2.57   During a tenant's temporary absence or following a permanent departure, the presence of a spouse or registered civil partner in the property makes good the tenant's failure to occupy and is treated as occupation by him or her (see para 1.15).[78] That situation continues for so long as the parties are married or their civil partnership subsists and lasts up to decree absolute or dissolution order.

2.58   If the landlord successfully takes possession proceedings against the tenant on one of the Housing Act 1985 grounds (chapter 3) and an order for possession is made, the remaining spouse or civil partner (or indeed a former spouse or civil partner having rights of occupation) can apply to stay or suspend the order.[79]

2.59   Other cohabitants – whether heterosexual or same sex – may also be able to claim protection. Depending on the specific facts, they may argue that their occupation is indicative of the tenant's intention to return and thereby the security of the absent tenant's tenancy is preserved. Otherwise, former spouses and cohabitants can apply under the Family Law Act 1996 for court orders permitting them to occupy

---

76   Ibid.
77   (1988) 20 HLR 576, CA.
78   Matrimonial Homes Act 1983 s1(6) as amended by Housing (Consequential Provisions) Act 1985 Sch 2 para 56(2), and Family Law Act 1996 s30(4)(b) as amended by Civil Partnership Act 2004 Sch 9 para 1.
79   HA 1985 s85(5).

and any such order works as a 'deemed' occupation by the departed tenant (see, generally, chapter 30).[80] Under section 85(5A) of the Housing Act 1985 a former spouse or civil partner or cohabitant with an occupation order granted under sections 35 and 36 of the Family Law Act 1996 will have the same rights to intervene in possession proceedings against a secure tenant as those described above in relation to spouses and registered civil partners.

2.60   If a possession order has been granted and has ended the tenant's tenancy, a spouse or civil partner, former spouse or former civil partner, or cohabitant enjoying the rights described above could apply under Housing Act 1985 s85 to 'postpone' the date on which possession is to be given and so revive the tenancy (see para 4.70). That would then make the tenancy available for the purposes of an application in family law proceedings for it to be transferred into the applicant's name.

The tenant has two homes

2.61   The tenant loses the benefit of secure status in a dwelling if it is neither his or her only nor principal home.[81] It is a question of fact in relation to people having two homes, which of them is the principal home.[82] In *Sutton LBC v Swann*[83] the tenant of a council flat purchased another home. At the other home he registered as a residential customer with the telephone company, gave his new address to his bank and mortgage lenders, gave that address as his residence to the local police and had the address on his firearms certificate changed accordingly. The trial judge's finding that his council flat had ceased to be his 'principal' home was not disturbed by the Court of Appeal. The practical application of the tenant condition in Housing Act 1985 s81 to a two-home tenant is well demonstrated by a series of noted first-instance decisions.[84]

---

80 Family Law Act 1996 ss35(13)(a) and 36(13)(a) as amended by Civil Partnership Act 2004 Sch 9 para 6 and *Gay v Enfield and Sheeran* (1999) 31 HLR 1126, CA.

81 HA 1985 s81.

82 See Thompson, 'The two-home tenant' (1986) 83 LS Gaz 2073 and the case-law on the two-home tenant under the Rent Acts discussed at para 14.14.

83 (1985) 18 HLR 140, CA.

84 *Camden LBC v Coombs* March 1988 *Legal Action* 17, *Marsh v Lewisham LBC* December 1989 *Legal Action* 14, *Miller v Falkirk DC* 1990 SLT (Lands Tr) 111, *Roxburgh DC v Collins* 1991 SLT (Sh Ct) 49 and (1991) 8 GWD 483 and *Lambeth LBC v Gent* July 2001 *Legal Action* 32.

Notice to the absent tenant

2.62   If the tenancy has become insecure as a result of the failure to fulfil the tenant condition in any of the circumstances described above, the landlord may end the tenancy by service of a notice to quit.

2.63   At common law such a notice is only proved to have been served if the landlord can show actual personal delivery (to the tenant, his wife or 'servant') or that the notice has otherwise actually come to the attention of the tenant. Plainly, this can prove difficult if the whereabouts of the absent tenant are unknown. If the tenancy agreement expressly makes provision for service of notice to quit by simple delivery to the premises or in some other way then such notice may be effectively given in that way.[85] If there is no such provision in the agreement there is presently no alternative statutory basis for even a local authority landlord to serve such a notice to quit other than in one of the ways sufficient at common law (see also paras 4.36–4.40).[86]

Tenant assigns

2.64   Security of tenure may be threatened if the tenant seeks to transfer the whole tenancy to a third party. As seen above (at para 2.40), *subletting* of the whole property brings to an end the security of tenure of the tenant (although not the tenancy itself).[87] The same provision operates to deprive the tenancy of secure status if the tenant 'parts with possession' otherwise than by subletting. However, if the tenancy is effectively transferred by an assignment there is no subletting and no parting with possession. The new tenant is 'in possession'.

2.65   Housing Act 1985 s91 provides that except in prescribed cases the secure tenancy is not capable of *assignment* at all. The three prescribed cases are:

- assignment by way of mutual exchange (in these circumstances the strict provisions of Housing Act 1985 s92 and Sch 3 must be complied with);
- assignment pursuant to a property transfer order made under Matrimonial Causes Act 1973 s24, Matrimonial and Family Proceedings Act 1984 s17, Civil Partnership Act 2004 Sch 5 Part 2 or Sch 7 or Children Act 1989 Sch 1;

---

85   *Wandsworth LBC v Atwell* (1995) 27 HLR 536, CA.
86   *Enfield LBC v Devonish and Sutton* (1997) 29 HLR 691, CA.
87   HA 1985 s93(2).

- assignment to a person who would have been qualified to succeed to the tenancy if the tenant had died immediately before the assignment.

2.66 The prohibition is one of substance rather than form. Thus, where two joint tenants purport, by deed of release, to transfer the tenancy from joint names into the sole name of one of them, that will be an attempted assignment and will fail.[88]

2.67 If an assignment takes place in one of the prescribed circumstances, the assignee receives the full secure tenancy (notwithstanding any prohibition on assignment in the tenancy agreement itself).[89] The landlord can then obtain possession only by serving a notice seeking possession (see above) and commencing possession proceedings on one of the grounds applicable to a secure tenant. In *Peabody Donation Fund Governors v Higgins*, the tenant assigned the tenancy to his daughter, who was his potential successor. The landlord claimed possession on the basis that the assignment was in breach of a specific clause in its tenancy agreement which prohibited assignment without the landlord's consent. While accepting that the secure tenancy had been transferred to the assignee, the Court of Appeal left open whether the assignment would give rise to a ground for possession on the basis of a breach of obligation of the tenancy.[90]

2.68 However, in the above circumstances, there is considerable doubt whether it is open to a landlord to grant a secure tenancy subject to a covenant against any one of the three classes of statutorily permitted assignment, since such a covenant arguably offends the Unfair Terms in Consumer Contracts Regulations 1999.[91] In any event, it is unlikely that the court in its discretion would consider it reasonable to enforce a tenancy condition which appears to be at variance with the statutory purpose.

---

88 *Burton v Camden LBC* (2000) 32 HLR 625, HL.
89 *Peabody Donation Fund Governors v Higgins* [1983] 1 WLR 1091; [1983] 3 All ER 122; (1983) 10 HLR 82, CA.
90 Ibid.
91 SI No 2083. The Regulations apply to tenancy agreements: *R (on the application of Khatun and others) v Newham LBC and Office of Fair Trading* [2004] EWCA Civ 55; [2005] QB 37; [2004] HLR 29. See also Office of Fair Trading, Guidance on unfair terms in tenancy agreements, OFT 356, September 2005 and Holbrook, 'Unfair terms in housing contracts' September 1999 *Legal Action* 26.

2.69   If the assignment is not made within the permitted three classes or the purported assignment is ineffective (for example, because no deed of assignment was used[92]), the tenancy is not transferred.

2.70   If the true tenant has left and the assigment was ineffective, the assignee will be without any right to occupy. He or she will be able to remain only until the landlord has taken the appropriate steps to recover possession. The landlord must first determine properly the tenancy of the original tenant (normally by service of a valid notice to quit, since the tenancy will no longer be secure) and then take proceedings for possession against the assignee as a trespasser.

---

92 *Croydon LBC v Bustin and Triance* (1991) 24 HLR 36, CA, *Newham LBC v Bennett* [1984] CLY 1960 (both cases of ineffective transfer from mother to son) and *Crago v Julian* [1992] 1 WLR 372, CA (spouse to spouse).

CHAPTER 3

Grounds for possession against secure occupiers

continued

Introduction

3.1 A landlord can bring a secure tenancy or secure licence to an end only by successful application to a court.[1] The prerequisite of an action to recover possession is service of a notice seeking possession in the pre-scribed form unless the court is prepared retrospectively to dispense with service of such a notice (see paras 4.11–4.42).[2]

3.2 The landlord brings the action for possession in the local county court (using Civil Procedure Rules (CPR) Part 55) as no costs can be recovered if the claim is started in the High Court.[3] The process starts with the issue of a claim form and particulars of claim (see chapter 21 for a full description of the procedure). Proceedings must be issued at a time when the notice seeking possession is still effec-tive (see para 4.32).

3.3 At the hearing of the claim the landlord must show that the neces-sary ground (or grounds) and conditions are made out. Before consid-ering these matters and the substantive merits, the court must also be satisfied about a number of technical issues (for example, that the notice was properly served). These are dealt with at para 4.10.

3.4 In this chapter references to secure tenancies also include secure licences unless the contrary is stated.

Possession by consent

3.5 The concept of a 'consent order' is not applicable in the case of secure tenants or licensees. Housing Act 1985 s84(1) prevents the making of any form of possession order until the court is satisfied that a ground and a condition for ordering possession are made out. The court can only be so satisfied if it hears the evidence or is presented with express admissions by the tenant.[4] For these purposes simple assent to a suspended possession order is not an admission of the landlord's grounds and any such order obtained 'by consent' will be set aside.[5] If

---

1   HA 1985 s82(1).
2   HA 1985 s83(1).
3   HA 1985 s110(3).
4   *Wandsworth LBC v Fadayomi* (1987) 19 HLR 512; [1987] 3 All ER 474, CA and see *R v Bloomsbury and Marylebone County Court ex p Blackburne* (1985) 2 EGLR 157, CA. Even where specific admissions have been made as to the facts, the issue of reasonableness must be specifically considered: see *Cobalt Housing Ltd v Devine* January 2005 *Legal Action* 28, Liverpool County Court.
5   *Hounslow LBC v McBride* (1999) 31 HLR 143, CA.

the tenant was present at the hearing, setting aside may be achieved either on appeal or on an application for judicial review.[6] However, once the hearing has started and evidence has been given, the tenant may, by agreeing to a consent order, impliedly admit that the grounds and conditions are made out on the evidence the court has heard.[7] If the tenant was not present at the hearing, application to set aside the order may be made under CPR 39.3.

Grounds and conditions

3.6   Once the court is seised of the matter (in the sense that all the technical requirements scrutinised in chapter 4 have been met) it must first be satisfied that a ground for possession is made out. Housing Act 1985 s84(1) provides that:

> The court shall not make an order for the possession of a dwelling-house let under a secure tenancy except on one or more of the grounds set out in Schedule 2.

3.7   If a ground within Housing Act 1985 Sch 2 cannot be established the proceedings must inevitably be dismissed. Each of the grounds is separately considered below (paras 3.10 onwards). The burden of proof is throughout on the landlord to show that the ground is made out on the balance of probabilities. Even if satisfied that a ground is made out, possession is not to be ordered unless the particular ground has been specified in the notice seeking possession (which was served before the proceedings were commenced) or the need for a notice seeking possession has been dispensed with. The routes available to a landlord who makes out an alternative ground are either (1) to seek permission of the court to amend the notice seeking possession to embrace the new ground,[8] or (2) to abandon the proceedings and serve a new notice seeking possession based on the new ground (perhaps with the intention of then consolidating the new proceedings with the current proceedings)[9] or (3) to seek permission of the court to dispense with the requirement for a notice seeking possession altogether.[10]

---

6   *R v Birmingham CC ex p Foley* March 2001 *Legal Action* 29, QBD (Admin Ct).

7   *R v Worthing BC ex p Bruce* (1994) 26 HLR 223, CA and *Morris v Barnet LBC* December 1995 *Legal Action* 18, CA.

8   HA 1985 s84(3).

9   *City of London v Devlin* (1997) 29 HLR 58, CA.

10   HA 1985 s83(1)(b). See para 4.41 below.

3.8 Furthermore, no order for possession may be made simply because a ground for possession has been established. The landlord must also prove that relevant conditions are made out. Each ground for possession carries with it a condition or set of conditions which must be satisfied before possession is ordered. Indeed, Housing Act 1985 s84(2) provides:

> (2) The court shall not make an order for possession –
> (a) on the grounds set out in Part I of that Schedule (grounds 1 to 8), unless it considers it reasonable to make the order,
> (b) on the grounds set out in Part II of that Schedule (grounds 9 to 11), unless it is satisfied that suitable accommodation will be available for the tenant when the order takes effect,
> (c) on the grounds set out in Part III of that Schedule (grounds 12 to 16), unless it both considers it reasonable to make the order and is satisfied that suitable accommodation will be available for the tenant when the order takes effect;
> and Part IV of that Schedule has effect for determining whether suitable accommodation will be available for a tenant.

3.9 Each of these conditions is considered below in relation to the relevant ground. If the landlord cannot show on the balance of probabilities that the conditions are satisfied, the claim for possession will be dismissed even though the grounds have been proved.

Ground 1 (first limb): rent arrears

3.10 This is the most common ground on which possession is sought against secure occupiers. The first part of ground 1 of Housing Act 1985 Sch 2 will be satisfied only if the landlord proves that 'rent lawfully due from the tenant has not been paid'.

3.11 In order to recover possession the landlord must also satisfy the court that the appropriate condition is met – in this case that it is reasonable to make the order.[11] Each element of both the ground and condition have to be proved to the satisfaction of the court.

The ground

3.12 In the usual case, the landlord proves the ground by putting in evidence of the rent payable under the tenancy agreement, particulars of

---

11 HA 1985 s84(2)(a).

the current rent due, the record of payments made by the tenant and copies of demands made for payments of arrears.[12]

3.13   For the purpose of preparing a defence to such proceedings, almost every word of ground 1 requires careful consideration.

'rent'

3.14   The rent in question is the rent due in respect of the relevant property. However, the term 'rent' is not defined in Housing Act 1985 Pt IV. It is suggested that 'rent' for these purposes does not include – in the absence of express provision to the contrary – service charges, water rates,[13] other amenity payments, insurance premiums, overpaid housing benefit or any other indebtedness which is not strictly rent.[14]

3.15   In addition to collecting basic 'rent', public sector landlords have a tendency to use the rent payment system to collect a variety of charges from tenants ranging from fees for communal TV aerials to tenants' association membership subscriptions, and from rent for separate garages to heating charges. It must be doubted whether all or any of these charges can properly be said to be part of the 'rent' for the premises let unless so described or defined expressly in the tenancy agreement.

3.16   On the other hand, in the Rent Act jurisdiction, where the amount of 'rent' has historically been crucial to the existence of security of tenure at all, courts have inclined to the view that 'rent' embraces the total monetary payment made to the landlord.[15] In *Dudley MBC v Bailey*[16] it was hoped that the Court of Appeal would provide an authoritative definition of 'rent' in the context of a public sector tenancy. However, the council in that case conceded that general rates owed by the tenant and normally collected with the rent were not part

---

12   See the requirement for a schedule of arrears in the particulars of claim: CPR PD 55 para 2.3.

13   The opportunity to determine finally whether water rates were part of rent arose in *Lambeth LBC v Thomas* (1998) 30 HLR 89, CA, but was not taken by the Court of Appeal although that court gave a strong indication that it would have found that 'rent' included water rates had it been necessary to decide the question.

14   See Ann McAllister and Siobhan McGrath, 'Grounds for possession: rent lawfully due' Parts 1–3 in December 1985 *Legal Action* 169, January 1986 *Legal Action* 9 and February 1986 *Legal Action* 21.

15   *Sidney Trading Co v Finsbury Corp* [1952] 1 All ER 460 at 461 and *Markworth v Hellard* [1921] 2 KB 755.

16   (1990) 22 HLR 424, CA.

of the rent and the case turned on other issues. The concession was in line with earlier decisions in the lower courts.[17] A subsequently noted county court decision has preferred the Rent Act 'total indebtedness' approach[18] and that is likely to be the approach most attractive to the Court of Appeal when the issue arises directly for determination.[19]

'lawfully due'

3.17   Rent must be lawfully due from the tenant. It is therefore open to the tenant to assert in a defence that the rent has been improperly fixed or increased and that accordingly the amount claimed is not 'lawfully' due. That involves a careful consideration of the contractual provisions for rent and rent increases in the tenancy agreement. Where the landlord is a local housing authority there may properly be an assertion that in breach of its statutory duty the council has not fixed a reasonable rent.[20] Although this is a straightforward assertion to make, it is exceptionally difficult to prove.[21] A successful defence of not 'lawfully' due may be raised if the rent increase was based on some misinterpretation by the landlord of the relevant housing finance legislation (as in *R v Ealing LBC ex p Lewis*[22]).

3.18   Similarly, the rent claimed is not lawfully due if the landlord has failed to observe any contractual or statutory requirements as to notice of increase.[23] Such requirements are strictly construed.[24] Furthermore, rent cannot normally be lawfully increased on account of any improvement work by the tenant.[25] In the case of a secure housing association tenant with a registered fair rent, the maximum rent recoverable will be that so registered. Any excess will not be 'lawfully due'.

3.19   Likewise, a rent is not payable and accordingly not lawfully due unless the landlord has given an address for service of notices in accordance with Landlord and Tenant Act 1987 s48 (see para 15.12) although the outstanding rent will immediately become lawfully due on the provision of such an address.

---

17 See *Trafford BC v Mullings* March 1990 *Legal Action* 12.

18 *Lewisham LBC v Simba-Tola* June 1993 *Legal Action* 14.

19 See *Lambeth LBC v Thomas* (1998) 30 HLR 89, CA.

20 HA 1985 s24. See *Wandsworth LBC v Winder (No 1)* [1985] AC 461; (1985) 17 HLR 196, HL.

21 *Wandsworth LBC v Winder (No 2)* (1987) 20 HLR 400, CA.

22 (1992) 24 HLR 484, QBD.

23 HA 1985 s102.

24 *Clements & O'Boyle v Brent LBC* March 1990 *Legal Action* 12.

25 HA 1985 s101.

'from the tenant'

3.20   Only the rent due from the tenant is relevant. Any rent owed by a previous occupier, former tenant or spouse/civil partner/cohabitant of the current tenant is irrelevant. For example, in *Notting Hill Housing Trust v Jones*[26] the defendant had received the secure tenancy on its transfer to her from her former husband pursuant to an order made in family proceedings. He owed arrears of rent. The tenant agreed to clear those arrears by instalments. Thereafter, she paid her current rent but failed to clear the arrears. The Trust brought possession proceedings based on non-payment of the old 'arrears'. The Court of Appeal dismissed the proceedings – the amount outstanding was not rent due from the present tenant, the defendant.

3.21   Likewise, a defendant who takes the tenancy by way of statutory succession following the death of the tenant or by an assignment starts with a 'clean slate' for the purpose of possession proceedings as against the present landlord and is only liable for rent accruing from the date of succession or assignment.[27] It should be noted, however, that any one of a number of joint tenants may be sued for the whole rent due from the commencement of their joint tenancy. There is no legal concept of one joint tenant's 'part' or 'proportion' of the rent.

'has not been paid'

3.22   If all arrears are cleared before the issue of proceedings, the court is not able to order possession under ground 1.[28] This is so, even though the landlord may prove that there were arrears as at the date of the notice seeking possession or that there is a history of poor payment. The landlord cannot seek to avoid this consequence by refusing to accept or by returning payments tendered shortly before the issue of proceedings even if they are substantially late.[29] There is no freestanding ground for possession in the case of secure tenants comparable to that available against assured tenants in Housing Act 1988 Sch 2 ground 11 (persistent late payment).

3.23   If arrears were outstanding at the date of issue of the proceedings but are cleared before the hearing or on the hearing date, the court

26 [1999] L & TR 397, CA.
27 *Tickner v Clifton* [1929] 1 KB 207, CA.
28 *Bird v Hildage* [1948] 1 KB 91, CA.
29 Ibid.

may still find the ground made out but is unlikely also to be satisfied that it is reasonable to make the order (see below).[30]

3.24   In spite of apparent arrears shown on the (often computer-generated) rent account, it may be that there are in fact no true arrears of rent or only a lesser amount than that shown. A number of possibilities should be carefully checked.

3.25   First, the tenant may have made payments not in fact recorded as received. These may either be very recent payments that had not reached the rent account by the date it was printed or earlier payments that the landlord has attributed to the wrong account. Many large landlords have an account holding substantial amounts in 'unattributed' receipts from current or former tenants. Second, the housing benefit authority (which might also be the landlord) may have awarded and paid housing benefit (see chapter 32) which has not been credited to the account. If the landlord is the benefit authority, the effect of an award of housing benefit will have been to 'rebate' the rent (ie, reduce the amount of it) whether or not the reduced level of rent has actually been adjusted on the rent account. Third, if the tenant has been having deductions made from welfare benefits by the Department for Work and Pensions (see para 3.40) those monies deducted may have been received by the landlord direct from the benefits office, but not yet applied to the account. Such 'direct deductions' are usually paid in a lump sum every 4 weeks in arrears. Fourth, the landlord may be charging an incorrect (higher) rent than that actually payable under the tenancy. All these possibilities repay careful consideration.

3.26   It is important to note that entitlement to housing benefit does not, of itself, serve to reduce or eliminate liability for rent. It is only when such benefit is awarded by the benefit authority, and (if the rent is not a rebated council rent) actually paid to the landlord, that liability for rent is satisfied (see paras 32.14–32.16). From that point in time the rent will have been 'paid' even if there is an administrative delay in attributing it to the particular tenant's rent account. If the landlord is the benefit authority itself, 'payment' is made by rebating the rent otherwise payable and showing only a net amount to be paid as rent. It appears from the forms of 'payment' in Social Security Administration Act 1992 s134(2) that the tenant's liability for the rent is satisfied by such a rebate, even if the local authority subsequently decides that there has been an overpayment of housing benefit. If the authority debits the amount of the overpaid housing benefit to

---

30 *Dellenty v Pellow* [1951] 2 KB 858, CA and *Haringey LBC v Stewart* (1991) 23 HLR 557, CA.

the rent account, this sum should not be treated as rent arrears and should be kept separate in the account. However, the council may recover the overpayment by weekly deductions from current housing benefit entitlement, so that the tenant will have to make up the shortfall in the rent from other resources.[31] Where the secure tenant of a registered social landlord has been overpaid housing benefit, and the overpayment has been recovered directly from the landlord, the landlord may seek to debit the amount of the overpayment to the tenant's rent account, with the result that the tenant will be placed in rent arrears and will be vulnerable to possession proceedings: see para 32.16.

3.27   However, there are other respects in which housing benefit issues may arise in ground 1 possession claims. First, delay in payment of benefit to the landlord by the benefit authorities is, of course, material in considering the reasonableness condition (see para 3.31). Second, delay by the landlord in processing the benefit claim – where the landlord is also the benefit authority – is likewise relevant to reasonableness. Third, 'arrears' may in fact have arisen where, after satisfaction of the rent liability by payment or credit of housing benefit, the benefit authority (which may or may not also be the landlord) has been advised of or discovered an overpayment and improperly sought to recover the overpayment by adjusting the tenant's rent account. It was previously arguable, in such a case, that there were no arrears of rent as the rent had already been paid[32] but the position would appear to have been settled by amendments to the Housing Benefit Regulations made in April 1997 and now incorporated in the consolidated Housing Benefit Regulations 2006, at least in relation to rent allowance payments (see further para 32.16).

3.28   It is strongly arguable that a court should delay considering whether or not a possession order should be made until outstanding housing benefit issues have been resolved since it is not possible to consider whether or not it is reasonable to make a possession order until the true figure for arrears is known. If it is the benefit authority itself claiming possession, it cannot expect the repeated indulgence of the court in granting adjournments while the benefit position is resolved. The court might well strike out a case in which the tenant had done everything he or she could to resolve a housing benefit problem but the landlord authority itself was not in a position to explain

---

31   Housing Benefit Regulations 2006 SI No 213 reg 102.

32   See *Thamesmead Town v Mighty* March 1998 *Legal Action* 12, *Church Commissioners v Akindele* March 1998 *Legal Action* 12 and *Hyde Housing Association v Brown* October 1999 *Legal Action* 24.

clearly what the true rent outstanding was.[33] It is, however, not for the judge in possession proceedings to determine entitlement to housing benefit.[34]

3.29   Even if there is prima facie an amount of rent owing, that may be matched or exceeded by an amount which the tenant is entitled to set off, for example, the cost of repair work which the tenant has had to undertake in response to the landlord's default in undertaking repairs or the damages awarded on a counterclaim.[35] Such a set-off will act as a complete defence to the claim for rent. These possibilities are discussed further at para 4.47.

3.30   If a landlord fails to prove any element of ground 1, proceedings founded solely on that ground must be dismissed.

The condition

3.31   Even if the court is satisfied that there has been a failure to pay rent lawfully due, it cannot make a possession order of any description (including a 'suspended' or 'postponed' order) unless also satisfied that in all the circumstances of the case it would be reasonable to do so.[36]

3.32   In such cases, if there is no evidence as to why it is reasonable for possession to be granted over and above the ordinary relief of a money judgment for the outstanding amount due, any form of possession order must be resisted. The tenant could invite the court to dismiss the possession claim but enter a judgment for a money claim made by the landlord, if the amount of the arrears claimed is agreed or has been proved. This gives the landlord the satisfaction of an order against the tenant in default, but it is arguable that no order for costs should be made against the tenant as a money claim could have been brought by ordinary small claim rather than by possession proceedings.

3.33   However, if the landlord contends that it would be reasonable to order possession, then in applying the 'reasonableness' test the court is required to have regard to all relevant factors. These will include the duration of the tenancy, the past rent record of the tenant, whether

33   *Lambeth LBC v Tagoe* August 2000 *Legal Action* 24.

34   *Southwark LBC v Kofi-Adu* [2006] EWCA Civ 281; May 2006 *Legal Action* 32.

35   See the 'forensic disaster' (of commencement of arrears possession proceedings against a tenant who then recovered over £50,000 on her counterclaim for damages for disrepair) in *Brent LBC v Carmel Murphy* (1996) 28 HLR 203, CA.

36   HA 1985 s84(2)(a).

the failure to pay rent is persistent, whether there have been earlier agreements to clear arrears, the conduct of the landlord in seeking or waiving amounts due and the personal circumstances of the tenant. *Woodspring DC v Taylor*[37] provides a good example of the application of these principles. The Court of Appeal held that it was not appropriate for an order to be made against long-standing tenants with a previous good rent record presently in financial difficulties, even though arrears of over £700 (in 1982) were proved. Where the root cause of the arrears of rent is the low income of the defendant, the court will need to consider the availability of, and entitlement to, social security benefits. In *Second WRVS Housing Society v Blair*[38] the Court of Appeal set aside an order for possession made against a young, single man who owed £1,200 rent (in 1985) and had been a tenant for only eight years. The county court judge had not adequately considered: (a) the possibility of arranging direct payment to the landlord of current rent from the housing benefit authorities; (b) the possibility of the social security office deducting small amounts from the tenant's welfare benefits and paying them direct to the landlord towards the arrears; and (c) the tenant's medical condition.

3.34   The Protocol for Possession Claims based on Rent Arrears (drafted by the Civil Justice Council) is in force from 2 October 2006 (see the CPR Practice Direction amendments, 42nd update). The text of the Protocol is set out in full in appendix D. The Protocol is a critical document for both the parties and the court in relation to any action for possession brought by a social landlord on the basis of rent arrears.

3.35   The aim of the Rent Arrears Protocol is to encourage more pre-action contact between the parties and to enable court time to be used effectively. The Protocol requires landlords to –

- contact the tenant as soon as reasonably possible once he or she falls into arrears to discuss the cause of the arrears, the tenant's financial circumstances, his or her entitlement to benefits and repayment of the arrears;
- attempt to agree an affordable sum for the tenant to pay off the arrears and (where appropriate) assist in arranging for direct payments to be made towards the arrears from the tenant's benefit entitlement;
- provide the tenant with a full rent statement;
- take reasonable steps to ensure that information has been appropriately communicated;

37   (1982) 4 HLR 95, CA.
38   (1986) 19 HLR 104, CA.

- assist the tenant in connection with his or her claim for housing benefit and establish effective liaison with the housing benefit department;
- refrain from taking possession action where the tenant has a reasonable expectation of eligibility for housing benefit and has provided all the evidence necessary for the claim to be processed;
- contact the tenant before the court hearing to discuss the current position with regard to the arrears and housing benefit;
- postpone the court proceedings where the tenant has reached an agreement to pay the current rent and arrears, so long as the tenant keeps to the agreement; and
- encourage the tenant to attend the court hearing.

3.36   If a landlord unreasonably fails to comply with the terms of the protocol the court may impose a sanction or sanctions in the form of costs and/or adjournment of the proceedings, or may strike out or dismiss the claim. If the tenant unreasonably fails to comply with the terms of the protocol, the court may take such failure into account when considering whether it is reasonable to make a possession order.

3.37   In addition, social landlords are expected to abide by guidance issued by central government or (in the case of registered social landlords) by the Housing Corporation in formulating their policies on taking possession proceedings. As far as local authorities are concerned, extensive good practice guidance has been published by the Department for Communities and Local Government (*Improving the Effectiveness of Rent Arrears Management*, June 2005, available at www.dclg.gov.uk). This document 'sets out the Government's view, supported by Housing Corporation guidance, which emphasises that social landlords should seek to maintain and sustain tenancies rather than terminate them, and that eviction should only be used as a last resort'. The guidance states that landlords can and should actively assist tenants with claims for housing benefit, including helping them to complete forms. Local authority housing officers should work with housing benefit colleagues to establish access to information systems and case records. Tenants should never be served with a notice seeking possession where there are unresolved housing benefit claims, unless it is clear that this is due to the tenant's failure to supply necessary information or unless the tenant is failing to pay personal contributions. The court's attention should be drawn to the guidance where the landlord's practices do not meet these standards or where proceedings have been brought without trying other methods of rent recovery.

3.38   In resisting rent arrear possession claims brought by *registered social landlords*, advisers may usefully refer to the Housing Corporation's Regulatory Circular 07/04 entitled *Tenancy Management: Eligibility and Evictions*. Section 3 of the circular contains clarification of the Corporation's expectations concerning evictions, in similar vein to the local authority guidance (reproduced at para 10.73 below). Reference may also be made to the Housing Corporation's *Performance Standards for Registered Social Landlords* for their constructive guidance on tackling rent arrears with measures short of possession proceedings. Although these documents only have statutory effect as 'guidance', the Housing Corporation expects them to be observed. Failure to follow these policies and procedures may be helpful on the question of the 'reasonableness' of the landlord's claim to possession.

3.39   Where the rent has been *withheld* because the amount due or outstanding is genuinely disputed, or because the tenant has a legitimate grievance over disrepair, the court would not usually find it reasonable to make an order, but is more likely to adjourn the proceedings with directions (for example, that a defence and counterclaim be entered in respect of the dispute or alleged repairing default). In *Haringey LBC v Stewart*,[39] the tenant withheld rent on account of alleged disrepair. At trial, his counterclaim for damages for disrepair was dismissed. In relation to the possession claim the tenant was then unable to repay the withheld rent amounting to over £1,000 (because it had been spent rather than set aside) and made no proposals as to payment of current rent and payment of the arrears. The Court of Appeal declined to interfere with a decision that it was reasonable to make an outright possession order.

3.40   Public landlords frequently bring possession proceedings in respect of rent arrears owed by tenants on very low incomes, including those on welfare benefits. The key issues on reasonableness in such cases are likely to be:

- Why did the landlord (if not itself a housing benefit authority) not arrange direct payment of housing benefit from the benefit authority to meet current rent, either with the tenant's consent or (once eight weeks' worth of arrears had accrued) as of right?[40]
- Why did the landlord not arrange with the Department for Work and Pensions the deduction at source of a small amount from the

---

39 (1991) 23 HLR 557, CA.
40 Housing Benefit Regulations 2006 SI No 213 regs 95–96 and see para 32.18.

tenant's welfare benefit to pay off the arrears[41] instead of bringing possession proceedings?

- Whether the landlord could have offered advice and assistance with claiming benefits, maximising other income and debt control and failed to do so.
- The fact that even if only a postponed possession order is made, the tenancy may, depending on the form of the order, automatically be lost on any breach of the payment terms (see paras 4.59–4.66).[42]

3.41   The most powerful submission available in such a case is that the tenant is paying (and is willing to keep paying) current rent and is paying (and willing to keep paying) whatever can reasonably be afforded towards the arrears. Where such a submission can be joined with an assertion that the arrears are in part the result of genuine housing benefit problems, possession is unlikely to be ordered.[43] Indeed, in these and other situations where the tenant is making genuine efforts to reduce the arrears, or where there have been difficulties with housing benefit, the court should be asked to consider granting a general adjournment of the claim, on the basis that it is not necessary, and therefore cannot be reasonable, to make any order for possession in these circumstances. The landlord may argue that it needs the potential sanction of a postponed possession order to secure continuing payment. However, unless the tenant has a history of broken arrangements to pay, the court may well accept that the landlord's interests are sufficiently protected by having liberty to restore the proceedings in the event of the tenant's breach of the terms of an adjournment; and that a postponed possession order would itself be a disproportionate response, bearing in mind the consequences of such an order (see paras 4.50–4.52).

3.42   A good example of the courts' approach to public sector possession claims for arrears of rent is afforded by *Brent LBC v Marks*.[44] In that case the tenant, having earlier fallen into arrears, was receiving housing benefit by way of rent rebate in respect of almost all her rent. The shortfall (water rates), together with a weekly sum of £2.50 in respect of the arrears, were, from September 1996, being deducted at source from her welfare benefits and paid over quarterly in arrears to

---

41   Social Security (Claims and Payments) Regulations 1987 SI No 1968 reg 35 and Sch 9.

42   See *Thompson v Elmbridge BC* [1987] 1 WLR 1425.

43   *Islington LBC v LaMarque* September 1991 *Legal Action* 14.

44   (1999) 31 HLR 343, CA.

the council landlord. In January 1997 the council served notice seeking possession and claimed possession under ground 1. In June 1997, HHJ Krikler granted possession suspended on payment of current rent plus £2.50 per week to meet the arrears of £1,500. On appeal, the Court of Appeal set the order aside and remitted the matter for rehearing. As it was clear that the social security office was paying the deducted amounts quarterly in arrears, the terms of the order requiring weekly payment unnecessarily put the tenant at risk of breach of the order. The relevant material about the history of the reduction of the arrears had not been properly put before the judge. As to the retrial, Butler-Sloss LJ indicated that the first main matter for the judge to deal with would be 'whether there should be an order for possession at all'. The council failed to recover its costs both in the county court and Court of Appeal.

3.43   The case also illustrates that in the public sector, if a possession order for arrears is to be made at all, an order may be postponed on terms requiring payment by the tenant of small instalments towards the arrears over a very long period. In *Lambeth LBC v Henry*[45] the Court of Appeal declined to set aside a suspended order made on terms as to payment of arrears by instalments which would need to run for over 20 years in order to clear the arrears.

3.44   Where a tenant has had difficulty in managing his or her financial affairs owing to a mental illness, he or she may be able to raise a defence under the Disability Discrimination Act 1995: see para 3.94.

Ground 1 (second limb): other breach of the tenancy agreement

3.45   Ground 1 of Housing Act 1985 Sch 2 further provides that (subject to it being reasonable in all the circumstances to grant possession) an order for possession can be made if 'an obligation of the tenancy has been broken or not performed'.

3.46   One of the most common obligations relied upon in such cases is the obligation in the tenancy agreement to pay additional sums together with the rent, such as water rates.[46] However, the obligation which is relied upon by the landlord must arise from an express or implied term of the tenancy agreement itself, and not from some col-

---

45   (2000) 32 HLR 874, CA.
46   *Lambeth LBC v Thomas* (1998) 30 HLR 89, CA.

lateral agreement (for example, the separate renting of a garage or a free-standing agreement to clear a previous tenant's arrears of rent[47]). A failure to comply with the conditions attached to a separate grant of permission to carry out improvements is, however, specifically brought within ground 1.[48]

3.47 The term breached must be a term of the tenancy itself, not a matter of mere personal obligation on the part of the tenant. On this basis landlords are unable to use this ground in respect of such matters as failure to comply with requirements to remain in the landlord's employment[49] or to participate in counselling, treatment or resettlement programmes.[50]

3.48 In preparing the defence, the tenancy terms should be carefully checked to see whether the term relied on by the landlord is in fact a term of the agreement applicable to the tenant's present tenancy. Public sector landlords often produce to the court the 'current version' of their standard tenancy agreement. However, the true tenancy agreement is the one originally entered into by the tenant, subject to the statutory procedure for variation.[51] A variation cannot be achieved simply by sending the tenant a 'fresh' tenancy agreement, even if after having received such a document the tenant remains in occupation and pays the rent.[52]

3.49 Once the correct document has been identified it is necessary to check the precise wording to see whether the conduct alleged against the tenant has actually been prohibited by the agreement.[53]

3.50 Additionally, the term relied upon by the landlord should be scrutinised carefully to see whether it is 'fair' for the purposes of the Unfair Terms in Consumer Contracts Regulations 1999. Useful guidance as to 'fairness' in this context is provided by the Office of Fair Trading in its *Guidance on Unfair Terms in Tenancy Agreements* (OFT 356, September 2005). If the term is unfair the court should reject any attempt to rely on it in ground 1 proceedings.[54]

---

47 *Notting Hill Housing Trust v Jones* [1999] 1 L & TR 397, CA.

48 HA 1985 s99(4).

49 *RMR Housing Society v Combs* [1951] 1 KB 486, CA.

50 *Paddington Churches Housing Association v Boateng* January 1999 *Legal Action* 27.

51 HA 1985 ss102 and 103.

52 *Palmer v Sandwell MBC* (1988) 20 HLR 74, CA and *Carolan and Hamnett v Warrington BC* June 2000 *Legal Action* 24.

53 *Lewisham LBC v Simba-Tola* (1992) 24 HLR 644, CA.

54 *R (Khatun Zeb and Iqbal) v Newham LBC* [2005] QB 37; [2004] HLR 29, CA, *Camden LBC v McBride* January 1999 *Legal Action* 26. See also Jon Holbrook, 'Unfair Terms in Housing Contracts' September 1999 *Legal Action* 26.

3.51 Many public landlords have in recent years introduced provisions into tenancy agreements which expressly prohibit acts of anti-social behaviour, domestic violence or racial harassment.[55]

3.52 Some public landlords have included among the obligations of their tenants a requirement to desist from any criminal activity (especially drug-dealing) at the premises let. This allows possession to be claimed even if the tenant is not actually convicted of an offence (in which case ground 2 below could have been relied upon). Any allegation of a criminal act needs to be made out on a higher than normal standard of proof, but if it is made out the usual order will be for possession.[56]

3.53 Another common provision is the prohibition contained in some tenancy agreements against the keeping of pets or other animals on the premises let. Proceedings under ground 1 based on this particular breach provide a good illustration of the distinction between the ground for possession and the reasonableness requirement. The tenant may well admit clear and continuing breach of the agreement by keeping an 'animal companion' but an order may be refused because in the particular circumstances it would not be reasonable to order possession (notwithstanding that the tenant intends to continue keeping the pet at the premises).[57] This may be the case particularly if there is good medical or social evidence of the effect that loss of the animal companion will have on the tenant.[58] In the absence of any such evidence, however, the court is likely to take the view that it is reasonable to evict a tenant who, despite having entered into a plain 'no pets' agreement, and having been given appropriate notice that the landlord intends to enforce the agreement, will not get rid of the animal.[59]

3.54 In other cases where the ground is proved, the condition of reasonableness is affected by considerations such as: whether the breach is continuing, persistent or repeated; the seriousness of the breach; its implications for the landlord; and the personal circumstances of the tenant. In *Wandsworth LBC v Hargreaves*[60] the tenant had allowed visitors to assemble fire bombs in his flat and throw them from the windows in clear breach of an express term of the tenancy (as to the

55 See *Kensington Housing Trust v Borkwood* July 2005 *Legal Action* 28.
56 *Bristol CC v Mousah* (1998) 30 HLR 32, CA.
57 *Bell London and Provincial Properties Ltd v Reuben* [1947] KB 157, CA.
58 *Corporation of London v Prior* (1996) 1 L & T Rev 1 pD8.
59 *Sheffield City Council v Jepson* (1993) 25 HLR 299, CA and *Green v Sheffield City Council* (1994) 26 HLR 349, CA.
60 (1994) 27 HLR 142, CA.

keeping of 'combustible materials' in the flats). Spilt petrol caused a fire which seriously damaged the flat. The Court of Appeal was not prepared to upset the trial judge's conclusion that notwithstanding the breach and the damage caused it was not reasonable to evict the tenant in the particular circumstances of that case.

3.55   It is, however, no part of the court's function in determining reasonableness to investigate whether the landlord's policy of including a particular term in a tenancy agreement is a good or valid one.[61]

3.56   Advisers may find it helpful to draw the attention of the court to the landlord's readily available alternative of injunction proceedings against the tenant, or particularly a member of the tenant's household who is the main perpetrator of the behaviour complained of, in respect of the alleged breach, rendering possession unnecessary.[62] However, they will need to be prepared to tackle the reverse contention that there are circumstances in which a postponed order can be more appropriate that an injunction enforceable by committal.[63]

3.57   Those defending tenants should always argue against the apparently attractive option of an order postponed or suspended on terms that there be no further breach. A postponed order can be resisted on the basis generally that it would not be reasonable in the circumstances to make any order at all. Alternatively, as in the case of rent arrears (see para 3.41), that the same objective can be met by adjourning the proceedings on terms (see paras 4.51–4.53), giving the landlord liberty to restore in the event of a further alleged breach. Even a postponed order would usually attract an award of costs against the tenant.

3.58   Those representing the tenant should argue that a postponed order in a 'breach of obligation' case should, where appropriate, only be made upon terms that it is not to be enforced without further permission of the court.[64] Without such an express restriction the landlord could obtain a warrant for possession, without a further hearing, simply by alleging breach. The court should be urged to adopt the form of order approved by the Court of Appeal in *Bristol CC v Hassan* (see para 4.62) suitably adapted for the purposes of a 'behaviour' case.

61 *Barking and Dagenham LBC v Hyatt* (1992) 24 HLR 406, CA.
62 *Sutton Housing Trust v Lawrence* (1987) 19 HLR 520, CA.
63 See Ralph Gibson LJ in *Sheffield City Council v Jepson* (1993) 25 HLR 299 at 303, CA.
64 See *Solon Co-op Housing Services Ltd v Headly* March 1997 *Legal Action* 11 and *Knowsley Housing Trust v McMullen* [2006] EWCA Civ 539, CA.

Ground 2: overview

3.59   Ground 2 (which deals with nuisance and criminal activity) was sub-stituted in its present wording – set out below – by Housing Act 1996 s144. The revised wording was intended to make it easier to recover possession from those guilty of anti-social behaviour. The ground is identical to ground 14 of the assured tenancy grounds for possession in Housing Act 1988 Sch 2, discussed below at para 10.88.

3.60   Because the factual background causing cases to be brought under this ground may require swift action by landlords, special provisions are made in relation to notices seeking possession which specify ground 2 among the grounds to be relied upon (see para 2.6). Proceedings can be commenced immediately after such a notice has been served[65] and possession can be ordered as early as the date on which the landlord has claimed for possession in the notice (ie, the date upon which the tenancy could have been brought to an end if it had not been secure). In a case of really serious nuisance or criminal-ity a landlord may simply issue proceedings immediately and invite the court to exercise its power to dispense with any notice seeking possession at all (see para 4.41).

3.61   A tenant might attempt to frustrate the landlord's intention to gain possession under ground 2, by exercising the statutory right to buy. If the application to buy has reached the stage at which the tenant would be enabled to compel completion, the tenant will ordi-narily be entitled to apply for an injunction requiring the landlord to complete the sale before the trial of any claim for possession under ground 2.[66] This could lead to a race between the tenant and the land-lord to secure a hearing for their respective claims first. It has been held that if the tenant's application falls for hearing on the same date as the possession claim, it will be for the judge to exercise a discre-tion as to which case to hear first;[67] and that the sequence of events and the seriousness of the allegations of misbehaviour are relevant factors which the court must take into account when considering whether the possession action or the injunction application should prevail.[68]

3.62   The issue now appears to have been resolved in favour of the land-

---

65   HA 1985 s83A(1).
66   HA 1985 s138(3).
67   *Bristol CC v Lovell* [1998] 1 WLR 446; [1998] 1 All ER 775, HL.
68   *Tandridge DC v Bickers* (1999) 31 HLR 432, CA.

lord by Housing Act 1985 ss121A[69] and 138(2A)–(2D).[70] Section 121A permits the court to make an order suspending the right to buy (a 'suspension order') for such period as is specified in the order. The grounds for making such an order are the same as the grounds for a demotion order (see para 8.61). Further orders can be made extending the period of suspension.[71] Where the conveyancing process is already well advanced, the landlord can still prevent completion of the right to buy taking place. Section 138(2A) provides that, where an application is pending before any court for a possession order under ground 2, a demotion order or a suspension order, the landlord is not bound to transfer the property to the tenant until the court application is determined.

Ground 2 (first limb): nuisance and annoyance

3.63   The first part of ground 2 of Housing Act 1985 Sch 2 is satisfied where:

> The tenant or a person residing in or visiting the dwelling-house –
> (a) has been guilty of conduct causing or likely to cause a nuisance or annoyance to a person residing, visiting or otherwise engaging in a lawful activity in the locality ...

3.64   Note that the ground imputes the tenant with responsibility for the actions of any others living in or visiting the property – not just members of the same household. In this sense the ground is one of 'strict liability' – its terms may be satisfied even in a case where the tenant did not know a co-resident or visitor was causing a nuisance or where, if the tenant had known, he or she would have been powerless to stop it.[72]

3.65   However, a casual caller guilty of causing annoyance may arguably not be 'visiting the dwelling-house' for the purposes of the ground if his or her visit is uninvited or positively unwelcome to the tenant. Otherwise tenants may be landed with responsibility for the activities of people actually coming to the property to cause nuisance to them, such as a violent ex-partner.

3.66   'Nuisance' is not restricted in this context to the meaning of the legal terms 'public nuisance' and 'private nuisance'.[73] Indeed, the

---

69   Inserted by Housing Act 2004 s192(2), with effect from 6 June 2005.
70   Inserted by Housing Act 2004 s193, with effect from 6 June 2005.
71   HA 1985 s121A(6).
72   *Portsmouth CC v Bryant* (2000) 32 HLR 906, CA.
73   *Harlow DC v Sewell* [2000] EHLR 122, February 2000 *Legal Action* 25, CA.

words 'or annoyance' add to and broaden the concept of nuisance. Both words are given their ordinary rather than their technical legal meanings. The necessary 'conduct' to be proved may possibly be constituted by one single act but is more likely to be shown through a number of examples of similar behaviour.

3.67   The use of the term 'guilty' does not impose a requirement that conduct be deliberate or culpable. In *Kensington and Chelsea RLBC v Simmonds*[74] the tenant's teenage son who resided with her had deliberately engaged in conduct amounting to nuisance. He was therefore 'guilty' of such conduct and ground 2 was satisfied. The Court of Appeal rejected the contention that the ground could be satisfied only if there was also some fault on the tenant's part, although it did hold that the existence or extent of any personal blame on the tenant's part would be relevant to the question of 'reasonableness' discussed below. That approach has likewise been applied to the revised wording of ground 2 by the Court of Appeal in *Portsmouth CC v Bryant*.[75]

3.68   In *Croydon LBC v Moody*,[76] a point was taken that the defendant tenant was so affected by mental illness as to have been incapable of being 'guilty' of the conduct complained of, which was simply a manifestation of his illness. However, as the conduct was also a breach of a tenancy term and the landlord was relying on ground 1 (which makes no reference to 'guilty' – see above), as well as ground 2, the issue did not need to be resolved. As to a possible defence under the Disability Discrimination Act 1995 in these circumstances, see para 3.94.

3.69   There is no need for the landlord to prove that any person was actually the recipient of nuisance or annoyance – it is sufficient if there is evidence of conduct that was *likely* to cause such nuisance or annoyance (so that the victim need not give evidence). Thus, the landlord may prove the ground using the evidence of those who simply saw or heard the misconduct complained of, for example, a police officer, an environmental health patrol team, the caretaker, or other 'professional' witnesses. Indeed, if the judge is prepared to give it sufficient weight, even pure hearsay evidence may satisfy the court that the ground is made out.[77]

3.70   A much wider group of potential victims than simply 'neighbours' is embraced by the ground. It extends to the protection of others living

74 (1997) 29 HLR 507, CA.
75 (2000) 32 HLR 906, CA.
76 (1999) 31 HLR 738, CA.
77 *Leeds City Council v Harte* April 1999 *Legal Action* 27, CA. See also *Solon South West Housing Association Ltd v James* [2004] EWCA Civ 1847; [2005] HLR 24 and *Washington Housing Company Ltd v Morson* [2005] EWHC 3407 (Ch).

in, visiting or otherwise lawfully conducting themselves in the locality. The term 'locality' is not defined by the Act. It was substituted for the word 'vicinity' which appeared in earlier drafts of the legislation and was thought too narrow. It is an ordinary English word requiring no special elaboration or definition. Any issue as to whether the matters complained of took place within the 'locality' of the dwelling is to be resolved as a question of fact on all the evidence.[78]

3.71　The victim cannot look to the ground in the hope of automatic redress against the tenant causing the nuisance. Even if its terms are satisfied, the landlord cannot be required to instigate proceedings in reliance upon it, unless there is an express term in the victim's tenancy agreement that the common landlord will bring proceedings. There is certainly no implied term which requires the landlord to take action under ground 2 in the case of neighbour nuisance. The affected neighbour accordingly cannot compel the landlord to act under this ground in the absence of an express agreement to do so.[79]

3.72　Even if the first limb of ground 2 is made out, the landlord must go on to show why it is reasonable that possession should be ordered to be given of the tenant's home.[80] This is the 'reasonableness condition' and must always be satisfied before an order under ground 2 can be made. There may be cases in which a judgment proceeds from a finding that ground 2 is made out, directly to a postponed possession order, thus missing the vital issue as to whether it is reasonable for *any* order to be made. The Court of Appeal has repeatedly emphasised the importance of the judge indicating in the judgment that the question of reasonableness has been expressly considered.[81]

3.73　In determining 'reasonableness' in ground 2 cases, the court is directed by Housing Act 1985 s85A(2) (inserted by the Anti-Social Behaviour Act 2003 s16) to consider in particular:

(a) the effect that the nuisance or annoyance has had on persons other than the person against whom the order is sought;
(b) any continuing effect the nuisance or annoyance is likely to have on such persons;
(c) the effect that the nuisance or annoyance would be likely to have on such persons if the conduct is repeated.

78　*Manchester City Council v Lawler* (1999) 31 HLR 119, CA.
79　*O'Leary v Islington LBC* (1983) 9 HLR 81, CA, *Hussain v Lancaster City Council* (1999) 31 HLR 164, CA and *Mowan v Wandsworth LBC* (2001) 33 HLR 56, CA.
80　HA 1985 s84(1).
81　For an example see *Manchester City Council v Green* January 1999 *Legal Action* 26, CA.

Essentially, this measure, which has the effect of structuring the court's discretion towards the interests of the victims or potential victims of the alleged behaviour, gives statutory effect to the approach of the Court of Appeal in anti-social behaviour cases in recent years (see para 3.78).

3.74   But while the court must give special prominence to the interests of the victims of the behaviour complained of, it nevertheless retains its discretion to consider other factors. It should also be invited to consider, among other issues, the seriousness and frequency of the nuisance; whether it is continuing, persistent or recently abated; warnings issued by the landlord; and the relevant personal circumstances of the tenant.[82] In *Woking BC v Bistram*[83] the nuisance proved was foul, abusive and menacing language. The trial judge refused to order possession on the basis that such language was commonplace in areas of council housing. The Court of Appeal held that (a) the finding as to use of similar language was not supported by any evidence; and (b) as the abuse had been continuing right up to trial it was reasonable for the protection of other tenants to grant possession. In *Solihull MBC v Reeman*[84] the trial judge had been satisfied that the tenant had caused nuisance and annoyance but found it not reasonable to order possession in view of the steps the tenant had taken to abate it and the fact that the tenant was an epileptic single man whom the council did not propose to rehouse if possession were granted. In *Stonebridge Housing Action Trust v Gabbidon*[85] where the home had been used for dealing in drugs, the judge was persuaded to suspend the order because the female defendant had not personally been involved in the dealing and there was no evidence of recent incidents. The judge also took into account the fact that there was a 7-month-old child in the household, The High Court on appeal refused to interfere with the judge's ruling: the claimant's contention that allowing the family to remain in occupation would set a precedent for other tenants was not supportable.

3.75   The court's attention on the 'reasonableness' issue might also be directed to the landlord's (and the victim's) alternative available remedies for nuisance including injunctions – especially in the light of the availability of draconian orders to control anti-social behaviour avail-

---

82   *Darlington BC v Sterling* (1997) 29 HLR 309, CA.
83   (1995) 27 HLR 1, CA.
84   June 1994 *Legal Action* 10.
85   [2002] EWHC 2091; (2003) 100(5) LSG 30 (Ch).

able under Housing Act 1996 Pt V Ch 3, Protection from Harassment Act 1997 s2 and Crime and Disorder Act 1998 s1 (anti-social behaviour orders (ASBOs)). However, the mere existence of these alternative remedies is no bar to the landlord seeking possession under ground 2 instead of, or in addition to, injunctive relief.[86] The fact that an ASBO has been made against the tenant or a member of his or her family can point in either direction, depending on the circumstances. In one case, the conduct which gave rise to the ASBO may be so serious that the making of an outright possession order, rather than a postponed or suspended order, may be self-evident, while in another case the ASBO may have served its purpose of restraining future misbehaviour, so that suspension might still be possible.[87] See para 3.81.

3.76 In considering 'reasonableness' where the nuisance has been caused not by the tenant but by another resident or a visitor, the court will need to be fully appraised of the extent to which the tenant has sought to modify or control that behaviour, whether by excluding the perpetrator or otherwise.[88]

3.77 Similarly, where the conduct on which the landlord relies is said to be a manifestation of the tenant's mental illness or personality disorder, the extent of those conditions and their 'treatability' will be crucial on the question of 'reasonableness' and the court will obviously need to have regard to medical evidence tendered.[89] Where it can be shown that such conduct was caused by a disability within the meaning of the Disability Discrimination Act 1995, this may be a powerful factor in persuading the court that it would not be reasonable to make a possession order: see para 3.94.

3.78 Historically, the Court of Appeal has been unwilling to interfere with the decisions of trial judges on 'reasonableness' issues. But in the context of modern concerns about anti-social behaviour, the Court of Appeal has, in a series of decisions, reversed judges who have not been satisfied that it was reasonable to order possession in public sector 'nuisance' cases or who have made only postponed or suspended

---

86 *Newcastle upon Tyne City Council v Morrison* (2000) 32 HLR 891, CA.

87 *Manchester City Council v Higgins* [2005] EWCA Civ 1423; [2006] 1 All ER 841, *Knowsley Housing Trust v McMullen* [2006] EWCA Civ 539, CA.

88 See *Kensington and Chelsea RLBC v Simmonds* (1997) 29 HLR 507, CA, *Gallagher v Castle Vale Housing Trust* [2001] EWCA Civ 944; (2001) 33 HLR 810 and *Portsmouth City Council v Bryant* (2000) 32 HLR 906, CA and *Knowsley Housing Trust v McMullen* [2006] EWCA 539.

89 *Croydon LBC v Moody* (1999) 31 HLR 738, CA and *Southwark LBC v Kennedy* [1998] CLY 2988.

orders rather than outright orders.[90] Indeed, the position may now be fairly said to have been reached that if ground 2 is made out in a serious case, something exceptional will be required on the part of the tenant to show why it would be unreasonable to order possession.

3.79   Instead, the focus in such anti-social behaviour cases is nowadays on whether the court can be persuaded to make a postponed rather than an outright order. The court will pay particular heed to whether the tenant acknowledges the seriousness of the conduct in question and, where the behaviour is that of a young person, to his or her efforts to co-operate with other agencies in seeking to bring about change. On the other hand, a tendency to minimise the alleged behaviour and its effects and to show no remorse will inevitably dispose the court against postponing the order.[91] Where there have been serious acts of harassment or intimidation, even a subsequent improvement in the conduct of the tenant's family will not prevent the court from making an outright order.[92] Again, the Court of Appeal has been prepared to upset suspended orders in such cases and replace them with outright orders[93] and (only very exceptionally) to substitute suspended orders for absolute orders.[94] It has repeatedly backed county court judges who have made outright possession orders in serious nuisance cases.[95]

3.80   The approach of the Court of Appeal to anti-social behaviour is evident in the case of *Manchester City Council v Higgins*.[96] Ms Higgins was a secure tenant and a single mother of three children, aged 15, 13 and 2. Her son, and, to a lesser extent, her elder daughter, caused distress to a widow who lived nearby with three sons, all of whom suffered from a mental disability. They swore at the neighbour and her children, bullied the children and damaged her property. The coun-

---

90 *Woking BC v Bistram* (1993) 27 HLR 1, *Darlington BC v Sterling* (1997) 29 HLR 309, *Bristol City Council v Mousah* (1998) 30 HLR 32, *West Kent Housing Association v Davies* (1999) 31 HLR 415 and *Newcastle upon Tyne City Council v Morrison* (2000) 32 HLR 891, CA.

91 See, eg, *Merton LBC v Mitchell* [2005] EWCA Civ 678.

92 *Solon South West Housing Association Ltd v James* [2004] EWCA Civ 1847; [2005] HLR 24.

93 *Canterbury CC v Lowe* (2001) 33 HLR 583, CA.

94 *Greenwich LBC v Grogan* (2001) 33 HLR 12, CA, *Gallagher v Castle Vale Housing Action Trust* [2001] EWCA Civ 944; (2001) 33 HLR 810, CA and *Moat Housing Group South Ltd v Harris and Hartless* [2004] EWCA Civ 1852; [2005] HLR 33; [2005] 3 WLR 691.

95 *Camden LBC v Gilsenan* (1999) 31 HLR 81, CA, *Waltham Forest LBC v Partridge* July 2000 *Legal Action* 28, *Westminster City Council v Garcia* August 2000 *Legal Action* 24, CA and *Lambeth LBC v Howard* [2001] EWCA Civ 468; (2003) 33 HLR 58, CA.

96 [2005] EWCA Civ 1423; [2006] 1 All ER 841.

cil warned her that if her son's behaviour did not change, it would have no alternative but to begin proceedings. That had no effect and the council obtained a 'without notice' injunction. Subsequently, the council obtained an ASBO against the son. He was then arrested after a further incident involving criminal damage, following which he was placed under supervision for two years for the offences of criminal damage and assault, but he continued to harass the neighbouring family.

3.81   The council began possession proceedings under grounds 1 and 2. In the county court, a recorder made a suspended or postponed possession order, but suspended it for 18 months. The Court of Appeal allowed the council's appeal. The discretion of the court to make a possession order under Housing Act 1985 s85 is unfettered, but it has to be exercised judicially. It follows that all the circumstances of the case which are material are to be borne in mind. If the misconduct by the tenant or by a member of the household is serious and persistent enough to justify an ASBO, that is strong but not conclusive evidence that the tenant would have forfeited any entitlement to retain possession. In one case, the facts giving rise to the making of an ASBO might be so serious that both the making of a possession order and the refusal to suspend it would be self-evident. In another case, the making of an ASBO might have served its purpose of restraining future misbehaviour, so that, in spite of past conduct, suspension of the order might still be possible. Since the court would already have found that it was reasonable to make a possession order, the question whether or not to suspend its execution has to be very much a question of the future. Previous unheeded warnings point one way; genuine remorse the other. The level of support available to a parent who is making proper efforts to control an errant child is relevant. However, there has always to be a sound basis for the hope that the anti-social behaviour will cease. Ultimately, given the respect for a tenant's home guaranteed by article 8 of the European Convention on Human Rights (ECHR), the question is whether an immediate possession order is necessary in order to protect the rights and freedoms of others, and is proportionate. In this case, the behaviour of Ms Higgins and her children, especially the son, had been quite intolerable. The son had shown himself unrepentantly anti-social. The mere fact that the ASBO would remain in force until the son attained the age of 16 would not give the neighbours sufficient protection. In the absence of any expression of remorse or any well-founded expectation of improvement, it was disproportionate not to make an immediate possession order. Ms Higgins was without remorse and totally indifferent to the effect her children's behaviour was having on her neighbours. She had forfeited her right to respect for her home. The recorder should have made an order for possession in 28 days.

3.82   On the other hand, in *Moat Housing Group South Ltd v Harris and Hartless*,[97] where the anti-social behaviour was far less serious, the Court of Appeal considered the absence of any prior warning or complaint by the landlords together with good school reports received by the tenant's children, the absence of any criminal records or any serious record of police involvement with the family and favourable testimonies which were given about the defendant, and suspended the possession order made in the county court.

3.83   What impact does the Human Rights Act 1998 have on the approach of the courts in relation to this ground? In particular, article 8(1) of the ECHR provides that everyone is entitled to the 'right to respect' for his or her home. However, the statutory requirement that the landlord prove both a ground for possession and that it is reasonable to order possession, is sufficient to achieve respect for a home – particularly given that article 8(2) qualifies the right to respect by reference to the wider interests of the community including, expressly, the need to control crime and disorder. In *Lambeth LBC v Howard*[98] Sedley LJ said that, while article 8 should not carry county courts to materially different outcomes from those which they had been arriving at in applying the condition of reasonableness, 'it can do no harm, and may often do a great deal of good, if the exercise is approached for what it is, an application of the principle of proportionality.' In *Kay v Lambeth LBC; Leeds CC v Price*,[99] Lord Brown stated:

> Of course, where the domestic law requires the court to make a judgment (most notably perhaps in those cases under Schedule 2 to the Housing Act 1985 where repossession can only be ordered if the court considers it reasonable), or to exercise a discretion, the judge will bear in mind that he is performing this task in the context of the defendant's article 8 right to respect for his home. [203]

3.84   But in cases where the court is deciding whether it is reasonable to make a possession order, the Court of Appeal has acknowledged that the concept of proportionality, which is inherent in article 8, is relevant to the exercise of the court's discretion. In *Gallagher v Castle Vale Housing Action Trust*,[100] an outright possession order was made

97 [2004] EWCA Civ 1852; [2005] 3 WLR 691.
98 [2001] EWCA Civ 468; (2001) 33 HLR 636, CA.
99 [2006] UKHL 10; [2006] 2 WLR 570.
100 [2001] EWCA Civ 944; (2001) 33 HLR 72.

against the tenant following complaints of nuisance. She argued that she was not personally to blame for the offensive conduct and had not acquiesced in it; the disturbance was caused by members of the family who were about to move out, and the nuisance would therefore cease. The Court of Appeal considered that the test of 'reasonableness' takes into account most of the issues that might be raised in an attempt to show that a possession order is a 'disproportionate' remedy. Nonetheless, an outright order should only be made in a very clear-cut case. The order was set aside and a two-year suspended possession order was substituted.

3.85 If the judge is satisfied that it is reasonable to grant an order for possession in a ground 2 case, it is not part of his or her function to require the housing authority to set out what arrangements will be available for the rehousing of the family after eviction.[101]

3.86 It is clear that ground 2 cases involving alleged nuisance can give rise to difficult issues of fact and law and that the risk of a possession order being made is such that the tenant should have a proper opportunity to prepare a defence and secure representation.[102]

Ground 2 (second limb): criminal activity

3.87 A landlord may additionally or alternatively rely on ground 2 where:

> The tenant or a person residing in or visiting the dwelling-house ...
> (b) has been convicted of –
>   (i) using the dwelling-house, or allowing it to be used, for immoral or illegal purposes, or
>   (ii) an arrestable offence committed in, or in the locality of, the dwelling-house.

3.88 Note that the ground is satisfied by the conviction (not mere arrest) of the tenant him or herself or of a co-resident or of a visitor. There is no definition of 'locality' for the purposes of the ground (see para 3.70 for discussion of its meaning in the context of ground 2) but 'arrestable offence' does have a specific definition in criminal law (see para 10.92).

3.89 There was little or no experience of use of the first part of this limb of ground 2 in the public sector in the early years following the introduction of security of tenure in 1980. In more recent years, convictions for use of premises to manufacture, store or trade illicit drugs have led to evictions. For guidance on judicial consideration

101 *Watford BC v Simpson* (2000) 32 HLR 901, CA.
102 *Bates v Croydon LBC* [2001] EWCA Civ 134; (2001) 33 HLR 792, CA.

of 'immoral' or 'illegal' purpose, reference may usefully be made to the developed case-law on the almost identically expressed wording found in the Rent Act 1977 for private tenants (para 15.20) and the Housing Act 1988 for assured tenants (see para 10.90).

3.90   The latter part of the second limb was an innovation introduced by the Housing Act 1996. It breaks the link between the acts of criminality and use of the dwelling which is the criminal's home. It 'may be particularly useful for a local authority which is concerned about drug dealing where the trafficking is taking place in the common parts of the estate rather than a house or flat'.[103]

3.91   The second limb of ground 2 is also subject to the condition that it must be shown to be reasonable in all the circumstances for a possession order to be made.[104] Here again, the court is directed to pay special attention to the effects of the behaviour in question on other people (see para 3.73), in so far as this consideration is relevant to the second limb. Other factors on reasonableness will include: the seriousness of the offence; the pattern of offending (if any); previous good character; the circumstances of the non-offending occupiers and the relationship (or lack of one) between the offence and the landlord-tenant relationship.

3.92   It may also be worthwhile to draw attention to the fact that it must follow from the conviction and sentence that the offender has subsequently received as much punishment as the criminal justice system thought appropriate. Such a case is likely to arise where a longstanding tenant (or fellow resident) has been found guilty of a one-off offence highly unlikely to be repeated.[105] However, if there has been a conviction of an offence or offences of any real seriousness, it would be an exceptional case in which not even a suspended order for possession were made, whatever sentence the criminal court imposed.[106]

3.93   In a case where the issue is as stark as whether the possession order should be outright or suspended, it is worth drawing the attention of the court to the increased risk of further offending if the criminal is evicted to live an insecure life on the streets or in transient accommodation as opposed to receiving the benefit of support services (such as that of the probation service), which can be more straightforwardly supplied to those with a fixed address.[107]

103   DoE Circ 2/97 para 28(iii).
104   HA 1985 s84(2)(a).
105   *Tower Hamlets LBC v Kellum* November 2000 *Legal Action* 22.
106   *Bristol City Council v Mousah* (1998) 30 HLR 32, CA.
107   *Greenwich LBC v Grogan* (2001) 33 HLR 140, CA.

Possession proceedings and the Disability Discrimination Act

3.94 Recent case law has explored the possibilities of invoking the Disability Discrimination Act 1995 (as amended by the Disability Discrimination Act 2005) by way of a defence of possession proceedings. A tenant or other occupier suffering from disability may argue that the Act protects him or her from eviction, other than in certain defined circumstances. The cornerstone of this argument lies in section 22(3)(c) of the Act, which renders it unlawful for a person managing premises to discriminate against a disabled person occupying those premises 'by evicting the disabled person or subjecting him to any other detriment'. A disabled person is defined for the purposes of the 1995 Act in section 1 as 'a person with a physical or mental impairment which has a substantial and long-term effect on his ability to carry out day-to-day activities'.[108]

3.95 Under section 24(1) of the 1995 Act, a person discriminates against a disabled person if:

(a) for a reason which relates to the disabled person's disability, he treats him less favourably than he treats or would treat others to whom that reason does not or would not apply; and

(b) he cannot show that the treatment is justified.

It is possible to justify treating a disabled person less favourably where another person (in this context, the landlord) considers that one of a number of conditions are met and that it is reasonable in all the circumstances to hold that opinion. One of the conditions (set out in section 24(3) of the 1995 Act) is that:

(a) in any case, the treatment is necessary in order not to endanger the health or safety of any person ...

3.96 Against this background, tenants in a number of cases have sought to raise a defence under the 1995 Act to possession proceedings. In *North Devon Homes Ltd v Brazier*,[109] possession proceedings were issued against an assured tenant on the grounds of nuisance. The cause of her behaviour was her psychotic illness. It was accepted that her bizarre

108 The definition carries a range of meanings which are more fully set out in Schedule 1 to the Act and in the Disability Discrimination (Meaning of Disability) Regulations 1996 SI No 1455. See also the Revised *Guidance on matters to be taken into account in determining questions relating to the definition of disability*, issued by the Secretary of State for Work and Pensions (May 2006).

109 [2003] EWHC 574; [2003] HLR 59, QBD.

and unwelcome behaviour was attributable to her mental illness and that she was unable to prevent herself behaving in an anti-social manner. The court upheld the tenant's argument that under the 1995 Act, discrimination is not a matter of direct comparison. It is irrelevant that a landlord would have treated a non-disabled person in the same way. Evicting the tenant would be lawful only if it were necessary in order not to endanger the health and well-being of the disabled person or anyone else (section 24(3)), and this was not proven on the evidence.

3.97   The defence will only be available where on the evidence the occupier's disability is the cause of the behaviour that has brought about the landlord's action: otherwise, the issue of discrimination does not arise.[110]

3.98   In *Manchester City Council v Romano and Samari*,[111] the Court of Appeal identified the factors that are relevant to a possible defence to possession proceedings on the basis of the 1995 Act, as follows:

- whether the person who complains about disability discrimination is a 'disabled person' within the meaning of the Act;
- whether there has been discrimination, ie, treating a disabled person less favourably for a reason which relates to his or her disability;
- whether the landlord's treatment of the tenant is justified. A decision to take possession proceedings may be justified only if, on the facts known to the landlord, such action is necessary in order not to endanger the health and safety of other occupiers, and it is reasonable for the landlord to take that view.

In relation to the test of necessity, the threshold of danger to health is relatively low and can encompass, for example, fatigue and stress arising from loss of sleep caused by noise nuisance. The Court of Appeal considered that Disability Discrimination Act issues should be raised as part of the tenant's argument that it is not reasonable to make a possession order, rather than by way of a separate claim for a declaration or injunction for breach of the Act.

3.99   A defence based on disability discrimination is not restricted to cases of alleged nuisance or anti-social behaviour. It may be that a tenant suffers from a mental illness which renders him or her unable to attend to the day-to-day activities of personal administration, such as budgeting, paying rent, claiming benefits or answering correspondence. Subject to medical evidence dealing with the specific effects of

110 See *Servite Houses v Perry* June 2004 *Legal Action* 30, Birmingham County Court.
111 [2004] EWCA Civ 834; [2005] 1 WLR 2775; [2004] HLR 47.

the illness, the tenant may argue, in possession proceedings based on rent arrears, that it cannot be reasonable to make a possession order.[112] There is, in such cases, no question of the discrimination being justified on grounds of health and safety.

3.100   While the reported decisions have to date concerned possession proceedings brought against secure or assured tenants on discretionary grounds, it seems that there is nothing to prevent disability discrimination arguments being used to defend a claim for possession where the court would ordinarily have no discretion, for example, in the case of an introductory or demoted tenancy, a non-secure tenancy, an assured tenancy where the claim is brought on a mandatory ground for possession or an assured shorthold tenancy.

Ground 2A: domestic violence

3.101   A new ground 2A was introduced by Housing Act 1996 s145 and has subsequently been amended by the Civil Partnership Act 2004. The ground can be satisfied where:

> The dwelling-house was occupied (whether alone or with others) by a married couple, a couple who are civil partners of each other, a couple living together as husband and wife or a couple living together as if they were civil partners and –
>
> (a) one or both of the partners is a tenant of the dwelling-house,
> (b) one partner has left because of violence or threats of violence by the other towards –
>   (i) that partner, or
>   (ii) a member of the family of that partner who was residing with that partner immediately before the partner left, and
> (c) the court is satisfied that the partner who has left is unlikely to return.

3.102   It is designed to deal with what might be broadly described as 'domestic violence', particularly where this has housing management implications for the landlord. The ground is most commonly relied upon where the landlord has rehoused the departed victim of violence, leaving the perpetrator under-occupying the former family home.

3.103   The ground has no application where there is no couple at all – as where the violence of a child causes a parent to leave.

3.104   The landlord must be able to prove not only that the dwelling had been home to a couple but both that (1) the partner who left did so

112 The argument succeeded in the county court case of *Liverpool City Council v Slavin* July 2005 *Legal Action* 28.

because of violence or the threat of violence (as distinct from some other unreasonable conduct); and that (2) he or she is unlikely to return. As to the first of these, it is not necessary for the landlord to establish that the violence was the sole cause of the partner's departure. However, it will not suffice simply to demonstrate that the violent behaviour was one of a number of factors that caused the departed partner to leave. It must be the main, substantive or significant reason why the victim left.[113]

3.105   The second of the conditions (unlikelihood of return) will be particularly difficult to satisfy if the departed partner wants to return if and when the partner remaining is evicted. If the departed partner is him or herself unwilling to give evidence the landlord may need to rely upon hearsay evidence – rendered admissible by the Civil Evidence Act 1995 – to establish these matters.

3.106   The ground arises not only through violence or threat directed to the departed partner but also to other family members. The term 'member of the family' is defined in Housing Act 1985 s113 (reproduced at para 2.30). The strict wording of the ground would not be satisfied if the family member was driven to leave ahead of the departing partner who only left sometime later. The requirement that the family member must be residing with the partner 'immediately' before the latter's departure suggests that only departure en masse is within the ground.

3.107   Special requirements concerning service of notices seeking possession apply if possession is to be sought on ground 2A. If the partner who has left is not the tenant (or one of the joint tenants), the landlord must serve a copy of the notice on that partner or show that it has 'taken all reasonable steps' to do so.[114] Likewise if permission is given to add ground 2A to a notice seeking possession after proceedings have started, the landlord must serve a special notice (complying with Housing Act 1985 s83A(6)) on the departed partner if he or she is not a party in the proceedings, or show that it has 'taken all reasonable steps' to do so.[115] The court cannot entertain a ground 2A claim unless these requirements are met. They can only be dispensed with if (a) the landlord has also specified ground 2 (nuisance – see above) in the notice seeking possession; and (b) it is just and equitable to do so.[116]

---

113 *Camden LBC v Mallett* (2001) 33 HLR 204, CA.
114 HA 1985 s83A(3).
115 HA 1985 s83A(4).
116 HA 1985 s83A.

3.108   Presumably, the rationale is that in all save the most urgent cases the departed partner should be forewarned that the former family home is at risk so that he or she might make any appropriate application under Family Law Act 1996 Pt IV for occupation or transfer orders before the tenancy is lost or may exercise the rights of intervention in the possession proceedings conferred on partners by Housing Act 1985 s85 (see para 2.60).

Ground 3: deterioration in condition

3.109   Schedule 2 ground 3 provides a remedy for the landlord where:

> The condition of the dwelling-house or any of the common parts has deteriorated owing to acts of waste by, or the neglect or default of, the tenant or a person residing in the dwelling-house and, in the case of an act of waste by, or the neglect or default of, a person lodging with the tenant or a sub-tenant of his, the tenant has not taken such steps as he ought reasonably to have taken for the removal of the lodger or sub-tenant.

The ground is subject to the condition that an order for possession may be made only if it would be reasonable to do so.[117]

3.110   Useful guidance on the construction of this provision is to be derived from cases on Rent Act 1977 Sch 15 case 3 (see para 15.22) and Housing Act 1988 Sch 2 ground 13 (see para 10.87). However, unlike the Rent Act case, ground 3 embraces deterioration in the condition of 'common parts'. This phrase is defined[118] as meaning:

> ... any part of a building comprising the dwelling-house and any other premises which the tenant is entitled under the terms of the tenancy to use in common with the occupiers of other dwelling-houses let by the landlord ...

and the ground may therefore cover the situation in which the tenant or other person residing in the dwelling-house has been responsible for damaging the lifts, stairways, rubbish chutes, communal lighting, etc, in the block of which the dwelling-house forms part. The acts or omissions must be proved on the balance of probabilities to have been the responsibility of the tenant or co-resident.

3.111   Note that in contrast to the amendments made by the Housing Act 1996 relating to ground 2 above, the wording of ground 3 has not been enlarged to make tenants responsible for damage caused by 'visitors'

---

117   HA 1985 s84(2)(a).
118   HA 1985 s116.

(although it does cover visitors who can properly be considered to be 'lodging with the tenant').

Ground 4: deterioration of furniture

3.112　Housing Act 1985 Sch 2 ground 4 provides:

> The condition of furniture provided by the landlord for use under the tenancy, or for use in the common parts, has deteriorated owing to ill-treatment by the tenant or a person residing in the dwelling-house and, in the case of ill-treatment by a person lodging with the tenant or a sub-tenant of his, the tenant has not taken such steps as he ought reasonably to have taken for the removal of the lodger or sub-tenant.

3.113　Although they have power to provide furniture for residents,[119] local authority landlords rarely do so. Most council and other public sector properties are let unfurnished. However, the ground extends to furniture provided by the landlord in the common parts of the property. Given the extended definition of 'common parts' in Housing Act 1985 s116 (set out at para 3.110 above), this would embrace vandalism by the tenant or co-resident in such places as the communal laundry or children's playing area.

3.114　Note that in contrast to the amendments made by the Housing Act 1996 relating to ground 2 above, the wording of ground 4 has not been enlarged to make tenants responsible for damage caused by 'visitors' although it will extend to those 'lodging with' the tenant.

3.115　Ground 4 is subject to the condition that even if the terms of the ground are established, an order may be granted only if it would be reasonable in all the circumstances.[120]

Ground 5: tenancy by deception

3.116　Housing Act 1985 Sch 2 ground 5 is satisfied if:

> The tenant is the person, or one of the persons, to whom the tenancy was granted and the landlord was induced to grant the tenancy by a false statement made knowingly or recklessly by –
> (a) the tenant, or
> (b) *a person acting at the tenant's instigation.*

---

119 HA 1985 s10.
120 HA 1985 s84(2)(a).

3.117　The ground extends not only to false representations known to be false at the time of making, but also to 'reckless' statements. Where a person completes an application form for housing on the basis that he or she will inform the council of any changes in their circumstances which might affect their need for housing, the subsequent failure to disclose new information to the council may amount to a false statement which induces the grant of a tenancy.[121] On the other hand, it cannot be applied where the landlord's essential complaint is that it would not have granted the tenancy if the tenant had given information for which in fact the landlord had failed to ask.[122]

3.118　The words in italics were added on 12 February 1997 by Housing Act 1996 s146. Previously, only statements attributable to the *tenant* (or one of the joint tenants) could satisfy the ground, so that if a partner induced the landlord to let the accommodation in the sole name of the other partner, the ground could not be relied upon. The effect of the amendment is to close that 'lacuna' and enable the landlord to rely on the ground in respect of a representation made by a third party. It is not enough, however, for the landlord just to prove that a third party made the relevant representation – it must additionally be shown that this was done at the instigation of the tenant.[123] Otherwise, ground 5 is not available where the current tenant is not the person to whom the tenancy was granted.[124]

3.119　In order to substantiate a ground 5 case the landlord must prove not only a false statement but also that the statement *induced* the grant of the tenancy. It is not necessary for the landlord to produce evidence from the actual decision-maker . In *Waltham Forest LBC v Roberts*,[125] the tenant had stated in her application for housing that she did not own any property, whereas she was in fact the joint owner of an undisclosed property. The Court of Appeal held that the correct approach was to ask whether the misstatement was material to the council's discharge of its public functions. Once the materiality of the misstatement had been established, it was a 'fair inference' of fact that the decision-maker had been influenced by it.

3.120　Even if the ground is proved, the landlord must also show that it is reasonable for possession to be ordered.[126]

3.121　When defending on reasonableness in such a case, the advocate

---

121　*North Herts DC v Carthy* [2003] EWCA Civ 20.

122　*Peterborough CC v Moran* September 1993 *Legal Action* 13.

123　*Merton LBC v Richards* [2005] EWCA Civ 639; [2005] HLR 44.

124　*Islington LBC v Uckac* [2006] EWCA Civ 340; [2006] 1 WLR 1303.

125　[2004] EWCA Civ 940; [2005] HLR 2.

126　HA 1985 s84(2)(a).

should remind the court that a local authority landlord already has a specific remedy if induced to grant the tenancy by the deception of an applicant for housing – prosecution under Housing Act 1996 s171 or s214. The loss of the home, it may be argued, would be 'excessive punishment' in all but the most exceptional cases. It should be noted too that the tenant may also be liable to prosecution for 'obtaining by deception' contrary to the Theft Act 1968.

3.122   In *Rushcliffe BC v Watson*[127] the tenant recorded on her application form that she had been a lodger in her former home. The landlord subsequently discovered that she had held a housing association tenancy. The entry on the form was unquestionably 'false' for the purposes of ground 5. The county court judge was satisfied that all the other elements of the ground were similarly proven and ordered possession. An appeal on the basis, inter alia, that it was not reasonable to render the tenant homeless by repossession was dismissed but the court stressed that a high burden of proof as to the ground itself was appropriate in view of the seriousness of an allegation that a tenant had made a knowing or reckless false statement.

3.123   However, if the burden of proof is met, so that it is clear that there has been flagrant and deliberate lying and deceitfulness, the expectation will be that possession will be ordered. In such a case it would be 'an affront to those who put forward their claims honestly, wait patiently and rely upon the local housing authority to deal fairly with their claims' if a judge in such a case was not satisfied that it was reasonable to order possession.[128] The possibility that the evicted tenant may be faced with a subsequent finding of intentional homelessness is no impediment to the court holding that it is reasonable to order possession in a ground 5 case.[129]

Ground 6: an illegal premium

3.124   The Housing Act 1985 permits assignment by way of exchange between secure occupiers[130] but payment of a premium renders both parties to any such exchange liable to possession proceedings based

---

127 (1992) 24 HLR 123, CA, and see also *Camden LBC v Burrell* June 1997 *Legal Action* 19.

128 *Shrewsbury and Atcham BC v Evans* (1998) 30 HLR 123, CA.

129 *Lewisham LBC v Akinsola* (2000) 32 HLR 414, CA.

130 HA 1985 s92 – see para 2.65.

on Housing Act 1985 Sch 2 ground 6. This applies where:

> The tenancy was assigned to the tenant, or to a predecessor in title of his who is a member of his family and is residing in the dwelling-house, by an assignment made by virtue of section 92 (assignments by way of exchange) and a premium was paid either in connection with that assignment or the assignment which the tenant or predecessor himself made by virtue of that section.

3.125　In this paragraph 'premium' means any fine or other like sum and any other pecuniary consideration in addition to rent. The wide definition of premium was presumably intended to catch not only those tenants who are induced to agree to 'swap' their homes by outright cash payments but also those offered other financial inducements by the other party to the swap – such as the purchase (at inflated values) of curtains and carpets left behind or the payment of removal expenses.

3.126　In order to recover possession the landlord must, in addition to proving the ground, show that it would be reasonable for an order for possession to be made.[131]

3.127　It should be noted that the ground is met whichever party to the assignment pays a premium and also extends to the current tenant where the assignment was carried out by a predecessor in title. In the latter case the predecessor must be a member of the tenant's family still living in the tenant's home. Thus if a notice seeking possession is served relying on this latter aspect of the ground, the claim can be defeated if the family member responsible moves permanently out of residence prior to the issue of proceedings.

3.128　Those defending tenants should carefully examine whether the mutual exchange (in relation to which a premium was paid or received) was in fact achieved by way of assignment under Housing Act 1985 s92 at all. Many social landlords still undertake exchanges by inviting each tenant to surrender his or her existing tenancy in order to take a fresh tenancy of his or her exchange-partner's home.[132] Such an exchange would plainly not be within the reach of this ground at all. Likewise it cannot be relied upon where the exchange took place before the statutory precursor of Housing Act 1985 s92 was first introduced on 26 August 1994 by the Housing and Building Control Act 1984.

131　HA 1985 s84(2)(a).
132　As in *Merton LBC v Richards*, n123 above.

Ground 7: non-housing accommodation

3.129   Ground 7 of Housing Act 1985 Sch 2 makes very specific provision for those residing in non-housing accommodation (for example, in a social service or educational facility) who are guilty of inappropriate conduct. It is met where:

> The dwelling-house forms part of, or is within the curtilage of, a building which, or so much of it as is held by the landlord, is held mainly for purposes other than housing purposes and consists mainly of accommodation other than housing accommodation, and –
> (a) the dwelling-house was let to the tenant or a predecessor in title of his in consequence of the tenant or predecessor being in the employment of the landlord, or of –
>   a local authority,
>   a new town corporation,
>   a housing action trust,
>   an urban development corporation,
>   ... or
>   the governors of an aided school,
>   and
> (b) the tenant or a person residing in the dwelling-house has been guilty of conduct such that, having regard to the purpose for which the building is used, it would not be right for him to continue in occupation of the dwelling-house.

The examples that legislators presumably had in mind were of 'misbehaviour' by resident staff (or their successors) accommodated within the buildings or grounds of schools, colleges and residential homes.

3.130   Note that the misconduct must be related to the purpose for which the main building is generally used. Note also that the dwelling occupied by the tenant must either be within the same building as the workplace or be within the 'curtilage' of that building. It is not sufficient simply to show that the tenanted dwelling is within the same grounds as that building.[133]

3.131   Whether the dwelling is within the 'curtilage' of another building is largely an issue of fact. Advisers will find helpful guidance in the case-law relating to applications for exercise of the right to buy, which turn on whether the property sought to be purchased is within the curtilage of another.[134]

---

133   *Dyer v Dorset CC* (1988) 20 HLR 490, CA and *Burns v Central Regional Council* 1988 SLT (Lands Tr) 46.

134   HA 1985 Sch 5 ground 5. See in particular *Barwick v Kent CC* (1992) 24 HLR 341, CA.

3.132   Likewise, assistance may be derived from judicial consideration of the term 'curtilage' in planning cases.[135]

3.133   If the accommodation has been provided to an employee who is required to occupy it for the better performance of his or her duties, the tenancy may not be secure at all.[136]

3.134   Possession may be ordered under ground 7 only if in all the circumstances it is reasonable for an order to be made.[137]

Ground 8: temporary accommodation

3.135   Not infrequently landlords temporarily rehouse secure tenants while works of repair or improvement are in progress at their homes. If the secure tenant is offered and accepts an alternative secure tenancy or licence of such accommodation while work is in progress, ground 8 of Housing Act 1985 Sch 2 deals with the situation if that tenant or his or her successor refuses to return 'home'. It is satisfied where:

> The dwelling-house was made available for occupation by the tenant (or a predecessor in title of his) while works were carried out on the dwelling-house which he previously occupied as his only or principal home and –
>
> (a) the tenant (or predecessor) was a secure tenant of the other dwelling-house at the time when he ceased to occupy it as his home,
>
> (b) the tenant (or predecessor) accepted the tenancy of the dwelling-house of which possession is sought on the understanding that he would give up occupation when, on completion of the works, the other dwelling-house was again available for occupation by him under a secure tenancy, and
>
> (c) the works have been completed and the other dwelling-house is so available.

3.136   Note that ground 8 is not concerned with requiring the tenant to move out for works to be done – that is covered by ground 10 (see para 3.141). Rather it concerns the tenant refusing to return to the former home when the work on that home is completed. It must be shown both that the tenant had agreed to move back (the term 'understanding' is used in the ground) and that the works have been completed.

3.137   The ground is subject to the condition that the grant of an order

135 See, eg, *Skerritts of Nottingham Ltd v Secretary of State for the Environment* [2001] QB 59, CA and *Morris v Wrexham BC* December 2001 *Legal Action* 22.

136 HA 1985 Sch 1 para 2 (see para 1.22 above).

137 HA 1985 s84(2)(a).

must be reasonable in all the circumstances.[138] Relevant factors will include: the circumstances under which the tenant was initially required to move; the terms of any understanding reached at that time with the landlord; and the length of time the tenant has been in the present property. The court may be particularly reluctant to disturb the tenant if works at the former home were scheduled to take a few months and were only completed some years later. For an example of the factual circumstances in which ground 8 could have been (but was not) deployed, see *Lambeth LBC v Gent*.[139]

Ground 9: overcrowding

3.138   Housing Act 1985 Sch 2 ground 9 is made out where:

> The dwelling-house is overcrowded, within the meaning of Part X, in such circumstances as to render the occupier guilty of an offence.

As to what may constitute 'overcrowding' for these purposes see the extracts from Housing Act 1985 Pt X reproduced at para 15.58.

3.139   Overcrowding is generally prohibited by Housing Act 1985 Pt X, but not all overcrowding renders the occupier guilty of an offence. In particular, overcrowding caused by visiting family members or natural growth in family size is excepted and a council may in any event license overcrowding[140] to prevent the occupier being liable to conviction. However, a council which places secure tenants in overcrowded property may itself be liable to conviction.[141]

3.140   If reliance is placed on this ground, the landlord need not satisfy the court on 'reasonableness' but must show that suitable alternative accommodation will be available to the tenant if an order is made.[142] Housing Act 1985 Sch 2 Pt IV para 3 makes special provision as to what is 'suitable alternative accommodation' for those against whom possession is sought on overcrowding grounds, in the following terms:

> 3. Where possession of a dwelling-house is sought on ground 9 (overcrowding such as to render occupier guilty of offence), other accommodation may be reasonably suitable to the needs of the tenant and his family notwithstanding that the permitted number of persons for that accommodation, as defined in section 326(3) (overcrowding:

---

138 HA 1985 s84(2)(a).
139 July 2001 *Legal Action* 32.
140 HA 1985 s330.
141 See *DPP v Carrick DC* (1985) 31 *Housing Aid* 5.
142 HA 1985 s84(2)(b).

the space standard), is less than the number of persons living in the dwelling-house of which possession is sought.

Of course, the accommodation must also be suitable in the other respects referred to in Housing Act 1985 Sch 2 Pt IV (see para 3.185).

Ground 10: landlord's works

3.141 Possession proceedings may be brought on ground 10 of Housing Act 1985 Sch 2 where:

> The landlord intends, within a reasonable time of obtaining possession of the dwelling-house –
> (a) to demolish or reconstruct the building or part of the building comprising the dwelling-house, or
> (b) to carry out work on that building or on land let together with, and thus treated as part of, the dwelling-house,
> and cannot reasonably do so without obtaining possession of the dwelling-house.

3.142 The landlord must not simply intend to carry out substantial work but in order to satisfy this ground must also show that the work cannot be carried out without obtaining possession of the dwelling-house. The landlord needs to establish that legal possession of the property and termination of the tenancy is necessary, not simply access to, or temporary occupation of, the premises by the landlord's contractors.

3.143 Unless the case is one of prospective complete demolition, it must be proved that either the tenant has refused to co-operate with the landlord's proposals for temporary displacement to other accommodation or that the landlord does not have and cannot secure any accommodation to provide a temporary dwelling for the tenant while works are in progress. That is because the ground cannot be made out if the tenant demonstrates a willingness to move out of the premises (for example, to stay with relatives) while work is in progress.

3.144 On the other hand, there will be cases in which the proposed works are so extensive as to amount to reconstruction, in which circumstances the recovery of possession seems sensible and the ground will be satisfied.

3.145 The Court of Appeal has held that in order to establish ground 10, the landlord must be in a position to (a) identify specifically the proposed works; and (b) show why it is necessary to recover possession in order for the works to be carried out.[143]

143 *Wansbeck DC v Marley* (1988) 20 HLR 247, CA.

3.146   Even if the ground is made out, possession cannot be ordered unless suitable alternative accommodation is available to the tenant and his or her family.[144] There is, however, no requirement that the landlord prove 'reasonableness', whether in the sense that it is reasonable for the landlord to want to carry out the particular works or that it is reasonable for the particular tenant to be compulsorily moved.

3.147   If the tenant is forced to give up possession he or she will usually seek permanent suitable accommodation rather than negotiate an 'understanding' for return to the original accommodation once work is completed as such an understanding opens the way to later proceedings under ground 8 (see para 3.135).

3.148   Tenants displaced as a result of ground 10 proceedings may be entitled to home loss payments.[145] A check should also be made to see if there is any specific provision in the tenancy agreement as to the compensation which may be payable.[146]

3.149   A tenant attached to his or her home in its present condition might frustrate the landlord's intentions for demolition or reconstruction by exercising the statutory right to buy. If the application to buy has reached the stage at which the tenant would be enabled to compel completion by injunction, the tenant will be entitled to complete the purchase if the application is heard before the trial of any claim for possession under ground 10.[147] If the injunction application and trial are listed on the same date, it will be for the judge to decide which matter to take first.[148]

Ground 10A: landlord seeking to sell with vacant possession

3.150   Housing and Planning Act 1986 s5 inserted[149] ground 10A into Housing Act 1985 Sch 2. It assists landlords who want to achieve vacant possession and thereafter sell property for redevelopment. Ground 10A provides that a court may order possession if suitable alternative accommodation is available (see para 3.185) and:

144   HA 1985 s84(2)(b).
145   Land Compensation Act 1973 s29 as amended by Housing and Planning Act 1986 s5(3).
146   *Borg v Southwark LBC* June 1987 *Legal Action* 19, CA.
147   *Dance v Welwyn Hatfield DC* [1990] 22 HLR 339, CA.
148   *Bristol City Council v Lovell* [1998] 1 WLR 446; [1998] 1 All ER 775, HL.
149   Housing and Planning Act 1986 Commencement (No 5) Order 1987 SI No 754. Effective date 13 May 1987; see DoE Circ 14/87.

The dwelling-house is in an area which is the subject of a redevelopment scheme approved by the Secretary of State or the Housing Corporation or Scottish Homes in accordance with Part V of this Schedule and the landlord intends within a reasonable time of obtaining possession to dispose of the dwelling-house in accordance with the scheme.

or

Part of the dwelling-house is in such an area and the landlord intends within a reasonable time of obtaining possession to dispose of that part in accordance with the scheme and for that purpose reasonably requires possession of the dwelling-house.

3.151   In order for the ground to become available, the dwelling must be in a 'redevelopment area'. Housing Act 1985 Sch 2 Pt V sets out the terms under which the secretary of state may designate such an area. The procedure requires an element of prior consultation with tenants[150] and allows the secretary of state to require information from the land-lords,[151] take into account a variety of factors[152] and grant conditional or outright approval.[153] If the scheme is approved conditionally, the landlord may rely on a notice seeking possession served on ground 10A even though the conditions are not satisfied at the date of service, so long as they are fulfilled at the date of the hearing.[154] Where the landlord is a registered social landlord, the Part V functions fall upon the Housing Corporation rather than the secretary of state.[155] The secretary of state's approach to Part V applications is set out in DoE (former Department of the Environment) Circular 14/87. The Corporation's approach is likewise described in its circulars.

3.152   In order to obtain possession on ground 10A, the landlord need not satisfy the court that an order is reasonably required. The only relevant condition is that suitable alternative accommodation is available.

3.153   Tenants displaced as a result of ground 10A proceedings may be entitled to home loss payments.[156] A check should also be made to see if there is any specific provision in the tenancy agreement as to the compensation which may be payable.[157]

---

150 HA 1985 Sch 2 Pt V para 2.
151 HA 1985 Sch 2 Pt V para 3(2).
152 HA 1985 Sch 2 Pt V para 3(1).
153 HA 1985 Sch 2 Pt V para 5(1).
154 HA 1985 Sch 2 Pt V para 5(3).
155 HA 1985 Sch 2 Pt V para 6.
156 Land Compensation Act 1973 s29 as amended by Housing and Planning Act 1986 s5(3).
157 *Borg v Southwark LBC* June 1987 *Legal Action* 19, CA.

Ground 11: charitable landlords

3.154   Housing Act 1985 Sch 2 ground 11 provides that a ground for possession arises where:

> The landlord is a charity and the tenant's continued occupation of the dwelling-house would conflict with the objects of the charity.

3.155   The condition which the landlord must also satisfy is that suitable alternative accommodation is available to the tenant[158] (see para 3.185). However, the landlord need not show that it is reasonable to require the tenant to move.

3.156   If the conflict with the objects of the charity is caused by the tenant's breach of the tenancy agreement, the tenant runs the risk that the landlord may in the alternative rely on ground 1 and secure possession without being required to provide alternative accommodation (see para 3.45).

3.157   In other cases the ground is likely to be satisfied as a result of a change in the tenant's circumstances (for example, where the charity's objects are single people and the tenant marries or has children) or by a change in the charity's objects.

Ground 12: tied accommodation

3.158   Housing Act 1985 Sch 2 ground 12 relates to what might be described as 'tied' or 'employment-related' accommodation and may be relied upon where:

> The dwelling-house forms part of, or is within the curtilage of, a building which, or so much of it as is held by the landlord, is held mainly for purposes other than housing purposes and consists mainly of accommodation other than housing accommodation, or is situated in a cemetery, and –
> (a) the dwelling-house was let to the tenant or a predecessor in title of his in consequence of the tenant or predecessor being in the employment of the landlord or of –
>   a local authority,
>   a new town corporation,
>   a housing action trust,
>   an urban development corporation,
>   ..., or
>   the governors of an aided school,
>   and that employment has ceased, and

---

158   HA 1985 s84(2)(b).

(b) the landlord reasonably requires the dwelling-house for occupation as a residence for some person either engaged in the employment of the landlord, or of such a body, or with whom a contract for such employment has been entered into conditional on housing being provided.

3.159   Clearly the ground is not restricted to the situation in which the same public body is both landlord and employer. It expressly incorporates situations where the landlord is a prescribed public body (see para 1.6) and the tenant is an employee of another or different authority.

3.160   It is not sufficient that the tenant or the person from whom the tenant derived title is an ex-employee of the landlord: the original letting must have been 'in consequence' of that employment. See the discussion on the similar Rent Act ground (para 15.32) and generally chapter 17 (Premises occupied by employees). As to the meaning of 'within the curtilage of' see paras 3.130–3.132.

3.161   Note that the landlord must already be employing the next person for whom the property is required or have a contract for the employment of that person. The property must also be 'reasonably required' by the landlord.[159]

3.162   Additionally, the landlord must satisfy the dual conditions that (a) there will be suitable alternative accommodation (see para 3.185) for the tenant and any family; and (b) it is reasonable to order possession in all the circumstances of the case.[160]

3.163   In considering whether it would be reasonable to order possession, the court will have regard to issues including the ex-employee's age and length of service, other accommodation possibilities for the new employee, and the nature of the accommodation of which possession is sought.

Ground 13: accommodation for the disabled

3.164   Special provision is made for the recovery of premises adapted for the disabled. Housing Act 1985 Sch 2 ground 13 applies where:

The dwelling-house has features which are substantially different from those of ordinary dwelling-houses and which are designed to make it suitable for occupation by a physically disabled person who requires accommodation of a kind provided by the dwelling-house and –

---

159 Compare with Rent Act 1977 case 8 discussed at para 15.32.
160 HA 1985 s84(2)(c).

(a) there is no longer such a person residing in the dwelling-house, and

(b) the landlord requires it for occupation (whether alone or with members of his family) by such a person.

3.165   Note that the special features must be 'substantially' different from those of an ordinary dwelling and they must have been 'designed' (in the technical sense) for the special needs of the physically disabled. A simple additional ground-floor lavatory does not fulfil those requirements.[161]

3.166   It should also be noted that the ground is not available where the premises are adapted for use by a mentally disabled tenant (recovery of possession in such cases would be sought under grounds 14 or 15). Furthermore, the landlord must show that possession is required for a new prospective tenant who is a physically disabled person with requirements for all or any of the particular special features presently provided.

3.167   If the ground is made out, the landlord must prove, in addition, that (a) suitable alternative accommodation is available (see para 3.185); and (b) it would be reasonable for a possession order to be made.[162]

Ground 14: special needs accommodation provided by housing associations and trusts

3.168   Housing Act 1985 Sch 2 ground 14 applies where:

> The landlord is a housing association or housing trust which lets dwelling-houses only for occupation (whether alone or with others) by persons whose circumstances (other than merely financial circumstances) make it especially difficult for them to satisfy their need for housing, and –
> (a) either there is no longer such a person residing in the dwelling-house or the tenant has received from a local housing authority an offer of accommodation in premises which are to be let as a separate dwelling under a secure tenancy, and
> (b) the landlord requires the dwelling-house for occupation (whether alone or with members of his family) by such a person.

3.169   Note that the limbs of paragraph (a) are expressed in the alternative. The second limb makes special provision for those reluctant to move on from 'half-way' houses or 'bridging' accommodation into perman-

---

161 *Freeman v Wansbeck DC* (1983) 10 HLR 54; [1984] 2 All ER 746, CA.
162 HA 1985 s84(2)(c).

ent public sector tenancies. That limb cannot be satisfied by the association or trust making available a secure or an assured tenancy with the same or another association or trust – only a local authority secure tenancy (and not an introductory tenancy) satisfies the provision. However, whichever limb is relied upon, the landlord must also show that a person with the appropriate special housing need would take the tenant's place.

3.170　　In order to succeed in reliance upon this ground the landlord must show that both the 'suitable alternative accommodation' (see para 3.185) and 'reasonableness' conditions are satisfied.[163]

3.171　　As to the position of housing association and housing trust tenants generally, see chapter 6.

Ground 15: special needs accommodation

3.172　Provision is made by Housing Act 1985 Sch 2 ground 15 for recovery of possession of one of a group of dwellings let to those with special needs. It applies where:

> The dwelling-house is one of a group of dwelling-houses which it is the practice of the landlord to let for occupation by persons with special needs and –
>
> (a) a social service or special facility is provided in close proximity to the group of dwelling-houses in order to assist persons with those special needs,
> (b) there is no longer a person with those special needs residing in the dwelling-house, and
> (c) the landlord requires the dwelling-house for occupation (whether alone or with members of his family) by a person who has those special needs.

3.173　The special needs dwellings must be in a 'group' within the ordinary meaning of that term. It is suggested that this requirement would not be met where the relevant dwellings said by the landlord to comprise the 'group' were spread throughout the area of the landlord's ordinary housing stock.[164]

3.174　　Limbs (a), (b) and (c) must all be satisfied. In order to succeed in recovering possession the landlord must also show that 'suitable alternative accommodation is available' (see para 3.185) and that the making of an order would be reasonable in all the circumstances.[165]

163　HA 1985 s84(2)(c).
164　*Martin v Motherwell DC* 1991 SLT (Lands Tr) 4, noted at September 1991 *Legal Action* 15.
165　HA 1985 s84(2)(c).

Ground 16: under-occupation

3.175   No ground for possession is available to the landlord in Housing Act 1985 Sch 2 simply on the basis that the original tenant no longer requires such extensive accommodation as at the date of the original letting.

3.176   However, if the present tenant is a statutory successor other than the deceased tenant's spouse or registered civil partner, ground 16 makes limited provision for recovery of the property by the landlord where:

> The accommodation afforded by the dwelling-house is more extensive than is reasonably required by the tenant and –
> (a) the tenancy vested in the tenant by virtue of section 89 (succession to periodic tenancy), the tenant being qualified to succeed by virtue of section 87(b) (members of family other than spouse or civil partner), and
> (b) notice of the proceedings for possession was served under section 83 *(or, where no such notice was served, the proceedings for possession were begun)* more than six months but less than twelve months after the date of the previous tenant's death.

> The matters to be taken into account by the court in determining whether it is reasonable to make an order on this ground include –
> (a) the age of the tenant,
> (b) the period during which the tenant has occupied the dwelling-house as his only or principal home, and
> (c) any financial or other support given by the tenant to the previous tenant.

3.177   Note therefore that ground 16 does not provide for recovery of possession from a widow or widower or surviving civil partner of the deceased tenant who is under-occupying. Nor does it apply to the under-occupying successor to a fixed-term tenancy.[166]

3.178   It can also be avoided if the late tenant had sufficient foresight to assign the tenancy to the successor in advance of his or her death rather than leaving it to be transmitted on death.[167] In such a case the new assignee tenant cannot be ousted under ground 16 (although ground 1 may be applicable if the assignment was made in breach of a prohibition against assignment: but see para 2.68 as to the possible unfairness of such a restriction).[168]

166 HA 1985 s90.
167 HA 1985 s91(3)(c).
168 *Peabody Donation Fund Governors v Higgins* [1983] 3 All ER 122; (1983) 10 HLR 82, CA.

3.179   Ground 16 sets a specific timetable for action by the landlord. The notice seeking possession must be served no earlier than six months from the date of death of the former tenant and no later than 12 months after the death. Note that the time runs from the actual date of death, not the date on which the landlord learned of the death (contrast this with Housing Act 1988 Sch 2 ground 7 – see para 10.44).

3.180   The words emphasised in ground 16 were added by Housing Act 1996 s147(3). It seems difficult to envisage a case in which the court could be persuaded in a ground 16 situation to exercise its discretion and dispense with a notice seeking possession when no notice had been given to the bereaved successor at all. More likely the new words will be relied upon by a landlord which is found to have served a technically defective notice (see para 4.11).

3.181   The landlord must not only satisfy each limb of ground 16 but also show that (a) suitable alternative accommodation is available (see paras 3.185 onwards); and (b) it would be reasonable for an order to be made.[169]

3.182   As to (a), because the present tenant is a successor he or she will take the fresh secure tenancy also as a successor unless the landlord can be persuaded to agree otherwise.[170] Such an agreement may provide sufficient 'encouragement' in negotiations to achieve a compromise at the door of the court in a ground 16 case where the defence is not strong and the successor is attracted by the offer of alternative accommodation which is not only suitable but which will also provide the opportunity for a further succession within the family.

3.183   As to (b), the reasonableness test, note that the second paragraph of ground 16 makes specific provision for identified factors to be taken into account by the court. In addition, the successor tenant may argue that, taking into account his or her rights under article 8 of the ECHR, it would be disproportionate to order possession, although a sense of proportionality is undoubtedly implicit in the general concept of reasonableness.[171]

3.184   It has been held that if the successor tenant has claimed the right to buy, the court, in considering reasonableness, should take into account the reasons why the landlord wishes to recover possession and the fact that the tenant may have established a right to purchase.[172] As to the specific factors which the court should consider in weighing

---

169 HA 1985 s84(2)(c).

170 HA 1985 s88(4).

171 *Newham LBC v Neal* [2003] EWCA Civ 541.

172 *Enfield LBC v McKeon* [1986] 2 All ER 730; (1986) 18 HLR 330, CA.

the legitimate claim by a tenant to exercise the right to buy against the landlord's well-founded claim for possession, see *Kensington and Chelsea RLBC v Hislop*[173] and *Basildon DC v Wahlen.*[174] Ultimately, it is a matter for the judge who had heard the evidence to balance the various factors.

Suitable alternative accommodation

3.185   In any proceedings based on grounds 9 to 16 the landlord must show that suitable alternative accommodation is available to the tenant and his/her family.[175]

3.186   Where the landlord is not the local housing authority the obligation is satisfied by production of a certificate issued by the housing authority to the effect that it will provide suitable accommodation before a specified date.[176]

3.187   Where the landlord is the housing authority or there is no certificate, the landlord must prove that suitable accommodation is available within the terms of Housing Act 1985 Sch 2 Pt IV paras 1 and 2 at the date of trial (earlier offers of other accommodation being irrelevant save possibly to any consideration of 'reasonableness'). Those paragraphs provide:

> 1. For the purposes of section 84(2)(b) and (c) (case in which court is not to make an order for possession unless satisfied that suitable accommodation will be available) accommodation is suitable if it consists of premises –
>
> (a) which are to be let as a separate dwelling under a secure tenancy, or
>
> (b) which are to be let as a separate dwelling under a protected tenancy, not being a tenancy under which the landlord might recover possession under one of the Cases in Part II of Schedule 15 to Rent Act 1977 (cases where court must order possession), or
>
> *(c) which are to be let as a separate dwelling under an assured tenancy which is neither an assured shorthold tenancy, within the meaning of the Housing Act 1988, nor a tenancy under which the landlord might recover possession under any of Grounds 1 to 5 in Schedule 2 to that Act*

---

173 [2003] EWHC 2944 (Ch); [2004] 1 All ER 1036; [2004] HLR 26.
174 [2006] EWCA Civ 326; May 2006 *Legal Action* 32.
175 HA 1985 s84(2)(b) and (c).
176 HA 1985 Sch 2 Pt IV para 4.

and, in the opinion of the court, the accommodation is reasonably suitable to the needs of the tenant and his family.

2. In determining whether the accommodation is reasonably suitable to the needs of the tenant and his family, regard shall be had to –
   (a) the nature of the accommodation which it is the practice of the landlord to allocate to persons with similar needs;
   (b) the distance of the accommodation available from the place of work or education of the tenant and of any members of his family;
   (c) its distance from the home of any member of the tenant's family if proximity to it is essential to that member's or the tenant's well-being;
   (d) the needs (as regards extent of accommodation) and means of the tenant and his family;
   (e) the terms on which the accommodation is available and the terms of the secure tenancy;
   (f) *if furniture was provided by the landlord for use under the secure tenancy, whether furniture is to be provided for use in the other accommodation, and if so the nature of the furniture to be provided.*

The words in italics were added by Housing Act 1988 Sch 17 para 65. As to the quality of security offered by an assured tenancy see chapter 10.

3.188   In applying these provisions, note that:

- 'family' is defined broadly;[177]
- if family members have different or conflicting views as to the suitability of the accommodation offered, the court should grant permission for them to be joined as parties to the proceedings in addition to the tenant;[178]
- the list of factors set out in paragraph 2 is not exhaustive;[179]
- the factors are not identical to those set out for Rent Act tenants in similar circumstances (although case-law developed in the Rent Act jurisdiction may provide useful aids to construction [see para 15.4], the Rent Act authorities must be approached with some caution);[180]
- it may be helpful to invite the judge to view the accommodation offered;

---

177 HA 1985 s113 as amended by Civil Partnership Act 2004 Sch 8 para 27, reproduced at para 2.30; and see *Stonebridge HAT v McKay* June 2006 *Legal Action* 37.

178 *Wandsworth LBC v Fadayomi* [1987] 3 All ER 474, CA.

179 *Enfield LBC v French* (1984) 17 HLR 211, CA.

180 Ibid at 216–217.

- if the alternative accommodation will be provided by a different landlord, and that landlord is a housing association or other registered social landlord, the court should be invited to direct that the tenancy of the accommodation be a secure rather than an assured tenancy;[181]

- paragraph 2(a) has no parallel in the Rent Act. It allows the court to consider the landlord's usual allocation policy for families of the same size, etc, as that of the tenant. Thus it will be open to the landlord to suggest in the case of a single person that its usual policy is to provide a small flat or bedsitter. The defence for a tenant faced with such an assertion relies upon showing that it is an unreasonable rule or that an exception should be made.

- where the local authority has elected to operate an introductory tenancy regime, it will be necessary to ensure that the new tenancy is secure rather than introductory. The court should ensure that the secure tenancy is not ended by the possession order on any date earlier than that on which the new tenancy is to begin (see Housing Act 1996 s124(2)).

Appeals[182]

3.189   Advisers should be aware that although a general right of appeal lies from the outcome of a trial in a possession case (from district judge to circuit judge or circuit judge to High Court judge), the appellate court is likely to be singularly reluctant to disturb findings made at first instance on issues of reasonableness and suitability of alternative accommodation.

3.190   Dicta in keeping with 'this court will only interfere with the exercise of the trial judge's discretion in such a case, if it can be shown to be plainly and utterly wrong'[183] are to be found liberally in reported cases: see para 3.78. Additionally permission to appeal is required in any case in which possession has been claimed.[184]

3.191   Furthermore, there can be no appeal on any matter of fact in a case turning on grounds 1 to 8,[185] although that is no impediment

---

181   HA 1988 s35(4)(e).

182   The procedure for appeals is regulated by CPR Part 52, discussed in more detail at paras 28.27 onwards.

183   Per Simon Brown LJ in *Kensington and Chelsea RLBC v Simmonds* (1997) 29 HLR 507.

184   CPR 52.3.

185   County Courts Act 1984 s77(6)(e).

to an appeal under one of those grounds on the basis that the judge failed to consider reasonableness or failed to consider whether the order for possession made should be suspended.[186]

3.192   For all these reasons every effort should be put into ensuring a successful outcome at the first hearing of a possession action.

Human Rights Act 1998

3.193   Although this chapter has been concerned with the circumstances in which a secure tenant of a local authority or other public landlord may lose his or her home, it may appear surprising that article 8(1) of the ECHR has played little part in the discussion of security of tenure or in the decisions of the courts since the advent of the Human Rights Act on 2 October 2000. Article 8(1) establishes that: 'Everyone has the right to respect for his private and family life, his home and his correspondence.'

3.194   This is not because the article is not 'engaged' by possession proceedings – quite the reverse. There could hardly be a more obvious interference with article 8(1) than an attempt to oust an individual from his or her home.[187] The explanation lies in the fact that the right to respect for the home is a 'qualified' rather than an absolute right. Article 8(2) provides that a proportionate interference with the right may be justified if it is:

> ... in accordance with the law and necessary in a democratic society in the interests of national security, public safety or the economic well-being of the country, for the prevention of disorder or crime, for the protection of health or morals, or for the protection of the rights and freedoms of others.

3.195   The House of Lords, in the leading case of *Kay v Lambeth LBC, Leeds CC v Price*[188] has held that article 8 is satisfied by the existence of domestic legislation which accords security of tenure to some, and not to others. In legislating for the provision of a scarce resource such as housing, Parliament must be taken to have satisfied the article 8(2) requirement of acting 'in the interests of ... the economic well-being of the country' and 'for the protection of the rights and freedoms of

---

186 *Gallagher v Castle Vale Action Trust Limited* [2001] EWCA Civ 944; (2001) 33 HLR 72, CA.

187 *R v Bracknell Forest BC ex p Johns and McLellan* (2001) 33 HLR 989, CA and *Lambeth LBC v Howard* [2001] EWCA Civ 468; (2001) 33 HLR 58, CA.

188 [2006] UKHL 10; [2006] 2 WLR 570, HL.

others'. Against that background, where a public authority has a right under domestic law to possession of property, it is not for the courts to question the exercise of that right in specific cases, other than on the normal principles of judicial review. For a full discussion of the relevance of the Human Rights Act 1998 to housing cases, see paras 5.31 onwards.

3.196   As the discussion earlier in this chapter has shown, the secure tenant is protected from arbitrary eviction. The 'hoops' through which a public landlord must pass (notice before proceedings, bringing court proceedings, proof of a 'ground' and proof of a 'condition') enable a court to ensure that the interference with the tenant's right to respect for his or her home only occurs where such action is justified. This is particularly true of those cases in which the landlord must satisfy the court that it is reasonable to order possession, and the court itself has power to 'suspend' any order for possession (which constitute the vast majority of the cases against secure tenants that are brought to court). In such cases:

> [a]s this court has said more than once, there is nothing in article 8, or in the associated jurisprudence of the European Court of Human Rights, which should carry county courts to materially different outcomes from those that they have been arriving at for many years when deciding whether it is reasonable to make an outright or a suspended order or no possession order.[189]

189 Sedley LJ in *Lambeth LBC v Howard* [2001] EWCA Civ 468; (2001) 33 HLR 58 at [31].

CHAPTER 4

Preparing the defence

General preparation

4.1   The preparation of the defence for a secure occupier should take place at the earliest possible opportunity. If instructed *at the last minute*, go immediately to para 4.74.

4.2   If instructed *well in advance* of any prospective or actual court hearing date, the adviser will need to take full instructions from the client (see the Instructions Checklist at appendix C).

4.3   In addition to taking the client's statement and assembling background material relating to the particular possession proceedings, the adviser will wish to gather together:

- a copy of the tenancy agreement;
- a copy of the notice seeking possession – if any (see para 2.4);
- the rent book/rent payment account;
- other relevant documents.

4.4   An early opportunity might usefully be taken to inspect the tenant's housing management file as held by the landlord, in order to secure copies of the above and other relevant documents. In the case of a local authority landlord an application for such access should:

- be made in writing;
- make reference to the Data Protection Act 1998;
- enclose a signed authority from the client;
- enclose a cheque for £10 (being the maximum fee currently payable for access).

4.5   Most local authority landlords will respond to such a request either by simply forwarding a photocopy of the entire file or by making it available at their offices with a copying facility. Other social landlords make similar provision for tenants (or their advisers) to inspect housing files. If the possession proceedings have already started, such documents would in any event be eventually obtained in the course of disclosure[1] and if the proceedings have not yet started but are contemplated, early disclosure of the documents would certainly accord with the principles of the *Practice Direction on Pre-action Protocols*[2] and the Rent Arrears Pre-Action Protocol (see para 3.34 and appendix D).

4.6   Depending upon the issues which arise in the client's statement, and after consideration of the documents, it may be necessary to undertake a housing benefit (or general welfare benefit) assessment and/or obtain a professional report on the condition of the property.

1   CPR Part 31.
2   See para 4 of the CPR *Practice Direction on Pre-Action Protocols*.

4.7   Full certificates for publicly funded legal representation should be applied for immediately if the tenant might meet the financial criteria and some prospect of resisting possession can be shown – as the litigation concerns an issue of vital importance, ie the tenant's continued occupation of his or her home.[3] Indeed, the Legal Services Commission's Decision-Making Guidance para 19.7(4) states:

> Legal Representation is likely to be granted where there is a substantive defence to the possession action, including a defence as to reasonableness of the possession order being made, ie, where the ground for possession has been made out but where the court must also assess whether it is reasonable in all the circumstances to make an order for possession,

If the adviser is instructed only a few days prior to the hearing, an emergency certificate should be obtained or granted under devolved powers (see chapter 24).

4.8   If a defence is to be submitted this should be in the appropriate form (N11), filed with the court, and properly served on the landlord in advance of the next hearing (see chapter 21 for possession procedure and appendix B for a precedent defence). The adviser instructed at a late stage will simply have to pass a copy to the landlord at court or apply for an extension of time in which to file a defence. In the latter case it would be sensible to have an outline or early draft of the defence available at court.

4.9   The following pages set out the so-called 'technical' defences and then the 'substantive' defences. Both can be successfully deployed to resist or defeat possession proceedings.

Technical defences

4.10   Although these defences are described as 'technical', at least in the short term[4] they have the potential to be as effective as the substantive defences in preventing the landlord from obtaining an order for possession against a secure occupier.

Defective notice

4.11   As seen above (at para 2.4) the proper notice (notice seeking possession) must normally be served on the tenant as a prerequisite to the commencement of possession proceedings. If the notice is deficient,

3   See Funding Code para 10.3.
4   See *City of London v Devlin* (1997) 29 HLR 58, CA.

the proceedings must fail unless the court exercises in the particular case its discretion to dispense with notice (see para 2.10).

4.12   A sample copy of a notice seeking possession in the current pre-scribed form for periodic secure tenancies is reproduced in appendix A. (The different prescribed form for fixed-term secure tenancies is not reproduced.) Every notice seeking possession should be carefully inspected with a view to discovering any possible deficiency.

Form

4.13   The notice must normally be in the form prescribed in regulations made by the secretary of state.[5] Those regulations are made by statutory instrument.

4.14   The prescribed form of notice is found in the Secure Tenancies (Notices) Regulations 1987,[6] as amended by the Secure Tenancies (Notices) (Amendment) (England) Regulations 1997,[7] and subse-quently by the Secure Tenancies (Notices) (Amendment) (England) Regulations 2004[8] and the Secure Tenancies (Notices) (Amendment) (Wales) Regulations 2005.[9]

4.15   These numerous references simply serve to demonstrate the importance of checking the actual notice against the prescribed form effective on the date on which the notice was given.

4.16   If the notice is *not* in the form prescribed at the date of service it may[10] be ineffective. However, because minor technical deficien-cies would otherwise invalidate notices, the 1987 Regulations con-tain a 'saving provision' that a notice seeking possession not in the prescribed form will be valid if 'in a form substantially to the same effect'.[11] The use of delegated legislation in this way to save otherwise

---

5   HA 1985 s83(2)(a).

6   1987 SI No 755. The earliest prescribed form was contained in the Secure Tenancies (Notices) Regulations 1980 SI No 1339, as amended by SI 1984 No 1224 and upheld in *Wansbeck DC v Charlton* 79 LGR 523; (1981) 42 P & CR 162, CA. Those regulations were saved for the purposes of the Housing Act 1985 by Housing (Consequential Provisions) Act 1985 s2(2). A revised form was prescribed by the Secure Tenancies (Notices) Regulations 1987 which came into force on 13 May 1987.

7   1997 SI No 71.

8   2004 SI No 1627.

9   2005 SI No 1226.

10   In *Swansea CC v Hearn* (1991) 23 HLR 284, CA a notice to quit served without the latest version of the statutorily prescribed information set out on it, but with the earlier version endorsed, was held effective.

11   Secure Tenancies (Notices) Regulations 1987 reg 2(1).

faulty notices has been held to be within the relevant powers of the secretary of state: *Dudley MBC v Bailey.*[12]

4.17 As that case was fought entirely on the point as to the lawfulness of the saving power (rather than on the faults in the notice actually served), there is little judicial guidance from it as to the degree of error necessary to remove a form from the category of 'substantially to the same effect' as that prescribed and into a category of invalidity.[13]

4.18 Arguably, a notice would differ in substance if the 'Notes for Guidance' contained in the body of the prescribed form were omitted from the notice actually served[14] or were only set out on the reverse[15] or on a separate sheet without (at the very least) an indication to 'see overleaf' or 'see attached'.

4.19 Similarly, the words 'name(s) of secure tenant(s)' in paragraph 1 of the prescribed form are crucial, as the later guidance notes distinguish secure tenants from other tenants and licensees. It should also be noted that the words 'Notice of Seeking Possession' and the statutory reference at the head are themselves an important part of the prescribed form. They enable the tenant to identify the statutory power under which it is alleged the notice has been given.

Name of tenant

4.20 The prescribed form has a space for the insertion of the tenant's name and the notice must be served on *that tenant.*[16] Practical difficulties may arise over the misspelling of names or the use of former names where the tenant has changed his or her name following marriage or otherwise. To guard against this difficulty most landlords will use the name as it appears on the original tenancy agreement.

4.21 If the tenancy is a joint tenancy then the reference on the form to the 'tenant' is a reference to all the joint tenants. All must therefore be named in the notice even if some are no longer in residence.[17]

---

12 (1990) 22 HLR 424, CA.

13 But see *Tadema Holdings v Ferguson* (2000) 32 HLR 866, CA in which a notice of rent increase has been held to be 'substantially to the same effect' as its prescribed form after an examination of its alleged defects.

14 See *Manel v Memon* (2001) 33 HLR 24, CA.

15 But see *Swansea CC v Hearn* (1991) 23 HLR 284 in which prescribed particulars were given on the reverse of a notice to quit, although this particular point does not appear to have been taken.

16 HA 1985 s83(1)(a). See *Enfield LBC v Devonish and Sutton* (1997) 29 HLR 691, CA.

17 *Newham LBC v Okotoro* March 1993 *Legal Action* 11.

Ground

4.22   The notice must 'specify the ground on which the court will be asked to make an order for possession'.[18] The ground specified must therefore correspond with the ground that is (1) pleaded in the particulars of claim; and (2) relied upon in court.

4.23   As to (1), landlords not infrequently fail to set out in their particulars of claim the ground on which possession is being sought, contrary to the relevant court rules (see chapter 21). As to (2), if a different ground for possession is made out at trial from that shown in the notice seeking possession, the proceedings must be dismissed[19] unless the court gives permission for an alternative ground to be read into the notice seeking possession by alteration or addition, or the court exercises a discretion to dispense with the requirement of notice altogether.[20]

4.24   Although the regulations do not define what is meant by 'specify', courts will interpret this to mean that the actual words of the ground as they appear in the statute must be set out or, in default, at least words giving all the salient elements of the ground relied upon.[21] It follows that the words used in the notice seeking possession must always be carefully checked against the actual statutory formulation of the ground in each case. If they are significantly different this may well invalidate the notice.

Particulars

4.25   The notice must, on its face, give 'particulars' of the ground for possession specified in it.[22] These particulars must give the tenant sufficient details of the circumstances that the landlord relies upon in asserting that a ground for possession is made out, since the function of the notice is to fire a 'warning shot' telling the tenant what the complaint is against him or her so as to enable the tenant to rectify it.[23] Clearly, the simple statement 'arrears of rent' is an insufficient particular.[24] Similarly 'various acts of nuisance' or 'instances of dilapida-

---

18   HA 1985 s83(2)(b).
19   See *Midlothian DC v Tweedie* 1993 GWD 1068, Sh Ct.
20   HA 1985 ss83–84 and see *Gedling BC v Brener* September 2001 *Legal Action* 23.
21   *Mountain v Hastings* (1993) 25 HLR 427, CA.
22   HA 1985 s83(2)(c).
23   *Torridge DC v Jones* (1986) 18 HLR 107; [1985] 2 EGLR 54, CA.
24   Ibid.

tion' would be inadequate.[25] In a nuisance case the Court of Appeal described the following particulars as 'obviously' insufficient:[26]

> The tenant frequently disturbs his neighbour, and on one occasion has threatened his neighbour with physical violence.

Likewise the use of the simple words 'major refurbishment scheme' in a claim for possession under ground 10 is deficient,[27] as is the bare repetition of the terms of a tenancy agreement where the ground alleged is breach of those terms.[28]

4.26   If insufficient particulars are given, the court cannot entertain the proceedings, which must, therefore, be struck out unless the notice is amended or the court finds it just and equitable to dispense with notice.[29] The court can give the landlord permission to amend the notice seeking possession for the purpose of improving the particulars,[30] but it should not be assumed that the discretion will be exercised in favour of such an amendment if application is made at a late stage in the proceedings.[31]

4.27   If particulars are given but they are *inaccurate*, the court may (according to the degree of inaccuracy) permit the matter to proceed or allow amendment of the notice seeking possession. Thus if the notice gives particulars that the 'arrears of rent are £x' and it is shown at trial that the landlord has innocently and in error included in that figure items which are not arrears of rent, the action can proceed, but the judge will take into account the nature and extent of the error in determining whether possession should be given.[32]

The dates

4.28   The prescribed form contains a space for completion of the specified date (see para 2.7) and for entry of the date of the notice itself (which should be the date of service). It is vital that these dates are carefully checked, first, to ensure that the dates have been entered and, secondly, to identify any errors. A form is not in the prescribed form or

---

25 *South Buckinghamshire DC v Francis* (1985) 11 CL 152 and *Slough BC v Robbins* December 1996 *Legal Action* 13.
26 *Camden LBC v Oppong* (1996) 28 HLR 701 at 703, CA.
27 *Waltham Forest LBC v England* March 1994 *Legal Action* 11.
28 *East Devon DC v Williams* December 1996 *Legal Action* 13.
29 *Torridge DC v Jones* (1986) 18 HLR 107; (1985) 276 EG 1253, CA.
30 *Camden LBC v Oppong* (1996) 28 HLR 701, CA.
31 *Merton LBC v Drew* July 1999 *Legal Action* 22.
32 *Dudley MBC v Bailey* (1990) 22 HLR 424, CA.

in a form to substantially the same effect if a material date has either been omitted[33] or incorrectly stated.[34]

4.29   The specified date must be no earlier than the date on which the tenancy or licence could have been brought to an end by notice to quit or notice to determine given by the landlord on the same date that the notice seeking possession was served.[35]

4.30   Accordingly, the adviser should check carefully the date of service and the minimum period of notice the landlord would have been required to give under contract, statute or common law. In the ordinary case of a weekly periodic tenancy the specified date must be no earlier than four weeks after the next rent day.[36] If the 'specified date' is too early the notice is bad on its face and the proceedings should be dismissed unless the court exercises a discretion to dispense with service of the notice in the landlord's favour. The Housing Act 1985 does not give the court power to amend the dates set out in the notice.

4.31   Unless the notice included ground 2 (nuisance) as one of the grounds specified in it, proceedings issued before the specified date should also be dismissed, as no claim should be issued until after the specified date has passed.[37]

Has the notice lapsed?

4.32   The notice is valid for only 12 months from the specified date.[38] It must be noted that the 12 months runs *not* from the date of service but from the specified date.

4.33   As the specified date is usually at least 28 days after the notice was served, it should be at about the end of the thirteenth month after service that the notice lapses (contrast the position for the notice seeking possession served in respect of an assured tenancy, para 10.16).

4.34   No proceedings can be brought in respect of a notice that has lapsed.[39] Thus, an action for possession started more than 12 months after the specified date is defective and should be struck out unless the court decides that it is just and equitable to dispense with notice.[40]

---

33   *Patel v Rodrigo* June 1997 *Legal Action* 23.
34   *Panayi v Roberts* (1993) 25 HLR 421, CA.
35   HA 1985 s83(5).
36   Protection from Eviction Act 1977 s5, as amended.
37   HA 1985 s83(4)(a).
38   HA 1985 s83(3)(b) and (4)(b).
39   HA 1985 s83(4).
40   *Edinburgh City Council v Davis* 1987 SLT 33, noted at June 1987 *Legal Action* 19.

4.35 For these purposes the proceedings 'begin' on the date the relevant county court issues the claim.[41]

Service

4.36 Housing Act 1985 requires that the notice seeking possession has been served by the landlord 'on the tenant'.[42] It is for the landlord to prove that the notice was served on the tenant.

4.37 Nothing in Housing Act 1985 Pt IV or in s617 (service of notices) assists with the form that service of the notice must take.[43] For the rules as to acceptable proof of service developed by the courts in relation to forms of service of notice to quit (in summary – personal service on the tenant, service on a wife of the tenant, or service on the servant of the tenant) see para 12.22.[44] The common law acceptance of service on the tenant's wife as service on the tenant must now be taken to extend to service on the husband or registered civil partner of the tenant.

4.38 In the absence of an express admission by the tenant of service of the notice seeking possession, the burden of proof remains on the landlord to show that the notice was properly served.

4.39 Although the surest route to proving service is personal delivery to the tenant, many landlords seek to rely on: postal service; putting the notice through a letterbox; or giving it to someone at the property to pass on to the tenant. None of these is reliable or offers conclusive evidence that the tenant was served. Local authority landlords cannot be assisted in establishing service by Local Government Act 1972 s233 (which permits service by post or hand delivery to the 'proper address', usually the last known address, of statutory notices), as a notice seeking possession is not served by the authority in its capacity as a local authority but rather in the capacity of landlord.[45]

4.40 To avoid these difficulties, the Court of Appeal has encouraged landlords of secure tenants to ensure that express provision for appropriate methods of service is made in the tenancy agreement itself.[46]

---

41 *Shepping v Osada* (2001) 33 HLR 13, CA. See also *Salford City Council v Garner* [2004] EWCA Civ 364; [2004] HLR 35, CA in relation to introductory tenancies.

42 HA 1985 s83(1).

43 See January 1982 *Housing* 27.

44 See *Enfield LBC v Devonish and Sutton* (1997) 29 HLR 691, CA.

45 See *Chesterfield BC v Crossley* June 1998 *Legal Action* 10 and *Eastbourne BC v Dawson* June 1999 *Legal Action* 23.

46 *Wandsworth LBC v Atwell* (1995) 27 HLR 536, CA and *Enfield LBC v Devonish* (1997) 29 HLR 691, CA.

Dispensing with notice

4.41   Until the changes introduced by the Housing Act 1996, a successful argument that a notice seeking possession was defective was fatal to the landlord's case. However, Housing Act 1985 s83(1)(b), as amended by the 1996 Act,[47] provides the court with the power to dispense with the need for a valid notice where it is 'just and equitable to do so'.

4.42   In *Braintree DC v Vincent*[48] the tenant was in a nursing home and her sons were occupying the property. The authority brought possession proceedings against the sons as trespassers. The judge joined the tenant to the proceedings, and an order was made on the basis that the property had ceased to be her only or principal home and on the alternative ground of rent arrears. In relation to the statutory ground, the judge considered that it was just and equitable to dispense with a notice. This decision was upheld in the Court of Appeal. Although it was 'obviously only in relatively exceptional cases where the court should be prepared to dispense with a section 83 notice', the circumstances were unusual in procedural terms. The tenant was only added as defendant at the insistence of the judge, and a notice of seeking possession would have been of no benefit to her. See also para 10.20, concerning the same power as it applies to assured tenancies (under Housing Act 1988 s8), and in particular *Curtis v Helena Housing Association Ltd* and *Revell v Knowsley Housing Trust*,[49] in which the claimant sought to dispense with the notice requirement following a large-scale transfer of the local authority's housing stock to a registered social landlord.

Defective claims

4.43   The usual rules as to drafting claims in civil litigation apply in possession proceedings against secure occupiers in the county court (see chapter 21). Common technical deficiencies in landlords' claims for possession in the public sector include:

- failure to join all joint tenants;
- failure to set out own title;
- failure to refer to the notice seeking possession;
- insufficient particulars given (particularly of 'reasonableness');[50]

---

47   HA 1996 s147.
48   [2004] EWCA Civ 415, CA.
49   [2003] EWCA Civ 496; [2003] HLR 63, CA.
50   See *Midlothian DC v Brown* 1990 SCLR 765 and *Renfrew DC v Inglis* 1991 SLT (Sh Ct) 83.

- failure to restrict the claim to the ground in the notice seeking possession.

4.44   The particulars of claim in possession proceedings must contain prescribed basic information about the premises and the tenancy agreement.[51] Moreover, if the claim is on the ground of non-payment of rent the particulars of claim will usually be in the relevant court form[52] and must contain prescribed particulars concerning the arrears and the circumstances of the parties.[53]

4.45   However, as landlords generally obtain permission to amend, reliance on defects in the claim will rarely provide a long-term defence. It has nevertheless been possible in some cases to have the whole proceedings struck out for failure to use and complete the normal form of particulars of claim for use in 'arrears' cases or otherwise give the prescribed particulars.

Action improperly brought

4.46   If the possession proceedings have been improperly brought (for example, the decision to bring them has been motivated by bad faith, abuse of power or dishonesty by the public sector landlord), the tenant may be able to secure an order of 'prohibition' restraining pursuit of the action. Such an order may be sought by an application for judicial review in the Administrative Court. It would be usual for the county court proceedings to be adjourned in such circumstances[54] to await the outcome of the Administrative Court action.[55] Alternatively, the county court may be asked to strike out the action as an abuse of process or the occupier could set up the unlawful action of the landlord by way of defence.[56]

Set-off

4.47   Secure tenants have a complete defence to an action for possession based on a failure to pay monies due to the landlord, if they can

---

51 CPR PD 55, para 2.1.
52 Form N119.
53 CPR PD 55, para 2.1.
54 HA 1985 s85(1).
55 *Avon CC v Buscott* [1988] QB 656; [1988] 1 All ER 841; (1988) 20 HLR 385, CA.
56 *Wandsworth LBC v Winder (No 1)* [1984] AC 461; [1984] 3 WLR 1254; (1984) 17 HLR 196, HL. See also *Kay v Lambeth LBC, Leeds City Council v Price* [2006] UKHL 10; [2006] 2 WLR 570, HL.

properly set off (for example, by a successful counterclaim under CPR Part 20) an amount payable by the landlord and equal to or greater than the amount claimed. Such circumstances usually arise from disrepair (see para 21.36) or a failure to pay housing benefit (see chapter 32). However, reliance should not be placed solely on the set-off by way of defence which relies on a counterclaim, as there is never a guarantee that the counterclaim will succeed.[57]

Substantive defences

Ground not made out

4.48   The first substantive line of defence for the secure tenant, assuming that the technical defences mentioned above have proved insufficient, is to argue that the ground asserted by the landlord is not made out on the evidence and on the balance of probabilities. The usual issues dealt with in possession proceedings on the grounds available against secure tenants and common methods of defending such cases are set out in the discussion of the individual grounds (see chapter 3).

Condition not made out

4.49   The second line of defence, assuming that the landlord has proved (or the tenant admits) that a ground has been made out, is to assert that there is insufficient evidence on the balance of probabilities to show that a necessary condition is satisfied. The conditions are discussed in chapter 3 together with the respective grounds to which they relate. The most common condition is that it is reasonable to order possession. It is for the landlord to satisfy the court that that is so.

Possession orders and eviction

Possession order inappropriate

4.50   It need not inevitably follow that, because both a ground and a condition could be made out, a possession order (whether immediate or suspended) should be made. Indeed, there are cases in which, despite it being shown that the landlord has acted reasonably in bringing

---

57   *Haringey LBC v Stewart* (1991) 23 HLR 557, CA.

possession proceedings which may establish both the ground and its associated condition, it is nevertheless worthwhile to give the tenant another 'chance'. The mechanism readily available to the court is the adjournment of the proceedings,[58] in all cases except those brought under grounds 9 to 11 inclusive (to which the explicit power to adjourn does not apply).

4.51　　The specific power to adjourn (additional to any other discretion in the court) arises in all cases relying on grounds 1 to 8 or grounds 12 to 16 contained in Housing Act 1985 Sch 2. In any of these cases the court may adjourn the proceedings for such period or periods as it thinks fit.[59] This has the substantial benefit to the claimant that the costs of the action are not usually awarded to one party or the other if the matter is adjourned.

4.52　　The safeguard for the landlord is that the court is free to make the adjournment conditional.[60] For example, the adjournment may be conditional upon the tenant paying the current rent plus £x towards the arrears. The check on excessive conditions is Housing Act 1985 s85(3)(a) which provides that conditions are not to be imposed if they would cause exceptional hardship to the tenant or would otherwise be unreasonable. A form of order for adjournment on terms meeting these points has been published[61] (and see appendix B).

4.53　　If the court cannot be persuaded to deal with the matter by way of adjournment, and decides to make a possession order, the adviser must take steps to avoid the making of an absolute order for possession which will terminate the tenancy.

Resisting an absolute possession order

4.54　　There are, of course, cases in which (the landlord having established both the grounds and conditions) the tenant is unable to resist the conclusion that a possession order must be made. If a possession order is made, the tenancy ends on the date on which the tenant is to give up possession in pursuance of the order.[62] The adviser should obviously seek to persuade the court to postpone for as long as possible the date on which possession is to be given.[63]

58　HA 1985 s85(1).
59　HA 1985 s85(1).
60　HA 1985 s85(3).
61　See J Platt and N Madge 'Suspended Possession Orders' (1991) 141 NLJ 853.
62　HA 1985 s82(2).
63　HA 1985 s85(2)(b).

4.55   There are, of course, cases in which (the landlord having established both the grounds and conditions) the tenant is unable to resist the conclusion that a possession order must be made. Then it will be necessary to persuade the court that the date for possession should be postponed, usually on condition that the tenant complies with certain specified terms; or, if the court is not prepared to postpone the possession date conditionally, so that the secure tenancy comes to an end on the date fixed, that execution of the order on or after that date should be suspended on terms.[64] For a general discussion of the jurisdiction of the court to postpone the date for possession and suspend execution of possession orders, see chapters 28 and 29.

Postponed possession orders

4.56   These orders have in the past been described as 'suspended possession orders'. The better view now is that they should be called 'postponed possession orders', since Housing Act 1985 s85(2) provides that the court may '*postpone* the date of *possession*'; or 'stay or *suspend* the *execution* of the order'. The term 'suspension' is therefore only used in relation to enforcement of the order after the possession order has taken effect and the tenancy has ended. For a detailed examination of suspended and postponed possession orders, see paras 29.3–29.6.

4.57   The court will usually only accede to an application to 'postpone' the order where postponement is on the basis of specified terms being complied with during the period of postponement. The court must impose conditions on any postponement relating to payment of rent and such further conditions as it thinks fit unless that would cause exceptional hardship or would otherwise be unreasonable.[65]

4.58   Where possible, advisers should seek to avoid any form of possession order, in view of the consequences to which even a postponed order gives rise. First, *costs* are usually awarded against the tenant on the making of the order for possession, whether postponed or otherwise. Although a tenant with a public funding certificate for legal representation has some protection against an award of costs, such protection is not absolute (see chapter 26) and for those without such protection, costs may cause considerable hardship. Second, the postponement may be on terms which – although they must not be unreasonable or cause exceptional hardship – may nevertheless cause some hardship. Third, where the order is made in form N28 (March 2006 – see para

64   HA 1985 s85(2)(b).
65   HA 1985 s85(3).

4.60 below) and the tenant breaches the terms of the order, even once, the tenant loses the tenancy and with it all benefits associated with 'secure' status, such as the right to buy, the right to assign and the right to succession.[66] He or she will then become a 'tolerated trespasser'.[67] See para 4.75 below. Fourth, in the event of a breach of the conditions, the landlord may proceed to apply for a warrant for possession.

4.59   If a postponed possession order is to be made, the form of wording of the order is critical. The court's practice may be to use court form N28 or N28A. However, the version of the Form N28 which was current during the period between October 2001 and March 2006 was seriously defective, in that it provided that the tenant was to give the claimant possession on a specified date and merely suspended enforcement of the order. Such an order brought the tenancy to an end on the specified date, whether or not there had been any breach of its terms. The effect of the decision in *Harlow DC v Hall*[68] is that all those tenants who had become subject to suspended possession orders since the adoption of Form N28 in October 2001 had lost their tenancies. They had become trespassers irrespective of whether they had breached the terms of the order or not, which was clearly not the court's intention.

4.60   Following the decision in *Harlow DC v Hall* HM Court Service provided an Interim Solution amending the terms of Form N28 pending a full revision of the form.[69] Under the amended N28 (March 2006), a date for possession is fixed in the order, but then postponed on the basis that the tenant keeps to the agreed payment terms. The effect of the amended order is to ensure that the giving of possession is postponed conditionally and will not actually come to pass unless the order is breached. The order itself is termed a 'postponed possession order'.

4.61   The correct form of the postponed possession order was further considered in the cases of *Bristol CC v Hassan; Bristol CC v Glastonbury*,[70] in which the Court of Appeal held that a judge is not obliged to set out a specific date for possession on the face of the order. It was therefore lawful for a court to make an order in the amended Form N28 (March 2006).

66   *Brent LBC v Knightley* [1997] 2 FLR 1; (1997) 29 HLR 857, CA.
67   *Thompson v Elmbridge BC* [1987] 1 WLR 1425; (1987) 19 HLR 526, CA.
68   [2006] EWCA Civ 156.
69   HMCS Business Information ref. BI/56/03/06 dated 17 March 2006 obtainable from the Debt and Housing Branch, Civil Family and Customer Services, HMCS, Department for Constitutional Affairs, 5th Floor, Selborne House, 54/60, Victoria Street, London SW1E 6QW.
70   [2006] EWCA Civ 656, CA.

4.62   In *Bristol CC v Hassan*, the Court of Appeal further considered[71] that it would be 'lawful and appropriate' for courts to adopt an alternative 'two stage' form of order, whereby a date for possession would not be fixed until the landlord had applied to the court for such a date following a breach. In the light of the 'very unsatisfactory position' of the tolerated trespasser, the Court of Appeal has endorsed a form of order which provides for possession to be postponed indefinitely on terms that, in the event of a breach of the order, the landlord may apply to the court on a 'without notice' basis to fix a date for possession. An order modelled on the *Hassan* order has been adopted with effect from 3 July 2006, bearing the title N28A. This form of order is set out in Appendix B (document no 10).

4.63   A new Section IV ('Orders fixing a date for possession') has been added to Practice Direction 55 of the CPR to complement the new form N28A, also with effect from 3 July 2006 (se appendix E). Where an order has been made in this form, and the conditions of postponement are breached, new para 10.2 provides that the landlord may apply to the court for an order fixing the date on which the tenant has to give up possession. At least 14 days before making such an application, the landlord must give written notice to the tenant of its intention to do so, and of its reasons for doing so. The notice must record, by reference to a copy of the rent account, in what respect the tenant has failed to comply with the order and must invite the tenant's response within 7 days. The application itself will be made without notice, but the landlord must atttach a copy of the tenant's reply (if any) and must state whether there is any outstanding housing benefit claim by the tenant. The district judge will normally determine the application without a hearing by fixing the date for possession as the next working day, unless he or she considers that a hearing is necessary, in which case a date of hearing will be arranged.

4.64   The exercise of fixing a date for possession will therefore be a paper procedure, although the judge may refer the landlord's application for an oral hearing where appropriate (eg, where the tenant has responded to the landlord's notice and has explained the reason for the breach). Only if the court then fixes a date will the tenancy end and the tenant become a trespasser (though it will still be possible to apply to the court to vary the possession order or suspend any warrant of possession at any time up to actual eviction).

4.65   It is a matter for the discretion of the judge at trial of the possession claim as to what form the order should take. In some circum-

71 Ibid para 39.

stances, for example, where the tenant has a particularly bad record of payment, the court may wish to make an order in accordance with Form N28 (March 2006).

4.66 It is clearly important for advisers and legal representatives to attempt to persuade the court that it should use form N28A rather than N28. Where an order is made in form N28 (March 2006), the secure tenancy ends on a single breach of the terms of the order and the tenant becomes a trespasser. Where form N28A is used, the secure tenancy does not end in spite of a breach or breaches unless and until the court fixes a date for possession following an application by the landlord.

4.67 Advisers will need to be alert to the position of those tenants who are already the subject of orders framed in the version of form N28 that was used between October 2001 and March 2006: such tenants will in fact already have lost their tenancy on the date specified in the order irrespective of any breach of the order, and should therefore be advised to make application to the court to vary the order by postponing the date for possession, adapting the wording of form N28A as a draft order.

4.68 Any postponed order should preferably be expressed to provide for automatic discharge on compliance with all its terms.[72]

4.69 If there is no such express provision, the fact of compliance with the terms of the postponement does not work a discharge of the order or revival of any lost tenancy,[73] so the adviser should be alert to the need for the tenant to apply for the discharge or rescission of the order as soon as all the terms are complied with.[74] Otherwise, the order will continue in existence and will apply again if the tenant misses a payment of rent or commits some other breach of the tenancy. If the tenant has complied with the terms of the order in full, application may be made to discharge the order under section 85(4). But where there has been any breach of the terms – even though the arrears under the order have now been cleared in full – it appears that section 85(4) does not assist.[75] In these circumstances it appears that the only way of discharging the order (and of reviving the lost secure tenancy) will be to apply to the court under section 85(2) to vary the original order by postponing further the date for possession. The terms of the

---

72 *Blaenau Gwent BC v Snell* March 1990 *Legal Action* 13; and see *Merton LBC v Hashmi* September 1995 *Legal Action* 13, CA.

73 *Marshall v Bradford MBC* [2001] EWCA Civ 594; [2002] HLR 22, CA.

74 HA 1985 s85(4).

75 *Swindon BC v Aston* [2002] EWCA Civ 1850; [2003] 35 HLR 42.

new order will be postponed possession on the basis of continued payment of current rent, since there are no longer any arrears. After a further period – perhaps three months – of compliance with that order, application may then be made to discharge it under section 85(4). Alternatively, it may be possible to argue that a new tenancy has been created, but this will not be the case merely because the landlord has continued to accept rent and used terminology in correspondence which implies a tenancy: the facts must 'force the conclusion' that a new tenancy has arisen.[76]

Preventing an eviction

4.70   Where an order for possession has been made, secure occupiers retain their secure status until the date on which they are to give up possession in pursuance of the order.[77] It is on that date that both security and the tenancy or licence end.

4.71   In the case of an *absolute order* for possession, the date on which the tenant is to give up possession will be clearly shown in the order itself or identified by a reference to 'X days from today's date' (usually 28 days from the date of hearing). An adviser instructed for the recipient of such an order which has not yet taken effect should always consider: (1) whether an appeal can be justified; (2) whether an application can be made to set it aside; or (3) whether circumstances have changed sufficiently since the order was made to enable a successful application to be made to postpone on terms the date for possession.[78]

4.72   In the case of a *postponed order* for possession made in court form N28 (see para 29.5), the date that both security and the tenancy end is the date on which the terms of the order are breached.[79] If the terms are not breached but are complied with, or if the order requires a further application to the court to fix a date for possession, the tenancy, and security with it, continue.

4.73   Once the date fixed by an order has passed (whether an outright order or a postponed order under which the date for possession has occurred), the landlord may apply to the court (by completing a

76 *Lambeth LBC v O'Kane, Helena Housing Ltd v Pinder,* [2005] EWCA Civ 1010; [2006] HLR 2, CA; see also *Hawkins v Newham LBC* [2005] EWCA Civ 451; [2005] HLR 42, CA.

77 HA 1985 s82(2).

78 *Ujima Housing Association v Smith* April 2001 *Legal Action* 21

79 *Thompson v Elmbridge BC* [1987] 1 WLR 1425; (1987) 19 HLR 526, CA, and *Leicester CC v Aldwinkle* (1992) 24 HLR 49, CA.

simple form) for the issue of a warrant for possession and its execution by a bailiff. The occupier should receive notice from the bailiffs (Form N54) giving the time and date on which they will attend to take possession.

4.74 Whether the order was expressed to be absolute or was postponed, the court can suspend or stay execution of the order or further postpone the date for possession on any grounds that it 'thinks fit'.[80] This can be done at any time before the moment of execution of the order by the bailiffs, even a matter of hours or minutes beforehand.[81] The procedure for making an application for a stay or postponement is described in chapter 29. Note that this procedure is not available where the possession order has been obtained under ground 9, 10, 10A or 11 contained in Housing Act 1985 Sch 2, but that in all other cases it is available even if the original date for possession has passed or a 'suspended' or postponed order has been breached.

The tolerated trespasser

4.75 The status of an occupier who has lost his or her tenancy and security as a result of a breach of a 'suspended' order (where the date for possession has been fixed) or expiry of an absolute order is described as a 'tolerated trespasser'.[82] Where a suspended possession order is in a form which brings a date for possession into effect automatically if its terms are not complied with, on a single breach of the terms, the tenancy ends at that instant.[83] The tenant loses the tenancy and all the rights which go with it, such as rights of succession, the right to buy and the landlord's implied repairing obligations under the Landlord and Tenant Act 1985.

4.76 The tolerated trespasser's former tenancy can be revived by a court order varying or discharging the original possession order. Where a postponed or suspended possession order is varied under Housing Act 1985 s85(2) and the date for delivery of possession is further postponed to a new date by court order, the revival is retrospective, and damages can be claimed for breaches of the repairing covenant which occurred during the period of 'tolerated trespass'.[84] There is no

---

80 HA 1985 s85(2).

81 *Islington LBC v Harridge* (1993) *Times* 30 June, CA.

82 See *Burrows v Brent LBC* [1996] 1 WLR 1448; [1996] 4 All ER 577; (1997) 29 HLR 167, HL.

83 HA 1985 s82(2); *Thompson v Elmbridge BC* [1987] 1 WLR 1425; (1987) 19 HLR 526, CA.

84 *Lambeth LBC v Rogers* (2000) 32 HLR 361, CA.

power to postpone the date of possession for the purpose of reviving a claim for damages for disrepair where the tenant has already left the property.[85] The Court of Appeal appears now to have discounted the view[86] that the secure tenancy can be revived by the landlord waiving breaches of the order: an application to the court to postpone the date of possession is required.[87]

4.77   If the 'tolerated trespasser' succeeds in an application to 'postpone' the date of possession in the *order* to a future date, the effect will be that the date for termination of the tenancy has not yet been reached and any tenancy which has been lost by the taking effect of the possession order at an earlier date will be revived.[88] The tenancy is revived only by an order which postpones the date for possession stated in the original order. An order which simply extends the life of the postponed possession order, where this was time limited, does not have this effect.[89] Where a warrant of possession has been issued, an order which stays or suspends the warrant on terms does not have the effect of reviving the tenancy, since it operates only to suspend *enforcement* of the order, and the occupier will remain a tolerated trespasser. Advisers who are assisting an occupier to apply for suspension of a warrant should consider including an application to vary the original order (by postponing the date for possession) in the same application notice.

Reinstating the tenant after eviction

4.78   Even if the order has been executed by the bailiff taking possession, it may still not be too late to set aside the possession order or the warrant or both. See chapter 29 for a full description of what can be done to reinstate the former tenant after eviction.

'Duty advocate' plan

4.79   This section of this chapter illustrates how an adviser might respond to the type of public sector possession case which occurs with great-

---

85   *Dunn v Bradford MDC* [2002] EWCA Civ 1137; [2003] HLR 15.
86   Expressed by Millett LJ in *Greenwich LBC v Regan* (1996) 28 HLR 469, CA.
87   *Marshall v. Bradford MDC* [2001] EWCA Civ 594; [2002] HLR 22, CA and *Dunn v Bradford MDC* [2002] EWCA Civ 1137; [2003] HLR 15.
88   *Lambeth LBC v Rogers* (2000) 32 HLR 361, CA.
89   *Richmond v Kensington & Chelsea RLBC* [2006] EWCA Civ 68; [2006] 8 EGCS 175.

est frequency (rent arrears) and where instructions are received *at the last moment.*

4.80   The proper preparation of a defence in a rent arrears case normally requires careful study and consideration. In particular, all the documents must be examined, statements taken and negotiations pursued. But too often tenants do not seek assistance until the last possible moment.

4.81   If instructed at 'the door of the court' the adviser should avoid the temptation of negotiating a 'postponed order' or 'suspended order' for current rent and a modest level of weekly payment off the arrears. After all, closer examination may establish that there are in fact no arrears at all.

4.82   If instructions are received literally at the last moment, the adviser should make an initial application for the case to be put back in the list and then take some brief particulars from the client. Although the court list may contain dozens of cases it does not always follow that there will be the opportunity to have a lengthy discussion – these cases can be processed very quickly in some courts.

4.83   The adviser should try to take a preliminary statement from the tenant covering the duration of the tenancy, the personal circumstances of the tenant, the circumstances surrounding the 'arrears', details of income and details of housing benefit received (see appendix C for a useful checklist).

4.84   If the tenant has any documents with him or her, or if copies can be obtained from the landlord's representative at court, the adviser should inspect:

- the notice seeking possession (see para 4.11);
- the claim form and the particulars of claim (see paras 4.43–4.45);
- the rent book/rent account; and
- any correspondence or other relevant documents.

4.85   If there is time, Legal Help and Help at Court forms should be completed at this stage so that upon return to court the adviser can undertake funded representation.

4.86   If it emerges that the arrears are disputed and/or the tenant is in hardship and/or there is disrepair, etc, the immediate objective should be the securing of an adjournment to another date. Before returning to make such an application in court the adviser should be briefed as to:

- the likely eventual defence;
- the tenant's circumstances;

- the possibility of an agreement to pay current rent during the adjournment;
- the possibility of an agreement to pay something off the alleged arrears during that time (without prejudice to any contention that nothing, or not the amount claimed, is owed);
- the reason why advice was not sought earlier;
- the minimum case management directions necessary to achieve the next stage in the action (for example, date by which a defence should be served).

4.87   The adviser may then return to court with the tenant and indicate to the landlord's representative that a request for an adjournment will be made. The adviser may then argue that he or she has just been instructed, those instructions reveal that the client has both an arguable defence (for example, that the arrears are disputed or it would not be reasonable to order possession) and/or that the tenant has a potential counterclaim and defence by way of set-off based on disrepair or failure to pay housing benefit, etc, and an adjournment is sought. It is usually helpful to be able to indicate that the tenant will submit to a condition that current rent be paid throughout the period of the adjournment,[90] but that further conditions would be unreasonable or would cause excessive hardship.[91] The adviser should invite the making of directions for a defence to be filed within (say) 21 days and for such other steps as may be appropriate, for example, disclosure, experts' reports, etc. The court should be addressed on the proper order as to the costs on the adjournment.

4.88   In most cases the above procedure ought to achieve an adjournment. If not, the adviser has to do his or her best to defend successfully on the day and obtain permission to appeal any adverse order made. In an appropriate case, an appeal may be entered against the refusal to adjourn, in addition to an appeal against the order made.[92]

4.89   Once the adjournment is secured, the adviser should make the necessary arrangements for full legal representation to be obtained and for all technical and substantive defences and counterclaims to be considered. If the matter is to be conducted by a solicitor, advisers should bear in mind the possible delays in obtaining a full public funding certificate and the importance of not exceeding the time allowed by the court for service of a defence.

90 HA 1985 s85(3).
91 HA 1985 s85(3)(a).
92 See *Janstan Investments Ltd v Corregar* (1973) 21 November, unreported, CA; *Spitaliotis v Morgan* [1986] 1 EGLR 51; (1985) 277 EG 750, CA and *Bates v Croydon LBC* [2001] EWCA Civ 134; (2001) 33 HLR 70, CA.

Special cases

Introduction

5.1   This chapter considers the position of four 'special' classes of occupier in public sector rented accommodation:

- subtenants of secure occupiers;
- homeless persons;
- non-secure tenants;
- non-secure licensees;

and considers in each case the prospects for defending possession proceedings brought against them.

Subtenants of secure occupiers

5.2   In advising those who claim to be, or are alleged to be, subtenants of secure occupiers it is necessary to consider the possibilities as to their true legal status in the property. The occupier may indeed be the *subtenant* of a secure tenant. But it is more often the case that the occupier is let into occupation as a *lodger*. This is usually what the secure tenant asserts because that tenant requires no permission from the head landlord to allow lodgers onto the premises[1] but may be in difficulties with his or her own landlord if he or she has sublet. The correct analysis of the legal position is therefore important and the first step is to determine whether the occupier is a lodger (or some other licensee) or a true subtenant.

Lodgers and other licensees

5.3   The occupier is a lodger in the secure tenant's home if he or she has *not* been provided with any exclusive part of the tenant's home for his or her own use. Even if the occupier does have his or her 'own room' he or she is a lodger if the secure tenant provides services which require unrestricted access to the occupier's room (such as changes of bed-linen, cleaning, removing refuse, etc).[2] Where the tenant exercises a high degree of control over the occupier's use of the room – for example, regarding decoration or visitors – this will also point towards a lodging situation. A true lodger is not a subtenant because he or she has no exclusive use of any property – such 'exclusive pos-

---

1   HA 1985 s93(1)(a).
2   *Huwyler v Ruddy* (1996) 28 HLR 550, CA. See also *Aslan v Murphy (No 2)* [1990] 1 WLR 766; [1989] 3 All ER 130, CA and *Crancour v De Silvaesa* (1986) 18 HLR 265, CA.

session' is one of the key hallmarks of a (sub)tenancy. In law, the lodger is a mere licensee of the tenant.

5.4 Secure tenants are free to take lodgers if they wish[3] but are usually required by the terms of their own tenancy agreements to inform the landlord if they do so.

5.5 The tenant may have allowed visiting family members to come and stay in his or her home or have had such people sharing with him or her from the outset of the tenancy. None of these occupiers has a subtenancy. That is either because they do not have exclusive possession (a prerequisite of tenancy – see above) or because there has been no intention to create a legal relationship,[4] or both. The lodger's position is precarious. He or she is liable to exclusion by the tenant at the end of any period of lodging without the need for a formal notice in any prescribed form. So that a lodger allowed to 'stay for a week' can be turned out at the end of the week and a lodger staying on a weekly basis can be given as little as a week's notice. This results from the exclusion of the lodger from the scope of the Protection from Eviction Act 1977 and is a consequence of the lodger sharing use of the premises with his or her licensor, the true tenant.[5]

5.6 In *Monmouth BC v Marlog*[6] a woman and her two children moved into a council house with its new tenant and she paid him £20 per week. She and her children had two of the three bedrooms, the tenant had his own bedroom and the use of the other rooms was shared. The Court of Appeal refused to disturb the county court judge's finding that the woman was only a licensee. The court described as 'ludicrous' any suggestion that the parties might have intended the creation of a subtenancy.

Subtenants of part

5.7 Secure tenants are free to sublet parts of their homes with the written consent of their landlord.[7] In practice many do not seek or obtain such consent even though it may not be unreasonably withheld.[8] However, whether or not consent of the head landlord has been obtained, any subletting is valid and enforceable as between tenant and subtenant.

---

3   HA 1985 s93(1)(a).
4   *Errington v Errington* [1952] 1 KB 290; [1952] 1 All ER 149, CA.
5   Protection From Eviction Act 1977 s3A(2)(a).
6   (1995) 27 HLR 30, CA.
7   HA 1985 s93(1)(b).
8   HA 1985 s94.

5.8   Such a subletting does not normally give the subtenant any security of tenure or protection under the Protection from Eviction Act 1977
as the 'landlord' (the secure occupier) will be resident (in the part not
sublet) and will be sharing accommodation with the tenant.[9]

Subtenants of the whole

5.9   It is not uncommon for secure tenants to move out of their homes
and put others in occupation on long or short-term arrangements.
Even if the secure tenant intends to return and resume occupation at
a later date, security of tenure is lost by the *subletting of the whole* and
cannot be regained.[10] In such circumstances, therefore, little is to be
achieved by the tenant displacing the subtenant and attempting to
regain occupation. It simply follows automatically from any subletting of the whole that secure status is lost and with it the statutory
'rights' (such as the right to buy) which flow from that status.[11]

5.10   In any dispute it is for the head landlord to prove the subletting of
the whole. It does not follow simply from the fact of occupation by a
third party that the tenant has sublet or otherwise parted with possession of the whole.[12] For further discussion of the effect of subletting
on the position of the secure tenant see para 2.40.

5.11   As between the secure tenant and the subtenant, the letting is
enforceable and, if made after 15 January 1989, may be an assured
tenancy. If made after 28 February 1997, it is likely to be an assured
shorthold tenancy.

The subtenant and the head landlord

5.12   The position of a subtenant may be placed in jeopardy by changes in
the relationship between the secure tenant and the landlord. If the
secure tenancy is brought to an end, for example, by the secure tenant giving notice to quit (see para 2.21), the landlord is able to proceed
directly for possession against the *sub*tenants on the basis that they
are trespassers[13] (see chapter 25 for the procedure involved) because

---

9 Protection from Eviction Act 1977 s3A(2)(a).
10 HA 1985 s93(2). Cf, *Poland v Earl of Cadogan* [1980] 3 All ER 544, CA and
    Waltham Forest CBHA v Fanning June 2001 *Legal Action* 33, QBD.
11 *Merton LBC v Salama* June 1989 *Legal Action* 25, CA, *Jennings v Epping Forest
    DC* (1993) 25 HLR 241, CA and *Muir Group Housing Association v Thornley*
    (1993) 25 HLR 89, CA.
12 *Hussey v Camden LBC* (1995) 27 HLR 5, CA, but see *Brent LBC v Cronin* (1998)
    30 HLR 43; September 1997 *Legal Action* 13, CA.
13 *Moore Properties v McKeon* [1976] 1 WLR 1278, CA.

normally their own subtenancy will have ended automatically with the ending of the tenant's tenancy.

5.13   Similarly, if the landlord seeks and obtains a possession order against the secure tenant, ending the tenancy by that means, it may rely on that primary possession order to recover vacant possession of the whole property – including the eviction of the subtenants by the court bailiff.[14]

5.14   The subtenant faced with proceedings asserting that he or she has become a *trespasser* could defend by showing that the interest of the secure tenant had not been properly determined by the landlord. This is especially relevant where the true tenant has died or simply 'disappeared' (see paras 2.27 and 2.52 respectively).

5.15   Subtenants of a secure tenant are not secure themselves because their immediate landlord is not a public sector body (see para 1.6). However, if the true tenant *surrenders* the premises to the landlord, the landlord accepting such surrender is bound by the tenancy of the subtenant.[15] (Note that the landlord is not bound by a subtenancy where the main tenant has given notice to quit rather than surrendered.[16]) The subtenant might in this way be elevated to the position of secure tenant of the landlord, providing he or she fulfils the conditions listed at para 1.3.[17] The most difficult of the conditions for the subtenant of *part* of the secure tenant's former home to establish will be that he or she occupies a dwelling which 'was let as a separate dwelling'.[18]

Homeless people

Placement in council-owned property

5.16   There are six common situations in which a public landlord might be providing temporary accommodation for homeless people in its *own* housing stock:

- while inquiries are being conducted to establish the circumstances of the homelessness of an applicant in apparent priority need;[19]

---

14   *R v Wandsworth County Court ex p Wandsworth LBC* [1975] 1 WLR 1314, CA and *Thompson v Elmbridge BC* [1987] 1 WLR 1425; (1987) 19 HLR 526, CA.

15   *Parker v Jones* [1910] 2 KB 32.

16   *Pennell v Payne* [1995] QB 192; [1995] 06 EG 152, CA.

17   *Basingstoke and Deane BC v Paice* (1995) 27 HLR 433, CA.

18   W Birtles, 'Sub-tenants: Problems for local authorities when properties are surrendered' *Local Government Chronicle* 18 September 1987, p12.

19   HA 1996 s188.

- while an applicant, having been declared intentionally homeless, is given an opportunity to secure his or her own accommodation;[20]
- pending the outcome of a referral made to another housing authority;[21]
- as a matter of discretion pending the outcome of a review or appeal;[22]
- when the local housing authority has accepted an obligation to house the applicant because he or she is eligible, in priority need and not intentionally homeless;[23]
- when the local authority exercises its discretion to accommodate an eligible person not in priority need who is not intentionally homeless.[24]

5.17   The occupier, whether a tenant or licensee, cannot achieve 'secure status' in respect of the public sector accommodation he or she occupies unless and until the local authority concerned notifies him or her that the occupancy is to be secure.[25]

5.18   Many homeless applicants are placed in short-life public sector accommodation awaiting redevelopment, and so are excepted from secure status for that reason also (see para 1.22). As there is no security of tenure, it is open to the landlord to determine the tenancy in the normal way by service of notice to quit and then to recover possession by proceedings.[26] If the tenancy (or licence) is not properly determined (for example, because the notice given is defective) it continues, and possession cannot be ordered.[27]

5.19   If the accommodation has been provided in a local authority hostel[28] on a licence, the occupier need only be given reasonable notice to end the licence. He or she need not be served with the minimum statutory notice usually required to determine a licence (see paras 12.8–12.9) and can be ejected from the hostel without a court order. That is because such a licence is expressly excluded from the protection of the Protection from Eviction Act 1977.[29]

---

20 HA 1996 s190(2)(a).
21 HA 1996 s200.
22 HA 1996 ss188(3) and 204(4).
23 HA 1996 s193.
24 HA 1996 s192(3) as inserted by the Homelessness Act 2002.
25 HA 1985 Sch 1 para 4 as substituted by HA 1996 Sch 17 para 3.
26 *Restormel BC v Buscombe* (1984) 14 HLR 91, CA.
27 *Eastleigh BC v Walsh* [1985] AC 809; [1985] 2 All ER 112; (1985) 17 HLR 392, HL.
28 Defined in HA 1985 s622.
29 Section 3A(8)(a) and see *Brennan v Lambeth LBC* (1998) 30 HLR 481, CA.

Placement in non-council-owned accommodation

5.20   Under arrangements made by the local authorities to whom they have applied for assistance, many homeless households are placed temporarily in the private rented sector in hostels, hotels or bed-and-breakfast accommodation. Where such accommodation is provided by way of interim accommodation pending the authority's decision on the household's application for accommodation[30] or under one of the authority's other duties or powers to provide temporary accommodation,[31] it does not attract the protection of even the minimum requirements of the Protection from Eviction Act 1977.[32]

5.21   It has been suggested,[33] however, that where the accommodation has been provided as a temporary home following the authority's acceptance of the full housing duty under section 193 of the Housing Act 1996, the occupier will be entitled to basic protection from eviction, ie, the service of a formal notice to quit[34] and the right not to be evicted without a court order.[35]

5.22   Under similar arrangements, a private landlord may provide self-contained accommodation to the homeless person in a house or flat. The general rule is that accommodation provided to homeless people under such arrangements in any of the situations described in the first four bullet points in para 5.16 does *not* attract security of tenure as 'assured' or even, at least for the first 12 months, as 'assured shorthold'.[36] A letting in the circumstances described in the last two bullet points in para 5.16 will be an assured shorthold.

5.23   As an alternative, the local authority may itself be the homeless person's 'landlord' in the private accommodation. In recent years, the phenomenon of 'short-term leasing' has been developed as a means of meeting the temporary accommodation needs of homeless households. Under this route, a local authority may take a lease or licence[37] of vacant privately owned property for use as temporary accommodation for the homeless. The council may then install – as its subtenant – the homeless applicant. Housing Act 1985 Sch 1 para 6 exempts

---

30   Under HA 1996 s188(1).

31   Eg, under HA 1996 s188(3), s190(2), s200(1) or s 204(4).

32   *Mohamed v Manek and Kensington and Chelsea RLBC* (1995) 27 HLR 439, CA, approved by a majority in *Desnousse v Newham LBC* [2006] EWCA Civ 547.

33   *Rogerson v Wigan MBC* [2004] EWHC 1677; [2005] 2 All ER 1000; [2005] HLR 10.

34   Under Protection from Eviction Act 1977 s5.

35   Under Protection from Eviction Act 1977 s3: see para 16.2.

36   HA 1996 s209(2) as substituted by the Homelessness Act 2002.

37   *Tower Hamlets LBC v Miah* (1992) 24 HLR 197, CA.

from secure status the tenancy granted to the homeless person, irrespective of the period for which it continues or the reasons why the homeless household is being accommodated.[38] The homeless person, at best, holds a non-secure subtenancy of the leased property.

5.24   Under another variant, the lease or licence from the private landlord is taken by a housing association or other registered social landlord. It then sublets to a homeless person nominated by the local authority in any of the situations described in the first four bullet points in para 5.16. Again, the homeless person has no security of tenure for a year unless the landlord notifies the tenant that the tenancy is to be regarded as an assured (or assured shorthold) tenancy.[39] A letting in the circumstances described in the last two bullet points in para 5.16 will be an assured shorthold.

5.25   Even where the tenant's immediate landlord is a housing association which has taken a lease or licence of the property from a local authority, and the tenant is a secure tenant of the housing association, he or she will have no protection against the local authority when the housing association's interest ends. In *Kay v Lambeth LBC*,[40] the council had granted a licence of a group of 'short-life' properties to a housing association, which was later replaced by individual leases. Eventually the council exercised a 'break clause' and terminated the leases. It was acknowledged that the occupier had been a secure tenant of the housing association. However, as soon as the housing association's interest came to an end, so also did the secure subtenancy. A challenge to that outcome on the basis of article 8 of the ECHR (right to respect for the home) also failed.

Non-secure tenants

5.26   There is a substantial number of public sector tenants who either never acquire security (for example, because they are excepted by Housing Act 1985 Sch 1 – see the list in para 1.22) or who have lost it in one of the ways described in chapter 2. They remain contractual tenants liable to pay rent and the other contractual obligations of both parties continue to bind them and be enforceable by either landlord or tenant. The landlord seeking to recover possession must

---

38 Provided that the statutory conditions are strictly complied with: *Hickey v Haringey LBC* [2006] EWCA Civ 373; June 2006 *Legal Action* 37, CA.

39 HA 1996 s209 as substituted by the Homelessness Act 2002.

40 [2006] UKHL 10; [2006] 2 WLR 570 and see also *Bruton v London and Quadrant Housing Trust* [2000] 1 AC 406, HL.

therefore determine the contractual tenancy and bring proceedings for possession.

5.27   There are broadly three lines of defence open to the non-secure tenant faced with a possession claim:

- *Defective notice to quit.* The tenant can successfully resist possession proceedings (if only temporarily) by showing that the contractual tenancy has not been properly determined because the notice to quit is defective. The circumstances in which this can be established are set out at paras 12.6 onwards.

- *Administrative law grounds.* The non-secure tenant may be able to defend on the grounds that the proceedings are improperly brought by the landlord, that is, that the public landlord is acting in abuse of its powers. Examples would include authorities motivated by bad faith or dishonesty, or otherwise acting unreasonably.[41] The onus is on the tenant to make out the allegation of abuse of power or breach of duty.[42]

- *Human Rights Act 1998 grounds.* See para 5.31.

5.28   Although normally an allegation that a public body is acting unlawfully on administrative law grounds should be made in proceedings brought by way of judicial review,[43] that requirement is disapplied where the public body has brought the proceedings itself and the illegality of the claimant's own action is being relied upon by the defendant.[44]

Non-secure licensees

5.29   Some public sector licensees never acquire secure status (for example, because they do not enjoy exclusive possession of their accommodation[45] or they are excepted by Housing Act 1985 Sch 1 – see the list in para 1.22) or lose it in one of the ways described above in chapter 2. They remain contractual licensees liable to pay their licence fee and the other contractual obligations of both parties continue to bind them and be enforceable by either licensor or tenant.

41   *Bristol DC v Clark* [1975] 3 All ER 976, CA, *Bristol CC v Rawlins* (1977) 34 P & CR 12, CA and *Sevenoaks DC v Emmott* (1979) 39 P & CR 404, CA.

42   *Cannock Chase DC v Kelly* [1978] 1 All ER 152, CA.

43   CPR Part 54.

44   *Wandsworth LBC v Winder* [1985] AC 461, HL.

45   *Westminster City Council v Clarke* (1992) 24 HLR 360, HL; and see paras 1.26–1.29.

5.30   The licensor seeking to recover possession must therefore determine the contractual licence and bring proceedings for possession
(except where the accommodation is a room in a 'public sector' hostel
– see para 5.19 – or where the licence was granted to squatters as
a temporary expedient[46]). Possession proceedings brought against
non-secure licensees may be defended on only one of three grounds:

- *Insufficient notice.* A licence can be determined only by the giving of contractual or reasonable notice.[47] 'What is a reasonable
  time depends on all the circumstances of the case and where the
  licence has been to occupy premises for residential purposes the
  reasonable time has reference to enabling the licensee to have an
  opportunity of taking his effects away from the property.'[48] The
  licensee given insufficient notice may have a short-term defence
  that longer notice should have been given. Any proceedings to
  recover possession on the basis that the licensee has become a
  trespasser (see chapter 25) can be started only *after* reasonable
  notice has expired.[49]

  Any notice given to determine a non-secure licence has to: (i)
  be in writing; (ii) contain the prescribed information; and (iii) be
  given not less than four weeks before it takes effect.[50] The only relevant licences not covered by the statutory rules are those granted
  to squatters as a temporary expedient[51] or to licensees of hostels
  provided by public sector landlords.[52]

- *Administrative law grounds.* The non-secure public sector licensee
  is as able as the non-secure public sector tenant to argue that the
  proceedings are improperly brought by the landlord authority (see
  above).[53]

- *Human Rights Act 1998 grounds.* (see next paragraph).

46 Protection from Eviction Act 1977 s3A.
47 *Minister of Health v Bellotti* [1944] KB 298, CA.
48 *GLC v Jenkins* [1975] 1 All ER 354 at 357C per Diplock LJ.
49 Ibid.
50 PEA 1977 s5(1B), as inserted by HA 1988 s32(2).
51 Protection from Eviction Act 1977 s3A(6).
52 Ibid s3A(8) and see *Brennan v Lambeth LBC* (1998) 30 HLR 481, CA.
53 *Cleethorpes BC v Clarkson* (1978) 128 NLJ 860, noted at July 1978 *LAG Bulletin*
    166, CA, *R v Wear Valley DC ex p Binks* [1985] 2 All ER 699, *Kensington and
    Chelsea RLBC v Haydon* (1984) 17 HLR 114, CA and *Wandsworth LBC v A*
    [2000] 1 WLR 1246, CA.

Human Rights Act 1998

5.31 This chapter has been concerned with the circumstances of occupiers who do not enjoy 'secure' status but are facing eviction by public authorities. The landlord or licensor does not need to give any reason or ground for the eviction, and there may be no question of any fault on the part of the occupier. When the Human Rights Act 1998 came into force in October 2000, it was generally anticipated that such occupiers, unable to invoke the full statutory protection from eviction available to those with secure status, might be able to fall back upon the basic protection of fundamental human rights provided by the European Convention on Human Rights (ECHR). Public bodies (which in this context includes both local authority landlords and the courts) are obliged to act in a way which is compatible with the convention: HRA 1998 section 6.

5.32 The convention rights which are most obviously relevant to housing cases are found in articles 6, 8 and 14 of the ECHR, together with article 1 of the First Protocol.

Article 6 of the ECHR provides:

> In the determination of civil rights and obligations ... everyone is entitled to a fair and public hearing within a reasonable time by an independent and impartial tribunal established by law ...

Article 8 of the ECHR, entitled 'Right to respect for private and family life', provides:

> (1) Everyone has the right to respect for his private and family life, his home and his correspondence.
> (2) There shall be no interference by a public authority with the exercise of this right except such as is in accordance with the law and is necessary in a democratic society in the interests of national security, public safety or the economic well-being of the country, for the prevention of disorder or crime, for the protection of health or morals, or for the protection of the rights and freedoms of others.

Article 14 of the ECHR provides:

> The enjoyment of the rights and freedoms set forth in this Convention shall be secured without discrimination on any ground such as sex, race, colour, language, religion, political or other opinion, national or social origin, association with a national minority, property, birth or other status.

Article 1 of the First Protocol provides:

> Every natural or legal person is entitled to the peaceful enjoyment of his possessions. No one shall be deprived of his possessions except in

the public interest and subject to the conditions provided for by law and by the general principles of international law.

5.33   The convention right which appears immediately relevant to possession proceedings is article 8. An order for possession does, of course, interfere with that right, and article 8 is engaged by possession proceedings. However, in a series of decisions, the courts have adopted a restrictive interpretation of article 8 rights in this context. The following is a chronological summary of the principal decisions in possession cases in which Convention arguments have been raised:

- *Poplar Housing and Regeneration Community Association Ltd v Donoghue*[54] concerned a possession claim against an assured shorthold tenant, following service of a Housing Act 1988 s21 notice. The Court of Appeal held that notwithstanding its mandatory terms, the right to possession contained in section 21(4) did not conflict with the tenant's right to family life under article 8. The section was clearly necessary in a democratic society in so far as there had to be a procedure for recovering possession of property at the end of a tenancy. The court would defer to parliament as to whether the restricted power of the court under that section was legitimate and proportionate.

- *Gallagher v Castle Vale Housing Action Trust.*[55] This was a possession claim against a secure tenant on the grounds of nuisance and annoyance to adjoining occupiers. The Court of Appeal doubted whether article 8 – and the associated concept of proportionality – made any significant difference to the way the court had always approached the question of the reasonableness of making a possession order. It did, however, reinforce the importance of only making an order depriving someone of his or her home in circumstances where a clear case was made out.[56] See para 3.84.

- *Southwark LBC v St Brice.*[57] The defendant applied to set aside a warrant which had been executed. The Court of Appeal held that the procedure which allowed the issue of a warrant for possession and arrangements for execution following non-compliance with a suspended possession order did not infringe articles 6, 8 or 14 of the ECHR. Proportionality had been considered when the possession order was made.

---

54 [2001] EWCA Civ 595; [2002] QB 48, CA.

55 [2001] EWCA Civ 944; (2001) 33 HLR 810, CA.

56 See also *Lambeth LBC v Howard* [2001] EWCA Civ 468; (2001) 33 HLR 636.

57 [2001] EWCA Civ 1138; [2002] 1 WLR 1537.

- *R (McLellan) v Bracknell Forest DC.*[58] This case concerned a possession claim against an introductory tenant (see chapter 8). It was held that, although an introductory tenant has the right to raise the question of whether the decision to evict him or her can be justified under article 8(2), the review procedure contained in Housing Act 1996 s129 taken together with the availability of judicial review provides adequate protection and is compliant with convention rights.[59]

- *Sheffield CC v Smart.*[60] The council claimed possession following complaints of nuisance against a non-secure tenant. In the view of the Court of Appeal, if such a tenant were entitled to have the court decide on the particular facts whether his or her eviction was disproportionate to the council's aim of managing its housing stock properly, the effect would be to convert non-secure tenancies into a form of secure tenancy. The balance of interests arising under article 8(2) had in all its essentials been struck by the legislature when enacting the current scheme for the housing of homeless persons and their eviction.

- *Michalak v Wandsworth LBC.*[61] This was a possession claim against a relative of a deceased secure tenant who did not qualify to succeed to the secure tenancy because the relationship was not in the list contained in Housing Act 1985 s113 (reproduced at para 2.30 above). The Court of Appeal held that although the provision was discriminatory in relation to a matter within the scope of article 8 and so article 14 was engaged, there was an objective justification for establishing a 'closed' list in section 113, that is, the need for certainty in determining which members of a secure tenant's family were eligible to succeed. Accordingly article 14 was not infringed. On a claim for possession against a non-successor, the county court was not required to investigate the individual circumstances of the defendant to ensure that the conditions in article 8(2) were satisfied. Those conditions were satisfied by the common law right to recover possession of property against a person who, under the relevant statutory scheme, had no right to remain following the death of the tenant.[62]

---

58 [2001] EWCA 1510; [2002] QB 1129.
59 See also *Merton LBC v Williams* [2002] EWCA Civ 980; [2003] HLR 20.
60 [2002] EWCA Civ 4; [2002] HLR 34.
61 [2002] EWCA Civ 271; [2003] 1 WLR 617.
62 See also *Sharp v Brent LBC* [2003] EWCA Civ 779; [2003] HLR 65 and *R (Gangera) v Hounslow LBC* [2003] EWHC 794 Admin; [2003] HLR 68.

- *Kensington and Chelsea RLBC v O'Sullivan.*[63] The council claimed possession against a wife after her husband had terminated his sole secure tenancy. The possession order did not violate any of Mrs O'Sullivan's rights under article 8. It was not open to her to argue that there was some defence to the possession proceedings based on an assertion that, although the council was otherwise entitled to possession, a possession order was not necessary for the protection of the rights and freedoms of others.

- *Harrow LBC v Qazi.*[64] The council brought a possession claim against a former joint secure tenant whose wife had terminated the tenancy by serving a notice to quit (see para 2.24). The House of Lords held unanimously that residential accommodation occupied by a former tenant whose tenancy has come to an end by operation of law is that person's 'home' within the meaning of article 8(1). However, it also held, by a majority (Lord Bingham and Lord Steyn dissenting) that the law, which enables a public authority landlord to exercise its unqualified right to recover possession, with a view to making the premises available for letting to others on its housing list, does not violate article 8. Contractual and property rights could not be defeated by a defence based on article 8. On 11 March 2004 the European Court of Human Rights (ECtHR) decided that Mr Qazi's application to the ECtHR was inadmissible.[65]

5.34   Although it appeared that the House of Lords' decision in *Qazi* represented the last word on the issue, there followed a decision of the ECtHR in the case of *Connors v UK.*[66] This was a case involving a gypsy family who had lived for some fourteen years on a site run by Leeds City Council. After termination of their licence, a possession order was made under the then County Court Rules (CCR) Ord 24. Considering the margin of appreciation, the ECtHR stated that in spheres such as housing, which play a central role in the welfare and economic policies of modern societies, it will respect the legislature's judgment as to what is in the general interest unless that judgment is manifestly without reasonable foundation. However, the vulnerable position of gypsies as a minority meant that special consideration

63 [2003] EWCA Civ 371; [2003] HLR 58.
64 [2003] UKHL 43; [2003] 3 WLR 792.
65 See also *Newham LBC v Kibata* [2003] EWCA Civ 1785; [2004] HLR 28 and *Bradney v Birmingham CC; Birmingham CC v McCann* [2003] EWCA Civ 1783; [2004] HLR 27.
66 Application no 66746/01: (2005) 40 EHRR 9; [2004] HLR 52.

should be given to their needs and their different lifestyle. There was a positive obligation on states to facilitate the gypsy way of life. The ECtHR referred to the seriousness of evicting Mr Connors and his family with consequent difficulties in finding a lawful alternative location for their caravans, in coping with health problems and young children and in ensuring the children's education. Such serious interference with article 8 rights required particularly weighty reasons of public interest by way of justification and the margin of appreciation to be afforded to the national authorities should be correspondingly narrowed. Even allowing for the margin of appreciation, the ECtHR was not persuaded that the necessity for a statutory scheme which permitted the summary eviction of Mr Connors and his family had been sufficiently demonstrated by the government. The ECtHR found that the eviction of Mr Connors and his family from the local authority site was not attended by the requisite procedural safeguards, namely, the requirement to establish proper justification for the serious interference with his rights, and consequently could not be regarded as justified by a 'pressing social need' or proportionate to the legitimate aim being pursued. There was, accordingly, a violation of article 8. The impact of this decision on possession claims in domestic courts was considered in *Kay v Lambeth LBC* (see next para).

Kay v Lambeth LBC and Leeds CC v Price

5.35   In *Kay v Lambeth LBC*, the council licensed 'short life' premises to London and Quadrant Housing Trust (LQHT) who purported to grant licences to those allowed into occupation. In fact those 'licences' created a relationship of landlord and tenant as between LQHT and the sub-occupants.[67] However, Lambeth gave notice to terminate the interest of LQHT and brought possession proceedings against Mr Kay and other occupiers as trespassers. Defences based upon article 8 were struck out and possession orders were made. The defendants appealed, relying upon the ECtHR decision in *Connors*, but the Court of Appeal[68] dismissed the appeal and held that *Connors* was only of assistance to the domestic courts in relation to cases involving gypsies.

5.36   In *Leeds CC v Price*, the council sought possession of land which had been unlawfully occupied two days earlier by the defendant

67 *Bruton v London and Quadrant Housing Trust* [2000] 1 AC 406, HL.
68 [2004] EWCA Civ 926; [2004] HLR 56.

trespassers, who were gypsies. The claim was transferred to the High Court for determination of the preliminary issue of whether the defendants could rely upon article 8. The judge, applying *Harrow LBC v Qazi* (see para 5.33), held that they could not and made a possession order. On appeal[69] the Court of Appeal held that:

- *Qazi* and *Connors* were inconsistent decisions;
- the Court of Appeal had been wrong in *Lambeth LBC v Kay* to suggest that the decision in *Connors* applied only in gypsy cases;
- the domestic courts should follow and apply *Qazi* until it had been reconsidered by the House of Lords in the light of *Connors,*

and granted leave to appeal to the House of Lords.

Kay and *Price* in the House of Lords[70]

5.37   The appeals were joined and heard together by an appellate committee comprising seven law lords which reconsidered *Qazi* in the light of *Connors*. The appeals were dismissed in both cases.

5.38   It was unanimously agreed that article 8 does not in terms give a right to be provided with a home and does not guarantee the right to have one's housing problem solved by the authorities.

5.39   Lord Hope, giving the leading speech of the majority, said that Strasbourg jurisprudence indicated that three requirements must be met under article 8(2). The first requirement is that the interference brought about by the possession claim is 'in accordance with the law'. The second requirement is that it has an aim that is identified as a legitimate one. Satisfaction of the housing needs of others is regarded as a legitimate aim for this purpose. The third requirement is that interference in pursuit of that aim is 'necessary in a democratic society'. The concept of necessity implies a pressing social need, and the measure employed must be proportionate to the legitimate aim pursued (at [66]). Lord Hope pointed out that *Connors* was the only case where the ECtHR had held that the making of a possession order against an occupier in favour of a public authority in accordance with the requirements of domestic property law had failed to meet the third requirement in article 8(2). 'It failed to do so in that case because the making of the order was not attended by the procedural safeguards that were required to establish that there was a proper

---

69 [2005] EWCA Civ 289; [2005] 1 WLR 1825; [2005] 3 All ER 573.
70 [2006] UKHL 10; [2006] 2 WLR 570.

justification for the interference with the applicant's right to respect
for his private and family life and his home.' It was the law itself that
was defective. In his opinion, it left untouched cases, such as *Qazi*,
where the judgment of parliament on issues of property law met the
third requirement of article 8.

5.40   Lord Hope explained that the effect of *Qazi* was that where an
order for possession was made by the court in accordance with domestic property law, the essence of the article 8(1) right to respect for the
home was not violated. So the question whether the interference was
permitted by article 8(2) was not a matter that needed to be considered by the county court. The law itself provided the answer to that
question. The only matter which the court needed to consider was
whether the requirements of the law and the procedural safeguards
which it laid down for the protection of the occupier (such as obtaining an order for possession) had been satisfied (at [72]). *Connors* was
a case 'of a special and unusual kind', where the interference with
the right to respect for the home which resulted from the making of
a possession order needed to be justified by a decision-making process that ensured that special consideration was given to the interests
safeguarded by article 8.

5.41   In the key passage in Lord Hope's speech, with which the other
members of the majority expressly agreed, he said:

> I agree ... that judges in the county courts, when faced with such
> a defence [based on article 8 principles], should proceed on the
> assumption that domestic law strikes a fair balance and is compatible
> with the occupier's Convention rights. (at [109])

> But, in agreement with [the majority] I would go further. Subject
> to what I say below, I would hold that a defence which does not
> challenge the law under which the possession order is sought as
> being incompatible with article 8, but is based only on the occupier's
> personal circumstances, should be struck out ... [If] the requirements
> of the law have been established and the right to recover possession is
> unqualified, the only situations in which it would be open to the court
> to refrain from proceeding to summary judgment and making the
> possession order are these:
>
> (a) if a seriously arguable point is raised that the law which enables
> the court to make the possession order is incompatible with article 8,
> the county court in the exercise of its jurisdiction under the Human
> Rights Act 1998 should deal with the argument in one or other of
> two ways: (i) by giving effect to the law, so far as it is possible to do so
> under section 3, in a way that is compatible with article 8, or (ii) by
> adjourning the proceedings to enable the compatibility issue to be
> dealt with in the High Court;

(b) if the defendant wishes to challenge the decision of a public authority to recover possession as an improper exercise of its powers at common law on the ground that it was a decision that no reasonable person would consider justifiable, he should be permitted to do this provided again that the point is seriously arguable: *Wandsworth LBC v Winder* [1985] AC 461. (at [110]).

He concluded that the decision in *Connors* was not incompatible with *Qazi*.

5.42   In the light of the above decision, it would seem that article 8 is of very limited application when it comes to defending possession claims. It is only in the rare cases, such as *Connors*, where it can be argued that the law itself is incompatible with convention rights, that it may provide a remedy. It is notable, however, that the House of Lords specifically endorsed the jurisdiction of the court, including the county court, to consider by way of defence the argument that a public authority has behaved improperly in seeking to evict the defendant, on the basis of its earlier decision in *Wandsworth LBC v Winder*.

CHAPTER 6

Housing associations and other registered social landlords

Introduction

6.1 Registered social landlords (RSLs) are those social landlords which are registered with, and regulated by, the Housing Corporation or Housing for Wales pursuant to the statutory scheme established by Part 1 of the Housing Act 1996. The vast majority of such landlords are housing associations and housing trusts.

6.2 Those who occupy RSL-owned property may do so as tenants or licensees and may fall within either the 'public sector' regime for security of tenure or the 'independent sector' regime. This chapter explains the protection available according to the type of arrangement under which the occupier is in residence.

Tenants of housing associations

6.3 Under the provisions of Housing Act 1985 s80 as originally enacted, tenants of all housing associations (whether registered or unregistered) were within the 'secure tenancy' regime described in chapter 1. The intention behind the Housing Act 1988, however, was to produce a situation in which all *new* housing association lettings would be on an assured tenancy basis rather than secure tenancies. Assured tenants have a more limited form of security of tenure than they would have enjoyed as secure public sector tenants and are placed in the same category of protection as tenants of private sector landlords albeit that most private landlords now grant assured *shorthold* tenancies (see chapter 9).

6.4 Subject to the limited exceptions described below, all housing association tenancies granted on or after 15 January 1989 are assured rather than secure tenancies.[1] They may be normal assured tenancies or assured shorthold tenancies, although the Housing Corporation in its statutory role of guiding the activities of housing associations[2] has indicated that associations that use assured shorthold tenancies as 'starter' tenancies should do so as part of a managed strategy for dealing with anti-social behaviour.[3]

6.5 The key to determining whether the tenant of a housing association is assured or secure is usually the date of grant of the tenancy. If

---

1   HA 1988 s35(4).
2   HA 1996 s36.
3   Housing Corporation Regulatory Circular 07/04, para 3.3.3. See also the Housing Corporation Regulatory Code and Guidance (August 2005) para 3.5.2.

that date falls on or after 15 January 1989 then the tenancy is likely to be assured. If that date falls on or before 14 January 1989 it will probably be secure. However, housing association tenancies granted on or after 15 January 1989 will be secure rather than assured if:

- The tenant was previously a secure occupier (whether as sole or joint secure tenant or as sole or joint secure licensee) of the same housing association.[4] Therefore a secure tenant can transfer to other property within the same housing association's stock without loss of secure status.

  or

- The tenancy was granted following the re-acquisition of defective property (which a former secure tenant had bought) under the procedure set out in Housing Act 1985 Pt XVI (formerly the Housing Defects Act 1984) pursuant to Housing Act 1985 s554(2A).[5] This embraces not only the original tenant who bought the defective house from the association, but also certain members of his or her family.[6]

  or

- The tenancy was granted pursuant to a contract to let made before 15 January 1989.[7] This exception demonstrates the importance of ascertaining not merely the date the tenancy commenced but also the date the agreement for the letting was made.

  or

- The tenancy is offered as 'suitable alternative accommodation' to a former secure occupier against whom a possession order has been made in proceedings taken under Housing Act 1985 s84(2)(b) or (c) and the court has directed that the new tenancy or licence should be secure.[8] This exception will be relevant to former tenants of a public sector body rehoused by a housing association in accommodation arranged by the former landlord (see para 3.185).

  or

- The tenant was a private sector protected or statutory tenant and the housing association has taken over from the private landlord.[9]

---

4   HA 1988 s35(4).
5   HA 1988 s35(4)(f)
6   HA 1988 Sch 17 para 61.
7   HA 1988 s35(4)(c).
8   HA 1988 s35(4)(e).
9   HA 1988 s34(5).

6.6   Further modifications to the normal rules as to whether the tenancy is secure or assured apply where the association is housing homeless families or is a housing co-operative. These are discussed separately below.

6.7   Of course, the general exceptions to secure or assured status (that prevent certain tenancies from enjoying security of tenure) also apply in the housing association sector. However, if one of those exceptions ceases to apply, whether the tenancy thereupon becomes secure or assured is determined according to the date of original letting and the application of any relevant transitional provisions.[10]

Defending housing association tenants

6.8   The first step is to work out (using the preceding paragraphs) whether the tenant facing a claim for possession holds an assured or a secure tenancy or has no security of tenure under either regime.

6.9   Wherever possible it should be argued that the tenancy is secure (rather than assured or unprotected) as this confers a greater degree of security of tenure (as well as the possibility of enjoying the full 'right to buy', etc).

6.10   The second step is to consider whether the association is acting in accordance with (or in breach of) the standards expected by the regulatory body, the Housing Corporation or Housing for Wales, in relation to the recovery of possession from the class of tenant in question.[11]

6.11   The relevant statutory guidance is contained in the Regulatory Code and Guidance (August 2005) issued by the Corporation and in particular in Housing Corporation Circular 07/04: *Tenancy management: eligibility and evictions*, published on 27 July 2004. The general management ethos of registered social landlords is set out, in plain English format, in the *Charter for housing association applicants and residents*.[12] Each tenant should have been provided by his or her association with a copy of the Charter: Regulatory Code and Guidance, para 3.5(b).

6.12   If a check of this material suggests that the association has not acted properly or fairly, that point can be raised with: (1) the association itself under its complaints procedure; (2) the Housing Corporation in its role as regulator; (3) the Housing Ombudsman Service; and/or (4) the court considering the possession claim.

---

10   See *Bhai v Black Roof Community Housing Association Limited* [2001] 2 All ER 685; (2001) 33 HLR 55, CA.
11   See paras 10.46 and 10.73 below.
12   Housing Corporation, September 2003.

6.13   Most particularly, where proceedings are brought under any of the discretionary grounds against a secure or assured tenant, the attention of the court can usefully be drawn to any relevant part of this management guidance from the Housing Corporation. The Regulatory Code and Guidance requires (in para 3.5c) that 'legal repossesion of a property is sought as a last resort'. Regulatory Circular 07/04 states that 'associations should act to support and sustain, rather than terminate, a tenancy: early intervention is essential' (para 1.2). Note also the Rent Arrears Protocol which ensures that social landlords offer tenants information, advice and assistance in applying for housing benefit, so that court proceedings are avoided wherever possible (see para 3.35).

6.14   Demonstrating a failure to comply with this guidance may be useful in persuading the court that it is not reasonable in all the circumstances to grant an order for possession.

Assured tenants

6.15   The principles for defending possession proceedings brought against assured tenants are set out in detail in chapter 10 (and see chapter 9 for assured shorthold tenants).

Secure tenants

6.16   The approach to defending secure tenants of housing associations and other public sector landlords is discussed in chapters 3 and 4.

Unprotected tenants

6.17   For the defences open to a tenant or licensee of a housing association facing eviction and unable to rely on any security of tenure, see paras 5.26–5.43.

Housing association licensees

6.18   Many housing associations make property available to occupiers on licence rather than by way of tenancy.[13] The first step for advisers assisting such an occupier is to determine whether what has been

---

13 See *Bruton v London & Quadrant Housing Trust* [2000] 1 AC 406; [1999] 3 WLR 150, HL; and *Kay v Lambeth LBC* [2006] UKHL 10; [2006] 2 WLR 570, HL.

granted is truly a licence or is in law a tenancy. If, despite its description, the licence is a tenancy, see para 6.3.

6.19   If the arrangement is a true licence (for example, because the services provided to the occupier by the association require unrestricted access to the premises) then the security of tenure it attracts is determined by the date on which it was granted. A licence granted by a housing association on or before 14 January 1989 may be a secure licence attracting considerable security of tenure (see para 1.26 for a discussion of the conditions for such a licence being secure). If the licence was granted on or before 14 January 1989 but does not fulfil the conditions for being a secure licence, see para 5.29 which deals with non-secure licensees.

6.20   If the licence was granted on or after 15 January 1989 it cannot be secure (unless it falls into one of the excepted categories set out at para 6.5). Nor can it be 'assured'. There is no such concept as an 'assured licence'. The occupier has only the most limited protection. See para 5.29 for the conditions governing the recovery of possession from such licensees.

Housing associations and the homeless

6.21   In discharging their statutory duties toward the homeless, local authorities are encouraged to seek the help and co-operation of housing associations[14] and RSLs are obliged by statute to provide reasonable help on request.[15] As a result, in many areas of the country, housing associations provide short-term temporary accommodation for homeless people where:

- investigations by the local authority under Housing Act 1996 Pt VII (Homelessness) are under way; or
- the person became homeless intentionally and is entitled only to short-term temporary accommodation; or
- the person is awaiting acceptance by a different housing authority to which he or she has been referred under the local connection provisions; or
- accommodation is being provided pursuant to the exercise of other local authority powers or duties under Part VII of the 1996 Act.

14   *Code of Guidance* (DTRL, 1996, revised 1997), para 21.24(a).
15   HA 1996 s213.

6.22 The occupier does not gain *secure* status in any of these situations as against the housing association (see further para 6.5 for the exceptional circumstances in which a tenancy granted by a housing association can now be secure). Nor, even if the accommodation is first provided on or after 15 January 1989 by way of grant of a tenancy, is it immediately *assured*. Such a tenancy is assured or an assured shorthold only if either: (a) the tenant is so notified by the association;[16] or (b) 12 months have expired since service on the tenant of the local authority's decision on the homelessness application or decision on review or appeal.[17]

6.23 In order to avoid the possible accrual of secure or assured status, many associations purport to grant licences, rather than tenancies, of temporary accommodation to homeless people. If the licence was granted before 15 January 1989 and it conferred rights of exclusive occupation, it will have become secure unless it was determined within 12 months of the local authority's homelessness decision. If granted on or after 15 January 1989 it is neither secure nor assured and attracts only the limited protection indicated at para 5.31.

6.24 Whether what has been granted to the homeless person pursuant to a temporary obligation is a licence or a tenancy is to be determined according to the usual legal principles.[18] The Court of Appeal has[19] resiled from the view that the usual principles can be modified in these cases.[20] Whether the arrangement is in law a tenancy or a licence can have important implications, principally because only a tenancy can have assured or assured shorthold status, but also in determining the correct method by which it may be ended.

Housing co-operatives and housing trusts

6.25 A tenancy or licence granted before 15 January 1989 is secure and covered by the provisions described in chapter 1 of this book if it is granted by:

- a housing trust which is a charity; or

16 HA 1996 s209, as substituted by the Homelessness Act 2002.
17 HA 1996 s209.
18 *Eastleigh BC v Walsh* [1985] 1 WLR 525; [1985] 2 All ER 112; (1985) 17 HLR 392, HL.
19 *Family Housing Association v Jones* [1990] 1 WLR 779; (1990) 22 HLR 45, CA, expressly not following *Ogwr BC v Dykes* [1989] 1 WLR 295; [1989] 2 All ER 880, CA.
20 *Ogwr BC v Dykes* [1989] 1 WLR 295; [1989] 2 All ER 880, CA.

- an unregistered housing association which is a co-operative housing association; or
- a registered housing association other than a co-operative housing association;[21] or
- a management co-operative exercising the functions of a public sector landlord.[22]

6.26   Accordingly, occupiers of property held by housing trusts which are not charities or held by registered housing co-operatives are not within the secure status regime. If a registered housing co-operative deregisters, however, the tenants must be notified that they have become secure.[23]

6.27   This requirement to notify a change of status simply illustrates the fact that the security of tenure of the occupiers may change from time to time depending upon which variant of association their landlord is at any particular time: see *Bhai v Black Roof Community Housing Association Limited.*[24]

6.28   Each of the above-mentioned variations in landlord type is closely defined by the Housing Act 1985 and the technical definitions may be found in the Act as follows:

- 'charity' (section 622);
- 'co-operative housing association' (section 5(2));
- 'housing association' (section 5(1));
- 'housing trust' (section 6);
- 'registered' (section 5(4)).

6.29   For tenancies granted on or after 15 January 1989, those granted by housing trusts, co-operatives and associations normally attract assured or assured shorthold status and so are governed by the regime described in Part II of this book. However, a 'fully mutual housing association' cannot grant an assured tenancy[25] and after 15 January 1989 it cannot grant a secure tenancy either. New tenants of fully mutual housing associations are therefore outside both schemes of security (see para 5.26 for their protection against eviction). The term 'fully mutual' is defined by Housing Act 1985 s5(2).

6.30   The tenants and licensees of housing management co-operatives and other similar bodies administering council property under

---

21 HA 1985 s80(1) and (2).
22 HA 1985 s80(4).
23 HA 1985 s80(3).
24 [2001] 2 All ER 865; (2001) 33 HLR 55, CA.
25 HA 1988 Sch 1 para 12(1)(h).

arrangements made within Housing Act 1985 s27B continue to be secure whatever the date of grant of their tenancies.

Other registered social landlords

6.31 As explained above, most RSLs are in fact housing associations and other similar bodies which were already subject to Housing Corporation supervision under previous statutory provisions. However, it is also open to not-for-profit private companies to apply for registration as RSLs under the Housing Act 1996. The tenants and licensees of RSLs will have broadly the same security of tenure (or lack of it) as would be granted to new tenants and licensees of private landlords. It may be expected, however, that the Housing Corporation will insist on the grant of full assured tenancies wherever possible and the use of comparatively 'generous' terms and conditions of tenancy.

Human Rights Act 1998

6.32 Advisers defending occupiers will wish to consider whether the housing association or other RSL with which they are dealing is or is not a 'public authority' for the purposes of Human Rights Act 1998 s6. In *Poplar HARCA v Donoghue*[26] the Court of Appeal rejected the proposition that all RSLs are automatically to be treated as public authorities. However, it found that Poplar HARCA (which had been set up by the local authority to take over parts of its stock) was a public authority in so far as it continued the function of making arrangements for the provision of short-term accommodation to those the council would previously have accommodated. Whether a particular RSL is or is not a public authority accordingly turns on both the nature of the RSL and the particular function in which it is engaged when accommodating the occupier. The test is whether it is exercising public functions. The existence of state funding, without more, is not sufficient to indicate that the RSL is a functional public authority.

6.33 In *R (on the application of Heather and others) v Leonard Cheshire Foundation*,[27] it was held that the Leonard Cheshire Foundation was not a public body, and its decision to close a residential home could not be challenged on public law grounds. In the light of more recent

26 [2001] EWCA Civ 595; [2002] QB 48, CA. See also para 5.31 ff.
27 [2002] EWCA Civ 366; [2002] 2 All ER 936.

judicial authority,[28] however, and of European law directives on procurement[29] it is now more likely that the courts will be prepared to
revisit the issue of RSLs as public bodies, especially in view of the fact
that in many areas, as a result of LSVT transfers (see para 1.11), housing associations are the only or main providers of social housing.

6.34   If the RSL is considered to be a public authority, a challenge may
be brought on judicial review principles, augmented by article 8 considerations, to the fairness or rationality of the RSL's decision to seek
possession in the particular case. In those circumstances, the county
court should be asked to adjourn the possession claim to permit an
application to be brought for judicial review. In *North British Housing
Association Ltd v Matthews*[30] the Court of Appeal held that, in dealing with possession proceedings brought on the basis of mandatory
ground 8 of the assured tenancy grounds for possession (see para
10.45), it was not open to the court to grant an adjournment of the
claim where the rent arrears had been caused by maladministration
on the part of the housing benefit authority. The court noted that the
landlord appeared not to have followed the Housing Corporation's
expectations in Regulatory Circular 07/04, since effective liaison
with the housing benefit authority would have disclosed the problem
with the tenant's benefit claim. The issue of a possible claim for judicial review of the landlord's actions was raised, but not dealt with, in
that case, and it remains open for argument before the Adminstrative
Court in another case. Alternatively, in accordance with the judgment
of Lord Hope in *Kay v Lambeth LBC*; *Leeds CC v Price*,[31] the tenant
may seek to defend the possession claim on the basis that the landlord is exercising its powers improperly in using ground 8: see paras
5.35–5.42 and 8.104.

---

28 See *Parochial Church Council of Aston Cantlow and Wilmcote with Billesley,
Warwickshire v Wallbank* [2003] UK HL 37; [2004] 1 AC 546, HL (liability for
chancel repairs to parish church dating from 1743: the Parochial Church
Council was not a 'core' public authority and was not carrying out public
functions when it demanded payment); and *R (on the application of Beer) v
Hampshire Farmers Markets Limited* [2003] EWCA Civ 1056; [2004] 1 WLR
233, CA (because of the close association between the Council and the market
company, and because of the public nature of markets, the market company
was acting as a public authority in making decisions concerning the grant of
licences to stallholders).

29 See Housing Corporation guidance for RSLs on the issue: *Application of
EC procurement directives to registered social landlords* (available at www.
housingcorplibrary.org.uk). See also note in November 2004 *Legal Action* 25.

30 [2004] EWCA Civ 1736; [2005] 1 WLR 3133; [2005] HLR 17.

31 [2006] UKHL 10; [2006] 2 WLR 570, HL.

Housing action trusts

Introduction

7.1   Housing action trusts (HATs) were set up to take over, revitalise, improve and regenerate certain specific areas of run-down local authority housing. The statutory basis of their operation is to be found in Housing Act 1988 Pt III. Only six[1] were in fact created due in part to the substantial finances that need to be raised for them to be able to undertake their work successfully. Five of these have already wound up (see para 7.14) and the sixth – Stonebridge HAT – will wind down in 2007.

7.2   Each individual HAT is established by a separate statutory instrument[2] for an area of land which is itself identified by a separate statutory order.[3] That area largely (but not necessarily exclusively) comprises tenanted local authority housing. The secretary of state, by further order, gives the HAT the housing management powers formerly held by the local authority in relation to that property[4] and may transfer ownership of the council property to the HAT.[5] The HAT thus becomes the 'new landlord' for existing council tenants and is free to grant new tenancies of, or otherwise dispose of, any empty property transferred to it from the local authority.

Effect on existing tenants

7.3   Tenants and licensees who have secure status – as described in the earlier chapters of this Part (or the status of *introductory* or *demoted* tenant mentioned in the following chapter) – retain that status following transfer of the freehold of their homes to a HAT. This is achieved by the addition of HATs to the statutory list of prescribed public landlords[6] (see para 1.6).

7.4   In order to obtain possession from a *secure* tenant the HAT therefore has to serve a notice seeking possession in the normal way (para 2.4) and take proceedings based on fulfilment of the grounds and conditions for possession (see chapter 3). The wording of the various grounds has been amended to make provision for HATs.[7] The

---

1   North Hull HAT; Waltham Forest HAT; Liverpool HAT; Castle Vale HAT; Tower Hamlets HAT; and Stonebridge HAT.
2   HA 1988 s62.
3   HA 1988 s60.
4   HA 1988 s65.
5   HA 1988 s74.
6   HA 1985 s80, as amended by HA 1988 s83(2).
7   HA 1988 s83(6).

procedure for recovery of possession from an *introductory* tenant or a *demoted* tenant is as described in the next chapter.

7.5 'Rent arrears' is the most common ground on which possession proceedings brought by HATs are based and there are two aspects of defending such cases which are particularly relevant to HATs.

Challenging the rent

7.6 The HAT can establish a ground for possession for rent arrears only if rent is 'lawfully due' from the secure tenant.[8] A HAT can lawfully make only a 'reasonable charge' for housing accommodation.[9] It is accordingly possible to raise a defence by showing that the charge levied is not reasonable.[10] This might be on the basis that the property let is in the midst of a 'building and redevelopment site' and therefore of reduced value. Alternatively, it might be that the rent has been substantially raised in advance of the improvement of the buildings and the local environment contrary to assurances[11] that rents would not be increased until improvement work had been carried out.

Old arrears

7.7 If the tenant is in arrear with rent at the date the property is taken over by the HAT, the liability for the arrears does not necessarily transfer to the HAT.[12] The tenant might be able to start with a 'clean slate' with the HAT. As long as no further arrears accrue, the tenant will be free from the risk of possession proceedings brought by either the HAT or the former council landlord (although obviously the former landlord can sue for the old rent arrears as a civil debt). If there are further arrears and the HAT takes possession proceedings it is important to make it clear to the court that the former arrears are not part of the HAT's claim. To find out whether liability for the arrears has been transferred it is necessary to consult the terms of the transfer order made by the secretary of state under Housing Act 1988 s74. This will be relatively easy as each order has been published as a statutory instrument.

---

8   HA 1985 Sch 2 ground 1.

9   HA 1988 s85(1).

10   *Wandsworth LBC v Winder (No 1)* [1985] AC 461; [1984] 3 WLR 1254, HL, and *Wandsworth LBC v Winder (No 2)* (1988) 20 HLR 400, CA.

11   *HATs: A consultation document*, DoE, October 1987, paras 20–21.

12   HA 1988 s74(4).

Access for renovation

7.8   In the course of its works to improve the property acquired, the HAT may need possession of dwellings for the purpose of renovation. For this purpose reliance will be placed on Housing Act 1985 Sch 2 ground 10 or 10A (see paras 3.141 and 3.150) in obtaining possession, although suitable alternative accommodation must be provided. Obviously, the more acceptable alternative (more acceptable to the tenant) would be for the HAT to offer temporary alternative accommodation while the works are undertaken and for the tenant thereafter to resume occupation of his or her home.

New tenants of housing action trusts

7.9   Tenancies granted by HATs are outside the lettings regime of the Rent Act 1977[13] and HATs are incapable of granting assured tenancies.[14] Accordingly, unless they fall into one of the exceptional categories described at para 1.22, all tenancies or licences granted by HATs are secure.[15] The HAT is, however, free to elect to operate an introductory tenancy regime. If it makes such an election its new tenants will initially be introductory tenants.[16]

7.10   As the HAT is one of the categories of organisation that local authorities can require to assist them in the discharge of their duties towards the homeless,[17] the exceptions from security applicable to temporarily housed homeless people (para 5.16) will be particularly relevant.

7.11   In defending possession proceedings against the new secure tenants of HATs the reader is referred to the other relevant chapters of this Part.

7.12   Advisers may find it possible to develop new lines of defence by paying close attention to the terms of the order establishing the trust,[18] the limited objects and powers of the trust[19] and the rules as to its constitution.[20] For example, it might be possible to establish in

---

13 Rent Act 1977 s14(h), as amended by HA 1988 s62(7).
14 HA 1988 Sch 1 para 12(1)(i).
15 HA 1988 ss4(f) and 80(1), as amended.
16 See chapter 8.
17 HA 1996 s213.
18 HA 1988 s62.
19 HA 1988 s63.
20 HA 1988 Sch 7.

a given case that a decision to take possession proceedings or serve a notice seeking possession was taken in excess of the powers of the trust and was thus ultra vires and a nullity.

7.13 HATs may also apply for a demotion order, which will have the effect of removing security of tenure from a secure tenant for a period of 12 months, during which he or she will have a probationary status similar to that of an introductory tenant: see chapter 8.

Winding-up of the trust

7.14 It is not intended that HATs retain control of areas of housing beyond the completion of their task of renovation and improvement. In time they will all be wound up. With the consent of the secretary of state, the HATs will dispose of the tenanted (and any empty) property to new landlords. The consultation requirements of Housing Act 1985 s105 and Housing Act 1996 s137 do not apply[21] and the tenants have no veto over the sale or transfer of their homes.

7.15 Instead, the HAT invites the local housing authority to consider whether it wishes to acquire any of the properties and the HAT then informs the tenants of its plans for disposal and their right to make representations.[22]

7.16 If the tenant of a house makes, or the majority of tenants in a block of flats make, representations that they wish to have a local authority landlord, the secretary of state must order the transfer of their homes to the local council.[23]

7.17 Unless the properties are transferred to another public body (for example, back to the local housing authority), the tenants lose their secure status and are likely to be assured tenants of the new landlord,[24] notwithstanding that the tenancy may originally have been granted long before the Housing Act 1988 was brought into force. Any property occupied by a secure or introductory tenant can, however, only be disposed of to a local authority or a registered social landlord.[25] With a local authority they would remain secure or introductory but with a registered social landlord they would become assured tenants.

21 HA 1988 s84(8).
22 *HATs: The struggle begins*, Shelter/LHU pamphlet, October 1988.
23 HA 1988 s84A, inserted by Leasehold Reform, Housing and Urban Development Act 1993 s125, as further amended by HA 1996 (Consequential Amendments) Order 1997 SI No 74.
24 HA 1988 s38.
25 HA 1988 s79(2), as substituted in part by HA 1996 Sch 3 para 11.

Human Rights Act 1998

7.18   As a result of their status as statutory corporations established by ministerial order, there can be little doubt that HATs are 'public authorities' for the purpose of Human Rights Act 1998 s6. They are, accordingly, subject to the requirement to observe 'the right to respect for the home' accorded to the occupiers of their housing by article 8(1) of the European Convention on Human Rights (ECHR).

7.19   Therefore, a HAT will be required to conduct itself in accordance with the human rights approach which is required of local authorities and other public bodies (see respectively paras 3.193, 5.31 and 6.32 for a discussion of that approach). In general, provided that HATs observe the procedural steps which the law requires in relation to its tenants, it will be taken to have acted in accordance with Convention rights. But, as *Gallagher v Castle Vale Action Trust Ltd*[26] demonstrates, where a HAT seeks possession against a secure tenant on a discretionary ground for possession, it will be required by article 8 ECHR to show that a possession order is a proportionate remedy in all the circumstances of the case. In that case, where the tenant was not herself responsible for the anti-social behaviour of members of her household, and where there was evidence that the perpetrators were about to move out of the home, it was held that an outright possession order should not have been made. A suspended possession order was substituted. The Court of Appeal doubted whether article 8 made a significant difference to the way the courts had always approached the question whether it was reasonable to make a possession order. It did, however, reinforce the importance of making an order depriving someone of his or her home only where a clear case was made out. For a full discussion of the relevance of the Human Rights Act 1998 to possession cases, see paras 3.193, 5.31 and 6.32.

26 [2001] EWCA Civ 944; (2001) 33 HLR 72, CA.

CHAPTER 8

Introductory and demoted tenancies

continued

INTRODUCTORY TENANCIES

Background

8.1 In 1995 the concerted efforts of some public sector landlords produced a commitment from central government to increase legal powers available to those landlords to deal with errant tenants guilty of 'anti-social' behaviour towards others.[1] The result was an array of new measures and amendments to existing housing law now to be found in Housing Act 1996 Pt V, which bears the title 'Conduct of Tenants'.

8.2 Chapter I of Housing Act 1996 Pt V sets out the arrangements for 'introductory tenancies'. It was brought into force on 12 February 1997. The voluntary adoption of its provisions by a local authority (or housing action trust (HAT)) allows that landlord to offer all its future lettings to new tenants on a 'probationary' or 'trial' basis. If the tenancy endures for 12 months (or, exceptionally, for 18 months where the trial period has been extended – see para 8.23), it becomes a 'secure' tenancy if it otherwise fulfils the requirements for attracting that status.

8.3 In the 'probationary' or 'trial' year, the introductory tenant enjoys no security of tenure and only modified statutory rights. The tenancy can be ended by a process which starts with the landlord giving suitable notice and possession can be recovered virtually 'as of right'. The underlying intention of the provisions is to enable public landlords to 'nip in the bud' anti-social behaviour among new tenants.

8.4 In the event, there is nothing in Housing Act 1996 Pt V Ch I (save its title) which confines the operation of the introductory tenancy scheme to a context of nuisance or nuisance-related issues. A public landlord may perfectly lawfully adopt the introductory scheme for other reasons (for example, to achieve quicker possession against new tenants in early default with rent) and may seek possession during the trial or probationary period for any reason at all. Not all local authorities or HATs favour the concept of introductory tenancies. Just before their amalgamation into the Local Government Association, the representative associations for local authorities published *Introductory Tenancies: Guidance for Local Authorities*,[2] with the intention of assisting those councils deciding to operate introductory tenan-

---

1   DoE, *Anti-Social Behaviour on Council Estates*, April 1995.
2   AMA/ADC/ALG, February 1997.

cies with practical matters of implementation. That guidance was subsequently expressly endorsed by the then Department of the Environment (DoE) in its own circular[3] outlining the new provisions. Authorities are advised to take particular care in using the sanctions associated with an introductory tenancy against vulnerable tenants:

> Landlords should ensure that introductory tenancies can never be used as a weapon against vulnerable individuals and ensure that there are safeguards to protect such tenants ... It is essential that landlords are fully alive to the special needs of vulnerable tenants and their relationship with the community as a whole.

Where problems have arisen between a vulnerable tenant and neighbours, eviction may not necessarily be the most appropriate action to take.[4]

8.5   This chapter does not purport to offer a description of every facet of the introductory tenancy, the specific rights that attach to it, or the more general rights of introductory tenants.[5] Its aim is to provide assistance in those circumstances where a person alleged to be an introductory tenant is faced with the prospect of repossession by his or her landlord. All references are to sections of the Housing Act 1996 unless otherwise stated.

8.6   The introductory tenancy scheme, by its very nature, creates the opportunity for discrimination in public sector housing. Two tenants of identical houses in the same street and paying the same rent may hold very different tenancies from their public sector landlord – one may have long-term security of tenure as a 'secure' tenant, the other may be (for an initial 12, or possibly 18, months) at risk of dispossession as an introductory tenant. The argument that this discrimination is in unlawful breach of article 14 of the European Convention on Human Rights has, however, been rejected by the courts.[6]

---

3   DoE Circ 2/97, *Introductory Tenancies and Repossession for Secure Tenancies*, 31 January 1997.

4   See Circ 2/97 paras 10–15. See also the joint DoH/DoE guidance *Housing and Community Care: Establishing a Strategic Framework*, January 1997.

5   Although the term 'tenancy' is used throughout this chapter it is possible to have an 'introductory licence' to which the provisions described in the chapter apply with like effect: HA 1996 s126.

6   *R (McLellan) v Bracknell Forest DC* [2001] EWCA Civ 1510; [2002] QB 1129, at para 104.

Strategy for defending possession proceedings

8.7 The adviser faced with a prospective or actual claim for possession against a person alleged to be an introductory tenant should consider first whether the tenancy is 'introductory' at all and (if it is), second, how best to use the procedures available to delay or prevent repossession. What steps to take should then be determined by the results of that consideration. Prior to the issue of proceedings the tenant will need advice and assistance (under the Legal Help scheme – see para 24.3) and once proceedings are issued should be able to obtain full publicly funded representation if financially eligible (see chapter 24).

Is the tenancy 'introductory'?

8.8 First, advisers need to establish whether the tenancy really is 'introductory', if that is the description being used by the landlord. Working through the following headings should enable that issue to be resolved. If that 'checking process' gives rise to an issue as to whether the tenancy is introductory then that could be resolved by an application by the tenant to the county court.[7] Such proceedings may well last so long as to take the alleged introductory tenant over the expiry of the trial period and into secure status by default. (but see para 8.46 as to the effect of the landlord starting possession proceedings before the expiry date).

The landlord

8.9 Only a local housing authority or a housing action trust may operate an introductory tenancy regime.[8] If the landlord claiming possession is a housing association or any other form of landlord, the tenancy cannot be 'introductory' at all (although it may be some other form of tenancy enjoying reduced statutory protection, such as an assured shorthold). Thus, if a housing association or other landlord acquires council or HAT stock with sitting introductory tenants, the tenancies will cease to have that status.

The election

8.10 The landlord must have 'elected' to operate the introductory tenancy regime.[9] That requires a decision of the trustees of a HAT or of the

---

7   HA 1996 s138.

8   HA 1996 s124(1).

9   HA 1996 s124(1).

relevant committee and/or full council of the local authority. No such election can have been made before 12 February 1997 when the statutory provisions were commenced and accordingly the date of the election should be identified and checked.

8.11 A tenancy can only be introductory if granted by that council or HAT *after* the election and at a date when the election is still in force. An election can be revoked at any time and can even be adopted again later.[10]

8.12 If it can be shown that the election was made improperly or is otherwise invalid or has been revoked, then that would provide a complete defence to any assertion that the tenant is an introductory tenant. The issue might be canvassed in judicial review proceedings or be raised by the tenant in defence to any actual proceedings for possession.[11]

8.13 A tenancy entered into (or adopted) *before* the date of election cannot be an introductory tenancy.[12] For these purposes a tenancy is 'adopted' if the council or HAT becomes the landlord under the tenancy following a disposal or surrender of the former landlord's interest.[13]

8.14 If a HAT becomes the landlord of a council's introductory tenant then that introductory tenancy continues as such, providing the trust elected to operate introductory tenancies before the acquisition.

The tenant

8.15 A tenant who is secure at the date of any election retains that status. Likewise, those who are secure tenants will not subsequently lose out by moving around in the social landlord sector.

8.16 The Housing Act 1996 provides that a tenancy is not an introductory tenancy if immediately before the new tenancy was entered into (or adopted) the tenant was a secure tenant of the same or other premises or an assured tenant (not a shorthold tenant) of a registered social landlord in respect of the same or other premises.[14]

8.17 If any one of several joint tenants satisfies either of the above conditions then the new tenancy will not be an introductory tenancy.[15]

---

10 HA 1996 s124(5).
11 See *Wandsworth LBC v Winder (No 1)* [1985] AC 461, HL.
12 HA 1996 s124(3).
13 HA 1996 s124(4).
14 HA 1996 s124(2).
15 HA 1996 s124(2).

The tenancy

8.18 Both periodic tenancies and periodic licences can be introductory.[16] A fixed-term tenancy or licence cannot be introductory.[17]

8.19 The tenancy is only an introductory tenancy if the tenancy would otherwise have been a *secure* tenancy but for the extant election to operate the introductory scheme.[18] Thus the landlord and tenant conditions of the Housing Act 1985[19] must be satisfied and the tenancy must not come within any of the exceptions to secure tenancy status in that Act.[20] For the prerequisites of 'secure' status see chapter 1.

8.20 Similarly, if an event occurs which would cause a secure tenancy to lose its status as such (for example, subletting the whole – see para 2.40), any introductory tenancy loses that status and reverts to a bare contractual tenancy.[21]

The trial period

8.21 A tenancy normally remains an introductory tenancy only until the end of the 'trial period' of one year. At the end of that period it ordinarily becomes secure without the need for further action by landlord or tenant (but see para 8.23). It is therefore crucial to establish the date at which the one year starts to run.

8.22 In the case of a tenancy granted by the council or HAT itself the period begins with whichever is the later of:

- the date on which the tenancy was entered into; or
- the date on which the tenant was first entitled to possession under the tenancy.[22]

Thus, if a tenancy agreement is signed on 14 August 2005 which entitles the tenant to possession on 20 August 2005, the trial period runs from the latter date and expires on 19 August 2006.

8.23 Where the introductory tenancy started on or after 6 June 2005, the landlord now has a power to extend the trial period by a further six months.[23] Where the landlord wishes to exercise this power,

---

16 HA 1996 s126.
17 HA 1996 s124(2).
18 HA 1996 s124(2).
19 HA 1985 ss80–81; see also para 1.3.
20 HA 1985 s79(4) and Sch 1; see also para 1.22.
21 HA 1996 s125(5)(a).
22 HA 1996 s125(2). And see *Salford City Council v Garner* [2004] EWCA Civ 364; [2004] HLR 35, CA.
23 HA 1996, s125A, inserted by HA 2004, s179.

presumably because there has been some breach of tenancy obligations but the landlord is prepared to give the tenant a chance to remedy the situation, it must serve a notice of extension on the tenant at least eight weeks before the original one-year expiry date. The notice must set out the reasons for the landlord's decision and inform the tenant of his or her right to request a review of that decision and the time allowed for making the request. The request must be made within 14 days beginning with the day when the notice of extension is served. The procedure on review is similar to that on review of a decision to seek possession (see para 8.39). The review is to be carried out and the tenant notified of the review decision before the original one-year expiry date.

8.24 An introductory tenant may of course be offered a further introductory tenancy by the same or another council or HAT before the year expires (for example, as a result of a successful early request for a transfer). In such circumstances the time served under the former tenancy counts towards the trial period of the new tenancy, providing that the former tenancy ended immediately before the grant of the new one.[24]

8.25 If a tenant has held more than two successive introductory tenancies then each period counts towards the trial period providing that:

- the most recent completed period ended immediately before the new introductory tenancy was entered into (or was adopted); and
- each period succeeded the other without interruption.[25]

8.26 Where the new introductory tenancy is held by joint tenants, time towards the trial period is calculated by reference to the tenant who has been an introductory tenant, without interruption, for the longest period.[26]

8.27 A housing association's assured shorthold tenant might successfully apply for a transfer to a local authority which is only operating introductory tenancies. Providing the housing association is a registered social landlord, the time served under the assured shorthold tenancy counts towards the trial period so long as the former assured shorthold tenancy ends immediately before the grant of the new tenancy.[27]

24 HA 1996 s125(3).
25 HA 1996 s125(3)(b).
26 HA 1996 s125(4).
27 HA 1996 s125(3).

Loss of introductory status

8.28 An introductory tenancy ceases to be such even before the end of the trial period if one of the following occurs:

- the circumstances are or become such that the tenancy could not otherwise be secure;
- the landlord ceases to be either a local authority or a HAT;
- the election in force when the tenancy was entered into (or adopted) is revoked; or
- the tenant dies and there is no one qualified to succeed.[28]

In any of these circumstances (other than revocation of the election), the tenancy itself continues but only as a bare contractual tenancy and it cannot resume introductory status.[29] Where the election is revoked, the tenancy may become secure.

8.29 However, if by the date of the occurrence of one of these developments, the landlord has already started possession proceedings, the tenancy has a deemed introductory status until those proceedings are concluded.[30]

8.30 Of course, the most common cause for the loss of introductory status is automatic conversion into a secure tenancy at the end of the one-year trial period or eighteen-month extended trial period. The landlord can only prevent that happening by the actual *issue* of court possession proceedings before the trial period expires. The date when the proceedings are issued by the court is crucial, and this will often be a few days later than the date when the landlord lodged the claim form with the court.[31] Such issue serves to preserve introductory status until the proceedings are determined.[32]

The repossession procedure

8.31 Assuming that consideration of the above factors has shown that the tenancy is indeed 'introductory', it will be necessary next for the adviser to check for proper observance by the landlord of the prescribed steps for recovery of possession. Those steps should be examined in turn and carefully scrutinised for error which may be relied on in defence of any proceedings.

---

28 HA 1996 s125(5).
29 HA 1996 s125(6).
30 HA 1996 s130(1)(b).
31 *Salford City Council v Garner* [2004] EWCA Civ 364; [2004] HLR 35, CA.
32 HA 1996 s130(1)(a).

Preliminary notice

8.32   Prior to issuing possession proceedings, the landlord must serve a notice on the tenant. The reference to 'service' would suggest that only a written notice suffices. Without service of such a notice the landlord cannot bring proceedings for possession and there is no jurisdiction in the court to dispense with service or waive any defect.[33]

8.33   No form of notice is prescribed but the notice must:[34]

- state that the court will be asked to make a possession order;
- set out the reasons for the landlord's decision to apply for a such an order;
- specify a date after which possession proceedings may be begun;
- inform the tenant of the right to request a review of the decision to seek an order;
- inform the tenant of the time within which such a request must be made; and
- inform the tenant that if he or she needs help or advice about the notice, and what to do about it, he or she should take it immediately to a citizen's advice bureau, a housing aid centre, a law centre or a solicitor.

Reasons

8.34   Where no reasons, inadequate reasons or plainly wrong reasons are given, the notice is invalid and the court cannot entertain the possession proceedings.[35] A notice with no reasons at all is plainly defective. It remains to be seen whether notices which are factually incorrect or contain sparse reasons (for example, '... because you have proved an unsatisfactory tenant') will be as readily struck down by the courts. In *Lambeth LBC v Dearie*[36] a possession order granted against an introductory tenant was set aside by a district judge. The reasons given in the notice were 'the tenant has failed to pay the rent due'. The court held this to be insufficient. These reasons did not enable the tenant to know precisely what had to be done to rectify the position or to exercise properly the right to review which was referred to in the notice. Generally a statutory duty to give reasons is construed to mean

---

33   HA 1996 s128(1).

34   HA 1996 s143E.

35   See by analogy *Torridge DC v Jones* (1986) 18 HLR 107, CA, and *Dudley MBC v Bailey* (1990) 22 HLR 424, CA.

36   April 2001 *Legal Action* 20.

that the reasons given must be proper, intelligible and adequate.[37] The Government circular advises landlords to give a 'full statement of reasons' which should include 'a case history of the sequence of events'.[38]

Dates

8.35 The date stated in the notice as the date after which possession proceedings may be begun must not be earlier than the date on which the tenancy could, if it were not an introductory tenancy, be brought to an end by notice to quit given on the same date as the notice of proceedings.[39] For a weekly periodic tenancy the earliest date is a date at least 28 days after service and that date must be the first or last day of a period of the tenancy.[40] The notice must also comply with any express terms of the tenancy as to the period of notice.

The request for review

8.36 Within 14 days of being served with the notice the tenant may request that the landlord review the decision to seek possession. The request need not be made in writing (although it would be sensible to ensure it was recorded in writing). There is no prescribed form, and no requirement to make the request in any particular manner.[41] There is no requirement to give grounds for seeking a review.

8.37 The period of 14 days begins with the day on which the notice is served.[42] Accordingly, if the notice is served on a Thursday the request for a review must be made by a week next Wednesday.[43] This 14-day time period cannot be extended by the landlord nor on application to a county court because a court has no discretion to extend a statutory time limit.[44]

---

37 Per Megaw J in *Re Poyser and Mills' Arbitration* [1964] 2 QB 467; [1963] 2 WLR 1309, approved by the House of Lords in *Save Britain's Heritage v Number1 Poultry Ltd* [1991] 1 WLR 153, HL.

38 DoE Circ 2/97 para 16. It also advises (para 17) that an explanation in a covering letter is not an adequate substitute.

39 HA 1996 s128(4).

40 Protection from Eviction Act 1977 s5.

41 *R (Chelfat) v Tower Hamlets LBC* [2006] EWHC 313 (Admin); April 2006 *Legal Action* 32.

42 HA 1996 s129(1).

43 *Trow v Ind Coope (West Midlands) Ltd* [1967] 2 QB 899; [1967] 3 WLR 633, CA.

44 *Honig v Lewisham LBC* (1958) 122 JPJ 302, CA.

Timing and procedure on review

8.38   The review must be dealt with speedily. It must be concluded (which includes notification of the result to the tenant) within the period between the service of the notice and the date specified in it for earliest commencement of proceedings.[45] That may be as short as 28 days. If the landlord misses this window of opportunity the chance may be lost – possibly for good if the trial year (or 18-month period) has meantime expired. If it has not expired the landlord can start again with a new notice. However, failure to conclude a review within the statutory period may not be fatal to the council's case. In *R (Chelfat) v Tower Hamlets LBC*,[46] the court in its discretion refused relief where the council had not conducted a review within the prescribed timescale as the tenant's request for a review had been directed to the housing benefits section of the council and not to the housing officer named in the notice. The council had subsequently agreed to a warrant of possession being suspended by consent to enable a review to be carried out, and against that background it would be wholly unjust to allow the tenant's application for judicial review. Since section 129(6) is silent as to the consequences of any failure to carry out a review within the time specified, the question of whether such a delay was fatal to the council's decision to seek possession would turn on the facts. If the failure was due to a genuine oversight capable of being remedied, there seemed to be no good reason to prevent a landlord from remedying the position and bringing a possession claim.

8.39   The Introductory Tenants (Review) Regulations 1997[47] are concerned with the procedure that is to be followed on a review.

- Regulation 2 provides that there is to be no oral hearing unless one has been expressly requested by the tenant within 14 days of the service of the Housing Act 1996 s128 notice of intention to seek possession. There is no power to extend that time limit. That notice need not advise the tenant of this right to request an oral hearing. The request for an oral hearing need not be made in writing.

- Regulation 3 provides that the review is to be carried out by a person who was not involved in the decision to apply for possession and if that person is an officer it must be a person senior to the officer who took the decision to serve the Housing Act 1996 s128 notice.

---

45 HA 1996 s129(6).
46 [2006] EWHC 313 (Admin); April 2006 *Legal Action* 32.
47 SI No 72.

- Regulation 4 provides that if no oral hearing has been requested in time, the tenant has a right to submit written representations within a fixed period of being notified of that right. This is based on the premise, therefore, that on receipt of a request for review the landlord will acknowledge it and invite written representations by a fixed date which must not be earlier than five clear days from the date the tenant receives this notice of the right to make representations.

- Regulations 5 and 6 deal with oral hearings. Where a request for an oral hearing has been made in time, the landlord must give the tenant notice of the date, time and place of the hearing, which cannot be less than five days after the landlord receives the tenant's request. If the notice is defective or short then the hearing may only proceed with the consent of the tenant or his or her representative. At a hearing the tenant has a right to:
  - be heard and to be accompanied and represented by another person (professional or otherwise);
  - call people to give evidence;
  - put questions to any person who gives evidence; and
  - make written representations.

  The tenant should be given sufficient opportunity to read any written material relied on by the council and to prepare his or her own case.[48]

- Regulations 7 to 10 deal with such matters as adjournments, postponements and non-attendance.

8.40 As is apparent from this description of the statutory review scheme, and of the regulations which flesh it out, the scheme makes no pretence of 'independence'. The review is carried out by the very landlord which has decided to give notice of intention to claim possession. In *R (McLellan) v Bracknell Forest BC*[49] it was contended that the review scheme was incompatible with the right to a fair and impartial determination of civil rights guaranteed by article 6(1) of the European Convention on Human Rights. The Court of Appeal decided that the requirements of article 6 were met because the Administrative Court's judicial review jurisdiction could be invoked to cure any deficiency in the review process in any particular case.

---

48 *R (on the application of McDonagh) v Salisbury DC* September 2001 *Legal Action* 23.

49 [2001] EWCA Civ 1510; [2002] QB 1129.

Outcome of the review

8.41   After the review has been completed, the landlord must notify the tenant of its decision and, if the decision to take possession proceedings still stands, then the landlord must give reasons for that decision.[50] The use of the word 'notify' would suggest that the notice and the reasons both have to be in writing.

8.42   Where the landlord decides, following a review, to allow the tenant an opportunity to remedy any breach of obligations, but the tenant does not do so, the landlord may take proceedings for possession without the need to serve a fresh notice. In *Cardiff City Council v Stone*,[51] the tenant had fallen into rent arrears. The council issued a section 128 notice of proceedings. Following a review, the tenant was informed that proceedings would not be taken if she cleared the arrears at the rate of £3 per week. The arrears later increased, and the council claimed possession on the basis of the original notice. The Court of Appeal rejected the argument that a second notice should have been served: this might deter a landlord from taking a humane 'wait and see' approach before issuing proceedings. In these circumstances the landlord should make it clear that it has upheld the decision to seek possession and is merely deferring proceedings to give the tenant a further chance to save his or her home.[52] Where the landlord serves a section 128 notice, and the tenant then commits breaches of a different nature from those specified in the notice, the landlord will normally be required to serve a second notice and hold a further review: this requirement may, however, be waived if the landlord has acted fairly and the tenant has suffered no prejudice.[53]

Possession proceedings

8.43   The landlord can only bring an introductory tenancy to an end (while it is an introductory tenancy) by obtaining a court order.[54]

8.44   Before commencing possession proceedings the landlord does not need to serve a notice to quit or a notice seeking possession (under the Housing Act 1985) – the notice procedure described above substitutes for those requirements. The landlord should use the normal

---

50   HA 1996 s129(5).
51   [2002] EWCA Civ 298; [2003] HLR 47.
52   *R (Forbes) v Lambeth LBC* [2003] EWHC 222 (Admin); [2003] HLR 49.
53   *R (Laporte) v Newham LBC* [2004] EWHC 227 (Admin).
54   HA 1996 s127(1).

procedure for possession in the county court set out in CPR Part 55 (see chapter 21).

Defending the proceedings

8.45 The court shall not make an order for possession unless satisfied that the provisions of Housing Act 1996 s128 apply.[55] Accordingly, the landlord needs to prove that:

- the tenancy was an introductory tenancy at the time when possession proceedings were begun; and
- a proper Housing Act 1996 s128 notice has been served; and
- the proceedings were begun after the date specified.

8.46 The effect of commencing the proceedings is to keep the introductory tenancy alive until the conclusion of the proceedings.[56]

8.47 It should be noted that the landlord does not need to prove that the post-notice review procedure has been properly observed or completed in order to recover possession. If the landlord can prove the three above-mentioned matters on the balance of probabilities, possession must be granted.

8.48 Advisers will want to explore the possibilities of running defences based on either or any of the following:

- the tenancy was not 'introductory' at the date the proceedings were issued (see para 8.8);
- the Housing Act 1996 s128 notice is defective or was not served (see paras 8.31–8.34);
- the proceedings were begun prematurely (see para 8.35);
- the proceedings were begun too late (ie, after the trial period had expired) (see para 8.30).[57]

If any of these defences succeed the proceedings should be dismissed, normally with costs.

Adjourning the proceedings

8.49 It is no part of the county court's function, in possession proceedings against an introductory tenant, to inquire into the reasons for the decision to give notice or the merits of the decision to take proceed-

---

55 HA 1996 s127(2).
56 HA 1996 s130.
57 *Salford CC v Entwhistle* October 2002 *Legal Action* 28; *Salford CC v Garner* [2004] EWCA Civ 364; [2004] HLR 35, CA.

ings. Likewise, the court is not concerned with the review process, its conduct or outcome – it has no jurisdiction to investigate compliance or otherwise with the review process or the general merits of the landlord's claim.[58] But, where the tenant asserts that the dicision to recover possession is improper or irrational, such matters may be raised in the county court by way of a defence[59] – see paras 5.41–5.42 and 8.104.

8.50 In those circumstances, a tenant wishing to challenge the initial decision to give notice, or challenge a decision on review, or to take issue with the procedure followed on review, must do so by way of judicial review in the Administrative Court (complaint might, of course, also be made to the local government ombudsman). Given the procedural complexity of the review procedure and the haste with which reviews are to be conducted it is inevitable that mistakes will be made. Where an application is to be made to adjourn possession proceedings in these circumstances, the court will need to assess the basis for the potential judicial review. To enable the court to take an informed view on this question, the authority should provide evidence setting out how the procedure was operated in the individual case. Such evidence should deal with the degree of independence of the review body from the person who took the original decision; the way the hearing was conducted; and the reason for taking the decision to continue the proceedings.[60]

8.51 To avoid any such challenge becoming 'academic', tenants will have to hold up the possession proceedings in the county court. That court has jurisdiction to grant a short adjournment if satisfied that there is a real chance of permission to proceed by way of judicial review being granted.[61] Having obtained such an adjournment, tenants will need to apply quickly for permission to proceed by way of judicial review and make an urgent application for a further stay of any possession proceedings until the full hearing of the judicial review.[62]

8.52 Even if there may be flaws in the decision-making procedure in the particular case, the court on judicial review will not grant a remedy where there is a lack of merit in the tenant's application. Where a tenant fell into rent arrears as a result of failing to provide information to

---

58 *Manchester City Council v Cochrane* (1999) 31 HLR 810, CA.
59 *Kay v Lambeth LBC; Leeds CC v Price* [2006] UKHL 10; [2006] 2 WLR 570, HL.
60 *R (McLellan) v Bracknell Forest DC* [2001] EWCA Civ 1510; [2002] QB 1129.
61 Ibid at 819 and see *R (McLellan) v Bracknell Forest DC* [2001] EWCA Civ 1510; [2002] QB 1129; (2001) 33 HLR 989, CA, at para 103.
62 As to the criteria on which such a stay may be granted see *West Glamorgan CC v Rafferty* [1987] 1 WLR 457 and *Avon CC v Buscott* [1988] QB 656, CA.

support a housing benefit claim, in the absence of good reasons for the failure his claim for judicial review was dismissed. The court noted that the role of a tenant was not a passive one. If he ignored correspondence and requests for further information, the failure lay at his door.[63]

8.53   If the application for judicial review fails, the possession proceedings are generally restored and possession granted. If the application for judicial review succeeds, the relevant decision to take the proceedings should be quashed and the authority directed to reconsider. If it then decides to withdraw the proceedings the tenant will become 'secure' (as more than 12 months will inevitably have passed since the grant of the tenancy). If it decides, this time lawfully, to proceed to recover possession it may apply for the proceedings in the county court to be restored. Any such reconsideration can take account of developments since the initial decision to evict.[64]

The possession order

8.54   If the court makes a possession order it cannot postpone the date for giving of possession for more than 14 days unless:

- possession by that date would cause exceptional hardship in which case the postponement can be for up to six weeks;[65] or
- the landlord consents to a longer period.

Save by consent, there is no scope for the making of 'suspended' possession orders. As the court has no discretion to stay or suspend execution of the order, a former introductory tenant left in possession does *not* become a 'tolerated trespasser', if not evicted, he or she may become a new tenant or licensee.[66]

Human Rights Act 1998

8.55   The Court of Appeal has held that the introductory tenant regime and its operation are not incompatible with articles 6, 8 or 14 of the Convention.[67]

---

63 *R (Chowdhury) v Newham LBC* [2003] EWHC 2837 (Admin); see also *Merton LBC v Williams* [2002] EWCA Civ 980; [2003] HLR 20.

64 *R (on the application of McDonagh) v Salisbury DC* September 2001 *Legal Action* 23.

65 HA 1980 s89.

66 See *Lambeth LBC v Azu* June 2002 *Legal Action* 25.

67 *R (Mclellan) v Bracknell Forest BC* [2001] EWCA Civ 1510; [2002] QB 1129; (2001) 33 HLR 989, CA.

DEMOTED TENANCIES

Background

8.56   The Anti-Social Behaviour Act 2003 introduced a new weapon in the armoury of social landlords to deal with serious nuisance behaviour. Section 14 of the Act gave new powers to social landlords to ask the court to 'demote' secure or assured tenancies to 12-month probationary tenancies.[68] If during the probation year the landlord has cause for complaint about the tenant's behaviour, the tenancy can be terminated by court order following a notice of proceedings, but without the need to prove a ground for possession.

8.57   A local authority, HAT or a registered social landlord (RSL) can apply to the county court for a demotion order, under:

- Housing Act 1985 s82A (local authority, HAT or RSL secure tenancy); or
- Housing Act 1988 s6A (RSL assured tenancy).[69]

8.58   Demotion involves the court making an order that:

- ends an existing secure or assured tenancy; and
- replaces it with a new tenancy which gives the tenant reduced security of tenure for a period of time; and
- carries forward any rent arrears or credits from the old rent account on to the new rent account.[70]

8.59   This chapter deals with the rules on demotion of both secure and assured tenancies. (For details of the assured tenancy scheme under the Housing Act 1988, see chapter 10.) While the grounds for demotion are identical in respect of both types of tenancy, there are major differences in the nature of the demoted tenancy which is created in either case.

---

68 With effect in England from 30 June 2004 and in Wales from 30 September 2004. See generally Jon Holbrook and Dean Underwood 'Defending demoted tenancy claims' September 2004 *Legal Action* 27 and October 2004 *Legal Action* 23; and Christopher Baker, 'Demoting Tenancies: Innovation or Exasperation?' Parts 1 and 2, *Journal of Housing Law*, September 2004 and November 2004.

69 Both sections were inserted in the respective Acts by Anti-social Behaviour Act 2003 s14(2).

70 HA 1985 s82A(3); HA 1988, s6A(3).

'Relevant landlord'

8.60 Only a local housing authority, housing action trust or registered social landlord is a 'relevant landlord' for these purposes, that is, one which can apply to demote a secure or assured tenancy.[71]

Grounds for a demotion order

8.61 The court must not make a demotion order unless it is satisfied that (1) the tenant or a person residing in or visiting the dwelling has engaged or threatened to engage in conduct which falls within either of the limbs set out below *and* (2) it is reasonable to make the order.[72] The same two-stage test applies in all cases.

The first limb: nuisance and annoyance

8.62 This limb relates to conduct:

(a) which is capable of causing nuisance or annoyance to any person; and

(b) which directly or indirectly relates to or affects the housing management functions of a relevant landlord.

8.63 It is immaterial where the conduct in question occurs.[73] Conduct which causes harassment to 'any person' – not only a neighbour – is included, but there must be a connection between the conduct and the landlord's 'housing management functions'. Housing management functions are defined broadly to include:

(a) functions conferred by or under any enactment; and

(b) the powers and duties of the landlord as the holder of an estate or interest in housing accommodation.[74]

8.64 Clearly, any behaviour which adversely affects tenants of the landlord or their household members or visitors, or the landlord's staff, relates to housing management functions. However, despite the reference to conduct which affects functions conferred by any enactment, it is suggested that the scope of this provision does not extend to the non-

---

71 HA 1985 s82A(1); HA1988, s6A(1).

72 HA 1985 s82A(4) in respect of secure tenancies; HA 1988, s6A(4) in respect of assured tenancies

73 HA 1996 s153A(5), inserted by Anti-social Behaviour Act 2003 s13(3).

74 HA 1996 s153E(11).

housing functions of a local authority, for example, in its capacity as highways authority.

The second limb: use of premises for unlawful purpose

8.65   This limb relates to conduct which consists of or involves using or threatening to use housing accommodation owned or managed by a relevant landlord (see para 8.60) for an unlawful purpose.[75]

8.66   It is not necessary to prove a conviction for the unlawful use of the accommodation (in contrast with the second limb of the comparable ground for possession for secure and assured tenancies – see paras 3.87 and 10.90).

Reasonableness

8.67   The court cannot grant a demotion order unless it is satisfied that it is reasonable to do so. The court has a broad discretion in assessing reasonableness, and some guidance in exercising its discretion may be derived from case-law decisions under the 'nuisance or annoyance' ground for possession in relation to secure and assured tenancies (see paras 3.72–3.78 and 11.10–11.14). There is no provision for a 'structuring' of discretion in which the court is specifically directed to consider the effects of the conduct on other persons, as there is in relation to the 'nuisance' grounds for possession: but Court of Appeal authorities have for many years taken this approach in cases involving evidence of anti-social behaviour.

Notice of intention to apply for a demotion order

8.68   Before applying for a demotion order, the landlord must serve a notice of its intention to do so. The procedure differs according to whether the tenancy is a secure tenancy or an assured tenancy.

Demotion claims against secure tenants

8.69   The landlord must first serve a notice in the prescribed form.[76] Where the landlord also intends to seek possession, two separate notices

75   HA 1996 s153B, inserted by Anti-social Behaviour Act 2003 s13(3).
76   HA 1985 s83(2) as amended by Anti-social Behaviour Act 2003 s14(3). See also the Secure Tenancies (Notices) (Amendment) (England) Regulations 2004 SI No 1627, and the Secure Tenancies (Notices) (Amendment) (Wales) Regulations 2005 SI No 1226.

must be served: the notice of seeking possession (see para 2.4) and the notice seeking demotion.

8.70 The notice of intended demotion must contain particulars of the conduct which has caused the landlord to seek to demote the tenancy. It must also specify a date after which proceedings may be begun.[77] That date must not be earlier than the date on which a notice to quit would expire:[78] since most secure tenants are weekly periodic tenants, a notice to quit would need to be at least 28 days long[79] following the date of service and expire on the first or last day of a tenancy period. There is no provision allowing proceedings to be begun immediately after service of the notice, as there is with regard to possession claims on nuisance grounds, but there is provision for dispensing with notice altogether.[80]

8.71 The notice has a 'life span' of 12 months beginning with the date specified in it: section 83(4A)(b). During that calendar year, proceedings may be issued based upon the notice; after that period, a fresh notice must be issued, unless the court is to be asked to dispense with the notice requirement.

Demotion claims against assured tenants

8.72 In the case of assured tenants, the landlord must serve a notice of intention to apply for demotion before the court can entertain proceedings,[81] but there is, strangely, no prescribed form of notice. However, the notice must:

- give particulars of the conduct complained of;
- state that proceedings will not begin before the date specified in the notice; and
- state that proceedings will not begin later than 12 months after the date of service.[82]

8.73 The notice period is shorter than that for secure tenancies: the date specified in the notice must be at least two weeks from the date of service of the notice, and the nominated date need not be the first or last day of a tenancy period. The 'life span' of the notice dates from the date of service, not from the date specified.

77 HA 1985 s83(4A)(a).
78 HA 1985, s83(5).
79 Protection from Eviction Act 1977 s5.
80 HA 1985 s83(1)(b).
81 HA 1988, s6A(5).
82 HA 1988, s6A(6).

8.74   In relation to both secure and assured tenants, the court may dispense with the notice requirements if it considers it just and equitable to do so.[83]

Applying for a demotion order

8.75   A landlord can seek a demotion order in possession proceedings as an alternative to a possession order, in which case the landlord should use the Claim Form N5 for possession; the claim will be governed by CPR Part 55.

8.76   Alternatively, a landlord may make a free-standing application for a demotion order without seeking possession. In this situation the landlord should use Form N6 (Claim Form for demotion of a tenancy) and specific particulars of claim (Form N122). The conduct of these stand-alone claims is governed by CPR 65 Pt III and the associated PD 65 Section III.

8.77   For further details of the procedure on applications for demotion see chapter 23.

Defending the proceedings

8.78   The court shall not make an order for possession unless satisfied that the provisions of Housing Act 1985 s82A(4) (in the case of secure tenancies) or Housing Act 1988 s6A(4) (in the case of assured tenancies) are satisfied. Accordingly, the landlord needs to prove that:

- the proper notice of intention to bring proceedings has been served (or the court agrees to dispense with such a notice);
- the proceedings were begun after the specified date and within the appropriate 12-month period;
- the tenant or a person residing in or visiting the dwelling has engaged or has threatened to engage in conduct which falls within one of the statutory limbs – see paras 8.62–8.66 above; and
- it is reasonable for a demotion order to be made.

8.79   Advisers should initially check that the form of the notice complies with the statutory requirements, that it was properly served and that the proceedings were not begun prematurely. Any irregularity may provide sufficient defence to the claim.

83   HA 1985 s83(1)(b); HA 1988 s6A(5)(b).

Substantive defences

8.80 Assuming that none of the more technical defences mentioned above is available, it may be open to the tenant to defend the claim on the basis that neither limb of the statutory ground has been made out on the evidence and on the balance of probabilities.

8.81 The first line of defence is to test the evidence concerning the alleged misconduct. As in possession proceedings based on anti-social behaviour, the adviser will need to take detailed instructions from the tenant and any other witnesses on every allegation particularised in the landlord's statement of case, and prepare the defence and witness statements accordingly. Where the tenant accepts general responsibility for the behaviour complained of, he or she should make the necessary admissions, explain any mitigating factors and emphasise his or her willingness to change. Where the tenant has not personally been responsible for the nuisance, but the conduct is that of a household member or visitor, the tenant must clearly set out the steps that he or she has taken to address the problem, including co-operating with any statutory or other agencies involved.

8.82 The second line of defence, assuming that the landlord has proved (or the tenant admits) that one of the limbs has been made out, is to assert that it is not reasonable to order demotion. It is for the landlord to satisfy the court that that is so. In applying the 'reasonableness' test, the court is required to have regard to all relevant factors. The witness statements should deal in detail with the tenant's own personal circumstances, including any health problems or other life experiences which have contributed to the present situation. In deciding whether to make an order, the court will be influenced by the tenor of Court of Appeal decisions in relation to the 'nuisance' ground for possession, and in particular the need to consider the interests of those affected by the behaviour. Even so, the objective will be to convince the court that demotion would be unnecessary and disproportionate, and that alternative measures – such as an undertaking to the court, or a willingness to engage in an acceptable behaviour contract – are sufficient to deal with the situation.

8.83 Assuming that the tenant is financially eligible, he or she may be able to obtain a public funding (legal aid) certificate to be represented in defending the proceedings. See generally chapter 24 (Public funding).

8.84 Where the application for demotion is made in possession proceedings, it will be one of the options which the court is considering at the conclusion of the evidence. In some cases, the range of choices

will effectively be between a demotion order and a postponed possession order. A demotion order may be presented by the landlord as a
less drastic alternative to a postponed order, as the tenant will have
the chance to regain his or her former security of tenure after a period
of good behaviour. On the other hand, it must be remembered that
under a postponed possession order, the court retains its discretion
up to the date of eviction, whereas it has no discretion to refuse a possession order sought against a demoted tenant (see below).

The effect of a demotion order

8.85   A demotion order – whether made in respect of a secure or assured
tenancy – has the following effects:

- the former secure or assured tenancy is terminated with effect
  from the date specified in the order;
- if the tenant remains in occupation of the dwelling after that date,
  a demoted tenancy is created with effect from that date;
- it is a term of the demoted tenancy that any rent in arrears or rent
  paid in advance at the termination of the secure or assured tenancy
  becomes payable or is credited under the demoted tenancy;[84]
- the parties to and period of the tenancy, the amount of the rent
  and the dates on which rent is payable are the same as under the
  former tenancy.[85]

8.86   But the nature of the demoted tenancy is different, depending on
whether the former tenancy was secure or assured. When a secure
tenancy is demoted, and the landlord is a local authority or a HAT,[86]
it becomes a *demoted tenancy* governed by Housing Act 1996 ss143A–
143P.[87] When an assured tenancy, or a secure tenancy with a RSL, is
demoted, it becomes a *demoted assured shorthold tenancy* governed by
Housing Act 1988 s20B.

Demoted tenancies (former secure tenancies)

8.87   The framework for demoted tenancies inserted at sections 143A–
143P of the Housing Act 1996 follows on from the introductory tenancy provisions in the same Act. The two statutory schemes are very

84   HA 1985 s82A(3); HA 1988 s6A(3).
85   HA 1985 s82A(5); HA 1988 s6A(8).
86   HA 1996 s143A(2).
87   Inserted by Anti-Social Behaviour Act 2003 Sch 1.

similar, as the demoted tenancy scheme has been closely modelled on introductory tenancies. The statutory framework also deals with matters such as succession, assignment, the right to carry out repairs and the provision of information.

8.88 The demoted tenancy will start on the date specified in the demotion order. If after one year from that date the landlord has not given notice of proceedings for possession, the tenancy will cease to be a demoted tenancy, and will become secure again.[88]

8.89 If, however, the tenant breaches the terms of his or her demoted tenancy, the landlord may give notice of possession proceedings within the one-year period. There is no prescribed form, but the notice of proceedings must:

- state that the court will be asked to make an order for possession;
- set out the landlord's reasons for seeking the order;
- specify the date after which possession proceedings may begin;
- inform the tenant of his or her right to request a review of the landlord's decision and the time within which the request must be made (ie, 14 days from the date of service).[89]

8.90 Although the basis for the demotion order in the first place lay in the anti-social behaviour of the tenant, the landlord's reasons for seeking possession of the demoted tenancy can relate to any breach of the tenancy conditions, such as rent arrears, or indeed to any other factor such as under-occupation.

8.91 The date specified in the notice must be not earlier than the date on which the tenancy could be brought to an end by a notice to quit.[90] In the usual case of a weekly tenancy, the earliest date will be the first or last day of a tenancy period which follows a period of 28 days from the date of the notice. The notice must also advise the tenant to take the notice immediately to a citizen's advice bureau, housing aid centre, law centre or solicitor if he or she needs help or advice.[91]

8.92 Where a landlord serves a notice of proceedings for possession on a demoted tenancy, the tenancy will continue as a demoted tenancy even if the 12-month anniversary of the start date goes by, until any of the following events occur:

- the notice of proceedings is withdrawn by the landlord;
- the proceedings are determined in favour of the tenant;

---

88 HA 1996 s143B.
89 HA 1996 s143E(2).
90 HA 1996 s143E(3).
91 HA 1996 s143E(5).

- a period of six months has gone by since the notice was served and no proceedings for possession have been brought;[92]
- the proceedings are determined in favour of the landlord (when the tenancy will come to an end on the date fixed for possession in the court order).

8.93   The effective extension of the demotion period by six months is achieved solely by the service of a valid notice of intended proceedings, and is not dependent (as in the case of introductory tenancies) on the issue of the possession claim.

8.94   The tenant has 14 days beginning with the date of service of the notice to request the landlord to review its decision[93] (the fourteenth day effectively being two calendar weeks less one day). If a tenant so requests, the landlord must carry out a review of the decision to seek an order for possession and notify the tenant of the outcome along with its reasons for the decision on review. The review must take place, and the decision must be notified, before the date specified in the notice as the date after which proceedings may be begun.[94] The decision on review must be made by a person of appropriate seniority who was not involved in the original decision, and the review must be conducted in accordance with the Demoted Tenancies (Review of Decisions) (England) Regulations 2004[95] or the Demoted Tenancies (Review of Decisions) (Wales) Regulations 2005.[96] In particular, the tenant may request an oral hearing.

8.95   If the tenant does not request a review within the 14-day period, or if the landlord on review decides to confirm its decision to seek possession, the landlord may thereafter start proceedings. The court must make an order for possession unless it thinks that the procedure relating to either the notice of proceedings or the review 'has not been followed'.[97] It has no power to investigate the landlord's reasons for bringing the proceedings. But, in contrast to the position in respect of introductory tenancies, where the court's role is restricted to ensuring that the correct notice has been served, here it appears that the court must be satisfied that all aspects of the procedure have been correctly observed, including the conduct of the review process.

92 HA 1996 s143B(4).
93 HA 1996 s143F(1).
94 HA 1996 s143F(6).
95 SI No 1679.
96 SI No 1228.
97 HA 1996 s143D(2).

8.96   A demoted tenant may therefore have a defence to the claim if:

- the notice of proceedings did not contain the requisite information;
- the notice was not served on the tenant;
- the period of the notice is insufficient;
- proceedings were started before the specified date;
- the landlord has not held a review despite the fact that the tenant requested one within the 14-day period allowed;
- the review has not been conducted by a person of appropriate seniority; or
- there has been some other material breach of the review regulations.

8.97   Where the tenant wishes to challenge the fairness or rationality of the decision to terminate the demoted tenancy, this should generally be done by proceedings for judicial review. In this event, the tenant should seek advice and legal representation as a matter of urgency and should make an application for public funding (legal aid) to cover the cost of the proceedings. It will be necessary to ask the county court to adjourn the possession claim to await the outcome of an application to the Administrative Court for permission to apply for judicial review. See paras 8.50–8.53 for further discussion of this strategy.

8.98   Where, however, the court makes an order for possession, it cannot postpone the date for giving of possession for more than 14 days unless:

- possession by that date would cause exceptional hardship, in which case the postponement can be for up to six weeks;[98] or
- the landlord consents to a longer period.

The court has no power to suspend a possession order unless the landlord consents. The demoted tenancy ends on the date on which the order requires the tenant to give up possession: see para 8.54 above, in relation to introductory tenancies.

Demoted assured shorthold tenancies

8.99   Former secure tenants of RSLs (demoted under Housing Act 1985 s82A) and former RSL assured tenants (demoted under Housing Act 1988 s6A) will have a demoted assured shorthold tenancy governed by section 20B of the 1988 Act. This tenancy is in most respects similar to a standard assured shorthold tenancy: see chapter 9.

98 HA 1980 s89(1).

8.100   The demoted assured shorthold tenancy will start on the date specified in the demotion order. If after one year from that date the landlord has not given notice of proceedings for possession, the tenancy will cease to be an assured shorthold tenancy.[99] The tenancy will then become assured, even where the original tenancy was a secure tenancy. Where notice of proceedings has been given within the demotion period, the tenancy continues to be a demoted assured shorthold tenancy even after the 12-month anniversary of the start date has gone by, and will remain such until one of the following events occurs:

- the landlord withdraws the notice of proceedings;
- the proceedings are determined in favour of the tenant (for example, where the landlord has served an invalid notice);
- a period of six months from the date of the notice has gone by and no proceedings for possession have been brought;[100] or
- the proceedings result in a possession order in favour of the landlord (as they usually will).

8.101   Where the RSL wishes to bring a demoted assured shorthold tenancy to an end, it may serve a notice requiring possession. For no obvious reason, the procedure in RSL cases is much less regulated than that governing demoted tenants of local authorities. The notice here will be a two months' notice under section 21(4) of the Housing Act 1988, which must expire on the last day of a period of the tenancy: see para 9.17. Moreover, a RSL is not obliged to offer its demoted tenants a right of review of its decision to seek possession. In practice, it is to be expected that RSLs will in fact offer a review.

8.102   Where the landlord brings proceedings for possession of a demoted assured shorthold tenancy, the court's role is restricted to examining the validity of the notice, and subject to being satisfied on this aspect, it must make an order for possession. Where the court makes an order for possession, it cannot postpone the date for giving of possession for more than 14 days unless:

- possession by that date would cause exceptional hardship, in which case the postponement can be for up to six weeks;[101] or
- the landlord consents to a longer period.

---

99 HA 1988 s20B(2).
100 HA 1988 s20B(4).
101 HA 1980 s89.

8.103   If the tenant believes that the RSL has made its decision to bring possession proceedings without sufficient evidence, or has failed to take account of relevant matters, or has failed to give the tenant the chance to respond to allegations against him or her, or has otherwise acted unfairly, there may be a challenge to the landlord's decision by way of judicial review. This is especially important where a review has not been offered, since it is difficult to see how such a procedure could be compatible with article 6 or 8 of the European Convention on Human Rights. While the law in this area is in a state of development, it is highly arguable that RSLs in general, or particular RSLs, will in future be held to be performing public functions,[102] and hence to be accountable as functional public authorities by way of judicial review. See paras 6.32–6.34.

8.104   Since the decision of the House of Lords in *Kay v Lambeth LBC* and *Leeds CC v Price*,[103] it is likely that such 'public law' points may also be taken by way of a defence to possession proceedings. Lord Hope confirmed that the county court has jurisdiction to deal with such challenges:

> ... if the defendant wishes to challenge the decisions of a public authority to recover possession as an improper exercise of its powers at common law on the ground that it was a decision that no reasonable person would consider justifiable, he shoud be permitted to do this provided again that the point is seriously arguable: *Wandsworth LBC v Winder* [1985] AC 461 (at 110).

---

102   See *Poplar Housing and Regeneration Community Association Ltd v Donoghue* [2001] EWCA Civ 595; [2002] QB 48; (2001) 33 HLR 73.
103   [2006] UKHL 10; [2006] 2 WLR 570, HL. See paras 5.35–5.42.

Independent sector tenants

Introduction to Part II

II.1   Outside the local authority sector, almost all new residential tenancies created on or after 15 January 1989 are assured or assured shorthold tenancies.[1] In practice, most private sector landlords aim to create assured shorthold tenancies whereas most landlords in the social sector wish to grant assured tenancies with security of tenure. There are, however, exceptions. Some social landlords grant assured shorthold tenancies in respect of temporary accommodation or as probationary tenancies. Also, before the implementation of Housing Act 1988 s19A on 28 February 1997, some private sector landlords inadvertently created assured tenancies because they failed to comply with the requirements in Housing Act 1988 s20. However, since 28 February 1997 almost all new tenancies are assured shorthold tenancies unless the landlord elects to create an assured tenancy (see para 9.6). In practice, in most cases, social landlords such as housing associations continue to grant assured tenancies with security of tenure.

II.2   The Housing Corporation has given general guidance to registered social landlords on evictions from housing association homes. The Corporation's *Regulatory Code and Guidance* and a circular *Tenancy Management: eligibility and evictions*[2] are available from www.housingcorp.gov.uk.

---

1   For tenancies granted by local authorities, see Part I. Occupiers of agricultural accommodation may enjoy 'assured agricultural occupancy' status.

2   Housing Corporation Regulatory Circular 07/04 July 2004. See too the ODPM non-statutory guidance *Improving the effectiveness of rent arrears management: good practice guidance* June 2005 and its report *The use of possession actions and evictions by social landlords* June 2005, both available at www.odpm.gov.uk.

Rent Act transitional provisions

II.3   Tenancies granted before 15 January 1989 by private sector landlords either enjoyed security of tenure under the Rent Act 1977 or lacked long-term security of tenure. There are still some 100,000 Rent Act protected or statutory tenants (see chapters 13 to 15).[3]

II.4   Housing Act 1988 s34 provides that no new Rent Act protected tenancies can be created after 15 January 1989, unless one of three exceptions applies:

- the tenancy is entered into in pursuance of a contract made before the Housing Act came into force; or
- the tenancy is granted to an existing Rent Act protected or statutory tenant by the same landlord. If there are joint tenants or joint landlords, it is sufficient for only one of the joint tenants to have been a protected tenant and for only one of the joint landlords to have been the landlord of the existing tenant or tenants. Although the wording of this section is not very clear, it is plain that parliament's intention was that this exception should apply even if the tenant has moved from other accommodation;[4] or
- before the grant of the new tenancy an order for possession was made on the ground of suitable alternative accommodation against a protected or statutory tenant[5] and in the possession proceedings relating to the earlier tenancy, the court directed that the tenancy of the suitable alternative accommodation should be held on a protected tenancy. The court should consider whether an assured tenancy would 'afford the required security'. If it would not, it may direct that the suitable alternative accommodation should be held on a protected tenancy. It is obviously important that representatives of Rent Act tenants in suitable alternative accommodation cases do all they can to ensure that the court directs that the new tenancy should be held on a protected tenancy. The higher rent which would be recoverable under an assured tenancy may mean that the

---

3   See *Cadogan Estates Ltd v McMahon* [2001] 1 AC 378; [2000] 3 WLR 1555; [2000] 4 All ER 897, HL per Lord Millett.

4   See *Laimond Properties Ltd v Al-Shakarchi* (1998) 30 HLR 1099; (1998) *Times* 23 February, CA, *Kotecha v Rimington* March 1991 *Legal Action* 15, *Singh v Dalby* September 1992 *Legal Action* 22, *Gorringe v Twinsectra* June 1994 *Legal Action* 11, *Giddy v Murray* March 1995 *Legal Action* 12 and *Secretarial Nominee Co Ltd v Thomas* [2005] EWCA Civ 1008; (2005) *Times* 20 September.

5   Under Rent Act 1977 s98(1)(a) or Sch 16 case 1 or Rent (Agriculture) Act 1976 Sch 4 case 1.

alternative accommodation would not be suitable 'to the means of the tenant' and/or it would be unreasonable to make a possession order.

CHAPTER 9

Assured shorthold tenancies

Introduction

9.1   Assured shorthold tenancies provide no long-term security of tenure and are subject to minimal rent control. Although, legally, they are a kind of assured tenancy, the lack of security of tenure means that, from a tenant's point of view, the adjective 'assured' is something of a misnomer.

9.2   Most private sector lettings since January 1989 have been assured shorthold tenancies. Until 28 February 1997, when amendments introduced by Housing Act 1996 ss96 to 100 came into force, landlords had to serve Housing Act 1988 s20 notices before the grant of tenancies informing prospective tenants that tenancies were to be assured shorthold tenancies. Failure to serve such notices, or service of invalid notices, resulted in the creation of assured tenancies. However, since 28 February 1997 the section 20 requirement has been abolished and, subject to the exceptions set out at para 9.6, all new tenancies are assured shorthold tenancies. This is the case even if they are granted orally or are periodic tenancies. Accordingly, when advising, it is vital to determine when the tenancy was granted or, if there have been a succession of assured shorthold tenancies, when the first assured shorthold tenancy was granted.

9.3   It should be noted that the Court of Appeal has held that the assured shorthold regime does not breach European Convention of Human Rights article 8 (respect for the home).[6]

Tenancies granted before 28 February 1997

Requirements for assured shorthold tenancies

9.4   Housing Act 1988 s20 stipulated four requirements for the creation of an assured shorthold tenancy:

- It must have been granted for a fixed term of not less than six months.[7]
- It must not contain any provision enabling the landlord to terminate the tenancy within six months of the beginning of the

---

6   *Poplar HARCA v Donoghue* [2001] EWCA Civ 595; [2001] 3 WLR 183.

7   See *Bedding v McCarthy* [1994] 41 EG 151; (1995) 27 HLR 103, CA. A tenancy granted for 'a term certain of one year ... and ... thereafter from month to month' is a tenancy granted for a term certain within the meaning of section 20(1)(a) which was capable of being an assured shorthold tenancy: *Goodman v Evely* [2001] EWCA Civ 104; [2002] HLR 53, CA.

tenancy. Housing Act s45(4) provides that a power of re-entry or forfeiture for breach of condition does not count as a provision enabling the landlord to determine the tenancy for this purpose.[8]

- Notice in the prescribed form must have been served[9] before the commencement of the tenancy stating that the tenancy would be an assured shorthold tenancy. The court has no power to dispense with service of this notice.[10] The form of the notice was prescribed by the Assured Tenancies and Agricultural Occupancies (Forms) Regulations 1988.[11] The omission of certain words from the prescribed form or the inclusion of incorrect details may render the notice invalid.[12] However, in view of the purposive approach adopted and sanctioned in *Manel v Memon*[13] and *Mannai Investment Co Ltd v Eagle Star Life Assurance Co Ltd*[14] a notice is likely to be valid if, notwithstanding any errors or omission, it was substantially to the same effect in accomplishing the statutory purpose of telling the proposed tenant of the special nature of an assured shorthold tenancy.[15]

---

8 See *Maryland Estates v Bar-Joseph* [1999] 1 WLR 83; [1998] 3 All ER 193, CA.

9 See *Yenula Properties Ltd v Naidu* [2002] EWCA Civ 719; [2003] HLR 18.

10 *Panayi v Roberts* (1993) 25 HLR 421; [1993] 28 EG 125, CA.

11 SI No 2203.

12 *Panayai v Roberts* (1993) 25 HLR 421; [1993] 2 EGLR 51 (notice failed to state date), *Clickex Ltd v McCann* (2000) 32 HLR 324; [1999] 30 EG 6, CA (dates in notice in conflict with dates in tenancy agreement), *Manel v Memon* [2000] 33 EG 74; (2001) 33 HLR 235, CA (omission of bullet points, exhortation to take legal advice and statement that tenant was not committed to take the tenancy), *London and Quadrant Housing v Robertson* September 1991 *Legal Action* 17; *Lomas v Atkinson* September 1993 *Legal Action* 16 (notice failed to include information about how to seek advice), *Mistry v Dave* June 1995 *Legal Action* 19 (notice gave no date for the end of the tenancy), *Symons v Warren* [1995] CLW 33/95 (failure to identify landlord properly and incorrect date), *Stevens v Lamb* March 1996 *Legal Action* 12 (failure to include landlord's name, address and telephone number), *Smith v Willson* November 1999 *Legal Action* 28 (error in date and use of notice of *protected* shorthold (HA 1980 s52)) and *Charalambous v Pesman* January 2001 *Legal Action* 26 (name and address of landlord omitted).

13 [2000] 2 EGLR 40, CA.

14 [1997] AC 749; [1997] 2 WLR 945, HL.

15 *Ravenseft Properties Ltd v Hall; White v Chubb; Kasseer v Freeman* [2001] EWCA Civ 2034; [2002] HLR 33. See too *Osborn and Co Ltd v Dior* [2003] EWCA Civ 281; [2003] HLR 45 (even if the particulars of the landlord are absent, a notice is still substantially to the same effect where the agent has signed and given its particulars), cf, *York and Ross v Casey* (1999) 31 HLR 209; [1998] 30 EG 110, CA.

- It would be an assured tenancy but for these three requirements being satisfied.[16] See para 10.3.

A further tenancy (or tenancies[17]) of the same or substantially the same premises granted to a former assured shorthold tenant is also an assured shorthold tenancy even if any of the first three requirements is no longer satisfied.

9.5   Housing Act 1988 s20(3) makes it impossible for a landlord to grant an assured shorthold tenancy to anyone who, immediately before the grant of a new tenancy, was an assured tenant of the same landlord. This is the case even if the premises in question are different.

Tenancies granted on or after 28 February 1997

9.6   Housing Act 1996 s96 and Sch 7 introduced a new Housing Act 1988 s19A and Sch 2A. They provide that all new tenancies entered into on or after 28 February 1997 which would otherwise have been assured tenancies are automatically assured shorthold tenancies lacking long-term security of tenure. This applies whether the tenancy is granted orally or by a written agreement. In other words, the requirement of a Housing Act 1988 s20 notice informing the tenant that the tenancy would be an assured shorthold tenancy has been abolished. There are, however, several exceptions which are set out in Housing Act 1988 Sch 2A. The new rule does *not* apply where:

- the new tenancy is granted pursuant to a contract made before the new provisions came into force;[18] or
- the landlord serves a notice before entering into the tenancy stating that the tenancy is not to be an assured shorthold tenancy;[19] or
- the landlord serves a notice after the grant of the tenancy stating that the tenancy is no longer an assured shorthold tenancy;[20] or
- there is a provision in the tenancy agreement stating that the tenancy is not an assured shorthold tenancy;[21] or

---

16 This is analogous to HA 1980 s52 which referred to 'a protected shorthold tenancy' as being 'a protected tenancy' which satisfied certain criteria.

17 *Lower Street Properties Ltd v Jones*(1996) 28 HLR 877; [1996] 48 EG 154, CA.

18 HA 1988 s19A(a).

19 HA 1988 Sch 2A para 1.

20 HA 1988 Sch 2A para 2.

21 HA 1988 Sch 2A para 3.

- the tenancy is an assured tenancy by succession, ie, a member of the family of a statutory tenant under the Rent Act 1977 or the Rent (Agriculture) Act 1976 became an assured tenant after the death of the original tenant;[22] or
- the tenancy was formerly a secure tenancy and became an assured tenancy, for example, on transfer of housing stock from a local housing authority to a housing association or other landlord;[23] or
- an assured tenancy came into existence on the ending of a long residential tenancy;[24] or
- the tenancy is granted to someone who immediately before its grant was an assured tenant (as opposed to an assured *shorthold* tenant) and is granted by someone who was the landlord under the old tenancy;[25] or
- in some cases, the tenancy or licence is an assured agricultural occupancy.[26]

Possession proceedings

9.7   Housing Act 1988 s21 as amended provides:

21 (1) Without prejudice to any right of the landlord under an assured shorthold tenancy to recover possession of the dwelling-house let on the tenancy in accordance with Chapter I above, on or after the coming to an end of an assured shorthold tenancy which was a fixed term tenancy, a court shall make an order for possession of the dwelling-house if it is satisfied –

(a) that the assured shorthold tenancy has come to an end and no further assured tenancy (whether shorthold or not) is for the time being in existence, other than an assured shorthold periodic tenancy (whether statutory or not); and

(b) the landlord or, in the case of joint landlords, at least one of them has given to the tenant not less than two months' notice *in writing* stating that he requires possession of the dwelling-house.

(2) A notice under paragraph (b) of subsection (1) above may be given before or on the day on which the tenancy comes to an end; and

22 Rent Act 1977 s2(1)(b) and Sch 1; HA 1988 s39 and HA 1988 Sch 2A para 4 as amended by Civil Partnership Act 2004 Sch 8.

23 HA 1985 Pt IV, HA 1988 s38 and HA 1988 Sch 2A para 5.

24 Landlord and Tenant Act 1954 Pt I, Local Government and Housing Act 1989 s186 and Sch 10 and HA 1988 Sch 2A para 6.

25 HA 1988 Sch 2A.

26 Rent (Agriculture) Act 1976, HA 1988 s24 and Sch 3 and HA 1988 Sch 2A para 9.

that subsection shall have effect notwithstanding that on the coming to an end of the fixed term tenancy a statutory periodic tenancy arises.

(3) Where a court makes an order for possession of a dwelling-house by virtue of subsection (1) above, any statutory periodic tenancy which has arisen on the coming to an end of the assured shorthold tenancy shall end (without further notice and regardless of the period) on the day on which the order takes effect.

(4) Without prejudice to any such right as is referred to in subsection (1) above, a court shall make an order for possession of a dwelling-house let on an assured shorthold tenancy which is a periodic tenancy if the court is satisfied –

(a) that the landlord or, in the case of joint landlords, at least one of them has given to the tenant a notice *in writing* stating that, after a date specified in the notice, being the last day of a period of the tenancy and not earlier than two months after the date the notice was given, possession of the dwelling-house is required by virtue of this section; and

(b) that the date specified in the notice under paragraph (a) above is not earlier than the earliest day on which, apart from section 5(1) above, the tenancy could be brought to an end by a notice to quit given by the landlord on the same date as the notice under paragraph (a) above.

(5) Where an order for possession under subsection (1) or (4) above is made in relation to a dwelling-house let on a tenancy to which section 19A above applies, the order may not be made so as to take effect earlier than –

(a) in the case of a tenancy which is not a replacement tenancy, six months after the beginning of the tenancy, and

(b) in the case of a replacement tenancy, six months after the beginning of the original tenancy.

(5A) Subsection (5) above does not apply to an assured shorthold tenancy to which section 20B (demoted assured shorthold tenancies) applies.

(6) In subsection (5)(b) above, the reference to the original tenancy is –

(a) where the replacement tenancy came into being on the coming to an end of a tenancy which was not a replacement tenancy, to the immediately preceding tenancy, and

(b) where there have been successive replacement tenancies, to the tenancy immediately preceding the first in the succession of replacement tenancies.

(7) For the purposes of this section, a replacement tenancy is a tenancy –

(a) which comes into being on the coming to an end of an assured shorthold tenancy, and

(b) under which, on its coming into being –
    (i) the landlord and tenant are the same as under the earlier tenancy as at its coming to an end, and
    (ii) the premises let are the same or substantially the same as those let under the earlier tenancy as at that time.

9.8   Housing Act 1988 s21 was amended by Housing Act 1996 s98(2) and (3) to make it clear that Housing Act 1988 s21 notices must be in writing. Subsections (5) to (7) were added by Housing Act 1996 s99. Subsection (5A) was added by the Anti-Social Behaviour Act 2003.

9.9   If the assured shorthold tenancy is for a fixed term, the ability of a landlord to recover possession depends upon whether or not the fixed term has expired.

During a fixed-term tenancy

9.10   During a fixed term, a landlord cannot rely upon Housing Act 1988 s21 (automatic right to possession on giving two months' notice), unless there is a contractual break clause in the tenancy allowing the landlord to recover possession before the expiry of the term.[27] If there is a 'break clause' in an assured shorthold tenancy, allowing the landlord to terminate the tenancy on giving notice after six months from commencement, service of a Housing Act 1988 s21 notice may be sufficient to activate the break clause.[28]

9.11   However, the normal grounds for possession against assured tenants apply (see para 10.22). Although the wording of the Act is far from clear, it seems that for a landlord to regain possession during a fixed term tenancy:

- the tenancy must contain a term allowing the landlord to re-enter or terminate the tenancy for breach of any covenant in the tenancy or if one of the grounds for possession against assured tenants exists;
- the landlord must serve notice of proceedings for possession in accordance with Housing Act 1988 s8 (see para 10.9); and
- the landlord must prove the existence of any of the following grounds for possession, namely, 2, 8, 10, 11, 12, 13, 14, 14A, 15 or 17 (ie, essentially 'tenant's default' grounds), and, if appropriate, that it is reasonable for an order to be made.

27 *Gloucestershire HA v Phelps* 10 February 2003, Gloucester County Court, May 2003 *Legal Action* 35.
28 *Aylward v Fawaz* (1997) 29 HLR 408, CA.

9.12   The tenant cannot apply for relief from forfeiture. Housing Act 1988 s5(1) sets out the only routes for bringing an assured tenancy to an end.[29]

During a periodic term

9.13   Before 28 February 1997 most landlords granted assured shorthold tenancies for the minimum period of six months, but then allowed the tenant to 'hold over' after the end of that period. In those circumstances, if the tenant continues to occupy premises as his or her only or principal home, a statutory periodic tenancy arises, but it remains an assured shorthold tenancy and lacks security of tenure. Alternatively, since 28 February 1997 the landlord may have granted an assured shorthold tenancy that was periodic from the outset.

9.14   All that a landlord need do to recover possession is to:

- prove that any fixed term tenancy has come to an end and that no new tenancy has been granted;
- give at least two months' notice to the tenant in accordance with Housing Act 1988 s21 that the landlord requires possession; and
- take court proceedings.

9.15   If landlords comply with these requirements, they are automatically entitled to possession. The court has no power to suspend possession orders, apart from Housing Act 1980 s89(1) which provides that orders for possession must take effect no later than 14 days after the court order unless exceptional hardship would be caused in which case the maximum period which may be allowed is six weeks. See para 28.1.

9.16   The Housing Act 1988 s21 notice:

- may be given before any fixed term expires or even at the beginning of the tenancy;[30]
- need not be in any particular form, although it must be in writing;[31]
- may be given by only one of several joint landlords.[32]

There is, however, no power to dispense with service of the notice.

---

29 See para 12.44. See also *Artesian Residential Investments Ltd v Beck* [2000] QB 541; [2000] 2 WLR 357, CA.

30 HA 1988 s21(2).

31 HA 1988 s21(1)(b) as amended by HA 1996 s98.

32 HA 1988 s21(4)(a).

9.17   It is important to check that:

- The notice gives at least two months' notice,[33] although no actual date need be specified provided that 'the tenant knows or can easily ascertain the date referred to'. ('The word "specified" ... means no more than "made clear".'[34])

9.18   • If the tenancy is a periodic tenancy, the date specified in the notice is (or the period of notice given in the notice expires on) 'the last day of a period of the tenancy'. The last day of a period of the tenancy may be the day before rent is due, but this is not automatically the case because a tenancy may provide for payment of rent on a day which is not the first day of the period of the tenancy.[35] In the past, uncertainty was caused by the dichotomy between Housing Act 1988 s21(1)(b) and s21(4)(a). Section 21(1)(b) merely provides that the landlord must give 'the tenant not less than two months' notice stating that he requires possession of the dwelling-house'. However, section 21(4)(a) provides that the date specified in a notice where there is 'a periodic tenancy' shall be 'the last day of a period of the tenancy'. There is no need for the two months' notice to expire on 'the last day of a period of the tenancy' if the notice is served *during* a fixed-term assured shorthold[36] but this requirement has to be satisfied if the notice is served during a periodic or statutory periodic assured shorthold tenancy. (See para 10.8 below.) In *Fernandez v McDonald*,[37] after the expiry of a fixed term assured shorthold tenancy, tenants remained in occupation as statutory periodic tenants from the 4th of each month to the 3rd of the following month. On 24 October 2002, the landlord gave them a notice headed 'Section 21(4)(a) Assured Shorthold Tenancy: Notice Requiring Possession Periodic Tenancy' stating 'I give you notice that I require possession of the dwelling house known as ... on 4th January 2003'. The Court of Appeal held that the notice did not comply with section 21(4)(a) and was defective.[38]

---

33 *Symons v Warren* [1995] CLW 33/95. See also *Mundy v Hook* (1998) 30 HLR 551; [1997] 3 CL 388.

34 *Lower Street Properties Ltd v Jones* [1996] 48 EG 154; (1996) 28 HLR 877, CA.

35 See, eg, *Baynes v Hall and Thorpe* Dewsbury County Court, 29 June 2005; November 2005 *Legal Action* 21

36 See, eg, Arden and Partington, *Housing Law*, (Sweet & Maxwell, 1994), para 1-223/4.

37 [2003] EWCA Civ 1219; [2004] 1 WLR 1027.

38 See too *Gracechurch International SA v Tribhovan and Abdul* (2001) 33 HLR 28, CA.

In order to avoid this problem, prudent landlords serve notices which include, after the date given, a rider which provides that the notice may also expire 'at the end of the period of your tenancy which will end next after the expiration of two months from the service upon you of this notice'.

In *Notting Hill Housing Trust v Roomus*[39] the Court of Appeal held that a section 21 notice which stated 'Possession is required (by virtue of section 21(4) of the Housing Act 1988) of [the property] which you hold as tenant at the end of the period of your tenancy which will end after expiry of two months from the service upon you of this notice' was valid because the phrase 'at the end of a tenancy' in a notice given pursuant to section 21 means 'after the end of the tenancy' and so complied with the requirements of section 21(4)(a):

9.19   • The date specified 'is not earlier than the earliest day on which ... the tenancy could be brought to an end by a notice to quit given by the landlord on the same date as the notice ...' (Housing Act 1988 s21(4)(b)). Accordingly, more than two months' notice is required where there is an express provision requiring a longer period of notice or the rental period is longer than two months, for example, where there is a quarterly tenancy, in which case three months' notice has to be given.

   • If the notice relates to a periodic tenancy, the section 21(4) notice includes reference to Housing Act 1988 s21 since section 21(4) provides that the court must be 'satisfied ... that the landlord ... has given ... notice ...stating that ... possession ... is required *by virtue of this section*' (emphasis added). A district judge, dismissing a possession claim, has held that a notice which failed to do this was defective.[40]

   • Proceedings have not been commenced before the date specified in the notice. The claim for possession in *Lower Street Properties Ltd v Jones*[41] was dismissed because proceedings were started the day before the Housing Act 1988 s21 notice expired. Schiemann LJ stated, it 'is implicit that the landlord cannot bring proceedings until after [the date specified in the notice]', although Kennedy LJ reached his decision on the grounds that the notice served stated that the 'landlord cannot apply for such an order before the notice

---

39 [2006] EWCA Civ 407; 29 March 2006.
40 *Adamson v Mather*, Harrogate County Court, 24 September 2004; November 2004 *Legal Action* 25.
41 (1996) 28 HLR 877; [1996] 2 EGLR 67.

has run out', and left open whether, with a different wording, proceedings could have been begun before expiry.

- If the tenancy is one to which Housing Act 1988 s19A applies (ie, it was granted after 28 February 1997 and none of the exceptions in Housing Act 1988 Sch 2A applies), then any possession order will not take effect earlier than six months after the grant of the original tenancy.[42]

9.20 There is no rule that section 21 notices expire or lapse or that landlords are deemed to waive their right to rely upon them if proceedings are not issued within a particular period after service of the section 21 notice. There may in theory be a gap of several years between service of a secton 21 notice and the issue of possession proceedings.[43]

Section 21 notices and HMOs

9.21 Housing Act 2004 s75 and s98 prevent section 21 notices being given where a house in multiple occupation (HMO) which is subject to mandatory licensing (section 75) or a property which is subject to selective licensing (section 98) is not licensed. These provisions came into force on 6 April 2006.

Section 21 notices and deposits

9.22 Housing Act 2004 s215(1) provides that if a tenancy deposit[44] has been paid in connection with an assured shorthold tenancy, no section 21 notice may be given in relation to the tenancy at any time when:

- the deposit is not being held in accordance with an authorised scheme;[45] or
- the initial requirements of such a scheme[46] have not been complied with in relation to the deposit.

This provision will only apply to assured shorthold tenancies granted after that section has been brought into force. At the time when *Defending Possession Proceedings* went to press it had not yet been implemented.

42 HA 1988 s21(5) as inserted by HA 1996 s99.
43 See, eg, *Paddington Churches HA v Khan* Willesden County Court; 29 October 2003; December 2004 *Legal Action* 18 (HHJ Copley reversing an earlier decision to the contrary noted at [2004] 3 CLD 328).
44 As defined in HA 2004 s212(8).
45 See HA 2004 s213(4).
46 See HA 2004 s213(4).

9.23   Section 215 provides:

Sanctions for non-compliance

(1) If a tenancy deposit has been paid in connection with a shorthold tenancy, no section 21 notice may be given in relation to the tenancy at a time when –

    (a) the deposit is not being held in accordance with an authorised scheme, or

    (b) the initial requirements of such a scheme (see section 213(4)) have not been complied with in relation to the deposit.

(2) If section 213(6) is not complied with in relation to a deposit given in connection with a shorthold tenancy, no section 21 notice may be given in relation to the tenancy until such time as section 213(6)(a) is complied with.

(3) If any deposit given in connection with a shorthold tenancy could not be lawfully required as a result of section 213(7), no section 21 notice may be given in relation to the tenancy until such time as the property in question is returned to the person by whom it was given as a deposit.

(4) In subsection (3) 'deposit' has the meaning given by section 213(8).

(5) In this section a 'section 21 notice' means a notice under section 21(1)(b) or (4)(a) of the Housing Act 1988 (recovery of possession on termination of shorthold tenancy).

Assured tenancies

continued

Introduction

10.1   Assured tenancies are lettings at market rents with security of tenure. There is no control over the rents at which such tenancies are initially let and subsequent rent regulation is minimal. The security of tenure provided is different from that provided by the Housing Act 1985 and the Rent Act 1977 and in many cases the grounds for possession are more widely drafted.

10.2   Statutory references in this chapter are to the Housing Act 1988 unless otherwise stated.

Definition of 'assured tenancy'

10.3   Housing Act 1988 s1 contains three prerequisites for the creation of an assured tenancy:

- The dwelling-house must be let as a separate dwelling. This is the well-known phrase which appears in Rent Act 1977 s1. The word 'dwelling' is not a term of art with a specialised legal meaning. It is 'the place where [an occupier] lives and to which he returns and which forms the centre of his existence ... No doubt he will sleep there and usually eat there; he will often prepare at least some of his meals there'.[1] However, there is no legislative requirement that cooking facilities must be available for premises to qualify as a dwelling. In deciding whether an occupant has security of tenure:

    > The first step is to identify the subject-matter of the tenancy agreement. If this is a house or part of a house of which the tenant has exclusive possession with no element of sharing, the only question is whether, at the date when proceedings were brought, it was the tenant's home. If so, it was his dwelling ... The presence or absence of cooking facilities in the part of the premises of which the tenant has exclusive occupation is not relevant.[2]

    If a tenancy comprises two or more separate units of accommodation which are let together to a tenant, there can be no assured tenancy.[3] Housing Act 1988 s3 provides that if a tenant enjoys exclusive occupation of some rented accommodation, with a right to share other accommodation with other people, apart from the

---

1   *Uratemp Ventures Ltd v Collins and Carrell* [2001] UKHL 43; [2002] 1 AC 301.

2   Ibid.

3   See, eg, *Horford Investments Ltd v Lambert* [1976] Ch 39, *St Catherine's College v Dorling* [1980] 1 WLR 66 and *Kavanagh v Lyroudias* [1985] 1 All ER 560.

landlord, the mere fact that the other accommodation is shared does not prevent the tenant from occupying the accommodation which is not shared as a separate dwelling.

- The tenant or, if there are joint tenants, each of the joint tenants, must be individuals. A genuine letting to a company cannot be an assured tenancy.[4] In such cases, the tenancy is unprotected and may be terminated either by the passing of time (if it is a fixed term tenancy) or by service of a notice to quit (if it is a periodic tenancy). If this is done, a landlord who brings possession proceedings is automatically entitled to possession without having to prove any ground for possession.

- The tenant or, if there are joint tenants, at least one of them, must occupy the premises as his or her only or principal home. This is the same wording as Housing Act 1985 s81, the 'tenant condition', which applies to secure tenancies (see paras 1.13–1.15). It is a more restrictive definition than the comparable provision in Rent Act 1977 s2(1)(a).[5] Although it is possible for tenants to occupy more than one home at the same time, a tenancy can only continue to be assured if it is in respect of the tenant's principal home. There is no reason why an assured tenant should not be temporarily absent from the premises in question, provided that they remain his or her main home.[6] If an assured tenant moves out permanently, the tenancy becomes unprotected and can be terminated by notice to quit. The landlord does not have to prove any ground for possession. This is well illustrated by *Ujima Housing Association v Ansah*[7] where an assured tenant sublet the entire flat on an assured shorthold tenancy on terms which were inconsistent with

---

4 *Hiller v United Dairies* [1934] 1 KB 57, CA, *Hilton v Plustitle Ltd and Rose* [1988] 3 All ER 1051, CA, *Kaye v Massbetter Ltd and Kanter* (1991) 39 EG 129; (1992) 24 HLR 28, CA and *Eaton Square Properties Ltd v O'Higgins* [2000] EGCS 118, CA. However, the court may decide that a letting to a company fails to represent the substance and reality of the transaction, is an artificial transaction or that the company is merely a nominee. See dicta in *Cove v Flick* [1954] 2 QB 326 (Note); [1954] 2 All ER 441, *Firstcross v East West Ltd* (1980) 7 HLR 577, CA and *Gisborne v Burton* (1988) 38 EG 129 and the passages in *AG Securities v Vaughan* [1990] 1 AC 417; [1988] 3 WLR 1205, HL; February 1989 *Legal Action* 21, concerning 'artificiality' and 'pretence'.

5 For more detailed consideration of these issues, see chapter 14.

6 *Crawley BC v Sawyer* (1987) 20 HLR 98, CA, *Sutton LBC v Swann* (1985) 17 HLR 140, CA, *Hussey v Camden LBC* (1995) 27 HLR 5, CA, *Hammersmith and Fulham LBC v Clarke* March 2001 *Legal Action* 28, CA and *Amoah v Barking and Dagenham LBC* March 2001 *Legal Action* 28, ChD.

7 (1998) 30 HLR 831, CA.

his remaining in occupation as his only or principal home. He left furniture in the flat, but no personal possessions. Ujima served a notice to quit and brought possession proceedings. The Court of Appeal held that Ujima was entitled to a possession order. The test introduced by the Housing Act 1988 was strict and, since the defendant was no longer in physical occupation, the onus was on him to establish that he was still occupying the flat as his principal home. He had granted the right to immediate occupation to others and was unable to return unless they voluntarily surrendered it to him. Viewed objectively, the defendant did not have the intention to preserve his occupation of the flat as his principal residence.[8]

10.4   If one spouse or civil partner ('A') is a sole assured tenant but moves out, occupation by the other spouse or civil partner ('B') as his or her only or principal home may preserve the assured tenancy. This is provided for by Family Law Act 1996 s30(4) as amended by Civil Partnership Act 2004 Sch 9 para 1 which states:

> B's occupation by virtue of this section –
> (a) is to be treated for the purposes of ... the Rent Act 1977 ... as occupation by A as A's residence, and
> (b) if B occupies the dwelling-house as B's only or principal home, it is to be treated, for the purposes of Housing Act 1985, Part I of the Housing Act 1988 ... as occupation by A as A's only or principal home.

Note the amendments made by Civil Partnership Act 2004 were brought into force on 5 December 2005 by Civil Partnership Act 2004 (Commencement No 2) Order 2005.[9]

10.5   A tenancy cannot be an assured tenancy if any of the exceptions listed in Housing Act 1988 Sch 1 applies. Many of these exceptions are similar to those set out in Rent Act 1977 Pt I.[10] They include:

- premises with high rateable values (ie, over £1,500 in Greater London and over £750 elsewhere) or, if granted after 1 April 1990, with a high rent (ie, a rent of more than £25,000 per annum);[11]
- tenancies at a low rent (ie, rent-free or less than two-thirds of the rateable value) or, if granted after 1 April 1990, at a rent of less than £1,000 per annum in London or less than £250 per annum elsewhere;[12]

8 See also *Waltham Forest CBHA v Fanning* July 2001 *Legal Action* 33.
9 SI No 3175 (C.136).
10 See, in particular, Rent Act 1977 ss4, 5, 8, 9, 10, 11, 12 (and Sch 2), 13 and 14.
11 References to Rating (Housing) Regulations 1990 SI No 434.
12 Ibid.

- business premises which are protected under Landlord and Tenant Act 1954 Pt II;
- licensed premises such as public houses;
- agricultural land or holdings;
- lettings to students by specified educational institutions;[13]
- holiday lettings where the tenant merely has 'the right to occupy the dwelling-house for a holiday';[14]
- lettings by resident landlords. This exception does not apply to purpose-built blocks of flats. For the exception to apply, the tenancy must have been granted by a landlord who, both at the time of the grant of the tenancy and at all times since, has had his or her 'only or principal home' elsewhere in the building. The schedule, like Rent Act 1977 Sch 2, provides that existing assured tenants cannot be deprived of security of tenure by accepting a new tenancy or moving to another part of the same building after a landlord has become a resident landlord. Similarly, there are periods of disregard after the sale of premises or the death of a landlord when the fact that there is no resident landlord living in the building does not mean that the 'resident landlord' exception ceases to apply;
- Crown tenancies, but not premises managed by the Crown Estate Commissioners; or
- tenancies granted by private landlords under arrangements made by local housing authorities in accordance with their functions under Housing Act 1996 ss188, 190, 200 or 204 (interim duties towards the homeless) within 12 months of the date of notification of the local authority's decision or the determination of any Housing Act 1996 s202 review or s204 appeal, unless the landlord notifies the tenant that the tenancy is to be an assured shorthold tenancy;[15]
- fully mutual housing associations.[16]

---

13 Assured and Protected Tenancies (Lettings to Students) Regulations 1998 SI No 1967 as amended.

14 But note *Buchmann v May* [1978] 2 All ER 993, CA and *R v Rent Officer for Camden ex p Plant* (1980) 257 EG 713; (1980) 7 HLR 15, QBD (where 'tenancies which were not genuine holiday lets' were found to be protected tenancies).

15 HA 1996 s209 as substituted by Homelessness Act 2002 Sch 1 para 19. HA 1988 s1(6), which formerly provided that tenancies granted by private sector landlords as a result of arrangements with local authorities to provide temporary accommodation for homeless people under HA 1985 ss63, 65(3) and 69(1), unless tenants are notified that they are to be assured tenants or one year has passed since receipt of a section 64 notification could not be assured tenancies, was repealed by HA 1996 Sch 19 Pt VIII. For the current provisions relating to private sector tenancies granted to homeless people, see chapter 5.

16 HA 1988 Sch 1 para 12(h).

If one of these exceptions applies, the tenant has no security of tenure. Once a notice to quit has been served and has expired, the tenant has no statutory protection, except for, in some cases, Protection from Eviction Act 1977 s3 which provides that it is unlawful for a landlord to evict such a tenant without taking court proceedings. The landlord has to prove only that the contractual tenancy has been terminated.

- local authority tenancies, or tenancies granted by the Commission for New Towns, residuary bodies within the meaning of Local Government Act 1985, the Residuary Body for Wales (Corff Gweddilliol Cymru), the disposal authorities, development corporations or housing action trusts.

If any of the categories in this exception applies, the tenancy is secure.

Termination of assured tenancies

Security of tenure

10.6   Housing Act 1988 s5 provides:

(1) An assured tenancy cannot be brought to an end by the landlord except by obtaining an order of the court in accordance with the following provisions of this Chapter or Chapter II below or, in the case of a fixed term tenancy which contains power for the landlord to determine the tenancy in certain circumstances, by the exercise of that power and, accordingly, the service by the landlord of a notice to quit shall be of no effect in relation to a periodic assured tenancy.

(2) If an assured tenancy which is a fixed-term tenancy comes to an end otherwise than by virtue of –
(a) an order of the court, or
(b) a surrender or other action on the part of the tenant,
then, subject to section 7 and Chapter II below, the tenant shall be entitled to remain in possession of the dwelling-house let under that tenancy and, subject to subsection (4) below, his right to possession shall depend upon a periodic tenancy arising by virtue of this section.

(3) The periodic tenancy referred to in subsection (2) above is one –
(a) taking effect in possession immediately on the coming to an end of the fixed term tenancy;
(b) deemed to have been granted by the person who was the landlord under the fixed term tenancy immediately before it came to an end to the person who was then the tenant under that tenancy;

    (c) under which the premises which are let are the same dwelling-house as was let under the fixed term tenancy;

    (d) under which the periods of the tenancy are the same as those for which rent was last payable under the fixed term tenancy; and

    (e) under which, subject to the following provisions of this Part of this Act, the other terms are the same as those of the fixed term tenancy immediately before it came to an end, except that any term which makes provision for determination by the landlord or the tenant shall not have effect while the tenancy remains an assured tenancy.

(4) The periodic tenancy referred to in subsection (2) above shall not arise if, on the coming to an end of the fixed term tenancy, the tenant is entitled, by virtue of the grant of another tenancy, to possession of the same or substantially the same dwelling-house as was let to him under the fixed term tenancy.

(5) If, on or before the date on which a tenancy is entered into or is deemed to have been granted as mentioned in subsection (3)(b) above, the person who is to be the tenant under that tenancy –

    (a) enters into an obligation to do any act which (apart from this subsection) will cause the tenancy to come to an end at a time when it is an assured tenancy, or

    (b) executes, signs or gives any surrender, notice to quit or other document which (apart from this subsection) has the effect of bringing the tenancy to an end at a time when it is an assured tenancy,

the obligation referred to in paragraph (a) above shall not be enforceable or, as the case may be, the surrender, notice to quit or other document referred to in paragraph (b) above shall be of no effect.

(5A) Nothing in subsection (5) affects any right of pre-emption –

    (a) which is exercisable by the landlord under a tenancy in circumstances where the tenant indicates his intention to dispose of the whole of his interest under the tenancy, and

    (b) in pursuance of which the landlord would be required to pay, in respect of the acquisition of that interest, an amount representing its market value.

'Dispose' means dispose by assignment or surrender, and 'acquisition' has a corresponding meaning.

(6) If, by virtue of any provision of this Part of this Act, Part I of Schedule 1 to this Act has effect in relation to a fixed-term tenancy as if it consisted only of paragraphs 11 and 12, that Part shall have the like effect in relation to any periodic tenancy which arises by virtue of this section on the coming to an end of the fixed term tenancy.

(7) Any reference in this Part of this Act to a statutory periodic tenancy is a reference to a periodic tenancy arising by virtue of this section.

Periodic tenancies

10.7   Housing Act 1988 s5 provides that a periodic assured tenancy can be brought to an end by a landlord only by means of an order of the court. Housing Act 1988 s5(1) makes it clear that notices to quit served by landlords have no effect upon periodic assured tenancies. However, a notice to quit served by a tenant terminates both the assured tenancy and the tenant's security of tenure.

Fixed-term tenancies

10.8   If a contractual, fixed-term assured tenancy is brought to an end, other than by an order of a court or by surrender, a periodic assured tenancy (called a 'statutory periodic tenancy') will generally come into existence immediately after the fixed-term tenancy has come to an end. In some ways this is similar to a Rent Act statutory tenancy,[17] but there are significant differences. The most important of these is the provision for fixing the terms of the statutory periodic tenancy. The basic rule is that the terms will be the same as for the former contractual assured tenancy.[18] However, Housing Act 1988 s6 provides a mechanism by which landlords and tenants may propose new terms.

Notice of intention to bring possession proceedings

10.9   Housing Act 1988 s8 as amended provides:

> (1) The court shall not entertain proceedings for possession of a dwelling-house let on an assured tenancy unless –
> > (a) the landlord or, in the case of joint landlords, at least one of them has served on the tenant a notice in accordance with this section and the proceedings are begun within the time limits stated in the notice in accordance with subsections (3) to 4B below; or
> > (b) the court considers it just and equitable to dispense with the requirement of such a notice.
> (2) The court shall not make an order for possession on any of the grounds in Schedule 2 to this Act unless that ground and particulars of it are specified in the notice under this section; but the grounds specified in such a notice may be altered or added to with the leave of the court.

---

17   Rent Act 1977 s2.
18   HA 1988 s5(3)(d) and (e).

(3) A notice under this section is one in the prescribed form informing the tenant that –

(a) the landlord intends to begin proceedings for possession of the dwelling-house on one or more of the grounds specified in the notice; and

(b) those proceedings will not begin earlier than a date specified in the notice in accordance with subsections (4) to 4B below; and

(c) those proceedings will not begin later than twelve months from the date of service of the notice.

(4) If a notice under this section specifies in accordance with subsection (3)(a) above Ground 14 in Schedule 2 to this Act (whether with or without other grounds), the date specified in the notice as mentioned in subsection (3)(b) shall not be earlier than the date of the service of the notice.

(4A) If a notice under this section specifies, in accordance with subsection (3)(a) above, any of Grounds 1, 2, 5 to 7, 9 and 16 in Schedule 2 to this Act (whether without other grounds or with any ground other than Ground 14), the date specified in the notice as mentioned in subsection (3)(b) above shall not be earlier than –

(a) two months from the date of service of the notice; and

(b) if the tenancy is a periodic tenancy, the earliest date on which, apart from section 5(1) above, the tenancy could be brought to an end by a notice to quit given by the landlord on the same date as the date of service of the notice under this section.

(4B) In any other case, the date specified in the notice as mentioned in subsection (3)(b) above shall not be earlier than the expiry of the period of two weeks from the date of service of the notice.

(5) The court may not exercise the power conferred by subsection (1)(b) above if the landlord seeks to recover possession on Ground 8 of Schedule 2 to this Act.

(6) Where a notice under this section –

(a) is served at a time when the dwelling-house is let on a fixed term tenancy, or

(b) is served after a fixed term tenancy has come to an end but relates (in whole or in part) to events occurring during that tenancy,

the notice shall have effect notwithstanding that the tenant becomes or has become tenant under a statutory periodic tenancy arising on the coming to an end of the fixed term tenancy.

10.10 A landlord wishing to bring possession proceedings against an assured tenant should first serve a notice, in prescribed form, informing the tenant that it is the landlord's intention to bring proceedings on one or more grounds specified in the notice. Courts have no jurisdiction to entertain claims for possession against assured tenants unless section 8 notices are served, or courts exercise their power to dispense with notice under section 8(1)(b) (see below).[19] The form of the notice, which is similar to that of notices seeking possession used against public sector secure tenants, is specified by the Assured Tenancies and Agricultural Occupancies (Forms) Regulations 1988[20] (Form 3) (see appendix A). A Housing Act 1988 s8 notice must specify the ground upon which possession is sought and give particulars of the ground.

The ground

10.11 The Regulations state that the landlord must 'give the full text of each ground which is being relied upon'. In *Mountain v Hastings*[21] the notice given by the landlord, under the heading 'Ground 8' simply stated, 'At least three months rent is unpaid', although later, under 'Particulars of Ground', it did state the total of arrears claimed. Ralph Gibson LJ said that although the full text of the ground as set out in Housing Act 1988 Sch 2 might not have to be repeated verbatim:

> ... the words used [must] set out fully the substance of the ground so that the notice is adequate to achieve the legislative purpose of the provision. That purpose ... is to give ... information ... to enable the tenant to consider what she should do and, with or without advice, to do that which is in her power and which will best protect her against the loss of her home.

The notice was defective because it had omitted the words, 'Both at the date of service of the Notice ... and at the date of the hearing' and the explanation that 'rent' means rent lawfully due from the tenant'. In the county court, it has been held that the omission of the words 'rent means rent lawfully due from the tenant' from a section 8 notice in which the landlord sought to rely upon ground 8 meant that the notice was not substantially to the same effect as that required by the prescribed form and the subsequent possession claim was dismissed.[22]

---

19 *Knowsley Housing Trust v Revell; Helena Housing Ltd v Curtis* [2003] EWCA Civ 496; [2003] HLR 63.

20 SI No 2203.

21 (1993) 25 HLR 427; [1993] 29 EG 96, CA. (Note that ground 8 has since been amended – eight weeks' or two months' arrears is now sufficient – see para 10.45.)

22 *Equity Housing Group Ltd v Boshir* Stockport County Court; 6 January 2005; March 2005 *Legal Action* 21.

10.12   Although Housing Act 1988 s8(2) provides that a court may alter or add to the grounds specified in a notice, in *Mountain v Hastings* (see above) the Court of Appeal held that there must be a valid notice before this power may be exercised. Section 8(2) is solely directed to the possibility of adding to or deleting grounds and cannot be used to cure a notice which is invalid because the only ground relied upon has not been properly set out.

Particulars

10.13   Particulars of the grounds relied upon have to be included, as well as reference to the ground itself. For example, if proceedings are to be issued under ground 11, it is not enough for the notice merely to state 'persistent rent arrears', without giving figures of arrears and dates of late payment.[23] A notice may however be valid even if it does not state a figure for the arrears if the amount due can be ascertained from the notice. In *Marath v MacGillivray*[24] the Court of Appeal stated that a landlord claiming possession under ground 8 could rely on a section 8 notice which did not specify a figure for the arrears provided that:

> ... it is made clear ... that more than three months rent is at the date of that notice unpaid and due and provided also that in some way or other that notice makes it clear either how much, or how the tenant can ascertain how much, is alleged to be due.

It is not necessary for the notice to contain a schedule of the arrears.

10.14   Courts have power to allow landlords to alter or add to the particulars relied upon in a notice, although such permission should only be given in circumstances where it would be just to do so. The nature and the extent of the addition or alteration should always be critical factors.[25]

Length of notice

10.15   Usually, notices of intention to bring possession proceedings against assured tenants have to give two weeks' notice, but in the case of

---

23 *Torridge DC v Jones* (1985) 18 HLR 107 (arrears of rent), *Kelsey Housing Association v King* (1995) 28 HLR 270, CA, *South Bucks DC v Francis* [1985] CLY 1900 (various acts of nuisance), *East Devon DC v Williams and Mills* December 1996 *Legal Action* 13 and *Slough BC v Robbins* December 1996 *Legal Action* 13; but cf, *Dudley MBC v Bailey* (1990) 22 HLR 424, CA.

24 (1996) 28 HLR 484, CA. (Note that ground 8 has since been amended – eight weeks' or two months' arrears is now sufficient – see para 10.45.)

25 HA 1988 s8(2) and *Marath v MacGillivray* (1996) 28 HLR 484, CA. Cf, HA 1985 s83(4) and *Camden LBC v Oppong* (1996) 28 HLR 701, CA.

grounds 1, 2, 5, 6, 7, 9 and 16 at least two months' notice or notice equivalent to the contractual period of the tenancy, whichever is longer, must be given. If ground 14 is relied upon, s8(4) provides no minimum period of notice, merely that the date specified in the notice shall not be earlier than the date of service of the notice.

Commencement of proceedings

10.16 With most grounds, the period specified in the notice must have expired before proceedings may be commenced. However, proceedings may be begun immediately after service if ground 14 (anti-social behaviour) is relied upon.[26] Proceedings must be started within 12 months of service of the notice, otherwise a new notice must be served.[27]

Service of notice

10.17 Housing Act 1988 s8(1)(a) provides that the notice must be 'served on the tenant'. If the tenancy agreement incorporates Law of Property Act 1925 s196, service may be effected by delivery to the premises. However, landlords cannot rely upon section 196 unless it is expressly incorporated into the tenancy agreement.[28] If there is no such provision in the tenancy agreement, the landlord must prove that the notice has been received by the tenant.

10.18 There is no need for a landlord of an assured tenant to serve a notice to quit as well as a notice of intention to bring proceedings.[29]

10.19 Housing Act 1988 s45(3) makes it clear that it is sufficient if just one out of two or more joint landlords gives notice.[30]

Dispensing with notice

10.20 Courts have power (except in relation to ground 8, ie, eight weeks' arrears) to dispense with service of a notice before the institution of possession proceedings if they consider it 'just and equitable' to do so.[31] This phrase is used in HA 1985 s83 and in different circumstances

---

26 HA 1988 s8(4).

27 HA 1988 s8(3)(c).

28 *Wandsworth LBC v Atwell* (1995) 27 HLR 536; [1996] 01 EG 100, CA and *Enfield BC v Devonish and Sutton* (1997) 29 HLR 691, CA.

29 HA 1988 s5(1).

30 See also HA 1988 Sch 2 Pt IV.

31 HA 1988 s8(1)(b). For a case in which the Court of Appeal decided that it was just and equitable to dispense with a notice, even though the trial judge was not asked to consider this, see *North British Housing Association v Sheridan* [2000] L & TR 115; (2000) 32 HLR 346, CA.

in Housing Act 1988 Sch 2 Pt I (see para 10.29) and Rent Act 1977 Sch 15 Pt II also (see para 15.46). It gives the court a wide discretion to review all factors which may affect or prejudice both the landlord and tenant, including matters which have occurred since the issue of proceedings.[32] In the context of secure tenancies, the Court of Appeal has stated that it is 'obviously only in relatively exceptional cases where the court should be prepared to dispense with' a notice seeking possession.[33] It may be that if a landlord has given written notice which does not comply with the regulations prescribing its form, or if oral notice is given, the court will consider that the tenant has not been prejudiced, and that it is 'just and equitable' to dispense with the requirement.[34] On the other hand, it may not be just and equitable if the tenant had no notification at all.

10.21   Applications to dispense with section 8 notices should not be heard at without notice hearings since judges must be in a position to weigh up all factors from both points of view.[35] In *Knowsley Housing Trust v Revell; Helena Housing Ltd v Curtis*,[36] a case where there was a stock transfer from a local authority to a registered social landlord after the issue of proceedings, the Court of Appeal held that the discretion under section 8(1)(b) is wide enough to allow substitution of the new landlord as claimant in the proceedings and dispensation of the section 8 notice where the reality is that the new landlord relies upon the same breach of the same term and the relief sought is no different. However it is not legitimate for courts to dispense with large numbers of such section 8 notices in one hearing without giving some consideration to any objection which might be taken by tenants with reference to the facts of their individual cases.[37]

---

32 Cf, *Bradshaw v Baldwin-Wiseman* (1985) 17 HLR 260, CA, *Fernandes v Parvardin* (1982) 264 EG 49, CA (Rent Act 1977 Sch 15 case 11 cases) and *Kelsey Housing Association v King* (1995) 28 HLR 270, CA.

33 *Braintree DC v Vincent* [2004] EWCA Civ 415; 9 March 2004, although in that case, where there were unusual facts, the Court of Appeal did find it just and equitable to dispense with a Housing Act 1985 s83 notice.

34 Cf *North British Housing Association v Sheridan* [2000] L & TR 115; (2000) 32 HLR 346, CA.

35 *Kelsey HA v King* (1996) 28 HLR 270, CA.

36 [2003] EWCA Civ 496; [2003] HLR 63.

37 See too *McShane v William Sutton Trust* (1997) 1 L & T Rev D67; December 1997 *Legal Action* 13.

Fixed-term assured tenancies

10.22 A fixed-term assured or assured shorthold tenancy can be terminated by the court during the fixed term if the landlord can prove that any of grounds 2, 8, 10, 11, 12, 13, 14, 14A, 15 or 17 exists and provided that the tenancy contains a provision entitling the landlord to rely on that ground (see Housing Act 1988 s7(6)).

10.23 In the past, a landlord wishing to determine a fixed-term tenancy would generally have relied on a forfeiture clause and the tenant would have been able to seek relief from forfeiture (for example, under County Courts Act 1984 s138 (see para 12.60) or Law of Property Act 1925 s146 (see para 12.48)). However, courts have no jurisdiction to grant relief from forfeiture where there is an assured tenancy. In *Artesian Residential Investments Ltd v Beck*[38] a fixed-term assured tenancy agreement included a proviso for re-entry and determination if the rent was at any stage 14 days in arrears. The defendant fell into rent arrears before the expiry of the term and the landlord brought possession proceedings relying on Housing Act 1988 Sch 2 grounds 8 and 10. A possession order was made, but the defendant later paid all the arrears and applied for suspension of the possession order, relying upon the relief from forfeiture provisions of County Courts Act 1984 s138. The Court of Appeal held that Housing Act 1988 s5(1) sets out the only routes for bringing an assured tenancy to an end. There is no need for a parallel claim for forfeiture to prevent the contractual tenancy continuing after the granting of an order for possession under the Act. Housing Act 1988 s5(1) makes it clear that an order for possession brings a tenancy to an end. This construction is also borne out by Housing Act 1988 s7(7) which provides that, when the court makes an order for possession on grounds relating to a fixed-term tenancy which has come to an end, any ensuing statutory periodic tenancy which arises on the ending of the fixed-term tenancy ends (without any notice or regardless of the period) on the day on which the order takes effect. Furthermore, Housing Act 1988 s7(3) is explicit, obliging the court mandatorily to make an order for possession if satisfied that any of the grounds in Schedule 2 is established subject to Housing Act 1988 s6. Section 7(6)(b) does no more than require provision for forfeiture to be included in the terms of the tenancy, and does not set up forfeiture as an independent ground for terminating the tenancy. As a matter of principle there is no room for applying Housing Act 1988 s138.[39]

38 [2000] QB 541; [2000] 2 WLR 357, CA.
39 See also ground 8, para 10.45.

10.24   Grounds 1, 3, 4, 5, 6, 7, 9 and 16 cannot be used against fixed-term assured tenants whose tenancies have not expired by effluxion of time (Housing Act 1988 s7(6)).

Grounds for possession

10.25   Housing Act 1988 s7 provides:

(1) The court shall not make an order for possession of a dwelling-house let on an assured tenancy except on one or more of the grounds set out in Schedule 2 to this Act; but nothing in this Part of this Act relates to proceedings for possession of such a dwelling-house which are brought by a mortgagee, within the meaning of the Law of Property Act 1925, who has lent money on the security of the assured tenancy.

(2) The following provisions of this section have effect, subject to section 8 below, in relation to proceedings for the recovery of possession of a dwelling-house let on an assured tenancy.

(3) If the court is satisfied that any of the grounds in Part I of Schedule 2 to this Act is established then, subject to subsections (5A) and (6) below, the court shall make an order for possession.

(4) If the court is satisfied that any of the grounds in Part II of Schedule 2 to this Act is established, then, subject to subsections (5A) and (6) below, the court may make an order for possession if it considers it reasonable to do so.

(5) Part III of Schedule 2 to this Act shall have effect for supplementing Ground 9 in that Schedule and Part IV of that Schedule shall have effect in relation to notices given as mentioned in Grounds 1 to 5 of that Schedule.

(5A) The court shall not make an order for possession of a dwelling-house let on an assured periodic tenancy arising under Schedule 10 to the Local Government and Housing Act 1989 on any of the following grounds, that is to say –

(a) Grounds 1, 2 and 5 in Part I of Schedule 2 to this Act;

(b) Ground 16 in Part II of that Schedule; and

(c) If the assured periodic tenancy arose on the termination of a former 1954 Act tenancy, within the meaning of the said Schedule 10, Ground 6 in Part I of Schedule 2 to this Act.

(6) The court shall not make an order for possession of a dwelling-house to take effect at a time when it is let on an assured fixed term tenancy unless –

(a) the ground for possession is Ground 2 or Ground 8 in Part I of Schedule 2 to this Act or any of the grounds in Part II of that Schedule, other than Ground 9 or Ground 16; and

(b) the terms of the tenancy make provisions for it to be brought to an end on the ground in question (whether that provision takes the form of a provision for re-entry, for forfeiture, for determination by notice or otherwise).

(7) Subject to the preceding provisions of this section, the court may make an order for possession of a dwelling-house on grounds relating to a fixed term tenancy which has come to an end; and where an order is made in such circumstances, any statutory periodic tenancy which has arisen on the ending of the fixed term tenancy shall end (without any notice and regardless of the period) on the day on which the order takes effect.

10.26   As well as serving a notice of intention to bring proceedings, or per-suading the court to dispense with such a notice, a landlord must also satisfy the court that one of the grounds for possession set out in Housing Act 1988 Sch 2 exists. Some of the grounds are similar in form to Rent Act 1977 and Housing Act 1985 grounds,[40] but others are not. As in the Rent Act 1977 and Housing Act 1985, some grounds for possession are mandatory, whereas others are discretionary, with a requirement that the landlord must convince the court that it is reasonable to make an order for possession as well as satisfying the ground for possession.

10.27   The jurisdiction of the court to make an order for possession under section 7 is limited. If the court is not satisfied that a ground under Schedule 2 has been established it does not have jurisdiction to make the order. A court is under a duty to determine whether the rele-vant ground has been established, whether or not it has been raised by the parties. Where a court lacks jurisdiction, it cannot be conferred merely by consent. To confer jurisdiction, an admission that a ground is satisfied, either express or implied, has to be clearly shown. Any consent order should clearly spell out in express terms the admission made by the tenant, or the court should ask the tenant what admis-sion was being made, so that there can be no room for confusion or doubt in the future.[41]

Some registered social landlords have standard form tenancy agree-ments which provide that they will only rely upon certain grounds for possession. In *North British Housing Association v Sheridan*,[42] where such a tenancy agreement set out in full the wording of the grounds that the landlord might rely upon, a tenant defended possession pro-ceedings by arguing that the landlord could not rely upon a ground that had been widened by the Housing Act 1996. The Court of Appeal

---

40 See chapters 3 and 15.

41 *Baygreen Properties Ltd v Gil* [2002] EWCA Civ 1340; [2003] HLR 12.

42 (2000) 32 HLR 346; [2000] L & TR 115, CA. See too *Charles Clay & Sons Ltd v British Railways Board* [1970] 2 All ER 463, ChD.

rejected this argument stating that it had not been the intention of the parties to the tenancy agreement 'to restrict the landlord for ever to the statutory grounds for possession as they stood in the 1988 Act and the intention must have been that, if the statutory grounds for possession (or other related provisions) were amended, neither party would be disentitled from relying on the amended provisions'. Any other construction 'would fossilise the agreement'.

Mandatory grounds for possession

Ground 1: Owner-occupiers

10.28   Not later than the beginning of the tenancy the landlord gave notice in writing to the tenant that possession might be recovered on this ground or the court is of the opinion that it is just and equitable to dispense with the requirement of notice and (in either case) –

(a) at some time before the beginning of the tenancy, the landlord who is seeking possession or, in the case of joint landlords seeking possession, at least one of them occupied the dwelling-house as his only or principal home; or

(b) the landlord who is seeking possession or, in the case of joint landlords seeking possession, at least one of them requires the dwelling-house as his, *his spouse's or his civil partner's* only or principal home and neither the landlord (or, in the case of joint landlords, any one of them) nor any other person who, as landlord, derived title under the landlord who gave the notice mentioned above acquired the reversion on the tenancy for money or money's worth.

Note: the words 'his, his spouse's or his civil partner's' were inserted in substitution for the words 'his or his spouse's' by Civil Partnership Act 2004 Sch 8. The amendment was brought into force on 5 December 2005 by Civil Partnership 2004 (Commencement No 2) Order 2005.[43]

10.29   This ground is similar to case 11 in Rent Act 1977 Sch 15 (see para 15.45), but much wider in its ambit. A landlord must:

- prove that at, or before, the grant of the tenancy the landlord gave notice in writing that possession might be recovered on this ground. The notice need not be in any particular form and may be included as a recital in any tenancy agreement provided that the agreement does not operate retrospectively; or

---

43   SI No 3175 (C.136).

- satisfy the court that 'it is just and equitable to dispense with the requirement of notice'. These words have 'a very wide importance' and mean that the court should take into account all of the circumstances, including questions of greater hardship, and not just the circumstances which surround a failure to give written notice.[44] If the court fails to consider relevant circumstances, any possession order may be set aside.[45] A tenant's persistent late payment of rent may be a relevant circumstance.[46] If oral notice was given when a tenancy was granted, it may be an important factor favouring dispensation, but it does not follow that oral notice is a prerequisite for such a decision. On the other hand, absence of oral notice is not a reason for restricting dispensation to circumstances where there is an 'exceptional case'.[47] Courts may consider circumstances affecting the landlord, the landlord's successors in title, the tenant's circumstances and the effect of the failure to give notice.[48] In one Rent Act case, where, prior to the granting of a tenancy, tenants were told orally that the premises were the landlord's home, that the landlord would be returning and there was no misunderstanding about this, the court considered that oral notice was just as effective as written notice and so dispensed with the formal requirements.[49] However, in another Rent Act case where no formal notice was given at the beginning of the tenancy because at that time the landlord had no intention of returning to the premises, it was not just and equitable to dispense with the requirement.[50] The fact that the parties signed what purported (wrongly) to be a temporary 'licence' agreement is not enough to

---

44 *Bradshaw v Baldwin-Wiseman* (1985) 17 HLR 260, CA, *Fernandes v Parvardin* (1982) 264 EG 49, CA, *Boyle v Verrall* (1997) 29 HLR 436; [1997] 1 EGLR 25, CA and *Wynne v Egan* June 1997 *Legal Action* 15, CA.
45 *Hegab v Shamash* June 1998 *Legal Action* 13, CA (judge correctly considered the fact that no tenancy had been intended because the defendant had intended to purchase the premises from the plaintiff and the fact that the landlord had later 'behaved in a disgraceful way' by illegally evicting the tenant and disobeying an injunction, but failed to take into account two matters: (a) the tenant had paid a deposit of £4,000 in relation to the proposed purchase, which had not been refunded and (b) the landlord had not paid the costs of the earlier proceedings concerning the illegal eviction.
46 *Boyle v Verrall* (1997) 29 HLR 436; [1997] 1 EGLR 25, CA.
47 Ibid. See also *Mustafa v Ruddock* (1998) 30 HLR 495; [1997] EGCS 87, CA.
48 *Bradshaw v Baldwin-Wiseman* (1985) 17 HLR 260, CA.
49 *Fernandes v Parvardin* (1982) 264 EG 49, CA. Cf, *White v Jones* (1994) 26 HLR 477, CA.
50 *Bradshaw v Baldwin-Wiseman* (1985) 17 HLR 260, CA.

make it 'just and equitable' to dispense with the need for a notice;[51] *and either*

- at some time before the grant of the tenancy, the landlord, or if there are joint landlords, at least one of them, had occupied the dwelling-house as his or her only or principal home.[52] A landlord's previous occupation may suffice even if it was only temporary or intermittent.[53] To satisfy this limb, the landlord need not give any reason for requiring possession; *or*
- the landlord (or at least one of them) 'requires the dwelling-house as his or his spouse's only or principal home'. The landlord need not show that the premises are 'reasonably' required, merely that the landlord 'bona fide wants' or 'genuinely has the immediate intention' of occupying the premises.[54] Premises need not be required as a permanent residence and fairly intermittent residence will be sufficient.[55]

This ground for possession is not available to a new landlord who acquired the premises 'for money or money's worth' from an original landlord who gave a notice that possession might be recovered under this ground. There is an equivalent provision in Rent Act 1977 Sch 15 case 11. All of the relevant case law relates to Rent Act 1977 Sch 15 case 9, but exactly the same principles apply. The purpose of this provision is to prevent an outsider buying up tenanted property and then evicting the tenant.[56] In this connection the word 'purchasing' means 'buying'.[57] It does not include 'inheriting',[58] acquiring through a family settlement,[59] a transfer to a family member 'in consideration

---

51   *Ibie v Trubshaw* (1990) 22 HLR 191, CA.
52   Note the contrast with the wording under Rent Act 1977 Sch 15 case 11.
53   *Naish v Curzon* (1984) 17 HLR 220, CA, *Mistry v Isidore* (1990) 22 HLR 281; [1990] 2 EGLR 97, CA and *Ibie v Trubshaw* (1990) 22 HLR 191, CA.
54   Cf, Rent Act 1977 Sch 15 case 9. See *Kennealy v Dunne* [1977] QB 837.
55   *Naish v Curzon* (1984) 17 HLR 220, CA and *Davies v Peterson* (1989) 21 HLR 63; [1989] 06 EG 130, CA.
56   *Fowle v Bell* [1946] 2 All ER 668 and *Epps v Rothnie* [1945] KB 562; [1946] 1 All ER 146.
57   *Powell v Cleland* [1948] 1 KB 262; [1947] 2 All ER 672.
58   *Baker v Lewis* [1946] 2 All ER 592, CA. Note, though, that where an owner said, before she died, that she wished her executors to offer a property for sale to the plaintiff, who then bought it, he was 'a landlord by purchase' and was not entitled to possession: *Amaddio v Dalton* (1991) 22 HLR 332.
59   *Thomas v Fryer* [1970] 1 WLR 845; [1970] 2 All ER 1, even though money was paid by one beneficiary under the will to the others.

of mutual love and affection'[60] or the granting of an intermediate lease with no premium.[61] A tenant will have a defence to proceedings under Housing Act 1988 Sch 2 ground 1 if his or her tenancy was in existence at the date when the premises were bought. The relevant date is the date of exchange of contracts, and not the date of completion.[62] However, owners are entitled to rely on ground 1 if they buy premises with vacant possession and subsequently let to tenants,[63] or if they buy premises with one sitting tenant who leaves and is then replaced by another tenant.[64] If landlords become 'landlords by purchase' they do not acquire the right to bring proceedings under Housing Act 1988 Sch 2 ground 1 even if a new contractual tenancy on different terms is created or there are minor changes in the subject matter of the tenancy, for example, by the addition or deduction of rooms.[65] Similarly if a 'landlord by purchase' dies, the person to whom the property is transferred acquires no greater right under ground 1 than the original landlord by purchase.[66]

Ground 2: Mortgagees

10.30   The dwelling-house is subject to a mortgage granted before the beginning of the tenancy and –

  (a) the mortgagee is entitled to exercise a power of sale conferred on him by the mortgage or by section 101 of the Law of Property Act 1925; and

  (b) the mortgagee requires possession of the dwelling-house for the purpose of disposing of it with vacant possession in exercise of that power; and

  (c) either notice was given as mentioned in Ground 1 above or the court is satisfied that it is just and equitable to dispense with the requirement of notice;

and for the purposes of this ground 'mortgage' includes a charge and 'mortgagee' shall be construed accordingly.

---

60 *Mansukhani v Stanley* (1992) *Times* 17 April.
61 *Powell v Cleland* [1948] 1 KB 262; [1947] 2 All ER 672.
62 *Emberson v Robinson* [1953] 1 WLR 1129 and *Newton and Wife v Biggs* [1953] 2 QB 211; [1953] 1 All ER 99.
63 *Epps v Rothnie* [1945] KB 562; [1946] 1 All ER 146.
64 *Fowle v Bell* [1947] KB 242; [1946] 2 All ER 668. See also *Newton and Wife v Biggs* [1953] 2 QB 211; [1953] 1 All ER 99 where the former owner sold premises to the plaintiff on condition that he was granted a tenancy. The new landlord was not a landlord by purchase.
65 *Wright v Walford* [1955] 1 QB 363; [1955] 1 All ER 207.
66 *Littlechild v Holt* [1950] 1 KB 1; [1949] 1 All ER 933.

10.31   This ground applies if, for example, the landlord/mortgagor has defaulted on instalments of the mortgage. The purpose of this ground is to enable the landlord's mortgagee, who has consented to a borrower letting or where the mortgage deed does not prohibit letting, to obtain the full vacant possession value when exercising a power of sale. Note, though, the suggestion by Lord Denning MR that the court's equitable powers may prevent a lender from obtaining possession, 'except when it is sought bona fide and reasonably for the purpose of enforcing the security'.[67]

For the principles to be applied when a landlord seeks to persuade the court to dispense with service of a notice prior to commencement of the tenancy see para 10.29.

Ground 3: Tenancy preceded by 'holiday let'

10.32   The tenancy is a fixed-term tenancy for a term not exceeding eight months and –
   (a) not later than the beginning of the tenancy the landlord gave notice in writing to the tenant that possession might be recovered on this ground; and
   (b) at some time within the period of twelve months ending with the beginning of the tenancy, the dwelling-house was occupied under a right to occupy it for a holiday.

10.33   This ground was designed to enable landlords who let premises on holiday lets during, for example, the summer, to be able to recover possession if they let them on longer lets during the winter. However, the ground as enacted operates in far wider circumstances than that. To rely on ground 3, a landlord must prove that:

• The premises were occupied at some time during the preceding 12 months for the purpose of 'a holiday'. Even if a landlord produces a copy of a 'holiday let agreement' relating to such a period, it may be possible for the tenant to prove that that agreement was 'a sham' or 'did not reflect the intention of the parties' to it.[68] However, it should be remembered that the burden of proving this lies on the tenant.

• The relevant tenancy was granted for a fixed period of not more than eight months. It is, however, arguable that ground 3 is available even where a tenant who initially agreed to rent the premises

---

67   *Quennel v Maltby* [1979] 1 WLR 318, CA approved in *Albany Home Loans v Massey* [1997] 2 All ER 609, CA.

68   See para 10.5 and *Buchmann v May* [1978] 2 All ER 993 and *R v Rent Officer for Camden ex p Plant* (1980) 257 EG 713; (1980) 7 HLR 15, QBD.

for eight months has held over and occupied the premises for a far longer period.

- Not later than the commencement of the tenancy the landlord gave written notice to the tenant that this ground for possession might be relied upon.

The court has no power to dispense with service of the notice required prior to the grant of the tenancy.[69]

Ground 4: Educational institutions

10.34 The tenancy is a fixed-term tenancy for a term not exceeding twelve months and –

(a) not later than the beginning of the tenancy the landlord gave notice in writing to the tenant that possession might be recovered on this ground; and

(b) at some time within the period of twelve months ending with the beginning of the tenancy, the dwelling-house was let on a tenancy falling within paragraph 8 of Schedule 1 to this Act.

10.35 This ground applies where, during the 12 months preceding the tenancy, the premises were let by a specified educational institution.[70] The term 'specified educational institution' includes universities, any other publicly funded institution providing further education and a number of associations and companies which have been specifically designated as such for Rent Act and Housing Act purposes, and for this purpose any registered housing association.

As with Housing Act 1988 Sch 2 ground 3, notice stating that this ground may be relied upon has to be served before the commencement of the tenancy.

Ground 5: Ministers of religion

10.36 The dwelling-house is held for the purpose of being available for occupation by a minister of religion as a residence from which to perform the duties of his office and –

(a) not later than the beginning of the tenancy the landlord gave notice in writing to the tenant that possession might be recovered on this ground; and

(b) the court is satisfied that the dwelling-house is required for occupation by a minister of religion as such a residence.

---

69 Cf, *Fowler v Minchin* (1987) 19 HLR 224, CA and *Springfield Investments v Bell* (1990) 22 HLR 440, CA.

70 See Assured and Protected Tenancies (Lettings to Students) Regulations 1998 SI No 1967 as amended.

This ground applies to premises which are 'held for the purpose of being available for occupation by a minister of religion as a residence from which to perform the duties of his office'. Notice that possession might be required under this ground must be served before the grant of the tenancy, and the landlord must satisfy the court that the property is required for occupation by a minister of religion as a residence. It is similar to Rent Act 1977 Sch 15 case 15.[71]

Ground 6: Demolition or reconstruction

10.37   The landlord who is seeking possession or, if that landlord is a registered social landlord or charitable housing trust, a superior landlord intends to demolish or reconstruct the whole or a substantial part of the dwelling-house or to carry out substantial works on the dwelling-house or any part thereof or any building of which it forms part and the following conditions are fulfilled –

(a) the intended work cannot reasonably be carried out without the tenant giving up possession of the dwelling-house because –

   (i) the tenant is not willing to agree to such a variation of the terms of the tenancy as would give such access and other facilities as would permit the intended work to be carried out, or

   (ii) the nature of the intended work is such that no such variation is practicable, or

   (iii) the tenant is not willing to accept an assured tenancy of such part only of the dwelling-house (in this sub-paragraph referred to as 'the reduced part') as would leave in the possession of his landlord so much of the dwelling-house as would be reasonable to enable the intended work to be carried out and, where appropriate, as would give such access and other facilities over the reduced part as would permit the intended work to be carried out, or

   (iv) the nature of the intended work is such that such a tenancy is not practicable; and

(b) either the landlord seeking possession acquired his interest in the dwelling-house before the grant of the tenancy or that interest was in existence at the time of that grant and neither that landlord (or, in the case of joint landlords, any of them) nor any other person who, alone or jointly with others, has acquired that interest since that time acquired it for money or money's worth; and

(c) the assured tenancy on which the dwelling-house is let did not come into being by virtue of any provision of Schedule 1 to the Rent Act 1977, as amended by Part I of Schedule 4 to this Act or, as the case may be, section 4 of the Rent (Agriculture) Act 1976, as amended by Part II of that Schedule.

---

71 See para 15.53.

For the purposes of this ground if, immediately before the grant of the tenancy, the tenant to whom it was granted or, if it was granted to joint tenants, any of them was the tenant or one of the joint tenants of the dwelling-house concerned under an earlier assured tenancy or, as the case may be, under a tenancy to which Schedule 10 to the Local Government and Housing Act 1989 applied, any reference in paragraph (b) above to the grant of the tenancy is a reference to the grant of that earlier assured tenancy, or as the case may be, to the grant of the tenancy to which the said Schedule 10 applied.

For the purposes of this ground 'registered social landlord' has the same meaning as in the Housing Act 1985 (see section 5(4) and (5) of that Act and 'charitable housing trust' means a housing trust, within the meaning of Housing Associations Act 1985, which is a charity, within the meaning of the Charities Act 1993.

10.38   This ground is available for a landlord who 'intends to demolish or reconstruct the whole or a substantial part of the dwelling-house or to carry out substantial works'. It is very similar to Landlord and Tenant Act 1954 s30(1)(f), which allows landlords of business tenants to oppose the grant of a new tenancy in similar circumstances.

10.39   It has been held that 'reconstruction' means 'a substantial interference with the structure of the premises and then a rebuilding, in probably a different form, of such part of the premises as has been demolished by reason of the interference with the structure'.[72]

10.40   The landlord must show that the intention to demolish or reconstruct will be fulfilled shortly after the date of the hearing.[73] There are two elements to the concept of intention: first, a genuine desire that the result will come about and, second, a reasonable prospect of bringing about that result. For example, in *Edwards v Thompson*[74] the landlord failed to prevent the grant of a new tenancy because she had not found a developer at the time of the hearing and 'there was a real possibility that [she] would not be in a position to carry out the entire development on the termination of the current tenancy ... She had failed to show that she had the means and ability; she had not established the necessary intention'. A landlord's case is stronger if planning permission has been obtained in advance of the institution

---

72   *Joel v Swaddle* [1957] 1 WLR 1094; [1957] 3 All ER 325 at 329 (removal of internal walls and replacement with reinforced steel joists amounted to reconstruction of a substantial part). See also *Barth v Pritchard* [1990] 20 EG 65 and *Cook v Mott* (1961) 178 EG 637, CA.

73   *Betty's Cafes Ltd v Phillips* [1959] AC 20; [1958] 2 WLR 513; [1958] 1 All ER 607, HL.

74   [1990] 29 EG 41, CA. See also *Capocci v Goble* (1987) 284 EG 230, CA.

of possession proceedings, but this is not essential if it can be shown that there is a reasonable prospect of getting consent.[75]

10.41   The landlord must also show that, because of one of four specified reasons, the intended work cannot reasonably be carried out without the tenant giving up possession of the premises. 'Possession' means 'putting an end to legal rights of possession' and not merely access. For example, in *Heath v Drown*[76] a business tenant successfully defeated the landlord's claim even though the front wall of the premises had to be entirely rebuilt and it would not be possible to occupy the premises while such work was carried out. It is not enough for the landlord to say that access is required, since most tenancies contain an express or implied[77] right of access to carry out repairs. The landlord must show that the work cannot be carried out while the tenancy still exists.

10.42   This ground for possession is not available to a landlord who has acquired his or her interest in the property by purchasing it after the grant of the tenancy.

When a possession order is made under this ground the landlord must pay a sum equal to the tenant's reasonable removal expenses.[78]

Ground 7: Death of the tenant

10.43   The tenancy is a periodic tenancy (including a statutory periodic tenancy) which has devolved under the will or intestacy of the former tenant and the proceedings for the recovery of possession are begun not later than twelve months after the death of the former tenant or, if the court so directs, after the date on which, in the opinion of the court, the landlord or, in the case of joint landlords, any one of them became aware of the former tenant's death.

For the purposes of this ground, the acceptance by the landlord of rent from a new tenant after the death of the former tenant shall not be regarded as creating a new periodic tenancy, unless the landlord agrees in writing to a change (as compared with the tenancy before the death) in the amount of the rent, the period of the tenancy, the premises which are let or any other term of the tenancy.

---

75   *Gregson v Cyril Lord* [1963] 1 WLR 41; [1962] 3 All ER 907, CA.

76   [1973] AC 498; [1972] 2 WLR 1306, CA and, for an example in the county court, *Sugarwhite v Afridi* [2002] 5 CL 425, Central London Civil Justice Centre. See too HA 1988 s16.

77   HA 1988 s16.

78   HA 1988 s11(1) – see below.

10.44 Although an assured tenancy may pass by will or on intestacy after the death of the tenant, the landlord may obtain possession if proceedings are brought within 12 months of the death of the tenant or the date upon which the landlord became aware of the death. 'Proceedings' means the issue of a court claim, not merely the service of a notice seeking possession.[79] No other reason for seeking possession need be given. This ground does not apply if a spouse or or civil partner, or person living with the tenant 'as his or her wife or husband or civil partner' succeeds to the tenancy as a result of the statutory succession provisions in Housing Act 1988 s17. The Act specifies that acceptance of rent after the death of the former tenant should not be regarded as creating a new tenancy unless the landlord has agreed in writing to a change in the terms of the tenancy, such as an increase in rent. The ground does not apply where the deceased tenant had a fixed-term tenancy.

Ground 8: Eight weeks' or two months' rent arrears

10.45 Both at the date of the service of the notice under section 8 of this Act relating to the proceedings for possession and at the date of the hearing –

(a) if rent is payable weekly or fortnightly, at least *eight* weeks' rent is unpaid;

(b) if rent is payable monthly, at least *two* months' rent is unpaid;

(c) if rent is payable quarterly, at least one quarter's rent is more than three months in arrears; and

(d) if rent is payable yearly, at least three months' rent is more than three months in arrears;

and for the purpose of this ground 'rent' means rent lawfully due from the tenant.

This is the first of three distinct grounds for possession based on rent arrears, although in practice many landlords plead all three in the alternative. Ground 8 was amended by Housing Act 1996 s101 to substitute eight weeks and two months in place of 13 weeks and three months. The amendments were brought into force by the Housing Act 1996 (Commencement No 7 and Savings) Order 1997[80] and apply whenever a Housing Act 1988 s8 notice is served after 28 February 1997.

---

79 *Shepping v Osada* (2001) 33 HLR 13; [2000] 30 EG 125, CA. See also *Tunbridge and Malling Housing Association v Reed* September 2001 *Legal Action* 24.

80 SI No 225.

10.46   Paragraph 3.1.4 of the Housing Corporation Regulatory Circular 07/04 *Tenancy Management: Eligibility and Evictions*,[81] which relates to housing associations provides:

> Before using ground 8, associations should first pursue all other reasonable alternatives to recover the debt. Where the use of ground 8 forms part of an arrears and eviction policy, tenants should have been consulted and governing board approval for the policy should have been given.

10.47   Under ground 8, two months' rent arrears (or eight weeks' arrears in the case of a weekly tenancy) give a landlord an automatic right to a possession order. However, the landlord must prove that there were eight weeks' or two months' arrears, both at the time when the notice of the landlord's intention to bring proceedings was served and at the date of the hearing. 'The date of the hearing' is the date when the claim is heard. It is not the date fixed for the hearing if, on that date, an adjournment is granted without a hearing taking place at all.[82]

10.48   A possession order cannot be made under ground 8 unless the landlord proves that a valid Housing Act 1988 s8 notice has been served.[83] There is no discretion to dispense with a section 8 notice if ground 8 is relied upon – see section 8(5).

10.49   Money which a defendant has been ordered to pay into court to abide the event is available 'on account of rent arrears' and ignoring such money would lead to an artificial and inequitable result when calculating arrears for the purpose of ground 8.[84] In *Day v Coltrane*,[85] a case where possession was sought under ground 8, the Court of Appeal held that an uncleared cheque delivered to the landlord at or before the hearing and which was accepted by him, or which he was bound by an earlier agreement to accept, was to be treated as payment on the date of delivery provided that it was subsequently paid on first presentation.

10.50   Delays on the part of a local authority in making housing benefit payments do not provide a defence to proceedings brought under ground 8.[86] In cases where arrears have been caused by delays in pay-

---

81   www.housingcorp.gov.uk, see November 2004 *Legal Action* 23.

82   *North British Housing Association Limited v Matthews* [2004] EWCA Civ 1736; [2005] 1 WLR 3133.

83   *Capital Prime Plus plc v Wills* (1999) 31 HLR 926, CA.

84   *Etherington v Burt* [2004] EWHC 95, QBD; 5 February 2004 (Fulford J).

85   [2003] EWCA Civ 342; [2003] 1 WLR 1379. See too *Homes v Smith* [2000] Lloyd's Law Rep Banking 139.

86   *Marath v MacGillivray* (1996) 28 HLR 484, CA.

ing housing benefit, it is worth considering issuing a witness summons to compel the appropriate official to attend at court to explain personally the reason for any delay.[87]

10.51   As ground 8 is mandatory, once the court is satisfied that the ground is proved, there is no power to adjourn or suspend.[88] In practice, where a tenant faces a claim for possession under ground 8, the only way for him or her to obtain time to pay rent arrears (or to sort out housing benefit) is to apply for an adjournment *before* evidence has been heard. The Court of Appeal considered such applications in *North British Housing Association Limited v Matthews*.[89] It held that:

- There is no doubt that it is a perfectly proper exercise of the court's discretion to adjourn, if a case has to be taken out of the list because there is no judge available, or because there has been over-listing, or because the defendant is prevented by ill health from attending court.
- The court retains jurisdiction to grant an adjournment before it is satisfied that the landlord is entitled to possession. It may be a proper exercise of discretion to adjourn the hearing before the court is satisfied that the landlord is entitled to possession, for example, where there is an arguable claim for damages which can be set off against arrears; where the tenant shows that there is an arguable defence based on accord and satisfaction or estoppel arising from an agreement whereby the landlord accepts an offer by the tenant to pay off the current rent and arrears at a certain rate in return for not pursuing the claim for possession; or where the court is satisfied that there is a real chance that the tenant would be given permission to apply for judicial review of the landlord's decision to claim possession because of abuse of power.
- However, it is not legitimate to adjourn to enable the tenant to pay off arrears and so defeat the claim for possession, unless there are exceptional circumstances, for example, if a tenant is robbed on the way to court, or if a computer failure prevents the housing benefit authority from being able to pay benefit due until the day after the hearing date. The fact that arrears are attributable to

---

87 See further chapter 32.
88 HA 1988 s9(6).
89 [2004] EWCA Civ 1736; [2005] 1 WLR 3133. See too cf, *Razack v Osman* [2001] 9 CL 426; December 2001 *Legal Action* 22. Cf, see, eg, *R v A Circuit Judge ex p Wathen* (1976) 33 P & CR 423, QBD, *Birmingham Citizens Permanent Building Society v Caunt* [1962] Ch 883, ChD, *Bristol CC v Lovell* [1998] 1 WLR 446, HL and *Hoffman v Cueto-Corondo and Filipe* April 2000 *Legal Action* 32.

maladministration on the part of the housing benefit authority is not an exceptional circumstance.

• Once the court has expressed the conclusion that it is satisfied that the landlord is entitled to possession, there is no power to grant an adjournment in any circumstances (see sections 7(3) and 9(6)). The court cannot be 'satisfied' within the meaning of section 9(6) until the judge has given a judgment and effect is given to that judgment in a perfected order of the court.

The Court of Appeal suggested that the Housing Corporation might consider it wise to expand its advice in Regulatory Circular 07/04[90] about the need for effective liaison between landlords and housing benefit departments right up to the time when a possession claim for rent arrears is heard. However, to date, no amendment to the Regulatory Circular has been made

10.52   As with all rent arrears grounds, it is important for advisers to consider whether or not there has been any breach of repairing obligations on the landlord's part. If there has, any damages awarded on a counterclaim based on the disrepair may be set off against arrears of rent and may result in the arrears being wiped out or reduced below the level of two months' arrears.

10.53   It is also important to check that the claimant has complied with the provisions of Landlord and Tenant Act 1987 s48, which require demands for rent to include the landlord's name and address, and that landlords supply tenants with details of an address in England and Wales where notices may be served. If landlords fail to comply with these provisions, rent is not due until the failure has been rectified.[91]

10.54   Assured tenancies may include contractual provisions for rent reviews. However, if such a clause is not in substance or reality a provision for the fixing of rent, but a provision for the landlord to recover possession otherwise than in accordance with the statutory scheme, it may not be enforceable. This is a question of fact. In *Bankway Properties v Penfold-Dunsford*,[92] the Court of Appeal found that such a clause permitting a landlord to increase the rent of a tenant in receipt

---

90   See www.housingcorp.gov.uk, see November 2004 *Legal Action* 23.

91   See *Dallhold Estate (UK) Pty Ltd v Lindsay Trading Properties Inc* [1994] 17 EG 148, CA, *Hussain v Singh* [1993] 31 EG 75, CA, but cf, *Rogan v Woodfield Building Services Ltd* (1995) 27 HLR 78; [1995] 20 EG 132, CA and *Drew-Morgan v Hamid-Zadeh* (2000) 32 HLR 216; [1999] 26 EG 156, CA.

92   [2001] EWCA Civ 528; [2001] 26 EG 164, CA. See too *Home 4 Rent Ltd v Killelea* St Helens County Court; 8 August 2003; *Housing Aid Update*, Issue 136, April 2004; June 2004 *Legal Action* 30 and *Shah v Mori* January 2004 *Legal Action* 30.

of housing benefit to £25,000 per annum was a mere device, which enabled the landlord, effectively when it chose, to recover possession. In those circumstances it was unenforceable and the landlord's claim based upon arrears was dismissed.

10.55   There is an argument that Housing Act 1988 Sch 2 ground 8 may conflict with articles 6, 8 and 14 of the European Convention on Human Rights and article 1 of the First Protocol to the convention. This is especially so when ground 8 proceedings are brought by a registered social landlord. In many cases rent arrears are caused solely by housing benefit problems, sometimes without the tenant being at fault in any way, for example, where housing benefit forms are lost by the local authority. It is hard to see how, in such circumstances, it is 'necessary', within the meaning of article 8(2), to deprive tenants of their homes. Further the legislation lacks any procedural safeguards which would allow tenants to challenge the decision to bring or continue proceedings.[93] Such a contention would be strengthened by reliance upon article 14 and a comparison with the rights of secure tenants (Housing Act 1985) who are not subject to a mandatory ground for possession based upon rent arrears. What is the 'objective and reasonable justification' for the distinction between assured and secure tenants of registered social landlords? How does it pursue a 'legitimate aim'?[94] The position is less clear cut if the claimant is a private landlord because the court would then have to balance the landlord's rights under article 1 of the First Protocol against the tenant's article 8 rights.

Discretionary grounds for possession

Ground 9: Suitable alternative accommodation

10.56   Suitable alternative accommodation is available for the tenant or will be available for him when the order for possession takes effect.

---

93 See, eg, the speech of Lord Hope in *Lambeth LBC v Kay; Leeds CC v Price* [2006] UKHL 10; [2006] 2 WLR 570; 8 March 2006, where he said that the making of a possession order in *Connors v UK* Application no 66746/01; [2004] HLR 52; (2004) *Times* 10 June; 27 May 2004, ECtHR failed to meet the third requirement in article 8(2). 'It failed to do so in that case because the making of the order was not attended by the procedural safeguards that were required to establish that there was a proper justification for the interference with the applicant's right to respect for his private and family life and his home.'

94 See *Larkos v Cyprus* (2000) 30 EHRR 597; (1999) 7 BHRC 244. See also *Dartmouth/Halifax County Regional Housing Authority v Sparks* (1993) 101 4th DLR 224.

As with Rent Act 1977,[95] the availability of suitable alternative accommodation, either at the time of the hearing or when the order is to take effect, is a ground for possession. Housing Act 1988 Sch 2 Pt III[96] gives further clarification as to the matters to be taken into account when determining whether or not accommodation is suitable.

1. For the purposes of Ground 9 above, a certificate of the local housing authority for the district in which the dwelling-house in question is situated, certifying that the authority will provide suitable alternative accommodation for the tenant by a date specified in the certificate, shall be conclusive evidence that suitable alternative accommodation will be available for him by that date.

2. Where no such certificate as is mentioned in paragraph 1 above is produced to the court, accommodation shall be deemed to be suitable for the purposes of ground 9 above if it consists of either –

   (a) premises which are to be let as a separate dwelling such that they will then be let on an assured tenancy, other than –

      (i) a tenancy in respect of which notice is given not later than the beginning of the tenancy that possession might be recovered on any of Grounds 1 to 5 above, or

      (ii) an assured shorthold tenancy, within the meaning of Chapter II of Part 1 of this Act, or

   (b) premises to be let as a separate dwelling on terms which will, in the opinion of the court, afford to the tenant security of tenure reasonably equivalent to the security afforded by Chapter I of Part I of this Act in the case of an assured tenancy of a kind mentioned in sub-paragraph (a) above, and, in the opinion of the court, the accommodation fulfils the relevant conditions as defined in paragraph 3 below.

3. (1) For the purposes of paragraph 2 above, the relevant conditions are that the accommodation is reasonably suitable to the needs of the tenant and his family as regards proximity to place of work, and either –

   (a) similar as regards rental and extent to the accommodation afforded by dwelling-houses provided in the neighbourhood by any local housing authority for persons whose needs as regards extent are, in the opinion of the court, similar to those of the tenant and his family; or

   (b) reasonably suitable to the means of the tenant and to the needs of the tenant and his family as regards extent and character; and

---

95 Section 98(1)(a).

96 Cf, Rent Act 1977 Sch 15 Pt IV. HA 1988 Sch 2 Pt III is very similar to the comparable Rent Act provisions, although the alternative accommodation should be let on an assured tenancy, rather than on a protected tenancy.

that if any furniture was provided for use under the assured tenancy in question, furniture is provided for use in the accommodation which is either similar to that so provided or is reasonably suitable to the needs of the tenant and his family.

(2) For the purposes of subparagraph (1)(a) above, a certificate of a local housing authority stating –

(a) the extent of the accommodation afforded by dwelling-houses provided by the authority to meet the needs of tenants with families of such number as may be specified in the certificate, and

(b) the amount of the rent charged by the authority for dwelling houses affording accommodation of that extent,

shall be conclusive evidence of the facts so stated.

4. Accommodation shall not be deemed to be suitable to the needs of the tenant and his family if the result of their occupation of the accommodation would be that it would be an overcrowded dwelling-house for the purposes of Part X of the Housing Act 1985.

5. Any document purporting to be a certificate of a local housing authority named therein issued for the purposes of this Part of this Schedule and to be signed by the proper officer of that authority shall be received in evidence and, unless the contrary is shown, shall be deemed to be such a certificate without further proof.

6. In this Part of this Schedule 'local housing authority' and 'district' in relation to such an authority, have the same meaning as in the Housing Act 1985.

10.57 When a possession order is made under this ground, the landlord must pay a sum equal to the tenant's reasonable removal expenses.[97]

Local authority certificate that accommodation available

10.58 Housing Act 1988 Sch 2 Pt III para 1 provides that a certificate from a local housing authority confirming that it will provide suitable alternative accommodation for the tenant is conclusive evidence that suitable alternative accommodation will be available[98] at the date specified in the certificate. The certificate must be from the housing authority for the area in which the relevant premises are situated, otherwise it is totally ineffective.[99] It seems that there is no requirement that the certificate provide details of the address or size of the suitable alternative accommodation. If, after issuing a certificate, a local authority failed to provide suitable alternative accommodation, the court would have power under Housing Act 1988 s9(2) to stay execution of the

97 HA 1988 s11(1) – see below.
98 *Wallasey v Pritchard* (1936) 3 LJNCCR 35.
99 *Sills v Watkins* [1956] 1 QB 250, CA.

order on an application by the tenant. There is no requirement that the certificate be in any particular form: a signed letter will suffice.

10.59   In view of the shortage of local authority accommodation, it is extremely rare for local authorities to provide certificates under paragraph 1. Accordingly, whether or not suitable accommodation is available is usually decided in the light of the guidelines in paragraphs 2 to 6.

No local authority certificate that accommodation available

10.60   If there is no local authority certificate the landlord must prove that the requirements set out below are satisfied (see HA 1988, Sch 2, Part III, paras 2–4).

Equivalent security of tenure

> 2 (a) ... premises which are to be let as a separate dwelling ... on an assured tenancy, other than [one under which] possession might be recovered on any of grounds 1 to 5 above, or ... an assured shorthold tenancy ... or ... premises ... let as a separate dwelling on terms which will ... afford to the tenant security of tenure reasonably equivalent to ... an assured tenancy ...

10.61   It is clear that the accommodation offered must be in a single building: accommodation offered in two separate houses cannot be suitable.[100] Similarly, the requirement is not satisfied if the premises offered consist of two separate parts of a building which are separated by another flat[101] or if the alternative accommodation involves sharing a kitchen.[102]

10.62   Housing Act 1988 Sch 2 Pt III para 2(b) provides that accommodation may be suitable even if it is not let on an assured tenancy, if the security of tenure provided is 'reasonably equivalent' to that provided by Housing Act 1988 Pt I Chapter I. In determining whether this condition is satisfied it is necessary to look strictly at the rights which the landlord of the alternative accommodation has to terminate the tenancy and not at common practice or the assurances given by the new landlord.[103] What is 'reasonably equivalent' security will depend

---

100 *Sheehan v Cutler* [1946] KB 339.
101 *Selwyn v Hamill* [1948] 1 All ER 70, CA.
102 *Cookson v Walsh* (1954) 163 EG 486.
103 Eg, *Sills v Watkins* [1956] 1 QB 250, CA, where the offer of alternative accommodation was a pre-1980 HA council tenancy with no security of tenure. Although in practice the council did not evict tenants without reason this offer did not comply with the statutory requirements.

on the facts. In one Rent Act case an unprotected fixed-term tenancy of 16 years was held to provide reasonably equivalent security.[104] In another, an unprotected fixed-term tenancy of ten years offered to a tenant aged 57 and her husband aged 58 was held to provide reasonably equivalent security.[105] It is not necessary for the alternative accommodation to be let by the same landlord. It is enough that it is available and suitable.

10.63   If the tenant against whom possession is sought occupies premises as a sole tenant, a joint tenancy or even joint ownership of a house cannot be suitable alternative accommodation since the other joint tenant or joint owner may unilaterally terminate the tenancy or force a sale.[106] It is not clear whether other premises owned by the tenant can amount to suitable alternative accommodation.[107]

Closeness to workplace

3 (1) The accommodation is reasonably suitable to the needs of the tenant and his family as regards proximity to place of work …

10.64   A 'place of work' need not be a factory or an office. It can be an area or the location in which the tenant's work is based.[108] The court should consider not only distance from work, but also the time which it would take to travel, the means of transport available and any inconvenience which would be caused.[109] The work may be unpaid.[110]

10.65   When considering the workplaces of other members of the tenant's family, the court can consider only those members actually residing with the tenant. The phrase 'member of family' is given its ordinary

---

104 *Fulford v Turpin* [1955] CLY 2324.

105 *Edwards v Cohen* (1958) 108 LJ 556.

106 *Barnard v Towers* [1953] 1 WLR 1203; [1953] 2 All ER 877, CA, *Greenwich LBC v McGrady* (1982) 6 HLR 36, CA, *Hammersmith and Fulham LBC v Monk* (1992) 39 EG 135; (1992) 24 HLR 203, HL and *Notting Hill Housing Trust v Brackley* [2001] EWCA Civ 601; [2001] 35 EG 106, CA.

107 See the conflicting dicta in *Barnard v Towers* [1953] 1 WLR 1203; [1953] 2 All ER 877, CA and *Standingford v Probert* [1950] 1 KB 377, CA.

108 *Yewbright Properties Ltd v Stone* (1980) 40 P & CR 402, CA.

109 Ibid. See also *Minchburn Ltd v Fernandez* (1987) 19 HLR 29; May 1985 *Legal Action* 66, CA, where alternative accommodation was held not to be suitable because it would have doubled the tenant's 30-minute walk to work to one hour. The needs of the particular tenant count, not those of a reasonable tenant.

110 *Dakyns v Pace* [1948] 1 KB 22.

meaning as understood by an ordinary person.[111] It has been held to include a son, daughter-in-law[112] and mother-in-law.[113] It will also now include a long-term gay or lesbian partner.[114] It is possible that a lodger may be counted as a member of the family.[115]

Rental and size

> 3 (1)(a) ... the accommodation ... is similar as regards rental and extent to the accommodation afforded by dwelling-houses provided in the neighbourhood by any local housing authority for persons whose needs as regards extent are ... similar to those of the tenant and his family; or ... reasonably suitable to the means of the tenant and to the needs of the tenant and his family as regards extent and character.

10.66 The landlord can satisfy this test in either of two ways. First, the landlord may produce a certificate from the local authority for the area in which the tenant rents his or her current accommodation setting out the kind of accommodation which would be provided for people of similar needs. The certificate should probably state the number of rooms which would be provided and give some indication as to the dimensions of such rooms.[116] A certificate which stated that local authority rents would be more than twice as high as the alternative accommodation offered did not show that the accommodation offered was similar as regards rental.[117] It is for a judge to decide, after considering the certificate, whether or not the accommodation offered is similar to that which the local authority would provide. In *Jones v Cook*[118] the Court of Appeal set aside a possession order where a judge had simply accepted the contents of a certificate which had stated that the property offered by the landlord was 'similar in extent to council-owned dwelling-houses which may be provided in the neighbour-

---

111 *Standingford v Probert* [1950] 1 KB 377, CA, *Scrace v Windust* [1955] 1 WLR 475, CA. See also, in another context, *Fitzpatrick v Sterling Housing Association* [2001] 1 AC 27; [1999] 3 WLR 1113, HL and *Ghaidan v Godin-Mendoza* [2004] UKHL 30; [2004] 3 WLR 113.

112 *Standingford v Probert* [1950] 1 KB 377, CA.

113 *Scrace v Windust* [1955] 1 WLR 475, CA.

114 *Fitzpatrick v Sterling Housing Association* [2001] 1 AC 27; [1999] 3 WLR 1113; [1999] 4 All ER 705 and *Ghaidan v Godin-Mendoza* [2004] UKHL 30; [2004] 3 WLR 113.

115 *Standingford v Probert* [1950] 1 KB 377, CA, cf, *Stewart v Mackay* 1947 SLT 250.

116 Per Edmund Davies LJ in *Macdonnell v Daly* [1969] 1 WLR 1482, CA, cf, *Wallasey v Pritchard* (1936) 3 LJNCCR 35.

117 *Turner v Keiller* 1950 SC 43 and *Robert Thackeray's Estate Ltd v Kaye* (1989) 21 HLR 160, CA.

118 (1990) 22 HLR 319, CA.

hood for families consisting of husband, wife and three children'.

10.67   If there is no local authority certificate (and it is comparatively rare for a landlord to obtain such a certificate), the court should consider whether the property offered is reasonably suitable. Accommodation may be suitable even though it is inferior to the accommodation currently occupied by the tenant.[119] It may also be suitable even though it is considerably smaller.[120] Part only of the accommodation currently rented by the tenant may amount to suitable alternative accommodation if at the time of the hearing the tenant is not occupying all of the accommodation let (for example, because part is sublet[121]) or because it is larger than the tenant requires.[122]

10.68   When the court considers the 'needs' of the tenant and the tenant's family, it should primarily consider their housing needs and not incidental advantages, such as the use of a stable and paddock.[123] The court may, however, take into account a tenant's professional needs, such as an artist using a room as a studio[124] or the need for a tenant to entertain business associates.[125] Accommodation may be unsuitable if it is too large,[126] if it is in disrepair,[127] if it lacks a bathroom and toilet,[128] if it means the tenant living with his estranged wife[129] or if

---

119 Per Lord Asquith in *Warren v Austen* [1947] 2 All ER 185, CA.

120 *Quick v Fifield* (1982) 132 NLJ 140 (less than half the size) and *Hill v Rochard* [1983] 1 WLR 478, CA.

121 *Parmee v Mitchell* [1950] 2 KB 199, CA, *Thompson v Rolls* [1926] 2 KB 426; [1926] All ER 257 and *Yoland v Reddington* (1982) 263 EG 157, CA.

122 *Macdonnell v Daly* [1969] 1 WLR 1482, CA (two out of three rooms) and *Mykolyshyn v Noah* [1970] 1 WLR 1271, CA (current accommodation less sitting room).

123 *Hill v Rochard* [1983] 1 WLR 478, CA, although such matters will be relevant when considering reasonableness. See also *Montross Associated Investments v Stone* March 2000 *Legal Action* 29, CA ('magnificent views' overlooking Hyde Park). On tenants' 'needs' generally, see H W Wilkinson 'What does a tenant need?' (1985) 135 NLJ 933 where there is a summary of the facts of some of the cases noted in the following footnotes.

124 *Macdonnell v Daly* [1969] 1 WLR 1482, CA.

125 *De Markozoff v Craig* (1949) 93 SJ 693, CA cf, *Stewart v Mackay* 1947 SLT 250 (tenant's inability to take in lodgers), *Wilcock v Booth* (1920) 122 LT 678 (loss of off-licence) and *Warren v Austen* [1947] 2 All ER 185, CA (unreasonable to make order where alternative accommodation not large enough to enable tenant to continue to take lodgers).

126 *Islington LBC v Metcalfe and Peacock* August 1983 *LAG Bulletin* 105.

127 If there is any question of disrepair in the alternative accommodation it is always wise for the tenant to obtain a full survey report.

128 *Esposito v Ware* (1950) 155 EG 383.

129 *Heglibiston Establishments v Heyman* (1977) 246 EG 567, CA.

it does not have a garden in which the tenant's children can play.[130] Accommodation in a shared house may be unsuitable for a tenant currently living alone.[131]

10.69   The court should take into account environmental factors. For example, in *Redspring Limited v Francis*[132] the alternative accommodation was on a busy traffic thoroughfare, had no garden, was next door to a fish shop and was near to a hospital, cinema and public house with the result that there were people 'coming and going' at all hours of the day and night, whereas the tenant's current accommodation was in a quiet and secluded residential street. However, environmental factors can be taken into account only so far as they relate to the character of the property. The proximity of the tenants' friends and cultural interests are not relevant here, although they clearly are relevant when the court comes to consider reasonableness.[133]

Furniture

3 (1)(b) ... if any furniture was provided for use under the assured tenancy in question, furniture is provided for use in the accommodation which is either similar to that so provided or is reasonably suitable to the needs of the tenant and his family.

Availability

... accommodation is available for the tenant or will be available for him when the order in question takes effect (see ground 9).

10.70   The suitable alternative accommodation must be available for the particular tenant.[134] In determining whether it is available, accommodation which was previously available is completely irrelevant,[135] although refusals by the tenant of previous offers of other accommodation may be considered when the court decides the question of reasonableness and may be relevant when the court considers costs. It is sufficient for the landlord to show that such accommodation is available even if it is to be rented from another person. It need not have been available when the Housing Act 1988 s8 notice was served or when proceedings were issued.

---

130 *De Markozoff v Craig* (1949) 93 SJ 693, CA, cf, in the public sector, *Enfield LBC v French* (1984) 17 HLR 211, CA.

131 *Barnard v Towers* [1953] 1 WLR 1203; [1953] 2 All ER 877, CA.

132 [1973] 1 WLR 134. See also *Dawncar Investments Ltd v Plews* [1993] 13 EG 110; (1993) 25 HLR 639, CA.

133 *Siddiqu v Rashid* [1980] 1 WLR 1018, CA.

134 *Topping v Hughes* [1925] NI 90.

135 *Kimpson v Markham* [1922] 1 KB 157.

Overcrowding

10.71 Accommodation shall not be deemed to be suitable to the needs of the tenant and his or her family if the result of their occupation of the accommodation would be that it would be an overcrowded dwelling-house for the purposes of Housing Act 1985 Pt X.[136] For the definition of overcrowding, see para 15.58.

10.72 It should be remembered that even if the court is satisfied that suitable alternative accommodation exists, the court must still consider whether it is reasonable to make a possession order. Failure to do this makes the possession order a nullity.[137]

Ground 10: Rent arrears

10.73 Some rent lawfully due from the tenant –
(a) is unpaid on the date on which the proceedings for possession are begun; and
(b) except where subsection (1)(b) of section 8 of this Act applies, was in arrears at the date of the service of the notice under that section relating to those proceedings.

Paragraph 3 of the Housing Corporation Regulatory Circular 07/04 *Tenancy Management: Eligibility and Evictions*[138] which relates to housing associations provides:

3 CLARIFICATION OF THE CORPORATION'S EXPECTATIONS: EVICTIONS

3.1 Financial circumstances

3.1.1 Housing Benefit. Possession proceedings for rent arrears should not be started against a tenant who can demonstrate that they have (1) a reasonable expectation of eligibility for housing benefit; (2) provided the local authority with all the evidence required to process a housing benefit claim; (3) paid required personal contributions towards the charges. Associations should make every effort to establish effective ongoing liaison with housing benefit departments and to make direct contact with them before taking enforcement action. A certificate should be obtained, if possible, to confirm that there are no outstanding benefit enquiries, according to Department of Work and Pensions good practice guidance.

---

136 HA 1988 Sch 2 Pt III para 4.
137 See chapter 11 and *Minchburn Estates v Fernandez (No 2)* (1986) 19 HLR 29, CA, *Treismann v Cotterell* September 1996 *Legal Action* 14 and *Hildebrand v Constable* September 1996 *Legal Action* 14.
138 See www.housingcorp.gov.uk.

3.1.2 Holistic debt advice. Tenants with rent arrears often face multiple debts.

Associations should refer tenants in arrears to holistic debt counselling services as soon as possible after the debt has arisen and should continue to do so during the recovery procedure. Possession action should not be taken where a tenant has maintained an agreement to pay the arrears.

See too the Rent Arrears Protocol referred to at para 3.35.

10.74　A landlord must prove that there were rent arrears both at the date when proceedings were begun and (unless the court considers it 'just and equitable' to dispense with service of a notice seeking possession) when the notice was served. In theory, a possession order may be made even if the arrears are paid off before the hearing, although in most circumstances there would be strong grounds for arguing that it would not be reasonable to make an order.[139]

10.75　If rent has been tendered to the landlord on a regular basis when it has become due, but has not been accepted by the landlord, there is a complete defence to the proceedings based on alleged rent arrears if the tenant pays into court all the rent which is due.[140] Accordingly, if a landlord refuses to accept rent, it is important that the tenant continues to tender rent regularly (for example, by sending cheques by recorded delivery) and saves any rejected rent in a separate bank or building society account so that the rent can be paid into court as soon as proceedings are issued.[141] Failure to provide a rent book does not disentitle the landlord from claiming that rent is lawfully due.[142]

10.76　When advising a tenant who faces a claim for possession based on rent arrears, it is important to check exactly what rent is lawfully recoverable, and, in particular, whether the landlord has been claiming too much rent. Note that if a landlord has failed to furnish the tenant with an address at which notices may be served, Landlord and Tenant Act 1987 s48 provides that any rent which would otherwise be due is to be treated as not being due before the landlord has rectified the failure.[143]

139　*Hayman v Rowlands* [1957] 1 WLR 317; [1957] 1 All ER 321, CA, *Sopwith v Stutchbury* (1983) 17 HLR 50, CA, but see *Lee-Steere v Jennings* (1988) 20 HLR 1, CA.

140　*Bird v Hildage* [1948] 1 KB 91, CA.

141　See CPR 37.3 which states that a defence of tender can only be relied upon if the amount tendered is paid into court.

142　*Shaw v Groom* [1970] 2 QB 504, CA.

143　See *Dallhold Estates (UK) Pty Ltd v Lindsay Trading Properties Inc* [1994] 17 EG 148, CA, *Hussain v Singh* [1993] 31 EG 75, CA, but cf, *Rogan v Woodfield Building Services Ltd* (1994) 27 HLR 78; [1995] 20 EG 132, CA and *Drew-Morgan v Hamid-Zadeh* (2000) 32 HLR 316; [1999] 26 EG 156, CA.

Advisers should also check whether there is any possibility of a counterclaim for breach of repairing obligations (see para 21.37), or whether there has been any failure by the relevant authorities to make payments of housing benefit (see para 32.9).

Ground 11: Persistent delay in paying rent

10.77   Whether or not any rent is in arrears on the date on which proceedings for possession are begun, the tenant has persistently delayed paying rent which has become lawfully due.

Even if there are no arrears on the date when possession proceedings are issued, persistent delay in paying rent that is due is a ground for possession. The phrase 'persistent delay' is not defined but is likely to have the same meaning as in Landlord and Tenant Act 1954 s30(1)(b), ie, one instalment of rent has been in arrears for a significant period of time or instalments have persistently been paid late, or both.[144]

10.78   It is important to check that the rent claimed was lawfully due – see paras 10.45 onwards (compliance with Landlord and Tenant Act 1987 s48, the possibility of a set-off for breach of repairing obligations, etc).

Ground 12: Breach of any obligation

10.79   Any obligation of the tenancy (other than one related to the payment of rent) has been broken or not performed.

The obligation must be one which is binding upon tenants in their capacity as tenants and not one of a personal nature or collateral to the agreement.[145] This can be determined by asking whether the obligation would be equally applicable if the tenancy were assigned to another person. For example, an obligation to remain in the employment of the landlord is a personal one, and breach of it cannot give rise to grounds for possession under ground 12. Similarly, a covenant that the tenant should give up possession by a particular date cannot be relied upon by a landlord since it is inconsistent with the provisions of the Housing Act 1988.[146]

---

144 See *Hopcutt v Carver* (1969) 209 EG 1069, CA and *Horowitz v Ferrand* [1956] CLY 4843.

145 *RMR Housing Society v Combs* [1951] 1 KB 486 [1951] 1 All ER 16, CA and *Paddington Churches Housing Association v Boateng* January 1999 *Legal Action* 27.

146 *Barton v Fincham* [1921] 2 KB 291, *Hunt v Bliss* (1919) 89 LJKB 174 and *Artizans,*

10.80   A court can make an order for possession provided that there has been a breach of an obligation under the tenancy agreement, even if it no longer exists at the date of the hearing: it is not confined to considering breaches which are existing at the time of the hearing.[147]

10.81   It is outside the scope of this book to consider in detail the meaning of covenants which may be found in tenancy agreements. The following brief points should, however, be noted.

Covenants against subletting

10.82   The exact wording of the covenant is important because the three forms of phraseology frequently used have different meanings. A 'covenant against subletting' without any further qualification is merely a prohibition against subletting the whole of the premises which are let.[148] It does not prohibit subletting of part or sharing the premises with licensees. A 'covenant against subletting the whole or any part of the premises' does prohibit the subletting of the whole or any part of the premises, but does not cover taking in lodgers or sharing the premises with anyone else who is not a formal subtenant. A covenant which is wide enough to cover all of these activities is one to the effect that the tenant 'cannot sublet the whole or any part of the premises or share occupation with any other person', or that 'the tenant can only use the premises as a private residence in his sole occupation'.[149] A tenant who has friends, who share living expenses, staying in the premises is not in breach of a covenant against parting with possession, taking lodgers or using premises for business purposes.[150] The mere fact that a name other than that of the tenant appears on the electoral register relating to the premises is not by itself evidence that anyone other than the tenant is living in the accommodation.[151]

Covenant against user for immoral purposes

10.83   This is basically designed to prevent prostitution. It does not prohibit two unmarried people living together.[152]

Labourers and General Dwellings Company Ltd v Whitaker [1919] 2 KB 301.

147 *Brown v Davies* [1958] 1 QB 117; [1957] 3 All ER 401, CA.
148 *Cook v Shoesmith* [1951] 1 KB 752, CA.
149 *Falgor Commercial SA v Alsabahia* (1986) 18 HLR 123, CA.
150 *Heglibiston Establishments v Heyman* (1977) 246 EG 567, CA. See also *Blanway Investments Ltd v Lynch* (1993) 25 HLR 378, CA.
151 *Metropolitan Properties Co Ltd v Griffiths* (1982) 43 P & CR 138, CA.
152 *Heglibiston Establishments v Heyman* (1977) 246 EG 567, CA.

Covenant against business user

10.84　This can have a wide meaning. It may include the carrying out of the activities of a political organisation on the premises[153] and the taking in of two paying lodgers.[154]

Unfair terms

10.85　If a term is unfair, it may breach the Unfair Terms in Consumer Contracts Regulations 1999.[155] These regulations (unlike the Unfair Contract Terms Act 1977) apply to tenancy agreements because landlords and tenants may be 'suppliers' and 'consumers' within the meaning of the Regulations.[156] A term is unfair if it has not been 'individually negotiated' and 'contrary to the requirement of good faith, it causes a significant imbalance in the parties' rights and obligations arising under the contract, to the detriment of the consumer'. Such a term is not binding on the tenant.[157]

Waiver of a breach

10.86　See para 15.17.

Ground 13: Waste or neglect

10.87　The condition of the dwelling-house or any of the common parts has deteriorated owing to acts of waste by, or the neglect or default of, the tenant or any other person residing in the dwelling-house and, in the case of an act of waste by, or the neglect or default of, a person lodging with the tenant or a subtenant of his, the tenant has not taken such steps as he ought reasonably to have taken for the removal of the lodger or subtenant.

For the purposes of this ground, 'common parts' means any part of a building comprising the dwelling-house and any other premises which the tenant is entitled under the terms of the tenancy to use in common with the occupiers of other dwelling-houses in which the landlord has an estate or interest.

153　*Florent v Horez* (1983) 268 EG 807, CA.

154　*Tendler v Sproule* [1947] 1 All ER 193, CA cf, *Lewis v Weldcrest Ltd* [1978] 1 WLR 1107; (1978) 247 EG 211, CA.

155　SI No 2083.

156　*R (on the application of Khatun) v Newham LBC* [2003] EWHC 2326 (Admin); [2005] QB 37.

157　Unfair Terms in Consumer Contracts Regulations 1999 paras 5(1) and 8.

This ground is similar to Rent Act 1977 Sch 15 case 3 but slightly wider, in that it applies not only to the premises let, but also to common parts.

10.88   It may apply even though there has been no breach of any term of the tenancy or of any common law duty.[158] The court should, however, take into account only neglect or waste which has taken place since the tenant became tenant of the premises. For example, in a Rent Act case where a son who was living with aged parents became a statutory tenant by succession after their death, it was wrong for the court to take into account his failure to do any works in the garden before their death.[159]

Ground 14: Nuisance or annoyance or criminal conviction

10.89 The tenant or a person residing in *or visiting* the dwelling-house –
  (a) has been guilty of conduct causing *or likely to cause* a nuisance or annoyance to a *person residing, visiting or otherwise engaging in lawful activity in the locality*, or
  (b) has been convicted of –
    (i) using the dwelling-house or allowing it to be used for immoral or illegal purposes, or
    (ii) an arrestable offence committed in, or in the locality of, the dwelling-house.

Paragraph 3 of the Housing Corporation Regulatory Circular 07/04 *Tenancy Management: Eligibility and Evictions*[160] which relates to housing associations provides:

> **3.2.1 Anti-Social Behaviour.** S.12 of the Anti-Social Behaviour Act 2003 places a statutory duty on housing associations to publish policies and procedures for tackling anti-social behaviour. These should show a commitment to using the full range of tools now available to tackle ASB. Eviction should be considered only when other interventions have failed to protect the wider community.

10.90 This ground was introduced by Housing Act 1996 s148 and replaced the more narrowly drafted ground 14 which originally appeared in Housing Act 1988 Sch 2. The *italics* denote the main changes between the old and the new grounds. It was brought into force by the Hous-

158 *Lowe v Lendrum* (1950) 159 EG 423 where it was also said that 'neglect' is used in the context of tenant-like conduct.
159 *Holloway v Povey* (1984) 15 HLR 104, CA.
160 www.housingcorp.gov.uk.

ing Act 1996 (Commencement No 7 and Savings) Order 1997[161] and applies where Housing Act 1988 s8 notices are served on or after 28 February 1997. It is identical in form to Housing Act 1985 Sch 2 ground 2 – see para 3.63.

10.91   It applies both to conduct of the tenant and the conduct of any person residing in or visiting the premises. There is no requirement that any person visiting the premises and causing a nuisance should be there lawfully. The ground is wide enough, for example, to encompass behaviour by a former partner of a tenant who has been excluded, but returns contrary to the tenant's wishes. The widening of the ground from conduct which *is* a nuisance or annoyance to neighbours to conduct which *is likely to cause nuisance or annoyance* is designed to meet two problems. First, the new ground avoids the apparent need for the landlord to produce neighbours as witnesses to whom nuisance or annoyance has been caused.[162] Second, the new ground covers nuisance or annoyance to people who are not neighbours, such as housing officers.

Arrestable offences are defined by Police and Criminal Evidence Act 1984 s24 and include all offences for which the sentence is fixed by law (for example, life imprisonment), offences for which adults may be sentenced with terms of imprisonment of five years or more, taking motor vehicles without authority and offences under Sexual Offences Act 1956 ss22 and 23 (causing prostitution of women and procuring girls under the age of 21).

Ground 14A: Violence to occupier

10.92   The dwelling-house was occupied (whether alone or with others) by *a married couple, a couple who are civil partners of each other*, or a couple living together as husband and wife, *or a couple living together as if they were civil partners* and –

(a) one or both of the partners is a tenant of the dwelling-house,
(b) the landlord who is seeking possession is a registered social landlord or a charitable housing trust,
(c) one partner has left the dwelling-house because of violence or threats of violence by the other towards –
   (i) that partner, or
   (ii) a member of the family of that partner who was residing with that partner immediately before the partner left, and

---

161 SI No 225.
162 But cf, *Frederick Platts Co v Grigor* [1950] 1 All ER 941, CA where it was held that the court can infer that nuisance or annoyance has been caused without hearing evidence from anyone affected.

(d) the court is satisfied that the partner who has left is unlikely to return.

For the purposes of this ground 'registered social landlord' and 'member of the family' have the same meaning as in Housing Act 1996 Pt I and 'charitable housing trust' means a housing trust, within the meaning of the Housing Associations Act 1985, which is a charity within the meaning of the Charities Act 1993.

10.93   Note: the words 'a married couple, a couple who are civil partners of each other,' and 'or a couple living together as if they were civil partners' were inserted in substitution for the words 'a married couple' and 'as husband and wife' by Civil Partnership Act 2004 Sch 8. The amendment was brought into force on 5 December 2005 by the Civil Partnership 2004 (Commencement No 2) Order 2005.[163]

10.94   This ground was introduced by Housing Act 1996 s149. It was brought into force by the Housing Act 1996 (Commencement No 7 and Savings) Order 1997[164] and applies where Housing Act 1988 s8 notices are served on or after 28 February 1997. It does not apply to private landlords, and is designed to enable registered social landlords or charitable housing trusts to recover possession where one partner has left because of violence or threats of violence and is unlikely to return. It is identical to HA 1985 Sch 2 Ground 2A – see para 3.101

10.95   There is no requirement that the partner who has left should give evidence to the effect that he or she is unlikely to return. It may be that such evidence would be advisable from the landlord's point of view unless the period of absence is long or there is other evidence which enables the court to draw that inference.

10.96   The term 'registered social landlord' is defined by Housing Act 1996 ss1 and 2. All housing associations on the register kept by the Housing Corporation under Housing Associations Act 1985 Pt I were automatically registered as social landlords. So far as registration since the implementation of the 1996 Act is concerned, bodies are eligible for registration as social landlords if they are:

- registered charities which are housing associations;
- societies registered under the Industrial and Provident Societies Act 1965 which are non-profit-making and established for the purpose of providing rented housing or hostels; or
- companies which are non-profit-making and established for the purpose of providing rented housing or hostels.

---

163 SI No 3175 (C.136).
164 SI No 225.

10.97 'Member of another's family' includes spouses, civil partners, people who live together as husband and wife or as if they were civil partners, parents, grandparents, children, grandchildren, brothers, sisters, uncles, aunts, nephews and nieces. Relationships of 'half-blood' are to be treated as relationships of the 'whole blood' and step-children are to be treated as children.[165]

10.98 A landlord seeking to rely upon this ground must satisfy the court that notice of proceedings for possession has been served on the partner who has left the home or that it has taken reasonable steps to do so or that it is just and equitable to dispense with the requirement of such a notice (see para 10.29).[166]

Where possession is sought under ground 14A, it is not sufficient that the alleged violence or threats of violence were merely one of a range of causes of equal efficacy in the victim's departure from the property. For the ground to be made out it has to be established that the alleged violence or threat of violence was the dominant, principal and real cause of the departure.[167]

Ground 15: Deterioration of furniture

10.99 The condition of any furniture provided for use under the tenancy has, in the opinion of the court, deteriorated owing to ill-treatment by the tenant or any other person residing in the dwelling-house and, in the case of ill-treatment by a person lodging with the tenant or by a subtenant of his, the tenant has not taken such steps as he ought reasonably to have taken for the removal of the lodger or subtenant.

Ground 16: Premises let to employees

10.100 The dwelling-house was let to the tenant in consequence of his employment by the landlord seeking possession or a previous landlord under the tenancy and the tenant has ceased to be in that employment.

This ground for possession is wider than case 8, the comparable Rent Act ground (see para 15.33). It applies whether or not the employer requires the premises for another employee. Normally, the employer and the landlord have to be the same person. However, if health service employees are employed by a health service body (for example, a health authority) but live in premises owned by the Department

165 HA 1996 s62 as amended by Civil Partnership Act 2004 Sch 8 para 51.
166 HA 1988 s8A, as inserted by HA 1996 s150.
167 *Camden LBC v Mallett* (2001) 33 HLR 20, CA.

of Health, the secretary of state, when bringing possession proceedings, may rely upon ground 16.[168]

Ground 17: Tenancy induced by false statement

10.101   The tenant is the person, or one of the persons, to whom the tenancy was granted and the landlord was induced to grant the tenancy by a false statement made knowingly or recklessly by –
(a) the tenant, or
(b) a person acting at the tenant's instigation.

This ground was introduced by Housing Act 1996 s102. It was brought into force by the Housing Act 1996 (Commencement No 7 and Savings) Order 1997 and applies where Housing Act 1988 s8 notices are served on or after 28 February 1997.

10.102   Ground 17 is identical to Housing Act 1985 Sch 2 ground 5 as amended (see para 3.116).

Demolition orders, etc

10.103 A tenant is not entitled to rely upon the protection of Housing Act 1988 or the Rent Act 1977 when a demolition order[169] is in force in relation to the premises. The effect of demolition orders is to remove security of tenure.[170] They do not, however, provide landlords with an automatic right to possession. Any tenancy must still be terminated in the normal way (for example, by notice to quit).[171] Local authorities have a statutory duty to rehouse residential occupiers who have been displaced from residential accommodation as a result of a demolition order, irrespective of whether they come within the category of 'priority need' within the meaning of Housing Act 1996 s189.[172] However, the making of a management order under Housing Act 2004 does not prevent the continuance of an assured tenancy or the continued operation of Housing Act 1988.[173]

---

168 National Health and Community Care Act 1990 s60(6) and Sch 8 para 10.
169 HA 1985 s270(3) as amended (recovery of possession after the making of a demolition order) and *Marela v Machorowski* [1953] 1 QB 565.
170 *Johnson v Felton* (1995) 27 HLR 65, CA.
171 *Aslan v Murphy (No 2)* [1990] 1 WLR 766; [1989] 3 All ER 130, CA.
172 Land Compensation Act 1973 s39(1).
173 HA 2004 s124.

10.104 Housing Act 1985 s582 restricts the recovery of possession of tenanted premises in a HMO or renewal area which have been compulsorily purchased by a local authority. The execution of any possession order may be suspended for a period of three years after the making of the compulsory purchase order – although this provision does not apply where it is the local authority that is seeking possession.[174]

Reasonableness

10.105 The criteria for establishing whether or not it is reasonable to make an order for possession against an assured tenant are the same as those used in proceedings against Rent Act protected tenants or Housing Act secure tenants (see chapter 11).

Other court orders

Removal expenses

10.106 Housing Act 1988 s11 provides:

(1) Where a court makes an order for possession of a dwelling-house let on an assured tenancy on Ground 6 or Ground 9 in Schedule 2 to this Act (but not on any other ground), the landlord shall pay to the tenant a sum equal to the reasonable expenses likely to be incurred by the tenant in removing from the dwelling-house.

(2) Any question as to the amount of the sum referred to in subsection (1) above shall be determined by agreement between the landlord and the tenant or, in default of agreement, by the court.

(3) Any sum payable to a tenant by virtue of this section shall be recoverable as a civil debt due from the landlord.

10.107 A landlord can only be compelled to pay removal expenses where possession is obtained on the grounds that the landlord wishes to demolish or reconstruct premises (ground 6) or where suitable alternative accommodation is available (ground 9).

Misrepresentation and concealment

10.108 If, after a possession order has been made, the court is satisfied that the landlord obtained the order 'by misrepresentation or concealment of material facts', the court may order the landlord to pay 'such sum

174 HA 1985 s582(7).

as appears sufficient as compensation for damage or loss sustained ... as a result of the order'.[175] Generally, a landlord who deprives a tenant of an assured tenancy by deceit is liable to a claim for damages,[176] and the tenant may be able to apply to set aside the possession order. This section, however, provides additional remedies where a landlord has obtained possession by misrepresentation or concealment. Housing Act 1988 s12 applies not only to misrepresentations made during the course of the hearing, but also to any made earlier which result in a tenant consenting to a possession order.[177]

10.109   There are few reported cases dealing with the quantum of damages. In *Neil v Kingsnorth*,[178] a case decided in 1988, a landlord converted a property into four flats and sold them off immediately after obtaining a possession order under Rent Act 1977 Sch 15 case 9. The tenant, who had found better accommodation by the date of the court hearing, obtained special damages of £180, general damages of £750 for worry and inconvenience and exemplary damages of £5,000. It seems that, unlike a claim founded in deceit, the court may, unless exemplary or aggravated damages are awarded, be limited by the wording of the section to considering the loss suffered by the tenant, and not any benefit accruing to the landlord, although tenants' advisers should bear in mind Lord Denning's comments that a statutory tenancy is a valuable asset[179] and the decision in *Murray v Lloyd*[180] where, in another context, damages for the loss of a statutory tenancy were assessed at a quarter of the vacant possession freehold value of the premises.

Adjournment, stays and suspension

10.110   If a court is satisfied that one of the mandatory grounds for possession applies, it has only the very limited power to adjourn,[181] stay or suspend an order for possession which is provided for by Housing

175   HA 1988 s12.

176   Under the tort of deceit. See *Mafo v Adams* [1970] 1 QB 548, CA.

177   *Thorne v Smith* [1947] KB 307, CA.

178   March 1988 *Legal Action* 21.

179   See remarks by Lawton LJ in *Drane v Evangelou* [1978] 1 WLR 455; [1978] 2 All ER 437 at 443, that to deprive a tenant of the roof over his or her head is one of the most serious torts imaginable. See also Clayton and Tomlinson 'Damages for loss of a Rent Act tenancy' January 1986 *Legal Action* 10.

180   [1989] 1 WLR 1060; [1990] 1 EGLR 274, ChD.

181   As to the power to adjourn in exceptional circumstances before a mandatory ground is satisfied, see para 10.51.

Act 1980 s89(1), ie, for 14 days, unless exceptional hardship would be caused, in which case the time for giving up possession may be delayed for up to six weeks. 'Exceptional hardship' is not defined by the Act and there have been no reported cases on its meaning. Otherwise, Housing Act 1988 s9 (see para 28.12) gives the court a discretion to adjourn proceedings, stay or suspend the execution of any order or postpone the date of possession for such period or periods as the court thinks fit, although when doing so the court must impose conditions relating to the payment of rent or rent arrears unless doing so would 'cause exceptional hardship ... or would otherwise be unreasonable'. This means that if a landlord satisfies the court that one of the discretionary grounds is proved, the court has exactly the same discretion as it has when making an order against a tenant enjoying the protection of the Rent Act 1977 or the Housing Act 1985.

10.111   A spouse or former spouse or civil partner or former civil partner who remains in occupation has the same rights in relation to adjournments, stays, suspensions and postponements as the tenant.[182]

---

182   HA 1988 s9(5). See chapter 30.

Reasonableness

Introduction

11.1   Issues concerning the reasonableness of the making of a possession order on discretionary grounds are considered in detail in chapter 3 – see especially 3.31 and 3.72. Readers are advised to consult that chapter first. This chapter considers particular factors concerning reasonableness which apply to assured and Rent Act tenants.

11.2   Landlords seeking possession on any of the discretionary grounds in Housing Act 1988 Sch 2 Pt II or Rent Act 1977 Sch 15 Pt I, as well as proving the ground for possession, must also satisfy the court that it is reasonable to make an order for possession. The question of reasonableness, which is an 'overriding requirement',[1] gives the court a very wide discretion.[2] Reasonableness must always be considered where a landlord has pleaded one of the discretionary grounds, so judgment cannot be entered in default in such cases.[3] Failure to consider reasonableness means that the judgment is a nullity,[4] even where the tenant consents to the possession order.[5] If the case is appealed because the county court judge failed to consider the question of 'reasonableness', it should normally be sent back to the county court for a new trial.[6] In *Cumming v Danson*[7] Lord Greene MR said:

---

1   See Megarry, *The Rent Acts*, 11th edn, Stevens, 1988, p387 and *Smith v McGoldrick* (1976) 242 EG 1047, CA.

2   *Bell London and Provincial Properties Ltd v Reuben* [1947] KB 157; [1946] 2 All ER 547, CA and *Plaschkes v Jones* (1982) 9 HLR 110, CA.

3   CPR 55.7(4). See too *Peachey Property Corporation Ltd v Robinson* [1967] 2 QB 543, CA, *Smith v Poulter* [1947] KB 339 and *Salter v Lask (No 1)* [1925] 1 KB 584.

4   *Shrimpton v Rabbits* (1924) 131 LT 478, *Minchburn v Fernandez (No 2)* (1987) 19 HLR 29, CA and *Verrilli v Idigoras* [1990] EGCS 3, CA.

5   See para 28.22 and *R v Bloomsbury and Marylebone CC ex p Blackburne* (1985) 275 EG 1273, CA (where a tenant consented to an order for possession in return for a payment of £11,000 – the order was set aside because the judge had not considered the question of reasonableness), *Hounslow LBC v McBride* (1999) 31 HLR 143, CA (in rent arrears case 'by consent' suspended possession order made without hearing evidence set aside), *R v Birmingham City Council ex p Foley* March 2001 *Legal Action* 29, QBD (nuisance suspended possession order 'by consent' set aside) and *Baygreen Properties Ltd v Gil* [2002] EWCA Civ 1340; [2002] 49 EG 126; [2003] HLR 12 (possession claim against assured shorthold tenant compromised at court by a consent order which provided that the landlord recover possession, all future proceedings be stayed, and the landlord pay the tenant £2,500 before she left the property, set aside).

6   *Smith v McGoldrick* (1976) 242 EG 1047, CA, but see a number of the cases noted at notes 43, 45 and 53. The Court of Appeal is increasingly substituting its own judgment as to reasonableness.

7   [1942] 2 All ER 653 at 655.

... in considering reasonableness ... it is, in my opinion, perfectly clear that the duty of the Judge is to take into account all relevant circumstances as they exist at the date of the hearing. That he must do in what I venture to call a broad commonsense way as a man of the world, and come to his conclusion giving such weight as he thinks right to the various factors in the situation. Some factors may have little or no weight, others may be decisive, but it is quite wrong for him to exclude from his consideration matters which he ought to take into account.

Relevant considerations

11.3   In considering reasonableness, courts should not be concerned with the propriety or impropriety of a landlord's policy or rules, but rather with 'the reasonableness in the particular case of ordering possession'.[8]

11.4   It has, however, been said that judges should only consider matters that have been expressly pleaded when taking into account reasonableness. In *Laimond Properties Ltd v Raeuchle*[9] the Vice-Chancellor indicated that a judge had been wrong to take into account matters which had not been pleaded. He should have constrained himself to those matters properly pleaded by the landlord to establish whether the order for possession should have been suspended. He said:

> In considering whether it is reasonable to make an order ... the judge should consider all the relevant circumstances: but that is not a consideration at large. It is, or should be, a consideration in accordance with the pleadings. In my judgment, the matters proposed to be relied upon by the landlord in support of the contention that it would be reasonable to make an order for possession ... must be pleaded by the landlord.

However, in practice landlords rarely follow this guidance and courts rarely penalise them for failing to do so.

11.5   There are many examples of circumstances which can be relevant:

- *The financial position of the parties.* For example, a financial gain which the landlord would receive from a possession order and the financial loss resulting to the tenant,[10] the fact that the landlord's

---

8   *Barking and Dagenham LBC v Hyatt* (1992) 24 HLR 406, CA.

9   (2001) 33 HLR 113, April 2000 *Legal Action* 31, CA.

10   *Cresswell v Hodgson* [1951] 1 All ER 710, CA, *Williamson v Pallant* [1924] All ER 623.

only motive is pecuniary gain,[11] loss of income to the tenant from subletting[12] or from taking paying guests.[13]

- *Hardship to people living with either party.* For example, overcrowding affecting the landlord's invalid sister and refugees living with them,[14] although the court may inquire as to the cause of such overcrowding.[15]
- *The length of time the tenant has lived in the premises.*[16]
- *Previous warnings by the landlord, breaches of agreements with the landlord, and earlier possession orders.*[17]
- *The landlord's reasons for wishing to obtain possession.*[18]
- *The health of the parties and their relatives.*[19]
- *The age of the parties.*[20]
- *In suitable alternative accommodation cases, the loss of amenities.* For example, a garden,[21] the importance of leisure activities and spiritual needs.[22]
- *The public interest.* In particular, in cases involving anti-social behaviour, the effect of the tenant's behaviour upon adjoining occupiers and the obligation of landlords towards other tenants.[23]

---

11 *Battlespring Ltd v Gates* (1983) 268 EG 355, CA.

12 *Yoland v Reddington* (1982) 263 EG 157, CA and *Amrit Holdings Co Ltd v Shahbakhti* [2005] EWCA Civ 339; [2005] HLR 30.

13 *Warren v Austen* [1947] 2 All ER 185, CA.

14 *Cumming v Danson* [1942] 2 All ER 653, CA. See also *Rhodes v Cornford* [1947] 2 All ER 601, CA.

15 *Wint v Monk* (1981) 259 EG 45, CA. See also *Hardie v Frediani* [1958] 1 WLR 318, CA.

16 *Battlespring v Gates* (1983) 268 EG 355, CA, *Minchburn v Fernandez (No 2)* (1986) 19 HLR 29, CA, *Hildebrand v Constable* September 1996 *Legal Action* 14, *Laimond Properties Ltd v Raeuchle* [2000] L & TR 319, December 1999 *Legal Action* 21, (2001) 33 HLR 113, CA and *Gallagher v Castle Vale Housing Action Trust* [2001] EWCA Civ 944; (2001) 33 HLR 72, CA.

17 *Laimond Properties Ltd v Raeuchle* December 1999 *Legal Action* 21; (2001) 33 HLR 113, CA. *Manchester City Council v Higgins* [2005] EWCA Civ 1423; [2006] 1 All ER 841.

18 *Minchburn v Fernandez (No 2)* (1986) 19 HLR 29, CA.

19 *Briddon v George* [1946] 1 All ER 609, *Hensman v McIntoch* (1954) 163 EG 322, *Williamson v Pallant* [1924] 2 KB 173; [1924] All ER 623 and *Croydon LBC v Moody* (1999) 31 HLR 738, CA.

20 *Battlespring v Gates* (1983) 268 EG 355, CA.

21 *Warren v Austen* [1947] 2 All ER 185, CA.

22 *Siddiqu v Rashid* [1980] 1 WLR 1018, CA.

23 *West Kent Housing Association v Davies* (1999) 31 HLR 415, CA, *Cresswell v Hodgson* [1951] 2 KB 92; [1951] 1 All ER 710, CA, *Woking BC v Bistram* (1995) 27 HLR 1, CA, *Wandsworth LBC v Hargreaves* (1994) 27 HLR 142, CA, *Grogan v Greenwich LBC* (2001) 33 HLR 140; (2000) *Times* 28 March, CA, *Portsmouth*

- *The conduct of the parties.* For example, a tenant's past failure to decorate or tend the garden,[24] or lies told by parties in court to substantiate their claim.[25] Where there is an admitted breach of covenant and the tenant intends to continue breaching the covenant, possession should only be refused in 'very special cases'.[26] It may be reasonable to make a possession order where the behaviour complained of is not that of the tenant, but that of other family members where the tenant has failed to prevent that behaviour,[27] but not necessarily against a tenant who is powerless to rectify the situation,[28] or where the person responsible for the anti-social behaviour has left.[29]
- *In rent arrears cases, whether or not the tenant is entitled to welfare benefits and, if so, whether or not they have been paid.*[30]

11.6 Particular factors relating to reasonableness apply to the various grounds for possession.

Rent arrears

11.7 In proceedings based on rent arrears, a judge who has found that a ground for possession is proved should first ask whether it is reasonable to make a possession order at all and then ask whether the order should be postponed or execution stayed or suspended under Housing Act 1988 s9 or Rent Act 1977 s100(2).[31]

11.8 In practice it is rare for the court to consider it reasonable to make an absolute order for possession unless there are substantial arrears. See, for example, *Woodspring DC v Taylor*[32] at para 3.33. It is very

City Council v Bryant [2000] EHLR 287; (2000) 32 HLR 906, CA and *Wallasey v Pritchard* (1936) 3 LJNCCR 35. See too the cases listed at note 43.

24 *Brown v Davies* [1958] 1 QB 117; [1957] 3 All ER 401, CA and *Holloway v Povey* (1984) 15 HLR 104, CA.

25 *Yelland v Taylor* [1957] 1 WLR 459; [1957] 1 All ER 627, CA.

26 *Sheffield CC v Green* (1994) 26 HLR 349, CA.

27 *Kensington and Chelsea RLBC v Simmonds* [1996] 3 FCR 246; (1997) 29 HLR 507, CA, *West Kent Housing Association v Davies* (1999) 31 HLR 415, CA and *Newcastle upon Tyne CC v Morrison* (2000) 32 HLR 891, [2000] L & TR 333, CA.

28 *Portsmouth City Council v Bryant* (2000) 32 HLR 906; [2000] EHLR 287, CA; cf *Knowsley HT v McMullen* [2006] EWCA Civ 539; (2006) *Times* 22 May.

29 *Gallagher v Castle Vale Housing Action Trust* [2001] EWCA Civ 944; (2001) 33 HLR 810, CA.

30 *Brent LBC v Marks* (1999) 31 HLR 343, CA and *Second WRVS Housing Society v Blair* (1987) 19 HLR 104, CA.

31 *Laimond Properties Ltd v Raeuchle* (2001) 33 HLR 113; April 2000 *Legal Action* 31, CA.

32 (1982) 4 HLR 95, CA.

unusual for any order for possession to be made if all the arrears have been paid into court before the hearing or if the arrears are very low,[33] although it may be reasonable to make an order if the tenant has a bad history of payment and, in particular, if proceedings based on rent arrears have been issued in the past.[34] The possibility of payment of housing benefit direct to the landlord may be an important factor when a tenant argues that it is not reasonable to make a possession order.[35] If arrears are in the region of a few hundred pounds, the court may adjourn on terms or make a suspended or postponed order for possession.[36] In *Laimond Properties Ltd v Raeuchle*[37] where, at the date of trial, there were arrears of £511.10 and the tenant had offered to pay £10 per week, Sedley LJ on granting permission to appeal, said that, in his experience:

> ... it would have been unique to find an outright order made in circumstances such as these, even against a tenant as difficult as this one where there was no history (and there was none) of breaches of the conditions upon which previous orders have been suspended. There was indeed no history of suspended possession orders.

11.9   If tenants have withheld rent because they believed that they had a counterclaim based on breach of the landlord's repairing obligations, but at court the tenants lose on that issue, it is normally not reasonable for the court to make an absolute order without giving tenants the opportunity to pay the arrears, although the position may be different if tenants fail to make any offer to pay off the arrears and have a history of non-payment.[38]

Breaches of obligation and anti-social behaviour

11.10   If possession proceedings are brought on the grounds of breach of an obligation in the tenancy, much depends on the seriousness of the breach and the tenant's intention. For example, if there is a breach which is 'trivial' and which 'cannot injure the plaintiff in any way at

---

33 *Hayman v Rowlands* [1957] 1 WLR 317; [1957] 1 All ER 321, CA, *Sopwith v Stutchbury* (1985) 17 HLR 50, CA, but see *Lee-Steere v Jennings* (1988) 20 HLR 1, CA.

34 *Dellenty v Pellow* [1951] 2 KB 858; [1951] 2 All ER 716, CA.

35 Cf, *Second WRVS Housing Society v Blair* (1987) 19 HLR 104, CA.

36 Suspended possession orders are described by Lord Denning MR as 'everyday practice' in *Hayman v Rowlands* [1957] 1 WLR 317; [1957] 1 All ER 321, CA.

37 [2000] L & TR 319, December 1999 *Legal Action* 21, CA.

38 *Lal v Nakum* (1982) 1 HLR 50, CA. See also *Lombard Realty Co v Shailer* [1955] CLY 2366 and *Haringey LBC v Stewart* [1991] 2 EGLR 252; 23 HLR 557, CA.

all' it will not be reasonable to make any order.[39] The same applies if a breach is committed in innocence, with the tenant believing that no breach was being committed.[40] Very occasionally it may be unreasonable for the court to make an order for possession even if the tenant intends to continue breaching the covenant, despite the fact that the covenant itself is reasonable.[41] Usually, however, tenants indicate that they will not breach the particular covenant in future and, if the past breaches have not been serious, the court makes an order which is suspended or postponed on condition that the tenant does not commit further breaches.[42]

11.11   Anti-Social Behaviour Act 2003 s16 introduced new Housing Act 1988 s9A which provides:

(1) ... if the court is considering ... whether it is reasonable to make an order for possession on ground 14 ...
(2) The court must consider, in particular –
   (a) the effect that the nuisance or annoyance has had on persons other than the person against whom the order is sought;
   (b) any continuing effect the nuisance or annoyance is likely to have on such persons;
   (c) the effect that the nuisance or annoyance would be likely to have on such persons if the conduct is repeated.

11.12   In serious anti-social behaviour cases involving nuisance to other tenants and/or drug-dealing, courts are increasingly making absolute possession orders.[43] It has been said that courts should not force

---

39 *Upjohn v MacFarlane* [1922] 2 Ch 256.

40 Ibid.

41 *Bell London and Provincial Properties Ltd v Reuben* [1947] KB 157; [1946] 2 All ER 547, CA and *Metropolitan Properties v Crawford and Wetherill* March 1987 *Legal Action* 20. See also *Tideway Investment and Property Holdings Ltd v Wellwood* [1952] Ch 791; [1952] 2 All ER 514, CA. Cf, *Sheffield City Council v Jepson* (1993) 25 HLR 299, CA.

42 See, eg, *Norwich City Council v Famuyiwa* [2004] EWCA Civ 1770; (2005) *Times* 24 January.

43 *Bristol City Council v Mousah* (1997) 30 HLR 32, CA, *Kensington and Chelsea RLBC v Simmonds* (1997) 29 HLR 507, CA, *West Kent Housing Association v Davies* (1999) 31 HLR 415; [1998] EGCS 103, CA, *Newcastle upon Tyne City Council v Morrison* (2000) 32 HLR 891; [2000] L & TR 333, CA, *Canterbury City Council v Lowe* (2001) 33 HLR 53; [2001] L & TR 14; January 2001 *Legal Action* 26, CA, *London and Quadrant Housing Trust v Root* [2005] EWCA Civ 43; [2005] HLR 28, *New Charter Housing (North) Ltd v Ashcroft* [2004] EWCA Civ 310; [2004] HLR 36 and *Manchester City Council v Higgins* [2005] EWCA Civ 1423; [2006] 1 All ER 841, cf, *Arena HA v Crossland* June 2002 *Legal Action* 26; 4 April 2002, Wigan County Court (assured tenant, arrested for possession of cannabis with intent to supply. District judge satisfied that the grounds for possession were proved but not that it was reasonable to order possession) and

neighbours to live alongside people who behave in a grossly offensive manner.[44] However, an outright possession order may not be appropriate where the anti-social behaviour was not caused by the tenant, but by a member of the tenant's family who has since left the premises, with the result that the chances of recurrence are reduced.[45]

11.13 Another exception to the practice of making suspended or postponed orders occurs where there has been breach of a covenant against immoral user (ie, prostitution). In such cases it has been held that it is prima facie reasonable to make an immediate order for possession.[46]

11.14 Where allegations that the tenant has neglected premises have been substantiated, it may be unreasonable to make an order for possession without giving the tenant an opportunity to put matters right.[47]

Landlord requiring occupation

11.15 In proceedings brought under Rent Act 1977 Sch 15 case 9, the overriding question of reasonableness has to be considered separately and independently from the question of whether or not the premises are reasonably required by the landlord (see below). The mere fact that it has been found that the landlord reasonably requires the premises does not mean that it is reasonable to make an order for possession: 'because a wish is reasonable, it does not follow that it is reasonable in a court to gratify it'.[48]

Tai Cymdogaeth Cyfngedig v Griffiths February 2003 *Legal Action* 36; 7 August 2002, Swansea County Court (defendant convicted of possessing significant amounts of amphetamine and cannabis resin on four occasions between July 2000 and May 2001 and once in November 2000 of possessing cannabis resin with intent to supply. HHJ Hickinbottom rejected the suggestion that any burden moves to the tenant to prove 'exceptional circumstances' to avoid a possession order, and, allowing the tenant's appeal, made a suspended possession order).

44 *Devon and Cornwall HA v Morgan* [2002] 3 CL 418, Plymouth County Court (campaign of bullying behaviour against neighbours, including threatening behaviour and throwing paint, rubbish and excrement into their garden. The existence of an ASBO was not a sufficient reason for declining to make a possession order).

45 *Gallagher v Castle Vale Housing Action Trust* [2001] EWCA Civ 944; (2001) 33 HLR 810, CA, cf, *London and Quadrant Housing Trust v Root* [2005] EWCA Civ 43; [2005] HLR 28 and *New Charter Housing (North) Ltd v Ashcroft* [2004] EWCA Civ 310; [2004] HLR 36.

46 *Yates v Morris* [1951] 1 KB 77 at 80 and 81, CA – although in *Yates* the order was in fact suspended.

47 *Holloway v Povey* (1984) 15 HLR 104, CA.

48 *Shrimpton v Rabbits* (1924) 131 LT 478.

Reasonableness and the Disability Discrimination Act 1995

11.16 The importance of the Disability Discrimination Act 1995 in the context of possession proceedings is considered in para 3.94. Readers should consider this whenever a tenant's behaviour is the result of a disability.

Appeals on questions of reasonableness

11.17 Although County Courts Act 1984 s77(6) excludes appeals against judges' findings of fact, it does not exclude, in a proper case, the possibility of an appeal against a finding of reasonableness.[49]

11.18 Reasonableness is above all a question of judgment based on the particular circumstances of each case. In the past it was generally difficult for a party who was dissatisfied with a judge's determination in respect of reasonableness to succeed on appeal[50] unless it could be shown that:

- there was no evidence to support the judge's determination; or
- the judge took into account irrelevant considerations or failed to take into account relevant considerations;[51] or
- no reasonable judge could have made such a finding.[52]

11.19 In recent years, however, there has been an increasing tendency for the Court of Appeal to overturn first instance decisions on

49 *Castle Vale Housing Action Trust v Gallagher* [2001] EWCA Civ 944; (2001) 33 HLR 810, CA.
50 Eg, *Pazgate Ltd v McGrath* (1984) 17 HLR 127 at 134, CA, *Lee-Steere v Jennings* (1988) 20 HLR 1, CA, *Rushcliffe BC v Watson* (1992) 24 HLR 124, CA, *Dawncar Investments Ltd v Plews* [1993] 13 EG 110; (1993) 25 HLR 639, CA, *Dame Margaret Hungerford Charity Trustees v Beazeley* [1993] 29 EG 100, CA, *Moray DC v Lyon* [1992] GWD 14–824, *Haringey LBC v Stewart* (1991) 23 HLR 557; [1991] 2 EGLR 252, CA and *Bristol CC v Grimmer* [2003] EWCA Civ 1582; 22 October 2003 where Hale LJ said that whether or not to make an outright possession order 'is pre-eminently a difficult judgment that has to be made by the judge who is hearing the evidence and seeing the parties'. Cf, *Mathews v Ahmed* (1985) CAT No 2, noted at (1985) 7 CL 3, *Sheffield CC v Jepson* (1993) 25 HLR 299, CA and *Westminster City Council v Garcia* August 2000 *Legal Action* 24, CA. See also County Courts Act 1984 s77(6).
51 See, eg, *Barking and Dagenham LBC v Hyatt and Hyatt* (1992) 24 HLR 406, CA and *Croydon LBC v Moody* (1999) 31 HLR 738, CA.
52 *Yoland v Reddington* (1982) 263 EG 157, CA.

reasonableness, even when they do not come within these limited categories.[53]

11.20   Where evidence has been given in a county court hearing which is relevant to the question of reasonableness, the Court of Appeal assumes that the judge had that evidence in mind when making an order even if it was not expressly referred to in the judgment.[54]

Article 8 and reasonableness

11.21   The Court of Appeal has doubted whether article 8 of the European Convention on Human Rights makes any difference to the way in which courts have always approached questions of the reasonableness of making a possession order. Article 8 does, however, reinforce the importance of only making an order depriving someone of his or her other home in circumstances where a clear case is made out.[55]

---

53 See, eg, *Bristol City Council v Mousah* (1997) 30 HLR 32, CA, *Grogan v Greenwich LBC* (2000) *Times* 28 March, CA, *Taj v Ali* [2000] 43 EG 183; (2001) 33 HLR 253, CA and *Newcastle upon Tyne City Council v Morrison* (2000) 32 HLR 891; [2000] L & TR 333, CA.

54 *Tendler v Sproule* [1947] 1 All ER 193, CA. See *Rhodes v Cornford* [1947] 2 All ER 601, CA, but cf, *Minchburn v Fernandez (No 2)* (1986) 19 HLR 29, CA and *Dame Margaret Hungerford Charity Trustees v Beazeley* [1993] 29 EG 100, CA.

55 *Gallagher v Castle Vale Housing Action Trust* [2001] EWCA Civ 944; (2001) 33 HLR 810, CA.

Termination of contractual tenancies

continued

Introduction

12.1 This chapter is relevant whenever a landlord is seeking a possession order against:

- unprotected tenants who lack any statutory security of tenure; or
- Rent Act protected tenants.

It is not relevant to secure or assured tenants who continue to occupy their homes as their only or principal residence.

12.2 Before a landlord can succeed in obtaining a possession order against an unprotected tenant or any Rent Act protected tenant, the original contractual tenancy must be terminated. If a landlord fails to prove that this has happened, the tenant has a complete defence to possession proceedings,[1] even if the landlord has grounds[2] for possession. If tenants have full Rent Act protection (ie, as protected tenants) and occupy the premises as their residence, the effect of the termination is to convert the tenancy into a statutory tenancy.[3]

12.3 The most common ways in which a contractual tenancy can be terminated are by expiry of a fixed-term tenancy, service of a notice to quit by a landlord or tenant, surrender, forfeiture and, in some circumstances, service of a notice of increase of rent. These various methods are considered in more detail in the following sections.

Expiry of fixed-term tenancies

12.4 If a tenancy is initially granted for a fixed period ('a fixed term') such as six months or one year, the contractual tenancy normally ends at the expiry of that period by the passing of time. If the tenancy is a protected tenancy,[4] any tenant who still occupies the premises as his or her residence automatically becomes a statutory tenant. If a fixed-term tenancy has expired, a landlord usually need not serve a notice to quit before bringing possession proceedings because the contractual tenancy has already been terminated.[5] Occasionally, however, the terms of the original contractual tenancy may be such that it continues even after the expiry of the initial fixed-term period. For example, if the tenancy agreement states that the tenancy is for a term

---

1 *Wallis v Semark* [1951] 2 TLR 222, CA.
2 See below and RA 1977 Sch 15 cases 1 to 20.
3 RA 1977 s2(1)(a).
4 RA 1977 s1 and see para 13.4.
5 RA 1977 s3(4) and *Morrison v Jacobs* [1945] KB 577.

'of one year, and thereafter from month to month until determined by notice to quit', the landlord will have to terminate the contractual tenancy after the expiry of the initial year before bringing possession proceedings.

12.5   Once a fixed-term tenancy has come to an end by the passing of time, the courts generally lean against implying a new contractual tenancy, unless there has been an express agreement for a new tenancy. The fact that a tenant continues to pay rent does not by itself imply a new contractual tenancy.[6] Occasionally, however, a landlord and a tenant may make an express agreement which will be construed either as commencing a new contractual tenancy or as a variation of the original tenancy, which means that a contractual tenancy continues to exist.[7] In such a case a landlord has to serve a notice to quit before starting possession proceedings.

Notice to quit by landlord or tenant

12.6   The most common way of terminating a contractual periodic[8] tenancy is by either the landlord or the tenant serving a notice to quit. Unlike surrender (see below), when both parties agree to the tenancy coming to an end, a notice to quit operates to terminate the contractual tenancy whether or not the other party agrees. If the tenancy has not been terminated in any other way, failure to serve a valid notice to quit is a complete defence to possession proceedings.[9] Similarly tenants have a complete defence to possession claims if court proceedings are issued before the expiry of the notice to quit.[10] A notice to quit should be strictly construed by the court. If invalid, it cannot be amended.[11] It is for a landlord seeking possession to prove that a valid notice to quit has been served.[12]

---

6   *Morrison v Jacobs* [1945] KB 577, cf, *Hartell v Blackler* [1920] 2 KB 161. See also *Longrigg, Burrough and Trounson v Smith* (1979) 251 EG 847, *Cardiothoracic Institute v Shrewdcrest Ltd* [1986] 3 All ER 633, *Westminster City Council v Basson* (1991) 23 HLR 225; [1991] 1 EGLR 277 and *Burrows v Brent LBC* [1996] 1 WLR 1448; [1996] 4 All ER 577, HL.

7   *Bungalows (Maidenhead) Ltd v Mason* [1954] 1 WLR 769.

8   That is, a tenancy which was not originally granted for a fixed period of time.

9   See, eg, *Plaschkes v Jones* (1982) 9 HLR 110 and *Franklyn v Tingey* (1975) BLT No 441A; (1976) 120 NLJ 767.

10   *Beaney v Branchett* [1987] 2 EGLR 115.

11   *Precious v Reedie* [1924] 2 KB 149.

12   *Lemon v Lardeur* [1946] KB 613.

12.7   Notices to quit have no application during a fixed-term tenancy unless the tenancy agreement contains a break clause which expressly provides that it may be terminated by a notice to quit. The normal method for a landlord to terminate a fixed-term tenancy before it expires is by forfeiture (see below). There is no need for a notice to quit where the tenancy has already become a Rent Act statutory tenancy.[13]

12.8   A notice to quit must comply both with the statutory requirements of Protection from Eviction Act 1977 s5 and with common law requirements.

Protection from Eviction Act 1977 s5

(1) Subject to subsection (1B) below no notice by a landlord or a tenant to quit any premises let (whether before or after the commencement of this Act) as a dwelling shall be valid unless –

(a) it is in writing and contains such information as may be prescribed, and

(b) it is given not less than 4 weeks before the date on which it is to take effect.

(1A) Subject to subsection (1B) below, no notice by a licensor or licensee to determine a periodic licence to occupy premises as a dwelling (whether the licence was granted before or after the passing of this Act) shall be valid unless –

(a) it is in writing and contains such information as may be prescribed, and

(b) it is given not less than 4 weeks before the date on which it is to take effect.

(1B) Nothing in subsection (1) or subsection (1A) above applies to –

(a) premises let on an excluded tenancy which is entered into on or after the date on which the Housing Act 1988 came into force unless it is entered into pursuant to a contract made before that date; or

(b) premises occupied under an excluded licence.

(2) In this section 'prescribed' means prescribed by regulations made by the Secretary of State by statutory instrument, and a statutory instrument containing any such regulations shall be subject to annulment in pursuance of a resolution of either House of Parliament.

(3) Regulations under this section may make different provision in relation to different descriptions of lettings and different circumstances.

13   RA 1977 s3(4) and *Morrison v Jacobs* [1945] KB 577.

Subsections (1A) and (1B) were inserted by Housing Act 1988 s32. Note that Protection from Eviction Act 1977 s5 does not apply to an agricultural holding, even if it includes a dwelling.[14]

12.9   Protection from Eviction Act 1977 s5 now applies to:

- all tenancies granted before 15 January 1989;
- all licences whenever created, apart from excluded licences;
- all tenancies granted on or after 15 January 1989, apart from excluded tenancies.

12.10   Tenancies and licences are excluded if:

- the occupier shares with the landlord or licensor accommodation which is part of his or her 'only or principal home'. However, a tenancy or licence is not 'excluded' if the accommodation shared consists only of storage areas or means of access, such as corridors or staircases;
- the occupier lives in the same building as the landlord or licensor and shares accommodation with a member of the landlord's or licensor's family. The definition of 'member of the family' which appears in Housing Act 1985 s113 applies. This includes spouses or civil partners, people living together as husband and wife or as civil partners, parents, children, grandparents, grandchildren, siblings, uncles and aunts;
- the tenancy or licence is granted as a temporary expedient to a person who entered the premises or any other premises as a trespasser;
- the tenancy or licence merely confers the right to occupy for a holiday;
- the tenancy or licence is not granted for money or money's worth;
- a licensee occupies a hostel provided by a local authority, development corporation, housing action trust, the Housing Corporation, a housing trust, etc;[15]
- The tenancy or licence is granted to provide accommodation to an asylum seeker through the National Asylum Support Service under Immigration and Asylum Act 1999 Pt VI.[16]

12.11   Protection from Eviction Act 1977 s5 applies to notices served by both landlords and tenants. However, the Notices to Quit etc (Prescribed

---

14   *National Trust v Knipe* [1997] 4 All ER 627; (1998) 30 HLR 449; [1997] 2 EGLR 9; (1997) *Times* 21 June, CA.

15   Protection from Eviction Act 1977 s3A inserted by HA 1988 s31.

16   See Immigration and Asylum Act 1999 Sch 14 para 73.

Information) Regulations 1988,[17] which specify what information must be included, apply only to landlords. Tenants' notices to quit must accordingly give four weeks' notice and be in writing, but need not follow any particular form.[18]

12.12 The requirement for a minimum of four weeks' notice does not mean 28 'clear' days.[19] In calculating the four weeks, one should include the day on which the notice to quit is served, but not the last day referred to in the notice to quit. A notice served on a Friday complies with Protection from Eviction Act 1977 s5 if it expires on a Friday four weeks later.[20]

12.13 The 'prescribed information' to be included in notices served by landlords is contained in the Schedule to the Notices to Quit etc (Prescribed Information) Regulations 1988:

> 1 If the tenant or licensee does not leave the dwelling, the landlord or licensor must get an order for possession from the court before the tenant or licensee can lawfully be evicted. The landlord or licensor cannot apply for such an order before the notice to quit or notice to determine has run out.

> 2 A tenant or licensee who does not know if he has any right to remain in possession after a notice to quit or notice to determine runs out can obtain advice from a solicitor. Help with all or part of the cost of legal advice and assistance may be available under the Legal Aid Scheme. He should also be able to obtain information from a Citizens' Advice Bureau, a Housing Aid Centre or a Rent Officer.

12.14 It has been held that an old, standard-form notice to quit which complied with the former regulations[21] but which was served after the introduction of the Notices to Quit etc (Prescribed Information) Regulations 1980,[22] was effective in terminating a tenancy, even though it did not follow the precise wording of the current regulations. Similarly, a notice to quit served on a tenant in 1989 which complied with the 1980 Regulations but not the 1988 Regulations was also held to be valid. The position might well be different if, for some reason,

---

17 SI No 2201.
18 See *Hounslow LBC v Pilling* [1993] 1 WLR 1242; [1994] 1 All ER 432, CA and *Laine v Cadwallader* [2001] L & TR 77; (2001) 33 HLR 397, CA.
19 *Schnabel v Allard* [1967] 1 QB 627.
20 Ibid, where a notice given on Friday 4 March to expire on Friday 1 April was held to be good.
21 Notices to Quit (Prescribed Information) (Protected Tenancies and Part VI Contracts) Regulations 1975 SI No 2196.
22 SI No 1624.

confusion or uncertainty was caused by using the old form rather than the current form.[23]

12.15   It has been held that it is possible for a landlord and tenant to waive the requirements of Protection from Eviction Act 1977 s5.[24]

Common law

12.16   A notice to quit must comply with the common law rules (see below) relating to validity. The first such requirement is that the notice must comply with any express provisions relating to service or validity which are contained in the tenancy agreement. Any such express provision overrides the rules, which are implied where there is no express provision. However, no express provision in the tenancy agreement can override Protection from Eviction Act 1977 s5. An express provision may, for example, state that a notice to quit should give more notice than usual[25] or less notice than usual. Similarly an express provision may provide that a notice to quit may be validly served in the middle of a rental period.[26] They may also restrict the circumstances in which a landlord may serve a notice to quit.

Clarity and timing

12.17   The main common law requirement is that a notice to quit should state with certainty when the notice expires. Landlords have a duty:

> ... to give notices in terms which are sufficiently clear and unambiguous in that the right date is either stated or can be ascertained by the tenant by reference to his tenancy agreement with the terms of which he must be taken to be familiar ...[27]

12.18   The time between the date on which notice is served and the date on which it purports to take effect should be at least as much as the rental period of the tenancy.[28] If the tenancy is a monthly tenancy, the notice to quit should give at least one month's notice. If the tenancy is a quarterly tenancy, the notice should give at least three months'

---

23   *Beckerman v Durling* (1981) 6 HLR 87, CA and *Swansea CC v Hearn* (1991) 23 HLR 284, CA, cf, *Shah v Emmanuel* December 1988 *Legal Action* 17.

24   *Hackney LBC v Snowden* (2001) 33 HLR 49, CA and *Lewisham LBC v Lasisi-Agiri* [2003] EWHC 2392 (Ch); [2003] 45 EGCS 175.

25   *Doe d Peacock v Raffan* (1806) 6 Esp 4.

26   *Charles Clay & Sons Ltd v British Railways Board* [1970] 2 All ER 463, ChD.

27   *Addis v Burrows* [1948] 1 KB 444; [1948] 1 All ER 177 at 182 per Evershed LJ.

28   *Doe d Peacock v Raffan* (1806) 6 Esp 4. See also *Manorlike Ltd v Le Vitas* [1986] 1 All ER 573, CA for the meaning of 'within three months'.

notice.[29] However, in addition to giving the correct length of time, it is vital that the notice expires on the correct day. A notice to quit a weekly tenancy may expire either on the same day as the date on which the tenancy commenced or on the date on which the rent is paid[30] or on the day before.[31] For example, if the tenancy began on the first day of the month or rent is payable on the first day of the month, the notice may validly expire on the first or last day of the month.[32] Any notice to quit expiring on any other day is completely invalid and the tenant will have a complete defence to possession proceedings.[33] The normal rule is that a contractual tenancy ends at midnight on the date on which the notice to quit expires.[34] The Civil Procedure Rules do not apply when calculating time in relation to service of a notice to quit.

12.19 Possession proceedings cannot be issued until the notice to quit has expired. It is usual for landlords to serve notices to quit which as well as giving a specific date also include the phrase 'or at the end of the period of your tenancy which will end next after the expiration of four weeks from the service upon you of this notice'. Such a saving clause is valid[35] provided that proceedings are not issued before the date on which the tenancy could have been validly determined.

12.20 Although the overriding consideration is that a notice to quit must be clear and unambiguous, it may well be that minor misdescriptions are not fatal. The question which a court should ask is: 'Is the notice quite clear to a reasonable tenant reading it? Is it plain that he cannot be misled by it?'[36] For example, a notice referring to 'The Waterman's Arms' which should have referred to 'The Bricklayer's Arms'

---

29 *Lemon v Lardeur* [1946] KB 613. A yearly tenancy can be determined by six months' notice.

30 *Crane v Morris* [1965] 1 WLR 1104 and *Harley v Calder* (1989) 21 HLR 214; [1989] 1 EGLR 88, CA. As to a yearly tenancy see *Sidebotham v Holland* [1895] 1 QB 378.

31 *Newman v Slade* [1926] 2 KB 328 and *Harley v Calder* (1989) 21 HLR 214; [1989] 1 EGLR 88, CA.

32 *Precious v Reedie* [1924] 2 KB 149 and *Queen's Club Gardens Estates v Bignell* [1924] 1 KB 117. Note the definition of 'month' in Law of Property Act 1925 s61(a).

33 *Precious v Reedie* [1924] 2 KB 149 and *Queen's Club Gardens Estates v Bignell* [1924] 1 KB 117.

34 *Bathavon RDC v Carlile* [1958] 1 All ER 801.

35 *Addis v Burrows* [1948] 1 All ER 177, *Bathavon RDC v Carlile* [1958] 1 All ER 801 and *Queen's Club Gardens Estates v Bignell* [1924] 1 KB 117.

36 *Carradine Properties Ltd v Aslam* [1976] 1 All ER 573 at 576 per Goulding J approved in *Mannai Investment Co Ltd v Eagle Star Life Assurance Co Ltd* [1997] AC 749, HL.

has been held to be valid.[37] Similarly, a notice served in 1974 stating that the tenant should give up possession in 1973 rather than 1975 has been held to be valid because it was clear to the tenant that there was a clerical error and the landlord intended the notice to refer to 1975.[38]

12.21   There are no common law requirements relating to signature of notices to quit. It is necessary only that a tenant should be able to ascertain who has sent the notice to quit. A notice to quit must include all of the premises let under the particular tenancy agreement. A notice to quit which purports to terminate a tenant's interest in only part of the property covered by the tenancy is completely ineffective.[39]

Service

12.22   A notice to quit may be served either by a landlord or tenant or by an authorised agent. In some circumstances a notice to quit may be given in the name of the agent[40] but it is more usual for notice served by an agent to state that it is served 'for and on behalf of' the landlord. One joint owner may validly serve notice to quit on behalf of other joint owners even if they are not named in the notice.[41] Similarly, one joint tenant may serve a notice to quit on the landlord and so determine the contractual tenancy even if the other joint tenant does not agree.[42] A notice to quit served by a landlord on only one out of several joint tenants is sufficient to determine the joint contractual tenancy.[43] It is not possible for a landlord to purport to terminate one joint tenant's interest in the premises without determining the interest of the other joint tenants.[44]

37   *Doe d Armstrong v Wilkinson* (1840) 1 A & E 743. Cf, *Jankovitch v Petrovitch* August 1978 *LAG Bulletin* 189, CA.

38   *Carradine Properties Ltd v Aslam* [1976] 1 All ER 573.

39   *Woodward v Dudley* [1954] Ch 283.

40   See *Lemon v Lardeur* [1946] KB 613.

41   *Doe d Aslin v Summersett* (1830) 1 B & Ad 135 and *Annen v Rattee* (1984) 17 HLR 323, CA. Cf, *Jacobs v Chaudhuri* [1968] 2 All ER 124, *Featherstone v Staples* [1986] 2 All ER 461, CA and *Leckhampton Dairies Ltd v Artus Whitfield* (1986) 130 SJ 225.

42   *Hammersmith LBC v Monk* [1992] 1 AC 478, HL, *Greenwich LBC v McGrady* (1982) 6 HLR 36, *Crawley BC v Ure* (1995) 27 HLR 524, CA and *Notting Hill Housing Trust v Brackley* [2001] EWCA Civ 601; [2002] HLR 212. Cf, *Harrow LBC v Johnstone* (1996) 28 HLR 83, CA, *Hounslow LBC v Pilling* 1993] 1 WLR 1242; [1994] 1 All ER 432, CA and *Hackney LBC v Snowden* (2001) 33 HLR 554; [2001] L & TR 60, CA.

43   *Doe d Bradford v Watkins* (1806) 7 East 551 and *Hammersmith and Fulham LBC v Monk* [1992] 1 AC 478; [1991] 3 WLR 1144; [1992] 1 All ER 1; (1992) 39 EG 135; (1992) 24 HLR 206.

44   *Greenwich LBC v McGrady* (1982) 6 HLR 36.

12.23   The notice to quit must be served on or before the date in the notice from which time starts to run, otherwise it is invalid and totally ineffective. It need not be served personally by handing it to the tenant. However, the common law rules on what is otherwise valid service are far from clear. There are few recent cases and many of the reported cases appear to conflict. It has been held sufficient to leave a notice to quit with a tenant's wife or servant even though it did not actually come to the tenant's attention before the time started running. On the other hand, service on a tenant's wife when she was not on the premises rented has been held to be bad service. The modern view seems to be that, unless Law of Property Act 1925 s196 applies (see below), a landlord must prove that any notice to quit left at the premises came to the attention of the tenant.[45]

12.24   If the tenancy was created by a written agreement it may provide that Law of Property Act 1925 s196 applies. Section 196 provides that a notice is 'sufficiently served if ... left at the last-known place of abode or business in the United Kingdom of the lessee ... [or] if it is sent by recorded delivery addressed to the lessee at his abode or business, office or counting house' if that letter is not returned through the Royal Mail undelivered. Section 196 does not apply to notices to quit unless the tenancy agreement expressly incorporates it.[46] Service is deemed to be made at the time at which the recorded delivery letter would arrive in the ordinary course of the post. Where Law of Property Act 1925 s196 applies, a notice may be validly served even though it is not received by the addressee.[47] Where a tenant rents a bed-sitting room, there is no need for the notice to be delivered to or fixed to the door of that room. It is sufficient for it to be delivered through the letter box in the main door on the ground floor of the building.[48]

12.25   The notice should be addressed to the tenant of the premises, and not to the sub-tenant, although it will operate to determine the sub-tenancy as well as the head tenancy.[49] If a tenant has died, the notice must be served either on the person who becomes legally entitled to

---

45   *Wandsworth LBC v Atwell* (1995) 27 HLR 536; [1996] 01 EG 100, CA and *Enfield BC v Devonish and Sutton* (1997) 29 HLR 691; (1997) 75 P & CR 288, CA.

46   Cf, though, *Wandsworth LBC v Atwell* (1995) 27 HLR 536, [1996] 01 EG 100, CA and *Enfield BC v Devonish and Sutton* (1997) 29 HLR 691; (1997) 75 P & CR 288, CA.

47   *Re 88 Berkeley Road, London NW9, Rickwood v Turnsek* [1971] Ch 648. See also *Cannon Brewery Co Ltd v Signal Press Ltd* (1928) 139 LT 384.

48   *Trustees of Henry Smith's Charity v Kyriacou* [1989] 2 EGLR 110; (1990) 22 HLR 66, CA.

49   *Mellor v Watkins* (1874) LR 9 QB 400 per Blackburn J. Cf, the effect of RA 1977 s137.

the tenancy or, if the tenant died without making a will, on the Public Trustee[50] or administrator of the estate (see para 18.1).

Statutory tenants and notices to quit

12.26   Although there is no need for landlords to serve notices to quit on Rent Act statutory tenants before starting possession proceedings (see above), such tenants remain liable for rent until any statutory tenancy has been validly determined,[51] even if they have moved out of the premises. This liability can be ended only by a possession order, voluntary agreement of landlord and tenant, or a notice to quit served by the tenant.

12.27   Rent Act 1977 s3(3) provides:

> Subject to section 5 of the Protection from Eviction Act 1977 (under which at least 4 weeks' notice to quit is required), a statutory tenant of a dwelling-house shall be entitled to give up possession of the dwelling-house if, and only if, he gives such notice as would have been required under the provisions of the original contract of tenancy, or, if no notice would have been so required, on giving not less than 3 months' notice.

12.28   A tenant cannot unilaterally determine a Rent Act statutory tenancy without serving a notice to quit and the normal strict requirements relating to notices apply.[52] Advisers should therefore caution tenants against simply departing without giving notice or reaching agreement with the landlord.

Acceptance of rent after service of a notice to quit

12.29   Acceptance of rent after a notice to quit has been served does not normally operate to create a new contractual tenancy.[53] In order to establish that a new contractual tenancy has been created a tenant has

---

50   Law of Property (Miscellaneous Provisions) Act 1994 s14 and Public Trustee (Notices Affecting Land) (Title on Death) Regulations 1995 SI No 1330. See also *Wirral BC v Smith and Cooper* (1982) 43 P & CR 312; (1982) 4 HLR 81, CA.

51   *Trustees of Smith's (Henry) Charity v Willson* [1983] 1 All ER 73, CA.

52   *King's College Cambridge v Kershman* (1948) 64 TLR 547, *Boyer v Warbey* [1953] 1 QB 234 and RA 1977 s5(1).

53   *Clarke v Grant* [1950] 1 KB 104, *City of Westminster v Basson* (1991) 23 HLR 225; [1991] 1 EGLR 277 and *Burrows v Brent LBC* [1996] 1 WLR 1448; [1996] 4 All ER 577, HL. An invalid agreement for an irrecoverable rent increase does not vary an existing tenancy agreement or amount to a new contractual tenancy: *Sopwith v Stutchbury* (1983) 17 HLR 50.

to establish that this was the intention of both landlord and tenant. Payment and acceptance of rent may, however, operate as a waiver on the landlord's part of any breach of any clause in the tenancy agreement (see below).

Notice of increase of rent

12.30 In some circumstances a notice of increase of rent may terminate a periodical Rent Act protected contractual tenancy in exactly the same way as a notice to quit.

12.31 Rent Act 1977 s49(4) provides:

> Where a notice of increase is served during a contractual period and the protected tenancy could, by a notice to quit served by the landlord at the same time, be brought to an end before the date specified in the notice of increase, the notice of increase shall operate to convert the protected tenancy into a statutory tenancy as from that date.

12.32 If a landlord wishes to increase the rent to take into account a new registration by the rent officer,[54] a notice of increase in the prescribed form must be served.[55] In addition, such an increase can normally take effect only if the tenancy is already a statutory tenancy or if the landlord can convert the contractual tenancy into a statutory tenancy. Rather than requiring the landlord to serve both a notice to quit and a notice of increase, a notice of increase which gives at least as much notice as would be necessary in a notice to quit, fulfils both functions.

12.33 If the notice of increase is invalid (for example, fails to comply with statutory requirements), purports to operate retrospectively, or does not give sufficient notice, it is ineffective in converting a contractual tenancy into a statutory tenancy. If tenants pay increases in rent after the service of invalid notices of increase, they are not estopped from maintaining that there is still a contractual tenancy.[56]

Surrender

Surrender by express agreement

12.34 A surrender is a voluntary agreement of both landlord and tenant that the tenancy should come to an end without the service of a notice to

---

54 See RA 1977 s72 and Pt III.

55 RA 1977 s49(2).

56 *Wallis v Semark* [1951] 2 TLR 222, CA.

quit. An express surrender must state an immediate intention that the tenancy should come to an end. It cannot operate to take effect in the future. Surrenders by express agreement must be made by deed,[57] although in some circumstances an oral agreement may be effective as a surrender by operation of law (see below).

12.35   If there are joint tenants all tenants must agree to the surrender.[58] A husband has no implied authority to surrender a tenancy on behalf of his wife.[59]

Surrender by operation of law

12.36   Even if there is no express surrender by deed, the law may consider that the landlord and tenant have behaved in an unequivocal way which is inconsistent with the continuance of the contractual tenancy. In such circumstances, if their behaviour makes it inequitable for one of the parties to claim that the tenancy still exists, the law will imply a surrender. In *Foster v Robinson*[60] Sir Raymond Evershed MR stated:

> It has been laid down that in order to constitute a surrender by operation of law there must be, first, an act or purported surrender invalid per se by reason of non-compliance with statutory or other formalities, and secondly, some change of circumstances supervening on, or arising from, the purported surrender, which, by reason of the doctrine of estoppel or part performance, makes it inequitable and fraudulent for any of the parties to rely upon the invalidity of the purported surrender.[61]

12.37   In *Mattey Securities Ltd v Ervin*,[62] when considering the circumstances in which a surrender by operation of law may occur, Bracewell J said:

> The conduct of the parties must unequivocally amount to an acceptance that the tenancy is ended for the doctrine to apply. Although a surrender by operation of law does not require that there is an intention of the

---

57   See Law of Property Act 1925 s52, Law of Property (Miscellaneous Provisions) Act 1989 s2 and *Ealing Family Housing Association v McKenzie* [2003] EWCA Civ 1602; [2004] HLR 21.

58   *Leek and Moorlands Building Society v Clark* [1952] 2 QB 788.

59   *Re Viola's Indenture of Lease, Humphrey v Stenbury* [1909] 1 Ch 244.

60   [1950] 2 All ER 342.

61   Ibid at 346, quoting from Foa, *General Law of Landlord and Tenant*, 7th edn, Hamish Hamilton, 1947, pp617–618. See also *Dibbs v Campbell* (1988) 20 HLR 374, CA.

62   [1998] 34 EG 91, CA.

parties to surrender the lease, it does however require that there is some unequivocal act which has the effect of estopping the parties from asserting that the lease is still extant.

12.38   In *Chamberlain v Scally*[63] it was held that for there to be an implied surrender there must be unequivocal conduct on the part of both the landlord and the tenant which is inconsistent with the continuance of the tenancy. There are three main examples of situations where there may be an effective surrender by operation of law.

12.39   First, where there is an agreement that the tenant should abandon the tenancy and that the landlord should resume possession of the premises.[64] It is necessary for the tenant to hand back the premises to the landlord. In *Hoggett v Hoggett and Wallis*[65] the tenant tried to surrender premises to the landlord while his wife was still living in them. This was not a valid surrender. Similarly, the mere departure by a tenant from the premises while rent is owing is not an implied surrender unless there is agreement.[66] In *Belcourt Estates Ltd v Adesina*[67] the Court of Appeal stated that there must either be relinquishment of possession and its acceptance by the landlord, or other conduct consistent only with the cesser of the tenancy and the circumstances must be such as to render it inequitable for the tenant to dispute that the tenancy has ceased or such as to render it inequitable for the landlord to dispute that the tenancy has ceased. Mere inaction, or acts of omission, cannot be unequivocal conduct. The position may be different if there has been a long absence and there are substantial rent arrears outstanding.[68]

12.40   Second, where there is a delivery of the key. Delivery of the key to the premises by the tenant to the landlord and its acceptance by the landlord may be a surrender by operation of law. However, it depends on the circumstances. In *Furnivall v Grove*[69] there was a surrender where a tenant handed back the key and a few days later the landlord

63   (1992) 26 HLR 26, CA.

64   *Phene v Popplewell* (1862) 12 CBNS 334.

65   (1980) 39 P & CR 121, CA. See too *Ealing Family Housing Association v McKenzie* [2003] EWCA Civ 1602; [2004] HLR 21 and *Hackney LBC v Ampratum Central London Civil Trial Centre* 7 April 2003; September 2003 *Legal Action* 25.

66   *Preston BC v Fairclough* (1982) 8 HLR 70, CA.

67   [2005] EWCA Civ 208; 18 February 2005.

68   *Preston BC v Fairclough* (1982) 8 HLR 70, CA, *R v Croydon LBC ex p Toth* (1986) 18 HLR 493 and *Chamberlain v Scalley* (1992) 26 HLR 26, CA.

69   (1860) 8 CB(NS) 496. See also *Phene v Popplewell* (1862) 12 CBNS 334 where the tenant delivered the key to the landlord who then painted out the tenant's name above the premises and instructed an auctioneer to put up a 'To let' sign.

demolished the building. On the other hand, in *Boynton-Wood v True-man*[70] a tenant handed the key of a cottage to his landlord so that repairs could be carried out. The court held that there was no surrender because there was 'no unequivocal act on the part of the tenant ... which would indicate that he was surrendering his tenancy'. In *Laine v Cadwallader*[71] tenants left and put the keys through the landlord's letter box. The landlord sued, among other things, for four weeks' rent in lieu of notice. The Court of Appeal held that the dropping off of the keys was not a surrender, but an offer to surrender. There was no express acceptance of the offer.

12.41   Third, where there is an agreement for a new lease. The creation of a new lease between landlord and tenant or between the landlord and some third party with the agreement of the tenant determines the original contractual tenancy.[72] This is the case even if the new lease is for a shorter period than the old lease[73] or if there is an agreement that instead of a tenancy the tenant should enjoy a rent-free licence for the rest of his or her life.[74] If the new lease is for some reason invalid, there is no surrender of the earlier lease unless the surrender has been effected by deed.[75] The new agreement must be more than a variation of the terms of the existing tenancy,[76] although an agreed increase in rent may, depending on the circumstances, take effect either as an implied surrender and regrant of a new lease, or as a vari-

---

70 (1961) 177 EG 191. See also *Proudreed Ltd v Microgen Holdings* [1996] 12 EG 127; (1995) *Times* 17 July, CA and *Borakat v Ealing LBC* [1996] EGCS 67, QBD.

71 [2001] L & TR 8, CA.

72 Eg, *Climping Park Ltd v Barritt* (1989) *Independent* 15 May, CA. In these circumstances a tenant is estopped from denying the validity of the new lease and so cannot deny the implied surrender of the old lease, for a landlord cannot validly grant a new lease without first procuring a surrender of the old lease: *Jenkin R Lewis & Son Ltd v Kerman* [1970] 1 All ER 833, but cf, *Rhyl UDC v Rhyl Amusements Ltd* [1959] 1 All ER 257 and *Ashton v Sobelman* [1987] 1 WLR 177 (agreement between freeholder and subtenant alone not sufficient).

73 *Phene v Popplewell* (1862) 12 CBNS 334.

74 *Foster v Robinson* [1951] 1 KB 149; [1950] 2 All ER 342, provided that it is a genuine transaction.

75 *Rhyl UDC v Rhyl Amusements Ltd* [1959] 1 All ER 257 and the cases reviewed therein by Harman J at 267.

76 *Smirk v Lyndale Developments* [1975] 1 All ER 690, although an agreement that a tenant will rent additional land or an extra part of premises and that the total should be held as one parcel with an increased rent does operate as an implied surrender and regrant: *Jenkin R Lewis & Son Ltd v Kerman* [1970] 1 All ER 833. Similarly the variation of the term (ie, length) of a lease so that it subsists for a longer period also operates as an implied surrender and regrant: *Re Savile Settled Estates, Savile v Savile* [1931] 2 Ch 210.

ation of the terms of the existing lease.[77] A request by the tenant that the landlord should relet the premises to someone else does not operate as a surrender if his wife is still in occupation of the premises.[78]

12.42   If a tenancy is surrendered and the tenant moves out with an intention to cease residing at the premises, that is the end of the tenancy. In these circumstances a surrender by operation of law takes effect irrespective of the parties' intentions.[79] No statutory tenancy can arise and there is no need for the landlord to bring possession proceedings. If, however, a landlord and a contractual protected tenant agree to the surrender of a tenancy, but the tenant continues to occupy the premises as a residence, the only effect of the surrender is to convert the contractual tenancy into a statutory tenancy.[80] The landlord still has to prove a Rent Act ground for possession, and, if appropriate, that it is reasonable for the court to make an order for possession (see below). This is the case even if the landlord, the tenant and a prospective purchaser all agree that the purchaser will acquire the property with vacant possession and that the tenant will not make any claim to occupy the premises against the purchaser.[81]

12.43   A surrender of a tenancy does not terminate any sub-tenancy which the tenant has previously created. The subtenant becomes a direct tenant of the landlord[82] even if the head tenancy contained a covenant against subletting without the landlord's consent.[83]

Forfeiture

Nature of forfeiture

12.44   Forfeiture is the procedure which allows a landlord to bring to an end a contractual fixed-term tenancy or lease before the fixed period of

---

77 Cf, *Jenkin R Lewis & Son Ltd v Kerman* [1970] 1 All ER 833 and *Gable Construction Co Ltd v Inland Revenue Commissioners* [1968] 2 All ER 968.

78 *Hoggett v Hoggett and Wallis* (1979) 39 P & CR 121, CA. See also *Fredco Estates v Bryant* [1961] 1 All ER 34 (where the landlord said that the tenant could use three extra rooms with no increase in rent. It was held there was no surrender) and *Coker v London Rent Assessment Panel* [2006] All ER (D) 297 May.

79 *Jenkin R Lewis & Son Ltd v Kerman* [1970] 1 All ER 833.

80 RA 1977 s2(1)(a) and *R v Bloomsbury and Marylebone CC ex p Blackburne* (1985) 275 EG 1273, CA.

81 *Appleton v Aspin and Plane* (1987) 20 HLR 182, CA.

82 *Mellor v Watkins* (1874) LR 9 QB 400.

83 *Parker v Jones* [1910] 2 KB 32.

time, for which the lease was originally granted, expires. Forfeiture of a fixed-term tenancy has the same effect as a notice to quit on a periodic tenancy (see para 12.6). If the tenancy is outside statutory protection, forfeiture means that the landlord is entitled to repossess the premises. If the tenancy has full Rent Act protection, forfeiture merely converts the contractual protected tenancy into a statutory tenancy. Forfeiture can take place only if there is an express provision in the lease allowing the landlord to 're-enter' or forfeit. In practice all leases contain such clauses. At common law there was no need for a landlord to bring court proceedings to forfeit a lease: an unequivocal act on the part of the landlord sufficed.[84] Most commonly this consisted of the landlord entering the premises and taking possession. However, Protection from Eviction Act 1977 s2 provides:

> Where any premises are let as a dwelling on a lease which is subject to a right of re-entry or forfeiture it shall not be lawful to enforce that right otherwise than by proceedings in the court while any person is lawfully residing in the premises or part of them.

As to whether premises are 'let as a dwelling', see *Pirabkaran v Patel*.[85]

12.45   The service of court proceedings claiming forfeiture is an unequivocal act which amounts to forfeiture.[86] In view of the various forms of relief available to lessees (see below), the lease is not actually terminated until a court order is made, but the effect of an order is that forfeiture takes effect from the date when proceedings were served.[87] If proceedings include a claim for an injunction to restrain the lessee from future breaches of covenant, however, the issue and service of proceedings is not an unequivocal act and so does not give rise to forfeiture.[88] A landlord claiming forfeiture in the county court must use a claim form in Form N6 and specify the daily rate of rent accruing.[89] When issuing proceedings, a landlord must notify any person who may be entitled to relief from forfeiture (see below).[90]

---

84 An agreement with an existing sub-tenant that the sub-tenant will change the locks is not sufficient to forfeit the headlease: *Ashton v Sobelman* [1987] 1 WLR 177.

85 [2006] EWCA Civ 685, 26 May 2006.

86 *Grimwood v Moss* (1872) LR 7 CP 360 and *Canas Property Co Ltd v KL Television Services Ltd* [1970] 2 QB 433; [1970] 2 WLR 1133.

87 *Borzak v Ahmed* [1965] 2 QB 320.

88 *Moore v Ullcoats Mining Co* [1908] 1 Ch 575.

89 CPR PD 55 para 2.3 and *Canas Property Co Ltd v KL Television Services Ltd* [1970] 2 QB 433; [1970] 2 WLR 1133.

90 CPR PD 55 para 2.4 (cf, CCR Ord 6 r3(2)).

12.46 Even before issuing proceedings for forfeiture, a landlord may have to comply with various requirements. If the landlord is claiming forfeiture due to rent arrears, the general rule is that there must be a formal written demand before proceedings are issued. In practice, however, this rule is usually excluded by a provision in the lease which gives the landlord a right to re-enter if there are arrears 'whether the rent has been lawfully demanded or not'. In addition, County Courts Act 1984 s139(1) provides that if six months' rent is owing at the commencement of the action and if there are insufficient goods on the premises to cover the arrears, proceedings may be issued without a formal demand for rent even if there is no corresponding provision in the lease. See too the special restrictions on the forfeiture of long leases for arrears of rent and service charges described in paras 12.51, 12.55 and 12.58.

12.47 If forfeiture proceedings are issued for breach of any other covenant in the lease, a notice must be served pursuant to Law of Property Act 1925 s146 before the issue of proceedings. Service of a Law of Property Act 1925 s146 notice by sending it to the property in question is good, even if it does not actually come to the attention of the lessee.[91]

12.48 Section 146 provides:

Restrictions on and relief against forfeiture of leases and underleases

(1) A right of re-entry or forfeiture under any proviso or stipulation in a lease for a breach of any covenant or condition in the lease shall not be enforceable, by action or otherwise, unless and until the lessor serves on the lessee a notice –
   (a) specifying the particular breach complained of; and
   (b) if the breach is capable of remedy, requiring the lessee to remedy the breach; and
   (c) in any case, requiring the lessee to make compensation in money for the breach;
   and the lessee fails, within a reasonable time thereafter, to remedy the breach, if it is capable of remedy, and to make reasonable compensation in money, to the satisfaction of the lessor, for the breach.

(2) Where a lessor is proceeding, by action or otherwise, to enforce such a right of re-entry or forfeiture, the lessee may, in the lessor's action, if any, or in any action brought by himself, apply to the court for relief; and the court may grant or refuse relief, as the court, having regard to the proceedings and conduct of the parties under the foregoing provisions of this section, and to all the other

---

91 *Van Haarlam v Kasner* [1992] 36 EG 135, ChD (lessee in prison).

circumstances, thinks fit; and in case of relief may grant it on such terms, if any, as to costs, expenses, damages, compensation, penalty, or otherwise, including the granting of an injunction to restrain any like breach in the future, as the court, in the circumstances of each case, thinks fit.

(3) A lessor shall be entitled to recover as a debt due to him from a lessee, and in addition to damages (if any), all reasonable costs and expenses properly incurred by the lessor in the employment of a solicitor and surveyor or valuer, or otherwise, in reference to any breach giving rise to a right of re-entry or forfeiture which, at the request of the lessee, is waived by the lessor, or from which the lessee is relieved, under the provisions of this Act.

(4) Where a lessor is proceeding by action or otherwise to enforce a right of re-entry and forfeiture under any covenant, proviso, or stipulation in a lease, or for non-payment of rent, the court may, on application by any person claiming as under-lessee any estate or interest in the property comprised in the lease or any part thereof either in the lessor's action (if any) or in any action brought by such person for that purpose, make an order vesting, for the whole term of the lease or any less term, the property comprised in the lease or any part thereof in any person entitled as under-lessee to any estate or interest in such property upon such conditions as to execution of any deed or other document, payment of rent, costs, expenses, damages, compensation, giving security, or otherwise, as the court in the circumstances of each case may think fit, but in no case shall any such under-lessee be entitled to require a lease to be granted to him for any longer term than he had under his original sub-lease.

(5) For the purposes of this section –

(a) 'Lease' includes an original or derivative under-lease; also an agreement for a lease where the lessee has become entitled to have his lease granted; also a grant at a fee farm rent, or securing a rent by condition;

(b) 'Lessee' includes an original or derivative under-lessee, and the persons deriving title under a lessee; also a grantee under any such grant as aforesaid and the persons deriving title under him;

(c) 'Lessor' includes an original or derivative under-lessor, and the persons deriving title under a lessor; also a person making such grant as aforesaid and the persons deriving title under him;

(d) 'Under-lease' includes an agreement for an under-lease where the under-lessee has become entitled to have his under-lease granted;

(e) 'Under-lessee' includes any person deriving title under an under-lessee.

(6) This section applies although the proviso or stipulation under

which the right of re-entry or forfeiture accrues is inserted in the lease in pursuance of the directions of any Act of Parliament.

(7) For the purposes of this section a lease limited to continue as long only as the lessee abstains from committing a breach of covenant shall be and take effect as a lease to continue for any longer term for which it could subsist, but determinable by a proviso for re-entry on such a breach.

(8) This section does not extend –

(i) To a covenant or condition against assigning, underletting, parting with the possession, or disposing of the land leased where the breach occurred before the commencement of this Act; or

(ii) In the case of a mining lease, to a covenant or condition for allowing the lessor to have access to or inspect books, accounts, records, weighing machines or other things or to enter or inspect the mine or the workings thereof.

(9) This section does not apply to a condition for forfeiture on the bankruptcy of the lessee or on taking in execution of the lessee's interest if contained in a lease of –

(a) Agricultural or pastoral land;

(b) Mines or minerals;

(c) A house used or intended to be used as a public-house or beer-shop;

(d) A house let as a dwelling-house, with the use of any furniture, books, works of art or other chattels not being in the nature of fixtures;

(e) Any property with respect to which the personal qualifications of the tenant are of importance for the preservation of the value or character of the property, or on the ground of neighbourhood to the lessor, or to any person holding under him.

(10) Where a condition of forfeiture on the bankruptcy of the lessee or on taking in execution of the lessee's interest is contained in any lease, other than a lease of any of the classes mentioned in the last subsection, then –

(a) if the lessee's interest is sold, within one year from the bankruptcy or taking in execution, this section applies to the forfeiture condition aforesaid;

(b) if the lessee's interest is not sold before the expiration of that year, this section only applies to the forfeiture condition aforesaid during the first year from the date of the bankruptcy or taking in execution.

(11) This section does not, save as otherwise mentioned, affect the law relating to re-entry or forfeiture or relief in case of non-payment of rent.

(12) This section has effect notwithstanding any stipulation to the contrary.

...

12.49   Law of Property Act 1925 s146 gives tenants two opportunities to resist forfeiture: first, an opportunity to remedy any breach which is capable of remedy and, second, to apply for relief from forfeiture.[92] It applies to breaches of all covenants except for non-payment of rent.[93] A landlord cannot avoid these provisions by dressing up a forfeiture as a surrender of the lease.[94] It should be noted that there are special provisions relating to service of notices where a landlord alleges that a lessee has been in breach of the lessee's repairing covenant.[95]

12.50   If the notice given under Law of Property Act 1925 s146(1) (above) does not state whether or not the breach is capable of remedy or, if it is remediable, does not require the lessee to remedy it within a reasonable time, the notice is invalid.[96] Breaches of 'positive covenants' (for example, to keep premises in repair) are normally capable of remedy if the lessee can comply with them within a reasonable time.[97] This applies even if the lessee is in breach of a continuing positive covenant. However, it is often more difficult to remedy a breach of a negative covenant.[98] For example, a breach of a covenant not to assign, sublet or part with possession is incapable of remedy because the assignment or subletting has already taken place and cannot be undone.[99] Breaches of covenant against immoral user (prostitution) cannot usually be remedied due to the stigma which attaches to the premises and the possible effect on property values,[100] although this is not an automatic rule,[101] particularly if the tenant does not know about the breach. A breach involving a criminal conviction cannot be remedied.[102]

---

92   *Expert Clothing Service and Sales v Hillgate House Ltd* [1986] Ch 340; [1985] 2 All ER 998 per Slade LJ.

93   Law of Property Act 1925 s146(11).

94   *Plymouth Corporation v Harvey* [1971] 1 WLR 549.

95   Leasehold Property (Repairs) Act 1938.

96   *Expert Clothing Service and Sales v Hillgate House Ltd* [1985] 2 All ER 998.

97   *Rugby School (Governors) v Tannahill* [1935] 1 KB 87 and *Expert Clothing Service and Sales v Hillgate House Ltd* [1985] 2 All ER 998.

98   But cf, *Savva v Houssein* [1996] 47 EG 138; (1997) 73 P & CR 150; (1996) *Times* 6 May, CA.

99   *Scala House and District Property Co v Forbes* [1974] QB 575.

100 *Rugby School (Governors) v Tannahill* [1935] 1 KB 87, *British Petroleum Pension Trust v Behrendt* (1985) 276 EG 199 and *Egerton v Jones* [1939] 2 KB 702.

101 *Glass v Kencakes Ltd* [1966] 1 QB 611.

102 *Hoffmann v Fineberg* [1949] Ch 245 (gaming club, no licence), *Ali v Booth* (1966) 110 SJ 708; (1966) 199 EG 641, CA (food hygiene offences) and *Dunraven Securities Ltd v Holloway* (1982) 264 EG 709 (Obscene Publications Act offences).

12.51   Commonhold and Leasehold Reform Act 2002 s168 provides that a landlord under a long lease of a dwelling may not serve a notice under s146(1) unless:

- it has been finally determined on an application under subsection s168 (4) that the breach has occurred;
- or the tenant has admitted the breach;
- or a court in any proceedings, or an arbitral tribunal in proceedings pursuant to a post-dispute arbitration agreement, has finally determined that the breach has occurred.

Commonhold and Leasehold Reform Act 2002 s76 defines 'a long lease'. The most common 'long leases' are shared ownership leases, leases granted for a term of years certain exceeding 21 years, and leases granted under the right to buy provisions of Housing Act 1985 Pt V and the right to acquire provisions of Housing Act 1996 s17.

Waiver of breach

12.52   If landlords waive particular breaches of covenant, they cannot rely on those breaches to bring proceedings for forfeiture. A landlord may waive a breach expressly or by implication. Waiver takes place where the landlord does an unequivocal act which recognises the continued existence of the lease after having knowledge of the ground for forfeiture. There are certain actions which amount to waiver of breach irrespective of the landlord's intention,[103] for example, a demand for or receipt of rent which accrues after knowledge of a breach giving a right to forfeit[104] even if the demand is made 'without prejudice',[105] or the commencement of proceedings seeking access to premises.[106] The knowledge or actions of agents[107] or employees such as porters[108] are deemed to be equivalent to direct knowledge of the landlord. Suspicion that there is a breach without actual knowledge of the facts is not enough to constitute waiver.[109]

---

103 *Central Estates (Belgravia) v Woolgar (No 2)* [1972] 3 All ER 610.
104 *Blackstone Ltd v Burnetts* [1973] 1 WLR 1487, *Van Haarlam v Kasner* [1992] 36 EG 135, ChD and *Iperion Investments Corporation v Broadwalk House Residents* [1992] EGLR 235, ORB.
105 *Segal Securities v Thoseby* [1963] 1 QB 887; [1963] 1 All ER 500.
106 *Cornillie v Saha and Bradford and Bingley BS* (1996) 28 HLR 561; 72 P & CR 147, CA.
107 *Central Estates (Belgravia) v Woolgar (No 2)* [1972] 3 All ER 610.
108 *Metropolitan Properties Co Ltd v Cordery* (1979) 251 EG 567.
109 *Chrisdell Ltd v Johnson and Tickner* (1987) 19 HLR 406, CA.

12.53   No demand for rent after proceedings have been issued can amount to waiver because the landlord has already acted unequivocally in issuing those proceedings. Similarly, there is no waiver of a breach even if the landlord knows about it but merely stands by without interfering while the lessee carries on with the conduct which amounts to the breach.

12.54   A continuing breach of covenant continually gives rise to new rights to forfeit and so waiver cannot affect future breaches.[110] Waiver operates to prevent a landlord from relying on a particular breach only, not on subsequent future breaches. Subletting is a 'one off' breach which only occurs at the time when premises are initially sublet. However, sharing premises may be a continuing breach which persists even after waiver.[111]

Long lessees, forfeiture and service charges

12.55 Housing Act 1996 s81 prevents landlords from exercising a right of re-entry or forfeiture of premises let as a dwelling for failure to pay service charges unless the amount claimed is either agreed or admitted by the lessee or has been determined by a court or an arbitral tribunal in accordance with Arbitration Act 1996 Pt I. 'Service charge' has the same meaning as in Landlord and Tenant Act 1985 s18(1), ie, sums payable 'directly or indirectly, for services, repairs, maintenance or insurance or the landlord's costs of management' and which vary according to the relevant costs. The importance of this provision is that it prevents freeholders from pressurising lessees who have a genuine dispute about service charges (or their mortgagees) into paying up rather than face forfeiture proceedings. It came into force on 24 September 1996[112] and applies to all proceedings begun on or after that date.[113]

12.56   The court has power to transfer a claim involving the reasonableness of service charges[114] to a leasehold valuation tribunal.[115]

---

110 *Segal Securities v Thoseby* [1963] 1 All ER 500 and *Houghton v Kemp* [1996] 12 CL 348.

111 *Metropolitan Properties Co Ltd v Crawford and Wetherill* March 1987 *Legal Action* 20.

112 HA 1996 s232(2).

113 See, eg, *Mohammadi v Anston Investments Ltd* [2003] EWCA Civ 981; [2004] HLR 8.

114 Landlord and Tenant Act 1985 s19.

115 Ibid s19(2A).

Relief from forfeiture

12.57   Even if a landlord establishes that a tenant has breached a covenant, the tenant may still be entitled to apply for relief from forfeiture. If the court grants relief, the tenant's contractual tenancy is restored to full effect and continues as if the landlord had not sought to forfeit.[116] Relief from forfeiture may be expressed to be conditional, for example, on the tenant not committing future breaches of covenant. There are several forms of relief which operate in different ways. The county court and High Court powers to grant relief from forfeiture differ.

Arrears of rent – long lessess

12.58   Commonhold and Leasehold Reform Act 2002 s166 provides that a tenant under a long lease[117] is not liable to pay rent unless the landlord has given a notice demanding payment. The notice must specify the amount of the payment and the date on which the tenant is liable to make it. The date on which the tenant is liable to make the payment must not be either less than 30 days or more than 60 days after the day on which the notice is given, or before the date on which payment would have been due under the lease. Any notice must be in the prescribed form, but may be sent by post.[118]

12.59   Landlords of long lessees[119] may not forfeit for failure to pay rent, service charges or administration charges unless the total amount unpaid exceeds 'the prescribed sum', or consists of or includes an amount which has been payable for more than 'a prescribed period'. The prescribed sum is currently £350 and the prescribed period is currently three years.[120]

---

116   *Hynes v Twinsectra* (1996) 28 HLR 183; [1995] 35 EG 136, CA.

117   For the meaning of 'long lease' see the Commonhold and Leasehold Reform Act 2002, summarised at para 12.51.

118   See too the Landlord and Tenant (Notice of Rent) (England) Regulations 2004 SI No 3096 and the Landlord and Tenant (Notice of Rent) (Wales) Regulations 2005 SI No 1355 (W.103) which contain additional requirements, namely notes for both lessees and lessors.

119   For the meaning of 'long lease' see the Commonhold and Leasehold Reform Act 2002, summarised at para 12.51.

120   See the Rights of Re-entry and Forfeiture (Prescribed Sum and Period) (England) Regulations 2004 SI No 3086 and the Rights of Re-entry and Forfeiture (Prescribed Sum and Period) (Wales) Regulations 2005 SI No 1352 (W.100).

Arrears of rent – county court

12.60 Procedure for forfeiture for non-payment of rent in the county court is governed by County Courts Act 1984 s138. The 1984 Act has been amended by Administration of Justice Act 1985 s55. Section 138 as amended provides:

Forfeiture for non-payment of rent

Provisions as to forfeiture for non-payment of rent

138(1) This section has effect where a lessor is proceeding by action in a county court (being an action in which the county court has jurisdiction) to enforce against a lessee a right of re-entry or forfeiture in respect of any land for non-payment of rent.

(2) If the lessee pays into court or to the lessor not less than 5 clear days before the return day all the rent in arrear and the costs of the action, the action shall cease, and the lessee shall hold the land according to the lease without any new lease.

(3) If –
  (a) the action does not cease under subsection (2); and
  (b) the court at the trial is satisfied that the lessor is entitled to enforce the right of re-entry or forfeiture,
  the court shall order possession of the land to be given to the lessor at the expiration of such period, not being less than 4 weeks from the date of the order, as the court thinks fit, unless within that period the lessee pays into court or to the lessor all the rent in arrear and costs of the action.

(4) The court may extend the period specified under subsection (3) at any time before possession of the land is recovered in pursuance of the order under that subsection.

(5) ... if –
  (a) within the period specified in the order; or
  (b) within that period as extended under subsection (4),
  the lessee pays into court or to the lessor –
    (i) all the rent in arrear; and
    (ii) the costs of the action,
  he shall hold the land according to the lease without any new lease.

(6) Subsection (2) shall not apply where the lessor is proceeding in the same action to enforce a right of re-entry or forfeiture on any other ground as well as for non-payment of rent, or to enforce any other claim as well as the right of re-entry or forfeiture and the claim for arrears of rent.

(7) If the lessee does not –
  (a) within the period specified in the order; or
  (b) within that period as extended under subsection (4),

pay into court or to the lessor –
(i) all the rent in arrear; and
(ii) the costs of the action,
the order shall be enforceable in the prescribed manner and so long as the order remains unreversed the lessee shall, subject to subsections (8) and (9A), be barred from all relief.

(8) The extension under subsection (4) of a period fixed by a court shall not be treated as relief from which the lessee is barred by subsection (7) if he fails to pay into court or to the lessor all the rent in arrear and the costs of the action within that period.

(9) Where the court extends a period under subsection (4) at a time when –
(a) that period was expired; and
(b) a warrant has been issued for the possession of the land,
the court shall suspend the warrant for the extended period; and, if, before the expiration of the extended period, the lessee pays into court or to the lessor all the rent in arrear and all the costs of the action, the court shall cancel the warrant.

(9A) Where the lessor recovers possession of the land at any time after the making of the order under subsection (3) (whether as a result of the enforcement of the order or otherwise) the lessee may, at any time within six months from the date on which the lessor recovers possession, apply to the court for relief; and on any such application the court may, if it thinks fit, grant to the lessee such relief, subject to such terms and conditions, as it thinks fit.

(9B) Where the lessee is granted relief on an application under subsection (9A) he shall hold the land according to the lease without any new lease.

(9C) An application under subsection (9A) may be made by a person with an interest under a lease of the land derived (whether immediately or otherwise) from the lessee's interest therein in like manner as if he were the lessee; and on any such application the court may make an order which (subject to such terms and conditions as the court thinks fit) vests the land in such a person, as lessee of the lessor, for the remainder of the term of the lease under which he has any such interest as aforesaid, or for any lesser term.

   In this subsection any reference to the land includes a reference to a part of the land.

(10) Nothing in this section or section 139 shall be taken to affect –
(a) the power of the court to make any order which it would otherwise have power to make as respects a right of re-entry or forfeiture on any ground other than non-payment of rent; or
(b) section 146(4) of the Law of Property Act 1925 (relief against forfeiture).

12.61   County Courts Act 1984 s138 provides three different forms of relief from forfeiture:

- If all the rent arrears and costs are paid to the lessor or into court at least five days before the return day, the action automatically ceases and the lease continues as if no proceedings had been issued.[121] The 'return day' is the date on the claim form even if that hearing is in fact only treated as a directions hearing and the action is adjourned for a full hearing at a later date.[122] If all arrears and costs are paid at least five days before the return day, the tenancy remains a contractual tenancy.

- At the hearing, if there is a claim based on arrears of rent, the court must automatically delay possession for at least four weeks. If during this period the lessee pays all the arrears and costs, there is again complete relief from forfeiture[123] and the tenancy continues as a contractual tenancy. The Court of Appeal has held that the words 'the lessee pays into court ... all the rent in arrear' used in County Courts Act 1984 s138(3) do not mean that the court can only order payment of the rent in arrears at the date of issue of the claim form. It is to be assumed that the lease continues after service of the claim, that the tenant remains under an obligation to pay the sum reserved in the lease as rent and that 'all the rent in arrear' means the rent payable up to the date stated in the order.[124] The court may, of its own motion, adjourn the hearing once for inquiry to ascertain the lessee's ability to pay rent, but it is normally wrong for there to be two such adjournments without the lessor's consent.[125] The period of postponement may be extended at any time before possession is actually recovered.[126]

- The lessee may apply to the court within six months of the landlord recovering possession (for example, by sending in the bailiff or otherwise) for relief against forfeiture.[127] Similar applications

---

121 County Courts Act 1984 s138(2).

122 *Swordheath Properties Ltd v Bolt* [1992] 38 EG 154, CA. See also County Courts Act 1984 s147.

123 County Courts Act 1984 s138(3).

124 *Maryland Estates v Bar-Joseph* [1998] 3 All ER 193; (1999) 31 HLR 269, CA.

125 *R v A Circuit Judge ex p Wathen* (1976) 33 P & CR 423 (tenant admitted arrears of rent, but said that he had an expectancy of money under a trust at an unknown future date).

126 County Courts Act 1984 s138(4).

127 County Courts Act 1984 s138(9A) reversing the effect of *Di Palma v Victoria Square Property Co Ltd* [1985] 2 All ER 676, cf, *Jones v Barnett* [1984] Ch 500; [1984] 3 All ER 129.

for relief where there has been peaceable re-entry may be made under County Courts Act 1984 s139(2), although in view of Protection From Eviction Act 1977 s2 (see above) this will rarely be applicable to residential premises.

Other breaches of covenants – county court

12.62 Law of Property Act 1925 s146(2) provides that a lessee may apply for relief from forfeiture and that the court may grant such relief, subject to whatever conditions it thinks fit. This does not apply where there are arrears of rent.[128] Although the most common way for lessees to apply for relief from forfeiture is to counterclaim in forfeiture proceedings which the landlord has issued, it is possible for lessees themselves to issue proceedings in which they claim relief. Indeed, that is the only way in which relief may be sought if a landlord peaceably re-enters premises which are 'not let as a dwelling' and so not protected by Protection from Eviction Act 1977 s2. Lord Templeman summarised the law in *Billson v Residential Apartments*,[129] by stating:

> A tenant may apply for ... relief from forfeiture under section 146(2) after the issue of a section 146 notice but he is not prejudiced if he does not do so. A tenant cannot apply for relief after a landlord has forfeited a lease by issuing and serving a writ, has recovered judgment and has entered into possession pursuant to that judgment. If the judgment is set aside or successfully appealed the tenant will be able to apply for relief in the landlord's action but the court in deciding whether to grant relief will take into account any consequences of the original order and repossession and the delay of the tenant. A tenant may apply for relief after a landlord has forfeited by re-entry without first obtaining a court order for that purpose, but the court in deciding whether to grant relief will take into account all the circumstances including delay on the part of the tenant.

12.63 Underlessees have, in all cases, including rent arrears cases, the right to apply for relief and to have leases vested in themselves instead of the lessees.[130] This operates by granting a new lease which comes into effect from the date when relief is given.[131]

12.64 If there are joint lessees of premises, all must apply together for relief under Law of Property Act 1925 s146.[132] The court may grant

---

128 Law of Property Act 1925 s146(11).
129 [1992] 1 AC 494; [1992] 2 WLR 15, HL.
130 Law of Property Act 1925 s146(4).
131 *Cadogan v Dimovic* [1984] 1 WLR 609.
132 *Fairclough (TM) and Sons v Berliner* [1931] 1 Ch 60.

relief in respect of part only of premises if, for example, the breaches of covenant are confined to one distinct part of the building.[133]

Equitable jurisdiction – county court

12.65   The court has a further equitable jurisdiction, wider than Law of Property Act 1925 s146(4), to grant relief to underlessees or mortgagees.[134] This jurisdiction does not, however, extend to lessees in rent arrears cases because of the inclusion of the words 'shall be barred from all relief' in County Courts Act 1984 s138(7).[135]

The High Court

12.66   Proceedings for forfeiture of leases of residential premises are normally brought in the county court, however large the arrears of rent,[136] because costs are not recoverable in the High Court[137] and because of the restrictions contained in Civil Procedure Rules Part 55.[138] Briefly, the High Court's powers to grant relief are contained in Common Law Procedure Act 1852 ss210–212. These provisions state that a lessee must seek relief within six months of the execution of judgment, although it appears that there is an equitable jurisdiction for the court to grant relief outside that period if there has been peaceable re-entry.[139] Law of Property Act 1925 s146 applies equally to High Court proceedings.

Principles on which relief is granted

12.67   The circumstances in which relief is granted vary considerably and the courts are reluctant to lay down general principles.[140] It is clear, however, that courts must take into account all relevant circumstances. The harm caused to a landlord by breach of covenant (for example, the effect on the value of the property[141]) is important. For

---

133 *GMS Syndicate Ltd v Gary Elliott Ltd* [1982] Ch 1.
134 *Abbey National BS v Maybeech* [1985] Ch 190; [1984] 3 All ER 262.
135 *Di Palma v Victoria Square Property Co Ltd* [1985] 2 All ER 676.
136 RA 1977 s141(3) and (5).
137 RA 1977 s141(4).
138 CPR 55.3 and PD 55 para 1.1.
139 *Thatcher v Pearce and Sons* [1968] 1 WLR 748.
140 *Leeward Securities Ltd v Lilyheath Properties* (1983) 271 EG 279; (1983) 17 HLR 35, CA and *Bickel v Duke of Westminster* [1977] QB 517 at 524 per Lord Denning MR.
141 *Central Estates (Belgravia) v Woolgar (No 2)* [1972] 3 All ER 610.

this reason relief was frequently refused where an unlawful subletting or assignment led to the creation of a Rent Act statutory tenancy
where there would not otherwise have been one and where it would
have been reasonable for a landlord to refuse consent to the subletting
or assignment.[142] Similarly, it is rare for relief to be given where the
covenant broken is a covenant against immoral user since the courts
take the view that a 'stigma' may attach to the property.[143] If a breach
has been brought to an end, or ended some time ago, the court is
more likely to grant relief.[144] If the breach complained of would not
have been a breach if the landlord had consented, it is relevant to consider whether the landlord could reasonably have withheld consent.[145]
Similarly, the intention of the lessee at the time of committing the
breach is important (for example, where the lessee had no intention
of breaching the lease, but the breach was brought about by a solicitor's mistake, relief was granted[146]). The landlord's conduct is also
relevant, and in a case where the conduct of the landlord throughout
had been to harass the lessee and in which the court held that the
landlord's conduct was unreasonable, relief was given without hesita-
tion.[147] The tenant's age and health may be relevant.

Forfeiture and Rent Act protection

12.68 A landlord who wishes to evict a Rent Act protected tenant for breach
of a covenant during a fixed-term tenancy has to go through two
stages, although both may be dealt with at the same hearing. First,
the court must consider whether the lease should be forfeited, and, if
appropriate, whether relief against forfeiture should be given.[148] If the
lease is forfeited, the tenancy becomes a statutory tenancy. The court
has then to consider whether a Rent Act ground for possession exists
(most commonly under case 1) and, if so, whether it is reasonable to
make an order for possession.[149]

---

142 *Leeward Securities Ltd v Lilyheath Properties* (1983) 271 EG 279; (1983) 17 HLR
35, CA and *West Layton Ltd v Ford* [1979] QB 593.

143 *British Petroleum Pension Trust v Behrendt* (1985) 276 EG 199.

144 *Scala House and District Property Co v Forbes* [1974] QB 575.

145 Ibid.

146 Ibid.

147 *Segal Securities v Thoseby* [1963] 1 All ER 500.

148 *Central Estates (Belgravia) v Woolgar (No 2)* [1972] 3 All ER 610. The position
is very different if the tenant is an assured tenant – see para 10.23.

149 See chapter 13 and *Wolmer Securities v Corne* [1966] 2 QB 243; [1966] 2 All ER
691.

The Rent Acts

13.1 Introduction

Introduction

13.1   This chapter only applies to tenancies granted before 15 January 1989, or, after that date, in the limited circumstances provided for by Housing Act 1988 s34 – see Introduction to Part II. There are nevertheless still more than 100,000 Rent Act regulated tenancies.[1]

13.2   The law relating to protected and statutory tenants' security of tenure and possession proceedings is an amalgam of the common law and protection superimposed on it[2] by the Rent Acts. Before the passing of the first Rent Act, landlords bringing possession proceedings had to prove only that they owned or had an interest in the premises in question and that they were entitled to possession. Normally, this involved proving that any occupant had never had permission to be on the premises, or, alternatively, that any such permission had been terminated in accordance with the provisions of the licence or tenancy. Apart from when landlords sought to forfeit fixed-term tenancies for breach of covenant, there was no question of a landlord having to prove any ground or reasons for seeking possession or that it was reasonable for the court to make an order.

13.3   Although landlords' and tenants' rights were very greatly modified by the Rent Acts, the old common law rules remain highly relevant to residential occupiers who wish to defend possession proceedings. If occupiers are outside full Rent Act or Housing Act protection the only defence that they may have to possession proceedings is likely to be that the landlord has failed to terminate the tenancy or licence in the proper way. Even if a tenant has full Rent Act protection, a landlord must prove that any occupant's contractual tenancy has been determined properly before relying on the Rent Act grounds for possession.[3] A landlord's failure to determine a contractual tenancy, for example, by serving an invalid notice to quit (see chapter 12), provides a complete defence even though there may be unanswerable Rent Act grounds for possession. For this reason, the common law rules relating to determination of tenancies are dealt with in detail (see paras 12.6–12.43).

13.4   The effect of most of the Rent Acts passed between 1915 and 1977

---

1   See *Cadogan Estates Ltd v McMahon* [2001] 1 AC 378; [2000] 3 WLR 1555, HL, per Lord Millett.

2   Common law rules have themselves been considerably modified, eg, the restrictions on forfeiture in Law of Property Act 1925 s146 and County Courts Act 1984 s138. See paras 12.48 and 12.60.

3   RA 1977 Sch 15 (see chapter 15). The position is different for assured and assured shorthold tenants. See chapters 9 and 10.

was to provide tenants who enjoyed full Rent Act status with two forms of rights, namely, control over recoverable rents and security of tenure. Rent Act 1977 s1 defines a protected tenancy as follows:

> Subject to this Part of this Act, a tenancy under which a dwelling-house (which may be a house or part of a house) is let as a separate dwelling is a protected tenancy for the purposes of this Act.

> Any reference in this Act to a protected tenant shall be construed accordingly.

13.5 The opening words of Rent Act 1977 s1 refer to the various exceptions to full Rent Act protection which are listed in Rent Act 1977 Pt I. Although it is outside the scope of this book to deal in detail with Rent Act security of tenure, the exceptions (in summary) are as follows:

- dwelling-houses with rateable values above certain limits (if granted before 1 April 1990) or where the rent is more than £25,000 per annum (if granted after 1 April 1990) (s4);[4]
- tenancies where no rent is payable or the rent is less than two-thirds of the rateable value (if granted before 1 April 1990) or less than £1,000 per annum in Greater London or £250 elsewhere (if granted after 1 April 1990) (s5);[5]
- some dwelling-houses let with other land (s6);
- tenancies where the tenant is obliged to pay for board or substantial attendances (s7);
- lettings by certain educational establishments to students (s8);
- holiday lettings (s9);
- agricultural holdings (s10);
- licensed premises (s11);
- some lettings by resident landlords (s12);
- landlord's interests belonging to the Crown, but not to the Crown Estates Commissioners (s13);
- landlord's interest belonging to a local authority, etc (s14);
- landlord's interest belonging to a housing association or housing co-operative (ss15 and 16); and
- assured tenancies (s16A) (see chapters 9 and 10).

13.6 Full Rent Act protection gives residential tenants the right to continue as 'statutory tenants'[6] even after their contractual tenancy has terminated, provided that they continue to occupy the premises 'as

---

4 As amended by the References to Rating (Housing) Regulations 1990 SI No 434.
5 Ibid.
6 See RA 1977 s2.

a residence'. However, this status of 'virtual irremovability' is qualified – landlords are given various 'grounds for possession'[7] which, if
proved, may enable the county court to make a possession order.

13.7   A landlord must always terminate a tenant's contractual tenancy (for example, by serving a valid notice to quit) *before* issuing
proceedings. Unless a tenant is already a statutory tenant, failure by
a landlord to terminate the contractual tenancy provides a complete
defence, even if the tenant is outside the protection of Rent Act 1977
or however overwhelming the Rent Act grounds for possession may
be. This is not, however, the case if the contractual tenancy has been
terminated at some time in the past and the tenant is already a statutory tenant (see chapter 14).

13.8   If statutory tenants cease to 'occupy premises as a residence' they
lose their Rent Act protection, and a landlord then only has to prove
that the contractual tenancy has, at some stage, been terminated.
However, statutory tenants do not cease to occupy as a residence (and
so may keep Rent Act protection) even though they are temporarily
absent or live in two different homes (see chapter 14).

13.9   There are two categories of grounds for possession: 'discretionary grounds'[8] and 'mandatory grounds'.[9] If a landlord proves that a
tenant's contractual tenancy has been terminated and that one of
the *mandatory* grounds for possession exists, there is an automatic
entitlement to an order for possession. However, where a contractual
tenancy has been terminated and one of the *discretionary* grounds for
possession exists, the landlord must in addition satisfy the court that
it is reasonable to make an order for possession (see chapter 11).

13.10   The Rent Act 1977 also provides for an intermediate category of
tenants and licensees who have the benefit of 'restricted contracts'.[10]
They are tenants and licensees who do not have full Rent Act security,
usually because their landlord comes within the 'resident landlord
exception'[11] or because their landlord provides board or substantial
attendances.[12] Tenants or licensees with restricted contracts enjoy
only minimal rights to delay the operation of a possession order (see
Rent Act 1977 ss102A–106A).

---

7 RA 1977 Sch 15.
8 RA 1977 cases 1 to 10 and the availability of suitable alternative
   accommodation.
9 RA 1977 cases 11 to 20.
10 RA 1977 s19.
11 RA 1977 s12.
12 RA 1977 s7. See, eg, *Otter v Norman* [1989] AC 129; [1988] 3 WLR 321, HL.

13.11   Even after a possession order has been made, the court may still have power to vary, stay, suspend or set aside the order (see chapter 29).

13.12   In chapters 14 and 15 of this book dealing with tenancies created before 15 January 1989, all references are to the Rent Act 1977 unless otherwise stated.

Statutory tenants ceasing to reside

General principles

14.1   After a contractual Rent Act protected tenancy has been determined, it becomes a statutory tenancy with continuing Rent Act protection provided that the tenant occupies the premises 'as his residence'.[1] Although there is no requirement in the Act that a contractual tenant should occupy premises as a residence, this is crucial for statutory tenants.

14.2   If a statutory tenant ceases to reside in the premises, Rent Act protection is lost completely and a landlord bringing possession proceedings need prove only ownership of the premises, the termination of the contractual tenancy and that the tenant no longer resides in the premises.[2] On the other hand, if a statutory tenant does not give up possession and cease to live in the premises, the only way in which the landlord can repossess is to prove one of the Rent Act grounds for possession, and, if appropriate, that it is reasonable to make an order for possession.[3]

14.3   Rent Act 1977 s2 provides for the creation of statutory tenancies:

> 2 (1) Subject to this Part of this Act –
>   (a) after the termination of a protected tenancy of a dwelling-house the person who, immediately before that termination, was the protected tenant of the dwelling-house shall, if and so long as he occupies the dwelling-house as his residence, be the statutory tenant of it; and
>   (b) Part I of Schedule 1 to this Act shall have effect for determining what person (if any) is the statutory tenant of a dwelling-house or, as the case may be, is entitled to an assured tenancy of a dwelling-house by succession at any time after the death of a person who, immediately before his death, was either a protected tenant of the dwelling-house or the statutory tenant of it by virtue of paragraph (a) above.
> (2) In this Act a dwelling-house is referred to as subject to a statutory tenancy when there is a statutory tenant of it.
> (3) In subsection (1)(a) above and in Part I of Schedule 1, the phrase 'if and so long as he occupies the dwelling-house as his residence' shall be construed as it was immediately before the commencement of this Act (that is to say, in accordance with section 3(2) of the Rent Act 1968).

---

1   RA 1977 s2.
2   There is no need in these circumstances to prove a Rent Act ground for possession or that it is reasonable to make an order for possession.
3   *Boyer v Warbey (No 1)* [1953] 1 QB 234; *Brown v Draper* [1944] KB 309; [1944] 1 All ER 246.

(4) A person who becomes a statutory tenant of a dwelling-house as mentioned in subsection (1)(a) above is, in this Act, referred to as a statutory tenant by virtue of his previous protected tenancy.

(5) A person who becomes a statutory tenant as mentioned in subsection (1)(b) above is, in this Act, referred to as a statutory tenant by succession.

14.4   There was no express requirement in the first Rent Acts[4] that a statutory tenant reside in the premises. However, in a series of cases it was decided that the protection given to a statutory tenant is 'a personal privilege which ceases when the tenant goes out of occupation'.[5] The object of the Acts was to protect tenants who occupied premises as their home,[6] not absentee tenants. The continuing importance of this principle is recognised by Rent Act 1977 s2(3).

14.5   In determining whether or not a tenant occupies premises as a residence, the first material date is the date of termination of the contractual tenancy.[7] Whether or not the tenant was living in the premises prior to the termination of the contractual tenancy is irrelevant. However, if the tenant is not residing in the premises when the contractual tenancy is terminated, a statutory tenancy cannot arise.[8] Even if a former protected tenant resumes residence after the termination of the contractual tenancy, it is impossible to reinstate Rent Act protection as a statutory tenant; it is lost forever.[9] In addition, the tenant must remain in residential occupation throughout the statutory tenancy. Accordingly, if the tenant sublets the whole of premises rented, the protection of a statutory tenancy is lost because it is impossible for the tenant to be in residential occupation.[10] However, it is not necessary for the tenant to reside in all parts of the premises all of the time. A landlord cannot claim that a tenant has ceased to be a statutory tenant of one part only of the premises and recover possession of that part.[11] Accordingly, a tenant who sublets parts of the premises

---

4   Eg, the Increase of Rent and Mortgage Interest (War Restrictions) Act 1915 and the Increase of Rent and Mortgage (Restrictions) Act 1920.

5   *Middleton v Baldock (TW)* [1950] 1 KB 657; [1950] 1 All ER 708.

6   *Skinner v Geary* [1931] 2 KB 546.

7   Ibid, and *John Brown v Bestwick* [1951] 1 KB 21; [1950] 2 All ER 338 and *Colin Smith Music v Ridge* [1975] 1 WLR 463.

8   *Brown v Bestwick* [1951] 1 KB 21; [1950] 2 All ER 338, cf, *Francis Jackson Developments v Hall* [1951] 2 KB 488.

9   *Brown v Bestwick* ibid.

10 Ibid, and *Ujima Housing Association v Ansah* (1998) 30 HLR 831, CA. See also RA 1977 Sch 15, Case 6 below and *Regalian Securities Ltd v Ramsden* [1981] 1 WLR 611; [1981] 2 All ER 65 at 74, HL.

11 *Berkeley v Papadoyannis* [1954] 2 QB 149.

from time to time, with a general intention to live in the future in the parts which are sublet, retains the statutory tenancy of the whole.[12]

14.6   'Residence' is not, however, interpreted in a narrow sense.[13] A statutory tenant need not occupy premises 24 hours per day, 365 days per year. It is accepted that tenants may be in residence for the purpose of the Rent Act even though they have been physically absent from premises for prolonged periods of 'temporary absence'. Similarly, it is well established that a tenant may maintain residence in two homes at the same time.

Temporary absence

14.7   Tenants must show two things to establish that they are still occupying, as a residence, premises from which they are temporarily absent.[14]

- *Some kind of physical presence.*[15] It is not enough merely to keep an inward intention to return. This intention must be clothed by outward and visible signs of the intention to return.[16] Tenants must leave behind deliberate symbols of their occupation and preserve the premises for their ultimate homecoming.[17] In some cases this requirement has been satisfied by tenants leaving behind furniture,[18] a caretaker to look after the premises[19] or relatives.[20] In practice, tenants intending to be absent for any length of time would be well advised to leave behind some personal items such as books, CDs, clothes, crockery and cutlery as well as furniture.
- *The tenant must at all times retain a definite intention to return.*[21] There must also be a practical possibility of the tenant fulfilling

---

12 Ibid, and *Herbert v Byrne (No 1)* [1964] 1 All ER 882.

13 *Skinner v Geary* [1931] 2 KB 546.

14 *Brown v Brash* [1948] 2 KB 247.

15 'Corpus possessionis'.

16 *Brown v Brash* [1948] 2 KB 247.

17 Ibid.

18 *Gofor Investments Ltd v Roberts* (1975) 29 P & CR 366, *Brown v Draper* [1944] KB 309; [1944] 1 All ER 246, *Hallwood Estates v Flack* (1950) 66 TLR (Pt 2) 368 and *Dixon v Tommis* [1952] 1 All ER 725.

19 *Brown v Brash* [1948] 2 KB 247 and *Amoah v Barking and Dagenham LBC* (2001) 82 P & CR DG6; March 2001 *Legal Action* 28, ChD.

20 *Dixon v Tommis* [1952] 1 All ER 725, *Roland House Gardens v Cravitz* (1975) 29 P & CR 432, *Warriner Ltd v Wood* (1944) 144 EG 81 and *Hammersmith and Fulham LBC v Clarke* (2001) 33 HLR 77; March 2001 *Legal Action* 28, CA.

21 'Animus possidendi'; *Cove v Flick* [1954] 2 All ER 441.

the hope of returning within a reasonable time.[22] It is not enough for this intention to be dependent on something else happening, such as the death of a parent.[23] The court should consider the tenant's intention both at the date of the expiry of the notice to quit and during the time since its expiry. It should focus on 'the enduring intention' of the tenant and not on 'fleeting changes of mind'. This is particularly true of an elderly tenant in poor health whose intentions 'may well have fluctuated from time to time and even from day to day'.[24] The reasons for a tenant's absence may be relevant and it is far easier to prove an intention to return if the initial absence is due to 'some sudden calamity' such as a sentence of imprisonment[25] or a flood.[26] Other reasons given for temporary absence have been illness of the tenant,[27] illness of relatives,[28] disrepair and pregnancy of the tenant's wife.[29] It is possible that a tenant's intention to return may override a purported assignment of the tenancy which is a nullity.[30]

14.8   It is a question of fact and degree in each case as to whether the absence is such that the tenant has ceased to occupy premises as a residence. The burden of proof initially lies on the landlord to show that the tenant is absent. Once a landlord has established this, it is for the tenant to show that a physical presence in the premises and an intention to return have been maintained.[31]

14.9   The following cases illustrate how long 'temporary absence' can be:

- *Wigley v Leigh*[32] – tenant's absence from 1940 to 1949. Initially she stayed with relatives because her husband was at war but she was then prevented from returning because she suffered from tuberculosis.

---

22 *Tickner v Hearn* [1960] 1 WLR 1406.

23 *Cove v Flick* [1954] 2 QB 326 (Note); [1954] 2 All ER 441.

24 *Hammersmith and Fulham LBC v Clarke* (2001) 81 P & CR DG20; March 2001 *Legal Action* 28, CA.

25 *Brown v Brash* [1948] 2 KB 247 and *Amoah v Barking and Dagenham LBC* (2001) 81 P & CR D12; March 2001 *Legal Action* 28, ChD.

26 *Bushford v Falco* [1954] 1 WLR 672; [1954] 1 All ER 957.

27 *Tickner v Hearn* [1960] 1 WLR 1406.

28 *Richards v Green* (1984) 11 HLR 1; (1983) 268 EG 443, CA.

29 *Atyeo v Fardoe* (1979) 37 P & CR 494.

30 *Bushford v Falco* [1954] 1 WLR 672; [1954] 1 All ER 957.

31 *Roland House v Cravitz* (1975) 29 P & CR 432 and *Amoah v Barking and Dagenham LBC* March 2001 *Legal Action* 28, ChD.

32 [1950] 2 KB 305; [1950] 1 All ER 73.

- *Dixon v Tommis*[33] – at the time of the hearing the tenant had been absent for six months and did not intend to return for three years. He left his furniture in the premises while his son and his son's family lived there.
- *Gofor Investments v Roberts*[34] – at the time of the hearing the tenants had been absent for five years and intended to return within 'three to five years'. They had been living in Morocco and Malta and had left their furniture and two sons in the premises.
- *Richards v Green*[35] – the tenant had been absent for two and a half years. He had been living at a house owned by his parents, initially because they had been ill, but after their death because he was clearing up the house and arranging for it to be sold.
- *Tickner v Hearn*[36] – absence of five and a half years by a tenant who was in a mental hospital suffering from schizophrenia. The mere fact that she was 'mentally unsound' did not mean that she was incapable of forming an intention to return to the premises.[37]

14.10　On the other hand, in *DJ Crocker Securities (Portsmouth) Ltd v Johal*[38] the Court of Appeal refused to overturn a judge's finding that a tenant had ceased to occupy a flat as his home. The tenant had returned to look after his father in Malaysia in 1977. Since then he had lived and worked in Malaysia with his wife and children, and between 1980 and 1988 had only spent between 9 and 26 days each year in the flat.

Occupation through other people

14.11　Although the presence of friends and relatives living in premises may be evidence of the absent tenant's intention to return,[39] it is not, as a general rule, possible for a tenant to maintain Rent Act protection through the residence of other people without an intention of returning.[40] However, an exception was that a husband was deemed

---

33　[1952] 1 All ER 725. See too *Brown v Draper* [1944] 1 All ER 246; *Hallwood Estates v Flack* (1950) 66 TLR (Pt 2) 368.

34　(1975) 29 P & CR 366.

35　*Richards v Green* (1984) 11 HLR 1; (1983) 268 EG 443, CA.

36　*Tickner v Hearn* [1960] 1 WLR 1406.

37　Cf, however, *Duke v Porter* (1987) 19 HLR 1; (1986) 280 EG 633, CA – absence of ten years. Held: tenant had ceased to occupy as a residence.

38　[1989] 42 EG 103. See also *Prince v Robinson* (1999) 31 HLR 89, CA.

39　*Dixon v Tommis* [1952] 1 All ER 725, *Roland House v Cravitz* (1975) 29 P & CR 432 and *Blanway Investments Ltd v Lynch* (1993) 25 HLR 378, CA.

40　*Collins v Claughton* [1959] 1 WLR 145; [1959] 1 All ER 95.

to be continuing to occupy premises as a residence even if he did not intend to return, if his wife was still living in the premises.[41] It was not, however, possible for a tenant who was a wife to maintain her own Rent Act protection by leaving her husband living in the premises.[42] That was changed by Matrimonial Homes Act 1967 s1.[43] The current provision is Family Law Act 1996 s30(4) as amended by the Civil Partnership Act 2004[44] which provides that one spouse's or civil partner's occupation is to be treated for the purposes of Rent Act 1977 as occupation by the other spouse (or civil partner) as the spouse's (or civil partner's) residence.[45] If the spouse (or civil partner) who is the tenant moves out and the statutory tenancy continues as a result of the non-tenant spouse's residence, the actual tenant remains liable for the rent, unless an order is made in accordance with Family Law Act 1996 Sch 7 para 11.[46]

14.12   Rent Act protection cannot, however, be maintained by the continuing occupation of a divorced ex-spouse of the tenant,[47] although Family Law Act 1996 Sch 7 does provide for the transfer of tenancies from one spouse to another.[48] Obviously, none of these problems of continuing occupation applies if the tenancy was originally granted

---

41 *Old Gate Estates v Alexander* [1950] 1 KB 311; [1949] 2 All ER 822, *Wabe v Taylor* [1952] 2 QB 735; [1952] 2 All ER 420, *Brown v Draper* [1944] KB 309; [1944] 1 All ER 246 and *Middleton v Baldock (TW)* [1950] 1 All ER 708.

42 *Collins v Claughton* [1959] 1 All ER 95.

43 Later re-enacted as Matrimonial Homes Act 1983 s1(6). Note that there is no protection unless at some time both spouses have lived in the premises as a matrimonial home: *Hall v King* (1988) 55 P & CR 307; [1987] 2 EGLR 121; (1987) 19 HLR 440, CA.

44 This provision was brought into force on 5 December 2005 by the Civil Partnership 2004 (Commencement No 2) Order 2005 SI No 3175 (C.136).

45 See para 10.4, where the relevant parts of the section are quoted.

46 *Griffiths v Renfree* (1989) 21 HLR 338; [1989] 2 EGLR 46, CA.

47 *Heath Estates v Burchell* (1980) 130 NLJ 548, *Metropolitan Properties Co Ltd v Cronan* (1982) 262 EG 1077 and *Crago v Julian* [1992] 1 WLR 372; [1992] 1 All ER 744; (1991) *Times* 4 December; [1991] EGCS 124, CA.

48 See also Matrimonial Causes Act 1973 s24. It is important that any application for a transfer of the tenancy is made promptly if the tenant spouse is not actually residing in the premises and the tenancy is a statutory tenancy. Occupation by a non-tenant spouse ceases to count as residence by the tenant on the making of the decree absolute unless the contrary is specifically ordered. In these circumstances the making of the decree absolute may terminate the statutory tenancy unless the order transferring the tenancy is made simultaneously. The court's power to transfer a statutory tenancy to another spouse is restricted to cases where the statutory tenancy is in existence at the date of the application for the transfer (*Lewis v Lewis* [1985] AC 828; [1985] 2 WLR 962).

in joint names because occupation by one joint tenant is sufficient to maintain a statutory tenancy.[49]

14.13   A Rent Act protected tenancy does not vest in the trustee in bankruptcy if the tenant is made bankrupt. Accordingly, there is nothing to prevent a statutory tenancy arising in the ordinary way.[50]

Residence in two homes

14.14   It has been recognised since the early days of the Rent Acts[51] that it is possible for a tenant to occupy two premises as residences at the same time. A tenant may maintain Rent Act protection in both homes or alternatively may maintain protection in one while owning the other.

14.15   The classic example is of a tenant who has one home in the town and another in the country.[52] The question 'to be answered by ordinary common sense standards, is whether the particular premises are in the personal occupation of the tenant as his or her home, or, if the tenant has more than one home, as one of his or her homes. Occupation merely as a convenience for ... occasional visits'[53] is not sufficient. It is not merely a question of what a tenant does in particular premises; the court should look at all the circumstances and the way in which the tenant leads his or her life.[54] Comparatively small amounts of occupation may be sufficient, as in *Langford Property Co v Athanassoglou*[55] where a tenant slept in his 'town house' twice a week and rarely ate there, and *Bevington v Crawford*[56] where tenants lived mainly in Cannes and spent approximately two or three months each year in their rented accommodation in Harrow. Tenants may occupy two homes as residences where they are in the course of moving from

---

49 *Lloyd v Sadler* [1978] QB 774; [1978] 2 WLR 721, CA. For further discussion of the position of spouses, former spouses and other cohabitants, see chapter 30.

50 Insolvency Act 1986 s283(3)(a), overruling *Smalley v Quarrier* [1975] 1 WLR 938; [1975] 2 All ER 688, *Eyre v Hall* (1986) 280 EG 193; (1986) 18 HLR 509. Note, however, that bankruptcy may provide a ground for possession – *Cadogan Estates v McMahon* [2001] AC 378; [2000] 3 WLR 1555, HL.

51 Eg, *Skinner v Geary* [1931] 2 KB 546. See too the more recent case of *Stephens v Kerr* [2006] EWCA Civ 187; [2006] All ER (D) 186 (Feb).

52 Eg, *Langford Property Co v Athanassoglou* [1948] 2 All ER 722.

53 *Beck v Scholz* [1953] 1 QB 570; [1953] 1 All ER 814 at 816.

54 *Regalian Securities Ltd v Scheuer* (1982) 263 EG 973.

55 [1949] 1 KB 29; [1948] 2 All ER 722.

56 (1974) 232 EG 191.

one home to another.[57] It is more difficult for a tenant to claim to occupy separate premises as residences when they are close together.[58] For example, in *Hampstead Way Investments v Lewis-Weare*[59] a tenant rented a flat half a mile from a house which he owned and in which his wife lived. He slept most nights in the rented accommodation but the House of Lords held that he did not occupy it as a residence. Similarly, the Rent Act does not provide protection for premises which are occupied only occasionally when the tenant is on holiday.[60]

57 *Herbert v Byrne* [1964] 1 All ER 882.

58 *Regalian Securities Ltd v Scheuer* (1982) 263 EG 973. See also *Swanbrae Ltd v Elliott* (1987) 19 HLR 86.

59 [1985] 1 WLR 164; [1985] 1 All ER 564, HL, cf, though, *Palmer v McNamara* (1991) 23 HLR 168; (1991) 17 EG 88, CA (comparable 'occupation as a residence' under RA 1977 s12 satisfied even though no cooker and landlord did not sleep in premises).

60 *Walker v Ogilvy* (1974) 28 P & CR 288.

CHAPTER 15

Grounds for possession against Rent Act tenants

continued

Introduction

15.1 The starting point for all grounds of possession is Rent Act 1977 s98, which provides:

> 98 (1) Subject to this Part of this Act, a court shall not make an order for possession of a dwelling-house which is for the time being let on a protected tenancy or subject to a statutory tenancy unless the court considers it reasonable to make such an order and either –
>   (a) the court is satisfied that suitable alternative accommodation is available for the tenant or will be available for him when the order in question takes effect, or
>   (b) the circumstances are as specified in any of the Cases in Part I of Schedule 15 to this Act.
> (2) If, apart from subsection (1) above, the landlord would be entitled to recover possession of a dwelling-house which is for the time being let on or subject to a regulated tenancy, the court shall make an order for possession if the circumstances of the case are as specified in any of the Cases in Part II of Schedule 15.
>   ...

15.2 The main distinction between the various grounds for possession is that if landlords rely on one of the 'discretionary' grounds, they must prove not only the existence of the ground for possession but also that it is reasonable to make an order for possession (see chapter 11).

15.3 The discretionary grounds are those set out in cases 1 to 10 and in Rent Act 1977 s98(1)(a) (ie, that 'suitable alternative accommodation' is available). The 'mandatory grounds' are those set out in cases 11 to 20 and statutory overcrowding;[1] in these cases the landlord has to prove only that the contractual tenancy has been terminated and that a ground for possession is satisfied.

Suitable alternative accommodation

15.4 This ground is fulfilled if 'the court is satisfied that suitable alternative accommodation is available for the tenant or will be available for him when the order in question takes effect'.[2]

15.5 Further guidance is given in Rent Act 1977 Sch 15 Pt IV, which provides:

> 3. For the purposes of section 98(1)(a) of this Act, a certificate of the local housing authority for the district in which the dwelling-

---

1 RA 1977 s101.
2 RA 1977 s98(1)(a).

house in question is situated, certifying that the authority will provide suitable alternative accommodation for the tenant by a date specified in the certificate, shall be conclusive evidence that suitable alternative accommodation will be available for him by that date.

4. Where no such certificate as mentioned in paragraph 3 above is produced to the court, accommodation shall be deemed to be suitable for the purposes of section 98(1)(a) of this Act if it consists of either –

   (a) premises which are to be let as a separate dwelling such that they will then be let on a protected tenancy (other than one under which the landlord might recover possession of the dwelling-house under one of the Cases in Part II of this Schedule), or

   (b) premises to be let as a separate dwelling on terms which will, in the opinion of the court, afford to the tenant security of tenure reasonably equivalent to the security afforded by Part VII of this Act in the case of a protected tenancy of a kind mentioned in paragraph (a) above,

   and, in the opinion of the court, the accommodation fulfils the relevant conditions as defined in paragraph 5 below.

5. (1) For the purposes of paragraph 4 above, the relevant conditions are that the accommodation is reasonably suitable to the needs of the tenant and his family as regards proximity to place of work, and either –

   (a) similar as regards rental and extent to the accommodation afforded by dwelling-houses provided in the neighbourhood by any local housing authority for persons whose needs as regards extent are, in the opinion of the court, similar to those of the tenant and of his family; or

   (b) reasonably suitable to the means of the tenant and to the needs of the tenant and his family as regards extent and character; and

   that if any furniture was provided for use under the protected or statutory tenancy in question, furniture is provided for use in the accommodation which is either similar to that so provided or is reasonably suitable to the needs of the tenant and his family.

   (2) For the purposes of sub-paragraph (1)(a) above, a certificate of a local housing authority stating –

   (a) the extent of the accommodation afforded by dwelling-houses provided by the authority to meet the needs of tenants with families of such number as may be specified in the certificate, and

   (b) the amount of the rent charged by the authority for dwelling-houses affording accommodation of that extent,

   shall be conclusive evidence of the facts so stated.

6. Accommodation shall not be deemed to be suitable to the needs of the tenant and his family if the result of their occupation of the accommodation would be that it would be an overcrowded dwelling-house for the purposes of Part X of the Housing Act 1985.

7. Any document purporting to be a certificate of a local housing authority named therein issued for the purposes of this Schedule and to be signed by the proper officer of that authority shall be received in evidence and, unless the contrary is shown, shall be deemed to be such a certificate without further proof.

8. In this Part 'local housing authority' and 'district' in relation to such an authority have the same meaning as in the Housing Act 1985.

A landlord may prove that alternative accommodation is suitable either by obtaining a certificate that the local authority will provide accommodation or by satisfying the various criteria set out in Rent Act 1977 Sch 15 Pt IV.

15.6   This ground for possession is very similar to Housing Act 1988 Sch 2 ground 9 (see para 10.56).

15.7   It should be noted that Housing Act 1988 s34 provides that in possession proceedings against a protected or statutory tenant based on the availability of suitable alternative accommodation, the court should consider whether the grant of an assured tenancy (see chapter 10) would provide reasonably equivalent security. If 'in the circumstances, the grant of an assured tenancy would not afford the required security', the court may direct that the tenancy of the suitable alternative accommodation should be held on a protected tenancy. The grounds for possession against assured tenants are wider than those against Rent Act protected tenants and so tenants' representatives should try to persuade the court to direct that any new tenancy should be a protected tenancy.

15.8   So far as rent is concerned, tenants' representatives should bear in mind that if the new tenancy is being offered on an assured tenancy, there will be minimal rent control and after a year or the termination of any fixed-term tenancy, the landlord will be able to seek a market rent.[3] Accordingly it may be necessary to adduce evidence about market rents or rents for assured tenancies determined by rent assessment committees in the area. Alternatively, a landlord may be persuaded to consent to a direction that the alternative accommodation should be held on a protected tenancy.[4]

3   HA 1988 s13.
4   HA 1988 s34.

Discretionary grounds

Case 1: Rent arrears or breach of obligations of tenancy

15.9   Where any rent lawfully due from the tenant has not been paid, or any obligation of the protected or statutory tenancy which arises under this Act, or –

(a) in the case of a protected tenancy, any other obligation of the tenancy, in so far as is consistent with the provisions of Part VII of this Act, or

(b) in the case of a statutory tenancy, any other obligation of the previous protected tenancy which is applicable to the statutory tenancy,

has been broken or not performed.

This is the most common ground for possession used by landlords of Rent Act tenants. They must prove either that there are rent arrears or that there has been a breach of a term or other obligation of the tenancy.

Rent arrears

15.10   A landlord must prove two things: first, that rent was lawfully due from the tenant and, second, that some rent remained unpaid, at the date of issue of the claim.[5] This applies only to rent which is due from the actual tenant against whom possession is claimed and not to that due from a predecessor of the present tenant.[6] Rent becomes lawfully due at midnight on the day when it is payable.[7] If rent has been tendered to the landlord on a regular basis when it has become due, but has not been accepted by the landlord, there is a complete defence to the proceedings based on alleged rent arrears if the tenant pays into court all the rent which is due.[8] Accordingly, if a landlord refuses to accept rent, it is important that the tenant continues to tender rent regularly (for example, by sending cheques by recorded delivery) and maintains a separate bank or building society account for any rent that has been rejected so that the rent can be paid as soon as court proceedings are issued. If the tenant has not tendered rent regularly and there are arrears outstanding when proceedings are issued, the mere fact that the tenant pays all the rent arrears and fixed costs

5   *Bird v Hildage* [1948] 1 KB 91.
6   *Tickner v Clifton* [1929] 1 KB 207.
7   *Aspinall v Aspinall* [1961] Ch 526.
8   *Bird v Hildage* [1948] 1 KB 91 and CPR 37.3.

into court before the hearing date does not deprive the landlord of the ground for possession under case 1, but it is unlikely that the court will consider it reasonable to make an order for possession (see para 11.1).

15.11   Failure to provide a rent book does not disentitle the landlord from claiming that rent is lawfully due.[9]

15.12   When advising a tenant who faces a claim for possession based on rent arrears, it is important to check exactly what rent is lawfully recoverable, and, in particular, whether the landlord has been claiming too much rent. This may happen where:

• A landlord has been charging more than a 'fair rent' registered by the rent officer.[10] A rent registration for furnished premises is binding even if a later tenancy of the same premises is unfurnished, and vice versa. Tenants who have paid more than the registered rent may claim back the difference for a period of up to two years before the claim.

• A landlord has increased the rent without complying with Rent Act 1977 s51. In general, any agreement between a landlord and a Rent Act protected tenant to increase the rent must comply with the provisions of section 51. Any such agreement must be in writing and contain wording pointing out that a tenant's security of tenure is not affected by refusing to enter into the agreement and referring to the tenant's right to apply to a rent officer. If a landlord unilaterally increases the rent or if an agreement does not comply with section 51, the increase is irrecoverable and the tenant can claim back the difference for a period of one year.

• A landlord has failed to serve a valid notice of increase. In some situations (for example, where a landlord wants to increase the rent following a new rent registration) a landlord must serve a formal notice of increase. Failure to do so means that the increase is not legally recoverable.

• A landlord has failed to furnish the tenant with an address at which notices may be served. In such circumstances, Landlord and Tenant Act 1987 s48 provides that any rent which would otherwise

---

9   *Shaw v Groom* [1970] 2 QB 504.
10   RA 1977 ss44, 45 and 57. See *Rakhit v Carty* [1990] 2 QB 315; [1990] 2 WLR 1107. Cf, *Metrobarn v Gehring* [1976] 1 WLR 776, *Kent v Millmead Properties Ltd* (1982) 10 HLR 13 and *Cheniston Investments Ltd v Waddock* (1990) 20 HLR 652, CA.

be due is to be treated as not being due before the landlord has rectified the failure.[11]

- A landlord has calculated the rent without taking into account the Rent Acts (Maximum Fair Rent) Order 1999[12] which limits increases in registered rents by reference to an arithmetical formula. On 20 January 2000 the Court of Appeal decided that the order was ultra vires and quashed it.[13] Although the House of Lords allowed the secretary of state's appeal and found that the order was valid on 7 December 2000,[14] in the intervening period many landlords served notices of increase purporting to bring the rent up to the full uncapped registered rent. The effect of the House of Lords decision is that the Rent Acts (Maximum Fair Rent) Order has been in force throughout the period and rents have been limited accordingly.

These provisions may mean that a landlord claiming rent arrears in fact owes the tenant money rather than vice versa. In such a situation a tenant may reclaim the balance by suing (or if proceedings have already been issued, by counterclaiming) or by withholding rent until all sums due have been recovered.[15]

15.13   Advisers should also check whether there is any possibility of a set-off and counterclaim for breach of repairing obligations (see para 21.33), or whether there has been any failure by the relevant authorities to make payments of housing benefit (see para 32.9). See too para 3.10.

Breach of any other tenancy obligation

15.14   This limb of case 1 is similar to Housing Act 1988 Sch 2 ground 12 (see para 10.79) and Housing Act 1985 Sch 2 Ground 1 (see para 3.10).

---

11   See *Dallhold Estates (UK) Pty Ltd v Lindsay Trading Properties Inc* [1994] 17 EG 148, CA, *Hussain v Singh* [1993] 31 EG 75, CA, but cf, *Rogan v Woodfield Building Services Ltd* (1994) 27 HLR 78; [1995] 20 EG 132, CA (RA 1977 s48 complied with where address for service of notices clear from tenancy agreement) and *Drew-Morgan v Hamid-Zadeh* (2000) 32 HLR 316, [1999] 26 EG 156, CA.

12   Rent Acts (Maximum Fair Rent) Order 1999 SI No 6.

13   *R v Secretary of State for the Environment, Transport and the Regions ex p Spath Holme Ltd* [2000] 3 WLR 141.

14   Ibid [2001] 2 AC 349; [2001] 2 WLR 15; [2001] 1 All ER 195, HL.

15   RA 1977 ss54 and 57.

15.15   It should be noted that the original provisions of the contractual tenancy continue to bind a statutory tenant so far as they are consistent with the provisions of the Rent Act 1977.[16] Breach of such obligations is a ground for possession, but see 'Waiver' below.

15.16   Where a clause in a tenancy agreement gives a landlord a right of re-entry if the tenant becomes bankrupt, and, after termination of the contractual tenancy, the tenant is made bankrupt, the landlord may rely upon case 1. Tenants are 'obliged' not to become bankrupt if they wish to remain in possession of their home. By becoming bankrupt tenants break 'an obligation of the previous protected tenancy' within the meaning of case 1(b).[17]

Waiver

15.17   The acceptance of rent by a landlord who has knowledge of a breach of covenant may amount to a waiver of that breach and thus prevent the landlord from relying upon case 1.[18] If the tenancy is contractual, acceptance of rent is a complete waiver of a breach even if the acceptance is qualified. However, if the tenancy is statutory, it is a question of fact in each case as to whether the breach has been waived.[19] A qualified acceptance of rent from a statutory tenant (for example, acceptance 'without prejudice') may mean that the landlord is still entitled to rely on the breach of covenant,[20] but an unqualified acceptance of rent by the landlord of a statutory tenant is as much a waiver of the breach as if it were a payment by a contractual tenant.[21]

15.18   Acceptance of rent by landlords' agents who have knowledge of a breach of covenant amounts to waiver.[22] Thus, the knowledge of a porter that there is someone other than a tenant living in the premises amounts to knowledge of the landlord.[23]

---

16 RA 1977 s3(1).

17 *Cadogan Estates Ltd v McMahon* [2001] AC 378; [2000] 3 WLR 1555; [2000] 4 All ER 897, HL.

18 *Carter v Green* [1950] 1 All ER 627. See too para 12.52.

19 *Oak Property Co Ltd v Chapman* [1947] KB 886; [1947] 2 All ER 1 and *Trustees of Smith's (Henry) Charity v Willson* [1983] 1 All ER 73.

20 Ibid.

21 *Carter v Green* [1950] 1 All ER 627, cf, *Trustees of Smith's (Henry) Charity v Willson* [1983] 1 All ER 73.

22 *Hyde v Pimley* [1952] 2 QB 506; [1952] 2 All ER 102.

23 *Metropolitan Properties Co Ltd v Cordery* (1979) 251 EG 567.

Case 2: Nuisance or annoyance, user for immoral or illegal purposes

15.19   Where the tenant or any person residing or lodging with him or any sub-tenant of his has been guilty of conduct which is a nuisance or annoyance to adjoining occupiers, or has been convicted of using the dwelling-house or allowing the dwelling-house to be used for immoral or illegal purposes.

Nuisance or annoyance

'Nuisance' and 'annoyance' are both used in the natural sense of the words. This ground may be satisfied by drunkenness, abusive behaviour, noise, obstructive behaviour towards other occupiers or violence.[24] Unknown people coming to the premises at all hours of the day and night may amount to an annoyance.[25] It is not necessary that the act which led to the annoyance should have taken place on the premises. For example, a married tenant who exercised 'undue familiarity' with the landlord's daughter in an alley some 200 yards away from the premises let was held to be guilty of 'annoyance'.[26] It is possible for the court to infer that annoyance or nuisance has been caused to adjoining occupants without direct evidence from them,[27] but it is more usual for the landlord to call adjoining occupants to give evidence. The word 'adjoining' does not mean that the premises must be physically touching the tenant's premises: it means that the persons affected by nuisance or annoyance must live near enough to be affected by the tenant's conduct, because, for example, they share a common entrance.[28]

Immoral or illegal purposes

15.20   'Immoral purposes' is the statutory formula for prostitution.[29] The mere fact that a tenant has been convicted of a crime which took place on the premises may not be sufficient to establish this limb of the ground for possession. It must be shown that:

---

24 Per Wood J in *Cobstone Investments Ltd v Maxim* [1985] QB 140; [1984] 2 All ER 635.

25 *Florent v Horez* (1983) 268 EG 807.

26 *Whitbread v Ward* (1952) 159 EG 494.

27 *Platts (Frederick) Co v Grigor* [1950] 1 All ER 941, CA.

28 *Cobstone v Maxim* [1984] 2 All ER 635.

29 *Yates v Morris* [1951] 1 KB 77.

... for the purpose of committing the crime, the premises have been used ... [It is] not enough that the tenant has been convicted of a crime with which the premises have nothing to do beyond merely being the scene of its commission.[30]

15.21 However, the ground may be satisfied even though a tenant has been convicted of an offence which does not specifically refer to 'using premises'.[31] Depending on the circumstances, a conviction for possession of cannabis or some other unlawful drug on the premises may amount to a ground for possession. There is, however, a difference between tenants having drugs in their immediate possession on the premises (for example, in a pocket or a handbag) and using the premises as a storage or hiding place.[32] Examples of other activities which may satisfy this ground for possession are using premises as a 'coiner's den' or as a deposit for stolen goods.[33]

Case 3: Neglect of or damage to premises

15.22 Where the condition of the dwelling-house has, in the opinion of the court, deteriorated owing to acts of waste by, or the neglect or default of, the tenant or any person residing or lodging with him or any sub-tenant of his and, in the case of any act of waste by, or the neglect or default of, a person lodging with the tenant or a sub-tenant of his, where the court is satisfied that the tenant has not, before the making of the order in question, taken such steps as he ought reasonably to have taken for the removal of the lodger or sub-tenant, as the case may be.

This ground is similar to ground 13 in Housing Act 1988 Sch 2 (see para 10.87).

15.23 There is no need for a landlord to give advance warning of an intention to issue proceedings relying on this ground,[34] although failure to do so may be relevant when the court considers reasonableness and costs. Where allegations that the tenant has neglected premises have been substantiated, it may be unreasonable to make an order for possession without giving the tenant an opportunity to put matters right.[35]

---

30 Per Scrutton LJ in *Schneiders & Sons v Abrahams* [1925] 1 KB 301 at 311.

31 *Abrahams v Wilson* [1971] 2 QB 88.

32 Ibid, per Widgery LJ. As to 'reasonableness' in such cases, see *Bristol CC v Mousah* (1997) 30 HLR 32, CA and the other cases referred to at para 11.10.

33 *Schneiders & Sons v Abrahams* [1925] 1 KB 301 and *Everett v Stevens* [1957] CLY 3062.

34 *Lowe v Lendrum* (1950) 159 EG 423, CA.

35 *Holloway v Povey* (1984) 15 HLR 104; (1984) 271 EG 195, CA.

Case 4: Ill-treatment of furniture

15.24   Where the condition of any furniture provided for use under the tenancy has, in the opinion of the court, deteriorated owing to ill-treatment by the tenant or any person residing or lodging with him or any sub-tenant of his and, in the case of any ill-treatment by a person lodging with the tenant or a sub-tenant of his, where the court is satisfied that the tenant has not, before the making of the order in question, taken such steps as he ought reasonably to have taken for the removal of the lodger or sub-tenant, as the case may be.

See notes under case 3 above.

Case 5: Notice to quit by tenant

15.25   Where the tenant has given notice to quit and, in consequence of that notice, the landlord has contracted to sell or let the dwelling-house or has taken any other steps as the result of which he would, in the opinion of the court, be seriously prejudiced if he could not obtain possession.

There must be a valid tenant's notice to quit before a landlord can rely on this ground for possession.[36] The words 'notice to quit' have their normal technical meaning (see para 12.6) and the disappearance of a tenant followed by a return by him of the keys did not amount to 'notice to quit'.[37] Similarly an agreement to move out is not sufficient.[38]

15.26   There are no recent cases on the meaning of 'serious prejudice'. In an old case decided on a section with different wording, it was held that there was no prejudice to a landlord where a proposed sale of the premises 'went off' without any liability for damages on the part of the landlord.[39]

Case 6: Subletting without the landlord's consent

15.27   Where, without the consent of the landlord, the tenant has, at any time after –

   (a) ...
   (b) 22nd March 1973, in the case of a tenancy which became a regulated tenancy by virtue of section 14 of the Counter-Inflation Act 1973;
   (bb) the commencement of section 73 of the Housing Act 1980, in the case of a tenancy which became a regulated tenancy by virtue of that section;

36   *De Vries v Sparks* (1927) 137 LT 441.
37   *Standingford v Bruce* [1926] 1 KB 466.
38   *De Vries v Sparks* (1927) 137 LT 441.
39   *Hunt v Bliss* (1919) 89 LJKB 174.

(c) 14th August 1974, in the case of a regulated furnished tenancy; or
(d) 8th December 1965, in the case of any other tenancy,
assigned or sublet the whole of the dwelling-house or sublet part of
the dwelling-house, the remainder being already sublet.

This ground gives protection to landlords against the risk of finding someone totally unknown to them irremovably installed in the
property.[40] The ground applies even if there is no prohibition against
assigning or subletting in the tenancy agreement. The word 'assigned'
includes a vesting assent (that is, a transfer of a lease made to imple-
ment the terms of a will) made by executors of a deceased tenant
which takes effect as an assignment.[41] It does not, however, apply
unless all of the premises rented have been disposed of by assigning
or subletting. In practice the ground normally applies only to subletting or assignment by a contractual tenant. If a statutory tenant
sublets the whole of premises, Rent Act protection is lost because the
tenant can no longer occupy the premises as a residence.[42] It is not
possible to assign a statutory tenancy (see above).

15.28 Consent to a subletting or assignment may be given implicitly,[43]
for example, by accepting rent for some time after acquiring knowledge of the subletting.[44] Consent may be given after the subletting
or assignment, at any time up to the issue of proceedings.[45] If the
tenancy agreement contains a provision that the tenant cannot assign
or sublet without the permission of the landlord, there is an implied
proviso that consent cannot be withheld unreasonably.[46]

15.29 It is not necessary for a landlord to prove that a subtenancy or
subtenancies have continued to exist right up to the date when proceedings were issued. It is enough that a tenant has at any time sublet
or assigned the whole of the premises.[47] However, there are likely
to be strong grounds for arguing that it is unreasonable to make an
order for possession if there is no subsisting subtenancy at the time

---

40 *Hyde v Pimley* [1952] 2 All ER 102.
41 *Pazgate Ltd v McGrath* (1985) 17 HLR 127.
42 See para 14.2. See also *Poland v Cadogan (Earl)* [1980] 3 All ER 544 dealing
    with similar provisions in the Leasehold Reform Act 1967 where the
    comparable wording is slightly different. It seems unlikely that statutory
    tenants who enjoy only personal rights in premises are able to create
    subtenancies of the whole, but cf, comments of Ormrod LJ in *Trustees of
    Smith's (Henry) Charity v Willson* [1983] 1 All ER 73.
43 *Regional Properties Ltd v Frankenschwerth* [1951] 1 KB 631; [1951] 1 All ER 178.
44 *Hyde v Pimley* [1952] 2 All ER 102.
45 Ibid.
46 Landlord and Tenant Act 1927 s19 and Landlord and Tenant Act 1988 s1.
47 *Finkle v Strzelczyk* [1961] 3 All ER 409.

when proceedings are issued. This ground for possession can enable a landlord to obtain possession against both the tenant and subtenant (notwithstanding the effect of Rent Act 1977 s137), provided that the court is satisfied that it is reasonable to make the order.[48]

15.30   Only tenants who have sublet after the various dates specified in case 6 are caught by this ground. Subparagraph (a) related to controlled tenancies and was repealed by the Housing Act 1980. Subparagraph (b) relates to tenancies which were brought into Rent Act protection by amendments to Rent Act 1977 s4 which provides the maximum rateable values for dwelling-houses falling within full Rent Act protection. Subparagraph (bb) relates to tenancies from the Crown Estates Commission which were brought into full Rent Act protection by the Housing Act 1980.

Case 7

15.31   Case 7 was repealed by Housing Act 1980 s152 and Sch 26. It related to controlled off-licences.

Case 8: Former employees

15.32   Where the dwelling-house is reasonably required by the landlord for occupation as a residence for some person engaged in his whole-time employment, or in the whole-time employment of some tenant from him or with whom, conditional on housing being provided, a contract for such employment has been entered into, and the tenant was in the employment of the landlord or a former landlord, and the dwelling-house was let to him in consequence of that employment and he has ceased to be in that employment.

In order to succeed under this ground a landlord must prove that:[49]

- *The tenant was in the employment of the landlord or a former land-lord at the time when the premises were let.*[50] 'Tenant' refers to the original contractual tenant. For example, if the son of the original tenant becomes a statutory tenant by succession,[51] the landlord can rely on this ground for possession if the father was in the land-lord's employment at the beginning of that contractual tenancy.[52]

---

48   *Leith Properties Ltd v Springer* [1982] 3 All ER 731, CA.
49   *Munro v Daw* [1948] 1 KB 125; [1947] 2 All ER 360 and *Benninga (Mitcham) Ltd v Bijstra* [1946] KB 58; [1945] 2 All ER 433.
50   *Fuggle (RF) Ltd v Gadsden* [1948] 2 KB 236.
51   RA 1977 Sch 1.
52   *Bolsover Colliery Co Ltd v Abbott* [1946] KB 8.

- *Premises were let in consequence of that employment.* This is a question of fact in each case.[53] The questions to be asked are: 'What was the reason for the landlord letting the premises to the tenant?' 'What was in the mind of the person who let the premises?' 'Was it let because of the tenant's employment or was there another reason?'[54] It is possible for premises to be let in consequence of employment even if there is no reference to the premises in the employee's contract of employment. If premises are let some time after an employee originally took the job, the letting may be in consequence of the employment or it may be treated as a separate 'independent' transaction.[55] If a former employer grants a new contractual tenancy after the tenant has stopped working for that employer, the new tenancy cannot be in consequence of that employment.[56] It is not necessary for it to be shown that the tenancy was granted as a result of any particular type of employment, only that it was in consequence of the relationship of employer and employee.[57] It is not possible for landlord and tenant to agree that a particular tenancy was not created in consequence of employment when the facts show clearly that the opposite was the case.[58]

- *Employment has ceased.* A tenant who has changed jobs (for example, from a farm worker to a laundry machine operator) but who is still employed by the same employer has not ceased to be in employment.[59]

- *The premises are reasonably required by the landlord for occupation as a residence by someone engaged in the whole-time employment of the landlord or someone with whom a contract of employment has been entered into which is conditional on housing being provided.* When the court considers whether or not the proposed new occupant is employed or whether a contract of employment has been entered into, the relevant date is the date of the court hearing.[60] Note that the premises must be reasonably required.[61]

53 *Long Eaton Co-op v Smith* [1949] 2 KB 144; [1949] 1 All ER 633 considering agricultural wages legislation.

54 *Braithwaite and Co Ltd v Elliot* [1947] KB 177; [1946] 2 All ER 537 at 539, cf, *Queen's Club Gardens v Bignell* [1924] 1 KB 117.

55 *Long Eaton Co-op v Smith* [1949] 2 KB 144; [1949] 1 All ER 633.

56 *Lever Brothers v Caton* (1921) 37 TLR 664.

57 *Munro v Daw* [1947] 2 All ER 360.

58 *Harvard v Shears* (1967) 111 SJ 683.

59 *Duncan v Hay* [1956] 1 WLR 1329.

60 *Benninga (Mitcham) Ltd v Bijstra* [1945] 2 All ER 433.

61 See comments on similar wording in case 9 at para 15.35.

15.33 A tenant may be entitled to compensation if a landlord obtains an order for possession under case 8 by deceit. See para 15.42.

Case 9: Premises required for occupation by a landlord or landlord's family

15.34 Where the dwelling-house is reasonably required by the landlord for occupation as a residence for –
(a) himself, or
(b) any son or daughter of his over 18 years of age, or
(c) his father or mother, or
(d) if the dwelling-house is let on or subject to a regulated tenancy, the father or mother of his wife or husband *spouse or civil partner,*
and the landlord did not become landlord by purchasing the dwelling-house or any interest therein after –
(i) 7th November 1956, in the case of a tenancy which was then a controlled tenancy;
(ii) 8th March 1973, in the case of a tenancy which became a regulated tenancy by virtue of section 14 of the Counter-Inflation Act 1973;
(iii) 24th May 1974, in the case of a regulated furnished tenancy; or
(iv) 23rd March 1965, in the case of any other tenancy.

Note: the words 'spouse or civil partner' were inserted in substitution for the words 'husband or wife' by Civil Partnership Act 2004 Sch 8.

This ground for possession has to be read in conjunction with Rent Act 1977 Sch 15 Pt III para 1, which provides:

> A court shall not make an order for possession of a dwelling-house by reason only that the circumstances of the case fall within Case 9 in Part I of this Schedule if the court is satisfied that, having regard to all the circumstances of the case, including the question whether other accommodation is available for the landlord or the tenant, greater hardship would be caused by granting the order than by refusing to grant it.

'Reasonably required'

15.35 Case 9 applies where the premises are reasonably required as a residence by the landlord or certain specified members of the landlord's family. The words 'reasonably required' mean more than a 'desire' on the landlord's part, but less than 'absolute necessity'.[62] The court should consider whether this requirement is reasonable on the landlord's part, and in doing so the tenant's interests are not relevant.[63]

---

62 *Aitken v Shaw* 1933 SLT 21 and *Kennealy v Dunne* [1977] QB 837.
63 *Funnell v Armstrong* [1962] EGD 319.

The tenant's interests should be taken into account when the overall questions of greater hardship and reasonableness are considered (see below). Matters which are relevant when considering whether the landlord's requirements are reasonable are, for example, the nature and place of the landlord's business, the size of the family, their actual residence or lack of it, their health, and 'innumerable other possible factors'.[64] The requirement need not be an immediate requirement.[65] It is perfectly proper for a landlord to seek possession under case 9 where the need for accommodation will exist in the ascertainable but not too far distant future.[66] However, possession has been refused in a case where a landlord stated that he required a basement for his daughter to live in on her marriage which might take place in two years' time,[67] and in a case where the trial judge had found that premises let to five surveyors were 'an investment property' which was not required by the landlord.[68] The landlord must need the premises 'with a view to living there for some reasonable period, definite or indefinite', and not for the purpose of sale[69] or for temporary accommodation while repairs are carried out in the landlord's own accommodation.[70] A landlord does, however, come within this ground for possession even if only part of the premises is required.[71]

15.36   The premises must be required for the landlord, or for the landlord's children, the landlord's parents or parents-in-law.[72] It has been said that this includes 'all normal emanations of' the landlord,[73] including a housekeeper who lived in the same household as the landlord and was paid to look after children after the landlord had separated from his wife.[74] It has also included the son of a landlord's wife, even though he was not the landlord's son and the landlord had not adopted him.[75] It does not, however, include someone who would

64 *Chandler v Strevett* [1947] 1 All ER 164 per Bucknill LJ.
65 Cf, *Aitken v Shaw* 1933 SLT 21.
66 *Kidder v Birch* (1983) 265 EG 773. See also *Alexander v Mohamadzadeh* (1986) 18 HLR 90; (1985) 276 EG 1258 (relevant date for deciding whether premises are required is date of hearing, not date of issue of proceedings).
67 *Kissias v Lehany* [1979] CLY 1625.
68 *Ghelani v Bowie* [1988] 42 EG 119, CA.
69 *Rowe v Truelove* (1976) 241 EG 533.
70 *Johnson-Sneddon v Harper* May 1977 *LAG Bulletin* 114.
71 *Kelley v Goodwin* [1947] 1 All ER 810.
72 But not step-children: *Towns v Hole* [1956] CLY 7493 and *Harty v Greenwich LBC and Done* [1956] CLY 7494.
73 *Richter v Wilson* [1963] 2 QB 426.
74 *Smith v Penny* [1947] KB 230.
75 *Theodotou v Potsos* (1991) 23 HLR 356; [1991] 2 EGLR 93; CA.

occupy premises as a separate household and not as part of the land-lord's household, for example, where it was intended that a couple should live in a separate self-contained flat in the same building as the landlord, in order to look after him.[76] Where premises are owned by joint landlords they must reasonably be required as a residence for *all* the joint landlords.[77] Personal representatives of the deceased landlord may be a 'landlord' for the purposes of case 9. Normally, it is necessary for the personal representatives to have a beneficial interest in the premises in order to come within this ground for possession, otherwise they are acting in breach of trust. However, in exceptional cases personal representatives who do not have a beneficial interest may reasonably require possession, for example, so that children of the original, deceased landlord may live in the premises.[78]

Landlord by purchase

15.37   Landlords are not entitled to rely on case 9 if they became landlords by purchasing the premises after specified dates.[79] (Counter-Inflation Act 1973 s14 (in subparagraph (ii)) is a reference to tenancies which came within full Rent Act protection when the rateable value limits in the Rent Act 1977 s4 were increased.)

15.38   See the explanation of the equivalent wording in Housing Act 1988 Sch 2 ground 1 at para 10.30.

'Greater hardship'

15.39   Tenants have a complete defence to possession proceedings brought under case 9 if they can prove that greater hardship would be caused to them by a possession order than would be caused to the landlord by refusing to grant the possession order. The burden of proving this lies on the tenant.[80] The court should consider how the balance of

---

76 *Richter v Wilson* [1963] 2 QB 426 and *Bloomfield v Westley* [1963] 2 All ER 337.

77 *Baker v Lewis* [1946] 2 All ER 592, *McIntyre v Hardcastle* [1948] 2 KB 82, but see *Bostock v Tacher de la Pagerie* (1987) 282 EG 999; (1987) 19 HLR 358, CA (legal estate owned by father who sought possession as residence for daughter who was equitable tenant in common of beneficial interest). Cf also, *Tilling v Whiteman* [1980] AC 1 (on case 11).

78 *Patel v Patel* [1982] 1 All ER 68, cf, *Sharpe v Nicholls* [1945] KB 382; [1945] 2 All ER 55 and *Parker v Rosenberg* [1947] KB 371; [1947] 1 All ER 87.

79 See para 15.33.

80 *Smith v Penny* [1947] KB 230, *Sims v Wilson* [1946] 2 All ER 261, *Kelley v Goodwin* [1947] 1 All ER 810, *Kidder v Birch* (1983) 265 EG 773, *Robinson v Donovan* [1946] 2 All ER 731, *Chandler v Strevett* [1947] 1 All ER 164 and *Manaton v Edwards* (1985) 276 EG 1256; (1985) 18 HLR 116, CA.

hardship will operate at the time when a possession order would take effect.[81] The 'greater hardship test' gives the court a very wide discretion to take into account all factors which may affect both landlord and tenant.[82] Matters which may be taken into consideration include:

- The availability of other accommodation for both landlord and tenant. Judges can apply their own knowledge of the difficulty in finding accommodation[83] but it is always advisable for tenants to be able to give evidence about the unsuccessful attempts which they have made to find other accommodation and any particular local accommodation difficulties. The fact that a tenant has taken no steps to look for other accommodation may be prejudicial.[84]
- The financial means of both parties, for example, the ability or inability of a tenant to buy a house.[85]
- The health of the parties, both physical and mental, and the nearness of relatives.[86]
- Hardship which may occur in the future, as well as present hardship.[87]
- The need for a tenant to sell or to store furniture on moving.[88]
- Hardship which may be caused to all people who may be affected by the grant or refusal of an order for possession including:

  ... relatives, dependants, lodgers, guests and the stranger within the gates but [the court] should weigh such hardship with due regard to the status of the persons affected and their 'proximity' to the tenant or landlord.[89]

The court should not, however, take into account trivial things such as 'the absence of a view of a neighbouring hill, river, tree or something pleasant of that kind'.[90]

---

81 *Wheeler v Evans* [1948] 1 KB 459 and *Kidder v Birch* (1983) 265 EG 773.

82 *Robinson v Donovan* [1946] 2 All ER 731.

83 *King v Taylor* [1954] 3 All ER 373 and *Bassett v Fraser* (1981) 9 HLR 105. See also *Manaton v Edwards* (1985) 276 EG 1256.

84 *Kelley v Goodwin* [1947] 1 All ER 810 and *Alexander v Mohamadzadeh* (1986) 18 HLR 90; (1985) 276 EG 1258.

85 *Kelley v Goodwin* [1947] 1 All ER 810.

86 *Thomas v Fryer* [1970] 2 All ER 1 and *King v Taylor* [1954] 3 All ER 373.

87 *Sims v Wilson* [1946] 2 All ER 261, *Wheeler v Evans* [1948] 1 KB 459 and *Bumstead v Wood* (1946) 175 LT 149.

88 *Sims v Wilson* [1946] 2 All ER 261.

89 *Harte v Frampton* [1948] 1 KB 73; [1947] 2 All ER 604.

90 *Coplans v King* [1947] 2 All ER 393.

15.40   There is a 'convention' that where the only issues before a court are questions of greater hardship and reasonableness, no order for costs should be made against the party who loses.[91]

15.41   It is hard for a landlord or tenant who is dissatisfied with a trial judge's finding in relation to greater hardship to succeed on appeal. The Court of Appeal takes the view that in all but exceptional cases greater hardship is a matter for the trial judge, and that findings made at first instance should not be upset.[92] Generally inferences made by judges about greater hardship are based on their findings of fact and no appeal can be made against a judge's findings of fact. There have, however, been successful appeals where tenants argued that the judge's inferences drawn from the facts were wrong and where the judge failed to consider the question of greater hardship properly. It appears that, contrary to the normal rule,[93] the Court of Appeal may be able to take into account material changes in circumstances which have occurred since the original hearing.[94]

Compensation for misrepresentation or concealment

15.42   Rent Act 1977 s102 provides:

> Where, in such circumstances as are specified in Case 8 or Case 9 in Schedule 15 to this Act, a landlord obtains an order for possession of a dwelling-house let on a protected tenancy or subject to a statutory tenancy and it is subsequently made to appear to the court that the order was obtained by misrepresentation or concealment of material facts, the court may order the landlord to pay to the former tenant such sum as appears sufficient as compensation for damage or loss sustained by the tenant as a result of the order.

This provision is similar to Housing Act 1988 s12 (see para 10.108), but, unlike Housing Act 1988 s12, only applies to two grounds for possession: cases 8 and 9.

Case 10: Overcharging of subtenant

15.43   Where the court is satisfied that the rent charged by the tenant –
(a) for any sublet part of the dwelling-house which is a dwelling-house let on a protected tenancy or subject to a statutory tenancy is or was

91 *Funnell v Armstrong* [1962] EGD 319.
92 *Coplans v King* [1947] 2 All ER 393 and *Hodges v Blee* (1987) 283 EG 1215.
93 *Goldthorpe v Bain* [1952] 2 All ER 23.
94 *King v Taylor* [1954] 3 All ER 373.

in excess of the maximum rent for the time being recoverable for that part, having regard to ... Part III of this Act, or

(b) for any sublet part of the dwelling-house which is subject to a restricted contract is or was in excess of the maximum (if any) which it is lawful for the lessor, within the meaning of Part V of this Act to require or receive having regard to the provisions of that Part.

Case 10 applies where a tenant overcharges a subtenant. It may come about in a number of ways, for example, by charging more than the registered rent,[95] where there has been a failure to comply with the statutory provisions relating to agreed increases in rent,[96] or where the tenant has charged a subtenant who enjoys a restricted contract more than the rent registered by a rent tribunal.[97] This ground for possession does not apply where the interest of the suboccupant is outside the protection of the Rent Act 1977 or where there is merely an arrangement to share the premises with other people.[98] If a subtenant is overcharged, the court may make an order for possession of the whole of the premises rented by the tenant or just that part to which the overcharging relates.[99]

15.44   There appears to be no reported authority on the position of a subtenant when a landlord has established that there has been overcharging within the meaning of case 10. In ordinary circumstances an order for possession against a tenant also operates against a subtenant, but it would seem that if the subtenancy is lawful, the subtenant would become a direct tenant of the landlord as a result of Rent Act 1977 s137.[100]

95 RA 1977 ss44 and 45.

96 RA 1977 s51.

97 RA 1977 s88.

98 *Kenyon v Walker* [1946] 2 All ER 595.

99 *Boulton v Sutherland* [1938] 1 All ER 488.

100 It is debatable whether or not a landlord would be able to rely on this ground against the subtenant – cf, *Leith Properties Ltd v Springer* [1982] 3 All ER 731, CA, where it was held that a landlord was entitled to rely on case 6 against a subtenant notwithstanding the effect of RA 1977 s137. Even if that reasoning does apply to proceedings under case 10, it is hard to imagine circumstances where it would be reasonable for the court to make an order against the subtenant.

Mandatory grounds

Case 11: Returning owner-occupier

15.45   Where a person (in this Case referred to as 'the owner-occupier') who let the dwelling-house on a regulated tenancy had, at any time before the letting, occupied it as his residence and –

(a) not later than the relevant date the landlord gave notice in writing to the tenant that possession might be recovered under this Case, and

(b) the dwelling-house has not, since –

  (i) 22nd March 1973, in the case of a tenancy which became a regulated tenancy by virtue of section 14 of the Counter-Inflation Act 1973;

  (ii) 14th August 1974, in the case of a regulated furnished tenancy; or

  (iii) 8th December 1965, in the case of any other tenancy,
  been let by the owner-occupier on a protected tenancy with respect to which the condition mentioned in paragraph (a) above was not satisfied, and

(c) the court is of the opinion that of the conditions set out in Part V of this Schedule one of those in paragraphs (a) and (c) to (f) is satisfied.

If the court is of the opinion that, notwithstanding that the condition in paragraph (a) or (b) above is not complied with, it is just and equitable to make an order for possession of the dwelling-house, the court may dispense with the requirements of either or both of those paragraphs as the case may require.

The giving of a notice before 14th August 1974 under section 79 of the Rent Act 1968 shall be treated, in the case of a regulated furnished tenancy, as compliance with paragraph (a) of this Case.

Where the dwelling-house has been let by the owner-occupier on a protected tenancy (in this paragraph referred to as 'the earlier tenancy') granted on or after 16th November 1984 but not later than the end of the period of two months beginning with the commencement of the Rent (Amendment) Act 1985 and either –

(i) the earlier tenancy was granted for a term certain (whether or not to be followed by a further term or to continue thereafter from year to year or some other period) and was during that term a protected shorthold tenancy as defined in section 52 of the Housing Act 1980, or

(ii) the conditions mentioned in paragraphs (a) to (c) of Case 20 were satisfied with respect to the dwelling-house and the earlier tenancy, then for the purposes of paragraph (b) above the condition in paragraph (a) above is to be treated as having been satisfied with respect to the earlier tenancy.

15.46 This ground for possession has been amended twice since the 1977 Act, first by Housing Act 1980 s66(1) which inserted subparagraph (c), and, second, by the Rent (Amendment) Act 1985 which inserted the provisions in brackets at the beginning and end of the case. Like cases 12 and 20 it should be read in conjunction with Rent Act 1977 Sch 15 Pt V, which was inserted by Housing Act 1980 s66(3) and Sch 7 and which provides:

Provisions applying to Cases 11, 12 and 20

1. In this Part of this Schedule – '
    mortgage' includes a charge and 'mortgagee' shall be construed accordingly;
    'owner' means, in relation to Case 11, the owner-occupier; and
    'successor in title' means any person deriving title from the owner, other than a purchaser for value or a person deriving title from a purchaser for value.

2. The conditions referred to in paragraph (c) in each of Cases 11 and 12 and in paragraph (e)(ii) of Case 20 are that –

    (a) the dwelling-house is required as a residence for the owner or any member of his family who resided with the owner when he last occupied the dwelling-house as a residence;

    (b) the owner has retired from regular employment and requires the dwelling-house as a residence;

    (c) the owner has died and the dwelling-house is required as a residence for a member of his family who was residing with him at the time of his death;

    (d) the owner has died and the dwelling-house is required by a successor in title as his residence or for the purpose of disposing of it with vacant possession;

    (e) the dwelling-house is subject to a mortgage, made by deed and granted before the tenancy, and the mortgagee –

        (i) is entitled to exercise a power of sale conferred on him by the mortgage or by section 101 of the Law of Property Act 1925; and

        (ii) requires the dwelling-house for the purpose of disposing of it with vacant possession in exercise of that power; and

    (f) the dwelling-house is not reasonably suitable to the needs of the owner, having regard to his place of work, and he requires it for the purpose of disposing of it with vacant possession and of using the proceeds of that disposal in acquiring, as his residence, a dwelling-house which is more suitable to those needs.

In Case 11, as with all the other grounds for possession in Rent Act 1977 Sch 15 Pt II (ie, cases 11 to 20) the phrase 'relevant date' is defined by Schedule 15 Pt III para 2, which provides:

2. Any reference in Part II of this Schedule to the relevant date shall be construed as follows –

(a) except in a case falling within paragraph (b) or (c) below, if the protected tenancy, or, in the case of a statutory tenancy, the previous contractual tenancy, was created before 8th December 1965, the relevant date means 7th June 1966; and

(b) except in a case falling within paragraph (c) below, if the tenancy became a regulated tenancy by virtue of section 14 of the Counter-Inflation Act 1973 and the tenancy or, in the case of a statutory tenancy, the previous contractual tenancy, was created before 22nd March 1973, the relevant date means 22nd September 1973; and

(c) in the case of a regulated furnished tenancy, if the tenancy or, in the case of a statutory furnished tenancy, the previous contractual tenancy was created before 14th August 1974, the relevant date means 13th February 1975; and

(d) in any other case, the relevant date means the date of the commencement of the regulated tenancy in question.

15.47   The purpose of case 11 was to allow owner-occupiers who intended to go away and then to return to their homes, to let the premises while they were away.[101] To rely on case 11 a landlord must prove that:

• *Prior to the granting of the tenancy in question, the landlord had at some time in the past occupied the premises as a residence.* The effect of the Rent (Amendment) Act 1985 is that it is not necessary for landlords to prove that they occupied the premises immediately before the granting of the tenancy.[102] Residence at any time in the past is sufficient. It is sufficient for such previous residence to have been temporary and intermittent, although visits to a house by a landlord to stay with a partner who lives there do not count as 'occupation as a residence'.[103] The landlord must previously have occupied the same premises as those which are let to the tenant

---

101 Griffiths LJ in *Bradshaw and Martin v Baldwin-Wiseman* (1985) 17 HLR 260 at 264; (1985) 49 P & CR 382; [1985] 1 EGLR 123.

102 Reversing the effect of *Pocock v Steel* [1985] 1 WLR 229. The Rent (Amendment) Act 1985 operates retrospectively and applies to tenancies created before it received royal assent: *Hewitt v Lewis* [1986] 1 All ER 927, CA.

103 *Naish v Curzon* (1984) 17 HLR 220; (1984) 51 P & CR 229; [1985] 1 EGLR 117, CA, *Mistry v Isidore* (1990) 22 HLR 281; [1990] 2 EGLR 97, CA and *Ibie v Trubshaw* (1990) 22 HLR 191, CA.

whom the landlord is seeking to evict: it is not sufficient for the landlord to have lived in other rooms in the same building.

- *Notice of intention to rely on case 11 was given before the commencement of the tenancy.* The schedule provides that such notice must be in writing, although no particular form is necessary. It has been said that it is 'of the utmost importance to a tenant that he should appreciate when he takes rented property whether or not he is obtaining security of tenure'.[104] Such notice must actually be received by the tenant, otherwise it has not been given in accordance with the terms of the schedule. It is not enough for the landlord merely to say that it was sent to the tenant if a tenant's evidence that it was not received is believed.[105] Alternatively the landlord may satisfy the court that it is just and equitable to dispense with service of the notice. The criteria which apply are the same as under Housing Act 1988 Sch 2 Pt I (see para 10.29).

- *All tenants to whom the premises have previously been let since the dates specified in case 11 have been given written notice.* Again there is a provision which entitles the court to dispense with this requirement if it is considered just and equitable to do so.

- *One of the requirements in subparagraphs (a), (c), (d), (e) or (f) in Rent Act 1977 Sch 15 Pt V is satisfied.* The most important of these is that the premises are 'required as a residence'. All that is required is that the landlord 'bona fide wants' or 'genuinely has the immediate intention' of occupying the premises.[106] The landlord need not require the premises as a permanent residence and fairly intermittent residence will be sufficient.[107] This is a question of fact in each case. It is sufficient if only one of two joint landlords requires the premises as a residence.[108] Another important use of case 11 would be where a landlord's place of work has changed and he or she wishes to sell the house with vacant possession in order to buy a new house which is more suitable, bearing in mind the

---

104 *Bradshaw and Martin v Baldwin-Wiseman* (1985) 17 HLR 260; (1985) 49 P & CR 382; [1985] 1 EGLR 123.

105 *Minay v Sentongo* (1983) 45 P & CR 190.

106 *Kennealy v Dunne* [1977] QB 837, cf, *Ghelani v Bowie* (1988) 42 EG 119, CA.

107 *Naish v Curzon* (1984) 17 HLR 220; (1984) 51 P & CR 229; [1985] 1 EGLR 117, where it was argued by the tenant that the landlord required the premises only for holidays and short visits, and *Davies v Peterson* (1989) 21 HLR 63; [1989] 06 EG 130, CA.

108 *Tilling v Whiteman* [1980] AC 1.

place of work.[109] The other situations in which possession may be obtained under case 11 arise following the death of the landlord or relate to rights of a mortgagee.

Case 12: Retirement homes

15.48   Where the landlord (in this Case referred to as 'the owner') intends to occupy the dwelling-house as his residence at such time as he might retire from regular employment and has let it on a regulated tenancy before he has so retired and –

(a) not later than the relevant date the landlord gave notice in writing to the tenant that possession might be recovered under this Case; and

(b) the dwelling-house has not, since 14th August 1974, been let by the owner on a protected tenancy with respect to which the condition mentioned in paragraph (a) above was not satisfied; and

(c) the court is of the opinion that of the conditions set out in Part V of this Schedule one of those paragraphs (b) to (e) is satisfied.

If the court is of the opinion that, notwithstanding that the condition in paragraph (a) or (b) above is not complied with, it is just and equitable to make an order for possession of the dwelling-house, the court may dispense with the requirements of either or both those paragraphs, as the case may require.

This ground for possession is similar in format to case 11. For the definition of 'relevant date' see Rent Act 1977 Sch 15 Pt III para 2 at para 15.45. Provisions as to the giving of written notice and the circumstances in which notice may be dispensed with are also similar to those relating to case 11.

15.49   Case 12 may be relied upon if:

- the owner has retired and requires the premises as 'a retirement home'; or
- the owner has died and the premises are required as a residence for a member of the family ('member of the family' is not defined and is wider than the definition in case 9); or
- the owner has died and a successor in title either requires the premises as a residence or wishes to dispose of them with vacant possession; or
- in some circumstances a mortgagee requires the premises for the purpose of disposing of them with vacant possession.

109 There must be a connection within a reasonable time between the proposed sale and purchase: *Bissessar v Ghosn* (1986) 18 HLR 486, CA.

Case 13: Out of season holiday lets

15.50   Where the dwelling-house is let under a tenancy for a term of years certain not exceeding 8 months and –

(a) not later than the relevant date the landlord gave notice in writing to the tenant that possession might be recovered under this Case; and

(b) the dwelling-house was, at some time within the period of 12 months ending on the relevant date, occupied under a right to occupy it for a holiday.

For the purposes of this case a tenancy shall be treated as being for a term of years certain notwithstanding that it is liable to determination by re-entry or on the happening of any event other than the giving of notice by the landlord to determine the term. This ground is almost identical to Housing Act 1988 Sch 2 ground 3 (see para 10.33).

It is important to note that, unlike cases 11 and 12, the court has no power to dispense with the requirement for service of notice prior to the grant of the tenancy.[110]

Case 14: Educational institutions

15.51   Where the dwelling-house is let under a tenancy for a term of years certain not exceeding 12 months and –

(a) not later than the relevant date the landlord gave notice in writing to the tenant that possession might be recovered under this Case; and

(b) at some time within the period of 12 months ending on the relevant date, the dwelling-house was subject to such a tenancy as is referred to in section 8(1) of this Act.

For the purposes of this Case a tenancy shall be treated as being for a term of years certain notwithstanding that it is liable to determination by re-entry or on the happening of any event other than the giving of notice by the landlord to determine the term.

15.52   This ground applies to any premises which, during the period of 12 months preceding the current tenancy, were let by a specified educational institution to a student who was pursuing or intended to pursue a course of study provided by that institution or by another specified educational institution.[111]

110 Cf, *Fowler v Minchin* (1987) 19 HLR 224; [1987] 1 EGLR 108, CA.

111 See RA 1977 s8 and the Assured and Protected Tenancies (Lettings to Students) Regulations 1998 SI No 1967 as amended.

It is almost identical to Housing Act 1988 Sch 2 ground 4 (see para 10.35). Notice in writing must have been given to the current tenant prior to the grant of the tenancy and the court has no power to dispense with service of that notice.

Case 15: Ministers of religion[112]

15.53   Where the dwelling-house is held for the purpose of being available for occupation by a minister of religion as a residence from which to perform the duties of his office and –

(a) not later than the relevant date the tenant was given notice in writing that possession might be recovered under this Case, and

(b) the court is satisfied that the dwelling-house is required for occupation by a minister of religion as such a residence.

Case 16: Agricultural employees

15.54   Where the dwelling-house was at any time occupied by a person under the terms of his employment as a person employed in agriculture, and –

(a) the tenant neither is nor at any time was so employed by the landlord and is not the widow of a person who was so employed, and

(b) not later than the relevant date, the tenant was given notice in writing that possession might be recovered under this Case, and

(c) the court is satisfied that the dwelling-house is required for occupation by a person employed, or to be employed, by the landlord in agriculture.

For the purposes of this Case 'employed', 'employment' and 'agriculture' have the same meanings as in the Agricultural Wages Act 1948.

The court cannot dispense with the requirement that notice must be served prior to the commencement of the tenancy. A term in a tenancy agreement that the tenant will vacate on 28 days' notice if the premises are required for another farm worker is not sufficient,[113] but a certificate of a fair rent which was handed to the tenant before the commencement of the tenancy and which stated that the tenancy was to be subject to case 16 has been held to be sufficient.[114]

112 Cf, HA 1988 Sch 2 ground 5, para 10.37 above.

113 See *Fowler v Minchin* (1987) 19 HLR 224; [1987] 1 EGLR 108, CA, where a possession order was refused.

114 *Springfield Investments v Bell* (1990) 22 HLR 440; [1991] 02 EG 157, CA.

Case 17: Redundant farmhouses

15.54A Where proposals for amalgamation, approved for the purposes of a scheme under section 26 of the Agriculture Act 1967, have been carried out and, at the time when the proposals were submitted, the dwelling-house was occupied by a person responsible (whether as owner, tenant, or servant or agent of another) for the control of the farming of any part of the land comprised in the amalgamation and

(a) after the carrying out of the proposals, the dwelling-house was let on a regulated tenancy otherwise than to, or to the widow of, either a person ceasing to be so responsible as part of the amalgamation or a person who is, or at any time was, employed by the landlord in agriculture, and

(b) not later than the relevant date the tenant was given notice in writing that possession might be recovered under this Case, and

(c) the court is satisfied that the dwelling-house is required for occupation by a person employed, or to be employed, by the landlord in agriculture, and

(d) the proceedings for possession are commenced by the landlord at any time during the period of 5 years beginning with the date on which the proposals for the amalgamation were approved or, if occupation of the dwelling-house after the amalgamation continued in, or was first taken by, a person ceasing to be responsible as mentioned in paragraph (a) above or his widow, during a period expiring 3 years after the date on which the dwelling-house next became unoccupied.

For the purposes of this Case 'employed' and 'agriculture' have the same meanings as in the Agricultural Wages Act 1948 and 'amalgamation' has the same meaning as in Part II of the Agriculture Act 1967.

Case 18: More redundant farmhouses

15.54B Where –

(a) the last occupier of the dwelling-house before the relevant date was a person, or the widow of a person, who was at some time during his occupation responsible (whether as owner, tenant, or servant or agent of another) for the control of the farming of land which formed, together with the dwelling-house, an agricultural unit within the meaning of the Agriculture Act 1947, and

(b) the tenant is neither –

(i) a person, or the widow of a person, who is or has at any time been responsible for the control of the farming of any part of the said land, nor

(ii) a person, or the widow of a person, who is or at any time was employed by the landlord in agriculture, and

(c) the creation of the tenancy was not preceded by the carrying out in connection with any of the said land of an amalgamation approved for the purposes of a scheme under section 26 of the Agriculture Act 1967, and

(d) not later than the relevant date the tenant was given notice in writing that possession might be recovered under this Case, and

(e) the court is satisfied that the dwelling-house is required for occupation either by a person responsible or to be responsible (whether as owner, tenant, or servant or agent of another) for the control of the farming of any part of the said land or by a person employed or to be employed by the landlord in agriculture, and

(f) in a case where the relevant date was before 9th August 1972, the proceedings for possession are commenced by the landlord before the expiry of 5 years from the date on which the occupier referred to in paragraph (a) above went out of occupation.

For the purposes of this Case 'employed' and 'agriculture' have the same meanings as in the Agricultural Wages Act 1948 and 'amalgamation' has the same meaning as in Part II of the Agriculture Act 1967.

Case 19: Protected shorthold tenancies

15.55   This ground for possession is now largely of historical interest only. Protected shorthold tenancies could only be granted between 1980 and 1989 for a fixed term of between one and five years. All new tenancies granted to former protected shorthold tenancies are automatically assured shorthold tenancies.[115]

Case 20: Lettings by armed forces personnel

15.55A   Where the dwelling-house was let by a person (in this Case referred to as 'the owner') at any time after the commencement of section 67 of the Housing Act 1980 and –

(a) at the time when the owner acquired the dwelling-house he was a member of the regular armed forces of the Crown;

(b) at the relevant date the owner was a member of the regular armed forces of the Crown;

(c) not later than the relevant date the owner gave notice in writing to the tenant that possession might be recovered under this Case;

(d) the dwelling-house has not, since the commencement of section 67 of the Act of 1980 been let by the owner on a protected tenancy with respect to which the condition mentioned in paragraph (c) above was not satisfied; and

115   HA 1980 ss51–55 and HA 1988 s34(3). See *Defending Possession Proceedings*, 4th edn, 1997, pp232–233.

(e) the court is of the opinion that –
  (i) the dwelling-house is required as a residence for the owner; or
  (ii) of the conditions set out in Part V of this Schedule one of those in paragraphs (c) to (f) is satisfied.

If the court is of the opinion that, notwithstanding that the condition in paragraph (c) or (d) above is not complied with, it is just and equitable to make an order for possession of the dwelling-house, the court may dispense with the requirements of either or both of these paragraphs, as the case may require.

For the purposes of this Case 'regular armed forces of the Crown' has the same meaning as in section 1 of the House of Commons Disqualification Act 1975.

15.56   Members of the regular armed forces may rely on this ground for possession only if they were members of the forces at the time when they acquired the premises and at the date when the tenancy began. The provisions relating to the giving of notice are similar to those in case 11. See para 15.45 for reasons in subparagraphs (c) to (f) of Part V which may found a claim for possession.

Other provisions entitling landlords to possession

Statutory overcrowding

15.57   Rent Act 1977 s101 concerns overcrowded dwelling-houses.

101 At any time when a dwelling-house is overcrowded, within the meaning of Part X of the Housing Act 1985 in such circumstances as to render the occupier guilty of an offence, nothing in this Part of this Act shall prevent the immediate landlord of the occupier from obtaining possession of the dwelling-house.

15.58   This section in effect provides an additional mandatory ground for possession. Statutory overcrowding is defined by Housing Act 1985 Pt X, which provides:

324 *Definition of overcrowding*
A dwelling is overcrowded for the purposes of this Part when the number of persons sleeping in the dwelling is such as to contravene –
(a) the standard specified in section 325 (the room standard), or
(b) the standard specified in section 326 (the space standard).

325 *The room standard*
  (1) The room standard is contravened when the number of persons sleeping in a dwelling and the number of rooms available as sleeping accommodation is such that two persons of opposite

sexes who are not living together as husband and wife must sleep in the same room.

(2) For this purpose –
   (a) children under the age of ten shall be left out of account, and
   (b) a room is available as sleeping accommodation if it is of a type normally used in the locality either as a bedroom or as a living room.

326 *The space standard*

(1) The space standard is contravened when the number of persons sleeping in a dwelling is in excess of the permitted number, having regard to the number and floor area of the rooms of the dwelling available as sleeping accommodation.

(2) For this purpose –
   (a) no account shall be taken of a child under the age of one and a child aged one or over but under ten shall be reckoned as one-half of a unit, and
   (b) a room is available as sleeping accommodation if it is of a type normally used in the locality either as a living room or as a bedroom.

(3) The permitted number of persons in relation to a dwelling is whichever is the less of –
   (a) the number specified in Table I in relation to the number of rooms in the dwelling available as sleeping accommodation, and
   (b) the aggregate for all such rooms in the dwelling of the numbers specified in column 2 of Table II in relation to each room of the floor area specified in column 1.

No account shall be taken for the purposes of either Table of a room having a floor area of less than 50 square feet.

TABLE I

Number of rooms	Number of persons
1	2
2	3
3	5
4	7½
5 or more	2 for each room

TABLE II

Floor area of room	Number of persons
110 sq ft or more	2
90 sq ft or more but less than 110 sq ft	1½
70 sq ft or more but less than 90 sq ft	1
50 sq ft or more but less than 70 sq ft	½

(4) The Secretary of State may by regulations prescribe the manner in which the floor area of a room is to be ascertained for the purpose of this section; and the regulations may provide for the exclusion from computation, or the bringing into computation at a reduced figure, of floor space in a part of the room which is of less than a specified height not exceeding eight feet.

(5) Regulations under subsection (4) shall be made by statutory instrument which shall be subject to annulment in pursuance of a resolution of either House of Parliament.

(6) A certificate of the local housing authority stating the number and floor areas of the rooms in a dwelling, and that the floor areas have been ascertained in the prescribed manner, is prima facie evidence for the purposes of legal proceedings of the facts stated in it.

Responsibility of occupier

327 *Penalty for occupier causing or permitting overcrowding*
(1) The occupier of a dwelling who causes or permits it to be over-crowded commits a summary offence, subject to subsection (2).

(2) The occupier is not guilty of an offence –
(a) if the overcrowding is within the exceptions specified in section 328 or 329 (children attaining age of 10 or visiting relatives), or
(b) by reason of anything done under the authority of, and in accordance with any conditions specified in, a licence granted by the local housing authority under section 330.

(3) A person committing an offence under this section is liable on conviction to a fine not exceeding level 2 on the standard scale and to a further fine not exceeding one-tenth of the amount corresponding to that level in respect of every day subsequent to the date on which he is convicted on which the offence continues.

328 *Exception: children attaining age of 1 or 10*
(1) Where a dwelling which would not otherwise be overcrowded becomes overcrowded by reason of a child attaining the age of one or ten, then if the occupier –
(a) applies to the local housing authority for suitable alternative accommodation, or
(b) has so applied before the date when the child attained the age in question,
he does not commit an offence under section 327 (occupier causing or permitting overcrowding), so long as the condition in subsection (2) is met and the occupier does not fail to take action in the circumstances specified in subsection (3).

(2) The condition is that all the persons sleeping in the dwelling are persons who were living there when the child attained that age and thereafter continuously live there, or children born after that date of any of those persons.

(3) The exception provided by this section ceases to apply if –
    (a) suitable alternative accommodation is offered to the occupier on or after the date on which the child attains that age, or, if he has applied before that date, is offered at any time after the application, and he fails to accept it, or
    (b) the removal from the dwelling of some person not a member of the occupier's family is on that date or thereafter becomes reasonably practicable having regard to all the circumstances (including the availability of suitable alternative accommodation for that person), and the occupier fails to require his removal.

329 *Exception: visiting family member*
Where the persons sleeping in an overcrowded dwelling include a member of the occupier's family who does not live there but is sleeping there temporarily, the occupier is not guilty of an offence under section 327 (occupier causing or permitting overcrowding) unless the circumstances are such that he would be so guilty if that member of his family were not sleeping there.

15.59   It has been held that a room with no natural lighting or ventilation was not a room generally used in the locality as a living or a bed-room,[116] and so it could not be taken into account when determining the number of rooms.

15.60   A 'room' is a room which can be used for living or sleeping in.[117] The relevant date when overcrowding must exist is the date of the trial and so a tenant has a complete defence if overcrowding has ceased by the time of the court hearing.[118] It is not necessary for there to be a conviction before a landlord can rely on this 'ground'.[119] All that a landlord need to do is to prove that the circumstances are such that a conviction for overcrowding could be obtained and that any contractual tenancy has been validly determined, normally by serving a notice to quit.

15.61   Where there is statutory overcrowding, the court has no power to suspend a possession order.[120]

Demolition orders, etc

15.62   See para 10.103.

---

116 *Patel v Godal* [1979] CLY 1620.
117 Ibid.
118 *Zbytniewski v Broughton* [1956] 2 QB 673; [1956] 3 All ER 348 – cf, *Henry Smith's Charity v Bartosiak-Jentys* (1992) 24 HLR 627; [1991] 2 EGLR 276, CA.
119 *Zbytniewski v Broughton* [1956] 2 QB 673; [1956] 3 All ER 348.
120 *Henry Smith's Charity v Bartosiak-Jentys* (1992) 24 HLR 627; [1991] 2 EGLR 276, CA.

Restricted contracts

15.63　A significant proportion of tenants or licensees[121] who moved into premises before 15 January 1989 and who did not enjoy full Rent Act protection occupied those premises under restricted contracts.[122] Many, but not all, tenants or licensees of resident landlords whose interests were created before 15 January 1989 and who were deprived of full Rent Act protection,[123] had restricted contracts. The other principal classes of tenants who had restricted contracts were those who were excluded from Rent Act protection because their tenancies included the provision of substantial attendances or small quantities of board by the landlord.[124]

15.64　Nowadays there are, however, virtually no tenants or licensees remaining with restricted contracts.[125] Housing Act 1988 s36 not only provided that no new restricted contracts could be created on or after 15 January 1989, but also stipulated that if the rent under a restricted contract was varied by agreement, it should be treated as a new contract, and could therefore no longer be a restricted contract. Accordingly, only tenants or licensees whose interests were created before 15 January 1989 and whose rents have not been varied by agreement can have restricted contracts. (A registration of a rent by a rent tribunal does not count as a variation by agreement.) For this reason this edition of Defending Possession Proceedings no longer deals with restricted contracts.[126]

121　Although RA 1977 s19(2) includes a reference to rent, it is clear that the term 'restricted contract' includes licensees with exclusive occupation of premises – *Luganda v Service Hotels Ltd* [1969] 2 All ER 692 (room occupied for three years in large hotel), *R v Battersea, Wandsworth, Mitcham and Wimbledon Rent Tribunal ex p Parikh* [1957] 1 All ER 352 (occupant described by landlord as 'paying guest'), but cf, *R v Paddington and St Marylebone Rent Tribunal ex p Walston Hotels Ltd* (1948) 152 EG 449 (no exclusive occupation) and *R v South Middlesex Rent Tribunal ex p Beswick* (1976) 32 P & CR 67 (a room in a YWCA hostel).

122　See RA 1977 s19.

123　RA 1977 s12 and Sch 2.

124　RA 1977 ss7 and 19.

125　However, for a recent case involving a tenant who originally had a restricted contract, see *Matthews v Rowe* (2001) 26 March, unreported, QBD.

126　See *Defending Possession Proceedings*, 4th edn, 1997, chapter 16.

Unprotected tenants and licensees

Introduction

16.1   If a tenant does not come within one of the forms of statutory protection provided by the Housing Act 1985, the Housing Act 1988 or the Rent Act 1977, landlords seeking possession need only commence proceedings and prove that they have some interest in the premises and that the contractual tenancy has been determined. It is likely that the only defence available in the short term to such a tenant is to allege that the contractual tenancy had not been determined at the date when proceedings were issued,[1] for example, because a notice to quit was defective. If the landlord is a public authority it may be possible to judicially review the decision to bring proceedings or defend on European Convention of Human Rights grounds, although the likelihood of 'human rights' arguments succeeding in the light of the decisions of the House of Lords in *Lambeth LBC v Kay* and *Leeds CC v Price* is remote.[2]

16.2   Protection from Eviction Act 1977 s3 makes it unlawful for landlords of many unprotected tenants and licensees to enforce their right to recover possession 'otherwise than by proceedings in the court'. Landlords who fail to comply with Protection from Eviction Act 1977 s3 commit a criminal offence contrary to section 1(2) of that Act and are liable to a claim for damages in tort. Section 3 has been amended by Housing Act 1980 s69(1) and by Housing Act 1988 ss30 and 31. It now applies to all unprotected tenancies and licences apart from excluded tenancies and excluded licences created on or after 15 January 1989. The categories of tenancies and licences which are 'excluded' are defined in Protection from Eviction Act 1977 s3A, as inserted by Housing Act 1988 s31 (see para 12.10). In brief, they are licences in hostels provided by social landlords, where accommodation is shared with a landlord or landlord's family, where the occupier is a former trespasser, where occupation is for a holiday and where occupation is rent-free.

---

1   For the termination of contractual tenancies, see chapter 12.
2   [2006] UKHL 10; [2006] 2 WLR 570. See paras 5.31–5.43; *Avon CC v Buscott* [1988] QB 656; [1988] 2 WLR 788; [1988] 1 All ER 841; (1988) 20 HLR 385, CA, and *Poplar HARCA v Donoghue* [2001] EWCA Civ 595; [2002] QB 48; [2001] 3 WLR 183.

Defences

16.3   A licensee has a complete defence to possession proceedings if the licence has not been terminated by the time that proceedings are issued,[3] or if a further licence has been created. A licence may simply be a temporary agreement that someone may be on or stay on the premises. In *Thomas v Sorrell*[4] Vaughan CJ stated, 'a dispensation or licence properly passeth no interest nor alters or transfers property in anything but only makes an action lawful, which without it has been unlawful'. It may be hard to draw the line between an owner who says, 'you can stay on the premises' and one who says, 'I do not agree to you staying on the premises, but I will refrain from evicting you until a certain date'.

16.4   If the licensee is a contractual licensee, the owner must observe the contractual provisions which the licence contains relating to termination. Whether or not there are contractual provisions in the licence, a licensee must be given reasonable notice:[5] there is no need for the notice itself to specify the particular time or indeed a reasonable time. However, a reasonable time must have elapsed between the giving of the notice and the issue of court proceedings.[6] The notice determines the licence immediately on service,[7] but does not become operative until the expiry of such a reasonable time, even if the notice contains a specified period of time which is too short. There are no set rules as to what is reasonable. The length of time depends on the circumstances in any particular case, and factors which may be taken into account are the length of time that the licensee has resided in the premises and the periods for which payments are made. A notice to terminate a licence must now comply with Protection from Eviction Act 1977 s5, as amended, unless the licence is 'excluded'. If a licence is excluded, notice may be given orally.[8] If there are joint owners, notice may be given by one of them acting alone.[9]

16.5   A former licensee whose licence has been determined but who remains on the premises is a trespasser. Accordingly, owners are entitled to damages for trespass without bringing evidence that they could or would have relet the property if the trespasser had not been

---

3   *GLC v Jenkins* [1975] 1 WLR 155; [1975] 1 All ER 354.
4   (1673) Vaugh 330.
5   *Minister of Health v Bellotti* [1944] KB 298; [1944] 1 All ER 238.
6   Ibid.
7   Ibid.
8   *Crane v Morris* [1965] 1 WLR 1104; [1965] 3 All ER 77.
9   *Annen v Rattee* (1985) 17 HLR 323; (1984) 273 EG 503.

there. The measure of damages is usually either the amount of loss suffered by the owner or the value to the trespasser of the use of the property for the period of occupation, and in a normal case this is the ordinary letting value of the property.[10]

---

10 *Swordheath Properties Ltd v Tabet* [1979] 1 WLR 285, [1979] 1 All ER 240; *Ministry of Defence v Thompson* [1993] 40 EG 148, (1993) 25 HLR 552, CA; and *Ministry of Defence v Ashman* (1993) 66 P & CR 195; (1993) 25 HLR 513, [1993] 40 EG 144, CA. See chapter 27.

CHAPTER 17

Premises occupied by employees

17.1   Employees who occupy residential premises owned by their employ-ers (ie, service occupiers) may be either tenants or licensees. Where it is necessary for the employee to live in the premises for the better performance of a job or where the employee is required to live in premises as a term of his or her contract of employment, it is likely that the employee is merely a licensee of those premises.[1] If this is not the case, an employee who has exclusive possession for a term and who pays rent is a tenant.[2] If the tenancy satisfies the normal requirements for full Rent Act or Housing Act protection[3] there is security of tenure, but subject to the possibility of possession pro-ceedings brought under Rent Act 1977 Sch 15 case 8 (see para 15.32), Housing Act 1985 Sch 2 ground 12 (see para 3.158) or Housing Act 1988 Sch 2 ground 16 (see para 10.100). If, however, employees are licensees, they have no security of tenure. Service licensees have only the limited protection that employers must bring court proceedings to evict them. Protection from Eviction Act 1977 s8(2) provides:

> For the purposes of Part I of this Act a person who, under the terms of his employment, had exclusive possession of the premises other than as a tenant shall have been deemed to have been a tenant and the expressions 'let' and 'tenancy' shall be construed accordingly.

17.2   This means that Protection from Eviction Act 1977 s1 (unlawful evic-tion and harassment of occupier) and section 3 of that Act (prohib-ition of eviction without due process of law) apply. Employers need prove only that they own or have an interest in the premises and that the rights of the employee (or ex-employee) to reside in the prem-ises have been determined, in accordance with either the contract of employment or any other agreement relating to the premises. A notice to terminate a service licence must comply with the require-ments of Protection from Eviction Act 1977 s5 unless it is an 'excluded licence'.[4] In some circumstances, where the occupation of a licensee

1   *Smith v Seghill Overseers* (1874–75) LR 10 QB 422; *Fox v Dalby* (1874–75) LR 10 CP 285 and *Glasgow Corporation v Johnstone* [1965] AC 609; [1965] 2 WLR 657.
2   *Royal Philanthropic Society v County* (1986) 18 HLR 83; (1985) 276 EG 1068.
3   One particular problem which tenants who are employees sometimes face is that often there is no rent payable and accordingly the tenancy is outside full RA protection due to RA 1977 s5 or cannot be an assured tenancy because of HA 1988 Sch 1 para 3. See *Heslop v Burns* [1974] 1 WLR 1241 and *Montagu v Browning* [1954] 1 WLR 1039.
4   HA 1988 ss30 and 31 (see para 12.10).

is expressed to be coterminous with employment and the licensee's employment has come to an end, no notice at all is necessary.[5]

17.3 If service licensees consider that they have been unfairly dismissed, an application may be made to an employment tribunal. Although the employment tribunal may recommend reinstatement, this is of little assistance in defending possession proceedings for tied accommodation. The employment tribunal cannot order reinstatement and the court considering possession proceedings is generally interested only in ascertaining whether or not the contract has been terminated, not whether it has been terminated fairly or unfairly. Applications for adjournments of such possession proceedings pending the hearing of an application to an employment tribunal are generally unsuccessful.[6]

---

5   *Doe d Hughes v Derry* (1840) 9 C & P 494; *Ivory v Palmer* [1975] ICR 340, CA, and *Norris v Checksfield* [1991] 1 WLR 1241; [1991] 4 All ER 327; (1991) 23 HLR 425, CA.
6   See, eg, *Whitbread West Pennines Ltd v Reedy* [1988] ICR 807; (1988) 20 HLR 642, CA (manager of public house dismissed).

CHAPTER 18

Death

18.1   A contractual tenancy does not terminate on the tenant's death unless the tenancy expressly states that that is to happen.[1] If the tenant leaves a will, the tenancy passes to the tenant's executors. However, if there is no will and the tenant dies intestate the tenancy passes to the Public Trustee until such time as letters of administration are taken out.[2] Unless there has been an automatic statutory succession, this applies to contractual Rent Act tenancies, secure tenancies, demoted and introductory tenancies and assured and assured shorthold tenancies, but not to Rent Act statutory tenancies.

18.2   If a landlord wishes to terminate a contractual tenancy vested in executors or administrators by serving a notice to quit, that notice must be served on the executors or administrators as the case may be. If letters of administration have not been taken out, the notice must be addressed to the personal representatives of the deceased and left at or posted to the last known place of residence of the deceased. In addition a copy must be served on the Official Solicitor and Public Trustee at PO Box 3010, London WC2B 6JS.[3] A Practice Note, originally issued by the Public Trust Office, which can be obtained by telephoning 020 7911 7100, describes how searches of the register can be made.

18.3   If a deceased tenant's contractual tenancy is not determined in this way, any sub-occupiers have a complete defence to possession proceedings which are issued before the tenancy has been determined.[4] In the long term, however, there is nothing to stop the landowner serving a valid notice to quit and then bringing new proceedings.

18.4   Although assured and assured shorthold tenancies can be inherited by will or on intestacy, the death of an assured tenant gives the landlord a ground for possession against anyone other than the deceased tenant's spouse or civil partner or anyone living with the 'original tenant as his or her wife or husband or civil partner'.[5]

18.5   In the ordinary course of events, a Rent Act statutory tenancy comes to an end on the death of the tenant since a dead person cannot occupy premises as a residence.[6] As a statutory tenancy is only

---

1   *Youngmin v Heath* [1974] 1 WLR 135.
2   Law of Property (Miscellaneous Provisions) Act 1994 s14.
3   Public Trustee (Notices Affecting Land) (Title on Death) Regulations 1995 SI No 1330 and *LS Gaz*, 17 January 2002, p31 and March 2002 *Legal Action* 16. See also *Wirral BC v Smith* (1982) 4 HLR 81; (1982) 43 P & CR 312, CA.
4   *Wirral BC v Smith* (1982) 4 HLR 81; (1982) 43 P & CR 312, CA.
5   HA 1988 Sch 4 para 2, as amended by Civil Partnership Act 2004 Sch 8 para 34. See also HA 1988 Sch 2 ground 7 (see para 10.44).
6   RA 1977 s2. See chapter 14 and *Skinner v Geary* [1931] 2 KB 546.

a personal right it cannot be left to another person through the deceased tenant's will.[7] However, Rent Act 1977 s2(1)(b) and Sch 1 Pt I, as amended by Housing Act 1988 s39, provide that a spouse or civil partner who was living with the tenant at the time of death or, if there was no such spouse or civil partner, a member of the tenant's family who had been living with the tenant for two years immediately before the death, can succeed to the tenancy. A spouse or civil partner who 'inherits' a tenancy in this way is called a 'statutory tenant by succession' and acquires a statutory tenancy. 'Spouse' is defined by Housing Act 1988 Sch 4 as including any person living with the deceased tenant as wife or husband. Any other member of the family who succeeds to a tenancy as a result of the death of a tenant on or after 15 January 1989 acquires an assured tenancy (see chapter 10). The succession provisions apply to both contractual and statutory tenancies.[8] Rent Act 1977 Sch 1 provides that any tenancy can be passed on twice if the first successor is a spouse.

18.6   Any spouse, civil partner or member of the original tenant's family who acquires a tenancy in this way takes over the tenancy with all the rights and obligations which existed on the tenant's death, for example, rent arrears or a suspended possession order.[9]

18.7   It is possible for a tenant to leave a contractual tenancy in a will to one person, but for another to be entitled to succeed to the tenancy in accordance with Rent Act 1977 Sch 1. In this situation any person who would be entitled to succeed to the tenancy acquires a statutory tenancy by succession and the contractual tenancy goes into 'abeyance' until the statutory tenancy comes to an end.[10]

---

7 *John Lovibond and Sons Ltd v Vincent* [1929] 1 KB 687.
8 *Moodie v Hosegood* [1952] AC 61; [1951] 2 All ER 582, HL.
9 *Sherrin v Brand* [1956] 1 QB 403.
10 *Moodie v Hosegood* [1952] AC 61; [1951] 2 All ER 582, HL, overruling *Smith v Mather* [1948] 2 KB 212; [1948] 1 All ER 704 and *Thynne v Salmon* [1948] 1 KB 482; [1948] 1 All ER 49.

Rental purchase agreements

Introduction

19.1   Rental purchase agreements[1] are happily now almost of historical interest only. The true rental purchase agreement is, in essence, a contract for the sale of a property with the purchaser allowed into possession paying the purchase price by instalments and with completion of the sale taking place, if ever, only following payment of the last instalment. It is inaccurate to describe the arrangement as a rental agreement as the purchaser is usually allowed into possession under the terms of the agreement for sale, not as tenant, but as licensee.

19.2   Normally, such agreements will be in written form, often of a pro forma nature. It is essential to study the document carefully as the terms can differ quite widely. The agreement will provide for a specified sum to be paid before completion can be called for. It will usually also specify the interest rate to be charged on the outstanding capital. A fixed weekly or monthly sum is generally specified which will either go directly towards repaying the capital borrowed or go towards satisfying the accruing interest, buildings insurance and other outgoings, with only part going towards repayment of the capital. Some agreements provide for completion to take place before payment of the whole capital sum but with the vendor granting a mortgage at the date of completion of the sale for the sum outstanding at the time. There are many permutations.

Rental purchase and evasion of security of tenure

19.3   Many ostensible rental purchase agreements were prepared not with the intention of selling the property to a willing purchaser but with the sole intention of avoiding the Rent Act or Housing Act protection otherwise given to tenants by the simple device of not creating a tenancy. Following *Street v Mountford*[2] it was thought that, where there was a bona fide rental purchase intended by the parties, no landlord/tenant relationship would be established. However, after *Bretherton v*

---

1   See generally B Hoggett 'Houses on the never-never: some legal aspects of rental purchase' (1972) 36 *Conv* 325; 'Houses on the never-never: some recent developments' (1975) 39 *Conv* 343; 'How to help the rental purchaser' June 1976 *LAG Bulletin* 133; L Burrows and R Murphy, *Rental Purchase – The Case for Change* (1990); Shelter and National Consumer Council, *Buying a Home on Rental Purchase; A Consumer View* (1989).

2   [1985] 2 WLR 877; [1985] 2 All ER 289, HL.

Paton[3] it seems that entering into possession even with the intention of purchasing the property does not bar the application of the *Street* principle where the occupier has exclusive possession paying a specified periodic payment. Normally, in such circumstances the tenancy will be protected under Rent Act 1977 or be an assured tenancy under Housing Act 1988.

19.4   Where it is felt that an arrangement is not caught by the principle in *Street* and it proves necessary to consider whether an arrangement is a bona fide rental purchase, advisers should consider the following points:

- Was there any expectation that the occupier would in fact purchase the property? If not, then this is likely to be decisive. It will be necessary to check the dealings between the parties *before* the document was signed. How was the property advertised, what conversation took place, did the owner really want to sell the property?
- Was the sale price inflated above market value or was the interest rate specified in the agreement inflated as compared to the then current mortgage rate?
- Is the term of repayment unduly long, either in itself or when compared with the length of any leasehold interest granted?
- Are there any clauses inconsistent with a bona fide contract for sale, for example, a prohibition against assigning, subletting or parting with possession in the agreement?
- Was there the usual investigation of title and the property as is normal before a purchase/sale?
- Have the parties' actions since the date of the agreement been more consistent with a tenancy than a bona fide sale?
- Were solicitors instructed by the occupier before entering into the agreement?
- Does the agreement contain terms that are unfair within the meaning of the Unfair Terms in Consumer Contracts Regulations 1999?[4] Although Unfair Contract Terms Act 1977 Sch 1 para 1 exempts land transactions from the provisions of that Act, there is no equivalent exemption from the Regulations. Under the Regulations an unfair term is one which, contrary to the requirement of good faith, causes a significant imbalance in the parties'

---

3   (1986) 18 HLR 257, CA; cf, *Sharp v McArthur* (1987) 19 HLR 364; see also *Martin v Davies* (1952) 7 HLR 119, CA, and *Francis Jackson Developments Ltd v Stemp* [1943] 2 All ER 601, CA.

4   SI No 2083.

rights and obligations to the detriment of the consumer.[5] Any term which is unfair is not binding upon the consumer.[6] Schedule 2 contains 'an indicative and non-exhaustive list of terms which may be regarded as unfair'.

19.5   Where an occupier wishes to dispute his or her description in the agreement he or she can either apply for a declaration by the county court that he or she is a tenant with statutory protection[7] or raise that proposition as a defence to possession proceedings.

Statutory and equitable protection

19.6   Assuming that the agreement in question is a bona fide rental purchase agreement, the court has a statutory discretion to protect the occupier from eviction under Housing Act 1980 s88:

> 88 (1) Where, under the terms of a rental purchase agreement, a person has been let into possession of a dwelling-house and, on the termination of the agreement or of his right to possession under it, proceedings are brought for the possession of the dwelling-house, the court may –
>   (a) adjourn the proceedings; or
>   (b) on making an order for the possession of the dwelling-house, stay or suspend execution of the order or postpone the date of possession;
> for such period or periods as the court thinks fit.

This is broadly similar to the protection given to mortgagors in default (see chapter 8) although there is no requirement that the occupier clear the arrears within a reasonable period.

19.7   The court can, but is not obliged to, grant relief on the condition that the occupier makes payments towards the arrears:

> (2) On any such adjournment, stay, suspension or postponement the court may impose such conditions with regard to payments by the person in possession in respect of his continued occupation of the dwellinghouse and such other conditions as the court thinks fit.[8]

The court has specific power to revoke or vary any condition which it has imposed.[9]

---

5   Reg 4.
6   Reg 5.
7   RA 1977 s141.
8   HA 1980 s88(2).
9   HA 1980 s88(3).

19.8   The definition of 'rental purchase agreement' is quite widely drafted:

> (4) In this section 'rental purchase agreement' means an agreement for the purchase of a dwelling-house (whether freehold or leasehold property) under which the whole or part of the purchase price is to be paid in three or more instalments and the completion of the purchase is deferred until the whole or a specified part of the purchase price has been paid.[10]

The definition requires the purchase price to be paid in at least three instalments so as not to protect purchasers who are allowed into possession in the more usual transaction after exchange of contracts when normally a ten per cent deposit is paid but before completion when the second and final instalment is made.

19.9   The court has some limited equitable jurisdiction to grant relief against forfeiture for breach of any terms of the agreement although the statutory discretion is much more extensive.[11]

Necessity for possession proceedings

19.10   Where a person is let into possession under a rental purchase agreement (as defined above) and continues to reside in the property after termination of the agreement or his or her right to possession under the agreement, then the provisions of Protection from Eviction Act 1977 will usually apply so as to require the owner to regain possession by court order.[12] An additional prohibition against eviction without court order is contained in Consumer Credit Act 1974 s92(2) in respect of regulated conditional sale agreements.

Other points

19.11   Payments under 'an agreement for the purchase of a dwelling under which the whole or part of the purchase price is to be paid in more than one instalment and the completion of the purchase is deferred until the whole or a specified part of the purchase price has been paid' qualify as 'rent' for housing benefit purposes.[13]

---

10   HA 1980 s88(4).
11   See references at n1 above and note at (1974) 37 MLR 705.
12   HA 1980 Sch 25 para 61.
13   Housing Benefit Regulations 2006 SI No 213 reg 12(1).

CHAPTER 20

Shared ownership

20.1   The last couple of decades have seen attempts to blur the edges between owner-occupation and renting. There is every reason to believe that the blurring will continue. Great efforts have been made to ease people into owner-occupation by use of shared ownership schemes.[1] These allow occupiers progressively to buy tranches of the homes that they occupy until the property is owned outright, or at least owned subject to a mortgage.

20.2   There are particular problems which face occupiers under such schemes, the principal one being that where part is owned subject to a mortgage and part is rented, there are potentially two separate claims for possession if the occupier defaults. It will be necessary to service both debts simultaneously in order to retain possession.

20.3   Under a typical shared ownership scheme, a freeholder agrees to grant a long lease to the occupier in return for a premium representing, for example, a quarter or half of the capital value of the property. The premium is raised by way of a mortgage from an institutional lender, or even from the freeholder. The occupier moves into the property and pays rent calculated by reference to the outstanding element not yet purchased.

20.4   In the above example the occupier will usually be an assured tenant since none of the exceptions in Housing Act 1988 Sch 1 are likely to apply. It is likely that the housing association in the example below will have specifically contracted (in the cases of shared ownership agreements entered into after 28 February 1997) into the grant of an assured tenancy rather than the presumed assured shorthold tenancy created after that date. Only where the rent payable under the tenancy is over £25,000 per annum or below £250 per annum (£1,000 in London) would the tenancy fall outside the Housing Act 1988 assured tenancy regime on grounds of rent level (see para 10.5). The tenant is, accordingly, at risk of possession proceedings under all the grounds in Housing Act 1988 Sch 2.

20.5   Additionally, since in purchasing the lease the purchaser executed a legal charge, there is also a risk of mortgage possession proceedings in the event of default under that agreement.

20.6   Occupiers under shared ownership agreements which fall within the scope of the Housing Act 1988 and the Administration of Justice Acts will be entitled to claim relief under either legislative regime in

1   The Department for Communities and Local Government website has a analysis of all the various schemes aimed at encouraging council and social tenants, key workers and some from council waiting lists into shared ownership: www.dclg.gov.uk.

the event of possession proceedings being brought by the relevant claimant.

20.7   Advisers will need to consider the particular agreement entered into by the individual being advised, as there are many differing forms of the shared ownership agreement.

20.8   Similarly, advisers will need to be alert to assess whether payments made by the mortgage-lender to the landlord who threatens forfeiture proceedings and hence the security are validly made. It is common for lenders to pay over money to the landlord simply because the landlord says that there are rent arrears and hence the risk of forfeiture. Such payments are then recorded as mortgage arrears and, in turn, put the borrower/tenant at risk of eviction by the lender. The assertion that the borrower is in mortgage arrears should be tested in correspondence and in possession proceedings if the borrower has ceased to pay rent to the landlord for legitimate reasons. It is clear that a mortgage-lender has the right to seek relief against forfeiture.[2]

Example

P agrees to buy a one-third share of a 99-year lease on a flat renovated by a housing association which has a market value of £180,000. The market rent for the flat is £1,200 per month. P takes a 99-year lease and borrows £60,000 from a bank, secured by way of legal charge on the leasehold title. P then makes mortgage repayments on the £60,000 borrowed and pays rent at the rate of £800 per month. Subsequently P agrees to purchase a further one-third share. P borrows an additional £60,000, and as a result the rent paid to the association is reduced to £400 per month but the mortgage repayments double. On buying the last third, P will then cease paying rent to the association and will continue to pay the mortgage repayments until the end of the term agreed with the bank at the time of the taking of the lease.

---

2   *Sinclair Gardens Investments (Kensington) Ltd v Walsh* [1996] QB 231; [1995] 3 WLR 524; [1995] 4 All ER 852; (1996) 28 HLR 338, CA. See para 12.57 onwards on relief from forfeiture.

Possession procedure

Procedure in possession proceedings

The need for possession proceedings

21.1　It is normal for landlords who wish to evict occupiers to take possession proceedings through the courts. In many circumstances landlords who take the law into their own hands by evicting people without first obtaining court orders risk prosecution under the Protection from Eviction Act 1977, with a fine and/or imprisonment and/or a claim for substantial damages, for breach of covenant for quiet enjoyment, trespass and/or unlawful eviction under Housing Act 1988 ss27 and 28. However, there are exceptions which advisers should bear in mind.

Trespassers

21.2　Court proceedings are not always necessary to evict trespassers. See chapter 25.

Excluded licences and tenancies[1]

21.3　Protection from Eviction Act 1977 s3A created categories of 'excluded tenancies and licences'. Housing Act 1988 s30 amended Protection from Eviction Act 1977 s3 (prohibition of eviction without due process of law). The combined effect of these sections is that if there is an excluded tenancy or licence, a landlord who evicts without a court order may not be committing a criminal offence under Protection from Eviction Act 1977 s1 (unlawful eviction and harassment), and if the tenancy or licence has been properly terminated (for example, by service of a valid notice to quit), the occupant has no civil redress.

21.4　　A tenancy or licence is excluded if:

- under its terms the occupier shares any accommodation with the landlord or licensor and the landlord or licensor occupies as his or her only or principal home 'premises of which the whole or part of the shared accommodation formed part';
- the tenant or licensee shares accommodation with a member of the family of the landlord or licensor and the landlord or licensor has his or her only or principal home in the building where the shared accommodation is situated;
- the tenant or licensee was originally a trespasser of premises but was granted a tenancy or licence as a temporary expedient;
- it confers on the tenant or licensee the right to occupy premises for a holiday only;

1　See chapter 16 and para 12.10.

- it is granted otherwise than for money or money's worth;
- the premises are in a hostel provided by a public sector landlord; or
- it is granted to provide accommodation to asylum-seekers through the National Asylum Support Service under Immigration and Asylum Act 1999 Pt VI.[2]

21.5 From the point of view of landlords, it may be wise to take possession proceedings even if they believe that there is an excluded tenancy or licence. There is not only the risk that the tenancy or licence may not in fact be excluded, but also, if the occupants are on the premises at the time of eviction, the possibility of a prosecution under Criminal Law Act 1977 s6 (using or threatening violence to secure entry). Prosecutions can be brought under Criminal Law Act 1977 s6 even if the occupants are trespassers. An offence may be committed under section 6 of that Act 'whether the violence in question is directed against the person or against property'.[3]

21.6 If a landlord is threatening to evict without obtaining a possession order and the occupants believe that they enjoy some form of security of tenure, the safest course of action is to seek an injunction without delay, pending an application for a declaration.

Possession procedure

21.7 Civil Procedure Rules 1998 (CPR) Part 55 applies to most claims for possession. The procedure set out in that part must be used where the claim includes a possession claim brought:

- by a landlord (or former landlord);
- by a mortgagee;
- by a licensor (or former licensor); or
- against trespassers.[4]

It applies to claims for possession begun on or after 15 October 2001.[5]

The full text of CPR Part 55 and its Practice Directions are set out in appendix E.

---

2 See Protection from Eviction Act 1977 ss3 and 3A, HA 1985 s622 and the Immigration and Asylum Act 1999 Sch 14 para 73.
3 Criminal Law Act 1977 s6(4)(a).
4 CPR 55.2.
5 Civil Procedure (Amendment) Rules 2001 SI No 256.

Issue of proceedings – which court?

21.8   Possession proceedings are usually started in the county court for the district where the property is situated.[6] A claimant may only start proceedings in the High Court if there are exceptional circumstances[7] such as:

- complicated disputes of fact;
- points of law of general importance; or
- in a claim against trespassers where there is a substantial risk of public disturbance or of serious harm to people or property which properly requires immediate determination.

21.9   The value of the property and the amount of any financial claim may be relevant circumstances, but they alone do not normally justify starting the claim in the High Court. The Practice Direction to CPR Part 55 points out consequences of issuing in High Court when not justified:

> If a claimant starts a claim in the High Court and the court decides that it should have been started in the county court, the court will normally either strike the claim out or transfer it to the county court on its own initiative. This is likely to result in delay and the court will normally disallow the costs of starting the claim in the High Court and of any transfer.[8]

21.10   If a claim is issued in the High Court it must be accompanied by a certificate stating the reasons for bringing the claim in the High Court, verified by a statement of truth.[9]

21.11   In addition there are substantive law provisions that provide that landlords who initiate proceedings in the High Court may be prohibited from recovering some or all of their costs.[10]

Challenging the decision to bring proceedings

21.12   Sometimes tenants wish to challenge the decision by a local authority or another type of social landlord to bring possession proceedings – either on *Wednesbury* unreasonability grounds or because European

---

6   CPR 55.3(1).
7   PD 55 para 2.1.
8   PD 55 para 1.2.
9   CPR 55.3(2).
10   HA 1985 s110(3), RA 1977 s141(4) and HA 1988 s40(4).

Convention on Human Rights (ECHR) rights have been breached. There are though considerable difficulties in raising 'human rights' challenges in possession claims in the light of the House of Lords decisions in *Leeds CC v Price; Lambeth LBC v Kay*.[11] If there are disputes of fact, such challenges should be made in the course of the country court proceedings, rather than by way of judicial review in the Administrative Court. Issues of fact can be explored in the county court, but not in the Administrative Court. A county court judge is able to take into account allegations that the institution of proceedings might have been unlawful and contrary to regulatory guidance when considering the issue of reasonableness.[12]

Claim forms

21.13   Claim forms in possession actions must be in the prescribed form.[13] They must be verified by a statement of truth.[14] It has been held, at first instance,[15] that a statement of truth in a possession claim form which had not been signed personally, but which bore the rubber stamp of a signature of an employee in the claimant's legal services department who had no personal knowledge of the case, had not been signed within the meaning of CPR 22.1. The requirement in CPR 22.1(a) for the statement of case to be signed is not a mere technicality or a matter of form. Courts need to be able to rely upon documents bearing statements of truth. It is essential that statements of case should be properly verified. See too PD 22.3.

21.14   In a claim against trespassers, if the claimant does not know the name of all the people in occupation, the claim must be brought against 'persons unknown' in addition to any named defendants.[16]

---

11   [2006] UKHL 10; [2006] 2 WLR 570. See too *Harrow LBC v Qazi* [2003] UKHL 43; [2003] 3 WLR 792 and paras 5.31 to 5.43.

12   *R (Mills) v Airways Housing Society Ltd* [2005] EWHC 328 (Admin); 14 January 2005.

13   PD 55 para 2.6 – Forms N119 (rent claims), N120 (mortgages) and N121 (trespassers).

14   CPR 22.1.

15   *Birmingham City Council v Hosey* December 2002 *Legal Action* 20, Birmingham County Court (HHJ MacDuff QC).

16   CPR 55.3(4). See chapter 25.

Particulars of claim

21.15   Particulars of claim must be filed and served with the claim form.[17] All particulars of claim must:

- comply with CPR Part 16, ie, they must contain a concise statement of the facts relied upon, and, if interest is sought, give details of the claim for interest;
- identify the land to which the claim relates;[18]
- state whether it is residential property;[19]
- state the ground on which possession is claimed;[20]
- give full details of any mortgage or tenancy agreement;[21]
- give details of every person who, to the best of the claimant's knowledge, is in possession of the property.[22]

21.16   There are additional requirements for particulars of claim where the claim relates to a tenancy of residential premises.[23] If the claimant alleges that there has been non-payment of rent, the particulars of claim must state:

- the amount due at the start of proceedings;
- in schedule form, the dates when arrears of rent arose, all amounts of rent due, the dates and amounts of all payments made and a running total of the arrears. In general the schedule should cover the preceding two years, or if the first date of default occurred less than two years before the date of issue, it should cover the period from the first date of default. However, if the claimant wishes to rely on a history of arrears which is longer than two years, this should be stated in the particulars and a full schedule should be exhibited to a witness statement;
- the daily rate of any rent and interest;
- any previous steps taken to recover arrears, with full details of any court proceedings;
- any relevant information about the defendant's circumstances, including details about benefits and payments direct.

21.17   The particulars of claim should also give the name of any person known to be entitled to apply for relief from forfeiture. In those cir-

---

17   CPR 55.4.
18   PD 55 para 2.1(1).
19   PD 55 para 2.1(2).
20   PD 55 para 2.1(3).
21   PD 55 para 2.1(4).
22   PD 55 para 2.1(5).
23   PD 55 para 2.3.

cumstances, the claimant must file a copy of the particulars of claim for service upon any person who is entitled to apply for relief from forfeiture.[24]

21.18 If the claimant is a mortgage lender who is seeking possession of residential premises, the particulars of claim must state:[25]

- whether a Class F land charge has been registered, or a notice under the Matrimonial Homes Act 1983 has been entered and whether a notice under the Family Law Act 1996 has been registered (if any of these things have been done, the claimant must serve notice of proceedings upon the person named in the charge or notice);
- the state of the mortgage account, including the amount of the advance, periodic payments and interest, the amount needed to redeem the mortgage, including solicitors' costs and administration charges;
- if the mortgage is a regulated consumer credit agreement, the total amount outstanding;
- the rate of interest payable.

21.19 If the claim is based on mortgage arrears, the particulars of claim must set out:

- in schedule form, the dates when the arrears arose, all amounts due, the dates and amounts of all payments made and give a running total of the arrears;
- details of all other payments to be made and claimed;
- any relevant information about the defendant's circumstances, including details about benefits and payments direct;
- any previous steps taken to recover arrears, with full details of any court proceedings.

21.20 There are additional requirements for particulars of claim where the claim is against trespassers.[26] The particulars of claim must state:

- the claimant's interest in the land;
- the circumstances in which the land was occupied without licence or consent.

21.21 The effect of a failure by a claimant to comply with these rules depends upon the circumstances. CPR 3.10 provides that where there has been an error of procedure, such as a failure to comply with a

24 PD 55 para 2.4. See also chapter 13.
25 PD 55 para 2.5.
26 PD 55 para 2.6. See chapter 25.

rule or practice direction, the error does not invalidate any step taken and the court may make an order to remedy the error. So, if a landlord issues proceedings in the wrong county court, it is likely that the court will simply transfer the claim to the correct court.[27] On the other hand, if the failure to comply with the rules has been deliberate, with the intention of obtaining an unfair advantage against the defendant, the court has power to strike out the claim.[28]

21.22   Particulars of claim in the usual form are reproduced in the precedents in appendix B.[29]

Hearing dates

21.23   On the issue of a possession claim form, the court should fix a date for the first hearing.[30] The hearing date should be not less than 28 days from date of issue[31] but the standard period between issue of the claim and the hearing should be not more than eight weeks.[32] Shorter periods apply to claims against trespassers (see para 21.25).

Service of the claim form

21.24   The normal Civil Procedure Rules as to service apply to ordinary possession claims. CPR Part 6 allows the court to arrange personal service, delivery by first class post, for the claim form to be left at the defendant's last known address, or service via the document exchange. Alternatively the claimant landlord may arrange service. Special rules apply to service of claims brought against trespassers.[33]

21.25   The period between service and hearing must be at least:

- two days where there is a claim against trespassers of non-residential land;
- five days where there is a claim against trespassers of residential premises;
- 21 days (all other possession claims).[34]

27 See, eg, *Cala Homes (South) Ltd v Chichester DC* [2000] CP Rep 28; (2000) 79 P & CR 430; and *Gwynedd CC v Grunshaw* [2000] 1 WLR 494; (2000) 32 HLR 610, CA.
28 CPR 3.4.
29 See also Forms N119, N120 and N121.
30 CPR 55.5(1).
31 CPR 55.5(3)(a).
32 CPR 55.5(3)(c).
33 See CPR 55.6 and chapter 25.
34 CPR 55.5(2) and (3).

21.26   However, those periods may be shortened.[35] The Practice Direction to Part 55 states that particular consideration should be given to shortening the period where:

- the defendant, or a person for whom the defendant is responsible, has assaulted or threatened to assault the landlord, a member of the landlord's staff, or another tenant;
- there are reasonable grounds for fearing such an assault; or
- the defendant, or a person for whom the defendant is responsible, has caused serious damage or threatened to cause serious damage to the property or to the home or property of another resident.[36]

Defences and counterclaims

21.27   The main text of this work sets out the substantive and technical defences which may be raised in response to an action for possession of residential property. The reader should refer to the main text for consideration of the issues which must always be reviewed in planning defences.

21.28   A defendant who wishes to defend must file a defence with the court and serve a copy upon the claimant within 14 days of service of the claim form.[37] A defendant to a possession claim who fails to file or serve a defence may still take part in the proceedings, but the failure to file or serve a defence may be taken into account when the court decides what costs order to make.[38] For example, if the first hearing is not effective and has to be adjourned because the tenant turns up without having filed or served a defence but obtains an adjournment by telling the court about a defence to the claim, it is likely that the court will order that tenant to pay the wasted costs of the adjourned hearing.

21.29   Defences to possession claims must be in the prescribed form annexed to the Practice Direction.[39]

21.30   CPR Part 10 (acknowledgment of service) does not apply to possession claims.[40] Similarly CPR Part 12 (default judgment) does not

---

35   CPR 3.1(2)(a).
36   PD 55 para 3.2.
37   CPR 15.2. However, this rule does not apply to claims against trespassers – see CPR 55.7(2).
38   CPR 55.7(2).
39   PD 55 para 1.5, N11, N11R or N11M.
40   CPR 55.7(1).

apply to possession claims.[41] This means that it is not possible for a claimant to obtain a possession order by default if the defendant fails to file or serve a defence.

21.31   In Consumer Credit Act cases, the borrower may apply for a time order in the defence or by making a application in the proceedings.[42]

21.32   The defence should answer each of the substantive points raised in the particulars of claim, as failure to respond to a point made is taken as admission of it. Moreover, any defence and, if appropriate, counterclaim must be sufficiently accurately drafted to withstand the test of a full trial.

21.33   Often the defendant will wish to raise a grievance arising from the breach of some duty or misconduct on the part of the landlord/owner. Most frequently this occurs in cases of disrepair and harassment. As such a complaint arises out of the subject matter of the proceedings, that is the tenancy (or other tenure), it may be raised by way of a counterclaim. For details of the law applicable to counterclaims for disrepair, readers are referred to Luba and Knafler, *Repairs: Tenants' Rights*,[43] and for counterclaims for harassment to Arden, Carter and Dymond, *Quiet Enjoyment*.[44] However, it should be noted that the following heads appear most commonly in counterclaims to possession proceedings (particularly those brought for rent arrears).

Disrepair

- Breach of an express repairing covenant in the tenancy agreement (see the terms of the tenancy agreement).
- Failure to repair the structure or exterior of the premises or the common parts.[45]
- Failure to repair (or maintain in proper working order) installations in the dwelling or serving the dwelling.[46]
- Failure to take reasonable care of the tenant and the tenant's property to prevent injury to either.[47]
- Negligence in construction of the dwelling, performance of repairing works or treatment of infestation, etc.
- Nuisance (where the disrepair is caused by a problem emanating from property retained by the landlord).

41 CPR 55.7(4).
42 PD 55 para 7.1.
43 3rd edn, LAG, 1999.
44 6th edn, LAG, 2002.
45 Landlord and Tenant Act 1985 s11, as amended.
46 Landlord and Tenant Act 1985 s11, as amended.
47 Defective Premises Act 1972 s4.

Harassment

- Trespass to land/trespass to the person/trespass to goods (tort).
- Breach of the covenant of quiet enjoyment (contract).
- Breach of Protection from Eviction Act 1977 s3 (for unprotected tenants).
- Intimidation (tort).
- Breach of Housing Act 1988 ss27 and 28 (unlawful eviction).

21.34   It is best for any counterclaim to be included in the same document as the defence. If that is done, the court's permission to bring a counterclaim against a claimant is not needed. However, if a tenant wishes to bring a counterclaim at a later stage, the court's permission is needed.[48] Any counterclaim should contain full particulars of the matters complained of.

21.35   If the defendant recovers damages on his or her counterclaim these may be set off, so as to reduce in whole or in part monies claimed by the claimant. In the case of counterclaims for disrepair, the application of a full set-off will amount to a complete defence to an action for arrears of rent. Accordingly, the body of the defence itself should plead the set-off, even though it may seek to set off an as yet unliquidated claim for damages in the counterclaim.[49]

21.36   An example of a defence (including counterclaims as appropriate) is given in appendix B.

Preparation for the hearing

21.37   Apart from claims against trespassers, claimants should file and serve all witness statements at least two days before the hearing. In arrears cases these should include evidence of the arrears up to the date of the hearing, if necessary by including a daily rate. However, this does not prevent a landlord bringing the position up to date at hearing.[50]

21.38   In mortgage possession claims, the claimant should, not less than 14 days before hearing, send a notice addressed 'to the occupiers' of the property giving details of the hearing. The claimant must produce a copy and evidence of service at the hearing.[51]

---

48 CPR 20.4.
49 *British Anzani (Felixstowe) v International Marine Management (UK) Ltd* [1980] QB 137; [1979] 3 WLR 451.
50 PD 55 para 5.2.
51 CPR 55.10.

21.39   Where the claimant has served the claim form and particulars of claim, the claimant must produce a certificate of service at the hearing.[52]

Adjournments

21.40   In view of the fact that tenants often do not seek legal advice until just before any hearing it is often necessary for their advisers to seek an adjournment at the initial hearing. Whether or not such an application is successful will depend on the particular circumstances of the case. If it is possible to draft a defence which shows that the tenant has a real prospect of successfully defending the claim, the court is far more likely to adjourn. Similarly if the case is one of many listed and (say) only five minutes has been allocated, practical list management may mean that the judge has no option but to adjourn. On the other hand, if the tenant's adviser/representative is not able to point to any defence, or only to a very weak defence, the court may choose to hear the case at the first hearing. In all cases the court is likely to want to know why the tenant delayed seeking advice.

21.41   In view of the Court of Appeal decision in *North British Housing Association Limited v Matthews*,[53] there are limitations on courts' powers to adjourn where landlords are seeking possession under mandatory grounds. See para 10.51. However, these limitations do not apply where possession is sought on a discretionary ground.[54]

21.42   Other factors which should be borne in mind include:

- the overriding objective, ie, the importance of dealing with cases justly – this includes ensuring that the parties are on an equal footing, saving expense, dealing with cases proportionately, ensuring that cases are dealt with expeditiously and fairly and allocating the appropriate share of the court's resources;[55]
- whether or not public funding has been granted to the defendant, and, if so, when;
- the risk of prejudice to either party;

---

52 CPR 55.8(6).
53 [2004] EWCA Civ 1736; [2005] 1 WLR 3133; [2005] 2 All ER 667.
54 *Milecastle Housing Ltd v Walton* High Court of Justice, Newcastle upon Tyne District Registry; 14 June 2005.
55 CPR 1.1.

- the extent to which the party applying for the adjournment has been responsible for creating the difficulty.[56]

In *Bates v Croydon LBC*,[57] a tenant facing a possession claim alleging 53 allegations of nuisance to neighbours sought an adjournment to obtain public funding. It was refused. The hearing date was then moved forward, with the result that she was given three days to read witness statements produced by the council and to prepare for the hearing. The Court of Appeal set aside the possession order. The defendant had been put on very short notice to deal with the documentation, exhibits and witness statements. She was required to respond in writing to lengthy details and then conduct her own case in person. While the court accepted the desirability of conducting litigation with proper dispatch, and was reluctant to review interlocutory decisions of district judges, the decision reached in this case was wrong. An adjournment was appropriate for Ms Bates to finalise her public funding application and enable her to be represented.

Hearings in private

21.43　European Convention on Human Rights article 6 normally requires a public hearing. However, CPR 39.2(3)(c) provides that a hearing may be in private if it involves confidential information (including information relating to personal financial matters) and publicity would damage that confidentiality. The Practice Direction to CPR Part 39 paras 1.1 to 1.5 states that the decision as to whether a hearing is held in public or private must be made by the judge, having regard to representations (para 1.4) and article 6(1) of the convention (para 1.4A). Mortgage possession claims, possession claims based upon rent arrears and applications to suspend warrants should, in the first instance, be listed as hearings in private (para 1.5). Are these provisions a breach of article 6? The answer is 'no'. Like many other convention provisions, article 6 does not provide an absolute right. It has to be balanced against other rights, such as the right to privacy given by article 8. CPR 39.2 and the Practice Direction to CPR Part 39 have been drafted specifically with article 6 in mind. They leave a discretion to the judge in each case. If that discretion is exercised reasonably,

---

56　See, eg, *McShane v William Sutton Trust* (1997) 1 L & T Rev D67, December 1997 *Legal Action* 13, a pre-CPR case which illustrates a Woolf-type approach, and *R v Kingston upon Thames Justices ex p Martin* [1994] Imm AR 172, QBD.

57　[2001] EWCA Civ 134; (2001) 33 HLR 70.

in accordance with the spirit of the convention, it is unlikely to be criticised. Indeed, taking into account the provisions of articles 8 and 14, it is possible that a tenant defending a rent arrears case would have been able to challenge the pre-CPR position where claims against tenants were held in public and claims by lenders against borrowers based upon mortgage arrears were held in private.

21.44   The legality of CPR 39.2(3)(c) and the Practice Direction to CPR Part 39, paras 1.5 to 1.7, were challenged unsuccessfully in *R (on the application of Michael John Pelling) v Bow County Court (No 2)*.[58] Dr Pelling claimed that these provisions were ultra vires and breached article 6 of the convention. Buxton LJ held that the general rule that hearings are to be in public[59] is not absolute. CPR 39.2(3) is facultative and permits certain limited exceptions. CPR 39.2 is not unlawful or ultra vires and does not breach articles 6 or 10.

At the hearing

21.45   At the first hearing, or any adjourned hearing, the court may either decide the claim or give case management directions.[60] If the claim is genuinely disputed, on grounds which appear to be substantial, directions should include allocation of the claim to a particular track or directions to enable it to be allocated.

Allocation to track

21.46   Possession claims should only be allocated to the small claims track if all the parties agree.[61] If a possession claim is allocated to the small claims track, the fast track costs regime applies but the trial costs are in the discretion of the judge and should not exceed the amount of fast track costs allowable in CPR 46.2 if the value were up to £3,000, ie, currently £350.[62]

21.47   In considering the appropriate track for a possession claim, the court should take into account:

---

58 [2001] UKHRR 165; [2001] ACD 1, QBD (Admin Ct).
59 See *Scott v Scott* [1913] AC 417, HL.
60 CPR 55.8(1).
61 CPR 55.9(2).
62 CPR 55.9(3).

- CPR 26.8, which refers to the financial value of the claim, the nature of the remedy sought, the likely complexity of facts, law or evidence, the number of parties, the value of any counterclaim, the amount of oral evidence, the importance of the claim to people who are not parties, the views expressed by the parties and the circumstances of the parties;
- the amount of any arrears of rent or mortgage instalments;
- the importance to the defendant of retaining possession; and
- the importance of vacant possession to the claimant.[63]

The financial value of the claim is not necessarily the most important factor. A possession claim may be allocated to the fast track even though the value of the property is in excess of £15,000.

Evidence at the hearing

21.48   If a possession claim has not been allocated to track, or has been allocated to the small claims track, any fact that needs to be proved may be proved by evidence in writing – ie, by a witness statement or a claim form with a statement of truth.[64] However, if that evidence is disputed and the maker of the witness statement is not present, the court will normally adjourn the claim so that oral evidence can be given.[65]

21.49   If the claim has been allocated to the fast track or the multi track, the normal rules as to evidence at trial apply – oral evidence should be given in public,[66] although it may well be that witness statements will be treated as evidence in chief and oral evidence will consist largely of cross-examination.

21.50   In *Moat Housing Group South Ltd v Harris and Hartless*[67] the Court of Appeal reviewed the use of hearsay evidence in possession claims based upon anti-social behaviour and gave guidance to the lower courts. It is now well established that hearsay evidence can be given at the trial of a possession action, but 'the willingness of a civil court to admit hearsay evidence carries with it inherent dangers'. Rumours abound in small housing estates, and it is much more difficult for

---

63   PD 55 para 6.1.
64   CPR 55.8(3).
65   PD 55 para 5.4.
66   CPR 32.2.
67   [2005] EWCA Civ 287; [2005] 3 WLR 691. See too *Washington Housing Company Ltd v Morson* [2005] EWHC 3407 (Ch), 25 October 2005.

judges to assess the truth of what they are being told if the original makers of statements do not attend court to be cross-examined on their evidence. In this case, the large volume of hearsay evidence presented the judge with an unusually difficult problem. It might have been better if he had started his judgment with an analysis of the direct oral evidence he received, and made more transparently clear his approach to the evidence of the absent named witnesses and anonymous witnesses. More attention should be paid by claimants to the need to state, by convincing direct evidence, why it was not reasonable and practicable to produce the original makers of statements as witnesses. If statements involve multiple hearsay, the route by which the original statement came to the attention of the person attesting to it should be identified as far as practicable. Anonymous hearsay is not generally admissible. See too *Solon South West Housing Association Ltd v James.*[68]

For the general procedural rules about the admissibility of hearsay evidence and the requirement (in some circumstances) to give notice of intention to rely on hearsay evidence, see the Civil Evidence Act 1995 and CPR 33.1 to 33.5.

Interim rent

21.51   While awaiting trial of the claim for possession, a landlord may apply for an order for interim rent.[69] Tenants often respond with an undertaking to pay current rent pending trial. No such order should be made, however, if there is a genuine dispute over the sum due or if a counterclaim is being pursued.[70] The court could not order that a tenant's defence be struck out under the County Court Rules and Rules of the Supreme Court merely because of failure to comply with an order to pay interim rent.[71] The position may be different under the CPR since Parts 1 and 3, when read together, give the courts a far wider discretion than the old rules.[72] Certainly failure to pay coupled with breach of an order to file a list of documents where there is no realistic prospect of the tenant ever paying current rent or arrears may justify striking out a defence and making a possession order[73]

---

68 [2004] EWCA Civ 1847; [2005] HLR 24.
69 CPR 25.6–25.9.
70 *Old Grovebury Manor Farm v Seymour* [1979] 1 WLR 263; [1979] 1 All ER 573.
71 *HH Property Co Ltd v Rahim* [1987] 1 EGLR 52; (1987) 282 EG 455, CA.
72 See in particular CPR 3.1(2)(m).
73 *Tower Hamlets LBC v Ellson* July 2000 *Legal Action* 28, CA.

– although in cases involving discretionary grounds, the court should still consider the question of reasonableness.[74]

21.52   In practice it is more common for courts to make an order for payment of current rent under the general case management powers[75] – for example, as a term of any adjournment.[76] Where financial terms are imposed as a condition of an adjournment, the onus lies on tenants to satisfy courts that they cannot comply with any condition before it is imposed.

21.53   Also, if a possession claim against a secure, assured, protected or statutory tenant is adjourned, the court must, unless it considers that to do so would cause exceptional hardship or would otherwise be unreasonable, impose conditions with regard to the payment of rent and arrears of rent (if any).[77] It would only be in an exceptional case that the court would accept a landlord's application for an interlocutory injunction and order the tenant to pay housing benefit into court, rather than require an application from the landlord for interim payments in the usual way.[78]

Possession Claims Online (PCOL)

21.54   PD 55b enables landlords and their representatives to start certain possession claims under CPR Part 55 by requesting the issue of a claim form electronically via the PCOL website. Where a claim has been started electronically, the claimant, the defendant and their representatives may take further steps in the claim electronically using PCOL. Parties may communicate with the court using the messaging service facility, available on the PCOL website. At present use of PCOL is limited to certain courts – details are available from www.possessionclaim.gov.uk.

21.55   Possession claims may be started online if:

- they are brought under Section I of CPR Part 55; and
- they include a possession claim for residential property by a landlord against a tenant, solely on the ground of arrears of rent (but not a claim for forfeiture of a lease); or

---

74 See chapter 11.

75 Eg, CPR 3.1(3).

76 See, under the old rules, *Agyeman v Boadi* (1996) 28 HLR 558; [1996] EGCS 14, CA.

77 RA 1977 s100(3), HA 1985 s85(3) and HA1988 s9(3).

78 *Berg v Markhill* (1985) 17 HLR 455; *Times* 10 May, 1085.

- they are brought by a mortgagee against a mortgagor, solely on the ground of default in the payment of sums due under a mortgage.

21.56   Landlords may request the issue of a claim form by completing an online claim form at the PCOL website and paying the appropriate issue fee electronically at the PCOL website or by some other means approved by Her Majesty's Courts Service. The particulars of claim must be included in the online claim form and may not be filed separately. It is not necessary for the landlord to file a copy of the tenancy agreement, mortgage deed or mortgage agreement with the particulars of claim. The particulars of claim must include a history of the rent or mortgage account, in schedule form setting out:

- the dates and amounts of all payments due and payments made under the tenancy agreement, mortgage deed or mortgage agreement either from the first date of default if that date occurred less than two years before the date of issue or for a period of two years immediately preceding the date of issue; and
- a running total of the arrears.

21.57   When the court issues a claim form it should serve a printed version of the claim form and a defence form on the defendant. The claim form should have printed on it a unique customer identification number or a password by which the defendant may access the claim on the PCOL website. Tenants may file defences (and if appropriate counterclaims) in written form. Alternatively, they may complete the relevant online form at the PCOL website, and, if, making a counterclaim, pay the appropriate fee electronically at the PCOL website or by some other means approved by Her Majesty's Courts Service.

21.58   Some applications may be made electronically. Landlords may also request the issue of warrants electronically. Tenants may apply electronically for the suspension of warrants, by completing an online application for suspension at the PCOL website and paying the appropriate fee electronically at the PCOL website or by some other means approved by Her Majesty's Courts Service. When an online application for suspension is received, an acknowledgment of receipt should automatically be sent to the defendant by the court, but that acknowledgment does not constitute a notice that the online application for suspension has been served.

Accelerated possession proceedings

Accelerated possession proceedings

22.1   The accelerated possession procedure which landlords can use against assured shorthold tenants after service of a Housing Act 1988 s21 notice was originally contained in County Court Rules (CCR) Ord 49 r6A. It was introduced on 1 November 1993 and has now been incorporated into Civil Procedure Rules 1998 (CPR) Part 55, with some amendments. CCR Ord 49 r6, which provided an accelerated possession procedure for use against assured tenants in certain limited circumstances has been repealed and has not been incorporated into CPR Part 55. The only possession procedure available to landlords against assured tenants is the standard one contained in CPR Part 55 Part 1.

22.2   The accelerated possession procedure only applies to claims brought under Housing Act 1988 s21 to recover possession against assured shorthold tenants.[1] The conditions set out in CPR 55.12 must be complied with. This means that the procedure can only be used where:

- the assured shorthold tenancy was entered into on or after 15 January 1989;
- the only purpose is to recover possession – no other claim (for example, rent arrears) can be made under the accelerated procedure;
- the tenancy did not immediately follow an assured tenancy which was not an assured shorthold tenancy;
- there has been an assured shorthold tenancy in accordance with Housing Act 1988 s19A (ie, granted on or after 28 February 1997) or s20(1)(a)–(c) (pre-28 February 1997 fixed-term tenancies granted for a term certain of not less than six months where notice was given prior to the grant of the tenancy);
- the tenancy is subject to a written agreement, or follows a tenancy where there was a written agreement; and
- a Housing Act 1988 s21(1) or s21(4) notice has been given.

22.3   Claims brought under the accelerated possession procedure must be started in the county court for the district in which the property is situated. The claim form:

- must be in the form set out in the Practice Direction;[2]
- must contain the information and be accompanied by the documents required in that form; and
- must have all sections completed.

---

1   CPR 55.11.
2   Form N5B.

22.4   A blank reply form should accompany every claim form issued under the accelerated procedure. It is crucially important that tenants who wish to defend proceedings brought under the accelerated procedure return the N11A reply form to the court within 14 days after service of the claim form.[3] In many cases it is necessary for solicitors to use Legal Help for this purpose. If they do not do so, the claim for possession will be treated as unopposed and a possession order may be made without any hearing. The defence must be set out in the reply form as specified in the Practice Direction.[4]

22.5   Common mistakes by landlords are:[5]

- for an agent to complete the statment of truth on the claim form;[6]
- for the landlord to fail to exhibit either the Housing Act 1988 s20 notice (ie, notice required before the grant of an assured shorthold tenancy commencing before 28 February 1997) or the Housing Act 1988 s21 notice (informing the tenant that the landlord will be seeking possession)[7] – the court has no power to dispense with either;
- to include a claim for rent arrears;
- for the Housing Act 1988 s20 notice[8] to be defective (see para 9.4 and the cases referred to there);
- for the Housing Act 1988 s21 notice to be defective (see para 9.16– 9.19 and the cases referred to there).[9]

22.6   Accelerated possession claims should be referred to a district judge, either on receipt of a defence, or on receipt of a request from the claimant after the expiry of 14 days from service of the claim form.[10] The judge can still consider any defence if the defence is received out of time but before the landlord's request is considered. If the defendant does not file a defence and no request for possession is received from the claimant within three months after service, the claim will be automatically stayed.

---

3   CPR 55.14.
4   Form N11A.
5   DETR research, *The Accelerated Possession Procedure: the experience of landlords and tenants* (1998), found a very high error rate among applications and that possession orders were only made on the initial consideration of the papers in 60% of cases.
6   See *Chesters Accommodation Agency Ltd v Abebrese* (1997) 94(33) LSG 27; (1997) 141 SJLB 199; (1997) *Times* 28 July, CA and CPR 22.1(6).
7   See RA 1977 s2.
8   Note that there is no requirement for a HA 1998 s20 notice if the tenancy was granted on or after 28 February 1997 – see HA 1988 s19A.
9   See HA 1988 s21(4).
10   CPR 55.15.

22.7   When considering accelerated possession claims, district judges should either:[11]

- make an order for possession without a hearing; or
- if they are not satisfied that the claim was served or that the claimant is entitled to possession, fix a hearing date and give case management directions – at least 14 days' notice of the hearing must be given; or
- strike out the claim if it discloses no reasonable grounds for bringing a claim. If the claim is struck out, reasons must be given with the order. In those circumstances, the claimant landlord may apply to restore the claim within 28 days.

22.8   The Court of Appeal has said that if a reply raises a case which, if true, would constitute an arguable defence, the judge has no discretion to make a possession order:

> [The accelerated possession procedure] is a robust machinery. It depends upon district judges rigorously considering the documents which have been filed. Some replies may be little more than a plea, however genuine, for mercy. But if, on the face of the reply, a matter has been raised which, if true, might arguably raise a defence; or if the documents filed by the claimant might arguably disclose a defect in his claim, then the district judge must necessarily be 'not satisfied' ...[12]

22.9   It is normal for the court to order that the tenant pay the landlord's costs on the claim form. If the tenant wishes to pay costs by instalments, the appropriate box on the form N11A should be completed and returned.[13]

Postponement of possession

22.10   Where a landlord is entitled to a possession order under the accelerated procedure, the court must make an order to take effect within 14 days, unless exceptional hardship would be caused to the tenant, in which case the court may delay the date for the giving up of possession for a maximum of six weeks.[14] Claimants may indicate, by not deleting the relevant paragraph in the claim form, that they are

11   CPR 55.16.
12   *Manel v Memon* (2001) 33 HLR 235; [2000] 33 EG 74; (2000) *Times* 20 April, CA. Although this was a case decided under CCR Ord 49 r6A the same principles apply to the accelerated possession procedure under CPR Part 55.
13   CPR 55.18.
14   HA 1980 s89.

content for the judge to consider postponing the date for possession without a hearing. In those cases judges may fix dates for possession in six weeks without a hearing.

22.11   Otherwise, if a defendant seeks postponement of the date for giving up possession on the ground of exceptional hardship, the judge must make an order for possession within 14 days, but direct a hearing on the issue of postponement. The hearing must be before the date on which possession is to be given up. If, at the hearing, the judge is satisfied that there will be exceptional hardship, he or she may vary the date on which possession must be given up – but to no more than six weeks after the date on which the original order was made.[15]

22.12   There is power for the court to set aside or vary a possession order made under the accelerated procedure on application within 14 days of service of the order, or on the court's own initiative.[16]

European Convention on Human Rights

22.13   It has been suggested that the accelerated possession procedure might fall foul of article 6 of the European Convention on Human Rights. In view of the firm line taken by the Court of Appeal in *Manel v Memon*,[17] it is hard to support this view. Article 6 only comes into play if the proceedings in question are decisive for private rights and obligations.[18] If the tenant accepts that there is no defence, there are no civil rights to be determined. If the tenant says that there is a defence, there is an entitlement to a public hearing.

15 PD 55 para 8.4 and HA 1980 s89.
16 CPR 55.19.
17 (2001) 33 HLR 235; [2000] 33 EG 74, CA.
18 *Ringeisen v Austria (No 1)* (1979–1980) 1 EHRR 455, ECtHR.

CHAPTER 23

Applications for demotion – procedure

23.1   The Anti-social Behaviour Act 2003 amended the Housing Acts 1985, 1988 and 1996 to give county courts power to change secure or assured tenancies into demoted tenancies, lacking the rights that are associated with secure and assured tenancies. See paras 8.87–8.103. Applications for demotion orders may be made by local housing authorities, housing action trusts and registered social landlords. The court can only grant a demotion order if:

- a notice seeking a demotion order has been served or it is just and equitable to dispense with that requirement;
- it is satisfied that the tenant or a person residing in or visiting the dwelling-house has engaged or has threatened to engage in conduct to which Housing Act 1996 s153A or s153B (anti-social behaviour or use of premises for unlawful purposes) applies; and
- it is reasonable to make the order.

23.2   A demotion order:

- terminates the secure or assured tenancy with effect from the date specified in the order;
- if the tenant remains in occupation, creates a demoted tenancy; and
- makes it a term of the demoted tenancy that any arrears of rent payable at the termination of the secure or assured tenancy become payable under the demoted tenancy.

23.3   The substantive law relating to demotion of tenancies is described in chapter 8.

23.4   A demotion order may be sought as an alternative to possession. In those circumstances, CPR Part 55, the normal procedure for possession claims, applies.[1] However, if the landlord only seeks demotion, CPR Part 65 applies, although the procedure is very similar to that provided for by CPR Part 55.

23.5   Demotion order claims must be made in the county court for the district in which the property to which the claim relates is situated.[2] However, in the light of CPR 3.10, issue in the wrong court is likely to be seen as an error of procedure which does not invalidate the step taken. In most cases judges would correct the error by transferring to the appropriate court.[3]

---

1   PD 65 para 5.1. See chapter 21.
2   CPR 65.12 and PD 65 para 6.1.
3   See, in another context, *Gwynedd County Council v Grunshaw* [2000] 1 WLR 494; [1999] 4 All ER 304, CA.

23.6   The claim form seeking demotion and the form of defence sent with it must be in the forms set out in the relevant practice direction.[4] Particulars of claim in Form N122 must be filed and served with the claim form.[5] The particulars of claim must:

- state whether the demotion claim is made under Housing Act 1985 s82A(2) or Housing Act 1988 s6A(2);
- state whether the claimant is a local housing authority, a housing action trust or a registered social landlord;
- identify the property to which the claim relates;
- provide details about the tenancy, including the parties, the period of the tenancy, the rent, the dates on which the rent is payable and any statement of express terms of the tenancy served on the tenant under s82A(7) or under s6A(10); and
- state details of the conduct alleged.[6]

23.7   Courts should fix hearing dates when they issue the claim form. The hearing date should be not less than 28 days from the date of issue of the claim form. The standard period between the issue of the claim form and the hearing should be not more than eight weeks. Defendants must be served with claim forms and particulars of claim not less than 21 days before the hearing date.[7] Courts may extend or shorten these times.[8] Particular consideration should be given to abridging time between service and the hearing if:

- the defendant has assaulted or threatened to assault the claimant, a member of the claimant's staff or another resident in the locality;
- there are reasonable grounds for fearing such an assault; or
- the defendant has caused serious damage or threatened to cause serious damage to the property or to the home or property of another resident in the locality.[9]

23.8   Defendants should file defences within 14 days after service of the particulars of claim, but they may still take part in any hearing even if they do not do so. However, courts may take such a failure to do so

---

4   PD 65 para 6.2 and PD 4 Table 1. The Forms are N6 and N11D.
5   CPR 65.15.
6   PD 65 para 7.1. See too PD 65 para 9.1 which provides that each party should wherever possible include all the evidence he or she wishes to present in his or her statement of case, verified by a statement of truth.
7   CPR 65.16.
8   CPR 3.1(2)(a).
9   PD 65 para 8.2.

into account when deciding what order to make about costs.[10] It is not possible for landlords to enter judgment in default if a tenant fails to file a defence.[11]

23.9   At the hearing, the court may decide the demotion claim, or give case management directions. Where the demotion claim is genuinely disputed on grounds which appear to be substantial, case management directions should be given. They should include the allocation of the demotion claim to a track or directions to enable it to be allocated.[12]

23.10   Any fact that needs to be proved by the evidence of witnesses may be proved by evidence in writing unless the demotion claim has been allocated to the fast or multi-track or the court directs otherwise.[13] The claimant's evidence should include details of the conduct alleged.[14] All witness statements should be filed and served at least two days before the hearing.

23.11   District judges have jurisdiction to try demotion claims.[15]

---

10   CPR 65.17(1).
11   CPR 62.17(2); cf CPR Part 12.
12   CPR 65.18(1).
13   CPR 65.18(3). See too CPR 32.2.
14   PD 65 para 6. See too *Washington Housing Company Ltd v Morson* [2005] EWHC 3407, ChD.
15   PD 2B para 11.1(b).

Public funding

Generally

24.1   With effect from April 2000 the responsibility for the provision of public money to assist litigants of low income passed from the Legal Aid Board to the Legal Services Commission. The expression 'legal aid' ceased to be used and was replaced by the expression 'public funding'. Different levels of support are now available as part of the Community Legal Service, which the Commission is statutorily charged with managing, and are paid for out of the Community Legal Service Fund.

24.2   In the context of housing litigation there are in effect three possible levels of service. These are: Legal Help, Help at Court and Legal Representation. Legal Help and Help at Court are services provided by solicitors and not-for-profit organisations who contract with the Commission and provide advice and assistance to a predetermined number of clients, either by reference to the number of 'case starts' a solicitor supplier has contracted to undertake during the contract period or, in the case of the not-for-profit supplier, by reference to a predetermined number of hours spent providing such advice and assistance. Legal Help and Help at Court are both described as 'controlled work'. Legal Representation, by contrast, is 'non-contracted work' provided to a client by a solicitor under a 'public funding certificate' which is applied for and awarded on a case-by-case basis. This effectively replaces the old legal aid certificate. Legal Representation may take the form of either Investigative Help or Full Representation and a solicitor can apply for either level depending on whether, at the time of the application, it is possible to estimate the prospects of successfully defending the proceedings. The most important difference between the levels of service is between Legal Help/Help at Court, on the one hand, and Legal Representation under a certificate, on the other. There is a significant overlap between work which can be carried out at either of these levels. Guidance on the full scope of Legal Help and Help at Court is contained in the General Civil Contract Specification.[1]

Using the Legal Help scheme

24.3   Advisers are able to give initial advice to those threatened with possession proceedings under the Legal Help scheme. Clients must be financially eligible both in terms of their level of income and their

---

1   Issued by Legal Aid Board in October 1999.

capital resources. The General Civil Contract specification[2] provides for the circumstances in which the supplier may continue to work on the client's case beyond an initial two hours. The supplier will, however, have to have documentary proof of the client's financial eligibility before working beyond this two-hour threshold. In practice, a solicitor supplier will be concerned to ensure that the work carried out is consistent with the amount that that supplier will be paid under the 'tailored fixed fee' scheme applicable to that firm. Under this scheme solicitors are paid a fixed amount for each case taken on. This replaced the previous arrangement where there was an initial limit of two hours paid work on each case.

24.4   Section 11 of the General Civil Contract specification provides detailed guidance in relation to housing cases. On possession claims it provides:[3]

Possession cases

16 The two-hour financial limit should normally be sufficient to allow you to take full instructions and to advise on the type of tenancy, the rights and obligations involved, and any available defences and counterclaims. You may write to the landlord in an attempt to settle the matter, and/or submit an application for Legal Representation. Your client may only seek help when notice of proceedings is received, in which case there may be greater opportunity for negotiation. However, if Legal Help is not sought until proceedings are issued and there is an imminent hearing date, an application for Emergency Representation will have to be made (provided there is a defence to the landlord's application for a possession order). Where negotiation is ongoing, an extension of 5–10 units (30 minutes to one hour) may be justified.

17 Advice may be sought on whether or not a proper notice has been served either to determine the tenancy or indicate proceedings will be issued. The two-hour financial limit should be sufficient to allow you to provide such Legal Help.

18 Even if there is no defence to the possession proceedings, you may still be able to negotiate the terms of any possession order. The landlord may agree not to pursue arrears of rent, and/or to allow more time for your client to vacate the premises. You may even be able to negotiate terms under which your client is allowed to remain under a suspended possession order, provided that the rent is paid regularly. An extension of about 10 units (one hour) may be justified to cover negotiations in these circumstances.

2   This can most conveniently be found in *Legal Services Commission Manual* Vol 2.

3   Para H3.5 – Financial limits.

Counterclaims for disrepair

19 In some circumstances, there may be a defence to possession proceedings based on the landlord's failure to keep the premises in repair. You will take full instructions on the condition of the premises in order to establish the value of any counterclaim, in addition to determining whether there is a defence to the proceedings. This can entail extra work. It may be that the amount of the damages that would be awarded for the disrepair would extinguish the landlord's claim for arrears of rent. The usual extensions in relation to disrepair may be appropriate and the calculation of quantum for the counterclaim should be noted on the file.

Accelerated possession proceedings

20 If a landlord is taking accelerated possession proceedings to obtain possession of premises let on an assured shorthold tenancy, an application for Legal Representation will not be appropriate because there is no court hearing. You will however go through the landlord's affidavit with your client. There are several reasons why objections could be made to the accelerated procedure. For example, there may be a dispute as to whether or not the correct notice of shorthold tenancy was served on the tenant before the tenancy commenced. If there is a dispute, you will need to help your client prepare a detailed reply for the court. This reply would raise the relevant issues and provide evidence to persuade the court that an immediate order for possession should not be made, and that the matter should be listed for an oral hearing. An extension of up to 5–10 units (30 minutes to one hour) would normally be sufficient to allow the application for Legal Representation to be made.

Defective notices

21 If there is a defence to the possession proceedings based on an incorrect notice, it would not be unusual for other problems to exist with the tenancy. There may be rent arrears and/or disrepair and/or welfare benefit problems. In cases where there is no defence, you may also have to provide Legal Help on homelessness. The amount of any extensions which could be justified will always depend on the number and extent of the issues arising.

...

Mortgage repossession

Claims by lenders against borrowers whose property is subject to a mortgage/legal charge

29 The two-hour financial limit should normally be sufficient to allow [an adviser] to take detailed instructions, identify the relevant issues and provide Legal Help as to the position, any defence, and relevant steps to be taken. The instructions taken will include details of the property, the nature of the loan, instalments, capital and interest outstanding. Legal Help will cover the nature of any proceedings

threatened or already issued, and of any defence/counterclaim which could be mounted. The financial limit will also cover the limited amount of correspondence usually necessary in identifying the issues and setting out your client's case. If additional correspondence is necessary, for example, where information is outstanding from the lender or negotiations are ongoing, an extension of up to 10 units (one hour) may be justified.

30 The following issues may arise when the client seeks advice of this nature:

(a) Arrears
Where, as in many cases this is the only issue in dispute you will normally write to the court to explain the borrower's position, unless the circumstances make Help at Court appropriate (see section 4). An immediate possession order is unlikely to be granted in the light of decision in *Cheltenham & Gloucester Building Society v Norgan*[4] as the Court can consider the remaining period of the mortgage as the reasonable period for repayment of arrears. If there is some dispute as to the level of arrears a modest extension of up to 10 units (one hour) may be appropriate

(b) Linked relationship breakdown or other disputes/litigation
This may be a factor justifying more extensive Legal Help, although an extension of more than ten units (one hour) is unlikely to be appropriate unless an application for Legal Representation in relation to the possession proceedings is made, in which case another 5 units (30 minutes) will be required. In most cases, you should be able to write to the Court to explain your client's position.

(c) Fraud
It may be alleged by your client that his or her signature has been fraudulently added to a document, usually by his or her cohabitant/spouse. An extension of not more than 5 units (30 minutes) would be appropriate to obtain a copy of the document, and to make the application for Legal Representation. If fraud is clear and unambiguous, you should write to the lender pointing this out before any application for Legal Representation is made.

(d) Duress/Undue Influence
If it is claimed that signatures have been obtained under duress/pressure, and/or, that inadequate independent advice has been given the guidelines laid down in *Royal Bank of Scotland v Etridge*[5] must be considered and noted.

If your client has had the benefit of independent advice from a solicitor before entering into the transaction, the lender is in a strong

4   [1996] 1 WLR 343; [1996] 1 All ER 449, CA.
5   [2001] UKHL 44; [2002] 2 AC 773, HL.

position. Your client will have difficulty in establishing duress/ undue influence in these circumstances. Where your client did not have advice from a solicitor some limited correspondence may be reasonable to establish whether any defence exists, and an extension of up to 10 units (one hour) may be justified.

Where a combination of two or more of the issues above arise, an extension of 10 to 20 units (one to two hours) may be justified prior to applying for Legal Representation.

(e) Arrears cases/Consumer Credit Act issues
The financial limit should generally be sufficient but an extension of not more than 10–20 units (one to two hours) may be necessary if the case is unusually complex and/or your client seeks to request time to pay and/or reduce interest charges.

(f) Addition of Parties
Where an occupant is not a party to the secured loan agreement he/ she may wish to apply to be added as a party to the proceedings. If there is sufficient benefit in so doing, it should be possible to consider the issues and apply for Legal Representation within the two-hour financial limit. An extension is therefore unlikely to be required.

(g) Counterclaims
Legal Help may be appropriate, for example, as to a negligent survey. An extension of up to 10 units (one hour) may be appropriate.

(h) Advice to tenants of borrowers
Legal Help may be provided to the tenant in relation to the mortgage and possible action against the borrower, if evicted. You should be able to investigate and consider the issues within the financial limit, and submit any application for Legal Representation.

(i) Help following issue of warrant for possession
If this is the first attendance on your client you will take full instructions so that you can consider any possibility of the judgement being set aside and/or making an application to set aside or suspend any warrant issued. If an application to set aside judgment can be made then an application for Legal Representation may be justified. An extension of up to 10 units (one hour) may be appropriate to allow you to take sufficient instructions. If none of these factors apply and the only issue is the amount of arrears, Legal Help should be restricted to the financial limit. If you decide that an application to the court to suspend the warrant is appropriate an extension of up to one hour (ten units) may be appropriate to provide ongoing Legal Help to your client.

(j) Sale by building society/bank in possession
Legal Help may be sought by clients against whom possession has been ordered and whose property is to be sold. Where it is suggested

the lender is pressing ahead with a sale at an undervalue it should possible in most cases to establish the approximate value of the property without a formal valuation report (for example, from an estate agent's valuation or client's estimate of the current market value) and to advise the borrowers of their rights. If undervalue can be established then an extension may be justified to enter into negotiations with the lender on value/conduct of sale and/or to obtain a formal valuation.

(k) Costs
Should judgment be obtained by a lender the costs will be added to the debt due under the mortgage/charge. Legal Help may be provided as to the possibility of assessing the lender's costs under section 70 Solicitors Act 1974. An extension of between 5–15 units (30 minutes to one and a half hours) may be appropriate to allow you to scrutinise and make representations in relation to the bill of costs.

Miscellaneous issues
Unlawful occupiers and trespassers
31 The two-hour financial limit will normally allow you to take instructions and advise. In many cases it will be no more than brief advice that the occupier/trespasser has no right to remain and possibly limited correspondence. Legal Help might be necessary to establish whether a tenancy/licence has been determined, whether possessory title can be alleged, or whether there is an ongoing licence to occupy. Should there be a defence to proceedings which have already been issued, then the two hour financial limit should be sufficient and allow you to make an application for Legal Representation.

Travellers
32 Advisers may be consulted by Gypsies/Romanies and other persons with a nomadic life-style including new travellers (sometimes referred to as new age travellers). Gypsies are a distinctive group under the Race Relations Act and anti-discrimination legislation will apply to them.

33 The two hour financial limit will usually allow you to take detailed instructions, to identify the relevant issues, provide Legal Help as to the legal position, and the appropriate response to any contact made by the owner of the land, the police or the local authority.

34 The following issues may arise in relation to gypsies and other travellers:

(a) Sites
Legal Help may be required as to the obtaining or keeping a pitch, the quality of services and evictions. Poor sites may contravene a local authority's duty under the Children Act to provide adequate conditions for children. You may be asked to write to the local authority. If ongoing correspondence takes place an extension of up to 20 units (two hours)

may be appropriate in this context. Where the poor quality of the site is in dispute action can be taken under the Environmental Protection Act 1990. The two hour financial limit will normally allow you to take instructions, identify the issues and advise your client. Whilst Legal Representation is not available Legal Help may be provided where it is reasonable to do so. The extensions for disrepair will apply
...

(c) Eviction by the Local Authority from Unoccupied sites or land forming part of the highway.
Travellers may be subject to Possession Proceedings under the Civil Procedure Rules Schedule 2 CCR 24 to evict them from caravan sites or other council owned property which they occupy as trespassers. The circular referred to above does not apply in this context as the council is exercising eviction powers rather than initiating removal directions. The financial two hour limit should be sufficient to allow you to consider any appropriate remedies, including judicial review. If judicial review is considered an extension of 5–10 units (30 minutes to one hour) may be appropriate to include applying for legal representation.
...

Advice in relation to a lease/notice of assured shorthold tenancy
40 The financial limit should normally be sufficient to allow you to take instructions and to advise on the terms and conditions of the lease or tenancy agreement. Where correspondence needs to be entered into a further extension of up to 5–10 units (30 minutes to one hour) may be justified.

Arrears of rent
41 The two hour financial limit will normally be sufficient to allow you to take full instructions and advise as to possible defences and action to be taken.

42 If proceedings have been issued in respect of a sum over £5,000 or for a lesser sum together with a claim for possession, and where there is a defence, an application for Legal Representation should be made within the financial limit.
...

Anti Social Behaviour Orders (ASBOs)
46 Twenty units (two hours) will normally be sufficient to enable you to take full instructions and advise on possible defences, the action to be taken and to make any necessary application for funding.

47 The initial twenty units (two hours) should, where the existing proceedings are the subject of a live certificate, cover any amendment to to extend the certificate's scope to include the ASBO application.

48 Where the existing proceedings are not publically funded, you should consider whether Legal Representation for the ASBO application is justified. If legal representation is not appropriate, Help at Court may be appropriate to provide mitigation for the client where the allegations are accepted.

...

24.5 Advisers should remember that the sentiments expressed by the Commission are by way of guidelines and it may well be appropriate in the circumstances of any case to exceed the timeframes suggested. The Legal Help scheme can be used to assist the client in applying for Legal Representation. Where it is not possible to assess the merits of any defence adequately it is always possible to apply for Legal Representation for Investigative Help.

Using the Help at Court scheme

24.6 The availability of Help at Court is separate from the availability of Legal Representation. Help at Court may be provided where the nature of the proceedings and the circumstances of the hearing and the client are such that representation is appropriate, but may not be provided where the contested nature of the proceedings or the nature of the hearing are such that it is more appropriate to consider Legal Representation (whether or not Legal Representation is likely to be granted in the particular case).[6] The same form is used for the Legal Help and Help at Court schemes and so if an adviser has been providing advice under the Legal Help scheme and it then proves necessary to represent at a hearing which falls within the criteria of cases for Help at Court, no further paperwork is necessary. However, it would be necessary to extend the financial limit on the Legal Help/Help at Court form to cover the costs of attending the hearing. The tests of financial eligibility for Legal Help and Help at Court are identical.

24.7 A non-exclusive list of types of hearing suitable for Help at Court appears in the General Civil Contract specification[7] and includes the following:

- where the client is a defendant to mortgage possession or other possession proceedings;
- where rent or mortgage arrears are not in dispute, it is unlikely that an immediate order for possession would be made and, in the

6 General Civil Contract Specification para 4.3.
7 Ibid.

absence of a defence to the proceedings, the only issue appears to be the terms on which a suspended order would be made;

- where the client is a defendant to possession proceedings on the grounds of mortgage or rent arrears where the claimant's claim for possession is not disputed but there is a dispute over the amount of arrears owed by the defendant;
- an application to suspend, or further suspend, a warrant for possession;
- to defend an application for a charging order absolute or to defend an application to enforce a charging order;
- an application to adjourn a court hearing;
- an application to set aside a default judgment or possession order based on mortgage or rent arrears.

Using the Legal Representation scheme

24.8　Legal Representation is designed to provide for the defendant the full range of services available from a solicitor when defending proceedings. This includes not just the services of the solicitor but also, where relevant, the cost of experts and counsel. As noted above, Legal Representation can be authorised by the Commission either for Investigative Help or for Full Representation. Where the prospects of success are clear then it is appropriate to apply for Full Representation.

24.9　　An application for Legal Representation is made to the Commission which will consider whether to award a 'public funding certificate'. This decision is made having regard to the Funding Code[8] and subordinate Decision Making Guidance[9] issued by the Commission.

24.10　　Section 10.3 of the Funding Code sets out the criteria for when Full Representation will be awarded in possession proceedings:

Prospects of success ˙
Full Representation will be refused if the client has no substantive legal defence to the proceedings or the prospects of successfully avoiding an order for possession (or, if the client is bringing proceedings, the prospects of obtaining such an order) are poor.

Cost benefit
Full representation may be refused unless the likely benefits of the proceedings to the client justify the likely costs, having regard to the prospects of success and all other circumstances.

8　Issued by the Legal Services Commission incorporating guidance issued by the Lord Chancellor under Access to Justice Act 1999 s23.

9　*Legal Services Commission Manual* Vol 3.

24.11 The Decision Making Guidance amplifies the terms of the Funding Code and, where relevant, advisers should quote the relevant paragraph in making an application for a public funding certificate. The Guidance says:

19.7 Cases concerning Possession of the Client's Home
Possession of Rented Property occupied by the Client
1. These cases come within section 10.3 of the Code. Legal Representation will be refused if the client has no substantive defence to the proceedings or the prospects of successfully avoiding an order for possession are poor.

2. Legal Representation will be refused in the absence of a substantive defence, (including where it applies, the defence that it would not be reasonable to make an order for possession), if the only issue to be placed before the court is whether an immediate order for possession is appropriate. If such a case Criterion 10.3.2 will not be satisfied.

3. Legal Representation to defend possession proceedings will be refused if the only defences available are technical ones. The landlord should be approached to seek a compromise. It is recognised, however, that in some cases it may be tactically advantageous to the client not to draw the defects to the landlord's attention, thus allowing the tenancy to continue longer. If no approach has been made, solicitors must explain their decision not to do so and why Legal Representation is justified with specific reference to the costs benefit test. Where Legal Representation has been granted, and the technical defects are capable of being cured within the proceedings solicitors must report this to the Regional Office immediately so a decision may be made whether to continue funding.

4. Legal Representation is likely to be granted where there is a substantive defence to the possession action, including a defence as to reasonableness of the possession order being made, ie, where the ground for possession has been made out but where the court must also assess whether it is reasonable in all the circumstances to make an order for possession.

Suspended possession orders in rent or mortgage cases
5. Legal Representation is unlikely to be granted where the probable order is a suspended possession order, eg, where the arrears are not in dispute, reasonableness is not likely to succeed as a defence, and the only issue is the terms on which a suspended possession order would be made. In these circumstances, Legal Help or Help at Court may be appropriate.

Possession: nuisance cases
6. Where possession is sought for anti social behaviour, Legal Representation is unlikely to be granted either where the conduct is admitted, or, where the proceedings have been issued as a result of breached undertakings, unless a defence can be raised as to

reasonableness. Examples of where Legal Representation may be appropriate are where the client's community care needs led directly to the breach or where the conduct complained of has ceased and is unlikely to reoccur. Legal Representation is likely to be granted where a substantive defence, including the issue of reasonableness, can be raised by the tenant.

6A. Where a demotion order is claimed in the alternative to a possession order or other than in a possession claim, the same considerations as set out in paragraph 6 above will apply to the grant of Legal Representation to defend those proceedings.

Client in rent arrears
7. Where the ground for possession is rent arrears, Legal Representation is unlikely to be granted if the arrears are the only issue, and are not in dispute, unless a defence can be raised on the issue of reasonableness. Whilst delay in payment (generated by the failure or delay of a local authority either to determine or pay housing benefit payment) is not a defence in itself, it may go to the issue of reasonableness where a reasonableness defence is being asserted.

8. Legal Representation is likely to be granted to a client who can show that no arrears of rent exist or who has a valid counterclaim which exceeds or significantly diminishes the alleged arrears, eg, damages for disrepair or quiet enjoyment.

Service charges
9. It would not be reasonable for Legal Representation to be granted where service charges arrears are the only issue in dispute as it is unlikely that an immediate order for possession would be made and, where there is a dispute, the proceedings can be referred to the Leasehold Valuation Tribunal (LVT). Legal Representation will be refused in any case where the LVT would provide an effective way of pursuing or defending the claim. The LVT would not be appropriate in a case where a determination needs to be made as to whether the freeholder is entitled to claim for the item of work under the lease (as distinct from the reasonableness of the cost of that item).

Accelerated possession procedure
10. Legal Representation will be refused in cases which fall within the accelerated possession procedure under Civil Procedure Rules Schedule 2 CPR Order 49 Rules 6 and 6A unless, following consideration of the papers, the matter is listed by the court for an oral hearing. The decision as to whether or not to hold an oral hearing is one taken by the court on the papers. Until there is a decision that the matter should be listed for an oral hearing it would not be reasonable to grant Full Representation as there is no need for representation (Criterion 5.4.5). Once the matter has been listed for an oral hearing Legal Representation may be applied for in the usual way.

11. Where issues arise as to:
- the nature of the tenancy;
- whether the case falls within the accelerated procedure;
- whether there is a defence;
- whether there is some defect in the application

solicitors should assist the client to make representations, either by the completion of the Form N11A or by preparing an affidavit under Legal Help, if appropriate.

Anti-social Injunctions
12. Legal Representation to defend an application for an anti-social injunction will generally only be granted where:
(a) There are very serious allegations;
(b) The allegations are denied wholly or substantially; and
(c) The matter cannot reasonably be dealt with by an undertaking.

However Legal Representation may be justified if there is some question of inability to defend (eg mental capacity). In such cases where the allegations made or issues raised are not sufficiently serious to justify Legal Representation or where mitigation is required at court, Help at Court may be appropriate.

Introductory tenancies
13. In relation to introductory tenancies Legal Representation will be refused unless the client can establish:
- the tenancy was not 'introductory' at the time the proceedings were issued;
- the section 128 notice is defective or was not served;
- the proceedings have been commenced prematurely; or
- that an adjournment is required under the principles set out in *Manchester CC v Cochrane* (1999) 31 HLR 810.[10]

14. In relation to an introductory tenancy an internal review should be sought before Legal Representation is applied for.

Suspension of Warrants for Possession
15. Legal Representation is unlikely to be granted to suspend a warrant for possession or execution if the application does not raise any significant issues of fact or law. Where there is a substantive defence to the possession proceedings or to the enforcement of the order Legal Representation may be granted. This would not include technical or procedural irregularities which only 'buy time' for the client. Examples of significant issues would be where:
(a) a non-party is trying to stop the eviction;
(b) the client is asserting that a new tenancy has been created;
(c) the landlord has waived the breach by subsequent acceptance of rent or other conduct;

---

10 *Manchester City Council v Cochrane* [1999] 1 WLR 809; (1999) 31 HLR 810.

(d) an application to set aside the original possession order can be made, eg, because the tenant was not present at the hearing;

(e) an application can be made to postpone the date of possession, which, if granted, would reinstate the tenancy.

Where Legal Representation is unlikely to be granted Legal Help may be available or, in appropriate cases, Help at Court.

Mortgage possession

16. Legal Representation is likely to be granted to the borrower to defend possession proceedings brought by the lender where there are substantial defences for consideration by the court, eg, where one or more of the following arise:

(a) allegations of fraud;

(b) allegations of duress or undue influence;

(c) where there are linked or (imminent) concurrent proceedings involving the borrower's spouse, co-habitee or trustee in bankruptcy;

(d) where the client is not a party but where it might be appropriate for the client to be joined to the action because the client does have a defence;

(e) where there is a substantive counterclaim.

17. Legal Representation is unlikely to be granted where:

– there is no substantive defence to a claim of arrears only;

– judgment has been entered and the representation is sought to set aside a warrant of possession in an arrears only case;

– duress or undue influence is alleged but at the relevant time the borrower received correct and appropriate legal advice from a solicitor;

– there is a procedural irregularity but no substantive defence.

18. In such cases, Legal Help should be used unless Help at Court is appropriate.

19. Legal Representation is likely to be granted to appeal if the District Judge exercised discretion unreasonably or misdirected him/herself in law. Legal Representation is likely to be refused if there is a lengthy delay before the client considered an appeal or only limited benefit to be gained.

20. Legal Representation is likely to be granted to pursue an action or counterclaim on the sale (including as to price or timing of the sale) where there are reasonable prospects of obtaining control of the sale and the quantum involved justifies the costs of representation.

...

19.11 Miscellaneous Proceedings

Alleged unlawful occupiers

1. Alleged [sic] possession proceedings brought on the basis that the client is an unlawful occupier fall within section 10.3 of the Code and

Legal Representation is likely to be granted where the client has a substantive defence or can show a triable issue which is likely to avoid the possession order, eg:
(a) the client asserts that a tenancy or licence exists which has not been validly determined;
(b) there is a intermediate undetermined tenancy or licence;
(c) there is a procedural irregularity which amounts to a defence;
(d) it is alleged that the occupier has acquired possessory title (twelve years' adverse possession);
(e) the client asserts that he has been given a licence to remain by the Local Authority. Legal Representation will only be justified if that licence has secure status.

NB: In the event of Legal Representation being granted a limitation to the initial summary hearing will be imposed – it is at that point that the court will decide whether there is a triable issue and only if that issue is likely to succeed will Legal Representation be continued.

2. Legal Representation is likely to be refused (unless a defence can be raised by way of estoppel) where the occupiers are within the classes of excluded occupiers in section 3(A) Protection from Eviction Act 1977, namely:
(a) persons who have entered the premises as trespassers (and their status has not changed) and an interim possession order under the Criminal Justice and Public Order Act 1994 is sought;
(b) persons occupying hostels where the status of the occupancy is not in issue;
(c) persons who have shared essential living accommodation with the landlord or the landlord's family throughout their occupancy;
(d) persons staying on in holiday lets when the holiday lease has expired and the status of the occupancy is not in issue;
(e) persons living rent free by agreement.

3. Where the dispute involving the alleged unlawful occupier does not relate to possession proceedings, the guidance for the particular issue should be followed, eg, harassment or wrongful eviction where such allegations are made.

...

Travellers
9. Legal Representation may be available for judicial review proceedings in relation to a local authority's decision, the facilities provided or for proceedings under the Mobile Homes Act.

10. Legal Representation is not available for any criminal or civil proceedings brought in the magistrates court under the Criminal Justice and Public Order Act 1994.

Objections to a lender's costs
11. Such cases will fall within the General Funding Code. Legal

Representation may be granted to cover attending the detailed assessment of the lender's solicitor's costs under section 70 of the Solicitors Act 1974 but only in cases where the costs and the reduction to be achieved are considerable. (This will be determined under Criterion 5.7.3)

24.12　It can be seen that the criteria for considering whether to grant Legal Representation to defend possession proceedings are reasonably generous. Particularly in the case of claims against tenants on discretionary grounds for possession the grant of legal representation is now the norm rather than the exception.

24.13　　Advisers need to apply for a public funding certificate on Forms CLSAPP1 and either CLSMEANS1 or 2. CLSMEANS2 is the financial form to be used for applicants in receipt of income support pension credit or income based jobseeker's allowance. CLSMEANS1 is used by others. For those in employment it is necessary for the employer to complete form L17 which gives details of the applicant's tax coding. Where an applicant cannot provide the completed form L17 then the Commission will require six wage slips if the applicant is paid weekly or two wage slips if paid monthly. Fewer slips will normally be acceptable only if they contain cumulative information covering the previous six weeks. In urgent cases Emergency Representation can be authorised either by a solicitor supplier if the firm has a housing franchise from the Commission or directly from the Commission. Emergency Representation is a form of Legal Representation and authorises work which needs to be done as an emergency before a Full Representation public-funding certificate can be obtained.

Advice to applicants for public funding

24.14　When assisting people who are considering applying for public funding it is important to advise them as to any likely financial contribution which they may be required to pay to the Commission each month. This is particularly important when applying for an emergency certificate as the applicant, when signing form CLSAPP1, undertakes to accept any offer of public funding which is made to him or her. Not to accept the offer will result in the Commission revoking the certificate and looking to the applicant to pay all of the costs which are paid to the solicitor and counsel by the Commission. Similarly, it is essential to advise the applicant to co-operate at all times with the Commission both before the grant of the full public funding certificate (if an emergency certificate has been granted) and also where a substantive public funding certificate has been issued. Failure to co-operate with the Commission can result in the certificate being revoked. In recent times the Commission has been much more active in seeking to recover costs paid than was previously the case. This advice can usefully be set out in the 'client care' letter sent to the applicant at the time of application, but there is no substitute for talking to the client about this.

The Legal Services Commission's statutory charge

24.15 Advice on the possible application of the statutory charge is import-ant as failure properly to advise the applicant is one of the greatest causes of complaints about solicitors. It is necessary to advise mort-gage-borrowers, in particular, of the possible application of the Legal Services Commission's statutory charge. In summary, the statutory charge arises in favour of the Legal Services Commission whenever any property is preserved or recovered in any proceedings in which a publicly funded litigant takes part except so far as regulations provide otherwise.[11] Accordingly, where a mortgage-borrower is successful in preserving the home, the charge arises unless he or she is awarded costs which are recovered and as a result no claim is made against the Community Legal Service fund. In *Parkes v Legal Aid Board*[12] the Court of Appeal held that where the right to possession of property is retained or extended, the statutory charge attaches to that property notwithstanding that the beneficial interests in the property were never in issue. Certainly, the Commission's practice is now to apply the statutory charge in virtually all cases where a mortgage-borrower has been successful in litigation where a public funding certificate has been granted.

24.16 The Legal Services Commission Manual[13] states:

When is property recovered or preserved?
The courts have said that:
(a) Property has been recovered or preserved if it has been at issue in the proceedings. It is recovered by the claimant or applicant if it is the subject of a successful claim. It is preserved by the defendant or respondent if a claim fails: see *Hanlon v The Law Society* [1980] 2 All ER 199; [1980] 2 WLR 756, HL.

---

11 Access to Justice Act 1999 s10(7).
12 [1997] 1 WLR 1547; [1996] 4 All ER 271, CA. See also M Thompson 'The Legal Aid Charge' [1997] Conv 47.
13 Vol 1 para 1D-022.

(b) What is at issue is a question of fact. The pleadings, affidavits and correspondence, judgment and/or order will show what property was at issue between the parties (*Hanlon*).

(c) The recovery or preservation of the **possession** of property can give rise to the charge. Even if the **title** to the property is not in issue, if the proceedings reduce it or restore it to the possession of its owner, he or she has recovered property: see *Curling v The Law Society* [1985] 1 All ER 705 and *Parkes v Legal Aid Board* [1994] 2 FLR 850. If as a result of the proceedings, the owner is able to unlock the value of the property, the charge arises.

24.17   While *Parkes* was a case involving an application for an order for sale under what is now Trusts of Land and Appointment of Trustees Act 1996 s14 which was successfully defended, the court went on to discuss the general application of the statutory charge in possession proceedings. However, what is not clear is whether the statutory charge can apply in the common case where a deferral of an eviction is obtained in an application to stay or suspend a warrant for possession. There are inevitably grey areas where advisers will need to be careful as to how court orders should be worded and subsequently in disputing the Commission's view that the statutory charge applies. It is worth noting that in *Parkes* the publicly funded person had preserved the right to possession potentially until her child, who was aged two, reached majority. The right to enjoy possession must be secured for a 'substantial period'. It was at one time the Commission's expressed view[14] that the statutory charge would not apply where there was a negative equity (in that the assisted person has only recovered or preserved a debt) although there appears to be a change in view, at least in some Legal Services Commission areas. It has also been observed that the statutory charge would not arise where an order for possession was postponed to enable the borrower to sell.[15]

24.18   Regulations provide that the statutory charge does not arise in respect of the cost to the Commission of work undertaken under the Legal Help or Help at Court schemes except in relation to potential family, clinical negligence or personal injury proceedings.[16] There is therefore no need for the adviser to consider whether to waive enforcement of the statutory charge because enforcement would cause grave hardship or distress to the client or would be unreasonably difficult

---

14 Letter from Legal Aid Board Area 4 to author, dated 30 June 1995.

15 See letter in June 1995 *Legal Action* 27.

16 Community Legal Service (Financial) Regulations 2000 SI No 516 reg 43(3). See also 'How the Access to Justice Act 1999 will affect the statutory charge' LSC Focus No 29 p11.

because of the nature of the property. Where the Commission has funded Legal Representation in proceedings which it considers to have significant wider public interest and where the statutory charge would apply, the Commission has a discretion to waive some or all of the amount of the statutory charge if it considers it equitable to do so.[17]

If, after getting Legal Help or Help at Court, the client goes on to receive help with Legal Representation under a public funding certificate, the statutory charge will arise in favour of the Commission in relation to property preserved after the issue of the certificate.[18]

24.19   In enforcing the statutory charge, the Commission has the same rights as are available to a chargee in respect of a charge given between parties.[19]

24.20   Where the statutory charge does apply, it is open to the client to ask the Commission to defer the enforcement of the statutory charge:

where (but only where):
(a) by order of the court or agreement it relates to property to be used as a home by the client or his dependents ...;
(b) the Commission is satisfied that the property in question will provide such security for the statutory charge as it considers appropriate; and
(c) as soon as it is possible to do so, the Commission registers a charge under the Land Registration Act 2002 to secure the amount in regulation 43 or as appropriate takes equivalent steps (whether in England and Wales or in any other jurisdiction) to protect its interests in the property.[20]

24.21   It should be noted that the Commission has only very limited discretion in relation to postponement of the enforcement of the statutory charge. Unless the property preserved is adequate security for the sums to be deferred, it would appear that the client will be at risk of the Commission seeking to enforce the monies secured by the statutory charge. Furthermore, the Commission may only defer enforcement of the charge if it appears to the Commission that it would be unreasonable for the assisted person to repay the amount of the charge.[21] The Commission may review the decision to defer enforcement and again, unless it appears to the Commission that it

---

17 Community Legal Service (Financial) Regulations 2000 SI No 516 reg 47.
18 Ibid reg 45.
19 Ibid reg 51.
20 Ibid reg 52(1).
21 Civil Legal Aid (General) Regulations 1989 SI No 339 reg 96A.

would be unreasonable for the assisted person to repay the amount of the charge, it shall proceed to enforce the charge.[22] If the Commission continues to defer enforcement of the charge it may also do so on such terms and conditions as to repayment of the amount of the charge by way of interim payments of either capital or interest or both, as appears to the Commission to be appropriate.[23]

24.22   The adviser must notify the Commission of the preservation or recovery of property using form CLSADMIN1. Where property which is preserved is jointly owned, the Commission requires both joint owners to execute the charge deed in form CLSADMIN1 in favour of the Commission. Failing this the Commission will only defer enforcement if the assisted person agrees to the matter being referred to the Commission's Debt Recovery Unit so that a judgment can be obtained against the assisted person. The Commission's position is then protected by a charging order which is capable of being registered as a restriction against the property.[24] This is far from satisfactory as additional costs are incurred which will increase the amount due to the Commission. The sum secured in the Commission's favour is the amount paid out to the client's solicitor and counsel and carries flat rate interest at the rate of 1 percentage point above the Bank of England base rate from the date the charge is first registered to the date of settlement.[25] The client can make interim payments towards discharge of the sums secured by the statutory charge.[26] Advisers are reminded of the duty to notify the Commission immediately of any property preserved so that the Commission can consider whether there are steps which need to be taken at that stage to safeguard the fund.[27] Unfortunately, this obligation is not always recognised and advisers put themselves at risk if, ultimately, the statutory charge cannot be postponed because of delay in the Commission being advised of property being preserved. The statutory charge will still arise where property is preserved in cases where a certificate has been discharged or revoked but where the client (or his or her personal representative or trustee in bankruptcy) has continued to defend the proceedings.[28]

---

22 Reg 96B(1).
23 Reg 96B(2).
24 See LSC *Focus* Issue 43 December 2003 addendum.
25 Community Legal Service (Financial) Regulations 2000 SI No 516 reg 53(1) and (3).
26 Ibid reg 53(2).
27 Community Legal Service (Costs) Regulations 2000 SI No 441 reg 20(1)(a).
28 Community Legal Service (Financial) Regulations 2000 SI No 516 reg 49.

24.23   Theoretically, the statutory charge may apply to contractual tenancies preserved[29] (though not to a statutory tenancy which is no more than a personal right) but only where the tenant has an interest in the property which is capable of being charged.[30] In practice there is little point in the Commission seeking to enforce as against the vast majority of assisted tenants.

29 See, eg, 'Legal aid – more about the statutory charge' (1985) 82 LS Gaz 1214.
30 Letter from Legal Aid Board Area 4 to author, dated 14 October 1994.

CHAPTER 25

Possession proceedings against trespassers and other unlawful occupiers

Generally

25.1   Historically, there was no need for landowners to bring court proceedings to evict trespassers. They were entitled to use 'self-help' and to evict trespassers without a court order.[1] However, to use the words of Lord Denning, this was a course 'not to be recommended' to landowners because of the 'possible disturbance' which might be caused.[2] Additionally, a landowner risks prosecution under Criminal Law Act 1977 s6 if violence to people or property is used or threatened for the purpose of securing entry to premises when there is someone present on those premises.[3] Also, if the trespassers are former tenants or licensees who are entitled to rely on Protection from Eviction Act 1977 s3 as amended,[4] a landlord using self-help risks prosecution. Advisers should, however, note Criminal Law Act 1977 s7 which creates a criminal offence where a trespasser fails to leave the premises if required to do so by or on behalf of a displaced residential occupier or a protected intending occupier of those premises.[5]

25.2   In possession proceedings against trespassers, landowners need prove only their title and an intention to regain possession.[6] If occupiers wish to claim some right of occupation which amounts to a defence (for example, a continuing licence or tenancy), the burden of proving its existence lies on them. The main defences likely to be advanced by people who face possession proceedings brought by landowners who claim that they are trespassers are:

- They have a tenancy or licence which has not been determined. As to termination of tenancies and licences, see chapters 12 and 16.

- Although the people in occupation of land do not themselves have a tenancy or licence, someone else, other than the landowner, has a tenancy or licence which has not been determined. Landowners

---

1   *R v Blankley* [1979] Crim LR 166, *McPhail v Persons, Names Unknown* [1973] Ch 447; [1973] 3 All ER 393, CA.

2   *McPhail v Persons, Names Unknown* [1973] Ch 447; [1973] 3 All ER 393, per Lord Denning MR at 396.

3   Unless the landowner is a displaced residential occupier or protected intending occupier – see Criminal Law Act 1977 ss6 and 7 and Criminal Justice and Public Order Act 1994 ss75 and 76.

4   Protection from Eviction Act 1977 as amended by HA 1988 ss30 and 31. See para 12.10 and chapter 16.

5   See Suzanne Tarlin 'Squatting and the criminal law' December 1977 *LAG Bulletin* 285.

6   *Portland Managements Ltd v Harte* [1977] QB 306; [1976] 1 All ER 225.

are not entitled to orders for possession unless they can prove that they have an immediate right to possession. This is not the case if there is an intermediate undetermined tenancy or licence. This situation most commonly arises where a tenant moves away or dies and someone else moves into the property without the landowner's permission (see para 2.52).

- The landowner has failed to comply with the necessary procedural requirements, for example, as to service of proceedings (see para 21.24). Sometimes this may succeed in delaying matters, giving occupiers time to find other accommodation, but it is unlikely to provide a long-term defence.

- The decision by a public body, such as a local authority, to bring possession proceedings can be challenged on administrative law grounds (for example, that it has failed to take into account relevant factors or has misdirected itself in law – see para 25.13) or on Human Rights Act 1998 grounds. Sometimes it will be necessary to seek an adjournment and apply for judicial review to quash the decision to bring proceedings, although there is the suggestion in *Poplar HARCA v Donoghue*[7] that county courts may summarily determine such issues and in *Lambeth LBC v Kay* and *Leeds CC v Price*[8] Lord Hope said that 'if the defendant wishes to challenge the decision of a public authority to recover possession as an improper exercise of its powers at common law on the ground that it was a decision that no reasonable person would consider justifiable, he should be permitted to do this provided again that the point is seriously arguable'.[9]

- Trespassers have acquired possessory title as a result of 12 years' adverse possession (Limitation Act 1980 s15(1)) or have rights under the Land Registration Act 2002 (see para 25.18).

25.3   Proceedings may be issued as ordinary possession claims. Alternatively they may be issued as 'a claim against trespassers' in accordance with Civil Procedure Rules (CPR) 55.1(b). (The summary procedure against those who entered into or remained in occupation without licence or consent contained in County Court Rules (CCR) Ord 24 or Rules of the Supreme Court (RSC) Ord 113 no longer exists.) Unlike CCR Ord 24 or RSC Ord 113 the standard possession procedure

---

7   [2001] EWCA Civ 595; [2002] QB 48; [2001] 3 WLR 183.

8   [2006] UKHL 10; [2006] 2 WLR 570; 8 March 2006; (2006) *Times* 10 March.

9   See too *Wandsworth LBC v Winder (No 1)* [1985] AC 461; [1984] 3 WLR 1254.

contained in CPR Part 55 applies to claims against trespassers, but with some modifications. CPR 55.1(b) provides that:

> a possession claim against trespassers' means a claim for the recovery of land which the claimant alleges is occupied only by a person or persons who entered or remained on the land without the consent of a person entitled to possession of that land but does not include a claim against a tenant or sub-tenant whether his tenancy has been terminated or not.

This means that a 'possession claim against trespassers' under the CPR is narrower than the equivalent provision in either the CCR or the RSC which could both be used against unlawful subtenants.[10]

25.4   The differences between a standard CPR Part 55[11] possession claim and a claim against trespassers are that in a claim against trespassers:

- proceedings may be issued in the High Court if there is a substantial risk of public disturbance or of serious harm to people or property which properly require immediate determination;
- if the claimant does not know the name of a person in occupation, the claim must be brought against 'persons unknown' in addition to any named defendants;[12]
- the particulars of claim must state the claimant's interest in the land or the basis of the right to claim possession, and the circumstances in which it was occupied without licence or consent;[13]
- service of the claim form must be effected against 'persons unknown' by attaching it to the main door of the property or some other part clearly visible and through the letter box in a sealed transparent envelope addressed to 'the occupiers' or by placing stakes in the land (if these methods are to be used, the claimant must supply the court with sufficient stakes and transparent envelopes);[14]
- CPR 15.2 (defendant who wishes to defend must file defence within 14 days) does not apply;[15]
- the time between service and the hearing must be at least two days (non-residential land) or at least five days (residential premises).[16]

---

10 See *Moore Properties (Ilford) Ltd v McKeon* [1976] 1 WLR 1278; [1977] 1 All ER 262, ChD.
11 See chapter 21.
12 CPR 55.3(4).
13 PD 55 para 2.6.
14 PD 55 para 4.1.
15 CPR 55.7(2).
16 CPR 55.5(2).

25.5 A licensee of premises (such as a short-life housing association) may bring a claim against trespassers provided that it has a right of effective control over land.[17]

25.6 Occasionally, after eviction, landowners are concerned that trespassers may move on to neighbouring land. If there is convincing evidence that there is a real danger that squatters may move onto land adjoining that already occupied, a possession order may be made to extend to that adjoining land.[18]

25.7 The Court of Appeal has held that in claims against trespassers (CPR 55.1(b)), separate unoccupied areas of land should be included in a possession order if, and only if, the landowner is entitled to an injunction quia timet against occupants in relation to the separate area.[19] The threshold requirement is for convincing evidence of a real danger of actual violation. The inclusion in a possession order of an unoccupied area should be exceptional. Factors to be considered are the imminence of the threat to move, the history of former illegal occupations and their frequency and timing, and evidence that the same people are involved. The necessary evidence should usually take the form of an intention to decamp to the other area, of a history of movement between the two areas from which a real danger of repetition can be inferred, or of such propinquity and similarity between the two areas as to command the inference of a real danger of decampment from one to the other.

25.8 Under the old summary procedure (CCR Ord 24 and RSC Ord 113) all that landowners could claim was an order for possession and

---

17 *Manchester Airport v Dutton* [2000] QB 133; [1999] 3 WLR 524; [1999] 2 All ER 675, CA; *Countryside Residential (North Thames) Ltd v Tugwell* [2000] 34 EG 87, CA. See also *Blackroof Community Housing Association v Charles* [1997] 6 CL 378, Lambeth County Ct (nothing in CCR Ord 24 to prevent a licensee bringing summary possession proceedings). Cf, *West Hampstead Housing Association v Church and others* (1983) 27 October, unreported, QBD (Goulding J) and *Family Housing Association v Gedge* December 1988 *Legal Action* 17. See also *Harper v Charlesworth* (1825) 4 B & C 574.

18 See *University of Essex v Djemal* [1980] 1 WLR 1301 and *Ministry of Agriculture v Heyman* (1990) 59 P & CR 48.

19 *Secretary of State for the Environment, Food and Rural Affairs v Drury* [2004] EWCA Civ 200; [2004] 1 WLR 1906; (2004) *Times* 15 March; 26 February 2004, *Ministry of Agriculture v Heyman* (1990) 59 P & CR 48, QBD and *University of Essex v Djemal* [1980] 1 WLR 1301, CA. For examples of injunctions granted to prevent trespass, see *Hampshire Waste Services Ltd v Persons Unknown* [2003] EWHC 1738 (ChD), 8 July 2003; September 2003 *Legal Action* 27 and *Northampton BC v Connors* 11 April 2003; [2003] All ER (D) 196; August 2003 *Legal Action* 31.

costs. They could not make any claim for mesne profits or damages. In view of the fact that claims against trespassers now come within CPR Part 55, there is no apparent reason why financial claims should not also be brought – although the concept of a money judgment against persons unknown is clearly problematic.

25.9   Under the old summary procedure, a body of case-law grew up to determine what might amount to a triable issue.[20] However, none of these cases applies to the new procedure under CPR Part 55 because it is not a summary procedure. If a defendant wishes to defend a claim against trespassers, the court will either try the case at the first hearing or give case management directions.[21]

25.10   At the hearing, anybody who is not a named party to the proceedings may apply to be joined and added as a defendant.[22] Unless occupants have a defence to the proceedings, there is no point in applying to be joined as a defendant since it merely opens up the likelihood of an order for costs. Orders for costs cannot be made against 'persons unknown', only against named defendants.

Orders

25.11   When dealing with claims against trespassers courts should normally make an order for possession to take effect 'forthwith' (ie, immediately).[23] The court can only make an order for possession to take effect on a specified later date, if all parties consent, or if the defendants are former service occupiers[24] or licensees under a rental purchase agreement (see chapters 17 and 19).

Damages for trespass

25.12   Landowners are entitled to seek orders for damages for trespass. There is no need for them to prove that they would have relet the

---

20 Eg *Henderson v Law* (1985) 17 HLR 237, *Cooper v Varzdari* (1986) 18 HLR 299 and *Filemart Ltd v Avery* [1989] 46 EG 92, CA.

21 See para 21.45.

22 CPR 19.4.

23 *McPhail v Persons, Names Unknown* [1973] 3 All ER 393, CA, *Swordheath Properties Ltd v Floydd* [1978] 1 WLR 550; [1978] 1 All ER 721 and *Mayor and Burgesses of Camden LBC v Persons Unknown* [1987] CLY 2183, CA; June 1987 *Legal Action* 19.

24 *McPhail v Persons Unknown* [1973] 3 All ER 393, CA.

premises. Damages are assessed according to the loss suffered by the landowner or the value of the premises to the trespassers, and in the absence of other evidence, this will normally be the ordinary letting value.[25]

Administrative law defences

25.13 Decisions of public bodies, such as local authorities, may be challenged in the courts on the grounds that:

- the decision is so unreasonable that no reasonable local authority could have come to the decision;
- the local authority failed to take into account relevant material when reaching its decision;
- the local authority took into account irrelevant material in coming to the decision;
- in making the decision the local authority misdirected itself in law;
- it has fettered its discretion by adopting a blanket policy without regard to the facts of the individual case;
- it has breached its obligations under the Human Rights Act 1998.

25.14 The usual method of challenging a decision for any of these reasons is to bring a claim for judicial review in the Administrative Court,[26] for a quashing order and/or mandatory order to compel the public body to comply with its obligations.[27]

25.15 A secure tenant with contractual rights may challenge the decision to bring proceedings relying on these administrative law grounds in the possession proceedings themselves.[28] However, where the defendant is a trespasser with no private law or contractual rights, the normal course of action is to make a claim for judicial review and seek an adjournment of the possession proceedings pending the outcome

---

25 *Swordheath Properties v Tabet* [1979] 1 WLR 285; [1979] 1 All ER 240, CA, *Ministry of Defence v Thompson* [1993] 40 EG 148, (1993) 25 HLR 552, CA and *Ministry of Defence v Ashman* (1993) 25 HLR 513; [1993] 40 EG 144, CA. See chapter 27.

26 CPR Part 54.

27 *Practice Note* [2000] 4 All ER 1071.

28 *Wandsworth LBC v Winder (No 1)* [1985] AC 461, HL, *Bristol DC v Clark* [1975] 1 WLR 1443; [1975] 3 All ER 976, *Cannock Chase Council v Kelly* [1978] 1 WLR 1; [1978] 1 All ER 152, CA and para 4.43.

of the claim for judicial review.[29] Courts dealing with possession proceedings are unlikely to be sympathetic to such applications for adjournments unless it can be shown that there is a real possibility of obtaining permission to bring a claim for judicial review and that steps are being taken expeditiously to obtain permission. Courts are particularly reluctant to allow squatters to use such tactics merely to delay proceedings. Trespassers should make applications for emergency public funding certificates for the judicial review as quickly as possible after it is known that a decision to take proceedings has been made. In some circumstances it may be possible to do this even before possession proceedings are served. Separate applications for emergency public funding certificates will be needed for the judicial review and the possession proceedings.

25.16   The fact that a local authority is in breach of its statutory obligations (for example, to provide accommodation to homeless people under Housing Act 1996 Pt VII) does not automatically provide a defence to possession proceedings.[30] However, breach of such statutory obligations may be extremely important when trying to prove that a local authority has been acting unreasonably.[31]

Enforcement

25.17   The High Court and County Courts Jurisdiction (Amendment No 2) Order 2001[32] provides that as from 15 October 2001 a possession order made against trespassers in a county court may be enforced either in the High Court or in a county court.

---

29 *Avon CC v Buscott and others* [1988] QB 656; [1988] 2 WLR 788; [1988] 1 All ER 841, CA and *Waverley BC v Hilden* [1988] 1 WLR 246; [1988] 1 All ER 807; [1988] 1 All ER 807. See also *R v Southwark LBC ex p Borrow* December 1988 *Legal Action* 17, but cf, *Hackney LBC v Lambourne* (1993) 25 HLR 172, CA, where the Court of Appeal struck out the tenant's 'administrative law defence'. See though the comments of Lord Hope in *Lambeth LBC v Kay* [2006] UKHL 10, noted at para 25.2.

30 *Southwark LBC v Williams* [1971] Ch 734; [1971] 2 WLR 467, *Kensington and Chelsea RLBC v Wells* (1973) 72 LGR 289 and *R v Barnet LBC ex p Grumbridge* (1992) 24 HLR 433, DC.

31 See, eg, *West Glamorgan CC v Rafferty* [1987] 1 WLR 457; [1987] 1 All ER 1005; (1986) 18 HLR 375, *Tower Hamlets LBC v Rahanara Begum* [2005] EWCA Civ 116; [2006] HLR 9, *Sharp v Brent LBC* [2003] EWCA Civ 779; [2003] HLR 65 and *R v Brent LBC ex p McDonagh* (1989) 21 HLR 494, DC.

32 SI No 2685.

Adverse possession

25.18   Limitation Act 1980 s15(1) provided that no action could be brought to recover any land after the expiration of the limitation period of 12 years. 'Limitation ... extinguishes the right of the true owner to recover the land, so that the squatter's possession becomes impregnable, giving him a title superior to all others.'[33] Time ran from the commencement of adverse possession. That required a degree of occupation or physical control, coupled with an intention to possess without the consent of the paper owner.[34] After 12 years' adverse possession, the paper proprietor of the land held it on trust for the squatter who might apply to be registered as proprietor of a new estate, where the registered land was freehold, or as proprietor of the registered estate where that estate was leasehold.[35]

25.19   However, the old law of adverse possession has been replaced by the Land Registration Act 2002. Under that Act, adverse possession of itself, for however long, does not bar the owner's title to a registered estate in land.[36] A squatter is entitled to apply to the Land Registry to be registered as proprietor after ten years' adverse possession.[37] If the application is not opposed by any of those notified, the squatter should be registered as proprietor of the land. Otherwise, adverse possession for ten years does not by itself give a right to registration. If any of the people notified opposes the application it should be rejected, unless the adverse possessor can bring him or herself within one or more of three conditions contained in Land Registration Act 2002 Sch 6 para 5. If the squatter's application for registration is refused but the squatter remains in adverse possession for a further two years, he or she is entitled to apply once again to be registered and should this time be registered as proprietor whether or not the registered proprietor objects. The purpose of the two-year period is to enable the paper owner to evict the squatter. Where the registered proprietor brings proceedings to recover possession from a squatter in that intervening period, the Act allows the squatter to establish certain limited defences. However, ten years' adverse possession by itself is not a defence. If a landowner obtains judgment for possession against someone who has been in adverse possession for ten

---

33   *Buckinghamshire County Council v Moran* [1990] Ch 623, 635; [1989] 3 WLR 152, CA.

34   *JA Pye (Oxford) Ltd v Graham* [2002] UKHL 30; [2003] 1 AC 419.

35   Land Registration Act 1925 s75.

36   Land Registration Act 2002 s96.

37   See s97 and Sch 6 and the Land Registration Rules 2003 SI No 1417.

years, that judgment ceases to be enforceable two years after the date of the judgment (section 98). If, in proceedings, a court determines that a squatter has a defence under section 98 or that a judgment for possession ceases to be enforceable under section 98(4), the court must direct the Land Registrar to register that person as proprietor of the estate. Most of the new provisions came into force on 13 October 2003.[38]

25.20   The Land Registration Act 2002 does not immediately affect the position of those who have already acquired possessory title prior to its implementation. Schedule 12 para 18 provides that where a registered estate in land is held in trust for a person by virtue of Land Registration Act 1925 s75(1) immediately before the coming into force of section 97, he or she is entitled to be registered as the proprietor of the estate. Similarly a person has a defence to any action for the possession of land if he or she is entitled under Sch 12 para 18 to be registered as the proprietor of an estate in the land. For three years after 13 October 2003 the squatter's unregistered interest will be an overriding interest whether or not he or she is in actual occupation and so will be binding on purchasers (Sch 12 para 7).

25.21   However, after three years have passed any squatter who has not been registered as owner will only continue to have an overriding interest if he or she remains in occupation and Sch 3 para 2 applies.

Interim possession orders

25.22   Criminal Justice and Public Order Act 1994 ss75 and 76 and amendments to CCR Ord 24 created a new form of interim possession order (IPO) which can only be granted against trespassers. Failure to comply with an IPO is a criminal offence (see below). CCR Ord 24 has largely been repealed. The procedure for IPOs is now contained in CPR Part 55.

25.23   The IPO procedure can only apply in limited circumstances. It can only be used if:

- the landowner is only claiming possession – an applicant cannot seek an IPO if there is a claim for another remedy (for example, damages);[39]

---

38   Land Registration Act 2002 (Commencement No 4) Order 2003 SI No 1725 (C.73).

39   CPR 55.21(1)(a).

- the applicant has an immediate right to possession and has had such a right throughout the period of unlawful occupation;[40]
- the defendants entered premises as trespassers[41] (it cannot be used against former licensees, tenants or subtenants). Criminal Law Act 1977 s12(1) states '(a) "premises" means any building, any part of a building under separate occupation, any land ancillary to a building, the site comprising any building or buildings together with any land ancillary thereto ...';
- the application is issued within 28 days of the date when the owner first knew, or ought reasonably to have known, that the defendants were in occupation.[42]

25.24 Landowners seeking IPOs should use Forms N5 (claim form)[43] and N130 which comprises both the application and the statement in support of the application. The written evidence (ie, the statement) must be made personally by the claimant (not by a solicitor or agent) unless the claimant is a corporate body in which case an authorised officer may make it. It includes an undertaking to re-instate the defendant and to pay damages if ordered by the court.

25.25 The court should list a hearing as soon as possible after the documents have been filed, but not less than three days after the date on which the application for an IPO is issued. 'Three days' means three clear days and Saturdays, Sundays, Bank Holidays, Christmas Day and Good Friday do not count.[44]

25.26 Service of Form N5, the completed Form N130 and a blank form of defendant's witness statement (Form N133) must take place within 24 hours after issue. This should be done by fixing a copy to the main door or other conspicuous part of the premises, and if practicable, inserting a copy in a sealed and transparent envelope addressed to the occupiers through the letter box in accordance with CPR 55.6. Failure to do so provides a defence to the proceedings.

25.27 In deciding whether or not to grant an IPO the court should have regard to whether or not the owner has given the undertakings in the prescribed Form N130 to reinstate the occupier and pay damages if the court subsequently finds that the IPO should not have been granted. Before making a final order, the court should have regard to whether or not the claimant has undertaken not to damage the

---

40 CPR 55.21(1)(b).
41 CPR 55.21(2).
42 CPR 55.21(1)(c).
43 See PD 55.13.
44 CPR 2.8.

premises or the defendant's belongings or to grant any right of occupation to any other person pending the final hearing.[45]

25.28   The court must make an IPO if:

- satisfied as to service;[46]
- the claimant is only seeking possession, has an immediate right to possession and has had such a right throughout the period of unlawful occupation and the defendant entered the premises as a trespassers;[47] and
- adequate undertakings have been given.[48]

25.29   A final hearing should be listed not less than seven days after the date on which the IPO is made.[49]

25.30   If an IPO is made in Form N134, it must be served upon the trespassers with a copy of the claimant's Forms N5 and N130 within 48 hours of it being sealed.[50] Under Criminal Justice and Public Order Act 1994 s76 it is a criminal offence to be 'present on the premises as a trespasser at any time during the currency of the order' but no offence is committed if the trespasser leaves the premises within 24 hours and does not return. Similarly no offence is committed if a copy of the order is not fixed to the premises.

25.31   If an IPO is made, the court fixes a return day which is not less than seven days after the initial hearing.[51] The IPO lapses on the return day. This means that once the return day has arrived, it is no longer a criminal offence for trespassers to be on the premises. At the return day hearing, the court may either make a final possession order, dismiss the claim, give further directions or enforce any of the claimant's undertakings. A final order for possession is made in Form N136.

25.32   If occupiers have vacated premises they may apply to set aside an IPO which has been made before the return day. Any such application should be supported by a witness statement.[52]

25.33   Local authorities at the initial stage of deciding whether and to whom to give a removal direction under Criminal Justice and Public Order Act 1994 s77 have to consider the relationship of their proposed

45 CPR 55.25.
46 See CPR 55.25(2)(a) and CPR 55.6(a).
47 See CPR 55.21.
48 See CPR 55.25(1).
49 CPR 55.25.
50 CPR 55.26.
51 CPR 55.27.
52 CPR 55.28.

action to various statutory and humanitarian considerations and make their decision accordingly. Such decisions should be reviewed by local authorities if there is a change in circumstances. They must strike a balance between the competing and conflicting needs of those encamped illegally and of residents in the area. A removal direction once made can only apply to people who were on the land at the time when the direction was made and, therefore, can only be contravened by such people.[53]

Interim possession orders and human rights

25.34 It is arguable that the IPO procedure does not constitute access to a fair hearing within the meaning of article 6 of the European Convention on Human Rights. Key elements of a fair hearing such as the right to participate effectively, equality of arms, the right to an adversarial hearing and the right to be present are all missing. Defendants have no right to be present unless a witness statement has been served in reply. Under the IPO procedure defendants are under a substantial disadvantage and do not have a proper opportunity to present their case or to comment upon the other party's evidence.[54]

---

53 *R v Lincolnshire CC ex p Atkinson* (1996) 8 Admin LR 529; [1995] NPC 145, QBD. See also *R v Wolverhampton MBC ex p Dunne* (1997) 29 HLR 745; [1997] COD 210, QBD and *R (Ward) v Hillingdon LBC* [2001] EWHC Admin 91; [2001] HRLR 40.

54 But see *R (Ward) v Hillingdon LBC* [2001] EWHC Admin 91; [2001] HRLR 40.

Costs

Costs in possession claims

26.1   In general, and with the important exception of mortgage possession claims, the normal rules about costs in the Civil Procedure Rules (CPR) apply to possession claims. This chapter accordingly considers rules relating to costs in landlord and tenant possession claims, but not the costs in mortgage possession claims – for those see chapter 37.[1]

26.2   The starting point is CPR 44.3 which states:

(1) The court has discretion as to –
  (a) whether costs are payable by one party to another;
  (b) the amount of those costs; and
  (c) when they are to be paid.
(2) If the court decides to make an order about costs –
  (a) the general rule is that the unsuccessful party will be ordered to pay the costs of the successful party; but
  (b) the court may make a different order.

In deciding about costs, the court must have regard to all the circumstances, including the conduct of the parties, whether a party has succeeded on part of his or her case, even if he or she has not been totally successful, and any payment into court or offer.[2]

26.3   Conduct includes conduct before the issue of proceedings, as well as conduct during the case. For example, failure to send a letter before action, which would have informed the tenant about the landlord's concerns and enabled him or her to respond without the need for litigation, may justify refusing an award of costs to the landlord.[3]

26.4   A pre-CPR example of circumstances in which a successful party was ordered to pay costs occurred in *Ottway v Jones*[4] where the plaintiff landlord established grounds for possession based on nuisance and annoyance but failed to convince the court that it was reasonable to make an order for possession, with the result that judgment on the claim was entered for the defendant. However, in view of the finding of nuisance the judge held that the successful defendant should pay the plaintiff's costs and this order was not disturbed by the Court of Appeal. There is no reason why that case would be decided any differently under the CPR.

---

1   Detailed consideration of the law of costs is outside the scope of this book. See CPR Parts 43 to 48 and the *Practice Direction relating to Costs*.
2   CPR 44.3(4).
3   *Brent LBC v Aniedobe* January 2000 *Legal Action* 25, CA. See too the Rent Arrears Protocol, paras 3.34–3.36.
4   [1955] 1 WLR 706; [1955] 2 All ER 585.

26.5   Costs may be awarded on either the standard basis or on the indemnity basis.[5] Where costs are awarded on the standard basis, the court should only allow those costs which are reasonable and proportionate to the matters in issue. Any doubt which the court may have as to whether costs have been reasonably incurred or are reasonable and proportionate in amount should be resolved in favour of the paying party. Where costs are assessed on the indemnity basis, the court need only be satisfied that they are reasonable. Issues of proportionality do not apply. Any doubt should be resolved in favour of the receiving party.[6] CPR 44.5 provides that the court must take into account all the circumstances when deciding whether to award costs on the standard or indemnity basis. The conduct of the parties is particularly relevant.[7] The most common type of possession claims where landlords seek indemnity costs are claims for forfeiture because leases often contain a contractual entitlement to such costs. In *Billson v Residential Apartments Ltd (No 1)*,[8] Lord Templeman stated that this practice was 'ripe for reconsideration', although in *Church Commissioners v Ibrahim*[9] the Court of Appeal held that landlords are not to be deprived of their contractual right to costs on an indemnity basis unless there is a good reason to do so.

26.6   When awarding costs the court may order detailed or summary assessment. If detailed assessment is ordered, the receiving party's solicitor (or costs draughtsman) prepares a detailed bill which is served upon the paying party. If the costs are disputed and agreement is not reached, a detailed assessment hearing should be listed for a district judge to decide the amount of costs.

26.7   If summary assessment is ordered, the judge who has heard the case immediately assesses costs, by considering the schedule of costs that the receiving party's solicitor should have served at least 24 hours before the hearing. Summary assessment is the norm for fast-track trials and for other hearings lasting not more than a day.[10] There are

5   CPR 44.4.

6   CPR 44.4.

7   See, eg, *Wailes v Stapleton Construction and Commercial Services Ltd* [1997] 2 Lloyd's Rep 112 – conduct described as 'disgraceful or deserving of moral condemnation' and *Baron v Lovell* (1999) *Times* 14 September (unreasonable conduct in litigation).

8   [1992] 1 AC 494; [1992] 01 EG 91, HL; see also *Copall v Fryxell* (1991) *Times* 31 December, QBD.

9   [1997] 1 EGLR 13; [1997] 03 EG 136, CA. See also *Gomba Holdings Ltd v Minories Finance (No 2)* [1993] Ch 171, CA (para 37.46 onwards).

10 See s13 of the *Practice Direction relating to Costs*.

fixed advocacy costs in fast-track trials, depending upon the value of the claim.[11] Summary assessment of costs is not possible where the receiving party is publicly funded.[12] It is common for judges when making a possession order against a defendant who is publicly funded, either to make no order for costs or to make an order for costs but to provide that that order should not be enforced until such time as a determination of the defendant's liability has been made in accordance with Access to Justice Act 1999 s11. A public funding certificate may thus be some protection against an order for costs but there is no absolute rule.

Fixed costs

26.8   Fixed costs apply to certain types of possession claims – unless the court orders otherwise. CPR 45.1 provides that fixed costs apply where:

- the defendant gives up possession and pays the amount claimed (if any) and the fixed commencement costs (CPR 45.1(2)(c));
- one of the grounds for possession is arrears of rent, the court gave a fixed date for hearing, a possession order is made (whether suspended or not) and the defendant has either failed to deliver a defence or the defence is limited to specifying proposals for payment of arrears (CPR 45.1(2)(d)); and
- the claim is brought under the accelerated procedure (CPR Part 55 Section 2) against an assured shorthold tenant, a possession order is made and the defendant has neither delivered a defence nor otherwise denied liability (CPR 45.1(2)(e)).

26.9   The amounts of fixed costs are set out in CPR 45.2A Table 2 and CPR 45.4A. They are as follows:

---

11   CPR 46.2 – currently £350 for claims up to £3,000, £500 for claims of more than £3,000 but not more than £10,000, and £750 for claims of more than £10,000.

12   See section 13.9 of the *Practice Direction relating to Costs.*

TABLE 2

Fixed costs on commencement of a claim for the recovery of land or a demotion claim

Where the claim form is served by the court or by any method other than personal service by the claimant	Where – ■ the claim form is served personally by the claimant; and ■ there is only one defendant	Where there is more than one defendant, for each additional defendant personally served at separate addresses by the claimant
£69.50	£77.00	£15.00

Costs on entry of judgment in a claim for the recovery of land or a demotion claim

45.4A(1) Where –

(a) the claimant has claimed fixed commencement costs under rule 45.2A; and

(b) judgment is entered in a claim to which rule 45.1(2)(d) or (f)[13] applies, the amount to be included in the judgment for the claimant's solicitor's charges is the total of –
(i) the fixed commencement costs; and
(ii) the sum of £57.25.

(2) Where an order for possession is made in a claim to which rule 45.1(2)(e) applies, the amount allowed for the claimant's solicitor's charges for preparing and filing –
(a) the claim form;
(b) the documents that accompany the claim form; and
(c) the request for possession,
is £79.50.

Proceedings begun in the High Court

26.10   If proceedings are issued in the High Court against a Rent Act protected tenant, a Housing Act assured tenant or a Housing Act secure tenant, a landlord is not entitled to recover any costs.[14]

---

13 Ie, demotion claims.
14 RA 1977 s141, HA 1985 s110 and HA 1988 s40.

Small claims track cases

26.11   It is rare for possession claims to be allocated to the small claims track.[15] However, if a possession claim is allocated to the small claims track, the fast track costs regime applies but the trial costs are in the discretion of the judge and should not exceed the amount of fast track costs allowable in CPR 46.2 if the value were up to £3,000 – ie, currently £350.[16]

---

15 See para 21.46.
16 CPR 55.9(3).

CHAPTER 27

Mesne profits and damages for trespass

27.1 If someone is in wrongful occupation of land, the owner of that land is entitled to damages. These may be referred to as damages for trespass, or, if the occupier is a former tenant whose tenancy has been terminated, as mesne profits. However, there can be no liability for mesne profits or damages for use and occupation until the tenancy has been determined. Until that time the tenant is liable to the landlord for rent. It is only after any tenancy has been terminated that any sub-occupier can become liable for damages for use and occupation.[1]

27.2 Until the introduction of CPR Part 55 it was not common for land owners to claim damages against trespassers because they could not be included in a claim brought under CCR Ord 24 or RSC Ord 113. This is no longer so because a claim for damages can be included in a possession claim against trespassers under CPR Part 55.[2] It has always been normal for landlords to claim mesne profits against former tenants from the date of termination of the tenancy until possession is given up. They are generally assessed as a lump sum figure for the period from termination of the tenancy until the date of the possession hearing and then as a daily sum until possession is actually given up.

27.3 The owner of land may either claim for the loss which has been suffered or for the value of the benefit which the occupier has received.[3] If the owner is claiming for the loss suffered, mesne profits are calculated according to the 'fair value of the premises'. In the absence of special circumstances, this may be calculated according to the ordinary letting value,[4] ie, the market value. The rent paid by the tenant before the tenancy was terminated may be the best evidence of this. It is not necessary for land owners to prove that they would have relet the premises if the defendant had not been on the premises.[5]

27.4 The position may be more complicated if the rent does not represent a fair value for the premises. The open market value may not be the appropriate rate for mesne profits where there are special circumstances, for example, where the property is not normally let on

---

1   *Braintree DC v Vincent* [2004] EWCA Civ 415; 9 March 2004, CA (Civ Div).
2   See chapter 25.
3   *Ministry of Defence v Thompson* [1993] 40 EG 148; (1993) 25 HLR 552, CA and *Ministry of Defence v Ashman* (1993) 66 P & CR 195; (1993) 25 HLR 513; [1993] 40 EG 144, CA (Civ Div).
4   *Swordheath Properties v Tabet* [1979] 1 All ER 240.
5   *Swordheath Properties v Tabet* [1979] 1 WLR 285; [1979] 1 All ER 240, CA (Civ Div) and *Viscount Chelsea v Hutchinson* (1996) 28 HLR 17; [1994] 43 EG 153, CA (Civ Div).

the open market.[6] In the case of homes provided to families of service personnel in the armed forces, more assistance may be gained by looking at what occupants would have had to pay for local authority housing than by looking at market rents.

6   See, eg, *Ministry of Defence v Ashman* (1993) 66 P & CR 195; (1993) 25 HLR 513; [1993] 40 EG 144, CA where the defendants would probably never have occupied the premises if they had had to pay the full market rent and the value to the wife (after her husband had left) was no more than she would have had to pay for suitable local authority housing if she could have been immediately rehoused.

CHAPTER 28

Possession orders

Occupiers without full Rent Act or Housing Act protection

28.1   At common law judges had a discretion to allow occupiers (other than trespassers) a reasonable time before a possession order took effect even if they had no security of tenure.[1] However, this discretion was largely taken away by the Housing Act 1980. Apart from various exceptions, orders for possession must now take effect not later than 14 days after the making of the order unless that would cause exceptional hardship, in which case the order can be postponed to a date which is not more than six weeks after the making of the order. Housing Act 1980 s89 provides:

> *Restriction on discretion of court in making orders for possession of land*
> 89 (1) Where a court makes an order for the possession of any land in a case not falling within the exceptions mentioned in subsection (2) below, the giving up of possession shall not be postponed (whether by the order or any variation, suspension or stay of execution) to a date later than fourteen days after the making of the order, unless it appears to the court that exceptional hardship would be caused by requiring possession to be given up by that date; and shall not in any event be postponed to a date later than six weeks after the making of the order.
> (2) The restrictions in subsection (1) above do not apply if –
>   (a) the order is made in an action by a mortgagee for possession; or
>   (b) the order is made in an action for forfeiture of a lease; or
>   (c) the court had power to make the order only if it considered it reasonable to make it; or
>   (d) the order relates to a dwelling-house which is the subject of a restricted contract (within the meaning of section 19 of the 1977 Act); or
>   (e) the order is made in proceedings brought as mentioned in section 88(1) above.

Housing Act 1980 s89 applies as much to orders made in the High Court as to those made in the county court.[2] The earlier decision of Harman J in *Bain and Co v Church Commissioners for England*,[3] that 'a court' meant 'a county court', was wrongly decided.

---

1   *Air Ministry v Harris* [1951] 2 All ER 862 (six months too long), *Sheffield Corp v Luxford* [1929] 2 KB 180 (one year too long), *Jones v Savery* [1951] 1 All ER 820 (one month reasonable).

2   *Hackney LBC v Side by Side (Kids) Ltd* [2003] EWHC 1813; [2004] 1 WLR 363; [2004] 2 All ER 373, QBD.

3   [1989] 1 WLR 24; (1989) 21 HLR 29, Ch D.

28.2   Gathering together all possible variations (including those not referred to in Housing Act 1980 s89), the position is as follows.

Trespassers

28.3   Courts must make an order to take effect immediately unless the trespassers are former restricted contract licensees, former service occupiers or both parties consent to a longer period (see chapter 25).

Proceedings brought by a mortgagee for possession

28.4   Courts have a wide discretion to adjourn, or to suspend or postpone the order (see para 35.10). For discussion of general procedure in mortgage possession actions, see chapters 35 and 36.

Forfeiture of a lease

28.5   In rent arrears cases any order forfeiting a lease must be suspended for at least 28 days. In proceedings for forfeiture based on other breaches of covenant, courts have a wide discretion to grant relief from forfeiture or to suspend the order (see paras 12.60 onwards).

The discretionary grounds within the Rent Act 1977, Housing Act 1985 and Housing Act 1988

28.6   Courts have a wide discretion to adjourn or postpone the date for possession (see below), although courts should not make totally indeterminate orders.[4]

Restricted contracts

28.7   If a restricted contract was created after 28 November 1980 the court may delay the order for possession by up to three months. The total time allowed cannot exceed three months.[5] In the case of a restricted contract created before 28 November 1980, it seems that whether or not the rent tribunal has exercised its power to delay the operation of

---

4   *Kidder v Birch* (1983) 46 P & CR 362; (1983) 265 EG 773 (no date given for possession, but statement that warrant should lie in the court office until the death of landlady's mother. Held: order bad and varied so that it would become operable only if the landlady's mother died within 12 months).
5   See Rent Act 1977 ss104 and 106A and *Bryant v Best* (1987) 283 EG 843, CA.

any notice to quit, in possession proceedings courts retain their common law powers to allow a reasonable period.[6]

Rental purchase agreements

28.8   There is a wide discretion to adjourn, stay or suspend (see chapter 19).

Mandatory grounds for possession against Rent Act, secure and assured tenants, and proceedings against assured shorthold, demoted and introductory tenants

28.9   If the court is satisfied that a landlord is entitled to possession on one of the mandatory grounds or because a Housing Act 1988 s21 notice served upon an assured shorthold tenant has expired, the court must make a possession order to take effect within 14 days unless exceptional hardship would be caused, in which case six weeks may be allowed[7] (see chapters 9, 10 and 15). The same applies to possession claims against introductory and demoted tenants (see chapter 8).

All other cases

28.10   The county court's discretion is limited by Housing Act 1980 s89 to a maximum of 14 days unless exceptional hardship would be caused. There is no definition of exceptional hardship.

Occupiers with security of tenure

28.11   Even if a landlord of a protected, statutory or assured tenant in the independent sector or a secure occupier in the public sector proves that one of the discretionary grounds for possession exists, the court may consider that it is not reasonable to make any order for possession.[8] For example, in rent arrears cases, if the arrears are low, the court may adjourn generally with liberty to restore on terms that the tenant pay current rent and a weekly or monthly sum towards the arrears, or merely make a money judgment order with a direction that the tenant pay off the arrears by instalments. Alternatively, if

---

6   See, eg, *Air Ministry v Harris* [1951] 2 All ER 862, *Sheffield Corp v Luxford* [1929] 2 KB 180, *Jones v Savery* [1951] 1 All ER 820.
7   HA 1988 s9(6).
8   See chapter 12, and, eg, *Woodspring DC v Taylor* (1982) 4 HLR 95, CA.

the court is not satisfied that it is appropriate to make an absolute order, it may make a postponed or suspended possession order.[9] Rent Act 1977 s100, Housing Act 1985 s85 and Housing Act 1988 s9(2), which are in almost identical terms, give the court a wide discretion to postpone the date on which possession should be given or to stay or suspend the execution of an order.

28.12   Housing Act 1988 s9 provides:

Extended discretion of court in possession claims

9 (1) Subject to subsection (6) below, the court may adjourn for such period or periods as it thinks fit proceedings for possession of a dwelling-house let on an assured tenancy.

(2) On the making of an order for possession of a dwelling-house let on an assured tenancy, or at any time before the execution of such an order, the court, subject to subsection (6) below, may –

(a) stay or suspend execution of the order, or

(b) postpone the date of possession,

for such period or periods as the court thinks just.

(3) On any such adjournment as is referred to in subsection (1) above or any such stay, suspension or postponement as is referred to in subsection (2) above, the court, unless it considers that to do so would cause exceptional hardship to the tenant or would otherwise be unreasonable, shall impose conditions with regard to payment by the tenant of arrears of rent (if any) and rent or payments in respect of occupation after termination of the tenancy (mesne profits) and may impose such other conditions as it thinks fit.

(4) If any such conditions as are referred to in subsection (3) above are complied with, the court may, if it thinks fit, discharge or rescind any such order as is referred to in subsection (2) above.

(5) In any case where –

(a) at a time when proceedings are brought for possession of a dwelling-house let on an assured tenancy, the tenant's spouse or former spouse, or civil partner or former civil partner, having home rights under Part IV of the Family Law Act 1996, is in occupation of the dwelling-house; and

(b) the assured tenancy is terminated as a result of those proceedings,

the spouse or former spouse or the civil partner or former civil partner, so long as he or she remains in occupation, shall have the same rights in relation to, or in connection with, any such adjournment as is referred to in subsection (1) above or any such stay, suspension or postponement as is referred to in subsection (2) above, as he or she would have if those home rights were not affected by the termination of the tenancy.

9   Form N28.

(5A) In any case where –

   (a) at a time when proceedings are brought for possession of a dwelling-house let on an assured tenancy –

     (i) an order is in force under section 35 of the Family Law Act 1996 conferring rights on the former spouse or former civil partner of the tenant, or

     (ii) an order is in force under section 36 of that act conferring rights on a cohabitant or former cohabitant (within the meaning of that Act) of the tenant,

   (b) that former spouse, former civil partner, cohabitant or former cohabitant is then in occupation of the dwelling-house, and

   (c) the assured tenancy is terminated as a result of those proceedings,

the former spouse, former civil partner, cohabitant or former cohabitant shall have the same rights in relation to, or in connection with, any such adjournment as referred to in subsection (1) above or any such stay, suspension or postponement as is referred to in subsection (2) above as he or she would have if the rights conferred by the order referred to in paragraph (a) above were not affected by the termination of the tenancy.

(6) This section does not apply if the court is satisfied that the landlord is entitled to possession of the dwelling-house –

   (a) on any of the grounds in Part I of Schedule 2 to this Act; or

   (b) by virtue of subsection (1) or subsection (4) of section 21 below.

Postponing or suspending possession orders

28.13 When postponing, suspending or delaying possession orders against protected, statutory, assured or secure tenants, the court must impose conditions with regard to the repayment of arrears (if any) unless this would cause exceptional hardship or would otherwise be unreasonable. The court may impose such other conditions as it thinks fit.[10]

28.14   The effect of a postponed possession order (ie an order which is conditional upon the defendant's complying with certain terms) depends upon the particular form in which the order is expressed. For details of the forms of order which a court may use, and of the difficulties caused by earlier versions of the court form N28, see paras 29.3 to 29.6.

28.15   The court may, either when it makes the initial order[11] or at any later time, discharge or rescind the order if the conditions originally

---

10 RA 1977 s100(3) as inserted by HA 1980 ss75 and 87(3).

11 See *Vandermolen v Toma* (1982–83) 9 HLR 91.

imposed have been complied with.[12] The normal form of suspended possession order in County Court Prescribed Form N28 used in suspended possession orders made before 1994 included the wording:

... the judgment(s) shall cease to be enforceable when the arrears of rent, mesne profits and costs ... are satisfied.

The Form N28 in use between 1994 and late 2001 provided:

When you have paid the total amount mentioned, the plaintiff will not be able to take any steps to evict you as a result of this order.

Accordingly most suspended possession orders in such claims automatically became unenforceable at the moment when any outstanding balance of arrears was paid.[13] These words are not included on Form N28 used in orders made between late 2001 and Spring 2006, although the new form of postponed possession order (form N28A) introduced from 3 July 2006 does contain a similar provision.

28.16   Spouses and civil partners of tenants (who are not joint tenants) have the same rights as tenants themselves to seek the suspension or postponement of orders until the making of a decree absolute or termination of civil partnership provided that they are still living in the premises.[14]

Criteria for postponing or suspending possession orders

28.17   It is clear that the court's powers under Rent Act 1977 s100(2), Housing Act 1985 s85(2) and Housing Act 1988 s9(2) must be exercised judicially, but (except in cases of immoral user, where, in general, the court's discretion to suspend should not be exercised[15] and serious anti-social behaviour/drug dealing where a postponed or suspended order is the exception[16]) there is little guidance as to circumstances in which orders should be postponed or suspended, or the factors to be taken into account.

28.18   In rent arrears cases, the fundamental purpose of a postponed or suspended possession order is to enable any arrears to be paid

12 RA 1977 s100(4) and HA 1980 s87(4). See also *Haymills Houses v Blake* [1955] 1 WLR 237; [1955] 1 All ER 592 and *Vale of Glamorgan DC v Grech* [1996] CLW May 3.

13 *Merton LBC v Hashmi* CAT 94/1147; September 1995 *Legal Action* 13, CA.

14 See chapter 30.

15 *Yates v Morris* [1951] 1 KB 77; [1950] 2 All ER 577, although in *Yates* the order was suspended.

16 *Bristol City Council v Mousah* (1997) 30 HLR 32, CA and the other cases referred to in para 3.78.

off within a reasonable time. Any postponement or suspension should be for a definite period and should not extend into the mists of time.[17]

28.19   In practice, unless there are large rent arrears, on the first occasion that a tenant is brought to court for arrears, it is usual, if the grant of an order is appropriate at all, for a possession order to be postponed or suspended on condition that the tenant pays the current rent when due *and* a regular amount towards the arrears.[18] Even if rent arrears are high, the court may take the view that the landlord is to some extent to blame in allowing large arrears to accrue without taking any action and that accordingly the tenant should be given the chance to pay off the arrears by instalments under a suspended possession order, although it should be remembered that if an assured tenant owes eight weeks' or two months' rent, ground 8 is mandatory. It is not uncommon for courts to make postponed or suspended orders which provide for arrears to be paid off over a few years.[19] The Court of Appeal has said that court practice is to be merciful to tenants and to give them a realistic opportunity to pay arrears. The question of whether it is appropriate for a tenant who owes substantial arrears to have the threat of losing his or her home hanging over him or her for years is a political question and does not go to the correctness of making an order.[20] Some courts take the realistic view that if a possession order is postponed or suspended, there is some likelihood of the landlord recovering arrears, whereas if an absolute possession order is obtained, practically, it is unlikely that the landlord will ever recover the arrears. Often though, courts are more prepared to postpone or suspend an order against a tenant with substantial arrears if the landlord is a local authority, rather than a private individual.

28.20   When considering what form of order should be made, the time the defendants have been tenants, their previous conduct, their age and health are all relevant factors.[21] The court should also take into account the level of arrears and the tenant's income and expenditure.

17 *Taj v Ali* (2001) 33 HLR 26; [2000] 43 EG 183, CA – judge wrong to make suspended possession order where arrears of £14,503 to be paid off at £5 per week, but cf *Lambeth LBC v Henry* (2000) 32 HLR 874, CA.

18 *Laimond Properties Ltd v Raeuchle* [2000] L & TR 319, CA. See too the Rent Arrears Protocol, para 3.34.

19 See, eg, *Lambeth LBC v Henry* (2000) 32 HLR 874, CA where the Court of Appeal refused to criticise a suspended possession order which provided for payment of arrears over a period of 23 years, cf, *Taj v Ali* (2001) 33 HLR 26; [2000] 43 EG 183, CA.

20 *Henry v Lambeth LBC* (2000) 32 HLR 874, CA.

21 *Woodspring DC v Taylor* (1982) 4 HLR 95, CA.

Again there is little guidance about the size of such payments, but there is a strong argument where a tenant is receiving income support or jobseeker's allowance that no suspended order should require the tenant to pay more than 5 per cent[22] of the personal allowance for a single claimant aged 25 or over towards the arrears. This is the limit of the amount which a benefit officer can deduct from the claimant's benefit and pay direct to the landlord towards satisfaction of arrears.[23] The basis of the argument is that since those drafting the regulations, taking into account the needs of claimants and the level of their benefit, consider that it is not reasonable for more than 5 per cent to be deducted when direct payments are made to the landlord, it would be unreasonable and contrary to Rent Act 1977 s100(3), Housing Act 1985 s85(3) and Housing Act 1988 s9(3) for the court to order the payment of a greater sum. Indeed, if the Department for Work and Pensions is already making deductions to go towards the arrears, it may well be unreasonable for the court to make any possession order at all because the landlord's interests are already being adequately protected.[24]

28.21   There is a tendency for advisers to view a suspended or postponed possession order as a victory, but it should be remembered that it is still a possession order and that if a tenant subsequently fails to comply with conditions imposed it can be difficult to argue that those conditions were not reasonable: also costs will usually be awarded. (For the particular dangers inherent in a suspended possession order made against a secure occupier see paras 29.6–29.8.) It is therefore particularly important to ensure that a tenant will be able to afford to make any proposed payments before agreeing to particular amounts.

Consent orders

28.22   It is a well-established principle that landlords and tenants cannot 'contract out' of the statutory protection provided by the Rent Act 1977, the Housing Act 1985 and the Housing Act 1988.[25] This rule can have important consequences where protected occupiers decide to compromise possession proceedings by agreeing to a 'consent order'. The court cannot make a 'consent order' against a protected,

22   From April 2006 £2.85 per week.
23   Social Security (Claims and Payments) Regulations 1987 SI No 1968 Sch 9 para 5(3) as amended.
24   *Woodspring DC v Taylor* (1982) 4 HLR 95, CA, *Second WRVS Housing Society v Blair* (1987) 19 HLR 104 and *Brent LBC v Marks* (1999) 31 HLR 343, CA.
25   *Barton v Fincham* [1921] 2 KB 291, *Mouat-Balthasar v Murphy* [1967] 1 QB 344; [1966] 3 WLR 695; [1966] 3 All ER 477, *Kenyon v Walker* [1946] 2 All ER 595.

assured or secure tenant unless there is either a concession by express admission that Rent Act or Housing Act protection does not apply or, alternatively, it is established that a ground for possession exists and, if appropriate, it is reasonable to make an order for possession.[26] Any order made without such a concession or without the establishment of a ground for possession and consideration of reasonableness, is a nullity and can be challenged by judicial review, even if both parties were legally represented and consented to it.[27] It may well be that a 'consent order' could be set aside at a later date if it were established that a concession that statutory protection did not apply was not made bona fide.[28]

28.23   In *R v Bloomsbury and Marylebone County Court ex p Blackburne*[29] possession proceedings based on rent arrears were settled on the basis that the tenant would consent to a possession order in return for payment of £11,000 plus costs. Both parties were legally represented. Subsequently the tenant changed his mind and successfully applied for an order of certiorari to quash the possession order.

28.24   In *Plaschkes v Jones*[30] an unrepresented tenant went to court intending to defend possession proceedings. However, at court he agreed to a possession order, being under the impression that he would be able to obtain a council house. He later found that he was not able to get a council house and the Court of Appeal allowed his subsequent appeal because the county court had not considered the question of reasonableness.

28.25   In *Hounslow LBC v McBride*[31] a claim against a secure tenant based upon non-payment of rent and serious criminal conduct causing nuisance or annoyance, the parties agreed that a suspended possession order should be made. At a brief hearing lasting no more than five minutes which was attended by solicitors, but not the defendant,

---

26 *R v Bloomsbury and Marylebone County Court ex p Blackburne* (1985) 275 EG 1273, CA, *R v Newcastle upon Tyne County Court ex p Thompson* (1988) 20 HLR 430, CA; *Wandsworth LBC v Fadayomi* [1987] 1 WLR 1473; [1987] 3 All ER 474; (1987) 19 HLR 512, CA, *Hounslow LBC v McBride* (1999) 31 HLR 143, CA (suspended possession order made by consent, without evidence or concession, in anti-social behaviour case set aside after issue of warrant) and *R v Birmingham CC ex p Foley* March 2001 *Legal Action* 29, QBD.

27 *R v Bloomsbury and Marylebone County Court ex p Blackburne* (1985) 275 EG 1273, CA.

28 See, eg, Atkins LJ's references to bona fides in *Barton v Fincham* [1921] 2 KB 291.

29 (1985) 275 EG 1273, CA.

30 (1982) 9 HLR 110.

31 (1999) 31 HLR 143, CA.

the district judge made the order sought. Before making the order she checked that the figure for the arrears was agreed and that the defendant understood the implications of the order. In a later affidavit it was stated that both solicitors 'assumed that the district judge would simply rubber stamp the order'. Later the council alleged that the defendant had broken the conditions of the suspended order and applied for a warrant of possession. Both the possession order and the warrant were set aside. Simon Brown LJ said that 'an order such as this is not in law capable of being consented to unless the terms of the Act are satisfied'. A distinction has to be drawn between a form of order which contains an admission about those matters on which the jurisdiction to make the order rests (for example, reasonableness) and an order such as this one which did not.

28.26 However, in *R v Worthing BC ex p Bruce*[32] an occupier unsuccessfully appealed against the refusal of his application for judicial review of the making of a consent order in possession proceedings. He had compromised his claim for a declaration and the council's counterclaim for possession when the action was part heard on terms that he would withdraw a 'right to buy' claim and give up possession. The Court of Appeal held that the implied admission in the consent order that the tenant was not a secure tenant taken together with the fact that the order was made by the judge after at least some evidence was heard, enabled the order to stand.

Appeals

28.27 If a possession order is made or refused by a district judge, an appeal lies to a circuit judge.[33] Permission to appeal is required. If permission is refused by the district judge, a further application for permission to appeal can be made to a circuit judge. Permission to appeal should only be given where the appeal has a real prospect of success or there is some other compelling reason why the appeal should be heard. The appellant's notice stating grounds of appeal should normally be filed within 21 days of the date on which the order appealed against was made.

28.28 If an order is made or refused by a circuit judge, permission to appeal to a High Court judge should be sought from the trial judge.

---

32 [1994] 1 EGLR 116; (1994) 26 HLR 223, CA. See also *Morris v Barnet LBC* December 1995 *Legal Action* 18, CA.
33 See generally CPR Part 52.

If permission is refused by the trial judge, it may be sought from a High Court judge. However, if a possession order is made in a claim allocated to the multi-track, appeals are heard by the Court of Appeal (see PD 52 para 2A).

28.29   There is no right of appeal on any question of fact if the court could only grant possession on being satisfied it was reasonable to do so.[34] However, this does not exclude, in a proper case, the possibility of an appeal against a finding of reasonableness.[35] As indicated in the text relating to each of the main schemes for security of tenure (see paras 3.189 and 11.17), it is, though, generally difficult to overturn any order where the issue is whether it was reasonable to award possession to the claimant.

28.30   Appeals should only be allowed where the decision of the lower court was 'wrong; or unjust because of serious procedural or other irregularity in the proceedings in the lower court'.[36] Re-hearings are the exception to the general rule that appeals are limited to a review of the decision of the lower court. To justify a re-hearing some injustice has to have occurred.[37]

28.31   Pending any appeal, an application should be made in the county court for a stay of the order for possession, as the mere lodging of an appeal does not act as a stay.[38] If a stay is refused by the judge whose decision is being appealed, application for a stay may be made to the appeal judge.

28.32   Different provisions apply to second appeals – for example, against a High Court judge's dismissal of an appeal from a circuit judge. They are outside the scope of this book – see the Access to Justice Act 1999 and CPR 52.13.

---

34 County Courts Act 1984 s77(6) and RA 1977 s99 as it applies to cases 16 and 9; HA 1985 s84(2)(a) and HA 1988 s7 as it applies to grounds 9–16.

35 *Gallagher v Castle Vale Housing Action Trust* [2001] EWCA Civ 944; [2001] All ER (D) 409 (Feb); (2001) 33 HLR 72, CA and *Hounslow LBC v McBride* (1999) 31 HLR 143, CA.

36 CPR 52.11.

37 See CPR 52.11(1)(b) and *Ealing LBC v Richardson* [2005] EWCA Civ 1798; [2006] HLR 13.

38 CPR 52.7.

CHAPTER 29

After the possession order

Status of tenancy after possession order

Absolute orders

29.1   Absolute (or outright) orders for possession terminate secure tenancies and statutory periodic assured tenancies on the date when it is
ordered that possession is to be given up, even if the operation of that
order has been delayed for a fixed period.[1] The conventional wisdom
is that such orders also terminate Rent Act 1977 tenancies and other
assured tenancies on the date specified in the order. It has been stated
that in this situation, once the date stated for the delivery up of possession has passed, the occupant is no longer a tenant. 'He has nothing
left but the limited interest granted to him by what may be described
as the indulgence of the court pursuant to [Rent Act 1977 s100(2)].
In effect he has a period of grace.'[2] One consequence of absolute (or
outright) orders for possession is that courts have no power to grant
injunctions to prevent future breaches of tenancy agreements after the
date on which possession is to be given up, because tenancies (and
therefore the obligation to comply with their terms) end on that date.[3]
However, it is perhaps arguable that absolute (or outright) orders for
possession against Rent Act tenants or assured tenants (other than
statutory periodic assured tenants) do not terminate statutory tenancies or contractual (as opposed to statutory periodic) assured tenancies
until the tenants move out and actually cease to occupy the premises.[4]

---

1   Housing Act 1985 s82(2) and Housing Act 1988 s7(7).

2   *American Economic Laundry v Little* [1951] 1 KB 400; [1950] 2 All ER 1186 at
1190, CA. See also *Mills v Allen* [1953] 2 QB 341; [1953] 3 WLR 356; [1953] 2
All ER 634 at 641, CA. In a case where an outright order for possession was
made under HA 1988 Sch 2 ground 8, but the landlord subsequently accepted
the tenant's offer to pay rent and £100 per month off arrears, the Court of
Appeal held that the landlord had done nothing to affect the legal relations
between the parties. No new or different terms were come to. The landlord had
no intention to create a new tenancy. The legal relations between the parties
were governed by the terms of the order until the landlord took a position
inconsistent with the order (*Stirling v Leadenhall Residential 2 Ltd* [2001] EWCA
Civ 1011; [2002] 1 WLR 4 99; [2001] 3 All ER 645, CA).

3   *Medina Housing Association ltd v Case* [2002] EWCA Civ 2001; [2003] 1 All ER
1084; [2003] HLR 37.

4   In relation to statutory tenancies, see Rent Act 1977 s2(1)(a), Chapter 14 and
Bristol CC v Hassan; Bristol CC v Glastonbury [2006] EWCA Civ 656 where
Brooke LJ stated that a statutory tenant 'would retain the status of statutory
tenant until possession was actually obtained.' (para 17). In relation to
contractual assured tenancies, the argument would rely, among other things,
on the absence of any equivalent to Housing Act 1985 s82(2) and Housing Act
1988 s7(7).

29.2 An agreement that an occupier may remain in premises after an absolute (or outright) possession order has been made (eg on terms that payments of rent and instalments towards arrears are made) is now unlikely to be construed as the grant of a new tenancy. The House of Lords in *Burrows v Brent LBC*[5] characterised such an agreement as one by which the landlord is merely agreeing to forbear from executing the order. It results in the occupier being in a form of 'legal limbo' as 'a tolerated trespasser'. That status continues until either the agreement is broken, in which case the landlord may apply for a warrant, or, if the occupant can rely upon Rent Act 1977 s100(2), Housing Act 1985 s85(2) or Housing Act 1988 s9(2), an application is made to discharge, rescind or modify the order, eg by applying retrospectively to postpone the date for possession (see paras 29.21 and 29.22). Occasionally, though, courts may decide that the conduct of both parties manifests an intention to grant a new tenancy (see para 29.8 below).

Suspended or postponed possession orders

29.3 The effect of suspended or postponed possession orders (eg with conditions that tenants pay current rent and a specified sum each week or month towards the arrears) depends on the type of tenancy and the wording of the order. As a result of recent case law, the position is complex and the wording of orders needs to be considered very carefully. The mere fact that an order was made at a time when most courts were using a particular version of Form N28 is not conclusive as to the wording of the order – the order itself must be examined.

(a) Orders made in Form N28 in use between 1993 and late 2001

The form of N28 introduced in 1993 and which commonly remained in use until late 2001, provided 'The court has decided that unless you make the payments as set out in paragraph 3, you must give the plaintiff possession of [property] on [date]'. These orders have always been described as 'suspended possession orders although the better view now is that they should be called 'postponed possession orders' since Housing Act 1985 s85(2) provides that courts may '*postpone* the date of *possession*' and 'stay or *suspend* the *execution* of the order'. However,

---

5 [1996] 1 WLR 144 8; [1996] 4 All ER 577. See also *Greenwich LBC v Regan* (1996) 28 HLR 4 69, CA and *Hackney LBC v Porter* (1997) 29 HLR 401; [1996] EGCS 119, CA.

in view of the fact that Form N28 itself described such orders as 'suspended' orders, and to avoid confusion, that term is still used in this paragraph. If a tenant has always complied with the terms of an order for possession in this form, any secure tenancy, assured tenancy or Rent Act statutory tenancy continues.[6] For example, a secure tenant continues to enjoy all the rights of a secure tenant, such as the right to buy, the right to mutual exchange etc. A spouse, civil partner or member of the family living with a tenant who dies may, depending on the type of tenancy, be entitled to succeed to the tenancy despite a suspended order against the tenant.[7] Similarly, tenants continue to enjoy the normal right to bring actions for breach of repairing covenants, whether express or implied, and protected or statutory tenants can apply to the rent officer for registration of a fair rent.

Where a tenancy which is subject to a suspended possession order is transferred from one spouse or civil partner to another under Family Law Act 1996 Sch 7 (formerly Matrimonial Homes Act 1983 Sch 1 para 3(1)), the possession order, as opposed to the conditions of the suspension, is not enforceable against the transferee. If landlords wish to evict in such circumstances, they should bring new proceedings.[8]

However, breach of the terms of a suspended possession order made in this version of Form N28 automatically brings a secure tenancy to an end. In *Thompson v Elmbridge BC*[9] the local authority had granted a secure tenancy to Mrs Thompson. She lived in the property with her husband. After arrears of rent had accrued, the council took possession proceedings and, in January 1985, obtained an order for possession in Form N28 suspended on terms that the defendant paid current rent and a further £10 per week off the accrued arrears. In August 1985 Mrs Thompson left the premises, but her husband continued to live there. He was unemployed and although some rent was paid by the DHSS, further arrears accrued. In January 1986 the local authority applied for a warrant for possession, presumably using Form N325. The warrant was issued without any further court hearing. Mr Thompson claimed that the tenancy was still continuing and that he, accordingly, had rights of occupation under Matrimonial Homes Act 1983 s1 (now Family Law Act 1996 s30). He applied to the court to suspend the warrant of possession and for an order under

6   *Sherrin v Brand* [1956] 1 QB 403; [1956] 2 WLR 131, CA.
7   *Sherrin v Brand* [1956] 1 QB 403; [1956] 2 WLR 131, CA, *Kyriacou v Pandeli* [1980] CLY 1648. See Rent Act 1977 s2(1)(b) and Sch 1, Housing Act 1985 ss87–90 and Housing Act 1988 s17.
8   *Church Commissioners v Al-Emarah* [1997] Fam 34; [1996] 3 WLR 633, CA.
9   (1987) 19 HLR 526, CA.

Matrimonial Homes Act 1983 Sch 1 (now Family Law Act 1996 Sch 7) transferring the tenancy to him. The Court of Appeal, in dismissing Mr Thompson's appeal against the refusal of his application, held that on the true construction of the order, the tenancy had come to an end on the first occasion when Mrs Thompson breached the terms of the suspended order by failing to pay current rent or instalments towards the arrears on time.[10]

Suspended possession orders in this form provided 'When you have paid the total amount mentioned the plaintiff will not be able to take any steps to evict you as a result of this order.' Although that provision means that once the order has been complied with, new proceedings are necessary if there is a new breach, it does not have the effect of resurrecting or reviving the former tenancy when the total has been paid.[11]

In view of Housing Act 1988 s7(7) it is clear that breach of a suspended possession order against a statutory periodic assured tenant also brings the tenancy to an end at the time of the breach. The position is, however, less clear in relation to other assured tenancies. This is not something which has been considered by the Court of Appeal. It is arguable that breach of such an order made against a contractual assured tenant does not bring the tenancy to an end because, apart from s7(7) which is of limited operation, Housing Act 1988 does not contain any equivalent of Housing Act 1985 s82(2) – the provision which expressly provides that 'the tenancy ends on the date on which the tenant is to give up possession in pursuance of the order.'

(b) Orders made in Form N28 in use between late 2001 and Spring 2006

29.4   The form of N28 introduced in late 2001 and which commonly remained in use until spring 2006, provided 'the court orders that ... the defendant give the claimant possession of [property] on or before [date].' After further paragraphs ordering payment of rent and costs, it provided 'This order is not to be enforced so long as the defendant pays the claimant the rent arrears and the amount for use and occupation [and costs] totalling £ by the payments set out below in

---

10 This is one of the reasons why it has always been better, where possible, to seek an order adjourning proceedings on terms. See para 28.11.

11 *Swindon BC v Aston* [2002] EWCA Civ 1850; [2003] HLR 42. But there may be a possibility of applying retrospectively to postpone the date for possession and so reviving the tenancy – see Rent Act 1977 s100(2), Housing Act 1985 s85(2) and Housing Act 1988 s9(2), and paras 29.21 and 29.22.

addition to the current rent.' The Form N28 itself described this as a 'suspended' order and that was the general understanding until the decision in *Harlow DC v Hall*.[12] In that case, the Court of Appeal held that this form of order in fact terminated secure tenancies and converted occupants into tolerated trespassers *even if they complied with the terms of the order*. The Chancellor stated

> ... the order required Mr Hall to give possession on 9th February 2005. ... it was suspended in the sense that it was to take effect on a specified future date, but the obligation to give possession on or before 9th February was not qualified by the postponement of its enforcement .... The distinction between suspending the execution of the order and postponing the date for possession is also made in s85(2). Accordingly it is ... plain that the date on which the tenant "is to give up possession ... in pursuance of the order" for the purposes of s.82(2) was 9th February 2005 whether or not the conditions prescribed by paragraph 5 for the postponement of its enforcement were observed. It follows that the secure tenancy had ended before ... 10th February 2005. (para 13)

Chadwick LJ stated

> it is not possible to treat the order made in the present case as an order which postpones the date on which possession is to be given beyond the date specified in paragraph 1.(para 26)

It may be that advisers instructed by former secure tenants against whom such orders were made will wish to consider applying to the court under CPR PD40B para 4.5 which provides 'The court has an inherent power to vary its own orders to make the meaning and intention of the court clear', or, alternatively, under Housing Act 1985 s85(2) retrospectively to postpone the date for possession.

Little consideration has been given to the effect of this form of order on assured tenancies (other than statutory periodic assured tenancies). Again, it is arguable that such an order made against a contractual assured tenant does not bring the tenancy to an end because, apart from s7(7), Housing Act 1988 does not contain any equivalent of Housing Act 1985 s82(2). However, the position is far from clear.

(c) Orders made in revised Form N28 in Spring and Summer 2006 and thereafter

29.5   In view of *Harlow DC v Hall*, the Department for Constitutional Affairs (DCA) advised courts to delete paragraph 5 in Form N28 and to substitute a new paragraph 1 in Form N28 in the following terms

12 [2006] EWCA Civ 156; (2006) *Times* 15 March.

1. The defendant give the claimant possession of (address of the property) on or before (date) provided that the date for possession will be postponed and the defendant's tenancy of the premises will continue, so long as the defendant pays the claimant the current rent and in addition the rent arrears and costs by the instalments set out below.

For secure tenants, the effect of this amendment is to revert to the pre-2001 position. Secure tenancies continue provided that tenants comply with the terms of the order, but immediately on breach such tenants become tolerated trespassers.

(d) Postponed orders made from Summer 2006

29.6   In *Bristol CC v Hassan; Bristol CC v Glastonbury*[13] the Court of Appeal held that courts do not have to use Form N28 and sanctioned a form of postponed order which allows a secure tenancy to continue even after breach of the terms of the possession order. A modified version of the form of order propounded by the Court of Appeal has now been adopted as new Form N28A – see appendix B. In summary, the Court of Appeal stated:

(1) It is not obligatory for the court to use Form N28 in any given case. CPR 4 provides that 'a form may be varied by the court or a party if the variation is required by the circumstances of a particular case.'

(2) Judges are not obliged to set out an absolute date for possession on the face of their orders. It was therefore lawful for judges to make orders in the revised Form of N28 set out in para 29.5 above.[14]

(3) The Court of Appeal referred to the 'very unsatisfactory position' of tolerated trespassers and stated that 'the courts possess more flexible powers for setting the terms of a postponed possession order than is generally appreciated'. It suggested that it is both 'lawful and appropriate' to make orders which do not specify a date for possession. Although it is not 'necessary or appropriate to give a fair wind to any procedure which will require a further hearing before a date for possession can be fixed, with all the

---

13   [2006] EWCA Civ 656; 23 May 2006. See too what was described by the Court of Appeal as 'an authoritative suggestion for different wording for a suspended possession order' in *Suspended Possession Orders* (1991) NLJ 853.

14   See too para 4.60, and for a review of the case law and practice developments, R Latham, 'Tolerated trespassers: the problem and the solution', May 2006 *Legal Action*, 35 and 'Tolerated trespassers: the interim solution', August 2006 *Legal Action*.

attendant expense and delay that this might involve, [it] would ... be sufficient for possession to be postponed on the terms that if a claimant landlord wishes a date to be fixed, it must write to the defendant giving details of the current arrears and its intention to request a date to be fixed at least 14 days before it makes that application. If the tenant does not respond, or if the landlord wishes to apply for a date to be fixed notwithstanding the tenant's response, it will then be at liberty to apply to the court on a "without notice" basis requesting a date to be fixed. With its application the landlord must submit to the court a copy of its letter (and the tenant's response, if any), together with a copy of the rent account since the date of the order postponing possession. Other evidence will seldom be required.' (para 37)

The importance of this form of postponed order is that it has the potential of virtually abolishing the status of 'tolerated trespasser'. However the Court of Appeal went on to state

What order the court will in fact make in any case will be a matter for the discretion of the judge on that occasion, although the [DCA] working party (and in due course the Rules Committee) will no doubt wish to prescribe or recommend simple forms of alternative order for the use of courts. If a tenant has a particularly bad record of payment, for instance, but is not yet deserving of an outright possession order, the court might wish to make an order along the lines of the current form N28, although the use of the phrase 'in addition to your current *rent*' would be inapposite since the contractual tenancy would have been brought to an end by the making of the order. (para 43)

Since the decision in *Bristol CC v Hassan* the Head of Civil Justice has amended PD55 and sanctioned two new forms of order – a modified Form N28 in similar form to that put forward by the DCA in Spring 2006 and a Form N28A in similar form to that set out in *Bristol CC v Hassan* which does not specify a date for possession. Breaches of orders in Form N28 result in secure tenants becoming trespassers. However, secure tenancies continue despite breaches of the terms of an order in Form N28A. If the tenant breaches the terms of an order in Form N28A and the landlord wants the court to fix a date for possession, the landlord can make an application to the court following a warning notice to the tenant. That notice must be sent at least 14 days and not more than three months before applying for an order. It must:

(1) state that the claimant intends to apply for an order fixing the date upon which the defendant is to give up possession of the property;

(2) record the current arrears and state how the defendant has failed to comply with the order (by reference to a statement of the rent account enclosed with the notice);

(3) request that the defendant reply to the claimant within seven days, agreeing or disputing the stated arrears; and

(4) inform the defendant of his or her right to apply to the court for a further postponement of the date for possession or to stay or suspend enforcement.

The application to the court to fix a date can be made on a 'without notice' basis, but the claimant must file the following documents with the application notice:

(1) a copy of the warning notice;

(2) a copy of the defendant's reply, if any, and any relevant subsequent correspondence between the claimant and the defendant; and

(3) a statement of the rent account showing the arrears that have accrued since the first failure to pay in accordance with the order or the arrears that have accrued during the period of two years immediately preceding the date of the application notice, where the first such failure to pay occurs more than two years before that date.

The application should be referred to a district judge who should normally determine the application without a hearing by fixing the date for possession as the next working day, but, if the judge considers that a hearing is necessary, a date should be fixed for the application to be heard and the defendant should be served with the application notice and supporting evidence.

It is particularly important that representatives try to persuade courts to use the new Form N28A in cases where tenants are in receipt of benefits since housing benefit problems and direct payments which are made in arrears frequently result in breach of the terms of postponed orders through no fault of the tenant. Even where the court has fixed a possession date, it is still possible to apply to the court to vary the possession order or suspend any warrant of possession at any time before actual eviction in accordance with Housing Act 1985 s85(2).

The amendments to PD55 came into force on 3 July 2006 and are set out in appendix E.

29.7   It is possible for landlords to apply to 'convert' suspended or postponed possession orders obtained on the ground of rent arrears into absolute or outright possession orders where there has been anti-social behaviour. In *Manchester City Council v Finn*,[15] the Court of Appeal referred to the words 'at any time' in Housing Act 1985 s85(2) and stated that a purposive construction has to be adopted. If a suspended order is still running, liberty to apply to the court is implicit, without the need to start new proceedings for possession. Courts can make a new order, even if the old order has not expired or if the new order would provide for possession to be given up forthwith. The court has, on such an application, to bear in mind the guidance given in cases such as *Sheffield City Council v Hopkins*,[16] as to the exercise of its discretion in such a situation, and should be astute to ensure that tenants are not taken by surprise. However, that does not necessarily extend to insisting that the proceedings be delayed by the equivalent of the extra time that would have been taken had the landlord had to begin new proceedings. Courts can ensure that any notice of application gives the grounds and particulars which put the tenant to no greater disadvantage than envisaged by Housing Act 1985 s84(3). Courts should determine any application to vary a possession order in exactly the same way as they would determine an original claim.

29.8   Former tenants may remain in occupation for many years after breaching the terms of suspended or postponed possession orders in Form N28. Courts are generally extremely reluctant to infer the creation of a new tenancy during the limbo period.[17] This is a question of fact for the trial judge. However, in *Swindon BC v Aston*,[18] viewed objectively, the conduct of both landlord and tenant was sensibly referable only to the existence of a new tenancy. That was confirmed by the way in which the landlord relied upon the terms of his 'tenancy agreement' to coerce Mr Aston into keeping the garden in proper order, and by the provision of a new tenancy agreement.

---

15   [2002] EWCA Civ 1998; [2003] HLR 41.
16   [2001] EWCA Civ 1023; [2002] HLR 12.
17   *Swindon Borough Council v Aston* [2002] EWCA Civ 1850; [2003] HLR 42. See too *Lambeth LBC v O'Kane; Helena Housing v Pinder* [2005] EWCA Civ 1010; [2006] HLR 2 (held: nothing in notice of variation of tenancy conditions and four notices of revision of rent and water charges 'to force the conclusion that the former landlord intended to create a new tenancy') and *Newham LBC v Hawkins* [2005] EWCA Civ 4 51; [2005] HLR 4 2, cf *PCHA v Depp* Central London Civil Justice Centre 6 October 2005; December 2005 *Legal Action* 21.
18   [2002] EWCA Civ 1850; [2003] HLR 42.

Setting aside the possession order

29.9   Civil Procedure Rules (CPR) 39.3 sets out the circumstances in which a party who fails to attend a trial may apply to set aside an order.[19] CPR 39.3 states:

> (3) Where a party does not attend and the court gives judgment or makes an order against him, the party who failed to attend may apply for the judgment or order to be set aside.
> (4) An application made under ... paragraph (3) must be supported by evidence.
> (5) Where an application is made under paragraph ... (3) by a party who failed to attend the trial, the court may grant the application only if the applicant –
> (a) acted promptly when he found out that the court had exercised its power to strike out or to enter judgment or make an order against him;
> (b) had a good reason for not attending trial; and
> (c) has a reasonable prospect of success at the trial.

29.10   Applications should be made on Form N244. The reference to the application being supported by 'evidence' in subparagraph (4) means that the tenant must either fill out Part C on the application form or (ideally) prepare a witness statement dealing with all three matters listed in subparagraph (5). In *Southwark LBC v Joseph,*[20] a case in which the council obtained an absolute order for possession and a money judgment for arrears of £6,617 in the secure tenant's absence, the Court of Appeal held that a court 'may not grant an application to set aside an earlier order unless' the requirements of CPR 39.3(5) are met. The first requirement is that the applicant explain his or her non-attendance at trial. In *Southwark LBC v Joseph* the tenant failed at that hurdle as there was no evidence of the reason for her non-attendance. In any event the judge had been entitled on the facts to find that there was no merit in any of the 'defences' that would have been advanced (because (a) as her tenancy had ended as a result of the earlier breach

---

19   As possession orders can generally only be made after landlords have proved their entitlement to possession by giving evidence, they are generally made at a trial. If a possession order is made on the hearing of an interlocutory application the comparable provision is CPR 23.11.

20   March 2000 *Legal Action* 29. For examples of successful applications, see *SLFHA v Hayden* Lambeth County Court; 14 July 2005; October *2005 Legal Action* 16 (deaf tenant with learning difficulties) and *Clapton Community Housing Trust v McGrath* 31 October 2003; January 2004 *Legal Action* 29 (tenant attended court but as result of information given to her left court and missed hearing) and *Lewisham LBC v Gurbuz* [2003] EWHC 2078 (Ch); 24 July 2003 (late notification of change of venue of trial led to a muddle plus triable issue).

of a suspended order, there were no repairing covenants of which the council was in default; (b) entitlement had not been established to the alleged unpaid housing benefit; and (c) none of the arrears was statute-barred because the council operated a running rent account in which payments made were first applied to satisfy the longest outstanding arrear).

29.11   It is not uncommon for local authority and registered social landlord housing officers to inform tenants that there is no need for them to attend possession hearings since suspended possession orders will be made in their absence. Such a statement (if accepted) may provide an explanation for tenants' absence which comes within CPR 39.3(5)(b).

29.12   Applications to set aside possession orders under CPR 39.3 can be made even after execution has resulted in the eviction of the tenant.[21]

29.13   Non-service of the claim form is a ground for setting aside any possession order.[22] However, it should be remembered that posting to the tenant's 'usual or last known residence'[23] is good service, even if the tenant does not receive it. Non-receipt is clearly a reason justifying non-attendance within CPR 39.3(5), but in such circumstances tenants must still be able to satisfy the court that they have acted without delay and that they have a defence which has a reasonable prospect of success.

29.14   In possession proceedings against secure tenants, evidence that a local authority has failed to credit housing benefit and that if this had been done arrears would have been significantly lower at the time when the possession order was made should give good grounds for applying to set aside a possession order.

29.15   An application to set aside a possession order does not operate automatically as a stay of execution. If a warrant is likely to be executed before the hearing of the application to set aside, a stay of execution should be obtained pending the hearing (see below).

29.16   If a possession order is set aside, the effect is the same as if the order had never been made.[24] Normally the court will give directions about the filing of a defence and other procedural matters.

21 See *Governors of Peabody Donation Fund v Hay* (1987) 19 HLR 145, CA, *Grimshaw v Dunbar* [1953] 1 QB 408, CA, *Ladup Ltd v Siu* (1984) 81 LSG 283; (1983) *Times* 24 November, CA and *Tower Hamlets LBC v Abadie* (1990) 22 HLR 264.

22 *White v Weston* [1968] 2 QB 647; [1968] 2 WLR 1459; [1968] 2 All ER 842, but see *Akram v Adam* [2004] EWCA Civ 1601 and *Hackney LBC v Driscoll* [2003] EWCA Civ 1037.

23 CPR 6.5.

24 See *Governors of Peabody Donation Fund v Hay* (1987) 19 HLR 145, CA and *Tower Hamlets LBC v Abadie* (1990) 22 HLR 264.

29.17   If the tenant did attend court, the most common ground for an application for a rehearing (perhaps under CPR 3.1(7) or more commonly by an appeal[25]) is the availability of fresh evidence, although this is circumscribed by the principles enumerated by Lord Denning in *Ladd v Marshall*,[26] where he said:

> In order to justify the reception of fresh evidence for a new trial, three conditions must be fulfilled: first it must be shown that the evidence could not be obtained with reasonable diligence for use at the trial: second the evidence must be such that, if given, it would probably have an important influence on the result of the case, although it need not be decisive: third the evidence must be such as is presumably to be believed, or in other words, it must be apparently credible, although it need not be incontrovertible.

Suspension of execution orders and postponement of the date for possession

29.18   If tenants have no prospect of having a possession order set aside the court may have power to suspend execution of the order. Where tenants enjoy statutory security of tenure and a possession order has been made under a discretionary ground, courts have wide powers to stay or suspend execution of any possession order or to postpone the date of possession (see chapter 28). Rent Act 1977 s100(2) gives such jurisdiction in the case of protected and statutory occupiers. Housing Act 1985 s85(2) applies to secure tenants while Housing Act 1988 s9(2) gives similar rights to assured tenants. These powers can be exercised after the making of a possession order 'at any time *before the execution* of such an order', even if an absolute possession order was originally made[27] or if the original order was made by consent.[28] Such an application 'is not in any way affected or fettered by the reasons given by [the district judge who heard the possession claim] ... on such an application the district judge can take all relevant circumstances into account as they appear at the time of the application. Those will

25 See chapter 28.
26 [1954] 3 All ER 745 at 748, CA.
27 *Plymouth CC v Hoskin* [2002] EWCA Civ 684; August 2002 *Legal Action* 32; 1 May 2002, *Payne v Cooper* [1958] 1 QB 174; [1957] 3 WLR 741; [1957] 3 All ER 335 and *Ujima Housing Association v Smith* October 2001 *Legal Action* 21, ChD, where the defendant was by the time of the application to suspend accepting her legal responsibility for serious damage to a shared kitchen and offering to pay £150 in compensation. This was a change of circumstances that justified suspension.
28 *Rossiter v Langley* [1925] 1 KB 741.

include any medical evidence which is before the court, any evidence as to the defendant's behaviour since the original order and the effect of an immediate order for possession which is not suspended upon the likelihood of the applicant being rehoused under the Housing Act 1996.' 'There is a continuing remedy in the county court.'[29]

29.19   In view of the words 'at any time before the execution of the order' in Rent Act 1977 s100(2), Housing Act 1985 s85(2) and Housing Act 1988 s9(3), such an application cannot, however, be granted if if tenants have already given up possession without the need for execution of the order. The words 'at any time before the execution of the order' in s85(2) have to be read subject to the qualification 'and for so long as execution is required to give effect to that order'.[30] Nor can such an application be used to obtain a complete rehearing of the case.[31] Where the court has made an absolute order under, for example, Rent Act 1977 Sch 15 case 8 or case 9 (see paras 15.32 onwards), the power can be used to delay possession so that the tenant has more time to find other accommodation, but it cannot be used to delay indefinitely the date when possession should be given up, even if the circumstances of landlord and tenant have changed.[32]

29.20   In view of the references to 'period or periods', it is clear that more than one application under Housing Act 1988 s9(2), Housing Act 1985 s85(2) or Rent Act 1977 s100(2) can be made.[33]

29.21   The powers under the 1985 and 1988 Housing Acts may also be used to resurrect former secure or assured tenancies which have come to an end as a result of breaches of suspended possession orders.[34] A successful application to postpone retrospectively a date for possession in a suspended possession order may enable an occupier to rely on contractual or statutory rights (such as repairs, right to buy, transfer of tenancy under the Family Law Act 1996) which were lost on breach.[35]

---

29 *Plymouth City Council v Hoskin* [2002] EWCA Civ 684; [2002] CP Rep 55; 1 May 2002.

30 *Dunn v Bradford MDC, Marston v Leeds City Council* [2002] EWCA Civ 1137; [2003] HLR 15.

31 *Goldthorpe v Bain* [1952] 2 QB 455; [1952] 2 All ER 23 at 25.

32 *Goldthorpe v Bain* [1952] 2 QB 455; [1952] 2 All ER 23.

33 *Sherrin v Brand* [1956] 1 QB 403; [1956] 2 WLR 131; [1956] 1 All ER 194 at 204 per Birkett LJ, *Vandermolen v Toma* (1982–83) 9 HLR 91 and *Westfield HA v Delin* 21 February 2002, Carlisle County Court.

34 *Thompson v Elmbridge BC* [1987] 1 WLR 1425, CA.

35 See, eg, *Routh v Leeds City Council* June 1998 *Legal Action* 11, CA, *Lambeth LBC v Rogers* (2000) 32 HLR 361, [2000] 03 EG 127, CA, *Marshall v Bradford MDC* [2001] EWCA Civ 594; [2002] HLR 22, CA, *Southwark LBC v Edem* [1999] 7 CLD 264 and *Lambeth LBC v Hudson* November 1999 *Legal Action* 28.

29.22   When postponing, suspending or staying possession orders against protected, statutory, assured or secure tenants, the court must impose conditions with regard to the repayment of arrears (if any), unless this would cause exceptional hardship or would otherwise be unreasonable.[36] The court may also, at any time, discharge or rescind a possession order if the conditions originally imposed have been complied with.[37] Spouses and civil partners of tenants (who are not themselves joint tenants) have the same rights as the actual tenant to seek the suspension or postponement of orders until, in the case of spouses, the making of a decree absolute, provided that they are still living in the premises.[38]

29.23   The court has a comparable jurisdiction where other statutory safeguards apply. For example, where a lease has been forfeited, a lessee may apply for relief even after eviction[39] provided that the application is made within six months of execution or the time when the landlord regained possession. In the case of mortgage-borrowers Administration of Justice Act 1970 s36 provides that the court may stay or suspend execution or postpone the date for delivery of possession 'at any time before the execution of [the] judgment or order'. That power may only be exercised if 'it appears to the court that ... the mortgagor is likely to be able within a reasonable period to pay any sums due'.[40]

29.24   There is no statutory power to stay, suspend or postpone the making of a possession order where there is no security of tenure.[41]

29.25   The court only has very limited power to suspend or delay the date for giving possession where the order is made under a mandatory ground.[42] Where an order for possession is made under a mandatory ground, that ground should be stated on the face of the order. It is not proper to return to the judge at a later date to find out the grounds on which he made the order. Accordingly, where an order for possession made under one of those grounds fails to state the ground on the face

36 See, eg, HA 1988 s9(3).

37 See, eg, HA 1988 s9(4).

38 See chapter 30.

39 Administration of Justice Act 1985 s55 (county court – cf, *Di Palma v Victoria Square Property Co Ltd* [1986] Ch 150; [1985] 3 WLR 207; [1985] 2 All ER 676, CA) or Common Law Procedure Act 1852 s210 (High Court).

40 See *Western Bank Ltd v Schindler* [1977] Ch 1; [1976] 3 WLR 341; [1976] 2 All ER 393 and *Cheltenham and Gloucester BS v Norgan* [1996] 1 WLR 343; [1996] 1 All ER 449; (1996) 28 HLR 443; (1996) 72 P & CR 46, CA. See too chapter 35.

41 See HA 1980 s89 (see para 28.1).

42 Eg, RA 1977 Sch 15 cases 11 to 19, HA 1985 Sch 2 grounds 9 to 11, HA 1988 Sch 2 grounds 1 to 8 and HA 1980 s89.

of the order, it should be regarded as having been granted on uncertain grounds. In such circumstances, a court can revisit the exercise of discretion by the previous judge.[43]

29.26　An application to suspend or postpone possession should be made either on Form N244 or N245. It should be supported by 'evidence'. This means that the tenant must either fill out Part C on the application form or (ideally) prepare a witness statement dealing with all matters relied upon.

Execution of a warrant for possession

29.27　If a tenant fails to give up possession as required by an absolute order, the landlord's normal remedy is to apply for a warrant of possession.[44] In the county court landlords follow the same procedure if they wish to enforce a suspended or postponed order for possession on a tenant's failure to comply with the terms of that order. An application for a warrant of possession is made by the landlord completing County Court Form N325.[45] A warrant cannot be issued before the date on which it is ordered that possession be given. If a warrant is issued in such circumstances, it is a nullity.[46]

29.28　A landlord cannot enforce a suspended or postponed possession order, if a tenant fails to comply with the terms of the suspension or postponement, without making an application for a warrant,[47] but (unless the original order specified that no warrant was to be issued without the permission of the court) a warrant in the county court is issued without any prior notice to the tenant and without a hearing. In this respect the county court procedure differs from that in the

---

43　*Diab v Countrywide Rentals 1 plc Independent* 5 November 2001; (2001) 10 July, unreported, ChD. See also *Capital Prime Plus plc v Wills* (1999) 31 HLR 926, CA.

44　CCR Ord 26 r17.

45　Note that the form must be properly completed. Failure to specify the amount of arrears currently outstanding may lead to the request for the warrant being refused or, if a warrant has been issued, to the warrant being set aside – *Westminster City Council v Mbah* June 1995 *Legal Action* 19, *South London Housing Association v Raxworthy* March 1996 *Legal Action* 11 (following *Hackney LBC v White* (1995) 28 HLR 219, CA), *Lambeth LBC v Johnson* December 1996 *Legal Action* 14 and *Westminster CC v Thomas* March 1997 *Legal Action* 12, but cf, *Tower Hamlets LBC v Azad* (1998) 30 HLR 241, CA and *Abbey National v Gibson* September 1997 *Legal Action* 15, CA.

46　*Tuohy v Bell* [2002] EWCA Civ 423; [2002] 1 WLR 2703; [2002] 3 All ER 975.

47　*R v Ilkeston County Court ex p Kruza* (1985) 17 HLR 539 and *Hasan Hanif v Robinson* (1994) 26 HLR 386, CA, and CCR Ord 26 r17(1).

High Court where leave to issue execution on a suspended or postponed order for possession on the grounds of an alleged breach of the terms of that order must not be given without allowing a tenant the opportunity to be heard.[48]

29.29 Tenants who fail to comply with possession orders theoretically commit a contempt of court. In extreme or exceptional cases landlords may apply to the court for penal notices to be attached to possession orders and, after re-service, apply to commit former tenants who still refuse to give up possession to prison for contempt of court.[49]

29.30 The sheriff's duty, on receiving a writ of possession, is to enforce it 'as soon as ... reasonably practicable', not 'at once'.[50]

29.31 Although tenants are not notified in advance of landlords' applications for warrants of possession in the county court, the bailiffs should notify occupiers of the time and date when they propose to call to evict them, using Form N54.

Warrants and the European Convention on Human Rights

29.32 Immediately after the passing of the Human Rights Act 1998, it was suggested that the failure of either the County Court Rules (CCR) or the CPR to provide automatic notification to a tenant of an application to issue a warrant for possession was a breach of articles 6 and 8 of the European Convention on Human Rights and article 1 of the First Protocol to the convention. Enforcement proceedings are certainly within the ambit of article 6.[51] The European Court of Human Rights has also stated, albeit in a case involving rather different issues, that applicants are 'entitled to expect a coherent system that would achieve a fair balance between the authorities' interests and [their] own; in particular, [they] should have ... a clear, practical and effective opportunity to challenge an administrative act that was a direct interference with [any] right of property'.[52]

29.33 It is also arguable that the absence of any requirement that the

---

48 RSC Ords 45 and 46. See *Fleet Mortgage and Investment Co Ltd v Lower Maisonette 46 Eaton Place Ltd* [1972] 2 All ER 737, *Practice Direction* [1972] 1 WLR 765; [1972] 1 All ER 576, *Civil Procedure 2006*, Vol 1 para sc46.4.1. For criticism of the county court procedure, see comments by the Court of Appeal in *Leicester CC v Aldwinkle* (1992) 24 HLR 49, CA.

49 *Tuohy v Bell* [2002] EWCA Civ 423; [2002] 1 WLR 2703 and *De Grey v Ford* [2005] EWCA Civ 1223; 30 September 2005.

50 *Six Arlington Street Investments v Persons Unknown* [1987] 1 WLR 188; [1987] 1 All ER 474, ChD.

51 See, eg, *Immobiliare Saffi v Italy* (2000) 30 EHRR 756, ECtHR.

52 *De La Pradelle v France* (1992) A 253-B.

tenant be given notice of an application to issue a warrant deprives him or her of a fair hearing within the meaning of article 6. That may not be significant if the warrant is issued shortly after a possession hearing and there has been no change of circumstances. However, if many years have passed, there are often changed circumstances which are relevant. Similar arguments apply in relation to article 8 and article 1 of the First Protocol. They might be bolstered by reliance upon article 14.[53] There is no apparent justification for the discrepancy between Rules of the Supreme Court (RSC) Ord 45 r3, RSC Ord 46 r3 and CCR Ord 26 r1(4), on the one hand, and CCR Ord 26 r17, on the other hand.

29.34   The Court of Appeal has, however, held that the procedure which allows the issue of a warrant of possession and the arrangements for execution following breach of a suspended possession order do not infringe tenants' rights under article 6, 8 or 14. Tenants' rights to possession of premises are determined, when suspended possession orders are made. The issue of the warrant of possession is simply a step authorised to be taken to enforce that order. It does not alter the legal status of the tenant or make any kind of decision in relation to his or her rights, and so is not required to be the subject of a separate hearing. Furthermore, although possession proceedings may interfere with tenants' right of respect for their homes, they are clearly in accordance with the law and are a legitimate and proportionate response to non-payment of rent.[54]

29.35   Bailiffs must, however, deliver Form N54 (Notice of Eviction) to all addresses where evictions are due to take place and hand it to the defendant personally or leave it at the property in an envelope addressed to the defendant(s) by name and 'any other occupiers'. The notice points out that in some circumstances the court can decide to suspend the warrant and explains the procedure to be followed.[55]

Effect of a warrant

29.36   When the bailiffs come to execute a county court warrant, or the sheriffs execute a High Court warrant, they can evict anyone they find on the premises, even if they were not a party to the possession proceedings or moved in after the possession order was made.[56] The

---

53   *Larkos v Cyprus* (1999) 7 BHRC 244.
54   *Southwark LBC v St Brice* [2001] EWCA Civ 1138; [2002] 1 WLR 1537; [2002] HLR 26.
55   Court Business, Issue 6.01, June 2001, available from the DCA, 020 7210 8581.
56   *R v Wandsworth County Court ex p Wandsworth LBC* [1975] 3 All ER 390.

only remedy for someone in the premises who was not a party to possession proceedings is to apply to be joined to the action and to set aside the order for possession. Obviously, such a course of action is likely to be successful only if there would have been a defence to the proceedings which has a real prospect of success and if there is a good reason why the applicant did not attend at the hearing.

29.37   At common law anyone entitled to possession, or anyone acting on his or her behalf, was entitled to use reasonable force to eject a trespasser.[57] By the time that a warrant is issued, the time for giving up possession should have expired and accordingly any occupiers are trespassers. Bailiffs are acting on behalf of the person entitled to possession and accordingly they are entitled to use reasonable force to execute the warrant.[58]

29.38   Permission to issue a warrant is required if six years have elapsed since the making of the possession order.[59] Applications for permission are normally made without notice with a witness statement in support, although the court may direct that the application should be served and heard on notice. Failure to obtain permission is an abuse of the process and any warrant obtained in such circumstances should be set aside.[60]

29.39   A county court or High Court warrant can be executed at any time within one year after it has been issued. If landlords want to rely on a warrant after that period an application must be made for it to be renewed.[61] For a discussion of warrants for possession in mortgage actions, see chapter 37 below.

Staying and suspending warrants

29.40   The mere fact that an application has been made to set aside a possession order or to suspend its operation does not automatically prevent a landlord from requesting the issue or enforcement of a warrant for possession. In some courts bailiffs may agree not to evict if an application to set aside or suspend a possession order has been made

---

57   *McPhail v Persons Unknown* [1973] Ch 447; [1973] 3 WLR 71, CA.

58   For a case in which the Court of Appeal held that an occupier may authorise the police to evict a trespasser, see *Porter v Commissioner of Police of the Metropolis* (1999) 20 October, unreported, CA. See also dictum of Cockburn CJ in *R v Roxburgh* (1871) 12 Cox CC 8.

59   CCR Ord 26 rr5 and 17(6) and RSC Ord 46 r2.

60   *Hackney LBC v White* (1996) 28 HLR 219, CA.

61   County Courts Act 1984 s111(2), CCR Ord 26 rr6 and 17.

– although as a matter of law a landlord may insist on the execution of a warrant unless a judge has ordered a stay. In the absence of clear written confirmation from the landlord or the court that a warrant will not be executed, tenants should apply to stay the warrant if eviction is likely to take place before the hearing of the application to set aside or suspend the order. CPR 3.1(2)(f) gives the court jurisdiction to stay execution. In addition County Courts Act 1984 s88 provides that:

> If at any time it appears to the satisfaction of the court that any party to any proceedings is unable from any cause to pay any sum recovered against him ... or any instalment of such a sum, the court may, in its discretion, stay any execution issued in the proceedings for such time and on such terms as the court thinks fit, and so from time to time until it appears that the cause of inability has ceased.

29.41 CCR Ord 25 r8 provides that the power to stay execution of a warrant may be exercised by a district judge, or, in some circumstances, by a proper officer of the court. Generally applications to suspend warrants for possession are heard by district judges. Form N245 is designed for such an application, but in practice Form N244 may also be used with a witness statement in support.

29.42 In accordance with the normal procedure governing applications, an application for a stay should be made on at least three days' notice to the landlord, unless it is particularly urgent, for example, the warrant is about to be executed. In general, if it is possible, it is better for time to be abridged under CPR 3.1(2)(a), allowing short notice to the landlord, than for the application to be made without notice.

29.43 If there is a substantial dispute over the amount of rent claimed to be owing and the tenant's compliance with the order, the application should be adjourned so that the up-to-date position can be established.[62] One cause of tenants' failures to comply with the financial provisions of suspended or postponed orders may be delays in receiving housing benefit. It may be that the service of a witness summons[63] on a senior official responsible for administering the scheme (in the local authority) compelling him or her to attend at the application and to explain the cause of the delay will not only be of assistance in making the application, but will also cause any benefit due to be paid rather rapidly.

29.44 The court, exercising its discretion to stay, suspend or postpone the date for possession under Rent Act 1977 s100(2), Housing Act 1985 s85

---

62 *Haringey LBC v Powell* (1996) 28 HLR 798, CA.
63 CPR 34.3.

or Housing Act 1988 s9(2) may take account of matters (for example, breaches of the terms of the tenancy agreement or anti-social behaviour) other than those relied upon as grounds for making the original possession order – although it is not always right to do so.[64] Whilst not attempting to fetter the discretion of district judges, the Court of Appeal has stated that the following points are relevant:

- The discretion should be used so as to further the policy of Housing Act 1985 Pt IV, reinforced by article 8 of the convention. The policy is only to evict after a serious breach of an obligation, where it is reasonable to do so, and where the tenant is proved to have breached any condition of suspension.
- The overriding objectives of the CPR, especially the need for applications to be dealt with in a summary and proportionate way, means that wider issues may not be able to be dealt with on an application to suspend or vary. They may need to be dealt with in some other way.
- The tenant should have clear evidence of what is alleged, especially where the allegations were not contained in the original claim.
- The fact that the landlord had or had not included the allegations as part of the original proceedings is relevant.
- The discretion to consider other allegations should generally be exercised more readily in respect of matters occurring after commencement of the proceedings.
- The court should also consider the practicalities of dealing with matters on the execution of a warrant.
- The fact that the tenant is at the mercy of the court and the responsibilities of a public landlord to its other tenants.

The list is not exhaustive. District judges have to exercise their discretion, bearing in mind the importance of the issue to the tenant, at risk of losing his or her home, and the responsibilities of social landlords to their other tenants. However, it would appear that the court cannot take into account allegations which have not been proved or admitted by the tenant.

29.45   Tenants outside the protection of the Rent Act 1977, the Housing Act 1985 and the Housing Act 1988 cannot apply to suspend the execution of a warrant for possession once it has been issued.[65]

---

64 *Sheffield City Council v Hopkins* [2001] EWCA Civ 1023; [2002] HLR 12. Cf, *Hammersmith and Fulham LBC v Brown* [2000] 5 CL 350 and *Islington LBC v Reeves* [1997] CLY 2715.

65 *Moore v Lambeth County Court Registrar* [1969] 1 WLR 141; [1969] 1 All ER 782.

After eviction

29.46   If execution has taken place, former tenants are unable to rely on the county court's general powers to suspend or stay judgments or orders[66] or to extend time or to allow for payment by instalments.[67]

29.47   Similarly, once eviction has taken place, the court no longer has any power to stay, suspend or set aside a warrant under Rent Act 1977 s100(2), Housing Act 1985 s85(2) or Housing Act 1988 s9(2), since those powers are expressly limited by the words 'at any time before the execution of the order'.[68] An application to set aside a warrant in these circumstances can only succeed if the possession order itself is set aside (see above), the warrant has been obtained by fraud or there has been an abuse of the process or oppression in its execution. In *Hammersmith and Fulham LBC v Hill*[69] the Court of Appeal held that there was an arguable case of oppression where representations by a housing officer deterred the tenant from seeking legal help or advice or otherwise making an application to stay the warrant before execution.[70]

29.48   The Court of Appeal has said that:

> [O]ppression may be very difficult if not impossible to define, but it is not difficult to recognise. It is the insistence by a public authority

---

66   County Courts Act 1984 s71.

67   CPR 3.1(2)(a) and (f). See *Moore v Registrar of Lambeth County Court* [1969] 1 All ER 782.

68   See *Scott-James v Bass Chehab* [1988] 41 EG 75, CA, *Leicester City Council v Aldwinkle* (1991) 24 HLR 49, CA, *Hammersmith and Fulham LBC v Hill* (1994) 27 HLR 368; [1994] 35 EG 124, CA and *Tower Hamlets LBC v Azad* (1998) 30 HLR 241, CA, but cf, *Islington LBC v Harridge* (1993) *Times* 30 June, CA, where it was held that an application was 'made' on the day before eviction when the application was lodged with the court and accordingly the court had power to hear it even though eviction had taken place prior to the hearing.

69   (1995) 27 HLR 368.

70   See also *Hackney LBC v Gabriel* December 1994 *Legal Action* 14 (warrant executed more than a year after issue), *Lewisham LBC v Clarke* December 1994 *Legal Action* 14 (where the council had misrepresented correspondence from the DSS which had affected payment of housing benefit), *Greenwich LBC v Minnican* December 1994 *Legal Action* 14 (local authority failed to arrange direct deductions from income support payments, as envisaged when the suspended possession order was made), *Haringey LBC v Innocent* June 1995 *Legal Action* 19 (bailiffs executing warrant gained entry to the former secure tenant's home but tenant re-entered using her back door key and resumed possession; held: the warrant had not been executed and the court still had power to stay or suspend the warrant) and *Westminster CC v Mbah* June 1995 *Legal Action* 19 (warrant set aside because application failed to state the amount of money remaining due (CCR Ord 26 r17(3A)).

on its strict rights in circumstances which make that insistence manifestly unfair. The categories of oppression are not closed because no-one can envisage all the sets of circumstances which could make the execution of a warrant oppressive.[71]

29.49   Recent years have seen a number of cases in which courts have decided what amounts to and what does not amount to 'oppression'. For example, in *Saint v Barking and Dagenham LBC*[72] a secure tenant failed to comply with the terms of a suspended possession order during a short period while he was held on remand in custody. Although he notified the council about his detention and whereabouts, they, without notice to him, applied ex parte for a warrant which was executed during his absence. The Court of Appeal set aside the warrant and directed his reinstatement. Peter Gibson LJ held that the conduct of the council in obtaining and executing the warrant had, in the circumstances, been 'oppressive'. The council had been under a duty 'promptly' to invite the applicant to renew his housing benefit under Housing Benefit (General) Regulations 1987[73] reg 72(14). That obligation required the council to send the renewal form to an address where it was likely to come to the applicant's attention (ie, his prison address). The council was relying on its own wrongdoing in obtaining the warrant to the extent that non-payment of housing benefit had caused the suspended order to be breached. Second, before the applicant's arrest his level of arrears had fallen below the level required to comply with the suspended order and when the warrant was applied for his outstanding debt was small (£336). In these circumstances, if he had been given an opportunity to apply to suspend the warrant of possession he should have succeeded.

29.50   Other examples of oppressive behaviour have included:

- continuing with execution of a warrant even though the tenant had paid the full amount of the arrears to the housing officer who attended with the bailiffs to execute the warrant;[74]
- execution of a warrant when the tenant was entitled to conclude that no further step would be taken until her housing benefit applications had been decided, against a background of maladministration that had been manifestly unfair;[75]

71   *Southwark LBC v Sarfo* (2000) 32 HLR 602 at 609, CA per Roch LJ.
72   (1999) 31 HLR 620,CA.
73   SI No 1971.
74   *East Staffs BC v Brady* January 1999 *Legal Action* 26.
75   *Southwark LBC v Sarfo* (2000) 32 HLR 602, CA.

- a housing officer not telling the defendant that a warrant had been applied for, even though the tenant had said that she was going abroad and had paid court costs and provided evidence of the renewal of her housing benefit claim;[76]
- eviction of a tenant amounted to oppression after (a) a letter claiming that the defendant was behind with his payments under the court order when he was still in fact ahead of schedule; (b) the issue of a warrant of possession one day before the expiry of the time allowed for the defendant to produce documents in support of his claim for housing benefit; (c) the issue of a warrant for possession at a time when the arrears which had accrued on the account were simply the result of an administrative decision to suspend the defendant's housing benefit; and (d) the failure to inform the defendant of his right to apply under s 85(2) at the time when the warrant was applied for.[77]

29.51　There is no reason why misleading information from a third party, such as a member of court staff, which deprives a tenant of the chance of taking steps to have execution of a warrant for possession stayed prior to execution, cannot amount to oppression thereby entitling the court to set aside execution of the warrant.[78]

29.52　On the other hand, in *Jephson Homes Housing Association v Moisejevs*[79] the Court of Appeal decided that if a possession warrant is obtained and executed against a secure tenant without fault on anyone's part, it cannot properly be set aside as oppressive or an abuse of process. Oppression cannot exist without the unfair use of court procedures. Something more than the mere use of the eviction process – some action on someone's part which was open to criticism – is required before the court's procedures can be said to have been unfairly used. An eviction cannot be regarded as oppressive or abus-

---

76　*William Sutton HT v Breen* March 2000 *Legal Action* 29.

77　*Barking and Dagenham LBC v Marquis* October 2002 *Legal Action* 28; (2002) 9 May, Ilford County Court.

78　*Hammersmith and Fulham LBC v Lemeh* (2001) 33 HLR 231; [2001] L & TR 423, CA (tenant who attended court to apply for suspension wrongly told by court staff that there was no warrant) and *Lambeth LBC v Hughes* (2001) 33 HLR 350, CA (council wrote to the defendant stating that the only way to stop eviction would be to pay all the arrears in full. Bailiff's letter giving date of eviction sent by second-class post arrived as the eviction was taking place).

79　[2001] 2 All ER 901; (2001) 33 HLR 594; [2001] 41 EG 186; (2001) *Times* 2 January; [2000] EGCS 123, CA. See too *Circle 33 Housing Trust v Ellis* [2005] EWCA Civ 1233; [2006] HLR 7.

ive merely because it is appreciated after the event that the tenant might usefully have applied to stay or suspend execution of the warrant. There is no requirement that a tenant should be given notice of a request for the issue of a possession warrant in all cases.[80] The absence of such a provision in the CCR was noted in *Peachey Property Corp Ltd v Robinson*.[81] There have been two new sets of Rules since then, without any such requirement being thought necessary. However, cases may arise when the landlord can properly be held to have acted oppressively if the tenant never received any notice whatever of the impending eviction.

29.53   Other examples where it has been held that execution of a warrant has *not* been oppressive include cases where:

- Shortly before the council made an application for a warrant the tenant took a lump sum of £400 to the council. A housing officer received it with the words 'that will do for now'. The tenant took no further step and made no further payment because he thought that the council would be in touch with him. The court found it 'difficult to believe' in all the circumstances that the tenant had genuinely formed the belief that he had simply to wait for the council to contact him. The judge preferred the evidence of the housing officer and rejected the allegation of 'oppressive' conduct. The Court of Appeal dismissed the tenant's appeal.[82]
- There was a dispute over housing benefit. The tenant had a poor rent record and there had been substantial non-compliance with a possession order.[83]

Warrants of restitution

29.54   Sometimes, particularly in squatting cases, occupiers move into premises after a warrant has been executed or the landlord has in some other way regained possession in accordance with the provisions of an order for possession. Unless there is some connection between the new occupiers and the people who were originally evicted, the landlord cannot apply for a further warrant in the same proceedings, but must issue further proceedings for possession.

---

80 But see Form N54, referred to at para 29.31.

81 [1967] 2 QB 543; [1966] 2 WLR 1386.

82 *Camden LBC v Akanni* (1997) 29 HLR 845, CA.

83 *Hackney LBC v Asik* March 2000 *Legal Action* 29, CA.

Once an order has been executed the proceedings are over and cannot be reactivated.[84]

29.55   The position is different if there is a 'close nexus' between the new
occupiers and any people who were dispossessed in earlier proceedings. If the further occupation is 'part and parcel of the same transaction'[85] the landlord is entitled to apply without notice for a warrant
of restitution in the county court or a writ of restitution in the High
Court.[86] The effect of a warrant of restitution is to enable the bailiff or
sheriff to evict any person in unlawful occupation of premises again
without the landowner having to issue new proceedings. A warrant
of restitution may be issued even though not all of the new occupiers
of the land were among the original defendants.[87] It is theoretically
possible for a landowner to apply to court to commit for contempt a
person who has re-entered premises unlawfully after an earlier eviction, but such an order should only be made in the most exceptional
circumstances.[88]

---

84   *Thomas v Metropolitan Housing Corp* [1936] 1 All ER 210, *Ratcliffe v Tait* (1664)
     1 Keble 216, *Lovelace v Ratcliffe* (1664) 1 Keble 785, *Doe d Pait v Roe* (1807) 1
     Taunton 55, *Clissold v Cratchley* [1910] 2 KB 244 and *Brighton BC v Persons
     Unknown* June 1991 *Legal Action* 13.
85   *Wiltshire CC v Frazer (No 2)* [1986] 1 WLR 109; [1986] 1 All ER 65 per Simon
     Brown J.
86   CCR Ord 26 r17(4) and RSC Ord 46 r3.
87   *Wiltshire CC v Frazer (No 2)* [1986] 1 WLR 109; [1986] 1 All ER 65.
88   *Alliance Building Society v Austen* [1951] 2 All ER 1068 where such an order was
     in fact granted. See too the cases noted at footnote 49.

CHAPTER 30

Domestic relationship breakdown in a rented home

Introduction

30.1   This chapter briefly outlines the steps which may be taken to maintain occupation of the family home where there has been a breakdown of the domestic relationship between the adult occupiers – most commonly between spouses or other cohabitants – and the home is rented. (For the parallel position on relationship breakdown where the family home is held on a mortgage, see chapter 39.) These few pages are only intended to highlight some of the issues.

30.2   Often a crisis in relation to occupation of the rented home (for example, the service of possession proceedings) arises at the same time as, or shortly after, a breakdown in the domestic relationship between occupiers. For example, as a result of the relationship breakdown one partner may have moved out, jeopardising security of tenure and/or leaving the other facing future financial difficulties in paying the rent, which will put the home at risk.

30.3   Where the landlord has not yet threatened possession proceedings there is usually time to get advice about immediate entitlement to remain in the home and any rights to obtain a transfer of the tenancy. Where very urgent action is needed (for example, to prevent violence or to prevent the loss of the tenancy), the client should be immediately directed to a source of specialist advice on family law.

30.4   Historically, some public and social landlords have found it difficult to deal with the housing consequences of relationship breakdown in rented housing stock. In 1999 the government published guidance intended to assist such landlords in devising appropriate policies.[1]

Preserving the tenancy[2]

30.5   The following paragraphs are concerned with the situation in which not only has the relationship broken down but one of the partners has *left* the family home.

---

1   *Relationship Breakdown: A Guide for Social Landlords*, DETR, 7 July 1999.
2   See Conway 'Protecting Tenancies on Marriage Breakdown' [2001] Fam Law 208 and Da Costa 'Keeping Alive the Tenancy in the Matrimonial Home' [1995] Fam Law 622.

Sole tenant in occupation

30.6   If the partner remaining in the family home is the sole tenant there should be little difficulty in preserving the home until the issues arising from the relationship breakdown are resolved. Where the breakdown of the relationship has caused financial difficulties this may trigger entitlement for the tenant to housing benefit or to higher payments of such benefit providing help with the payment of rent. If, however, possession proceedings are threatened or have been launched, the appropriate chapters of this book should assist in avoiding dispossession.

Sole tenant has left

30.7   In this scenario there are twin concerns for the partner remaining in possession. The first is to prevent the departed tenant from ending the tenancy. The second is to ensure that the tenancy retains any security of tenure and survives any possession proceedings brought by the landlord. In the longer term, once those matters have been addressed, the partner remaining may seek to have the tenancy transferred into his or her sole name as part of the legal arrangements made to resolve the consequences of the relationship breakdown.

30.8   If the remaining occupier is a *spouse* or *civil partner* of the sole tenant he or she enjoys legal rights of occupation (and associated benefits) by virtue of the 'home rights' conferred by Family Law Act 1996 s30 for as long as the marriage or civil partnership lasts. Any question of occupation thereafter should be addressed in the legal proceedings to end the marriage or partnership.

30.9   The *cohabitant* of the departed tenant who remains in occupation, by contrast, has no such automatic rights to continue to occupy the home but can apply to the court for an 'occupation order' under Family Law Act 1996 s36. If granted, that confers rights equivalent to the home rights enjoyed by a spouse or civil partner.[3]

30.10   If there is any risk that the departed sole tenant may end the tenancy without other arrangements being in place for the continued occupation of the former family home, the non-tenant partner may need to move very quickly to obtain a court order to prevent the tenant from either giving notice to quit or surrendering the tenancy. Such a pre-emptive injunction is – for obvious reasons – normally sought without notice to the tenant until after the injunction is granted.

3   *Gay v Enfield LBC* [2000] 1 WLR 673; [1999] 3 All ER 795.

Where the partners are married, the family court has jurisdiction to grant such an injunction under Matrimonial Causes Act 1973 s37(2)(a). Where the partners are unmarried, the jurisdiction will be based on the court's power to grant interim relief in proceedings under the Family Law Act 1996 or the Children Act 1989 (brought to obtain an occupation order or to achieve a transfer of the tenancy from the tenant partner).[4]

30.11   If no such protection is obtained from the court, the sole tenant could simply end the tenancy by giving notice to quit or by agreeing a surrender with the landlord (although the latter would be unusual as the presence of the former partner will prevent the tenant giving vacant possession).[5] This may happen very fast – for example, because the landlord is prepared to waive any requirements as to length or formality of the notice to quit.[6] Once the tenancy has been ended it will plainly not be available for the purpose of being transferred from one partner to the other. It will also be too late for even a spouse or civil partner to set aside the termination of the tenancy.[7] The owner would be able to seek possession against the remaining former partner as a trespasser.

30.12   If the departed tenant's tenancy is continuing, the remaining partner needs to ensure that the tenancy is safeguarded until other arrangements can be made. For example, if the tenant's rent is not being paid, the remaining partner could pay it. If the remaining partner is a spouse or civil partner, any payments he or she makes are treated by law as though they had been made by the tenant and must be accepted as such.[8] Likewise, a payment of rent made by a cohabitant with an occupation order (see para 30.9) is treated as made by the tenant.[9] Housing benefit may be claimed by the occupying partner if the person legally liable to pay for the family home is not paying.[10]

30.13   Although the sole tenant is not physically present, the continued occupation by the former partner may operate to preserve any secur-

---

4   *Greenwich LBC v Bater* [1999] 4 All ER 944; [1999] 2 FLR 993, CA and *Re F (Minors)* [1994] 1 WLR 370; (1993) 26 HLR 354, CA.

5   But see *Sanctuary Housing Association v Campbell* [1999] 1 WLR 1279; (2000) 32 HLR 100, CA.

6   *Hackney LBC v Snowden* (2001) 33 HLR 554; [2001] L & TR 6, CA.

7   *Harrow LBC v Johnstone* [1997] 1 WLR 459; (1997) 29 HLR 475, HL and *Newlon Housing Association v Al-Sulaimen* [1999] 1 AC 313; [1998] 4 All ER 1; (1998) 30 HLR 1132, HL.

8   Family Law Act 1996 s30(3).

9   Family Law Act 1996 s36(13).

10 Housing Benefit Regulations 2006 SI No 213 reg 8.

ity of tenure the tenant enjoyed. Where the remaining occupier is the tenant's spouse or civil partner, his or her own occupation is deemed to be occupation by the tenant for the purposes of preserving security of tenure as a protected, assured, secure, demoted or introductory tenant.[11] The same 'deemed occupation' arises if the remaining partner is a cohabitant who has successfully applied for an occupation order (see para 30.9).[12]

30.14 The remaining partner may also have to intervene in any possession proceedings taken against the sole tenant in order to preserve the home.

30.15 If those possession proceedings are based on the proposition that any security of tenure has been lost by failure of the sole tenant – who has left – to occupy the premises as his or her home, the remaining partner may be able to defend successfully on the basis that there is continuing deemed occupation by a spouse or civil partner with home rights or by a cohabitant with an occupation order (see para 30.13).

30.16 If the possession proceedings are based on one of the grounds for possession which requires the court to be satisfied that suitable alternative accommodation is available, this may involve (consequent upon a relationship breakdown) the provision of separate units of housing for the tenant and his or her partner. Any spouse, civil partner or cohabitant anxious that he or she should be adequately housed if possession is ordered against the tenant in these circumstances should apply to be joined as a party to the proceedings.[13]

30.17 If the proceedings result in the termination of a secure tenancy (see chapter 1), the spouse or civil partner – and any former spouse, civil partner or cohabitant who has an occupation order – has the same rights as the former tenant to seek a stay or suspension in the execution of the possession order.[14] Similar provisions are available if the court has terminated an assured tenancy[15] or terminated a protected or statutory tenancy[16] but no equivalent rights are available following termination of an introductory tenancy or an otherwise unprotected tenancy.

---

11 Family Law Act 1996 s30(4).
12 Family Law Act 1996 s36(13).
13 *Wandsworth LBC v Fadayomi* [1987] 1 WLR 1473; [1987] 3 All ER 474, CA.
14 HA 1985 s85(5) and (5A).
15 HA 1988 s9(5) and (5A).
16 RA 1977 s100(4A) and (4B).

Joint tenant remaining in occupation[17]

30.18 The first priority for the joint tenant who remains in occupation of a family home held on a joint tenancy is to ensure that the other joint tenant does not bring the joint tenancy to an end. Although the other joint tenant, acting alone, cannot end the joint tenancy by means of a surrender, a joint tenancy can be ended by that tenant giving the landlord a notice to quit. The other joint tenant need not even inform or consult the one in occupation before giving such notice.[18] The effect of a valid notice to quit is to bring the whole joint tenancy to an end,[19] which obviously leaves the former partner in occupation as a trespasser and entitles the landlord to possession.[20]

30.19 If there is any risk that the departed joint tenant may end the tenancy without other arrangements being in place for the continued occupation of the former family home, the joint-tenant partner may need to move very quickly to obtain a court order to prevent the other joint tenant from giving notice to quit. Such a pre-emptive injunction is – for obvious reasons – normally sought without notice to the other joint tenant until after the injunction is granted. Where the partners are married, the family court has jurisdiction to grant such an injunction under Matrimonial Causes Act 1973 s37(2)(a). Where the partners are unmarried the jurisdiction may be based on the court's power to grant interim relief in proceedings under the Family Law Act 1996 or the Children Act 1989 (brought to obtain an occupation order or to achieve a transfer of the tenancy from joint to sole names).[21]

30.20 If a joint tenant has already given a notice to quit it should be checked as to its validity. A notice not complying with the relevant contractual or statutory requirements is not effective to terminate the tenancy (because the agreement of all joint tenants is needed to waive any defect).[22] If it is a valid notice it terminates the tenancy and cannot be set aside, even in matrimonial proceedings.[23]

---

17 Jenrick and Bretherton 'Joint Tenancies: Continuing Implications for Housing and Family Law' [2000] JHL 8.

18 *Notting Hill Housing Trust v Brackley* [2001] EWCA Civ 601; [2002] HLR 10.

19 *Hammersmith and Fulham LBC v Monk* [1992] 1 AC 478; [1990] 3 WLR 1144, HL.

20 *Greenwich LBC v McGrady* (1983) 81 LGR 288; (1983) 46 P & CR 223, CA.

21 *Greenwich LBC v Bater* [1999] 4 All ER 944; [1999] 2 FLR 993, CA.

22 *Hounslow LBC v Pilling* [1993] 1 WLR 1242; (1993) 25 HLR 305, CA.

23 *Harrow LBC v Johnstone* [1997] 1 WLR 459; (1997) 29 HLR 475, HL and *Newlon Housing Association v Al-Sulaimen* [1999] 1 AC 313; [1998] 4 All ER 1; (1998) 30 HLR 1132, HL.

30.21 See para 12.6 onwards for further discussion concerning the validity of notices to quit.

30.22 Of course, if the landlord is prepared to grant the remaining party a new sole tenancy with equivalent security of tenure, there is no difficulty caused by either partner giving notice to quit.

30.23 It may be possible for the two joint tenants to 'regularise' matters either by the departed tenant completing a deed of release or by both joint tenants assigning the tenancy into the sole name of one of them. In either case, the remaining joint tenant becomes the sole tenant. However, these options may not be available in respect of some tenancies. There have been particular difficulties with secure joint tenancies in this regard.[24]

30.24 If the departing joint tenant fails to make any contribution towards the rent, the remaining joint tenant may obtain assistance from the housing benefit scheme both towards his or her own 'share' of the rent and towards the share of the former partner (see chapter 32).

30.25 The joint tenant may rely on his or her own occupation as meeting any necessary conditions of residence for retention of security of tenure (for example, the continued occupation by one of several joint secure tenants maintains the 'security of tenure' of a secure or assured tenancy).[25]

30.26 In any possession proceedings, the joint tenant may defend in just the same way as a sole tenant.

Transferring the tenancy[26]

30.27 In the longer term, the sensible outcome following a relationship breakdown is often the making of a court order for transfer of the tenancy (if that is needed) into the sole name of the partner remaining in the home. Jurisdiction to make such orders is available both in Matrimonial Causes Act 1973 s24 (for spouses) and in Family Law Act 1996 s53 (for spouses, civil partners and cohabitants). Alternatively, where the parties are parents, an order can be made for a transfer of the tenancy for the benefit of a child.[27] Procedural rules make provision for notice to be given to the landlord. The housing statutes themselves

---

24 *Burton v Camden LBC* [2000] 2 AC 399; [2000] 2 WLR 427; [2000] 1 All ER 943, HL and Blandy 'Secure Tenancies and Relationship Breakdown Revisited' [2000] JHL 47.

25 HA 1985 s81, HA 1988 s1.

26 See Bridge 'Transferring Tenancies of the Family Home' [1998] Fam Law 26.

27 Children Act 1989 Sch 1 para 15.

make provision for the consequences of such transfer orders being made (see, for example, Housing Act 1985 s91(3)(b) in relation to orders for transfer of secure tenancies). Any competent family law specialist should be familiar with the process involved in securing an order for the transfer of the tenancy.

Homelessness

Introduction

31.1   A full description of the law relating to homelessness is beyond the scope of this book and readers seeking a detailed treatment are accordingly referred to Arden and Hunter's *Homelessness and Allocations*.[1] However, the following pages describe how homelessness law affects those people subject to actual or potential possession proceedings.

31.2   The substantive law relating to homelessness is now contained in the Housing Act 1996 as amended by the Homelessness Act 2002. All statutory references in this chapter are accordingly to Housing Act 1996 Pt VII (Homelessness) unless otherwise stated.

31.3   In outline, Housing Act 1996 Pt VII requires the local housing authority to 'secure that accommodation is available' to a homeless person who is eligible for assistance and in priority need, unless the authority is satisfied, following the making of inquiries, that the person became homeless intentionally.[2]

31.4   In the exercise of their functions under Housing Act 1996 Part VII, authorities are bound to have regard to guidance given by the Secretary of State. At the time this book went to press, a new edition of the Homelessness Code of Guidance was due for publication.[3] Although authorities are expected to comply with the guidance in the Code, they may depart from it if such departure is justified in a particular case.[4]

Eligibility

31.5   The scope of Housing Act 1996 Pt VII is restricted to 'eligible persons' which is defined to debar most 'persons subject to immigration control' and some other 'persons from abroad' from help under the Act.[5]

---

1   7th edn, LAG, 2006.
2   HA 1996 s193(2).
3   See the DCLG website, www.dclg.gov.uk.
4   *R v Croydon LBC ex p Jarvis* (1994) 26 HLR 194, QBD. Compare *R v Newham LBC ex p Ugbo* (1993) 26 HLR 263, QBD.
5   HA 1996 ss185 and 186, together with the Allocation of Housing and Homelessness (Eligibility) (England) Regulations 2006 SI No 1294.

Preventing homelessness

31.6   Each housing authority is required to have its own homelessness advisory service or to contract with others to provide such a service.[6] A primary function of such a service is to provide the advice and information necessary to prevent homelessness. The Department for Communities and Local Government has issued guidance on ways of preventing homelessness, for example, by negotiation with the applicant's landlord or by exploring the scope for mediation.[7] The Guidance emphasises (para 2.11) that local authority approaches to homelessness prevention should not be inspired by a 'gatekeeping' mentality. Advice on other housing options should never replace or delay a statutory homelessness assessment where the authority has reason to believe that someone is homeless or threatened with homelessness.

31.7   Additionally, Homelessness Act 2002 ss1–3 require authorities to conduct homelessness reviews and formulate homelessness strategies. These reviews and strategies must be available for inspection and purchase[8] and must address the prevention of homelessness in the council's district.[9]

Threatened homelessness

31.8   All those against whom possession proceedings are initiated ultimately run the risk of homelessness. Local housing authorities have a statutory duty to assist people who apply to them for accommodation and are being 'threatened with homelessness'. Where an applicant who is in priority need is threatened with homelessness, the authority is obliged to take reasonable steps 'to secure that accommodation does not cease to be available for his occupation'[10] unless it can satisfy itself that the applicant became threatened with homelessness intentionally. For the duty to be triggered it must be likely that a person will become homeless within 28 days.[11] However, authorities are required to consider taking action at an earlier stage where possible.

31.9   It is for the authority to decide whether the occupier is threatened with homelessness within the meaning of Housing Act 1996 s175(4).

---

6   HA 1996 s179(1).
7   *Homelessness prevention: a guide to good practice*, DCLG, June 2006.
8   Homelessness Act 2002 ss2(3) and 3(9).
9   Homelessness Act 2002 ss2(2)(a) and 3(1)(a).
10   HA 1996 s195(2).
11   HA 1996 s175(4).

In calculating whether the occupier is within 28 days of homelessness, authorities must work back from the hypothetical or actual future date on which the occupier may or will be evicted.[12] If an occupier is not threatened with homelessness any decision on an application will be premature and unlawful.[13]

31.10   Even if there are more than 28 days to go before any possession order could be executed, an occupier faced with prospective or actual proceedings might be accepted as threatened with homelessness on the ground that it will shortly become unreasonable for him or her to remain in possession.[14] Some authorities are prepared to accept that those faced with possession proceedings on mandatory grounds, or an inevitable possession order in other circumstances, are threatened with homelessness earlier than 28 days before a possession order will take effect or following the expiry of a valid notice.

31.11   Once the occupier is accepted as threatened with homelessness the authority must either 'take reasonable steps to secure that accommodation does not cease to be available for his occupation' (where the occupier is in priority need and not intentionally threatened with homelessness) or 'furnish advice and assistance' to help maintain accommodation (where the occupier is not in priority need or became threatened with homelessness intentionally).[15] There is also a power to take steps to secure that accommodation does not cease to be available to a person unintentionally threatened with homelessness who does *not* have a priority need.[16]

31.12   The first of those duties is usually interpreted as a duty initially to try to keep for the applicant his or her existing accommodation and then, if that fails, to secure alternative accommodation.[17]

31.13   Where the possession proceedings are taken or threatened by a private owner or registered social landlord, the advice and assistance which an authority is required to provide by Housing Act 1996 s195 might include legal advice on the merits of the claim; possible defences; other legal advice; the provision of representation in court by the council's own lawyers;[18] counselling; mediation; financial assistance; welfare benefits advice and much else besides.

12   *R v Newham LBC ex p Khan* (2001) 33 HLR 29, QBD (Admin Ct).
13   *R v Rugby BC ex p Hunt* (1994) 26 HLR 1, QBD.
14   HA 1996 s175(3).
15   HA 1996 s195(2) and (5).
16   HA 1996 s195(6) inserted by Homelessness Act 2002 s5.
17   HA 1996 s195(4).
18   Local Government Act 1972 s222.

31.14   If the possession proceedings have been initiated by the local authority, the occupier can at least expect some assistance as to what steps should be taken if a possession order is made.

Homelessness

31.15   In essence, a person is homeless if there is no accommodation which that person is entitled to occupy.[19] However, the definition of statutory homelessness also provides:

> A person shall not be treated as having accommodation unless it is accommodation which it would be reasonable for him to continue to occupy.[20]

The Act provides that it is not reasonable for a person to continue to occupy accommodation if it is probable that this will lead to violence against him or her, or another member of the household.[21] But in other cases, in assessing whether it is reasonable for a person to remain in accommodation, the authority may have regard to the general housing circumstances in its area.[22]

31.16   In some situations an occupier involved in possession proceedings may in fact already be statutorily homeless and therefore entitled to some immediate assistance from the local authority. Occupiers are homeless unless the authority is satisfied that it is reasonable for them to continue in occupation of their accommodation.[23] The authority might accept that it is not reasonable to continue in occupation if faced by a strong case for mandatory possession and the risk of court costs (see para 31.9).

31.17   Where a person's existing accommodation is not affordable – for example, because of a housing benefit restriction or because of a severe deterioration in a mortgage borrower's financial circumstances – he or she may be statutorily homeless even before possession proceedings have been initiated or completed.[24] Where, following a careful assessment of the applicant's financial situation, it is evident that the loss of the home is inevitable, then it is strongly arguable that it is

---

19 HA 1996 s175(1).
20 HA 1996 s175(3).
21 HA 1996 s177(1) and (1A).
22 HA 1996 s177(2).
23 HA 1996 s175(3). See *R v Kensington and Chelsea RLBC ex p Hammell* (1988) 20 HLR 666, CA.
24 Homelessness (Suitability of Accommodation) Order 1996 SI No 3204.

not reasonable for him or her to continue to occupy the property and that he or she is already statutorily homeless. Subject to the questions of eligibility, priority need and intentionality being resolved in the applicant's favour, a local authority would then find itself obliged to provide alternative accommodation before proceedings have been concluded or even started. In this context it is worth reminding local authorities of the following observation by Kennedy J in the case of *R v Hillingdon LBC ex p Tinn*:

> As a matter of commonsense, it seems to me that it cannot be reasonable for a person to continue to occupy accommodation when they can no longer discharge their financial obligations in relation to that accommodation ... without so straining their resources as to deprive themselves of the ordinary necessities of life, such as food, clothing, heat, transport and so forth.[25]

31.18 An application for homelessness assistance should be made at the earliest opportunity to try to resolve the question of what rehousing duty, if any, falls on the housing authority. In this way, the legal costs of possession proceedings may be avoided, not to mention the trauma of the applicant being evicted.

31.19 All squatters (ie, those occupying property without authorisation of the owner) are already homeless persons within the meaning of Housing Act 1996 s175. The fact that the owner has chosen to evict them by court proceedings rather than by physically dispossessing them does not alter their status.

31.20 A possession order cannot usually be enforced other than by execution by a court bailiff acting on a warrant for possession. It has been held in both the High Court[26] and the Court of Appeal[27] that homelessness occurs at the point of actual eviction, rather than the date when the possession order takes effect. In the 28 days prior to the eviction the occupier is 'threatened' with homelessness (see para 31.7).

31.21 The type of assistance the authority must provide to a homeless person varies depending upon whether the applicant is in priority need[28] and/or intentionally homeless.[29]

---

25 (1988) 20 HLR 305 at 308.
26 *R v Newham LBC ex p Khan* (2001) 33 HLR 269.
27 *R v Newham LBC ex p Sacupima* [2001] 1 WLR 563; (2001) 33 HLR 2, CA.
28 HA 1996 s189.
29 HA 1996 s191.

Priority need

31.22 The following persons (in England) have a priority need for accommodation:[30]

- a pregnant woman or a person with whom she resides or might reasonably be expected to reside;
- a person with whom dependent children reside or might reasonably be expected to reside;
- a person who is homeless or threatened with homelessness as a result of an emergency such as flood, fire or other disaster;
- a person aged 16 or 17 (with certain exceptions where the young person is already owed a duty by social services);
- a person under 21 who was (but is no longer) looked after, accommodated or fostered at any time between the ages of 16 and 18;
- a person who is vulnerable as a result of:
  - old age, mental illness or handicap or physical disability or other special reason (or a person with whom such a person resides or might reasonably be expected to reside);
  - having been looked after, accommodated or fostered;
  - having been a member of Her Majesty's regular naval, military or air forces;
  - having been imprisoned or held in custody;
  - ceasing to occupy accommodation because of violence from another person or threats of violence from another person which are likely to be carried out.

31.23 A person is considered 'vulnerable' for the purpose of priority need if he or she is less able when homeless to fend for him/herself than an ordinary homeless person, so that injury or detriment would result to him or her when a less vulnerable person would be able to cope without harmful effects.[31] The assessment is a composite one, but there must be a risk of injury or detriment. The assessment is carried out on the basis that the applicant is street homeless.[32]

---

30 HA 1996 s189(1) together with the Homelessness (Priority Need for Accommodation) (England) Order 2002 SI No 2051 and the Homeless Persons (Priority Need) (Wales) Order 2001 SI No 607. Note that there are some differences between the classes of priority need under the England and the Wales orders respectively.

31 *R v London Borough of Camden ex p Pereira* (1999) 31 HLR 317, CA and *R v Waveney DC ex p Bowers* [1983] QB 238; (1983) 4 HLR 118, CA.

32 *Osmani v LB Camden* [2004] EWCA Civ 1706; [2005] HLR 22, CA.

Interim accommodation

31.24   Where the authority has reason to believe that an applicant may be homeless, eligible for assistance and in priority need, it has an immediate statutory duty to provide suitable interim accommodation pending the outcome of its inquiries[33] and to take reasonable steps to prevent the loss of or damage to the applicant's personal property if he or she is unable to protect or deal with it.[34] The threshold of proof necessary to trigger the interim accommodation duty is a low one. The test is not whether the authority is 'satisfied' that the three conditions exist, only that it has reason to believe that they may exist.

Intentional homelessness

31.25   The homeless (including those in priority need) will not qualify for the 'full' housing duty if they are found to have become homeless 'intentionally'. In these circumstances the duty is limited to securing accommodation for the applicant's use for such period as the authority considers will give him or her 'a reasonable opportunity of securing accommodation for his occupation'.[35] At most the applicant will receive short-term temporary accommodation together with advice and assistance in looking for alternative accommodation.[36] In those circumstances it is clearly important to avoid, where possible, the prospect of the person faced with possession proceedings being found intentionally homeless.

31.26   A person is intentionally homeless:

> ... if he deliberately does or fails to do anything in consequence of which he ceases to occupy accommodation which is available for his occupation and which it would have been reasonable for him to continue to occupy.[37]

31.27   This definition is, however, qualified so that:

---

33 HA 1996 s188(1).
34 HA 1996 s211.
35 HA 1996 s190(2).
36 HA 1996 s190. In deciding how long a period will give the applicant a 'reasonable opportunity', the authority must consider the particular needs and circumstances of the applicant: *Conville v LB Richmond upon Thames* [2006] EWCA Civ 718, CA.
37 HA 1996 s191(1).

... an act or omission in good faith on the part of a person who was unaware of any relevant fact shall not be treated as deliberate.[38]

The 'good faith' test is a subjective one, that is, whether the applicant honestly had no knowledge of the circumstances, whether or not another person acting reasonably would have done so. The distinction was made by the Court of Appeal in the context of a mortgage default case:

> It is not enough simply to find that he was a hopeless businessman or that the venture was ill advised, but it is necessary to look at all the circumstances to decide whether on the one hand, he honestly believed he was acting sensibly, or on the other, he knew perfectly well the risk he was taking, namely that his house might be repossessed.[39]

Only in the latter case can the applicant be classified as intentionally homeless.

31.28   A person can be found intentionally homeless only if he or she satisfies all limbs of the definition at para 31.26 above. He or she must have deliberately done or failed to do something in consequence of which accommodation is lost. If it would not have been reasonable to have continued to occupy the property, then the applicant cannot be intentionally homeless.

31.29   Where a person has lost his or her home because of financial difficulties, authorities must pay careful attention to the question whether the accommodation was affordable. An applicant's actions may not amount to intentional homelessness where he or she has lost his or her home, or was obliged to sell it, because of rent or mortgage arrears resulting from particular financial difficulties, and the applicant was genuinely unable to keep up the rent or mortgage payments even after claiming benefits.

31.30   Advisers must be aware that local authorities are given a 'very substantial measure of appreciation' in deciding whether a person who has been evicted for non-payment of housing costs has become homeless intentionally or whether the failure to pay was genuinely attributable to inadequacy of resources to cover the necessities of life.[40] It is vital therefore to be able to justify every item of the applicant's expenditure.

31.31   Where it is feared that the partner with financial control in a relationship may be found intentionally homeless, it is advisable for a

38   HA 1996 s191(2).
39   *R v Wandsworth LBC ex p Onwudiwe* (1994) 26 HLR 302.
40   *R v Brent LBC ex p Baruwa* [1997] 3 FCR 97; (1997) 29 HLR 915, CA.

clearly separate application to be made to the authority under Housing Act 1996 Pt VII by the 'non-responsible' partner. The authority is required to investigate whether the partner had acquiesced in the deliberate failure to make the appropriate payments before he or she can be found to be 'intentionally' homeless.[41]

31.32 Similar difficulties can arise where a mortgage borrower decides to sell the property in advance of the lender taking possession proceedings, where the borrower knows or believes that there is no prospect of defending the lender's claim at court. Many authorities find applicants who sell the property in such circumstances intentionally homeless. It should be stressed, in representations to the authority, that the borrower had no reasonable prospect of preventing disposession and reference should be made to the test of whether it would have been reasonable to continue to occupy the property.[42] It is wise before sale of the property to approach the authority to explain the financial circumstances and discuss any alternative options.

31.33 Three further points of importance arise. First, it is obvious that any form of 'consent' order should be avoided in possession proceedings (even if it is possible for such an order to be made – see paras 3.5 and 28.22) since this at least raises the inference for the authority that the homeless person has brought about his or her own homelessness.[43]

31.34 Second, it does not automatically follow that an occupier against whom a possession order has been made on a 'fault' ground is intentionally homeless; the authority is required to make its own inquiries[44] and to satisfy itself as to the true facts of the case. For example, if the ground on which possession was granted was 'nuisance', the authority must itself investigate who caused or was responsible for the nuisance.[45] The council cannot fetter its discretion in the application of the definition of intentionality[46] by unquestioningly adopting the findings of the court which dealt with the possession action.

31.35 Third, occupiers not infrequently panic and leave the premises before they are legally required to do so. This may occur either at the stage at which possession proceedings are threatened or under

---

41 *R v North Devon DC ex p Lewis* [1981] 1 WLR 328; [1981] 1 All ER 27.

42 See *R v Eastleigh BC ex p Beattie (No 1)* (1982–83) 10 HLR 134 and *(No 2)* (1984) 17 HLR 168, *R v Hammersmith and Fulham LBC ex p Duro-Rama* (1983) 9 HLR 71; 81 LGR 702 and *R v Hillingdon LBC ex p Tinn* (1988) 20 HLR 305.

43 *R v Wandsworth LBC ex p Henderson* (1986) 18 HLR 522, QBD.

44 HA 1996 s184.

45 *Devenport v Salford City Council* (1983) 8 HLR 57, CA.

46 HA 1996 s191.

way or otherwise before the time allowed by the possession order has expired. If in leaving they bring to an end their interest in the property (for example, by notice to quit or surrender) they become homeless. In such circumstances it is open to a local authority to find that, notwithstanding that the applicants would have become homeless in due course, they are 'intentionally homeless' because it would have been reasonable for them to have remained in the property as at the date they left it.[47] Consideration should be given to the possibility of challenging any such finding.

31.36   Acts or omissions made in good faith where someone was genuinely unaware of a relevant fact must not be regarded as deliberate.[48] A general example would be a situation where a person gave up possession of accommodation in the belief that they had no legal right to continue to occupy the accommodation and, therefore, it would not be reasonable for them to continue to occupy it.

31.37   A more acute illustration of the 'early departure' problem arises where the local authority has actually advised the tenant to stay in possession and resist the possession proceedings. Although the authority cannot properly advise defending in hopeless cases,[49] it may assert that a person renders him or herself intentionally homeless as a result of ignoring appropriate advice to 'stay put'.[50]

31.38   If met with a decision of 'intentionally homeless' the applicant should be immediately referred to an adviser specialising in housing law.

Deemed applications

31.39   In order to be considered for assistance as 'homeless', people displaced by possession proceedings must apply to the local authority. If those people make an application at a stage when they are actually homeless and in priority need they must be accommodated by the authority while inquiries are made into the circumstances of their homelessness.[51]

---

47   *Din v Wandsworth LBC* [1983] 1 AC 657; [1981] 3 WLR 918; [1981] 3 All ER 881; (1982) 1 HLR 73, HL.

48   HA 1996 s191(2).

49   *R v Portsmouth City Council ex p Knight* (1983) 10 HLR 115, QBD and *R v Surrey Heath BC ex p Li* (1984) 16 HLR 79, QBD.

50   *R v Penwith DC ex p Hughes* August 1980 *LAG Bulletin* 187.

51   HA 1996 s188.

31.40   In order to avoid even this interim housing duty to an applicant who is a tenant or licensee of the authority, but whom the authority is now evicting, some local authorities have created the device of a 'deemed application' as a bluff to use against secure occupiers whom they themselves have subjected to possession proceedings. A typical letter in such cases runs (after reciting the threat of proceedings) as follows:

> ... and at the same time we will treat you as having applied for rehousing as a person threatened with homelessness. Despite being in priority need you will be classified as intentionally homeless and will be accommodated at your present address only until the date stated by the judge in the possession order. Thereafter no application for accommodation by you will be accepted and you will be homeless.

Faced with this sort of quite improper conduct, the tenant should take up the matter with a councillor and/or the local government ombudsman. The 'deemed application' is a nullity[52] and the person eventually threatened with homelessness or made homeless should apply to the authority for assistance in the ordinary way. Failure by the authority to accept the application would be challengeable by judicial review.

Local connection

31.41   In certain limited circumstances an authority which has accepted a duty to house an unintentionally homeless person in priority need may refer him or her to a different authority which will provide the accommodation. The conditions for referral of the case to another authority are met if (and only if) the applicant (and any household member) has no local connection with the authority; and the applicant (or any household member) has a local connection with the district of a second authority; and the applicant (or any household member) will not run the risk of violence in that other district.[53]

31.42   A person has a local connection with the district of a local housing authority if any of the following circumstances apply:

- because she or he is, or in the past was, normally resident there, and that residence is or was of his or her own choice;
- because she or he is employed there;

52   *R v East Northamptonshire DC ex p Spruce* (1988) 20 HLR 508, QBD.
53   HA 1996 s198.

- because of family associations; or
- because of special circumstances.[54]

31.43　If a person has no local connection with any authority in England, Wales or Scotland, the authority to which he or she has applied must take responsibility for discharging the housing duty.[55]

31.44　The local connection provisions may be invoked only when the first authority has accepted that it owes a duty to house the homeless person. It would be unlawful for an authority to refuse to entertain an application on the basis of a want of local connection, and the authority must continue to accommodate the applicant pending a referral to another borough. Authorities must consider in each case whether in all the circumstances it is appropriate to make the referral and should always be prepared to consider special circumstances for not referring to another authority.[56]

Protection of property

31.45　It is important to note that local authority duties towards the homeless extend to the protection of property and powers are available to assist the non-priority homeless in this respect.[57] Assistance should be sought once loss of possession has become inevitable. The effect of a possession order will be that the defendant loses a home, while these property protection powers and duties prevent the defendant's loss of all his or her belongings too.[58] Of course, the council is entitled to levy a reasonable charge for transport and storage.[59]

Housed as homeless

31.46　Local authorities and others may seek recovery of possession of accommodation into which a homeless person has been placed in discharge of statutory duties arising under Housing Act 1996 Pt VII. For the 'security of tenure' of such people see paras 5.16–5.24.

54　HA 1996 s199(1).
55　*R v Hillingdon LBC ex parte Streeting (No 2)* [1980] 1 WLR 1425; [1980] 3 All ER 413, CA.
56　*R v Harrow LBC ex p Carter* (1994) 26 HLR 32, QBD.
57　HA 1996 s211.
58　See *Deadman v Southwark LBC* (2001) 33 HLR 75; (2000) *Times* 31 August, CA.
59　HA 1996 s211(4).

Housing benefit

Introduction

32.1   Many occupiers faced with possession proceedings are in that situation as a result of failure to make rental or other payments to the landlord or licensor.

32.2   The housing benefit scheme is designed to assist those on low incomes in meeting their liabilities for housing costs. The benefit is claimed from – and payable by – the local housing authority for the area in which the property is situated. Housing benefit is not available to owner-occupiers (financial assistance for mortgage borrowers is outlined in chapter 36).

32.3   In outline, the statutory scheme[1] provides that recipients of income support or income-based jobseeker's allowance are eligible for assistance with up to 100 per cent of their housing costs and others on low income are eligible to receive proportionate help. In a number of local authority areas, however, housing benefit is paid on the basis of a flat-rate 'local housing allowance': the local authorities in question are known as 'pathfinder authorities'.[2] This book does not have scope for a full description of the workings of the housing benefit scheme, for which see Zebedee, Ward and Lister's *Guide to Housing Benefit and Council Tax Benefit*.[3] However, there are a number of aspects of the housing benefit scheme which touch directly on possession proceedings.

Maximising housing benefit to clear arrears

32.4   If there are arrears and the occupier is presently (or has recently been) on a low income, the starting point should be to check that housing benefit is being paid or has been paid and that the correct amount is being, and has been, received.

32.5   Once the appropriate current housing benefit entitlement has been established, it may be possible to use the housing benefit scheme to make inroads into the outstanding arrears.

32.6   First, *backdating* should be considered. If there has been some potential entitlement in the past for which the occupier failed to claim,

---

1   Contained in the Social Security Contributions and Benefits Act 1992 and Housing Benefit Regulations 2006 (HB Regs 2006) SI No 213.
2   For a list of pathfinder authorities, and for details of the housing benefit regime in pathfinder areas, see Sch 10 to the Housing Benefit Regulations 2006.
3   29th edn forthcoming (Shelter, 2006).

application should be made for the backdating of the current award of benefit. This may produce a lump sum of arrears of housing benefit which can be applied to meeting the debt. The local authority has power to backdate for up to 12 months if good cause is shown for not having initiated a claim at an earlier date.[4] 'Good cause' is undefined and might be established by a variety of circumstances ranging from ill-health to earlier inaccurate advice. The adviser should not hesitate to present the individual claimant's explanation as one amounting to good cause.

32.7   Second, the occupier may be able to apply for a *discretionary housing payment*. The scheme for payment of discretionary housing payments (which are strictly not housing benefits) is contained in the Discretionary Financial Assistance Regulations 2001[5] made under the Child Support, Pensions and Social Security Act 2000. Guidance[6] issued to local authorities on 16 March 2001 by the Department for Work and Pensions (DWP) sets out both a description of the scheme and an indication of the breadth of the discretion to assist with unmet housing costs.

32.8   If possession proceedings have already been started they should be adjourned pending the outcome of an application for backdating of housing benefit or for discretionary housing payments if that is possible. It is not generally possible to secure such an adjournment where a court is satisfied that mandatory Housing Act 1988 Sch 2 ground 8 is satisfied in respect of an assured tenant. If the requisite level of rent arrears has been proved in such a case, the court must order possession even if the arrears have accumulated for want of housing benefit to which the tenant is entitled.[7] The Protocol for Possession Claims based on Rent Arrears (in force 2 October 2006) requires social landlords to make direct contact with the relevant housing benefit department and to ensure that difficulties are resolved wherever possible without court proceedings. The full text of the Protocol is set out in appendix D. See also paras 3.34 to 3.36.

---

4   HB Regs 2006 reg 83(12).
5   SI 2001 No 1167.
6   *Guidance for Local Authorities on the Operation of Discretionary Housing Payments*, March 2001.
7   *North British Housing Association v Matthews* [2004] EWCA Civ 1736; [2005] 1 WLR 3133.

'Arrears' resulting from delayed payment

32.9 Not infrequently, landlords initiate possession proceedings based on arrears which are entirely, or mainly, the result of late or delayed payment of housing benefit to the occupier by the local authority. Once a claim has been submitted, it is essential for the claimant, or someone cting on his or her behalf, to check that it has been received by the authority, that it is being processed and that all necessary evidence of personal and financial circumstances has been provided. All too often, claims are 'lost' in the system and it is essential to keep track of them. Where the claimant supplies documents (such as wages slips) in connection with the claim, he or she should obtain a note of acknowledgment from the housing benefit office to confirm receipt.

32.10 Once the occupier has claimed housing benefit from the local authority, the latter should, within 14 days, make a decision on the claim (provided that the claimant has provided all necessary evidence).[8] If it is not possible to determine a claim for benefit in respect of a private tenant (or tenant of a registered social landlord) within 14 days, and provided that the claimant has not without good cause failed to provide evidence of his or her circumstances, the local authority should make payments on account of prospective entitlement.[9] Each of these duties on the authority is mandatory and capable of enforcement in proceedings for judicial review.[10]

32.11 Where the claimant in such a case is the local authority itself, the occupier may be properly advised to respond to any possession proceedings based on arrears either by inviting the court to strike out the proceedings as an abuse of process[11] or by entering a defence and counterclaiming for breach of statutory duty. The private law duty in respect of which breach can be asserted arises only after a decision to make a payment of housing benefit has been taken.[12] If the problem is in securing such a decision, the tenant may seek to defend the claim on the basis that it is an improper exercise of power for the authority to bring proceedings in these circumstances, or alternatively request an adjournment of the possession claim and apply for judicial review.[13]

8 HB Regs 2006 reg 89(2).
9 HB Regs 2006 reg 93(2).
10 See *R v Liverpool City Council ex p Johnson* (1994) 23 June, unreported, QBD, and *R v Haringey LBC ex p Ayub* (1993) 25 HLR 566, QBD.
11 *Lambeth LBC v Tagoe* August 2000 *Legal Action* 24.
12 *Haringey LBC v Cotter* (1997) 29 HLR 682, CA.
13 *Wandsworth LBC v Winder* [1985] AC 461, *Kay v LB Lambeth, Leeds CC v Price* [2006] UKHL 10, para 110.

32.12   Where the claimant is a private landlord or registered social landlord, the local authority could be joined as a third party (under Part 20 of the Civil Procedure Rules 1998 (CPR)) if there has been an actionable breach of duty.[14] Alternatively, the senior officer responsible for housing benefit could be summonsed to give evidence relating to the occupier's entitlement to housing benefit and reasons for non-payment of it.[15] Either step should prompt the authority into payment of the correct benefit and a back payment. If the whole proceedings have been caused by local authority failures in dealing with the defendant's housing benefit claim, that authority should be joined as a third party (as a second claimant or defendant) simply for the purpose of obtaining an order that it pay all the costs.[16]

'Arrears' resulting from overpayment

32.13   Since the introduction of the modern housing benefit scheme in 1988, local authorities have had the power to recover overpayments of housing benefit from both the claimant *and* any other person to whom such benefit was paid (which may include the landlord – see para 32.16 below).[17] If recovery is made by deducting an amount from future benefit entitlement, the tenant faces the possibility of being unable to pay the rent in full and of subsequent arrears arising. However, many authorities seek to recover the past overpayment in a lump sum. The issue then arises as to whether the 'debt' in such sum can constitute 'arrears' in any proceedings for possession based on arrears. The answer depends on whether the landlord is the local authority.

Council tenants

32.14   Typically, a local authority pays housing benefit to its own tenants by way of credit to the rent account (ie, a 'rent rebate'). The rent due is directly 'paid'[18] in this way in whole or in part and the occupier's rent liability is met at least to the extent of that credit or payment. Inevitably, there are errors or mistakes and tenants are paid too much

---

14 CPR Part 19.
15 CPR Part 34.
16 CPR 48.2 and *Asra Greater London Housing Association v Cooke* June 2001 *Legal Action* 31.
17 HB Regs 2006 regs 99–107.
18 See the definition of 'pay' in Social Security Administration Act 1992 s134(2).

benefit or paid benefit to which they are not entitled. The regulations prescribe careful procedures to regulate recovery and ensure notification in such cases.[19] However, local authorities, on discovering an overpayment, not infrequently 'seize' back from the occupier's rent account the benefit overpaid and then issue rent account statements showing tenants 'in arrears' by that amount. This activity is improper for the following reasons:

- some overpayments are irrecoverable[20] and the authority has a discretion as to whether to recover any overpayment even if it is recoverable;[21]
- before taking any recovery action, the authority is obliged to issue written notification of the decision that there has been an overpayment, that it should be recovered and details of the method selected for recovery;[22]
- the permitted methods of recovery of overpaid housing benefit do not include debiting the amount of the overpayment to the occupier's rent account.

32.15   If possession proceedings are initiated against an occupier for such 'paper arrears', the defence should be that 'the amount alleged is not rent lawfully due' but is overpaid housing benefit (see para 3.27), and that the county court in possession proceedings is not the appropriate venue for recovery. The effect of the statutory definition of 'payment' in this context is that the amount of benefit awarded extinguishes liability for that much rent, ie, the rent lawfully due is and has been paid in that amount. The council cannot resurrect a liability for rent which has been extinguished. For that reason the *DWP HB/CTB Overpayments Guide* emphasises the distinction between a recoverable overpayment of housing benefit and arrears of rent (see paras 4.97–4.104 of the *Guide*).

Other tenants

32.16   Similar difficulties can occur when housing benefit payments have been made direct to private landlords or registered social landlords and are subsequently discovered to have been overpayments. If a local authority exercises its power to seek recovery from the landlord,[23] and

---

19 HB Regs 2006 reg 102.
20 HB Regs 2006 reg 100.
21 Social Security Administration Act s75(1).
22 HB Regs 2006 reg 90 and Sch 9 para 15.
23 Social Security Administration Act 1992 s75(3)(a) and HB Regs 2006 reg 101.

the landlord repays the money, the tenant's adviser needs to consider carefully the legal consequences. Regulation 95(2) of the Housing Benefit Regulations 2006 provides that:

> Any payment of rent allowance made to a landlord pursuant to this regulation or to regulation 96 (circumstances in which payments may be made to a landlord) shall be to discharge, in whole or in part, the liability of the claimant to pay rent to that landlord in respect of the dwelling concerned, except in so far as –
>
> (a) the claimant had no entitlement to the whole or part of that rent allowance so paid to his landlord; and
>
> (b) the overpayment of rent allowance resulting was recovered in whole or in part from that landlord.

It has, however, been suggested that it is 'strongly arguable' that this provision is ultra vires.[24]

32.17   Whether the occupier is a social or private sector tenant or licensee, the authority is required properly to notify a decision to recover an overpayment. Until such proper notification is given the overpayment is not legally recoverable.[25]

Direct payments of housing benefit

32.18   The housing benefit scheme contains a series of provisions under which benefit can be paid directly to a private landlord or registered social landlord. These are obviously relevant to possession proceedings because:

- failure by a landlord to apply for the direct payment facility may be helpful in establishing that it is not 'reasonable in all the circumstances' for the court to make a possession order in proceedings based on rent arrears on a discretionary ground;
- a tenant's offer to the landlord to arrange for all future housing benefit to be paid direct may encourage a compromise in the proceedings;
- an undertaking by the occupier to the court to apply for direct payments to meet future rent might persuade the court to grant any necessary adjournment;

---

24 See CPAG's *Housing Benefit and Council Tax Benefit Legislation* 18th edn, p447 (in relation to the equivalent provision in reg 93(1) of the Housing Benefit (General) Regulations 1987, now superseded by the Housing Benefit Regulations 2006).

25 *Warwick DC v Freeman* (1995) 27 HLR 616, CA and *R v Thanet DC ex p Warren Court Hotels Ltd* (2001) 33 HLR 32, QBD (Admin Ct).

- where direct payments have been operating but there has been an overpayment, the landlord might repay the authority and claim that the occupier is 'in arrears' (see para 32.16 above).

These provisions are in addition to those permitting direct payments toward rent arrears to be made by the DWP by deduction from income support and other social security benefits.[26]

32.19   The local authority *must* pay housing benefit direct to the landlord where:[27]

- direct deductions are already being made from income support by the DWP towards rent arrears; or
- eight or more weeks' worth of rent is outstanding (except where it is in the overriding interest of the claimant for direct payments not to be made).

Additionally, the authority *may* agree to pay housing benefit direct where:[28]

- the claimant requests direct payments; or
- the landlord requests direct payments and the claimant agrees; or
- payment direct is in the interests of the claimant and his or her family; or
- the tenant has left owing rent arrears and there is an outstanding payment of housing benefit attributable to that tenant and that accommodation.

32.20   Where direct payments are to be made, both the occupier and the landlord are informed in writing by the authority.[29]

32.21   Usually upon receipt of the direct payment the landlord applies the housing benefit in satisfaction of all or part of the occupier's rent liability. Difficulties can arise if subsequently it is discovered that the amount of housing benefit has been overpaid (see para 32.16).

---

26 See para 3.40.
27 HB Regs 2006 reg 95(1).
28 HB Regs 2006 reg 96(1).
29 HB Regs 2006 reg 90 and Sch 9 para 11.

Mortgages

Mortgages

Introduction

33.1   In 1904, an appeal judge said, 'No one, I am sure, by the light of nature ever understood an English mortgage of real estate'.[1] In 1986, the Law Commission, in more reserved tone, commented in its introduction to Working Paper No 99 on reform of land mortgages:[2]

> The English law of land mortgages is notoriously difficult. It has never been subjected to systematic statutory reform, and over several centuries of gradual evolution it has acquired a multi-layered structure that is historically fascinating but inappropriately and sometimes unnecessarily complicated.

33.2   It is clear that the current state of the English law of mortgages is inadequate. This was recognised by the Law Commission which in November 1991 published its recommendations for the reform of the law regulating land mortgages.[3] The defects in the law have become all the more important given the great social impact of its subject matter. Between 1994 and 2004 the owner-occupied share of the residential market increased from 67 per cent to 71 per cent.[4] About two-thirds of these properties are subject to one or more mortgages. Between 1980 and 2005 the number of mortgage possession actions started in the county courts in England and Wales rose from 27,105 to 115,353.[5] The number of repossessions by members of the Council of Mortgage Lenders (which comprises all the major lenders) in 2005 came to 10,250 and at the end of 2005 there were 59,700 mortgage borrowers between three and six months in arrears.[6]

33.3   It is against this backdrop that this Part is written, to try to explain the law and practice of mortgage possession actions and how advisers can help prevent loss of occupation by borrowers and their families.

Nature of legal mortgages

33.4   A lender who has secured its loan on property by way of mortgage has a considerable advantage over an unsecured lender and is not solely

---

1   *Samuel v Jarrah Timber and Wood Paving Corporation* [1904] AC 323 at 326 per Lord MacNaughten.
2   *Land Mortgages*, Law Commission Working Paper No 99, HMSO, 1986.
3   *Transfer of Land – Land Mortgages*, Law Com No 204 HC5, HMSO, 1991.
4   See www.dclg.gov.uk.
5   Lord Chancellor's Department, *Judicial Statistics: Annual Report 1991*, Cm 1990 and *Judicial Statistics: Annual Report 2005*, May 2006.
6   Council of Mortgage Lenders, press release, 3 February 2006.

dependent on the solvency of the borrower to recover the money lent. A mortgagee (ie, lender) has a number of options open as methods of enforcing the security. The lender may sue the borrower on the personal covenant in the mortgage deed, may appoint a receiver to collect rent due from any tenants in the property, or seek a foreclosure order from the court. However, in practice, large institutional lenders usually seek to obtain possession of the property and sell with vacant possession to recover the money owed to them.[7] Part IV of this book primarily deals with the law and practice related to this last method of enforcement. Throughout, the terms 'lender' and 'borrower' will be used in place respectively of the more technical terms 'mortgagee' and 'mortgagor', except where a term of art is to be used. The lender will, of course, almost invariably be a building society, bank or similar institution rather than an individual.

33.5   Since 1925, legal mortgages have only been capable of being made in one of two ways.[8] The first is the granting of a lease by the freehold owner to the lender for a term of 3,000 years. Where the property is leasehold, the lease granted in favour of the lender is for a term equivalent to the owner's interest, less one day. In both cases there is included a provision for 'cesser on redemption', that is for the lease to terminate on redemption of the loan. The second (and much more usual) way is a charge by deed expressed to be by way of legal mortgage. This is commonly known as a legal charge. Although the borrower remains the holder of the legal estate, with the lender obtaining no legal term as such, the lender is by statute given the same powers and remedies as a lender whose loan is protected by the creation of a lease in the lender's favour.[9]

33.6   In practice, modern institutional lenders invariably rely on mortgages by way of legal charge as they are simpler to use. The legal charge is an agreement whereby a particular property is used as security to ensure that a borrower complies with the terms of a loan from the lender without the transfer of possession or title by the borrower to the lender. In the event of default by the borrower, the lender is given various statutory powers in respect of the property and, generally,

---

7   See *Alliance & Leicester plc v Slayford* [2000] EWCA Civ 257; [2001] 1 All ER (Comm) 1 and M Thompson, 'The Cumulative Range of Mortgagee's Remedies' [2002] Conv 53 for a discussion as to the interrelationship between the different remedies open to a lender.

8   Law of Property Act 1925 ss85(1) and 86(1). See also *Lavin v Johnson* [2002] EWCA Civ 1138 and C McNall, 'Truth Suppressed? "Purported Conveyance by Way of Mortgage"' [2003] Conv 326.

9   Ibid s87(1).

additional contractual powers are reserved to the lender in the mortgage deed. The borrower is usually made responsible in the charge deed for the maintenance and insurance of the building, and is made personally liable for payment of the mortgage money and the lender's legal costs and expenses in enforcing the security. Advisers should look at the terms of the charge deed (and any collateral agreement) for the details in each case. In the case of loans from fringe banks and similar lenders, it is essential to obtain a copy of the loan agreement as well as the legal charge so that all the terms of the loan are clear. Usually, a copy will be forthcoming on request.

Types of mortgage

33.7   There are, most commonly, two different forms of modern mortgage used by individuals for the securing of a loan, whether for the initial purchase of a property or for a subsequent loan. It is important for advisers to clarify which the borrower has entered into. The first is the *capital repayment* (or annuity) mortgage. This usually requires a monthly repayment to the lender, part of which is repayment of the capital borrowed and the balance of which is interest. In this way the capital is repaid gradually over the term of the loan. The second common form of mortgage is the *interest-only* mortgage in which, usually, two monthly payments are required: one is to the lender and comprises interest on the capital borrowed, and the second is to a financial institution which over the term of the mortgage (through investment) creates a lump sum payment which should be adequate to pay off the capital sum borrowed. Perhaps the most common of these 'capital vehicles' is the endowment insurance policy. During the term, the benefit of the policy is usually formally assigned to the lender and it is a condition of the loan that the premiums are paid on the policy. However, sometimes the policy may not have been the subject of a deed of assignment when the mortgage was taken out and as a result the policy remains the borrower's and can be disposed of at the borrower's discretion. Some endowment mortgages are 'with profits' and are designed to give the borrower a small additional lump sum at the end of the term, over and above the money needed to pay off the loan and redeem the mortgage. A 'with profits' endowment mortgage requires higher monthly instalments. Unfortunately, in recent years, a significant number of borrowers have been told by their endowment policy companies that the policies will be inadequate to pay off the capital sum borrowed. Borrowers in this situation should be encouraged to contact the Financial Services Authority for advice.[10]

33.8   Other forms of interest-only mortgage are now available. One is the *pension* mortgage, where the owner's private retirement pension is used as security for repayment of the capital borrowed. Personal equity plans (PEPs) and Individual Savings Accounts (ISAs) can also be used as investment 'wrappers' to secure a mortgage. In all cases the capital is paid out of the lump sum which becomes payable to the borrower when the pension plan, PEP or ISA matures. No formal assignment of the pension, PEP or ISA can be made, and so lenders are really relying on their right to possession as security in the event of the capital not being repaid at the end of the agreed term. As with endowment mortgages, the borrower is required to pay interest on the outstanding capital throughout the term. Numerically these types of mortgage are becoming more significant as the push to develop private pension and personal finance plans continues.

33.9   A recent development is the *'flexible'* mortgage which seeks to blur the distinction between capital and interest only loans. In essence this is an interest-only mortgage which allows the borrower to make capital payments ostensibly at any time, with the payment instantly reducing the balance due and upon which interest payments are calculated. Some of these 'flexible' mortgage 'products' are designed to combine the borrower's other personal finances with the mortgage debt, in effect so that the mortgage is used as a bank account. The aim is to ensure maximum financial benefit for the borrower. However, in this way all of the borrower's indebtedness is secured in favour of the lender by the mortgage. Such mortgages commonly also include provisions where the borrower is permitted to have mortgage payment 'holidays' where no payments are required for a specified period.

10 See www.fsa.gov.uk.

CHAPTER 34

Lender's right to possession

34.1   As the legal charge gives the lender a notional lease of the property, the lender is, subject to any agreement to the contrary contained in the deed, entitled to take possession of the property as soon as the deed has been executed.[1] It is not necessary for the borrower to be in default. However, if someone other than the borrower has a right to possession in priority to that of the lender, the latter would be prevented from taking possession (see para 40.2). The fact that a lender may have entered into a sub-charge does not strip the lender, as principal chargee, of its right to possession. Both principal chargee and sub-chargee have rights to possession.[2] Obviously modern institutional lenders do not want possession of the property as they are anxious to ensure that they receive the regular repayments agreed with the borrower. The exercise of this right to possession is normally only a preliminary step to enforcing the security by way of sale with vacant possession in case of financial or other default under the mortgage. Unless the mortgage deed requires it, notice of proceedings for possession need not be given,[3] although a number of warning letters are usually sent by a lender. It is not necessary for lenders to obtain a possession order in order to take possession,[4] except in cases regulated by the Consumer Credit Act 1974. Where, however, a property is occupied a lender would be guilty of an offence under Criminal Law Act 1977 s6 if it recovered possession other than through the courts. In practice, to ensure an ability to sell as mortgagees in possession, lenders do seek orders for possession. The extent to which parliament has modified this common law right to possession is discussed in chapter 35.

34.2   Some charge deeds contain a clause effectively creating a notional tenancy between the lender and the borrower. This is now not common. Such a clause is called an 'attornment clause'. If the agreement contains such a clause then the lender must first terminate the tenancy before exercising its right to possession.[5] Such clauses are not used in modern institutional mortgage deeds. The legal charge may expressly state when the lender is able to seek possession from the borrower.

---

1   Law of Property Act 1925 s95(4) and *Four-maids Ltd v Dudley Marshall (Properties) Ltd* [1957] Ch 317; [1957] 2 All ER 35 and generally R J Smith 'The Mortgagee's Right to Possession – the Modern Law' [1979] Conv 266.
2   *Credit & Mercantile plc v Marks* [2004] EWCA Civ 568; [2005] Ch 81.
3   *Jolly v Arbuthnot* (1859) 4 De G & J 224.
4   *Ropaigealach v Barclays Bank plc* [2000] QB 263; [1999] 3 WLR 17; [1999] 4 All ER 235, CA.
5   *Hinckley and Country Building Society v Henny* [1953] 1 WLR 352.

CHAPTER 35

Courts' powers to allow borrowers to remain in their home

continued

Legal regulation of mortgages – overview

35.1   On 31 October 2004 major changes were introduced to the legal regulation of residential mortgages. The Financial Services and Markets Act 2000 brought significant elements of mortgage lending and mortgage administration under the control of the Financial Services Authority (FSA). Regulations issued under the 2000 Act introduced the new concept of the 'regulated mortgage contract'. For full details see para 35.87. The 2000 Act also set up the Financial Ombudsman Service as a dispute resolution body whose function is to investigate and resolve complaints about regulated activities as an alternative to the courts, including those relating to the sale, granting and administration of mortgages. The 2000 Act does not, however, apply to mortgages, which are not 'regulated mortgage contracts' such as 'buy to let' mortgages or second charges nor to mortgages that were entered into pre 31 October 2004. The Consumer Credit Act 2006, which received Royal Assent on 30 March 2006, will also, once implemented, make changes to the powers available to the courts when dealing with possession proceedings by lenders.

35.2   Mortgages entered into pre 31 October 2004 will, so far as court-based regulation is concerned, be regulated by the provisions of the Administration of Justices Acts 1970 and 1973 unless they fall within the definition of 'regulated agreement' within the meaning of the Consumer Credit Act 1974 in which case they will be regulated by that legislation.[1]

35.3   Mortgages which are entered into post 31 October 2004 but before the date of implementation of the changes to the Consumer Credit Act 1974 brought about by the Consumer Credit Act 2006 and which fall within the definition of 'regulated mortgage contract', will be regulated by the FSA. In the event of possession proceedings, the courts have the powers available in the Administration of Justice Acts 1970 and 1973 again unless the agreement falls within the 1974 Act when that legislation will apply.

35.4   Mortgages entered into after implementation of the Consumer Credit Act 2006 changes to the 1974 Act and which are 'regulated mortgage contracts' will be regulated by the FSA and, in the event of possession proceedings, by the court powers in the 1970 and 1973 legislation. The majority of mortgages that fall outside the definition of 'regulated mortgage contract' will be regulated by the provisions of

---

1   Administration of Justice Act 1970 s38A inserted by Consumer Credit Act 1974 Sch 4 para 30.

the Consumer Credit Act 1974 as amended by the Consumer Credit Act 2006.[2] The small residue of residential mortgages which do not qualify as 'regulated mortgage contracts' and which also fall outside the provisions of the Consumer Credit Act 1974 will have possession proceedings regulated by the 1970 and 1973 Acts.

35.5   As has been indicated above (see chapter 34), the lender has an immediate legal right to possession of the mortgaged property. The court, when considering an application by the lender for an order for possession, has only limited inherent and statutory power to prevent the lender from obtaining possession or to delay repossession.

Inherent power

35.6   The High Court has an inherent discretion in possession proceedings to grant a short adjournment only (for example, 28 days) so as to allow any default to be remedied or for the loan to be paid off.[3] It has also been stated that the court's equitable powers extend to preventing a lender from taking possession 'except when it is sought bona fide and reasonably for the purpose of enforcing the security and then only subject to such conditions as the court thinks fit to impose'.[4]

35.7   This is a proposition of equity promulgated by Lord Denning MR in 1979 which has since been approved in the Court of Appeal[5] and gives scope for borrowers to argue, for instance, that if there is some other method of enforcing payment of arrears (such as an agreed attachment of earnings order) then no order for possession should be granted. This would be particularly useful in cases where the lender's capital is not significantly at risk because there is plenty of equity in the property (ie, the sale value of the property substantially exceeds the outstanding debt). The courts have also accepted an equitable jurisdiction, which potentially may assist borrowers, through the doctrine of 'unconscionable bargain' where the court can set aside the legal charge or clauses within a charge on the basis that they are 'unconscionable', 'unfair' or 'unreasonable', where the lender 'has imposed the objectionable terms in a morally reprehensible manner

---

2   Consumer Credit Act 1974 s16(6C) as inserted by Financial Services and Markets Act 2000 (Regulated Activities) Order 2001 SI No 544 reg 90(1).

3   *Birmingham Citizens' Permanent Building Society v Caunt* [1962] Ch 883.

4   *Quennel v Maltby* [1979] 1 WLR 318; [1979] 1 All ER 568 at 571e, CA.

5   *Albany Homes Loans v Massey* [1997] 2 All ER 609; (1997) 29 HLR 902, CA. See also M P Thompson, 'The Powers and Duties of Mortgagees' [1998] Conv 391.

... in a way which affects his conscience'.[6] Browne-Wilkinson J gave as the classic example of such a bargain, a case 'where advantage has been taken of a young, inexperienced or ignorant person to introduce such a term which no sensible well-advised person or party would have accepted'.[7] It seems that there has to be some element of morally reprehensible behaviour, involving abusive inequality of bargaining power such as to 'shock the conscience of the court'.[8] There is obviously a very clear overlap between this, the extortionate credit bargain and the unfair relationship provisions of the Consumer Credit Act 1974 and the Unfair Terms in Consumer Contracts Regulations (see paras 35.53 and 35.73). While of obviously limited application, in appropriate cases this equitable jurisdiction may prove to be an additional basis of challenge.[9]

Statutory powers

35.8   There are two mutually exclusive statutory regimes which may be available to assist a borrower in default under the mortgage. In the case of residential mortgages the court has powers to grant relief either by virtue of the Administration of Justice Acts 1970 and 1973 or, alternatively, under the Consumer Credit Act 1974. A regulated mortgage contract within the meaning of the Financial Services and Markets Act 2000 which is entered into after 31 October 2004 is an 'exempt agreement' and as such is outside the scope of the Consumer Credit Act 1974 and hence will be governed by the Administration of Justice Acts 1970 and 1973.[10] Where the mortgage is a 'regulated agreement' within the meaning of the Consumer Credit Act 1974 (for which see para 35.31), the provisions of that Act apply in place of those of the Administration of Justice Acts.[11] Where the mortgage relates to

---

6   *Multiservice Bookbinding Ltd v Marden* [1979] Ch 84 at 110F.

7   *Multiservice Bookbinding Ltd v Marden* [1979] Ch 84.

8   See *Creswell v Potter* [1978] 1 WLR 255, *Backhouse v Backhouse* [1978] 1 All ER 1158, *Lloyds Bank Ltd v Bundy* [1974] 3 All ER 757, CA and *Alec Lobb (Garages) Ltd v Total Oil GB Ltd* [1983] 1 All ER 944.

9   See *Credit Lyonnais Bank Nederland v Burch* [1997] 1 All ER 143, CA. Cf, *Portman Building Society v Dusangh* [2000] 2 All ER (Comm) 221, CA. See also L McMurty, 'Unconscionability and Undue Influence: An Interaction?' [2000] 64 Conv 573.

10   Financial Services and Markets Act 2000 (Regulated Activities) Order 2001 SI No 544 reg 90.

11   Administration of Justice Act 1970 s38A inserted by Consumer Credit Act 1974 Sch 4 para 30, Consumer Credit Act 1974 (Commencement No 8) Order 1983 SI No 1551 and County Courts Act 1984 s21(9).

non-residential property then there is statutory power to grant relief only if the agreement in question is 'a regulated agreement' within the Consumer Credit Act 1974.

35.9   Occasionally, the court may make the mistake of treating consumer credit loans in the same way as loans to which the Administration of Justice Acts apply. It is important to remind district judges of the difference when dealing with consumer credit loans and to emphasise the fact that the court's powers under the Consumer Credit Act 1974 are wider than those under the Administration of Justice Acts.

Administration of Justice Acts 1970 and 1973

35.10   Administration of Justice Act 1970 Pt IV, together with Administration of Justice Act 1973 s8, sets out the court's principal powers to assist borrowers who are in default.[12] Administration of Justice Act 1970 s36(1) provides:

> Where the mortgagee under a *mortgage* of land which consists of or includes a *dwelling-house* brings an action in which he claims possession ... not being an action for *foreclosure* in which a claim for possession ... is also made, the court may exercise any of [its] powers ... if it appears to the court that in the event of its exercising the power the mortgagor *is likely* to be able within a *reasonable period* to pay any *sums due* under the mortgage or to remedy a default consisting of a breach of any other obligation arising under or by virtue of the mortgage. [Authors' emphasis: the phrases are considered below.]

Section 36(2) provides that the court:

(a) may adjourn the proceedings, or
(b) on giving judgment, or making an order, for delivery of possession ... or at any time before execution of such judgment or order may:
    (i) stay or suspend execution of the judgment or order, or
    (ii) postpone the date for delivery of possession,
    for such period or periods as the court thinks reasonable.

By Administration of Justice Act 1970 s36(3) any order made in exercise of any section 36(2) powers may be made:

> ... subject to such conditions with regard to payment by the mortgagor of any sum secured by the mortgage or the remedying of any default as the court thinks fit.

---

12 See generally R J Smith, 'The Mortgagee's Right to Possession – The Modern Law' [1979] Conv 266 and A Clarke, 'Further Implications of s36 of the Administration of Justice Act' [1983] Conv 293.

The court is empowered by Administration of Justice Act 1970 s36(4) to vary or revoke any condition imposed under section 36(3) but not the period of any postponed possession order.[13]

35.11   Administration of Justice Act 1970 s36 is qualified by Administration of Justice Act 1973 s8(2) which states:

> A court shall not exercise ... the powers conferred by section 36 ... unless it appears to the court not only that the mortgagor is likely to be able within a reasonable period to pay any amounts regarded ... as due on account of the principal sum secured, together with the interest on those amounts, but also that he is likely to be able by the end of that period to pay any further amounts that he would have expected to be required to pay by then on account of that sum and of interest on it ...

35.12   In effect, before exercising any of its powers it must appear to the court not only that the borrower is likely to be able to pay off the missed monthly payments within the reasonable period, but also that it is likely that by the end of that reasonable period the borrower will also have paid off the payments which have fallen due during that period. This will usually mean being able to show that the borrower can resume payment of the current instalments and can make regular payments towards the arrears so that at the end of the reasonable period the arrears will have been discharged. However, the section would also be satisfied if the borrower can pay off the arrears over the reasonable period and discharge the payments that have fallen due over that period by a payment at the end of that period[14] or, alternatively, pay the current instalments and discharge the arrears by a lump sum payment at the end of the reasonable period.

35.13   The court's powers apply equally to endowment mortgages, where there is no obligation to repay the capital originally borrowed until the end of the loan period, as they do to annuity (or repayment) mortgages, where part of each monthly repayment is capital and part interest.[15] By analogy, interest only loans would also be included. Administration of Justice Act 1970 s36 powers can also be exercised whether or not there is default under the mortgage deed itself, for example, breach of some collateral agreement.[16]

13   *Secured Residential Funding v Greenhill* noted at *Current Law Week* 22 October 1993, Bournemouth County Ct, HHJ Darwell-Smith.

14   *Governor & Company of the Royal Bank of Scotland v Elmes* April 1998 *Legal Action* 11.

15   *Bank of Scotland v Grimes* [1985] QB 1179; [1985] 3 WLR 294, CA.

16   *Western Bank Ltd v Schindler* [1976] 2 All ER 393; [1977] Ch 1; [1976] 3 WLR 341, CA and generally C Harpum, 'A Mortgagee's Right to Possession and the Mischief Rule' (1977) 40 MLR 356.

35.14   Administration of Justice Act 1973 s8(1) restricts the way in which the court can exercise its Administration of Justice Act 1970 s36 powers. It provides that only where a borrower is entitled to repay the capital by instalments or otherwise to defer payment of it in whole or in part and there is also provision for earlier payment of the capital either on default by the borrower or demand by the lender, then the court may treat as due in respect of capital such sums as the borrower would have been expected to repay but for the provision in the mortgage for earlier repayment. Section 8(1) will not apply where deferral is granted as a mere indulgence by the lender, lacking contractual force, unless it is enforceable by estoppel.[17] Where an agreement to secure a bank overdraft provides that money owed shall only become payable on demand, then there is no agreement to defer payment and so the agreement falls outside the scope of Administration of Justice Act 1973 s8.[18] These are sometimes described as 'all monies' charges. In such cases the court retains the more limited power under Administration of Justice Act 1970 s36 to suspend enforcement of a possession order to enable the borrower to pay off the entire debt over a reasonable period. In such cases the court, however, has no contractual term to refer to by way of guidance as to what the reasonable term should be and therefore will have to determine this in isolation.

35.15   A reasonable time must be given to the borrower to comply with a demand for repayment before the lender is permitted to claim possession unless it is clear that, even if given a reasonable period, the borrower will not be able to pay off the mortgage debt.[19]

'Mortgage'

35.16   As indicated in chapter 33 there is no significant practical difference between a legal mortgage and a legal charge. Administration of Justice Act 1970 s39(1) confirms that the expression 'mortgage' includes a 'charge' and that 'mortgagor' and 'mortgagee' should be similarly construed.

'Dwelling-house'

35.17   Administration of Justice Act 1970 s39(1) defines 'dwelling-house' as meaning any building or part of a building which is used as a

---

17   *Rees Investments Ltd v Groves* [2002] 1 P & CR DG9; (2001) 27 June, unreported, ChD, Neuberger J noted at April 2002 *Legal Action* 22.

18   See *Habib Bank Ltd v Tailor* [1982] 3 All ER 561; [1982] 1 WLR 1218, CA.

19   *Sheppard & Cooper v TSB Bank plc (No 2)* [1996] 2 All ER 654, ChD.

dwelling. Section 39(2) of the 1970 Act amplifies this by expressly providing that the fact that part of the premises occupied as a dwelling is used as a shop, as an office or for business, trade or professional purposes, does not prevent the premises from being a dwelling-house. It follows, therefore, that a mixed business/residential user is covered by the 1970 Act. The relevant time for determining whether land consists of, or includes, a dwelling-house is the date the lender claims possession.[20] The fact that the property may be used as a dwelling for someone other than the borrower does not prevent the security from being a dwelling-house and so within scope of the 1970 Act. However, if the occupier is in occupation in breach of a term of the mortgage, this amounts to a breach within the meaning of Administration of Justice Act 1970 s36(1).

'Foreclosure'

35.18   Although it is often said that a property is being foreclosed by a lender, in practice the common form of enforcement is that of taking possession and subsequent sale.

35.19   Foreclosure of residential mortgages is very rare as it is more complex than enforcement by possession and sale. The latter is usually sufficient as a method of enforcement. Foreclosure is technically quite different from the obtaining of possession and subsequent sale in that it involves the extinction of the borrower's equitable right to redeem the mortgage on the property and the vesting of the legal estate absolutely in the lender. An example will illustrate the difference.

EXAMPLE

X borrows £120,000 by way of a mortgage from C Ltd. X repays £40,000 before C Ltd obtains possession and sells it for £140,000. X would receive £60,000 after redemption of the existing mortgage of £80,000. If C Ltd foreclosed on the property, instead of taking possession and selling, X would lose the equity of £60,000. C Ltd would become the absolute owner of the property worth £140,000 and X would receive nothing.

35.20   In view of the draconian nature of foreclosure, the courts are reluctant to grant foreclosure orders absolute and they put procedural obstacles in the way of a lender seeking such an order. Briefly, the

---

20 *Royal Bank of Scotland v Miller* [2001] EWCA Civ 344; [2001] 3 WLR 523, CA.

procedure to obtain such an order is as follows. Once repayment of the mortgage money has fallen due, for example, on breach of any term in the mortgage or after calling-in by the lender (ie, an express and unconditional demand is made for payment) and it remains unpaid, the lender can apply for a foreclosure decree nisi. This order directs the taking of accounts between the lender and the borrower as to money paid during the term of the mortgage, and provides that if the borrower pays the remaining outstanding money by a particular date then the mortgage is redeemed and the debt discharged. If the mortgage is not redeemed by that date, then the lender can apply to be granted a foreclosure order absolute. The lender then becomes the legal owner and the property is transferred to it. At the request of any person interested the court has the power[21] to order sale of the property instead of foreclosure. Normally, such an order for 'judicial sale' would be granted so as to ensure that the borrower receives the balance of the sale price once the lender has been paid off. The court's dislike of foreclosure is such that, on occasion, even after a foreclosure order absolute, it will 'open' the foreclosure. As a result of this, and the efficacy of other methods of enforcement, foreclosure is rarely used by lenders[22] although it may be pleaded as part of the lender's claim for relief in addition to claims for sale and/or possession.

35.21   It seems likely that foreclosure is no longer possible in the case of 'regulated agreements' within the meaning of the Consumer Credit Act 1974 (see para 35.51) as section 113(1) of that Act prevents a lender from obtaining any greater benefit by enforcing any security provided in relation to a regulated agreement than would be the case if no such security had been given. No authority on the point has been found but in view of the very restricted use of foreclosure, the point may happily remain academic.

35.22   The Administration of Justice Acts add, to some limited degree, to the court's powers in cases where foreclosure is claimed. In effect, where foreclosure alone is claimed, the only statutory (as opposed to common law or inherent) power is adjournment. If the claim is for foreclosure and possession, there appears to be power to adjourn the foreclosure claim and to adjourn the possession claim or stay, suspend execution or postpone any order for possession.[23]

---

21 Law of Property Act 1925 s91(1), (2).
22 For a note on foreclosure in commercial mortgages, see E Bannister, 'Foreclosure – A Remedy out of its Time?' (1992) EG 28 March.
23 Administration of Justice Act 1970 s36 and Administration of Justice Act 1973 s8(3). See generally S Tromans, 'Mortgages: Possession by Default' [1984] Conv 91.

'Is likely'

35.23   The question of whether a borrower is likely to be able to pay any sums due within a reasonable time is one of fact for the judge on the evidence before him or her, whether in a witness statement or by way of oral evidence.[24] For this reason it is essential that the borrower(s) attend the possession hearing, otherwise it is likely that there will be no evidence before the district judge to allow him or her to exercise the court's statutory powers, although the district judge may of his or her own volition ask about the last payments or in some other way seek evidence from the lender's representative. It may be reasonable to adjourn proceedings in order to determine, at a later date, whether there has emerged in the interim any prospect of the borrower being able within a reasonable period to pay sums due under the mortgage, for example, where a student borrower is working for qualifications which would result in employment adequate to ensable the borrower to discharge the arrears.[25]

'Reasonable period'

35.24   One crucial question, which has to be asked in each case, is what is the 'reasonable period'? It has been stated, obiter, that in making the assessment the court must 'bear in mind the rights and obligations of both parties, including [the lender's] right to recover the money by selling the property, if necessary, and the whole past history of the security'.[26] More important, however, is the approach to the length of the period during which arrears are to be cleared. Local practice can vary. For many years some district judges adopted a restrictive view of what 'reasonable period' meant and periods of 12 months or two or three years were common. However, in *Cheltenham & Gloucester Building Society v Norgan*[27] the Court of Appeal reviewed the authorities and concluded that when assessing a 'reasonable period' it was appropriate for the court to take account of the whole of the remaining part of the original term of the mortgage. The court stated that in determining the 'reasonable period' the court 'should take as its

---

24   *Royal Trust Company of Canada v Markham* [1975] 3 All ER 433; [1975] 1 WLR 1416, CA and *Western Bank Ltd v Schindler* [1976] 2 All ER 393; [1977] Ch 1; [1976] 3 WLR 341, CA.

25   *Skandia Financial Services Ltd v Greenfield* [1997] CLY 4248.

26   *Centrax Trustees v Ross* [1979] 2 All ER 952 at 957 per Goulding J.

27   [1996] 1 All ER 449; [1996] 1 WLR 343, CA. See also J Morgan, 'Mortgage Arrears and the Family Home' (1996) 112 LQR 553 and M Thompson, 'Back to Square Two' [1996] Conv 118.

starting point the full term of the mortgage and pose at the outset the question: would it be possible for the mortgagor to maintain payment-off of the arrears by instalments over that period?'.[28] The court listed a number of considerations which are likely to be relevant when establishing what is a reasonable period. They are:

> '(a) How much can the borrower reasonably afford to pay, both now and in the future? (b) If the borrower has a temporary difficulty in meeting his obligations, how long is the difficulty likely to last? (c) What was the reason for the arrears which have accumulated? (d) How much remains of the original term? (e) What are the relevant contractual terms, and what type of mortgage is it, ie when is the principal due to be repaid? (f) Is it a case where the court should exercise its power to disregard accelerated payment provisions (section 8 of the 1973 Act)? (g) Is it reasonable to expect the lender, in the circumstances of the case, to recoup the arrears of interest: (1) over the whole of the original term, or (2) within a shorter period, or even (3) within a longer period, ie by extending the repayment period? Is it reasonable to expect the lender to capitalise the interest or not? (h) Are there reasons affecting the security which should influence the length of the period for payment?'[29]

35.25   It is clear from the judgment that the existence of equity in the security to protect the lender (see para 35.26) is a significant factor in determining whether the court will exercise its discretion in the borrower's favour. Following this case, district judges have tended to adopt a much more generous interpretation of the reasonable period. Although, no doubt mindful of certain obiter dicta in *Norgan* to the effect that the court should be less sympathetic if a borrower has once failed to meet payments calculated by reference to the balance of the contractual term, it is not universal practice to use the balance of the term as the starting point in assessing the reasonable period. In the case of regulated mortgage contracts (for which see para 35.87) the FSA's stated position is that in appropriate cases the remaining term of the mortgage will be the reasonable repayment period.[30]

35.26   Where there is sufficient equity in the property (ie, the surplus value of the property arrived at after deducting the money outstanding under any mortgages), it is hard to see what risk there is to the lender in deferring possession to the lender. It can be useful to clarify with the lender before the hearing therefore whether it accepts that

---

28 [1996] 1 All ER 449 at 458.

29 Ibid at 463a.

30 Mortgage Conduct of Business sourcebook (MCOB) 2003 13.3.6, see para 35.104.

there is equity or to produce evidence to prove the amount of equity to show that the lender is not at risk. The Legal Help scheme (see para 24.3 for further discussion) can be used to pay for the cost of a valuer's report as to the valuation. An estate agent's valuation may be helpful as a guide although the Court of Appeal has commented that such valuations should be treated with 'reserve'.[31] Institutional lenders often have property valuations which bear little relationship to a genuine valuation based, as they are, on general statistics relating to market trends or even 'drive by' valuations. Where there is likely to be a dispute as to the value of the property, and therefore the level of equity, then this of itself may be sufficient to persuade the Legal Services Commission to grant a public funding certificate (see chapter 24). In such cases it should be pointed out that in practice the courts are influenced greatly by the valuation evidence.

35.27 Where, however, there is no equity (ie, there would be a shortfall if the property were sold) it is possible to argue that the lender's interests are better served by a delay in possession being given up, particularly where there is some prospect of the market improving. The contrary view is that on a falling market it is in the lender's interest to allow sale to proceed at the earliest opportunity so that the loss to the lender is minimised.

35.28 See chapter 42 for the situation where the borrower wishes to sell the property in order to pay off the loan.

'Sums due'

35.29 Most mortgage deeds enable the lender to 'call in' the loan at any time or else provide that the capital money in total becomes immediately payable in the event of any default. As originally drafted, Administration of Justice Act 1970 s36 enabled the court to give relief to the borrower only if it were likely that he or she could pay any sums due under the mortgage. The court's power to give relief was therefore available in such cases only if the borrower could pay off any arrears and the outstanding capital which had invariably also become payable. To resolve this anomaly, Administration of Justice Act 1973 s8(1) redefined 'sums due' to make it clear that in the case of instalment mortgages or mortgages where payment was deferred in whole or part, the financial default to be considered at the hearing was limited to the normal instalments due but unpaid and that the provision for earlier repayment of capital contained in the mortgage deed was to be ignored.

31 *Bristol & West Building Society v Ellis* (1997) 29 HLR 282; 73 P & CR 158, CA.

35.30 It is not clear from the wording of Administration of Justice Act 1970 s36 and Administration of Justice Act 1973 s8, when read together, whether it is proper for the court in 'instalment mortgage' cases to take into account interest which accrues on arrears (and other payments which fall due as a result of being in arrears) in determining a borrower's ability to pay off 'any sums due' over the reasonable period. It is suggested that, given the wording of Administration of Justice Act 1973 s8(1), the borrower should only be required to show that he or she is likely to be able to pay off the arrears built up by the hearing date and not that he or she can pay off those arrears plus any interest and other payments which may accrue over the reasonable period.[32]

Consumer Credit Act 1974

35.31 Where a 'regulated agreement' within the meaning of Consumer Credit Act 1974 is secured by a legal charge, then the provisions of that Act apply in place of those in the Administration of Justice Acts.[33] Basically, an agreement under which an individual is supplied with credit not exceeding £25,000[34] is a regulated agreement unless the agreement falls within the Act's 'exempt agreement' provisions.[35]

35.32 Amendments made to the Consumer Credit Act 1974 by the Consumer Credit Act 2006 s2, when implemented, will remove the financial limit rendering all loans under regulated agreements within the provisions of the 1974 Act. The Consumer Credit Act 2006 received Royal Assent on 30 March 2006 but its provisions will be brought into force over time.

35.33 Loans which otherwise would be within scope of the Consumer Credit Act 1974 are 'exempt agreements' in the following circumstances. All loans by local authorities secured on land are exempt.[36]

---

32 For an interesting article on this and other points relating to the practice of mortgage possession proceedings, see D J Parmiter, 'Wrongly Dispossessed?' LS Gaz 29 April 1992.

33 See note 11.

34 The limit of £25,000 was substituted for £15,000 from 1 May 1998 by Consumer Credit (Increase of Monetary Limits) (Amendment) Order 1998 SI No 996. Previously £15,000 was substituted for £5,000 from 20 May 1985 by the Consumer Credit (Increase of Monetary Limits) Order 1983 SI No 1878.

35 See Consumer Credit Act 1974 ss8 and 16.

36 See 'Mortgage Sales Guidance for Local Authorities and Registered Social Landlords' issued by DCLG for regulation of local authority mortgage lending – www.dclg.gov.uk/index.asp?id=1161631.

Also, loans by building societies and the various banks, insurance companies, friendly societies and charities specified in the Consumer Credit (Exempt Agreements) Order 1989[37] are exempt provided the loans are secured on land and are for the purchase of land, or the provision of a dwelling or business premises. Additionally, loans by these lenders are exempt where they are for:

- the alteration, enlargement, repair or improvement of a dwelling or business premises, provided the lender has already lent for the purchase of land or the provision of a dwelling or business premises; or, alternatively,
- the alteration, enlargement, repair or improvement of a dwelling, such work to be undertaken by a housing association or other specified body.

In either case, to be exempt, the loan must be secured on the property in question.

35.34   Loans which are 'regulated mortgage contracts' (see para 35.87) entered into after 31 October 2004 are exempt agreements[38] as, following the implementation of the Consumer Credit Act 2006, will be loans in excess of £25,000 entered into wholly or predominately for the purpose of a business carried on or intended to be carried on by the borrower.[39] The secretary of state will also have power by order to provide for exemption where the borrower is a person who has a 'high net worth', ie, had an income in the previous financial year in excess of a prescribed amount.[40]

35.35   Happily, in practice it is usually clear whether a loan falls within scope of the Consumer Credit Act 1974 because of the explicit references to the Act in the documentation.

35.36   The provisions of the Consumer Credit Act 1974 are notoriously complicated, dealing as they do with a multitude of different types of credit transaction. The Act seeks to prescribe the way in which regulated agreements are entered into. Failure to observe any of these rules renders the agreement 'improperly executed' and so unenforceable without a court order.[41] Additionally, the loan agreement must be in a prescribed form[42] and the Act lays down provisions for copies of the unexecuted agreement to be given to the borrower and a

---

37   SI No 869 as substantially amended.
38   Consumer Credit Act 1974 s16(6C).
39   Ibid s16B.
40   Ibid s16A.
41   Ibid s65.
42   Ibid s60 and Consumer Credit (Agreements) Regulations 1983 SI No 1553.

prescribed procedure for the execution of the agreement.[43] The sanction for non-compliance with the formality provisions of the 1974 Act is that the agreement is deemed not to have been 'properly executed' and is enforceable only by way of a court order under Consumer Credit Act 1974 s127.[44] The provisions of the 1974 Act are not simple and reference should be made to the standard works on consumer credit law for details.[45]

35.37   In the context of possession proceedings, the Consumer Credit Act 1974 affords a borrower some protection from enforcement of the loan and mortgage. The lender can only enforce through a particular procedure in which the court has specific powers to give relief. The lender under a regulated agreement must serve a default notice before being entitled 'to recover possession of any ... land' or 'to enforce any security'. The default notice must be in a prescribed form and specify the nature of the breach of the agreement being alleged.[46] If the borrower complies with the notice, the breach is treated as never having occurred.[47] The terms of the default notice must be accurate. If the amount claimed by the creditor to remedy non-payment was in excess of the sum necessary to remedy such a breach, that default notice would be invalid and any subsequent proceedings liable to be struck out.[48]

Time orders

35.38   Receipt of a default notice by the borrower entitles him or her to apply to the court for a time order by means of which the court can reschedule payment of money owed under the agreement. The time order provisions are dealt with below. Following a default notice, application[49] is by way of a Part 8 claim under the Civil Procedure Rules (CPR). Alternatively the borrower can seek a time order in any possession action which the lender brings, following the expiry of the default notice, either in his or her defence or by application notice

---

43   Ibid ss58, 61, 62 and 63.

44   Ibid s65(1).

45   See Goode, *Consumer Credit Law & Practice* (5 Vols), Butterworths, and Goode, Consumer Credit Reports (3 Vols), Butterworths.

46   Consumer Credit Act 1974 ss87 and 88 and Consumer Credit (Enforcement, Default and Termination Notices) Regulations 1983 SI No 1561.

47   Consumer Credit Act 1974 s89.

48   *Worcester Lease Management Services Ltd v Swain & Co* [1999] 1 WLR 263, CA.

49   CCR Ord 49 r4(5).

in the proceedings.[50] In most cases it will be advisable to seek a time order at the earliest possible date.[51]

35.39   Assuming that the borrower does not pay off the arrears or remedy any other default within the period specified in the default notice, then the lender will be at liberty to issue a possession claim against the borrower. A mortgage securing a regulated agreement is specifically enforceable only by an order of the court.[52] The time order provisions,[53] together with the supplementary powers of Consumer Credit Act 1974 ss135 and 136, give the court powers to assist the borrower greatly in excess of those in the Administration of Justice Acts.

35.40   Consumer Credit Act 1974 s129(1) provides:

> If it appears to the court just to do so –
> ...
> (b) on an application made by a debtor ... under this paragraph after service on him of –
>   (i) a default notice, or ...
> (c) in an action brought by a creditor ... to enforce a regulated agreement or security, or recover possession of any ... land to which a regulated agreement relates,
> the court may make an order under this section (a 'time order').

It is clear from the wording of the section that, in the case of proceedings brought by the lender to recover possession, the court has the discretion to make a time order even if the borrower has not sought one or even if the borrower is not present in court. The only requirement is that it should appear to the court 'just to do so'. Form N440 in CPR Part 4 may be used in a time order application. See precedent at appendix B for a consumer credit defence and Part 20 claim.

35.41   Consumer Credit Act 1974 s129(2) provides:

> A time order shall provide for one or both of the following, as the court considers just –
> (a) the payment by the debtor ... of any sum owed under a regulated agreement or a security by such instalments, payable at such times, as the court, having regard to the means of the debtor ... and any surety, considers reasonable;

---

50   CPR PD 55 para 7.1.

51   See generally D McConnell, 'Time Orders on loans secured against property' January 1990 *Legal Action* 19, R Leszczyszyn, 'Time Orders Revisited' (1990) *Adviser* No 20 p22, E James, 'Time orders and the Consumer Credit Act' March 1991 *SCOLAG* p40 and F Ratcliffe, 'Tinkering with time orders' September 2005 *Legal Action* 6.

52   Consumer Credit Act 1974 s126.

53   Ibid ss129 and 130.

(b) the remedying by the debtor ... of any breach of a regulated agreement (other than non-payment of money) within such period as the court may specify.

35.42   The court is required by the section to order payment of any money owed by instalments or the remedying of other default if it wishes to make a time order. However, expressly, having determined to exercise its discretion to grant a time order, the court must have regard only to the means of the debtor (and any surety) when considering the size and rate of instalments. It is not legitimate to look to possible hardship caused to the lender or its investors. Equally, there is no requirement that the arrears or any other monies owed be paid off within a 'reasonable period' or even by the end of the original contractual loan period. The court is given absolute discretion.

35.43   The court's power under Consumer Credit Act 1974 s129(2)(a) enables it to order payment by instalments of 'any sum owed', ie, already owed. Only in the cases of hire-purchase and conditional sale agreements may the courts deal with sums which fall due for payment in the future.[54]

35.44   In mortgage cases, this seemed to rule out the rescheduling of anything other than the total of instalments missed by the date of the hearing. However, many legal charges provide that as soon as default occurs then the whole loan becomes immediately payable. Alternatively, in cases where the whole loan does not automatically become due on default, lenders may have 'called-in' the loan before issuing proceedings. In other words, demand by letter for immediate payment of the outstanding loan may have been made in pursuance of rights given to the lender in the legal charge. This calling-in letter is distinct from the statutory default notice.

35.45   Allied to the time order provisions, is the related but distinct power to impose conditions or to suspend operation of an order. Section 135 of the 1974 Act provides:

(1) If it considers it just to do so, the court may in an order made by it in relation to a regulated agreement include provisions –
(a) making the operation of any term of the order conditional on the doing of specified acts by any party to the proceedings;
(b) suspending the operation of any term of the order either –
(i) until such time as the court subsequently directs, or
(ii) until the occurrence of a specified act or omission.

35.46   This subsection empowers the court to suspend any order for possession it may make, whether conditionally on payment of specified

---

54   Ibid s130(2).

instalments by the borrower or until a particular event (for example, default in an instalment order, or the date the property is sold or the borrower rehoused by a local authority). Where a court finds it appropriate to make a time order, the enforcement of any order for possession granted can be suspended so long as payment of the instalments under the time order is made.

35.47 It is specifically stated that any person, 'affected by a time order'[55] or 'affected by a provision'[56] included in an order under Consumer Credit Act 1974 s135, may apply to the court for a variation or revocation in the case of a time order or a variation in the case of a section 135 order. These are particularly useful provisions as they allow a lender to make application to the court for a variation of the terms of a time order where, for example, a time order has been granted on favourable terms to allow the borrower to overcome temporary difficulties. In this way it can be argued that the lender would not be prejudiced by the granting of a time order on terms generous to the borrower, as the lender would be able to come back to court to have those terms varied.

35.48 Finally, Consumer Credit Act 1974 contains a rather cryptic provision in section 136 under the heading of 'Power to vary agreements and securities'. The section reads:

> The court may in an order made by it under this Act include such provision as it considers just for amending any agreement or security in consequence of a term of the order.

35.49 For some years it was not clear as to how the time order provisions were to be construed. However, in *Southern & District Finance plc v Barnes*[57] the Court of Appeal (in hearing three linked appeals and in reviewing conflicting county court decisions) gave general guidance on the time order provisions as follows. When a time order is applied for, the court must first consider whether it is just to make it. This involves consideration of all of the circumstances of the case including the position of the lender as well as that of the borrower. When a time order is made it should normally only be made for a stipulated period on account of temporary financial difficulty. The court must consider what instalments would be reasonable, both in amount and their timing, having regard to the borrower's means. If, despite being

---

55 Ibid s130(6).

56 Ibid s135(4).

57 (1995) 27 HLR 691; [1995] Con Cred LR 62, CA. See also A Dunn, 'Footprints on the sands of time: Sections 129 and 136 Consumer Credit Act 1974' [1996] Conv 209 and R Rosenberg, 'Calling Time' *Quarterly Account* Issue 63 p11.

given more time, the borrower will be unable to resume payment of the total indebtedness by at least the amount of the contractual instalments, no time order should be made. In such circumstances it is more equitable to allow the regulated agreement to be enforced. When a time order is made following financial default, the 'sum owed' means every sum which is due and owing; in the context of possession proceedings, that usually comprises the total indebtedness. The court may vary the contractual interest rate under Consumer Credit Act 1974 s136. Where a time order is made governing the whole of the outstanding balance due under the loan, there will be consequences for the term of the loan, the rate of interest or both. If justice requires the making of a time order the court should suspend any possession order so long as the terms of the time order are complied with.

35.50   Some further guidance can be gleaned from the judgments. Once it is accepted that it is just to make a time order, it appears to be legitimate to assess what the borrower can afford in the temporary period of relief which he or she is being given and to fix this as the rate of payment due to the lender. Variation of the interest rate to give efficacy to this rate of payment is permissible. It is worth noting that the Court of Appeal in this case expressly approved the approach of one circuit judge who reduced the interest rate under the loan agreement to nil and ordered the total indebtedness to be repaid over a period exceeding the original contractual term. In *Director General of Fair Trading v First National Bank plc*[58] the circuit judge's approach was approved. However, it was also observed that 'time orders extending over long periods of time are usually better avoided'.

35.51   It is important to recognise that the time order provisions are distinct from the 'extortionate credit bargain' or the 'unfair relationship' provisions contained in Consumer Credit Act 1974 ss 137 to 140 and 140A to 140C. The new 'unfair relationship' provisions will replace the 'extortionate credit bargain' provisions in sections 137 to 140 and apply to agreements entered into after the relevant commencement date prescribed in the Consumer Credit Act 2006. They will also apply to agreements already entered into which continue in existance beyond 12 months from the commencement date.[59] It is possible for the 'extortionate credit bargain' provisions or the 'unfair relationship' provisions to be used in addition to an application for a time order in the same proceedings or independently from a time order application.

---

58 [2001] UKHL 52; [2002] 1 AC 481; [2001] 3 WLR 1297, HL.
59 Consumer Credit Act 2006 s69 and Sch 3 para 14

35.52   It is sensible to emphasise to district judges hearing possession actions relating to regulated agreements that they have powers which are distinct from and much wider than those under the Administration of Justice Acts with which they are more familiar. In particular, the absence of any requirement to clear arrears within the 'reasonable period' should be stressed. It is important to reflect on the fact that loans taken out for the initial purchase of a property (which is the case with the majority of first mortgages) have been seen by parliament to warrant different treatment from loans taken out for consumer purposes which happen to be secured on a borrower's home.

Extortionate credit bargains

35.53   The extortionate credit bargain provisions of the Consumer Credit Act 1974, as originally enacted, will be replaced by the 'unfair relationship' provisions of the Consumer Credit Act 2006 once implemented. At the time of going to print, the date for this was not certain although it was anticipated that it would be in April 2007.

35.54   The provisions of Consumer Credit Act 1974 at sections 137 to 140 give the courts powers to go far beyond the fairly limited options available under sections 129 to 136 to give a borrower time to remedy financial default. The extortionate credit bargain provisions enable the court, in appropriate cases, in effect to rewrite the agreement between lender and borrower. Consumer Credit Act 1974 s137(1) provides:

> If the court finds a credit bargain extortionate it may reopen the credit agreement so as to do justice between the parties.

35.55   The expression 'credit agreement' is defined as meaning 'any agreement ... between an individual (the "debtor") and any other person (the "creditor") by which the creditor provides the debtor with credit of any amount', and 'credit bargain' as being (i) the credit agreement or (ii) where one or more other transactions are to be taken into account in computing the total charge for credit the credit agreement and those other transaction, taken together (section 137(2)).

35.56   Consumer Credit Act 1974 s138 provides:

> (1) A credit bargain is extortionate if it –
>   (a) requires the debtor or a relative of his to make payments ... which are grossly exorbitant, or
>   (b) otherwise grossly contravenes ordinary principles of fair dealing.

(2) In determining whether a credit bargain is extortionate, regard shall be had to such evidence as is adduced concerning –
    (a) interest rates prevailing at the time it is made,
    (b) the factors mentioned in subsections (3) to (5), and
    (c) any other relevant considerations.
(3) Factors applicable under subsection (2) in relation to the debtor include –
    (a) his age, experience, business capacity and state of health; and
    (b) the degree to which, at the time of making the credit bargain, he was under financial pressure, and the nature of that pressure.
(4) Factors applicable under subsection (2) in relation to the creditor include –
    (a) the degree of risk accepted by him, having regard to the value of any security provided;
    (b) his relationship to the debtor; and
    (c) ...

35.57 It is noteworthy that these provisions expressly are *not* limited to loans which fall within the financial limit of the 1974 Act and can apply to loans of any amount. The power of the court is not limited to an examination of the terms of the credit agreement itself. The court is required to consider whether the credit bargain as a whole is extortionate. Although, in terms, Consumer Credit Act 1974 s137 only enables the credit agreement (not bargain) to be reopened, section 139(2)(b) (see below) enables the court to relieve the debtor or any surety of any obligation imposed by the credit bargain or indeed 'any related agreement'.

35.58 Under Consumer Credit Act 1974 s138, the court must look at the interest rates prevailing at the time the bargain was entered into. The comparison must be like with like and it is inappropriate to consider general market rates in the case of a loan where only a fringe lender would have lent money.[60] While the interest rate charged is of importance, the legislation does require the court to consider various subjective factors in carrying out its assessment. There is no express requirement that the lender should have had knowledge of these subjective factors although there is some suggestion that there is a requirement that the lender must have taken advantage of the borrower.[61]

35.59 Lenders, with some justification, seek to emphasise the fact that in considering both the level of payments required and business conduct the statute requires the court to be satisfied that the payments

---

60 *A Ketley Ltd v Scott* [1980] Con Cred LR 37.
61 *Davies v Directloans Ltd* [1986] 1 WLR 823.

required are grossly exorbitant or that the bargain grossly contravenes ordinary principles of fair dealing before intervening. There is little authority on the interpretation of the word 'grossly' in this context. It has been held that sums are not 'grossly exorbitant' merely because they are in excess of what the court would consider 'fair due and reasonable' under Consumer Credit Act 1974 s139(2).[62]

35.60   An excessive rate of interest may, of itself, be sufficient to render the payments grossly exorbitant.[63] A rate of interest which may be legitimate for an unsecured loan may be exorbitant for an advance which is fully secured.[64] In considering the degree of risk that the loan poses for the lender 'it is not what the real risk is, ascertained after the event, which has to be looked at, but how the matter would present itself to the lender at the time of the loan ...'.[65]

35.61   Even if the amounts payable are in all respects legitimate there may be other features of the transaction which grossly contravene principles of fair dealing either taken with objectively high rates of payment or taken on their own. The mere fact that the transaction is unwise or improvident on the debtor's part does not render the bargain extortionate.[66] When considering 'ordinary principles of fair dealing' advisers also need to look at 'Guidelines of the Office of Fair Trading: Guidelines for lenders and brokers' published by the Director General of Fair Trading, as these comment on practices relating to 'secured lending to non-status borrowers'.[67] For a comprehensive source for cases in this area see Goode, Consumer Credit Reports.[68]

35.62   Consumer Credit Act 1974 s139(1) provides:

A credit agreement may, if the court thinks just, be reopened on the ground that the credit bargain is extortionate –
(a) on an application for the purpose made by the debtor or any surety to the High Court, county court or sheriff court; or
(b) at the instance of the debtor or surety in any proceedings to which the debtor and creditor are parties, being proceedings to enforce the credit agreement, any security relating to it ...

62 *First National Securities Ltd v Bertrand* [1980] Con Cred LR 5.
63 *Samual v Newbold* [1906] AC 461.
64 *Verner-Jeffreys v Pinto* [1929] 1 Ch 401.
65 *Carringtons Ltd v Smith* [1906] 1 KB 79.
66 *Wills v Wood* (1984) Con Cred LR 7, CA.
67 Revised November 1997.
68 Published in three volumes by Butterworths. See also the helpful summary of cases at R Rosenberg, 'When is an Agreement Extortionate?' *Quarterly Account* 54 Winter 1999/2000 p11. See also *Grangewood Securities v Ellis* (2000) 9 November, Milton Keynes County Court noted at *Quarterly Account* Issue 59 p21.

(c) at the instance of the debtor or surety in other proceedings in any court where the amount paid or payable under the credit agreement is relevant.

Section 139(2) provides:

In reopening the agreement, the court may, for the purpose of relieving the debtor or surety from payment of any sum in excess of that fairly due and reasonable, by order –
(a) direct accounts to be taken ... between any persons,
(b) set aside the whole or part of any obligation imposed on the debtor or a surety by the credit bargain or any related agreement,
(c) require the creditor to repay the whole or part of any sum paid under the credit bargain or any related agreement by the debtor or a surety, whether paid to the creditor or any other person,
(d) direct the return to the surety of any property provided for the purposes of the security, or
(e) alter the terms of the credit agreement or any security instrument.

35.63   It can been seen that the court is given almost limitless powers to adjust the legal relationships between the debtor, his or her creditor and any surety. However, Consumer Credit Act 1974 s139(4) restricts this by providing that 'an order under subsection (2) shall not alter the effect of any judgment'. Advisers therefore need to be alive to the possibility of any application to set aside any earlier judgment. That application will be made under CPR 39.3, and advisers must be conscious of the need to act promptly, to have a good reason for not attending the trial, and to have a good prospect of success at trial. Advisers also need to consider the nature of the judgment obtained. A possession order obtained by a lender does not prevent a borrower who has remained in possession from subsequently applying for relief from future liability to make payments under the credit bargain.[69]

35.64   It has been assumed that the court has the jurisdiction to reopen a loan agreement even after the loan had been repaid.[70] The relevant limitation period within which a borrower must make application to have the transaction reopened is 12 years from the date the bargain was entered into although it seems that the period for the reclaiming of payments made is six years.[71]

35.65   Consumer Credit Act 1974 s171(7) provides:

If, in proceedings referred to in section 139(1), the debtor or any surety alleges that the credit bargain is extortionate it is for the creditor to prove the contrary.

---

69 *Rahman v Sterling Credit Ltd* [2001] 1 WLR 496, CA.
70 *Davies v Directloans Ltd* [1986] 1 WLR 823.
71 See *Rahman v Sterling Credit* [2001] 1 WLR 496, CA.

35.66 However, commentators have suggested that there is an 'evidential burden' on the borrower to adduce sufficient evidence properly to raise the issue. A mere assertion that the bargain is extortionate is insufficient. Once this is raised, it is for the lender to discharge the legal or 'persuasive' burden of proof to satisfy the court on the balance of probabilities that the bargain is not extortionate. In one case it was held that the burden on the lender is 'sufficiently discharged by showing that the bargain was on its face a proper and not an extortionate commercial bargain and that the [lender] acted in a way that an ordinary commercial lender would be expected to act'.[72]

35.67 Advisers must be concerned to identify whether there has been any deceit or non-disclosure of relevant facts by the borrower when the loan was taken out, as this may be fatal to any application for reopening the credit bargain.[73]

Unfair relationships

35.68 The Consumer Credit Act 2006 revokes the 'extortionate credit bargain provisions' contained in ss139 to 140 of the Consumer Credit Act 1974 and once implemented will replace them with a new power in the court to interfere with the lender-borrower relationship where it is assessed as being 'unfair'. Consumer Credit Act 2006 s19 introduces a new section 140A into the 1974 Act:

140A *Unfair relationships between creditors and debtors*
(1) The court may make an order under section 140B in connection with a credit agreement if it determines that the relationship between the creditor and the debtor arising out of the agreement (or the agreement taken with any related agreement) is unfair to the debtor because of one or more of the following –
(a) any of the terms of the agreement or of any related agreement;
(b) the way in which the creditor has exercised or enforced any of his rights under the agreement or any related agreement;
(c) any other thing done (or not done) by, or on behalf of, the creditor (either before or after the making of the agreement or any related agreement).
(2) In deciding whether to make a determination under this section the court shall have regard to all matters it thinks relevant (including matters relating to the creditor and matters relating to the debtor).

---

72 *Coldunell Ltd v Gallon* [1986] 1 QB 1184, CA.
73 *First National Securities Ltd v Bertrand* [1980] CCLR 5 and *Premier Finance Co v Gravesande* [1985] Con Cred LR 1.

(3) For the purposes of this section the court shall (except to the extent that it is not appropriate to do so) treat anything done (or not done) by, or on behalf of, or in relation to, an associate or former associate of the creditor as if done (or not done) by, or on behalf of, or in relation to, the creditor.

(4) A determination may be made under this section in relation to a relationship notwithstanding that the relationship may have ended.

(5) An order under section 140B shall not be made in connection with a credit agreement which is an exempt agreement by virtue of section 16(6C).

35.69   Section 16(6C) exempts regulated mortgage contracts (see para 35.87) from the provisions of the Consumer Credit Act 1974.[74]

35.70   However, even 'exempt agreements' within the meaning of the Consumer Credit Act 1974 s16 fall within scope of the 'unfair relationship' provisions.[75]

140B   *Powers of court in relation to unfair relationships*

(1) An order under this section in connection with a credit agreement may do one or more of the following –

(a) require the creditor, or any associate or former associate of his, to repay (in whole or in part) any sum paid by the debtor or by a surety by virtue of the agreement or any related agreement (whether paid to the creditor, the associate or the former associate or to any other person);

(b) require the creditor, or any associate or former associate of his, to do or not to do (or to cease doing) anything specified in the order in connection with the agreement or any related agreement;

(c) reduce or discharge any sum payable by the debtor or by a surety by virtue of the agreement or any related agreement;

(d) direct the return to a surety of any property provided by him for the purposes of a security;

(e) otherwise set aside (in whole or in part) any duty imposed on the debtor or on a surety by virtue of the agreement or any related agreement;

(f) alter the terms of the agreement or of any related agreement;

(g) direct accounts to be taken, or (in Scotland) an accounting to be made, between any persons.

(2) An order under this section may be made in connection with a credit agreement only –

---

74 Financial Services and Markets Act 2000 (Regulated Activities) Order 2001 SI No 544 reg 90.

75 Consumer Credit Act 1974 s16 (7A) inserted by Consumer Credit Act 2006 s22(2).

> (a) on an application made by the debtor or by a surety;
> (b) at the instance of the debtor or a surety in any proceedings in any court to which the debtor and the creditor are parties, being proceedings to enforce the agreement or any related agreement; or
> (c) at the instance of the debtor or a surety in any other proceedings in any court where the amount paid or payable under the agreement is relevant.
>
> (3) An order under this section may be made notwithstanding that its effect is to place on the creditor, or any associate or former associate of his, a burden in respect of an advantage enjoyed by another person ...

35.71 If the debtor or surety alleges that the relationship is unfair it is for the lender to prove to the contrary.[76] The Act also entitles a party to any proceedings mentioned in section 140B(2) to have any person who might be the subject of an order under section 140B made a party to the proceedings.[77] An application by the borrower or surety under section 140B(2)(a) may only be made in the county court.[78]

35.72 The unfair relationship provisions have been deliberately drafted in a way which gives the county court considerable discretion and it remains to be seen how the courts will develop the jurisprudence.

Unfair contract terms

35.73 The Unfair Terms in Consumer Contracts Regulations 1994[79] and 1999[80] can in some ways be seen as complementing the powers available to the court under the 'extortionate credit bargain' provisions and the 'unfair relationship' provisions of the Consumer Credit Acts 1974 and 2006. The regulations are made pursuant to the European Communities Act 1972 and were introduced in order to comply with EC Directive 93/13. The purpose of the Directive was 'to approximate the laws, regulations and administrative provisions of the Member States relating to unfair terms in contracts concluded between a seller or supplier and a consumer'. The 1994 Regulations were implemented

---

76 Ibid s140B(9)
77 Ibid s140B(8).
78 Ibid s140B(2), (4).
79 SI No 3159.
80 SI No 2083. See J Holbrook, 'Unfair Terms in Housing Contracts' September 1999 *Legal Action* 26.

with effect from 1 July 1995. The 1999 Regulations revoked the 1994 Regulations with effect from 1 October 1999. It appears that the 1994 Regulations were not retrospective and apply to consumer contracts concluded between 1 July 1995 and 30 September 1999.[81] The 1999 Regulations apply to consumer contracts concluded on or after 1 October 1999.

35.74   The 1994 Regulations applied to consumer contracts where 'either a good or a service is provided'. While there was a question mark as to whether they applied to mortgages, given that there must be some doubt as to whether the lender had provided 'a good or service', the argument that the financial services element within mortgages brought them within the 1994 Regulations has generally been accepted.[82] Regulation 4 of the 1999 Regulations is broader in scope and applies the regulations 'in relation to unfair terms in contracts concluded between a seller or supplier and a consumer'. However, the regulations do not apply if the contractual term reflects a mandatory statutory or regulatory provision. The term 'consumer' is defined as meaning 'any natural person who, in contracts covered by these Regulations, is acting for purposes which are outside his trade, business or profession'.[83]

35.75   Regulation 5(1) of the 1999 Regulations provides: 'A contractual term which has not been individually negotiated shall be regarded as unfair if, contrary to the requirements of good faith, it causes a significant imbalance in the parties' rights and obligations arising under the contract, to the detriment of the consumer.' The criteria by which the assessment as to 'good faith' is to be made is not defined in the 1999 Regulations although it was in 1994 Regulations Sch 2. This provided that 'regard shall be had in particular to: (a) the strength of the bargaining positions of the parties; (b) whether the consumer had an inducement to agree to the term; (c) whether the goods or services were sold or supplied to the special order of the consumer; and (d) the extent to which the seller or supplier has dealt fairly and equitably with the consumer.' Given that these matters are contained in the preamble to the Directive they must remain a good aid to construction.

35.76   Unfair Terms in Consumer Contracts Regulations 1999 reg 5(2) states '[a] term shall always be regarded as not having been indi-

---

81   See *Paragon Finance plc v Nash & Staunton* [2001] EWCA Civ 1466; [2002] 1 WLR 685.

82   See *Falco Finance Ltd v Gough* [1999] CCLR 16. See also S Bright and C Bright, 'Unfair Terms in Land Contracts: Copy Out or Cop Out' (1995) 111 LQR 655.

83   Unfair Terms in Consumer Contracts Regulations 1999 reg 3.

vidually negotiated where it has been drafted in advance and the consumer has therefore not been able to influence the substance of the term'. Regulation 8 provides that 'an unfair term in a contract concluded with a consumer by a seller or supplier shall not be binding on the consumer' and goes on to say that '[t]he contract shall continue to bind the parties if it is capable of continuing in existence without the unfair term'.

35.77 Schedule 2 to the 1999 Regulations contains 'an indicative and non-exhaustive list of terms which may be regarded as unfair'. In the context of mortgage lending the following are worthy of note:

> Terms which have the object or effect of ...
>
> (e) requiring any consumer who fails to fulfil his obligation to pay a disproportionately high sum in compensation;
>
> ...
>
> (i) irrevocably binding the consumer to terms with which he had no real opportunity of becoming acquainted before the conclusion of the contract;
> (j) enabling the seller or supplier to alter the terms of the contract unilaterally without a valid reason which is specified in the contract
>
> ...

Schedule 2 to the 1999 Regulations does qualify this latter term so as to allow a supplier of financial services to 'alter the rate of interest payable by the consumer or due to the [supplier], or the amount of other charges for financial services without notice where there is a valid reason, provided that the supplier is required to inform the other contracting party or parties thereof at the earliest opportunity and that the latter are free to dissolve the contract immediately'.

35.78 Apart from providing that an unfair term is not binding on a borrower, the regulations also enable the Director General of Fair Trading to seek an injunction against anyone using or recommending the use of unfair terms.[84]

35.79 These regulations, particularly in relation to secured loans from secondary lenders, have not perhaps been considered enough by advisers and it is hoped that we will see greater development in this area. Provisions which have been found unfair by the courts include dual interest rates where a concessionary rate is lost, computation of interest on a flat-rate basis over the term of a loan irrespective of the amounts paid off the capital, and the calculation of a redemption

---

84 Ibid reg 12. See *Director General of Fair Trading v First National Bank plc* [2001] UKHL 52; [2002] 1 AC 481; [2001] 3 WLR 1297, HL.

figure by applying the Rule of 78[85] and the provision of a deferred settlement date of six months.[86]

35.80 Unfair Terms in Consumer Contracts Regulations apart, whilst a lender has considerable discretion as to the rate of interest charged in relation to a loan, the mortgage agreement is subject to an implied term that this discretion will not be exercised for an improper purpose, dishonestly, capriciously, arbitrarily or so unreasonably that no lender would have acted in that way.[87] The FSA 'Fairness of Terms in Consumer Contracts – Statement of Good Practice'[88] issued in May 2005 also provides useful commentary on fairness in the context of a lender's unilateral right to vary interest rates.

35.81 On 24 February 2005 the Law Commission issued its report Unfair Terms in Contracts (Law Com No 298) which proposes reform of the law in this area.[89]

Regulation of mortgage lending by the Financial Services Authority

35.82 The Financial Services Authority ('FSA') was set up by the Government under the Financial Services and Markets Act 2000 to regulate the activities of persons involved in financial services in the UK. In January 2000 it was announced that the FSA would be responsible for mortgage regulation and in 2001 this was extended to cover those advising and arranging mortgages as well as the conduct of lenders. The regime set up by the FSA for the regulation of residential mortgages came into effect on 31 October 2004.[90] The Financial Services and Markets Act 2000 also set up the Financial Ombudsman Ser-

---

85 Consumer Credit Act 1974 s95 and Consumer Credit (Rebate on Early Settlement) Regulations 1983 SI No 1562 provide for a statutory rebate in cases where a regulated agreement is repaid before the end of the contract period. With effect 31 May 2005 the 'Rule of 78' was replaced by the formula set out in the Consumer Credit (Early Settlement) Regulations 2004 SI No 1483. See also R Rosenberg, 'Good-Bye to Rule of 78' *Quarterly Account* Issue 76 p4.

86 See *Falco Finance Ltd v Gough* April 1999 *Legal Action* 13, cf, *Kindlance Ltd v Murphy* (1997) unreported, No 625, High Court Northern Ireland. S Bright, 'Attacking Unfair Mortgage Terms' [1999] Conv 360.

87 See note 81.

88 See www.fsa.gov.uk.

89 See www.lawcom.gov.uk.

90 Mortgages: Conduct of Business Sourcebook (Amendment) Instrument 2004 and Financial Srvices and Markets Act ('FSMA') 2000 ss138, 145, 156 and 159(1).

vice[91] ('FOS') for the resolution of some types of dispute 'quickly and with a minimum of formality'.[92]

35.83 The regulatory role of the FSA and the FOS is not a simple alternative to the use of the courts and advisers will need to have regard to the statutory regimes of the Administration of Justice Acts 1970 and 1973 which set out the courts powers in relation to possession claims by lenders. The authority of the FSA and the power of the FOS may, however, be an important adjunct when seeking to influence the way that a mortgage lender is responding to a borrower whose loan falls within the scope of the 2000 Act.

35.84 Financial Services and Markets Act 2000 ss19 and 22 impose a 'general prohibition' on any person carrying on an activity regulated by the Act without appropriate authorisation from the FSA. An activity is a 'regulated activity' within the meaning of the 2000 Act if it is carried on by way of a business and if it is a 'specified' activity.

35.85 The Financial Services and Markets Act (Regulated Activities) Order 2001[93] Chapter XV deals with 'Regulated Mortgage Contracts'.

35.86 Entering into a 'regulated mortgage contract' as a lender is a 'specified' activity.[94] 'Administrating' a regulated mortgage contract is also a specified kind of activity.[95]

35.87 A 'regulated mortgage contract' means a contract under which –

(i) a person ('the lender') provides credit to an individual or to trustees ('the borrower'); and
(ii) the obligation of the borrower to repay is secured by a first legal mortgage on land (other than timeshare accommodation in the United Kingdom, at least 40 per cent of which is to be used, or is intended to be used, as or in connection with a dwelling by the borrower or (in the case of credit provided to trustees) by an individual who is a beneficiary of the trust, or a related person.[96]

35.88 'Administrating' a regulated mortgage contract means 'either or both of –

(i) notifying the borrower of changes in interest rates or payments due under the contract, or of other matters of which the contract requires him to be notified; and

---

91 FSMA 2000 Part XVI.
92 FSMA 2000 s225
93 SI 2001 No 544.
94 Reg 61(1).
95 Reg 61 (2).
96 Reg 61(3)(a).

(ii) taking any necessary steps for the purposes of collecting or recovering payments due under the contract from the borrower;

but a person is not treated as administering a regulated mortgage contract merely because he has, or exercises, a right to take action for the purposes of enforcing the contract (or to require that such action is or is not taken).'[97] 'Credit' includes a cash loan and any other form of financial accommodation.[98]

35.89   In terms of the requirement that the borrower must use or intend to use at least 40 per cent of the property '... the area of any land which comprises a building or other structure containing two or more storeys is to be taken to be the aggregate of the floor area of each of those storeys'.[99] A 'related person' is defined as being the borrower or beneficiary's spouse or civil partner or 'a person (whether or not of the opposite sex) whose relationship with that person has the characteristics of the relationship between husband and wife' or the borrower or beneficiary's parent, brother, sister, child, grandparent or grandchild.[100]

35.90   It follows that loans secured on commercial properties, 'buy to let' mortgages, loans to limited companies and second mortgages are outside scope of regulation by the 2000 Act. A regulated mortgage contract which would otherwise fall within the scope of Consumer Credit Act 1974 is an 'exempt agreement' for the purposes of the 1974 Act and as such outside the provisions of that legislation save for the requirement that the mortgage is enforceable only following court order.[101]

35.91   Part III of the 2000 Act sets up a requirement for persons engaged in mortgage lending activities to be authorised by the FSA. Part V enables the FSA to regulate the performance of authorised persons. An agreement entered into in relation to a regulated activity by a person when not authorised is unenforceable by that person and any money paid or property transferred to that person is recoverable.[102]

35.92   The FSA is charged with regulatory control of a myriad of different financial services and has issued a 'Handbook' which contains over 30 'sourcebooks' setting out the rules governing regulated persons in different fields. If a lender fails to comply with the rules it

97 Reg 61(3)(b).
98 Reg 61 (3)(c).
99 Reg 61(4)(b).
100 Reg 61(4)(c).
101 Reg 90(2).
102 FSMA 2000 s26.

runs the risk of regulatory and disciplinary action by the FSA. A borrower who can show that s/he has suffered loss as a result of a contravention of a rule may sue the authorised person for damages.[103] However such a contravention does not render the transaction void or unenforceable.[104] In the Handbook, *Rules* issued by the FSA are identified by a suffix 'R' to a particular paragraph. *Guidance* issued by the FSA is identified by a suffix 'G'. Guidance is generally designed to throw light on a particular aspect of regulatory requirement but is not of itself binding. The Handbook also contains commentary which identifies evidential provisions which tend to show compliance with a particular rule. These paragraphs contain suffix 'E'.[105] The 'Mortgage: Conduct of Business sourcebook'[106] ('MCOB') was issued in its final form in October 2003 and came into effect on 31 October 2004[107] affecting mortgages entered into on or after that date. It governs the relationships between the lender and borrower including any intermediaries. It consists of 13 chapters governing every facet of the life of a mortgage. Chapter 13 of MCOB deals with arrears and repossession.

The Mortgage Conduct of Business Rules (MCOB)

35.93 The Rules cover all aspects of the mortgage lender/borrower relationship effectively from the cradle to the grave and, indeed, beyond, as they also regulate mortgage shortfalls. Advisers would do well to create a link to the Handbook on their computer as a 'favourite' for easy access. The most relevant Chapters in relation to mortgage repossession cases are Chapter 11, which deals with 'Responsible Lending', Chapter 12 on 'Charges' and more importantly Chapter 13, which deals with 'Arrears and Repossessions'.

35.94 In relation to 'responsible lending', MCOB 11.3.1 R requires a lender to 'be able to show that before deciding to enter into a regulated mortgage contract with a customer or, on making a further advance on a regulated mortgage contract, account was taken of a customer's

---

103 FSMA 2000 s150(1).

104 FSMA 2000 s151(2).

105 See generally 'Reader's Guide: an introduction to the FSA Handbook', chapter 6: status of provisions, July 2005.

106 www.fsahandbook.info/FSA/html/handbook/MCOB.

107 *Mortgages: Conduct of Business Sourcebook Instrument 2003* issued by FSA under FSMA 2000 s153(2).

ability to pay'. Furthermore a lender 'must make an adequate record that it has taken account of the customer's ability to pay for each regulated contract that it enters into and each further advance is that it provides on a regulated contract. The record must be retained for a year from the date at which the regulated mortgage contract is entered into or the further advance provided.' Particular guidance is given in relation to cases involving self-certification of income in MCOB 11.3.2 R.

35.95   MCOB 11.3.4 R deals in more detail with the requirements for a 'responsible lending policy'. A lender must put in place, and operate in accordance with, a written policy setting out the factors it will take into account in assessing a customer's ability to pay. Further, more detailed guidance is given in MCOB 11.3.5 G to 11.3.8 G as to the evidence needed to satisfy a lender that the borrower has the ability to repay the loan being sought. The lender should take account of a prospective borrower's actual or reasonably anticipated income or both when deciding whether to enter into the loan. The lender should consider whether the borrower will still be able to meet the payments at the end of any initial discounted repayment period and whether the borrower can service the debt payments due on any associated repayment vehicle such as an endowment policy.

35.96   MCOB 12 seeks to regulate 'early repayment charges', 'arrears charges' and 'excessive charges'. Guidance at 12.2.1 G reaffirms earlier obligations in MCOB as to appropriate disclosure at pre-application stage, at offer stage and general product disclosure to make charges transparent to customers. Chapter 12.2.1 is expressly intended to reinforce 'these requirements by preventing a [lender] from imposing unfair and excessive charges'.

35.97   MCOB 12.3.1 R deals with 'early repayment charges'. It requires a lender to 'ensure that any regulated mortgage contract that it enters into does not impose, and cannot be used to impose, an early repayment charge other than one that is (1) able to be expressed as a cash value and (2) a reasonable pre-estimate of the costs as a result of the customer repaying the amount due under the regulated mortgage contract before the contract has terminated'.

35.98   MCOB 12.4.1 R regulates 'arrears charges'. A lender 'must ensure that any regulated mortgage contract that it enters into does not impose, and cannot be used to impose, a charge for arrears on a customer except where that charge is a reasonable estimate of the cost of additional administration required as a result of the customer being in arrears'. However this would not prevent a mortgage term under which a defaulting borrower may be transferred from a fixed or discounted interest rate to some other generally applicable standard variable interest rate.[108]

35.99   MCOB 12.5.1 R requires a lender 'to ensure that any regulated mortgage contract that it enters into does not impose, and cannot be used to impose, excessive charges upon a customer'. The concept of 'excessive charge' is not further defined.

35.100   MCOB 13 deals with 'Arrears and Repossessions'. The chapter seeks to control both the administration of a regulated mortgage contract during its lifetime and also the recovery of any mortgage shortfall debt after repossession and sale.

MCOB 13.1 'Dealing fairly with customers in arrears: policy and procedures'

35.101 A lender is obliged to 'deal fairly with any customer who (a) is in arrears on a regulated mortgage contract; or (b) has a mortgage shortfall debt'.[109] A lender must also 'put in place, and operate in accordance with, a written policy (agreed by its governing body) and procedures for complying with [its duty to deal fairly]'.[110] Guidance provides that:

(1) A [lender] should ensure that its written policy and procedures include:
   (a) using reasonable efforts to reach an agreement with a customer over the method of repaying any payment shortfall or mortgage shortfall debt, in the case of the former having regard to the desirability of agreeing with the customer an alternative to taking possession of the property;
   (b) liaising, if the customer makes arrangements for this, with a third party source of advice regarding the payment shortfall or mortgage shortfall debt;
   (c) adopting a reasonable approach to the time over which the payment shortfall or mortgage shortfall debt should be repaid, having regard to the need to establish, where feasible, a payment plan which is practical in terms of the circumstances of the customer;
   (d) granting, unless it has good reason not to do so, a customer's request for a change to:
      (i) the date on which the payment is due (providing it is within the same payment period); or
      (ii) the method by which payment is made;
      and giving the customer a written explanation of its reasons if it refuses the request;

---

108 MCOB 12.4.1 R(2).
109 MCOB 13.3.1R (1).
110 MCOB 13.3.1 R (2).

(e) giving consideration, where no reasonable payment arrangement can be made, to the customer being allowed to remain in possession to effect a sale; and

(f) repossessing the property only where all other reasonable attempts to resolve the position have failed.[111]

35.102 Expressly, MCOB states that contravention of these procedures may be relied on as tending to show contravention of the obligation to operate in accordance with the duty to deal fairly.[112] This would therefore permit ultimately for a complaint to be made to the FOS. The duty to have an adopted policy to deal with arrears and mortgage shortfall debts 'does not oblige a [lender] to provide customers with a copy of the written policy and procedures. Nor, however, does it prevent a [lender] from providing customers with either these documents or a more customer-orientated version'.[113]

35.103 In relation to a lender's obligation, to try to reach an agreement with a borrower over repayment of arrears, lenders are advised that 'customers:

(1) should be given a reasonable period of time to consider any proposals for payment that are put to them; in addition, and depending on the individual's circumstances, a [lender] may wish to do one or more of the following with the agreement of the customer:
(a) extend the term of the regulated mortgage contract; or
(b) change the type of the regulated mortgage contract; or
(c) defer payment of interest due on the regulated mortgage contract or mortgage shortfall debt; or
(d) treat the payment shortfall as if it was part of the original amount borrowed;
(2) should be given adequate information to understand the implications of any proposed arrangement; ...[114]

35.104 In terms of the requirement to adopt a reasonable approach as to the length of time a borrower should be given to clear arrears, MCOB guidance provides:

... The FSA takes the view that the determination of a reasonable repayment period will depend upon the individual circumstances. In appropriate cases this will mean that repayments are arranged over the remaining term of the regulated mortgage contract.[115]

---

111 MCOB 13.3.2 E.
112 MCOB 13.3.2 E (2).
113 MCOB 13.3.3 G.
114 MCOB 13.3.4 G.
115 MCOB 13.3.6 G.

Lenders are advised that if they intend to outsource aspects of customer relationships (including debt collection) the FSA will continue to hold them responsible for the way in which this work is carried on.[116]

MCOB 13.3. 'Record keeping: arrears and repossessions'

35.105 A lender who is also involved in the administration of a regulated mortgage contract is obliged to make and retain an adequate record of its dealings with borrowers in arrears (or who have a mortgage shortfall debt) to enable it to show that it has complied with the obligations imposed by MCOB Chapter 13. A lender is required to retain a record for one year from the date on which the relevant payment shortfall or mortgage shortfall debt was cleared.[117]

> The record should contain, or provide reference to, matters such as:
> (1) the date of first communication with the customer after the account was identified as being in arrears;
> (2) in relation to correspondence issued to a customer in arrears, the name and contact number of the employee dealing with that correspondence, where known;
> (3) ... [*This paragraph deals with business mortgages*]
> (4) information relating to any new payment arrangements proposed;
> (5) the date of issue of any legal documents;
> (6) the arrangements made for the sale after the repossession (whether legal or voluntary); and
> (7) the date of any communication summarising the customer's outstanding debt after sale of the repossessed property.[118]

MCOB 13.4.1 R 'Arrears: provision of information to the customer'

35.106 A lender is required to provide a comprehensive package of information to a borrower in arrears.

> If a customer falls into arrears on a regulated mortgage contract, a [lender] must as soon as possible, and in any event within 15 business days of becoming aware of that fact, provide the customer with the following in a durable medium:
> (1) the current FSA information sheet on mortgage arrears;
> (2) a list of the due payments either missed or only paid in part;

---

116 MCOB 13.3.8 G.
117 MCOB 13.3.9 R.
118 MCOB 13.3.10 G.

(3) the total sum of the payment shortfall;

(4) the charges incurred as a result of the payment shortfall;

(5) the total outstanding debt, excluding charges that may be added on redemption; and

(6) an indication of the nature (and where possible the level) of charges the customer is likely to incur unless the payment shortfall is cleared.[119]

MCOB 13.4.5 R 'Steps required before action for repossession'

35.107 Before issuing possession proceedings a lender must provide the information listed in para 35.106, ensure that the borrower is informed of the need to contact the local housing authority to establish whether s/he is 'eligible' for local authority housing if the property is repossessed and 'clearly state the action that will be taken with regard to repossession'.[120] It is far from clear what this last requirement means in practice.

MCOB 13.5 R 'Statements of charges'

35.108 Many lenders have adopted punitive policies of levying additional charges on borrowers in arrears and the MCOB seeks to ensure that at least the borrower is made aware of the extent of the charging.

> Where an account is in arrears, and the payment shortfall or mortgage shortfall debt is attracting charges, a [lender] must provide the customer with a regular written statement (at least once a quarter) of the payments due, the actual payment shortfall, the charges incurred and the debt.[121]

Charges that trigger the requirement for regular statements include all charges and fees levied directly as a result of the account falling into arrears. This includes charges such as monthly administrative charges, legal fees and interest. If interest is applied to the amount of the arrears, as it is applied to the rest of the mortgage, a lender need not send a written statement, unless other charges are also being made. If interest is applied to the amount of the arrears in a different manner to the rest of the mortgage then a written statement will be required.[122]

---

119 MCOB 13.4.1 R.

120 MCOB 13.4.5 R.

121 MCOB 13.5.1 R.

122 MCOB 13.5.2 G (1).

MCOB 13.5 R 'Pressure on customers'

35.109 MCOB also seeks to protect borrowers from the more unpleasant forms of debt collection.

35.110 'The rules state that a [lender] must not put pressure on a customer through excessive telephone calls or correspondence, or by contact at an unreasonable hour'.[123] Guidance suggests that a reasonable hour will usually fall between 8 am and 9 pm. Putting pressure on a borrower includes the use of documents which resemble a court summons or other official document, or are intended to lead the borrower to believe that they have come from or have the authority of a court. It also includes the use of documents containing unfair, unclear or misleading information intended to coerce the borrower into paying.[124]

MCOB 13.6 R 'Repossessions'

35.111 Lenders are required to dispose of repossessed properties and to deal with the consequences of sale in a reasonable manner.

> A [lender] must ensure that, whenever a property is repossessed (whether voluntarily or through legal action) and it administers the regulated mortgage contract in respect of that property, steps are taken to:
> (1) market the property for sale as soon as possible; and
> (2) obtain the best price that might reasonably be paid, taking account of factors such as market conditions as well as the continuing increase in the amount owed by the customer under the regulated mortgage contract.[125]

35.112 Guidance suggests that:

> ... it is recognised that a balance has to be struck between the need to sell the property as soon as possible, to reduce or remove the outstanding debt, and other factors which might prompt the delay of the sale. These might include market conditions ... but there may be other legitimate reasons for deferring action. This could include the expiry of a period when a grant is repayable on re-sale, or the discovery of a title defect that needs to be remedied if the optimal selling price is to be achieved.[126]

123 MCOB 13.5.3 R.
124 MCOB 13.5.5 G.
125 MCOB 13.6.1 R.
126 MCOB 13.6.2 G.

'If the proceeds of sale are less than the debt'

35.113 A lender is obliged to ensure that, as soon as possible after the sale of a repossessed property, the borrower is informed in a 'durable medium' of the size of the mortgage shortfall and, where relevant, whether the debt might be pursued by another person, for example a mortgage indemnity insurer.[127] Durable medium is defined as paper or electronic medium such s floppy disc, CD Roms etc.

35.114   If a lender intends to seek to recover the shortfall the borrower must be told of this fact and this notification must take place within six years of the date of sale.[128] Guidance suggests that a lender is not obliged to seek to recover a mortgage shortfall debt,[129] 'for example where the sums involved make action for recovery unviable'.

'If the proceeds of sale are more than the debt'

35.115 A lender is obliged to ensure that reasonable steps are taken, as soon as possible after the sale, to inform the borrower in a durable medium of the surplus and subject to the rights or any other lender to pay the surplus to the borrower.[130]

Dispute Resolution

35.116 The Financial Services and Markets Act 2000 s225 provides for the setting up of the FOS to investigate complaints about lenders (although it also covers those involved in the administration of regulated mortgage contracts).

35.117   Complaints are to be determined according to what the Ombudsman considers to be 'fair and reasonable in all the circumstances of the case'.[131] The FSA Handbook sets out an elaborate Complaints Dispute Resolution procedure entitled 'Dispute Resolution: Complaints'.[132]

> 35.118 The procedure provides that a complainant must first seek redress through the lender's internal complaint's procedure. The FOS cannot look into a complaint until either the lender has issued its

---

127 MCOB 13.6.3 R.

128 MCOB 13.6.4 R.

129 MCOB 13.6.5 G

130 MCOB 13.6.6 R.

131 FSMA 2000 s228.

132 www.fsahandbook.info/FSA/html/handbook/DISP.

final response to the complaint or eight weeks have elapsed from the date the complaint was received by the lender.[133] If the FOS upholds a complaint it may either make a money award against the lender (to a maximum of £100,000) or a direction that the lender takes such steps in relation to the complaint as the FOS considers just and appropriate (whether or not a court could order those steps to be taken) or both.[134] It remains to be seen to what extent the court will itself grant a stay in possession proceedings, under CPR 26.4(2)(b), to allow negotiations to take place between the parties or to allow the FOS time to investigate a complaint.

35.119 For the purpose of awards financial loss includes consequential or prospective loss.[135] The FOS can also award a sum which reflects some or all of the costs reasonably incurred by the complainant although 'it is not anticipated that awards of costs will be common since in most cases complainants should not need to have professional advisers to bring complaints to the Financial Ombudsman Service'.[136] The FOS website can be found at www.financial-ombudsman.org.uk and the FOS Technical Advice Desk on 020 7964 1400.

133 DISP 2.3.1 R.
134 DISP 3.9.1.G.
135 DISP para 3.9.3 G.
136 Dispute Resolution: Complaints para 3.9.11 G.

CHAPTER 36

Preventing the lender from obtaining possession – raising the necessary money

Introduction

36.1   In practice, mortgage possession actions can normally only be successfully defended by raising enough money to satisfy the lender or, failing that, persuading the court that it is right to exercise one of the statutory powers described in chapter 35. In common with most debt cases, this involves minimising the borrower's expenditure and maximising the borrower's income.

36.2   Where the borrower is working, the question of income maximisation is largely one of ensuring that he or she is in receipt of any possible relevant additions to wages, income support, working tax credit, child tax credit, maintenance and child support payments, child benefit, etc. If the borrower is unemployed, it is important to ensure that benefit payments are correct and complete. Any potential tax rebates should be claimed and any unfair dismissal, redundancy or discrimination claims considered.

36.3   It is also worth checking whether the borrower is protected by any mortgage protection plan (where an insurance company has agreed to make part or all of the mortgage repayments for a limited period of time following the borrower becoming sick or unemployed). See para 36.6 below. Detailed consideration of these options is really outside the scope of this chapter and readers are encouraged to go online to National Debtline[1] which has a range of leaflets and advice on all aspects of debt. However, a brief synopsis of options relating to cutting mortgage costs may be useful here.

Reducing mortgage costs

36.4   Although in law most lenders have quite wide-ranging powers to lend money as they wish, lenders often say that options for rescheduling the loan are not available, possible or practical. It will be necessary to persevere and show that by the lender reducing the current mortgage costs, eg by rescheduling over a longer term (see para 36.7 below) or by altering the level and/or frequency of repayment, it will be possible for the borrower to meet future commitments.

---

1   www.nationaldebtline.co.uk; tel: 0808 808 4000.

Reduction of repayments

36.5   Lenders (especially 'responsible lenders' such as local authorities, building societies and banks) should be prepared to accept interest-only payments and defer capital repayments within repayment mortgages at least in the short term. This should prevent further arrears accruing providing payments are made, although the lender may require that the unpaid capital elements be paid off when normal repayments are resumed. In relation to regulated mortgage contracts (see para 35.87) the Financial Services Authority requires lenders to deal fairly with any borrower in arrears.[2] Lenders must also operate within their written policy for complying with this obligation. Financial Services Authority guidance suggests that lenders may wish to defer payment of interest due on a regulated mortgage contract or treat any arrears as if they were part of the original amount borrowed.[3] An unreasonable response to such a request might found the basis for a complaint to the Financial Ombudsman Service.[4] See para 35.116. Many financial institutions are also sensitive to bad press publicity where the lender is obviously acting insensitively.

36.6   Where the borrower took out a mortgage protection policy (to pay the mortgage instalments in the event of unemployment or sickness), it is important to lodge the necessary claim form with insurers as soon as possible. Many of these policies set down a very short time-scale within which a claim should be made. Do not, however, be put off lodging the claim after the time specified, as the insurers can extend the time at their discretion. Complaints about insurance policies can be lodged with the Financial Ombudsman Service. Mortgage protection policies are commonly taken out with second mortgages or 'secured loans'. Payments received under a mortgage protection policy which are used by claimants receiving income support or income-based jobseeker's allowance claimants to pay housing costs not covered by the Department for Work and Pensions are not treated as the claimant's income.[5] Similarly payments which these claimants actually receive from other sources (rather than being paid directly by a third party to the lender) and which are actually used to make payments towards a secured loan which does not qualify for

2   Mortgage Conduct of Business sourcebook (MCOB) 13.3.1 R (1)(b).
3   MCOB 13.3.4 G (1) (c) and (d).
4   www.financial-ombudsman.org.uk/.
5   Income Support (General) Regulations (IS Regs) 1987 SI No 1967 Sch 9 para 29 and Jobseeker's Allowance Regulations (JSA Regs) 1996 SI No 207 Sch 7 para 30.

assistance under the benefit regulations, are ignored unless the claimant has used insurance policy payments for the same purpose.[6]

Extension of term

36.7   In any repayment mortgage case, it may be possible to extend the term of the loan so as to reduce the capital element and thus the amount of the monthly repayment. This option need not be pursued if the lender is prepared to accept interest only for a period. Extending the term of the loan involves entering into a new mortgage arrangement and it may be possible, as part of that process, to have the existing arrears 'capitalised', by the lender wiping out the arrears and increasing the outstanding capital by an equivalent amount. In this way the borrower can be given a fresh start. Care, however, should be taken in pre-October 1995 loan cases to try to ensure that the new agreement will not be treated as a post-October 1995 loan in the case of future claims for income support and jobseeker's allowance.

36.8   Again the Financial Services Authority encourages lenders in relation to regulated mortgage contracts[7] to consider extending the term of the regulated mortgage contract.[8]

Changing type of mortgage

36.9   In the case of an endowment mortgage, it is worth considering whether there would be a reduction in monthly payments by switching to a repayment mortgage. The amount of interest paid each month would remain the same but the monthly repayments of the capital (over the remainder of the term or over an extended term) may be less than the payments of the life insurance premium. The amount of capital originally borrowed from the lender could be reduced by the surrender or sale value of the life insurance policy. If the life insurance policy has been going for some years, more will be raised by selling the policy to an endowment policy investor. The borrower should contact a reputable insurance broker for details of how the policy could be sold on. It can be difficult to sell policies which have been in existence for only a few years. If the lender agrees to a new

6   IS Regs 1987 Sch 9 para 30(a)–(d) and JSA Regs 1996 Sch 7 para 31.
7   Para 35.87.
8   MCOB 13.3.4 G (1) (a).

loan, a mortgage protection policy may have to be taken out to cover the possibility of the borrower's death before the end of the loan term. Where an endowment mortgage borrower is told by the endowment policy insurance company that the sums likely to be realised at the end of the term of the policy are less than the amount needed to pay off the mortgage loan, the borrower would probably be better advised to negotiate with the lender to make additional payments towards the shortfall, as if those payments were capital repayments, rather than taking out an additional endowment or similar policy cover to pay off the shortfall. Again the Financial Services Authority advice in relation to regulated mortgage contracts[9] is that lenders may wish to consider changing the type of the regulated mortgage contract.[10] Borrowers who have been advised that their endowment policy is unlikely to be enough to pay off the capital borrowed and who feel that they may have been missold the policy should contact the Financial Services Authority.[11]

Remortgaging

36.10 Where there are two or more mortgages (one of which is likely to be with a 'fringe' mortgage company which charges high rates of interest), or even where there is one high interest rate loan, it is worth trying to persuade one of the mainstream lenders (such as a bank or building society) to 'remortgage' the loan.[12] This involves redemption of the existing loan(s) and replacement with a new mortgage agreement. It is easier to persuade a building society or bank to remortgage the defaulting borrower if, at the time of the new mortgage, the local housing authority agrees to enter into a form of mortgage guarantee which would indemnify the lender in the event of the bank or building society suffering a loss because of the default.[13] It is worth arguing that the lender has in the future nothing to lose, as the money will be recovered either following repossession and sale or, if there is any shortfall, by the local authority meeting the shortfall under the terms of the guarantee. Extreme caution should be exercised when considering whether to remortgage with institutions other than building

9   Para 35.87.
10   MCOB 13.3.4 G(1) (b).
11   See www.fsa.gov.uk.
12   Building Societies Act 1986 Part I.
13   See HA 1985 s442 as amended by HA 1996.

societies (or other similar lenders) as the terms offered may well be disadvantageous over a period of time. The costs of remortgaging may also be considerable, as they include not only surveyors' and solicitors' costs but also the commission charged by the mortgage broker who arranges the remortgage. However, it is worth seeking specialist advice from a reputable mortgage broker as lenders are keen to attract new customers, often on initially advantageous terms.

36.11   Where a borrower is 'threatened with homelessness', ie, it is 'likely that he will be homeless within 28 days',[14] it is useful to remind the housing authority of its duty[15] to 'take reasonable steps to secure that accommodation does not cease to be available for [the borrower's] occupation'. It is arguable that this duty may extend to requiring the authority to use one or more of its powers in Housing Act 1996 Pt VII to try to prevent dispossession. This duty, however, arises only where the authority is satisfied that the borrower is in priority need and not intentionally threatened with homelessness. See chapter 31

Repurchase by local authorities

36.12   In practice, it is quite common for a defaulting borrower who has purchased his or her previously council-owned property to request the local authority to buy the property back. Local authorities purchasing properties which have previously been bought under the 'Right to Buy' provisions of the Housing Act 1985 receive government subsidy.[16]

Financial help from the Department for Work and Pensions

36.13   For a detailed analysis of the rules relating to mortgage interest payments by the Department for Work and Pensions for people eligible for income support and jobseeker's allowance, reference should be made to the current year's edition of the Child Poverty Action Group's Welfare Benefits and Tax Credit Handbook. By way of overview the following should be observed. The Department is required in most cases to pay interest on loans for the purchase or repair or improve-

---

14   HA 1996 s175(4).
15   HA 1996 s195(2).
16   Local Authorities (Capital Finance) (Amendment) Regs 1999 SI No 501.

ment (as defined) of the home, where the borrower is in receipt of income support or income-based jobseeker's allowance.[17] There is no obligation on the Department to pay the capital element in the monthly loan repayment or the monthly premium on the insurance policy in endowment mortgages, or to assist in maintaining the private pension contribution in cases of pension mortgages.

36.14   The Department makes reduced payments during the first weeks of the claim unless the claimant or his or her partner is aged over 60. For loans taken out before 2 October 1995 nothing is paid for the first eight weeks, 50 per cent of the housing costs are paid for the next 18 weeks, and full housing costs after 26 weeks. For loans taken out after 1 October 1995 nothing is paid for the first 39 weeks but full housing costs are paid after 39 weeks. For post-October 1995 loans the more generous 26-week provision applies where the claimant is a single parent and carer. Complicated 'add back' provisions apply to those who were receiving financial assistance before 2 October 1995.

17 IS Regs 1987 regs 17(e) and 18(f), Sch 3 paras 7 and 8 and JSA Regs 1996 reg 83(f), Sch 2 paras 14 and 15.

Procedure and tactics

Venue for proceedings

37.1   Proceedings for possession of a dwelling-house must be brought in
the county court for the district in which the land is situated unless an
enactment provides otherwise or the claimant believes that there are
exceptional circumstances warranting the issue of the proceedings in
the High Court.[1] Where the loan is one regulated by the Consumer
Credit Act 1974, proceedings must be brought in the county court.[2]
The claim may be brought in the High Court if the claimant files,
with the claim form, a certificate stating the reasons for bringing
the proceedings in the High Court verified by a statement of truth.
Circumstances which may, in an appropriate case, justify starting a
claim in the High Court are if: (1) there are complicated disputes of
fact; (2) there are points of law of general importance; or (3) the claim
is against trespassers and there is a substantial risk of public disturbance or of serious harm to people or property which properly require
immediate determination.[3] The value of the property and the amount
of any financial claim may be relevant circumstances but these factors alone will not normally justify starting the claim in the High
Court.[4] If a claimant starts a claim in the High Court and the court
decides that it should have been started in the county court, the court
will normally either strike out the claim or transfer it to the county
court of its own initiative. The court will normally disallow the costs
of starting the claim in the High Court or of any transfer.[5] In practice
it is much more common for proceedings to be brought in the county
court, and the procedure and tactics discussed in this chapter apply to
proceedings in that court unless otherwise indicated.

Claim form

37.2   Proceedings are brought by claim form with attached particulars of
claim which are endorsed with the hearing date.[6] The hearing date
cannot be less than 28 days from the date of issue[7] and the standard

---

1   CPR 55.3 but see CPR 3.10 and *Gwynedd County Council v Grunshaw* [2000] 1
WLR 494; (2000) 32 HLR 610, CA.
2   Consumer Credit Act 1974 s141(1).
3   PD 55 para 1.3.
4   Ibid para 1.4.
5   Ibid para 1.2.
6   CPR 55.4 and 55.5.
7   CPR 55.5(3)(a).

period between the issue of the claim form and the hearing should not be more than eight weeks.[8] The defendant must be served with the claim form and the particulars of claim not less than 21 days before the hearing.[9] The proceedings are for recovery of the property and are not an action to enforce the mortgage.[10] The stage of borrower default at which lenders issue proceedings varies but can be when as little as two months' arrears have accrued. In practice, proceedings are brought to enforce payment with the deterrent that failure to pay will result in possession being lost. The proceedings are in the same form whether the claimant is a first or subsequent mortgagee.

37.3   Depending on the terms of the mortgage deed, before issuing the claim the lender may send a 'calling-in' letter. This specifies the amount required to be paid by the borrower to redeem the loan. The mortgage deed may require the lender to make such a formal demand for the outstanding loan before it becomes payable in whole. Alternatively, the mortgage deed may provide that the whole outstanding loan becomes due immediately on default in which case the calling-in letter is not necessary.

37.4   The particulars of claim attached to the claim form are required[11] to specify certain details relating to the loan including, among others, the amount of the loan, any periodic payment, any payment of interest required to be made and in schedule form show the dates and amounts of all payments due and payments made under the mortgage agreement for the period of two years immediately preceding the date of issue of the proceedings.[12] If the lender wishes to rely on a history of arrears which is longer than two years this must be stated in the particulars of claim and a full (or longer) schedule exhibited to a witness statement.[13] Details of any other payments required to be made as a term of the mortgage (such as for insurance premiums, legal costs, default interest, penalties, administrative or other charges) must also be specified as must details of any other sums claimed, stating the nature and amount of any such charge. The lender must also specify

8   CPR 55.5(3)(b).

9   CPR 55.5(3)(c).

10   *R v Judge Dutton Briant ex p Abbey National Building Society* [1957] 2 QB 497; [1957] 2 All ER 625. In the High Court an action by a bank against a customer for recovery of an overdraft secured by a legal charge is not a mortgage action within RSC Ord 88 – *National Westminster Bank v Kitch* [1996] 4 All ER 495, CA.

11   PD 55 para 2.5 and Form N120.

12   PD 55 para2.5(3).

13   PD 55 para 2.5A.

whether any of those payments are in arrears and whether these are included in the amount of any periodic payment. However, failure to provide the required specified information may not justify refusing to grant a possession order.[14] The claim form must be verified by a statement of truth.[15] In the normal way, the defendant(s) has 14 days within which to file any defence. An acknowledgment of service is not required.[16]

37.5   Generally, the only defence available will be to seek the benefit of the court's powers under the Administration of Justice Acts or the Consumer Credit Act 1974 (see chapter 35). Although it is important to file a formal defence if any unusual point is to be argued, the courts will allow a defendant to seek such relief without any formal pleadings being served.[17] It remains to be seen to what extent the courts will stay proceedings under CPR 26.4 to allow any complaint concerning a regulated mortgage contract (see para 35.87) to be investigated by the Financial Ombudsman Service. It is not possible to obtain a default judgment in possession proceedings.[18] Usually, all that will be applicable is a short defence claiming the protection of the Administration of Justice Acts or Consumer Credit Act 1974. See appendix B for a precedent. Form N11M, the defence form which is sent out by the court with the possession summons, must be used.[19] This enables the borrower to give a complete picture of his or her finances as the form is really little more than an income and expenditure statement. An application for a time order under Consumer Credit Act 1974 s129 may be made in the defence or by application notice in the proceedings.[20]

37.6   Where, after proceedings have been issued, the borrower pays off the arrears, the proper course is to adjourn the proceedings generally so that the lender can apply to reinstate the proceedings if further arrears accrue. This saves further legal costs which are likely to be added to the borrower's mortgage debt.[21]

---

14 *Nationwide Anglia Building Society v Shillibeer* [1994] CLY 3295.

15 CPR 22.1.

16 CPR 55.7.

17 See *Redditch Benefit Building Society v Roberts* [1940] Ch 415; [1940] 1 All ER 342, CA and CPR 55.7(3).

18 CPR 55.7(4).

19 PD 55 para 1.5.

20 PD 55 para 7.1. See also Form N440.

21 *Halifax plc v Taffs* April 2000 *Legal Action* 15; [2000] CLY 4385, CA. See also *Greyhound Guaranty Ltd v Caulfield* [1981] CLY 1808.

Parties to proceedings

37.7 It is, it seems, necessary to join as defendants not only to the borrower(s) but also those people in occupation who are known to claim a right to remain.[22] An occupier who is not a legal owner (the property being in the sole name of the borrower) he or she does not have the absolute right to be joined as defendant. Where a spouse or civil partner has registered a Class F land charge, or a notice or caution pursuant to Family Law Act 1996 s31, he or she has the right to be notified of the action being brought by the lender against his or her spouse, and should be sent a copy of the particulars of claim.[23] He or she does not have to be joined as defendant by the lender from the outset. Whether or not any such charge, notice or caution has been registered, a 'connected person' who is not a defendant may apply to be joined as a defendant 'at any time before the action is finally disposed of in that court' and shall be made a defendant with a view to meeting the borrower's liabilities provided that the court 'does not see any special reason against it' and the court is satisfied that he or she may be able to persuade the court to exercise any of its powers under the Administration of Justice Act 1970.[24] The expression 'connected person' in relation to any person means that person's spouse, former spouse, civil partner, former civil partner, co-habitant or former co-habitant.[25] In such circumstances, the court can only refuse the application to be joined if there are 'special reasons' against the applicant being joined in the action. Where a person has registered his or her rights of occupation under the Family Law Act 1996 as a land charge or at the Land Registry then the lender is also obliged to serve notice of the claim on that person.[26]

37.8 Obviously, it is quite possible that a deserted spouse or civil partner may not hear about the proceedings until the bailiffs come to execute a warrant for possession, but it would be possible for him or her to apply at that stage to be joined as a defendant and to claim relief. Occupiers (such as tenants) who wish to be joined as defendants to argue any point should apply without notice by letter to the court and attend the hearing.[27] Alternatively, they could simply attend

---

22 *Brighton and Shoreham Building Society v Hollingdale* [1965] 1 All ER 540.
23 Family Law Act 1996 s56.
24 Ibid s55.
25 Ibid s54(5).
26 Ibid s56.
27 CPR 19.3.

the hearing and ask to be joined as defendant then. The court rules require a lender to send to the mortgaged property, not less than 14 days before the hearing, a notice addressed to the occupiers stating that possession proceedings have been commenced, giving the name and address of the claimant, of the defendant and of the court and specifying the case number and the hearing date.[28] The lender is also required to produce at the hearing a copy of the notice and evidence that the notice has been served.[29] An occupying tenant (who may well have no right to remain as against the lender) may need to apply to be joined as defendant so as to obtain a possession order for the purpose of application to the local housing authority for assistance under the homelessness provisions of Housing Act 1996 Pt VII. Advisers should consider the practice of the local housing authority before making any application because a tenant renders himself or herself at risk as to costs. It is likely, however, that a lender would not usually take steps to recover costs against the tenant but would rely on recovery of costs against the security of the property (see para 37.47 below). However, a tenant wishing to be joined in the proceedings as a named defendant should be advised of this theoretical risk.

37.9   The fact that the borrower is bankrupt does not mean that he or she has no right or power to address the court in possession proceedings. Both the order and warrant are directed to the named defendants and as such they have locus standi to raise issues which are relevant to the exercise of any Administration of Justice Act discretion.[30] The trustee in bankruptcy of a bankrupt borrower should only be joined as party if the court so directs.[31]

Evidence

37.10   The claim for possession is heard in private (unless the court directs to the contrary).[32] Evidence may be given by witness statement without specific court order except where the case is allocated to the fast or multi-track or the court otherwise orders.[33] Usually, institutional lenders make use of this facility as it is easier and more cost-effective to give

28   CPR 55.10(3).
29   CPR 55.10(4).
30   *Nationwide Building Society v Purvis* [1998] BPIR 625, CA.
31   *Alliance Building Society v Shave* [1952] Ch 581.
32   PD 39 para 1.5.
33   CPR 55.8(3).

evidence by witness statement than to incur the expense of attendance at court of management personnel. Pro forma witness statements are generally produced, which do little more than confirm the contents of the particulars of claim. The mortgage deed is usually exhibited to the witness statement, as is any calling-in letter. Where relevant, an up-to-date search certificate of HM Land Registry or Land Charges Department will also be exhibited to ascertain if any notice, caution or Class F land charge has been registered to protect a civil partner or spouse's rights of occupation under matrimonial legislation.

37.11 However, it is possible on the application of any party to obtain an order requiring the maker of the witness statement to attend court for cross-examination. If the maker of a witness statement does not attend the hearing and the borrower disputes material evidence in the statement, the court 'will normally adjourn the hearing so that oral evidence can be given'.[34] The borrower may wish to require attendance of the maker of the witness statement where, for example, the lender is claiming arrears of payments which include separate interest charges on missed monthly payments so as to have this clarified for the court. Advisers can then argue that only bona fide missed payments should be taken into account in considering whether to postpone an order or not. Borrowers should seek the attendance of the makers of witness statements only if there is some good reason, in view of the formidable position which lenders have in connection with costs and expenses (see para 37.48 below). The witness statement is usually sent by post to the borrower before the hearing. However, a witness statement must be served at least two days before the hearing.[35]

37.12 The court is entitled to accept material adduced as evidence informally by the borrower or his or her representative even if that does not strictly comply with the laws of evidence.[36] If the lender disputes what the borrower has said then formal evidence would need to be called.

37.13 Advisers may wish to request, in place of the attendance of the maker of the witness statement, an order from the court that the claimant file a detailed witness statement setting out all sums claimed to be due and a copy of the account from the inception of the loan so as to expose to the court the full details of the claim.

---

34 PD 55 para 5.4.
35 CPR 55.8(4).
36 *Cheltenham & Gloucester Building Society v Grant* (1994) 26 HLR 703, CA. See also M Thompson, 'A Very Wide Discretion?' [1995] Conv 51.

Hearings and orders for possession

37.14   As stated above (para 37.10), the hearing of the action is normally in private and before the district judge.[37] Given the numbers of possession claims being listed for hearing, in practice the court may well only expect to be able to spend a matter of minutes on each case.[38] If any substantive argument is raised, then it is likely that the case will be adjourned to another date. In such cases the borrower should offer to make some payment towards the mortgage in the interim. If the case is to be defended then the court should proceed to deal with the case or give case management directions to include, 'where the claim is disputed on grounds which appear to be substantial', allocating to track.[39] In deciding allocation to track the matters to which the court shall have regard include Civil Procedure Rules 1998 (CPR) 26.8, the level of arrears, the importance to the defendant of retaining possession and the importance of vacant possession to the claimant.[40] The financial value of the property is not necessarily the most important factor in deciding the track for a possession claim and the court may direct a possession claim to be allocated to the fast track even though the value of the property is in excess of £15,000.[41] In practice, it is rare for an 'undefended' claim to be allocated to a track. As with many hearings in private, practice and procedure vary. Normally, the lender's solicitor outlines the history of the case and advises on any change in circumstances since the date of the witness statement.

37.15   The original legal charge and a search for the purpose of identifying any rights registered under the Family Law Act 1996 may be produced for examination by the district judge and a certificate of service if, unusually, the claimant has served the claim form and particulars of claim.[42] There is strictly no need for the *original* charge certificate to be produced as office copies of the register and documents filed at the Land Registry are admissible under Land Registration Act 2002.[43] The lender is obliged to produce at the hearing a copy of the 'Dear

---

37   Originally Administration of Justice Act 1970 s38(3) (repealed by County Courts Act 1984 s148(3)) and now CPR PD 39 para 1.5.

38   For a study of possession proceedings see J Nixon et al, *Housing cases in county courts*, Policy Press, 1996.

39   CPR 55.8(1) and (2).

40   CPR 55.9.

41   PD 55 para 6.1.

42   CPR 55.8(6).

43   PD 33.

Occupier' notice as well as evidence that the notice has been served.[44] Failure to produce these can be grounds for an adjournment. Where no valid search has been made it is for the claimant to satisfy the court that there are no people who should be notified in accordance with Family Law Act 1996 s56.

37.16   The borrower will then be asked to comment on the lender's case and to justify the court's exercise of any statutory power to postpone the giving up of possession. It is important to ensure that the court has the essential information needed to assess the case including the current balance outstanding, the arrears, the monthly instalment, the remaining term of the mortgage and the last payment made and the amount. Where there is equity available to protect the lender then this should be made clear. It is obviously essential that the borrower attends the hearing so as to give evidence to support any claim for statutory relief. Evidence which can be of use includes a letter of confirmation from the Department for Work and Pensions concerning payment of mortgage interest, evidence of future regular employment from a new employer, or a loan from friends or relatives, proof of remortgage facilities and an estate agent's valuation of the property. Where relief by way of a time order is being sought, realistic statements of income and expenditure should be available.

37.17   If, when arranging the mortgage, the borrower was required to pay for a mortgage indemnity policy, taken out by the lender to protect it in the event of a shortfall on sale following the borrower's eviction, this should be made clear to the district judge if there is any doubt about extent of the security. Since such a policy indemnifies the lender (either entirely or to a pre-set figure), the lender will not normally be prejudiced by giving any benefit of the doubt to the borrower. The existence of such a policy should be clear from the mortgage offer letter which would have been sent to the borrower at the time the loan was taken out (as the paying for the policy would have been one of the 'special' conditions of the advance).

37.18   As stated above, local practice varies but the courts since *Norgan*,[45] when considering possible orders for postponed possession, are now much more flexible in assessing how long to give the borrower to pay off the arrears. Advisers should obviously seek to argue for as long a period as is viable so that the amount of money required to be paid monthly towards the arrears is minimised. That said, advisers need

---

44 Section 67.
45 *Cheltenham & Gloucester Building Society v Norgan* [1996] 1 WLR 343; [1996] 1 All ER 449, CA.

to bear in mind observations in the judgment in *Norgan* that if the borrower is given the period most favourable to the borrower and still defaults, it will be easier for the lender to argue against the borrower being given a further postponement, in any future application by the borrower.[46] In cases falling within the Consumer Credit Act 1974, it is important to ensure that the district judge is aware that, when considering an application for a possession order, there is no statutory restriction requiring the arrears to be paid off within a 'reasonable period'. In addition, it is important also to ask him or her to consider making a time order (see para 35.38) as well as suspending any order for possession granted in favour of the lender.

37.19   Any order giving statutory relief is likely to require the borrower to pay a stated amount per month in addition to the normal monthly instalment. The usual postponed order for possession in mortgage cases is set out as county court Form N31. Effectively, the number of months it will take to clear off the arrears at £x per month is the 'reasonable period' referred to in Administration of Justice Act 1970 s36(1) (see chapter 35).

37.20   Courts generally lean against making absolute orders unless the borrower either fails to attend the hearing or is unable to make any proposals which meet the statutory criteria. Usually the court will, unless the security is insufficient or threatened, be concerned not unnecessarily to grant an absolute order in favour of the lender. Where the court does not feel able to exercise its discretion then an order for possession in 28, or possibly 56, days is given in favour of the lender.

37.21   Where the borrower's financial position is uncertain (for example, where he or she has recently applied for a job or where a fresh claim has been made for income support and the amount of help to come from the Department for Work and Pensions by way of income support is not clear), it is possible to ask for an adjournment for a short period to allow the issues to be clarified. Borrowers should, if at all possible, offer to make some payments in the interim.

37.22   Where an endowment mortgage borrower has defaulted in maintaining payments under the endowment policy it is common for lenders, where they become aware of this, to 'switch' the mortgage from an interest-only loan to a capital and interest loan. This, particularly where the mortgage has been running for some time, results in a substantial increase in the monthly payments expected from the borrower. Advisers must check carefully whether the legal charge provides for this. A lender will no doubt seek to argue that there must

46 Ibid at 459.

be a term implied into the mortgage agreement that allows for this 'switching'. Where the legal charge does specifically regulate the circumstances in which this conversion can take place it is difficult to see how such a term can be implied where the particular circumstances of the borrower's case do not meet the requirements of the express term in the legal charge. In any event it is arguable that, even if there is no 'capital vehicle' in place to repay the original loan, the loan can be repaid from the sale of the security if there were insufficient funds available to the borrower at the end of the mortgage term. It would be open to the lender to make application to the court if there was a change in circumstances such as to put the lender at risk.[47]

37.23   If the borrower is not able to persuade the district judge to grant a postponed order for possession because the borrower is not able to meet the current payments and clear the arrears over a reasonable period, some district judges have adopted a practice of granting a postponed order for possession effective some time in the future. This might be, for instance, an order for possession in three months' time. The rationale for this would seem to be that this gives a borrower who is not able to meet the statutory criteria for relief a period of time in order to improve his or her situation. If this proves to be the case, the borrower can apply to the court at that stage for a variation of the order for possession so that it is then further postponed on terms. Alternatively, the court may direct that there be a review hearing in, say, three months to ensure that the case is reassessed automatically.

37.24   In general, an order for possession should not be made against one of two borrowers where it would not advantage the lender because the other borrower is entitled to remain in possession. This will, for example, arise where a husband has no defence to the claim but the wife has an arguable defence based on her consent to the charge being obtained by undue influence. In such circumstances, however, the court should not grant a possession order against the husband alone but should adjourn the proceedings as against the husband with liberty to restore should the wife leave the property or an order for possession be made against her.[48]

37.25   Where it is clear that some form of statutory relief is to be given to the borrower, advisers should argue, where the Administration of Justice Acts apply, for an adjournment on terms as to specified

---

47 See *Household Mortgage Corporation plc v Etheridge* April 1997 *Legal Action* 13.

48 *Albany Home Loans Ltd v Massey* [1997] 2 All ER 609, CA. See also M P Thompson, 'The Powers and Duties of Mortgagees' [1998] 62 Conv 391.

monthly payments by the borrower instead of a postponed order for possession. The advantage is that in the event of default a further hearing would be required if adjournment was originally ordered; whereas a lender would be able to apply immediately for a warrant for possession without further hearing if the terms of a postponed order were breached. Many district judges are unwilling to adjourn on terms as they feel that this is insufficient by way of incentive to the borrower to pay and/or that by building in this extra step in the proceedings all that is being done is to increase the legal costs which will usually be added to the mortgage debt.

37.26   By contrast, in the High Court, execution of an order for possession because of a breach of a suspensory term cannot take place without the defendant being given an opportunity to be heard.[49]

37.27   The court should not normally in a mortgage claim attach to a postponed order for possession a requirement that the warrant for possession should not be executed without permission of the court,[50] although in practice it is not unknown for such a requirement to be added.

37.28   A borrower is not barred from making an application for a further postponement of an order or warrant just because a similar application has been refused before, although the court can dismiss such an application if it is an abuse of process.[51]

37.29   Where a borrower is not able to satisfy the court that it should grant him or her any statutory relief, then the lender is entitled to possession of the property. This may put the borrower in practical difficulty if some time is required to obtain alternative accommodation (either privately or from the local housing authority) and the lender is not willing to defer, by consent, the obtaining of physical possession. The county court has sufficient jurisdiction to postpone execution of the warrant for possession for a reasonable period.[52] However, it is clear that this power must be used judicially and the limits of this jurisdiction are unclear.

---

49 *Fleet Mortgage and Investment Co v Lower Maisonette 46 Eaton Place Ltd* [1972] 2 All ER 737 and *Practice Direction* [1972] 1 All ER 576.

50 *Royal Trust Co of Canada v Markham* [1975] 3 All ER 433, CA.

51 *Abbey National Mortgages v Bernard* (1996) 71 P & CR 257; [1995] NPC 118, CA.

52 See *Kelly v White, Penn Gaskell v Roberts* [1920] WN 220 noted most recently in notes to County Courts Act 1984 s21 in *The County Court Practice 1997*, Butterworths, p27.

Counterclaims

37.30   The existence of a counterclaim for damages against a lender does not prevent the latter from exercising its common law right to possession. Even where a meritorious counterclaim exists (for example, for negligence or breach of warranty arising out of a survey report on the condition of the mortgaged property), this does not allow the court to exercise its Administration of Justice Act discretion, as damages received by virtue of the counterclaim would not necessarily extinguish arrears by the end of a 'reasonable period'.[53] The position may be different, however, where the claim against the lender is by way of a set-off and if the existence and prospects of success can be regarded as enabling the sums due to be paid within a reasonable period[54] or where the counterclaim is for rescission of the mortgage.[55] The situation of mortgages governed by the Consumer Credit Act 1974 may be different, in that the court's power to assist the borrower is not qualified by having to be satisfied that the arrears and accruing payments will be paid up to date by the end of a 'reasonable period'.

Money judgments

37.31   The practice of the major institutional lenders varies but some lenders include, as part of the relief claimed, a request for judgment for the entire debt due as at the date of the hearing. The witness statement in support forms the evidence for that claim as well as for the order for possession. The rationale behind this is that a money judgment makes it easier for the lender to take subsequent enforcement action (if, for example, the property is sold for less than the money judgment obtained). However, the court has the discretion under County Courts Act 1984 s71(2) to suspend payment of the entire debt. In the usual case the money judgment is postponed on the same terms as the order for possession.[56] There are instances where it would be right to depart from the practice of granting a money judgment (where,

---

53   See *National Westminster Bank plc v Skelton* [1993] 1 All ER 242, CA, *Citibank Trust v Ayivor* [1987] 1 WLR 1157, *Barclays Bank plc v Tennet* (1984) 6 June CAT 242 noted at [1985] CLY 5, *Midland Bank plc v McGrath* [1996] EGCS 61, CA and A Pugh-Thomas, 'Mortgagees and Counterclaims' LS Gaz 27 April 1988, p28.

54   See *Ashley Guarantee plc v Zacaria* [1993] 1 All ER 254, CA.

55   See *Barclays Bank plc v Waterson* (1988) Manchester County Ct, noted at [1989] CLY 2505.

56   *Cheltenham & Gloucester Building Society v Grattidge* (1993) 25 HLR 454, CA.

for example, the borrower produces evidence of the sale of the mort-gaged property taking place within a reasonable period[57]). The money judgment, in cases where a postponed order for possession is also obtained, does not appear on the judgment register as a county court judgment unless and until terms of the suspension are breached and the lender takes steps to enforce the order for possession. The Register of Judgments, Orders and Fines Regulations 2005[58] reg 9(d) exempts from registration as a county court judgment 'an order for the payment of money arising from an action for the recovery of land (whether for costs, payments due under a mortgage, arrears of rent or otherwise) until the creditor takes any step to enforce the order ...'. It is not an abuse of process for a lender to seek possession first before subsequently choosing the alternative remedy of seeking a money judgment.[59] Accordingly, it is not improper for a lender who has been met with a successful *Barclays Bank v O'Brien* defence (for which see para 41.4) choosing after disclaiming the security of the legal charge to sue on the personal covenant in the legal charge with a view as an unsecured creditor to bankrupt the mortgage borrower even if this might result in the trustee in bankruptcy applying for an order for sale.[60] A lender's claim for a money judgment is not res judicata simply because no money judgment was requested in previ-ous unopposed proceedings in which a possession order was obtained where in those proceedings a money claim was made.[61] However, a claimant who had obtained a money judgment as well as a possession order based on an 'all monies' legal charge cannot subsequently issue fresh proceedings against the defendant seeking a money judgment in relation to a guarantee entered into by the defendant before the previous proceedings. The claimant's cause of action had merged in the earlier judgment.[62]

---

57 *Cheltenham & Gloucester Building Society v Johnson* (1996) 28 HLR 885, CA.

58 SI No 3595.

59 *Zandfarid v BCCI* [1996] 1 WLR 1420.

60 *Alliance & Leicester plc v Slayford* [2000] EWCA Civ 257; [2001] 1 All ER (Comm) 1; (2001) 3 HLR 66, CA.

61 *UCB Bank plc v Chandler* [1999] EGCS 56, CA.

62 *Lloyds Bank plc v Hawkins* [1998] Lloyd's Rep Bank 379, CA. See also P Mostyn, 'No interest for mortgagees after money judgment' [1998] NLJ 1728 for a discussion of the case and an argument that lenders are, post-judgment, restricted to interest on the judgment debt at the statutory judgment rate rather than any contractual rate. See also *Director General of Fair Trading v First National Bank plc* [2001] UKHL 52; [2002] 1 AC 481; [2001] 3 WLR 1297, HL.

Appeals

37.32   Appeals from a district judge lie to the circuit judge.[63] The procedure is set out in CPR Part 52 and Practice Direction 52. Appeals from the circuit judge lie to the High Court in most cases. The old distinction between interlocutory and final orders has now gone and, accordingly, it can now in practice be more difficult to appeal certain orders by district judges, such as refusals to suspend warrants. CPR 52.11(3) provides that '[t]he appeal court will allow an appeal where the decision of the lower court was (a) wrong or (b) unjust because of a serious procedural or other irregularity in the proceedings in the lower court'. However, an appeal court will be reluctant to interfere with the exercise of discretion unless it can be shown that the judge had (1) misunderstood the facts, (2) taken account of irrelevant matters, (3) failed to exercise the discretion, or (4) made a decision that no reasonable judge could have made.

37.33   Permission to appeal is required from the judge whose order it is proposed to appeal or from the appeal judge. The appellant's appeal notice must be filed within 21 days of the order under appeal. The lodging of an appellant's notice does not stay enforcement of the order under appeal.[64] An undertaking not to seek to enforce the order under appeal should be sought from the claimant or a stay should be sought from the district judge or the circuit judge pending appeal. There are special rules relating to second appeals, that is an appeal from a circuit judge hearing a case on appeal from the district judge.

37.34   Where a borrower has unsuccessfully applied to a district judge for the suspension of a warrant and has been evicted, if subsequently the borrower is successful on appeal to the circuit judge, he or she is entitled to be reinstated into the property. A circuit judge hearing an appeal can exercise all the jurisdiction which the district judge had. If the circuit judge reverses the decision of the district judge he or she should restore, as near as possible, the position as it would have been had the district judge made the order now made by the circuit judge.[65]

---

63   See Access to Justice Act 1999 (Destination of Appeals) Order 2000 SI No 1071.

64   CPR 52.7.

65   *Hyde Park Funding Ltd v Ioannou* [1999] CLY 4382, Cty Ct.

Warrants for possession

Pre-execution

37.35 Where an absolute order for possession has been granted at the hearing and any period of postponement has expired or where the terms of any postponed order have been broken, the lender is free to apply without notice for the issue and execution of a warrant for possession. No further hearing is required and this does not breach European Convention on Human Rights article 6.

37.36 It is often only when the occupiers receive notification of the proposed eviction by the bailiffs that advice is sought. At this stage advisers should consider applying to set aside the original possession order, if there are grounds for doing so under CPR 39.3, before execution of the warrant, for example, where the borrower did not attend the hearing because of non-receipt of the summons or illness. See para 29.9 above. Applications should be made in Form N244, preferably with a supporting witness statement and if possible with a draft defence (see precedent at appendix B). Where occupiers are not parties to the proceedings they may wish to make an application to be joined as defendants as well as applying to have the order for possession set aside. An application to be joined as a party may be made on notice using Form N244 and should also be supported by evidence setting out the occupier's interest in or connection with the claim.[66] Where a tenant occupies part of the property he or she may only be able to have judgment set aside in respect of the part he or she occupies.

37.37 A borrower in breach of a postponed order for possession can apply to have the order itself further postponed, or alternatively to have the warrant for possession suspended on terms. Administration of Justice Act 1970 s36 may be used to stay or suspend execution of an order for possession 'at any time before execution of such ... order'.[67] Similar scope is given to the court in respect of regulated agreements within the meaning of the Consumer Credit Act 1974.[68] Any application for such a further stay or suspension should usually be made on notice to the lender on Form N244. It is advisable to make such an application (see precedent at appendix B) pending negotiations if there is any doubt as to whether a lender will agree to a stay.

---

66 PD 19 paras 1.3 and 1.4.
67 See *R v Bloomsbury and Marylebone County Court ex p Villerwest Ltd* [1976] 1 All ER 897, CA, *R v Ilkeston County Court ex p Kruza* (1985) 17 HLR 539 and *Hawtin v Heathcote* [1976] CLY 371, Cty Ct.
68 Consumer Credit Act 1974 s135.

Post-execution

37.38 Once the bailiff has executed the warrant and the borrower has been displaced, the court's statutory powers are exhausted.[69] However, the court's power to set aside judgment granting the order for possession and the subsequent warrant for possession and then to suspend the warrant for possession may still be of assistance.[70] See para 29.47 for a discussion as to the circumstances where the warrant for possession will be set aside on grounds of fraud, oppression or abuse of process by the lender. A party to proceedings who through no fault of his or her own did not have notice of a hearing until after it had already commenced, but who then made no attempt to apply to have the hearing recommenced could not later expect the court to set aside judgment given against him or her.[71] Where the borrower can raise the money to redeem the mortgage prior to exchange of contracts on the lender's sale the court may restrain the lender from selling although separate proceedings for an injunction to restrain sale would need to be brought. The borrower's equity of redemption is extinguished when the lender enters into a contract for sale, rather than at the time of completion, although it is unclear what the situation would be where the borrower has grounds to have the original order set aside or where the warrant was obtained by fraud or there has been abuse of the process or oppression in its execution such as to justify the warrant being set aside.[72] Where a lender is concerned about the risk of a borrower making some sort of application to the court which would have the effect of putting off a prospective buyer, the appropriate step is for the lender to apply for an order for sale under Law of Property Act 1925 s91 where, taking the property by virtue of the court order, would absolutely protect the buyer.[73]

37.39 Where, however, an occupier is evicted by the bailiff and claims to have an independent right to remain as against the lender, for example, as an occupier with a tenancy binding on the lender or as an occupier with a superior equitable interest (for which see paras

---

69 *Cheltenham & Gloucester Building Society v Obi* (1996) 28 HLR 22, CA and *Mortgage Agency Services Number Two Ltd v Bal* [1998] EWCA Civ 1186; (1998) 95(28) LSG 31, CA.

70 CPR 39.3. See also *Governors of Peabody Donation Fund v Hay* (1987) 19 HLR 145, *Hammersmith and Fulham LBC v Hill* (1995) 27 HLR 368, CA and *Cheltenham & Gloucester Building Society v Obi* (1996) 28 HLR 22, CA.

71 CPR 39.3 and *National Counties Building Society v Antonelli* [1995] NPC 177, CA.

72 *National Provincial Building Society v Ahmed* [1995] 38 EG 138, CA.

73 *Arab Bank plc v Mercantile Holdings* [1994] Ch 71.

38.1 and 40.7), he or she may apply to have judgment set aside or stayed so far as he or she is concerned and to be allowed to defend the proceedings.[74]

Responsibilities of mortgagee in possession

37.40   In the context of residential mortgages, the lender will be seeking possession of the borrower's home with a view to evicting the borrower and selling with vacant possession. For a discussion on the responsibilities imposed on the lender when selling, see para 42.14. A borrower will be concerned about the time it takes for the sale to be concluded and the fact that interest continues to accrue until the final redemption of the mortgage following sale. The common law 'Duty to account' imposed on a mortgagee in possession may be of some assistance to borrowers in these circumstances. The extent of this liability has not been considered recently by the courts, and many of the old cases do not readily lend themselves to giving guidance to the position where modern institutional lenders take possession for the sole purpose of disposing of the premises with vacant possession. The duty to account operates in the borrower's favour by allowing the borrower, on redeeming the mortgage, to set off against monies due to the lender under the mortgage any rent or other profits received during the period of the lender's possession of the mortgaged property. If necessary, the court can order the taking of accounts in redemption proceedings.

37.41   A mortgagee who goes into possession of the mortgaged property, and thereby excludes the mortgagor from control of it, is bound to account to the mortgagor, not only for the rents and profits which he or she actually receives, but also for the rents and profits which, but for his or her wilful default or neglect, he or she might have received; ie, for everything which he or she has received, or might or ought to have received, while he or she continued in possession.[75]

37.42   A lender who refuses to rent out the property will also be liable to account for rent that could have been received. In the seventeenth-century case of *Anon*[76] it was held that the lender's liability to account on the basis of wilful default included the refusal to rent to a tenant

---

74   *Minet v Johnson* (1890) 63 LT 507 and *Hawtin v Heathcote* [1976] CLY 371.
75   *Halsbury's Laws* Vol 32 para 698.
76   (1682) 1 Vern 45.

who was capable of paying the going rent for the property. The short note of the case states:

> A Mortgagee shall not account according to the value of the land, viz. He shall not be bound by any proof that the land was worth so much, unless you can likewise prove that he did actually make so much of it or might have done so, had it not been for his wilful default: as if he turned out a sufficient tenant, that held it at so much rent, or refused to accept a sufficient tenant that would have given so much for it.

The burden of proof is on the person alleging wilful default in not letting the property,[77] and the onus shifts to the lender where that person shows that the property can be let or has been let, and it is then up to the lender to show that he or she has been vigilant in attempts to let the property.

37.43   While the leading textbook on the law of mortgages considers that this duty to account for notional rent does not arise where possession has been taken with a view to sale within a reasonable period,[78] the authority upon which the proposition is based does not in fact support that assertion.[79]

37.44   The courts have been more restrictive in terms of imposing obligations on a mortgagee in possession in relation to repair of the property. It appears that there is some general obligation not to be negligent in relation to protection of the repossessed property, with the lender being under a duty to take reasonable steps to protect the property against vandalism.[80]

37.45   One of the practical problems which can be a cause of further animosity between the lender and borrower is in deciding what items in the property are fixtures and hence should be left in situ when the borrower leaves, and what items are the borrower's and can lawfully be removed when the borrower gives up possession. In *TSB Bank plc v Botham*[81] the Court of Appeal gave guidance on whether tap fittings, extractor fans, mirrors, 'white goods' and the like were part of the fixtures and as such the lender's to dispose of with the security on sale or were the borrower's to remove.

---

77 *Brandon v Brandon* (1862) 10 WR 287.

78 W Clark, *Fisher and Lightwood's Law of Mortgages*, 11th edn, Butterworths, 2002, para 19.67 and 1st supplement, 2003.

79 *Norwich General Trust v Grierson* [1984] CLY 2306.

80 See generally Fisher and Lightwood, note 78, *Norwich General Trust v Grierson* ibid and H Markson, 'Liability of lenders in possession' (1979) 129 NLJ 334.

81 [1996] EGCS 149; 73 P & CR (D) 1, CA. See also S Elwes, 'When do chattels form part' (1995) 11 IL & P 141.

Costs

37.46   Advisers should, throughout, be conscious of the advantageous position which lenders have concerning legal and other costs. In other
types of litigation the normal rule is that costs follow the event. In
mortgage cases the lender is, prima facie, entitled to all its 'costs,
charges and expenses' reasonably and properly incurred in preserving the security or recovering the mortgage debt, including the costs
of possession proceedings.[82] Costs of possession proceedings themselves will be allowed as being part of these 'just allowances',[83] even
without mention of an order for costs in the court order. However,
where the court orders detailed assessment of the lender's costs in
a possession action that assessment will be on a standard basis and
then it seems the lender is restricted, in the absence of terms to the
contrary in the deed, to those standard basis costs.[84] Usually, however, the lender's position is strengthened by such contrary terms in
the mortgage deed. The court has no authority to assess the lender's
costs unless requested to do so by the lender.[85]

37.47   In practice, lenders normally seek a specific order that there be 'no
order as to costs' (or 'costs to be added to security') or simply make
no reference as to the costs at the hearing, relying on a mortgagee's
apparent right to add costs to the security. It appears that a mortgagee
may be entitled to charge, in addition to any standard basis costs, the
sum required to make them up to the solicitor and own client costs
which it will be charged by its solicitor (if there is a right to do so in
the mortgage deed).[86]

37.48   However, it is arguable that a lender is entitled to recover only
what its own solicitor could properly charge following an assessment
under the Solicitors Act 1974. Under that Act[87] the amount which may
be allowed in the county court on assessment must not exceed the
amount which would have been allowed in respect of that item on a
standard basis. Where the rights of the lender as to costs are extended

---

82   *Drydon v Frost* (1838) My & C 670, *National Provincial Bank of England v Games*
(1886) 31 Ch D 582, CA and *Sandon v Hooper* (1843) 6 Beav 246.

83   *Wilkes v Saunion* (1877) 7 Ch D 188.

84   *Re Adelphi Hotel (Brighton)* [1953] 2 All ER 498 and *Re Queen's Hotel Co Cardiff
Ltd* [1900] 1 Ch 792.

85   *Principality Building Society v Llewellyn* [1987] CLY 2940 and *Bank of Ireland
Home Mortgages Ltd v Bissett* [1999] 11 CL 53.

86   *Gomba Holdings (UK) Ltd v Minories Finance Ltd (No 2)* [1992] 4 All ER 588;
[1993] Ch 171; [1992] 3 WLR 723, CA.

87   Solicitors Act 1974 s74(3).

by the terms of the mortgage deed, then that agreement may be unaffected by the Solicitors Act 1974 and assessment of the lender's costs conducted on the basis specified in the mortgage deed.[88] However, where the court assesses a lender's bill in accordance with an indemnity provision in the legal charge this can only fix the upper limit of the borrower's liability. In separate proceedings the borrower may be able to have that sum reduced if costs were unreasonable or improperly incurred and any clause providing to the contrary would be contrary to public policy.[89] In practice, it is usual for lenders to secure indemnification of all costs and expenses (including all solicitors' and estate agents' costs) from sale receipts when the mortgage is redeemed on sale.

37.49   While it is clear from the above that the lender is in a strong position as regards costs, the borrower can ask the court to restrict the lender's claim for costs in a number of ways. CPR PD 48 para 1.3 effectively restates the decision in the leading case of *Gomba Holdings (UK) Ltd v Minories Finance Ltd (No 2)*[90] and sets out the principles which apply. The lender's prima facie entitlement to the costs of the possession proceedings does not exclude the court's jurisdiction to regulate the payment of litigation costs. Even where the mortgage deed provides for the lender's costs to be paid on the indemnity basis, the court has the discretion to override that contractual provision and to disentitle the lender from receiving those costs. This can be done where the costs proposed to be claimed by the lender have been unreasonably incurred or where they are unreasonable in amount.

37.50   Walton J put it this way: 'The court might very well take the view that, in the circumstances of any particular case, [the contractual right to costs on an indemnity basis] was a contractual provision which it ought to overlook and it ought not to give effect to.'[91]

37.51   The court may order that the disputed costs are assessed under CPR 48.3.[92]

---

88   *Tarrant v Speechly Bircham* [1986] CLY 3193. See also 'Costs' (1992) EG 4 April for a short commentary on *Primeridge Ltd v Jean Muir Ltd* [1992] 1 EGLR 273 on the importance of the correct wording in mortgage deeds if the lender is to ensure that costs will be paid on an indemnity basis.

89   *McLeod v Royal Bank of Scotland* LS Gaz 29 November 1995, p27.

90   [1992] 4 All ER 588; [1993] Ch 171; [1992] 3 WLR 723, CA.

91   *Bank of Baroda v Panessar* [1987] Ch 335; [1987] 2 WLR 208 at 224D. See also *Gomba Holdings (UK) Ltd v Minories Finance Ltd (No 2)* [1992] 4 All ER 588; [1993] Ch 171; [1992] 3 WLR 723, CA, and C Evans, 'The New Rules are Working!' [2000] *Adviser* 79.

92   PD 48 para 50.4(3).

37.52   Where the lender has acted unreasonably in relation to the bringing of proceedings or in relation to some aspect of the proceedings, it is advisable to ask at the hearing for the court expressly to direct, as part of the order, that the lender 'be not at liberty to add any costs to the security' in relation to the proceedings or the particular hearing in question.

37.53   Additionally, the borrower, as the paying party to the proceedings, is entitled to ask the court to subject the lender's solicitor's costs to detailed assessment under Solicitors Act 1974 s70. The borrower has the absolute right to ask the court to subject the bill to detailed assessment if objection is made within one month of delivery of the bill.[93] Outside this period the court may grant an order for detailed assessment on such terms as it thinks fit.[94] However, no order for assessment will be granted after the expiry of 12 months from the bill's delivery in the absence of 'special circumstances',[95] and no order can be made at all more than 12 months after payment.[96] This would seem to be the case under the Solicitors Act 1974 even if the borrower has not been told of the amount of the costs claimed by the lender's solicitors. Unfortunately, borrowers are very often not told of the fact that the bill has been delivered, or of the amount claimed and debited to the borrower's account. However, it has been held that a paying client against whom a solicitor brings proceedings for non-payment of a bill is at common law entitled to challenge the reasonableness of the bill even if the 12-month period allowed by the Solicitors Act 1974 has elapsed.[97]

37.54   An application under Solicitors Act 1974 s70 should be made by claim form unless it is made in pending proceedings in which case it should be made by application within those proceedings. The county court has jurisdiction where the amount of the bill does not exceed £5,000 and all or part of the work to be the subject of court scrutiny was carried out in the county court. Otherwise the High Court has jurisdiction.[98]

37.55   Under the Solicitors Act 1974 the party asking for the assessment of the costs will have to pay for the costs of the assessment proceedings unless he or she is able to persuade the court to reduce

93 Solicitors Act 1974 s70(1).
94 Ibid s70(2).
95 Ibid s70(3).
96 Ibid s70(4).
97 *Turner & Co v O Palomo SA* [2000] 1 WLR 37, CA.
98 Solicitors Act 1974 s69(3).

the amount of the costs to be paid by one-fifth of the sum claimed.[99] However, it is possible to identify a part only of the bill for scrutiny by the court and so restrict the risk of the consequences of the 'one-fifth rule'. It would, however, seem that the district judge has some discretion under Solicitors Act 1974 s70(10) to disregard the one-fifth rule where there are 'any special circumstances'. It is advisable to ask the lender to provide details of its solicitor's bill of costs as soon as it is received, itemising the number of letters written and received, phone calls made and received, the time spent, the status of the fee earner in the case and the hourly rate claimed as well as the work undertaken. Details of the amount of the disbursements involved should also be identified. From this it may be possible to assess whether Solicitors Act 1974 assessment is advisable.

37.56   Subject to the terms of the mortgage deed, a borrower is not personally liable for such costs[100] and does not have to pay them directly. They will be added to the security as part of the mortgage and paid out of the proceeds of the sale.[101] Lenders are entitled to add costs to the security even against a borrower with a public funding certificate and this will not be contrary to Access to Justice Act 1999 s11 which restricts awards of costs against publicly funded parties,[102] as technically the costs are recovered from the security and not the borrower.

---

99 Ibid s70(9).
100 *Sinfield v Sweet* [1967] 3 All ER 479.
101 *National Provincial Bank of England v Games* (1886) 31 Ch D 582, CA.
102 *Saunders v Anglia Building Society (No 2)* [1971] 1 All ER 243, HL.

Tenants of borrowers

Introduction

38.1   At common law, a borrower had no power to grant a tenancy which was binding on the lender. Since 1925 borrowers have been given statutory power to grant certain types of lease.[1] However, this statutory power can be excluded by the terms of the mortgage deed and in practice the power to grant tenancies is invariably excluded either absolutely or on terms that the property cannot be let without prior written approval.

38.2   Providing a borrower remains in control of the property and does not get into arrears, the lender may not be interested in any third party occupation. In recent years, many institutional lenders have advanced money under 'Buy to Let' mortgages specifically to enable their borrowers to rent out properties. It is clear that, irrespective of whether the tenancy is binding on the lender, as between the borrower/landlord and the tenant, the tenancy will be binding on the former, if only by estoppel.[2] However, when a lender seeks possession, the position of a tenant is normally dependent on whether the tenancy was granted before or after the mortgage deed was executed.[3]

Tenancies granted prior to the date of the mortgage

Registered land

38.3   In common with any other purchaser of a legal interest, a mortgagee takes the property subject to any interests which qualify as 'overriding interests' within the meaning of Land Registration Act 2002 Sch 3 para 2. Certain tenancies qualify as overriding interests.

38.4   A lease granted for a term not exceeding three years where the tenant is in possession is effective to create a legal interest.[4] Such a tenancy need not be registered at HM Land Registry to bind the lender and will qualify as an overriding interest being the right of a person in actual occupation unless inquiries have been made and

---

1   Law of Property Act 1925 s99.

2   *Dudley and District Benefit Society v Emerson* [1949] 2 All ER 252, CA and *Chatsworth Properties v Effiom* [1971] 1 All ER 604, CA.

3   For an inventive article on the possibility of civil and criminal action against lenders for harassment of residential tenants, see D Barnsley, 'Harassment of Tenants by Mortgagees' [1991] JSWL 220; see also S Robinson, 'Helping Tenants of Defaulting Landlords' (1991) March *Adviser* 23. See also *Berkshire Capital Funding Ltd v Street* (2000) 32 HLR 373, CA and *Woolwich Building Society v Dickman* [1996] 3 All ER 204; (1996) 28 HLR 661, CA.

4   Law of Property Act 1925 s54(2).

these rights are not disclosed.[5] The fact that tenants may have signed a form of consent subordinating their rights as tenants to those of the lender to enable the borrower landlord to obtain the mortgage does not prevent the tenants subsequently relying on their tenancy as an overriding interest which binds the lender.[6]

38.5 In addition, a lease for a term not exceeding seven years also qualifies as an overriding interest[7] and, provided it is in writing, will be valid and binding on the lender whether or not the tenant is in occupation. In the case of registered land, the mortgage is completed and becomes effective on the date it is executed although tenancies which are created after completion of the advance but before registration at HM Land Registry will be binding on the lender.[8] This applies even if the tenancy is granted in breach of a term of the legal charge.[9]

Unregistered land

38.6 The tenancy of a person who went into occupation prior to the mortgage will be binding on the lender if validly created, that is if the tenancy either was created formally by deed or was one capable of being created orally, ie, for a term not exceeding three years taking effect in possession at the best rent which can be reasonably obtained without taking a fine.[10] This will include weekly and monthly tenancies. Given the provisions of the Land Registration Act 2002 in relation to compulsory registration of land, in practice it is uncommon to find unregistered titles.

Pre-mortgage binding tenancies

38.7 Although it is conceivable that a borrower may have been able to allow tenants into a property in anticipation of the completion of the initial purchase, in practice cases where a tenant has an interest binding

---

5 Land Registration Act 2002 Sch 3 para 2, *Barclays Bank Ltd v Stasek* [1957] Ch 28, *Bolton Building Society v Cobb* [1965] 3 All ER 814; [1966] 1 WLR 1, *Woolwich Equitable Building Society v Marshall & Long* [1952] Ch 1; [1951] 2 All ER 769, ChD and *Barclays Bank plc v Zaroovabli* [1997] Ch 321; [1997] 2 All ER 19, ChD.

6 *Woolwich Building Society v Dickman* [1996] 3 All ER 204, CA. See also J Morgan, 'Mortgages v Occupiers: Overriding Interest in an Age of Consent' [1997] Conv 402.

7 Land Registration Act 2002 Sch 3 para 1.

8 *Abbey National Building Society v Cann* [1991] 1 AC 56; [1990] 1 All ER 1085; [1991] 1 AC 56, HL and *Pourdanay v Barclays Bank plc* [1997] Ch 321, ChD.

9 *Barclays Bank plc v Zaroovabli* [1997] Ch 321.

10 Law of Property Act 1925 s54(2) and *Universal Permanent Building Society v Cooke* [1952] Ch 95, CA.

on a lender are more likely to arise with second or subsequent mortgages. The effect of a binding tenancy is that the lender cannot take possession as against the tenant unless, for example, the tenancy was granted following a notice under Housing Act 1988 Sch 2 ground 2 (for which see para 10.31). So long as the borrower is allowed to retain the property as against the lender he or she is entitled to claim the rent and to sue for possession against the tenant.[11] If the lender claims possession in accordance with its common law right then the tenant is bound to pay the rent to the lender.[12] This includes any rent due but unpaid to the borrower at the time of the lender's demand.[13] Where the lender takes possession and gives notice to the tenant requiring rent to be paid to it, the tenant cannot set-off against the rent a personal claim he or she has against the borrower.[14] A borrower executing a second mortgage deed, after the granting of a tenancy, to correct the terms of an earlier deed entered into before the granting of the tenancy does not replace the earlier deed so as to result in the tenancy being binding on the lender.[15]

Tenancies granted after the date of the mortgage

38.8   As indicated above (see para 38.1), most mortgage deeds exclude the borrower's statutory power to grant leases, either absolutely or without the lender's specific permission. It has been held that a tenancy granted in breach of such a term in the mortgage deed is not binding on the lender under the Rent Act 1977 although it remains binding as such on the borrower.[16] The principle applies equally to tenancies under the Housing Act 1988. The statutory tenant's 'status of irremovability' granted to a protected tenant on the ending of the contractual tenancy does not bind the lender if the original contractual tenancy was granted in breach of a term in the mortgage deed.[17] As a result,

---

11 Law of Property Act 1925 1925 ss99 and 141 and *Trent v Hunt* (1853) 9 Exch 14.
12 *Rogers v Humphreys* (1835) 4 Ad & El 299.
13 *Moss v Gallimore* (1779) 1 Doug KB 279.
14 *Reeves v Pope* [1914] 2 KB 284.
15 *Walthamstow Building Society v Davies* (1990) 22 HLR 60, CA.
16 *Dudley and District Benefit Society v Emerson* [1949] 2 All ER 252; [1949] Ch 707, CA. Cf, *Abbey National plc v Yusuf* June 1993 *Legal Action* 12.
17 *Britannia Building Society v Earl* [1990] 2 All ER 469; [1990] 1 WLR 422, CA. For a commentary see S Bridge, 'The Residential Tenant and the Mortgaged Reversion' [1990] Conv 450. See also *Mann v Nijar* (2000) 32 HLR 223, CA and *Sadiq v Hussain* [1997] NPC 19, CA.

the occupying tenant has no claim to remain once the lender exercises its right to possession. Until and unless something takes place to change the relationship, the tenant is, as against the lender, a trespasser. The lender is not entitled to demand payment of any arrears of rent due from the tenant to the borrower at the date the lender takes possession from the borrower.[18] Where a tenant is required by the lender to pay rent to it, the tenant can raise this as recognition of a tenancy as a defence to any claim by the borrower for the payment of rent.[19]

38.9　　The fact that the lender knew that a borrower was proposing to rent out the property for which mortgage finance was being sought does not prevent the lender from relying on a clause prohibiting the granting of a tenancy.[20]

38.10　　The occupier's tenancy, however, becomes binding on the lender if the lender does something expressly or by implication to recognise the tenant as its tenant.[21] As the original tenancy between the borrower and the tenant is a nullity so far as the lender is concerned, any tenancy created between the tenant and the lender must take effect as a new tenancy. An example of this arose where a lender's solicitor wrote to the borrower's tenant informing him that he should not pay any more rent to his 'former landlords' and making new arrangements for payment of rent.[22] The test is not one of intention but of objectivity – what would a reasonable person understand the relationship to be? In this case the court held that, by writing to the borrower's tenant in such terms, the lender was estopped from denying that it had accepted him as its tenant.

38.11　　Mere knowledge of an unauthorised post-mortgage tenancy, coupled with a failure to take steps to evict the tenant, does not have the effect of creating a new tenancy with the lender.[23] Acceptance of rent by the lender from the borrower's tenant creates a yearly tenancy between the two parties, although the terms of the tenancy are not necessarily the same as the tenancy from the borrower but are such as are agreed or inferred from conduct.[24] However, a lender's requirement that payment of rent should in future be made to a receiver appointed under a legal charge as a formal agent for the borrower (as

18　*Kitchen's Trustee v Madders* [1950] Ch 134; [1949] 2 All ER 1079, CA.
19　*Underhay v Read* (1888) 20 QBD 209, CA.
20　*Lloyds Bank plc v Doyle* April 1996 *Legal Action* 17, CA.
21　See *Stroud Building Society v Delamont* [1960] 1 All ER 749.
22　*Chatsworth Properties v Effiom* [1971] 1 All ER 604, CA.
23　*Taylor v Ellis* [1960] Ch 368 and *Parker v Braithwaite* [1952] 2 All ER 837.
24　*Keith v R Gancia & Co Ltd* [1904] 1 Ch 774, CA.

is normally the case with receivers) does not create a landlord-tenant relationship.[25]

38.12   The mere fact, however, that a receiver has been appointed does not in an appropriate factual context prevent a court from concluding that a tenancy has arisen with the lender as landlord.[26] Where a first mortgagee has acted in such a way as to have created a tenancy between itself and occupying tenants, a second mortgagee in possession proceedings is entitled to a possession order but subject to the rights of the tenants until such time as those rights are determined.[27]

38.13   It has been argued that the lender may act in such a way that, although falling short of creating a tenancy at common law, an equitable estoppel is raised precluding it from treating the tenant as a trespasser, relying on the normal equitable principles relating to estoppel.[28] It is thought that, for this to happen, a lender who knew of the tenancy would have to act or refrain from acting at a time when the tenant was prejudicing him or herself (over and above paying rent) in reliance on that action or inaction. The essence of this would be that the lender was giving the tenant a false sense of security which resulted in the tenant acting reasonably in the circumstances but to his or her detriment. No direct authority is, however, known on the point.

38.14   The definition of 'mortgagor' in the Administration of Justice Acts as including 'any person deriving title under the original mortgagor'[29] does not include the borrower's tenant so as to enable that tenant to seek the protection of the Acts as if he or she were the borrower.[30] Where, however, a tenant does pay the rent to the lender to avoid eviction, he or she may deduct the amount actually paid to the lender from any future rental payments to the borrower.[31]

38.15   Under the Consumer Credit Act 1974 it would be open to a tenant, who is joined as a defendant, to seek to persuade the court to exercise its discretion to make a time order and to postpone any order for possession. The court is empowered[32] to make a time order and to postpone a possession order of its own volition where it is 'just to

25 *Lever Finance Ltd v Needleman's Tr* [1956] Ch 357 and Law of Property Act 1925 s109(2).
26 *Mann v Nijar* (2000) 32 HLR 223, CA.
27 *Berkshire Capital Funding Ltd v Street* (1999) 78 P & CR 321, CA.
28 See A Walker, 'Tenants of Mortgagors' (1978) 128 NLJ 773.
29 Administration of Justice Act 1970 s39(1).
30 See *Britannia Building Society v Earl* [1990] 2 All ER 469, CA.
31 *Johnson v Jones* (1839) 9 Ad and El 809 and *Underhay v Read* (1887) 20 QBD 209, CA.
32 Consumer Credit Act 1974 ss129(1), (2) and 135.

do so' in actions brought for possession of land to which a regulated agreement relates. It is clear that a time order must be directed at the borrower, requiring payment by the borrower. However, in the face of potential proceedings by the tenant for breach of covenant for quiet enjoyment (see para 38.19), the borrower may be persuaded to meet the payments required under the time order.

38.16 Where a borrower seeks consent from the lender to let out the security, it may in exceptional circumstances be possible to imply a term that the lender's consent would not be unreasonably refused.[33]

38.17 A tenant whose tenancy is invalid as against the lender is still, during the period of a contractual as opposed to a statutory tenancy, a person interested in the equity of redemption and has the right to take a transfer of the mortgage on paying off the loan.[34] Similarly, as a person entitled to redeem the mortgage, the tenant can ask the court to order sale of the property with a view to buying it.[35]

38.18 Where occupiers are occupying the property under a tenancy which is not binding on the lender, it has been held to be inappropriate for the lender to use the shortened procedure against squatters under Civil Procedure Rules 1998 (CPR) Part 55 to obtain an order for possession. The correct procedure is by way of an orthodox possession claim.[36]

38.19 A tenant evicted by a lender as a result of possession being obtained against the borrower may be able to sue the borrower landlord for breach of the limited covenant for quiet enjoyment implied into the tenancy agreement.[37] A similar right to claim damages for breach of an express covenant for quiet enjoyment may arise where there is a written lease.[38] However, there may well be practical difficulties in enforcing a monetary judgment against the borrower/landlord unless other assets can be identified.

38.20 Tenants threatened with eviction in these circumstances should consider applying to be joined as defendants to the possession proceedings with a view to claiming damages against the landlord/borrower

---

33 *Starling v Lloyds TSB Bank plc* [2000] EGLR 101, CA, and *Citibank International plc v Kessler* [1999] Lloyd's Rep Bank 123.

34 *Tarn v Turner* (1888) 39 Ch D 456, CA as considered in *Britannia Building Society v Earl* [1990] 2 All ER 469; [1990] 1 WLR 422, CA.

35 Law of Property Act 1925 s91(2) and *National Westminster Home Loans v Riches* [1995] 43/95 CLW 2.

36 *London Goldhawk Building Society v Eminer* (1977) 242 EG 462. See CPR 55.5.

37 *Stalker v Karim* June 1994 *Legal Action* 12 and *Sutherland v Wall* [1994] CLY 1448.

38 *Carpenter v Parker* (1857) 3 CBNS 206.

within those proceedings under CPR 19.1. Where an expedited hearing resulting in judgment can be arranged, or where it is possible to obtain judgment in default, it would be possible to register a charging order against the title. Assuming that there is sufficient equity, the judgment would be satisfied on the lender selling the property.

Assured tenancies

38.21   The Housing Act 1988 introduced a new mandatory ground for possession available to a borrower/landlord or a lender against assured tenants.[39] There is no corresponding ground under the Rent Act 1977. The ground provides that the court must make an order for possession where:

- the mortgage was granted before the beginning of the tenancy;
- the lender is entitled to exercise a power of sale conferred by the deed or under Law of Property Act 1925 s107;
- the lender requires possession of the dwelling-house for the purpose of disposing of it with vacant possession;

and either:

- notice was given by the landlord not later than the beginning of the tenancy that possession might be required under this ground; or
- the court considers it is just and equitable to dispense with the requirement of notice.

For further discussion see para 10.31.

38.22   Assured tenancies created after the mortgage and in breach of a prohibition on the granting of tenancies are not binding on the lender but are, however, binding on the borrower (see para 38.8 above). This ground for possession specifically empowers a lender to permit a borrower to create a tenancy without running the risk of the tenant claiming security of tenure by virtue of the lender's permitting the tenancy to arise.

---

39 HA 1988 Sch 2 ground 2: see para 10.31.

Domestic relationship breakdown

Introduction

39.1   The two most common causes of mortgage default are reduction of income following loss of employment and relationship breakdown. Where partners separate, it may be inevitable that the home has to be sold if neither can afford to maintain the property on his or her sole income. However, where it is possible for one partner to maintain the property there are two additional problems for the remaining partner to consider over and above the continuing problem of paying for any existing mortgage. The first is preventing sale of the property by the other party and the second is preventing the property being used as security for further loan finance with the corresponding increased risk of eviction by a lender to obtain possession.

Sole ownership

39.2   Where the property is in the sole legal ownership of the departed partner the latter is free to sell or raise further mortgage finance. As a result, where the couple are married or have entered into a civil partnership under the Civil Partnership Act 2004, it is important for the remaining spouse or civil partner as soon as possible to register his or her statutory right to occupy the home ('home rights') under the Family Law Act 1996 s30. In the case of registered land this should be done by way of a notice registered at HM Land Registry, or a class F land charge if the title is unregistered. If in doubt an index map search should be made to check if the property is registered or not. This is done by sending District Land Registry Form SIM to the Land Registry for the area in which the property is situated. Land Registry Practice Guide 10, 'Official Searches of the Index Map', provides more information on the process.[1] No fee is payable on filing Form SIM. Land Registry Practice Guide 11 deals with obtaining a copy of the register in relation to any title.

39.3   Application for the registration of home rights is made on form HR1. No fee is payable. Since 28 May 2001 HM Land Registry practice has been automatically to notify the registered proprietor that an entry relating to the family home has been made. This is, according to HM Land Registry, to ensure compliance with the registered proprietor's rights under the Human Rights Act 1998. Advisers must therefore ensure that people registering home rights are aware of this process.

1   See www.landreg.gov.uk.

39.4   The effect of registration of home rights is, in practice, that the legal owner is unable to sell or mortgage the property until the notice or charge is vacated. It is important to note that taking this step has no effect on any prior mortgage and any arrears which may accrue under that loan. However, where such home rights have been registered a lender is required to give notice to the remaining spouse or civil partner of any possession proceedings brought,[2] to name that person in the particulars of claim and to file at court a copy for service on that person. Such a person may then apply to be joined as defendant with a view to persuading the court to exercise its statutory powers.[3] A 'connected person' has the right to make the mortgage repayments in respect of the home and should do so if he or she can, in order to avoid loss of possession.[4] 'Connected person' in relation to any person means that person's spouse, former spouse, civil partner, former civil partner, co-habitant or former co-habitant.[5] He or she has the right to seek to be joined as a party 'at any time before the action is finally disposed of in that court'[6] and will be made a party if the court does not see 'a special reason' against him or her being joined *and* if the court is satisfied that he or she may be able to meet the legal owner's mortgage liabilities either with or without the court exercising its Administration of Justice Acts powers.

39.5   An occupier who does not fall within the definition of 'connected person' has no right to contest the possession proceedings or to pay the mortgage instalments on behalf of the legal owner. Where, however, he or she has an equitable interest in the property which has priority over the interest of the lender, this protects him or her against dispossession (see chapter 40).

Joint ownership

39.6   Where the property is in joint legal ownership, the departed partner obviously cannot sell or obtain further mortgage finance without the remaining partner's agreement because he or she would have to execute the necessary mortgage deed or transfer form. It would, however, be open to the partner to seek a court order requiring sale of the property or, indeed, any other order that the court may think fit

2   Family Law Act 1996 s56.
3   Ibid s55.
4   Ibid s30(3).
5   Ibid s54(5).
6   Ibid s55(3).

to make in relation to the property.[7] Given the abolition by the Trusts of Land and Appointment of Trustees Act 1996[8] of the presumption of a trust for sale where land is owned jointly the court is given wide discretion as to whether, on application following relationship breakdown, the home should be sold or its occupation regulated. For an analysis of the law on this topic see para 42.27. In the case of married couples the court has the normal wide-ranging power to transfer property as part of its matrimonial jurisdiction on divorce or judicial separation and similar powers are available under the Civil Partnership Act 2004.[9] As joint owners, both partners remain equally liable under the mortgage deed and are normally both joined as defendants in any proceedings brought by a lender.

39.7   Difficulties can arise where one joint legal owner forges the signature of the other on a deed creating a legal charge. In the case of unregistered land the beneficial interest of the owner who has created the forgery passes to the lender, leaving the legal estate being held on trust by the joint legal owners for the innocent legal owner and the lender. The lender would be able to seek a court order for sale under the Trusts of Land and Appointment of Trustees Act 1996. With registered land, the legal charge is effective if registration at HM Land Registry is completed. The innocent joint legal owner's beneficial interest may, however, qualify as an overriding interest if he or she is in actual occupation. See para 40.9. For further detail reference should be made to one of the major works on land law.[10]

---

7   Trusts of Land and Appointment of Trustees Act 1996 s14.
8   Ibid ss4 and 5 and Sch 2.
9   Civil Partnership Act 2004 ss66, 72 and Sch 5.
10   See, eg, K Gray and S Gray, *Elements of Land Law*, 4th edn, Butterworths, 2004.

Rights of equitable owners

Introduction

40.1   This chapter considers those cases where the legal title to a property is vested in the name of one or more people (the legal owners) but where another person has an interest in the property which is recognised in equity but falls short of being a legal interest. The most common example of this is where a matrimonial home is in the sole legal ownership of one spouse but where the other has an equitable interest. Such an occupier, who is not a legal owner, may defeat a lender's possession claim by relying on an equitable interest.

40.2   A legal charge is treated as a legal interest in land. So a lender who advances money secured by a legal charge is treated as a purchaser of a legal interest in the property which is being used as the security. In the case of unregistered land it is a basic principle of English land law that a bona fide purchaser for value of a legal estate (which includes a mortgage lender) takes that estate subject to any equitable interests in the property of which the lender has notice, whether actual or constructive.[1] In the case of registered land, a purchaser takes the property subject to entries on the land register and any 'overriding interests', which can include the rights of people in actual occupation except where inquiry is made of them and their rights are not disclosed in circumstances where they could reasonably have been expected to do so.[2] The application of these general principles in the context of residential mortgages is considered in more detail below. In certain circumstances, therefore, occupiers who are not legal owners but who have some form of equitable interest in the property can effectively prevent the lender from obtaining possession. In this way the defaulting legal owner may retain occupation under the protection of the equitable owner, without even making any further financial payments. The following is a brief outline only of what is a complicated area of residential land law.

Creation of equitable interests

40.3   The courts have found it difficult to be consistent when deciding whether an occupying non-owner has acquired an equitable interest in a property. Many of the cases seem to depend on whether the judge feels that the justice of the situation demands intervention as against

---

1   Law of Property Act 1925 ss199(1) and 205(1).
2   Land Registration Act 2002 Sch 3 para 2(b).

the legal owner and third parties. Sir Nicolas Browne-Wilkinson, who decided many of the leading cases, even said:

> I do not think that the principles lying behind these decisions ... have yet been fully explored and on occasion it seems that such rights are found to exist simply on the ground that to hold otherwise would be a hardship to the Plaintiff.[3]

40.4   No apology is made for not analysing the extensive case-law in detail; for a full explanation, reference must be made to the standard works on land law as well as family law, where many of the decisions have been reached in the context of relationship breakdown.[4] However, by way of example only, the courts have held that a non-legal owner has acquired an equitable interest by:

- paying directly for the purchase of a property which was conveyed into the legal owner's sole name;[5]
- contributing towards the deposit paid on the purchase;[6]
- helping with the construction of the house;[7]
- regular and substantial direct financial contributions to the mortgage.[8]

40.5   Great weight is attached to financial contribution or direct contribution of money's worth.[9] Indirect financial contribution to the

---

3   *Re Sharpe* [1980] 1 WLR 219 at 223D.

4   See generally K Gray and S Gray, *Elements of Land Law*, 4th edn, Butterworths, 2004; P Sparkes, *A New Land Law*, 2nd edn, Hart Publishing, 2003; and S Cretney, J Masson and R Bailey-Harris, *Principles of Family Law*, 7th edn, Sweet & Maxwell, 2003.

5   *Pettitt v Pettitt* [1970] AC 777, HL. A resulting trust does not, however, arise from the fact that money was lent to facilitate a purchase: see *Hussey v Palmer* [1972] 1 WLR 1286, CA and *Pettitt v Pettitt* [1969] 2 All ER 385; [1970] AC 777, HL. See also *Midland Bank plc v Cooke* [1995] 4 All ER 562, CA, where the court held that where an equitable owner had established an interest by direct contribution the court will assess the assumed beneficial proportion by investigating the whole course of dealings between the parties.

6   See *Gissing v Gissing* [1971] AC 886, HL and *Burns v Burns* [1984] 1 All ER 244 at 264; [1984] Ch 317, CA.

7   *Cooke v Head* [1972] 1 WLR 518, CA.

8   *Gissing v Gissing* [1971] AC 886, HL.

9   See *Lloyds Bank plc v Rosset* (1990) 22 HLR 349; [1991] 1 AC 107, HL, M P Thompson, 'Establishing an Interest in the Home' [1990] Conv 314, S Gardner, 'A Woman's Work' (1991) 54 MLR 126, D Hayton, 'Equitable Rights of Cohabitants' [1990] Conv 370 and P Sparkes, 'The Quantification of Beneficial Interests: Problems arising from Contributions to Deposits, Mortgage Advances and Mortgage Instalments' [1991] OJLS 39. See also *Ivin v Blake* [1995] 1 FLR 70 and A Lawson, 'Direct and Indirect Contributions to the Purchase Price of a Home' [1996] Conv 462.

purchase of the property may result in the acquisition of an equitable interest, for example, by pooling of resources or in some other way relieving the legal owner from expenditure on the property.[10] Alternatively, where the non-legal owner has acted to his or her detriment on the basis of assumed joint ownership, then the court may be prepared to recognise some equitable interest.[11]

Nature of equitable interests

40.6   The courts have also not been consistent in defining the nature of the interest accruing to the occupying non-owner who successfully argues that he or she has some form of equitable interest. The court may hold that the occupier is a tenant in common under a resulting or constructive trust. If this is the case, the legal owner holds the property jointly on his or her behalf and on behalf of the non-legal owner.[12] An alternative basis for granting relief may be to find that the non-legal owner has rights under an irrevocable licence conferring some property interest that is binding on the legal owner and lender.[13]

Binding equitable interests

Legal ownership in one name

40.7   The legal considerations to be applied in deciding whether an equitable owner's interest in a property (which is vested legally in another person) binds third parties differ, depending on whether the land is registered or unregistered.

40.8   In the case of *registered* land, a lender taking a legal charge takes it

---

10   *Grant v Edwards* [1986] 2 All ER 426, CA, J Warburton, 'Interested or Not?' [1986] Conv 291.

11   *Midland Bank Ltd v Dobson* [1986] 1 FLR 171, *Coombes v Smith* [1986] 1 WLR 808, *Re Basham (decd)* [1986] 1 WLR 1498, M P Thompson, 'Estoppel and Clean Hands' [1986] Conv 406 and J Montgomery, 'A Question of Intention' [1987] Conv 16. See also *Drake v Whipp* [1996] 1 FLR 826, CA.

12   *Oxley v Hiscock* [2004] EWCA Civ 546; [2004] 3 WLR 715 and 'Resulting and Constructive Trusts of Land: The Mist Descends and Rises' [2005] Conv 79, *Kingsnorth Finance Co v Tizard* [1986] 2 All ER 54; [1986] 1 WLR 783 and *Grant v Edwards* [1986] 2 All ER 426; [1986] Ch 638.

13   *Re Sharpe* [1980] 1 WLR 219 and see *Bristol and West Building Society v Henning* [1985] 2 All ER 606; [1985] 1 WLR 778, CA, and noted at [1985] Conv 361. See generally references at notes 4 and 11.

subject to the interests specified in the land register and to any over-riding interests.[14]

40.9   Land Registration Act 2002 Sch 3 defines what interests can constitute an overriding interest of a person in occupation and includes:

Interests of persons in actual occupation

2 An interest belonging at the time of the disposition to a person in actual occupation, so far as relating to land of which he is in actual occupation, except for –

(a) ...

(b) an interest of a person of whom inquiry was made before the disposition and who failed to disclose the right when he could reasonably have been expected to do so;

(c) an interest –

(i) which belongs to a person whose occupation would not have been obvious on a reasonably careful inspection of the land at the time of the disposition, and

(ii) of which the person to whom the disposition is made does not have actual knowledge at that time.

40.10   The wording differs slightly from the comparable provision in the previous legislation.[15] The aim of the legislation is clearly to protect occupiers of property where the fact of their occupation would alert a purchaser as to the possibility of unrecorded interests on the land register and, as a result, the necessity to make further inquiry. It follows that the interests of an actual occupier 'override' the legal charge taken by the lender except in cases where either the actual occupier has unreasonably failed, on inquiry, to disclose his or her own entitlement or the relevant occupation was neither reasonably discoverable by nor actually known to the lender. The inclusion of the wording 'could reasonably have been expected to do so', which did not appear in the previous legislative definition of 'overriding interest', would seem to suggest that there is now some duty of candour on an occupier to assert a right (but still only if inquiry is made).

40.11   In *Williams & Glyn's Bank Ltd v Boland*,[16] the House of Lords held that the beneficial interest under a trust of an occupying spouse, acquired by way of substantial contribution to the initial purchase price of the house, is such an overriding interest capable of binding a lender. Whether someone is in 'actual occupation' is a question of fact.[17] Vicarious occupation through, for example, a spouse

---

14   Land Registration Act 2002 s29(1) and (2) and Sch 3.

15   Land Registration Act 1925 s70(1)(g).

16   [1981] AC 487; [1980] 3 WLR 138; [1980] 2 All ER 408, HL.

17   *Lloyds Bank plc v Rosset* [1989] Ch 350, CA.

or other relative or even a limited company[18] qualifies.[19] Protection only applies to the part actually occupied although in the context of residential mortgages this provision might have limited impact. A child cannot be a person in occupation for this purpose.[20] The relevant date for considering whether someone is in occupation is the date of execution of the mortgage, not the date of registration at HM Land Registry.[21] Where the mortgage financed the initial purchase of the property and the purchase and the mortgage were simultaneous, the courts have been loath to allow an equitable owner's rights to take precedence over the lender's legal interest where the equitable owner knew, at the time, that the mortgage was being taken out. In such circumstances the courts have concluded that the equitable owner intended that his or her interest be postponed to that of the lender and so is estopped from claiming priority.[22] This postponement of the equitable owner's interest applies even to a subsequent remortgage taken out by the legal owner without the equitable owner's knowledge but limited to the extent of the original mortgage.[23] Where, however, the mortgage was genuinely granted after the property's acquisition to a borrower in whom the legal estate had already vested, where the beneficial owner was unaware of the creation of the legal charge, then that occupier's equitable interest binds the lender.[24]

40.12   In the case of *unregistered* land, a mortgage lender advancing money on land by way of legal charge takes the security subject to any equitable interests in the property of which it has notice, whether actual, constructive or imputed. Actual notice is self-explanatory. Constructive notice is notice which the lender would have obtained 'if such enquiries and inspections had been made as ought reasonably to have been made' by the lender.[25] Imputed notice is the actual

---

18 *Stockholm Finance Ltd v Garden Holdings Inc* [1995] NPC 162.

19 *Abbey National Building Society v Cann* [1991] 1 AC 56, HL.

20 *Hypo-Mortgage Services Ltd v Robinson* [1997] 2 FLR 71, CA.

21 See *Abbey National Building Society v Cann* [1991] 1 AC 56; (1990) 22 HLR 360, HL.

22 See *Paddington Building Society v Mendelsohn* (1985) 50 P & CR 244, CA, M P Thompson, 'The retreat from Boland' [1986] Conv 57 and *Bristol and West Building Society v Henning* [1985] 2 All ER 606; [1985] 1 WLR 778, CA. See also M Welstead, 'The Mistress and The Mortgage' [1985] CLJ 354. See generally Gray, note 4.

23 *Equity Home Loans Ltd v Prestridge* [1992] 1 WLR 137; (1991) 24 HLR 76, CA.

24 *Williams and Glyns Bank v Boland* [1981] AC 487; [1980] 2 All ER 408; [1980] 3 WLR 138, HL.

25 Law of Property Act 1925 s199(1)(ii)(a).

or constructive notice of the lender's agent, although only so far as notice was received by the agent in the case of the lender obtaining the mortgage.[26] It is not clear as to when a lender is fixed with constructive notice or the lengths to which a lender has to go to discharge its duty to make reasonable inquiry. However, it seems that the courts require not inconsiderable inquiries to be made. In one case it was held that a lender's agent visiting the property at a prearranged time was insufficient inquiry to discharge an obligation to find out whether a matrimonial home was occupied by a spouse who might have an equitable interest.[27] As with registered land, the courts have proved unwilling to allow a beneficial owner to bind a lender where he or she knowingly was to benefit from the legal owner's borrowing money by way of mortgage, although the courts' reasoning is open to question.[28]

40.13   In practice, however, the question of whether an equitable owner's interest or right binds a lender is most likely to arise in cases of mortgages entered into *after* the initial purchase of the property.

40.14   Where a lender has taken a mortgage on a property which is subject to equitable rights in priority to its rights under the mortgage, the lender will wish to consider whether to dispute the assertion that there is a binding equitable interest on the assumption that the claim is being fabricated in an attempt to prevent eviction.[29] Advisers should therefore test the evidence supporting the claim as to the equitable interest at an early stage. Similarly advisers will need to assess whether there would be any basis for a lender to be able to argue that the beneficial owner's conduct constitutes an estoppel so as to give the lender's rights priority.[30] If these are not viable responses, it would remain open to the lender to apply for an order for sale under Trusts of Land and Appointment of Trustees Act 1996 s14.[31] Alternatively, it is open to the lender to sue the legal owner for repayment of the loan by virtue of any covenant to repay contained in the mortgage deed.

---

26 Ibid s199(1)(ii)(b).
27 *Kingsnorth Finance Co v Tizard* [1986] 2 All ER 54; [1986] 1 WLR 738. See also P Luxton, 'Clandestine co-owners: an occupational hazard for mortgagees?' (1986) NLJ 771 and M P Thompson, 'The purchaser as private detective' [1986] Conv 283. See also *Lloyds Bank plc v Carrick* [1996] 4 All ER 630, CA.
28 See *Bristol and West Building Society v Henning* [1985] 2 All ER 606; [1985] 1 WLR 778, CA and M P Thompson, 'Relief for first mortgagees?' (1986) 49 MLR 245.
29 *Midland Bank plc v Dobson* [1986] 1 FLR 171.
30 See note 22.
31 *Bank of Baroda v Dhillon* (1997) 30 HLR 845; [1998] 1 FLR 524, CA and S Pascoe, 'The Further Decline of Overriding Interests' [1998] Conv 415.

If the borrower is made bankrupt, his or her trustee in bankruptcy could seek a court order for sale of the property under Trusts of Land and Appointment of Trustees Act 1996 s14.[32] See para 43.9.

Legal ownership in several names

40.15 Different legal considerations apply where the title to the mortgaged property is held legally in joint names. Although there was initially some doubt, following the decision in *Boland*, the House of Lords, in *City of London Building Society v Flegg*,[33] confirmed that a lender who advances money on the security of a property where the legal title is vested in two or more people as trustees for sale, is free from the concern of whether or not other people may have equitable interests under such a trust[34] as in *Boland*. By virtue of the 'overreaching' provisions of the Law of Property Act 1925,[35] such a lender takes its interest by virtue of the mortgage free from all beneficial claims. The equitable owner's interests theoretically attach to the capital money realised when the property is sold. Notice of beneficial interests in unregistered land and actual occupation in registered land is irrelevant.

40.16 It has been argued that a distinction needs to be drawn between people who have a beneficial interest behind a trust (where 'overreaching' will apply) and people who have a right to occupy the property under a form of estoppel licence (where overreaching would not apply).[36]

Mortgage consent forms

40.17 In an effort to avoid the risk of being landed with a binding equitable owner, most lenders now require adult occupiers (intending or actual)

---

32 See *Alliance & Leicester plc v Slayford* [2000] EWCA Civ 257; [2001] All ER (Comm 1); (2001) 33 HLR 66 and M P Thompson, 'The Cumulative Range of a Mortgagee's Remedies' [2002] Conv 53.

33 [1988] AC 54; (1987) 19 HLR 484, HL. See also W Swadling, 'The Conveyancer's Revenge' [1987] Conv 451 and S Gardner, 'Bleak House Latest – Law Lords Dispel Fog?' (1988) 51 MLR 365.

34 Law of Property Act 1925 ss2 and 27. See also Gray, note 4.

35 Ibid s36(1). See M P Thompson, 'Dispositions by Trustees for Sale' [1988] Conv 108, M P Thompson, *Co-ownership*, Sweet & Maxwell, 1988, p136, *Re Sharpe* [1980] 1 WLR 219 and Gray, note 4.

36 See M P Thompson, 'Dispositions by Trustees for Sale' [1988] Conv 108, M P Thompson, *Co-ownership*, Sweet & Maxwell, 1988, p136, *Re Sharpe* [1980] 1 WLR 219 and Gray, note 4.

who are not to be joined as parties to the mortgage deed to execute forms of consent or undertaking prior to completion of the mortgage. These are intended to postpone any legal or equitable rights they may have, until after those of the lender. Executing such a form may act either as an estoppel preventing the equitable owner from seeking to rely on his or her interest or have the effect of postponing such rights to those of the lender.[37]

---

37 *Woolwich Building Society v Plane* [1997] EWCA Civ 2372, *Woolwich Building Society v Dickman* [1996] 3 All ER 204, CA and *Skipton Building Society v Clayton* (1993) 25 HLR 596.

CHAPTER 41

Undue influence

Introduction

41.1   The courts have historically sought to protect people who have acted to their detriment because of undue pressure put upon them. In recent years there has been a burgeoning trend of borrowers (or sureties) claiming that a mortgage is voidable, and hence unenforceable, because of misrepresentation or because of 'undue influence' put upon them, either by the lender directly or more commonly by a third party for whose benefit finance is being sought. In this context the expression 'surety' is intended to include joint owners who allow their interest in property to be used as security for another joint owner for whose benefit a loan is taken out as well as a person who puts up property as security for another where that person is not themselves putting anything forward as security for the loan.

41.2   Litigation in this field has been extensive since the 1980s. The House of Lords has had cause to consider the law on two separate occasions with the lead cases being *Barclays Bank v O'Brien* and *CIBC Mortgages v Pitt*[1] in 1994 and *Royal Bank of Scotland v Etridge (No 2)*[2] in 2001. This chapter is simply designed to introduce advisers to the issues. For a comprehensive analysis of the law reference should be made to leading texts on land law and mortgages.[3]

Lender misconduct

41.3   The instances where a borrower or surety will allege that a bank or other mortgage lender has misrepresented or pressured a borrower or surety into signing a legal charge are limited. Before the transaction will be set aside, it will be necessary to show that unfair advantage has been taken in the sense that the transaction was to the manifest disadvantage of the victim.[4] Where, however, there is actual undue influence (as contrasted with constructive undue influence, for which see below) then manifest disadvantage does not need to be shown.[5] There is no general duty on a bank to advise a potential borrower/surety as

1   [2001] UKHL 44; [2002] 2 AC 773.
2   [2002] AC 773, HL.
3   K Gray and S Gray, *Elements of Land Law*, 4th edn, Oxford University Press, 2005, pp1649–1659 and W Clark, *Fisher and Lightwood's Law of Mortgage*, 11th edn, Butterworths, 2003, pp353–362.
4   *National Westminster Bank plc v Morgan* [1985] AC 686, HL.
5   *O'Hara v Allied Irish Banks Ltd* [1985] BCLC 52.

to the nature of a relevant transaction although the situation is likely to be different where the borrower/surety is an existing customer.[6] Where the lender is taken to be under a duty and its explanation is inadequate, the security may not be enforceable.[7] Where the principal debtor was acting as the lender's agent, the lender is fixed with the misrepresentation or undue influence practised by him or her.[8] In practice, however, cases are rare in which the lender simply leaves the principal debtor to extract from the surety his or her signature by whatever means he or she may choose.

Misconduct of principal debtor

41.4   In recent years, the courts have in some cases sought to impose liability on lenders for the misconduct of a principal debtor where that person could reasonably have been expected to have had influence over a prospective mortgage borrower or surety. Most of the cases have involved wives being prevailed upon to enter into second mortgages on the matrimonial home, with the principal debtor being their husbands. This development culminated in the leading cases of *Barclays Bank plc v O'Brien* and *CIBC Mortgages v Pitt*[9] where the House of Lords sought to define the circumstances in which a lender will be deemed to be on notice of undue influence or misrepresentation perpetrated in order to induce a borrower to enter into the mortgage or a joint owner to put up his or her interest as surety, such as to enable the borrower or surety to apply to the court to have the transaction declared ineffective to charge that person's interest in the property used as security. While, commonly, the case involved second mort-

---

6   *Cornish v Midland Bank plc* [1985] 3 All ER 513, CA. See generally A Ward, 'The Liability of UK Banks for Financial Advice – Recent Developments' (1996) 11 JIBL 472, *Barclays Bank v Khaira* [1992] 1 WLR 623, *Midland Bank v Perry* (1987) Fin LR 237, *Verity v Lloyds Bank* [1995] NPC 148 and L Wise, 'Biting the Hand that Lends?' SJ, 9 February 1996.

7   *Barclays Bank plc v O'Brien* [1994] 1 AC 180, HL.

8   *Kings North Trust Ltd v Bell* [1986] 1 WLR 119 and *Barclays Bank plc v Kennedy* (1989) 58 P & CR 221, CA.

9   [1994] AC 200. See generally M Thompson, 'The Enforceability of Mortgages' [1994] Conv 140, J Lehane, 'Undue Influence, Misrepresentation and Third Parties' (1994) 100 LQR 167B, Fehlberg, 'The Husband, the Bank, the Wife and her Signature' (1994) 57 MLR 467, P Sparkes, 'The proprietary effect of undue influence' [1995] Conv 250, B Fehlberg, *Sexually Transmitted Debt*, Clarendon Press, 1997 and S Gardner, 'Wives' Guarantees of their Husbands' Debts' [1999] LQR 1.

gages on jointly owned property, the principles apply equally where a sole owner or a beneficial co-owner is prevailed upon by a principal debtor to secure finance made available to that person. Where the lender is taken to be on notice of the principal debtor's misconduct then the lender is not able to enforce the mortgage but the lender's rights against the principal debtor remain unaffected. In this way the surety may be able to resist possession proceedings by the lender although advisers should be aware that where the surety and the principal debtor are joint owners then, ultimately, possession is at risk if the principal debtor is bankrupted and an order for sale sought by the trustee in bankruptcy or where the lender may be able independently to seek an order for sale under the Trusts of Land and Appointment of Trustees Act 1996.[10] See para 43.9.

41.5   The following is an attempt to summarise the situation following *O'Brien* and *Pitt* in the light of the refinements of the principles superimposed by the House of Lords in *Etridge (No 2)*. A mortgage may be unenforceable against the innocent party for misrepresentation by the principal debtor to the innocent party so long as the misrepresentation would have been sufficient to make a contract voidable if that misrepresentation had been made by the lender. An innocent misrepresentation suffices.[11] The mortgage may also be set aside if there has been undue influence exercised resulting in the surety entering into the transaction. A lender having actual knowledge of the facts entitling the surety to apply to set aside is very rare. A lender is put on inquiry wherever a person offers to stand as surety for the debts of a spouse or any other person involved in some non-commercial relationship (whether heterosexual, homosexual or platonic, whether or not involving cohabitation[12]) of which the lender is aware. The relationship of employer-employee falls within this definition.[13] The transaction must not appear to be to the surety's advantage.[14]

41.6   The requirement that the transaction is not to the innocent borrower/surety's financial advantage will often be fulfilled in the case where the borrower is being asked to stand as surety for the

10   *First National Bank plc v Achampong* [2003] EWCA Civ 487; [2004] 1 FCR 18. See M P Thompson, 'Undue Influence before Etridge' [2003] Conv 314.

11   *TSB v Camfield* [1995] 1 All ER 951; (1994) 27 HLR 205, CA.

12   *Massey v Midland Bank plc* [1995] 1 All ER 929

13   *Credit Lyonnais Bank Nederland NV v Burch* [1997] 1 All ER 144, CA. See H Tijo, 'O'Brien and Unconscionability' (1997) 113 LQR 10.

14   *Royal Bank of Scotland v Etridge (No 2)* [2002] AC 773, HL. See M P Thompson, 'Wives, Sureties and Banks' [2002] Conv 174 and G Andrews, 'Undue Influence – Where's the Disadvantage?' [2002] Conv 456.

principal debtor's debts and where no direct financial gain is being obtained by the former. This was the case in *O'Brien* and such cases are described in the case-law as 'surety cases'. Where, however, the transaction is ostensibly a joint borrowing by the borrower/surety and the principal debtor , then there will be no constructive notice to the lender even if the stated purpose (as in *Pitt*) was false. These are called 'joint loan cases'. Cases where a spouse becomes surety for the debts of a company whose shares are held by her and her husband, even when the surety is a director or secretary, cannot be equated with joint loans.[15]

41.7 A lender may be put on notice, even if the loan being sought is ostensibly a joint borrowing, if the advantage to be gained by the borrower/surety is out of proportion to the risk being undertaken.[16] Knowledge possessed by solicitors acting for a lender, the principal debtor and surety in a remortgage (as to the purpose for which monies were to be used) is not imputed to the lender. The knowledge has not come to the solicitors as solicitors for the lender as such.[17]

41.8 Where the lender is put on inquiry it must take 'reasonable steps' to bring home to the surety the risks involved in the transaction proposed.[18] In *Etridge (No 2)* the House of Lords drew a distinction between transactions entered into prior to the ruling in that case (ie, 11 October 2001) and those after.

41.9 In pre-*Etridge* transactions Lord Nicholls, in *Etridge (No 2)*, indicated that the duty on lenders was as set out in *O'Brien*. Reasonable steps would have been taken if the lender had received from a solicitor confirmation that the surety had been advised of the risks involved in the transaction. The lender would also have satisfied the requirement by advising that the surety obtain independent legal advice and this would also have been satisfied if it had insisted that the surety attend a private meeting (without the third party being present) with a representative of the lender at which the surety was warned as to the risks.

---

15 *Royal Bank of Scotland v Etridge (No 2)* [2001] UKHL 44; [2001] 4 All ER 449, HL.
16 *Goode Durrant Administration v Biddulph* (1994) 26 HLR 625, *Barclays Bank v Sumner* [1996] EGCS 65 and *Bank of Scotland v Bennett* [1997] 1 FLR 801.
17 *Halifax Mortgage Services Ltd v Stepsky* [1996] Ch 207; (1995) 28 HLR 522, CA, *Scotlife Home Loans (No 2) v Hedworth* (1996) 28 HLR 771, *National Westminster Bank plc v Beaton* (1997) 30 HLR 99, CA and *Woolwich plc v Gomm* (2000) 79 P & CR 61, CA, S Nield, 'Imputed Notice' [2000] Conv 196, *Northern Rock Building Society v Archer* (1999) 78 P & CR 65, CA and M P Thompson, 'Constructive Notice of Undue Influence' [1999] Conv 510.
18 [2002] 2 AC 773.

41.10   In post-*Etridge (No 2)* transactions a more taxing protocol is required to be followed, involving again the requirement for advice from a solicitor. The steps to be taken by a lender are:

- The lender must make direct contact with the surety to identify the solicitor whom the surety will instruct and to advise that the role of that solicitor will be to ensure that any later consent to the transaction cannot be disputed.
- The lender must receive the surety's nomination of solicitor.
- The lender must disclose to the solicitor all relevant information in respect of the principal debtor's financial position and the extent, purpose and terms of the proposed transaction. A copy of the loan application form should be provided to the solicitor.
- The solicitor and the surety must meet in the absence of the principal debtor. At that meeting, the solicitor must advise in suitably non-technical language about the nature and implications of the transaction. The relevant documents must be explained, as must the implications if the lender has to take enforcement action – ie, repossession and/or bankruptcy. The advice must cover the extent of the surety's liability under the transaction and the fact that the transaction is optional. The solicitor must check that the surety wishes to proceed and indicate to the surety that the lender will be advised that these issues have been covered and that the transaction is being entered into in the knowledge of this.

41.11   Receipt by the lender of written confirmation that these steps have been taken from the solicitor in question protects the lender from any future allegation of undue influence or misrepresentation. Clearly, however, the solicitor involved in this process runs the risk of a claim of negligence if the surety suffers loss as a result of the transaction because s/he will owe a duty of care to the surety.

The relief available to the surety

41.12   A surety who successfully raises an *O'Brien* defence will be able to resist the claim for possession based on the legal charge.

41.13   It is not possible to 'partly' escape from the consequences of a transaction in part where, for example, a surety knew that he or she was guaranteeing a certain sum whereas the mortgage which he or she was induced to enter into secured a much larger debt.[19] In such

---

19   *TSB Bank plc v Camfield* [1995] 1 WLR 430; [1995] 1 All ER 951, CA. See A Phang, 'Partial Rescission for Misrepresentation Rejected' [1995] 111 LQR 555.

circumstances the whole transaction must be set aside. Where, however, a loan arrangement comprises several transactions, for example, a loan agreement with a separate later side letter, it is possible to sever the objectionable transaction leaving the other uncontaminated part enforceable.[20] A lender granting a remortgage which would otherwise be voidable by the surety has a 'right of subrogation' in relation to a previous charge which was not voidable and can claim possession based on the element of the remortage referrable to the previous mortgage.[21] A remortgaging lender in such circumstances is entitled to the same security as the original lender but cannot be subrogated to an amount greater than the mortgage which has been discharged by the remortgage.[22] Where a mortgage, which is voidable because of undue influence, is discharged and a new mortgage created between the same parties the new mortgage is itself voidable.[23]

The lender's response

41.14   A surety who delays asserting an *O'Brien* defence (for example, by acknowledging the legal charge in matrimonial ancillary relief proceedings) may be barred from raising it in subsequent possesssion proceedings by the lender.[24] There is nothing improper in a lender, met with an *O'Brien* defence, seeking a money judgment against the principal debtor with a view to bankruptcy of the principal debtor and subsequent sale by the trustee in bankruptcy of the security.[25]

20 *Barclays Bank plc v Caplan* [1998] 1 FLR 532, ChD.
21 *Halifax plc v Omar* [2002] EWCA Civ 121; [2002] 2 P & CR 377, *Halifax Mortgage Services Ltd v Muirhead* (1997) 76 P & CR 418, CA.
22 *Cheltenham & Gloucester plc v Appleyard* [2004] EWCA Civ 291; [2004] 13 EGCS 127.
23 *Yorkshire Bank plc v Tinsley* [2004] EWCA Civ 816; [2004] 1 WLR 2380. See M P Thompson, 'Replacement Mortgages' [2004] Conv 399.
24 *First National Bank plc v Walker* [2001] 1 FCR 21, CA.
25 *Alliance & Leicester plc v Slayford* [2000] EWCA Civ 257; [2001] 1 All ER (Comm) 1. See M P Thompson, 'The Cumulative Range of a Mortgagee's Remedies' [2002] Conv 53.

Taking instructions from the borrower/surety

41.15   Obviously much will depend on the circumstances of each case, although there are a number of common issues which will need to be considered when considering an *O'Brien* defence:

- Did the principal debtor exert real pressure or misrepresent matters to the borrower/surety? What exactly was said and done? Did the borrower/surety rely on the principal debtor for financial decisions and rely unquestioningly on him or her?
- What educational or business background does the borrower/surety have?
- How was the transaction explained by the principal debtor? Were half-truths or inaccuracies involved?
- Where, when, how and before whom was the document signed? Is there a certificate confirming that the implications were made known to the borrower/surety?
- Did the client have any advice from the lender or from anyone else and, if so, who and what was the advice? Was the extent of present and prospective future financial liability made clear? Was the principal debtor present when the advice was given? Did the borrower/surety understand the advice?
- Did the lender insist on legal advice being obtained as a precondition to the loan?
- Did the borrower/surety receive legal advice, and if so from whom and what was that advice?
- Did the borrower/surety understand the nature of the transaction?
- Was the transaction in relation to a guarantee or a joint loan? What did the lender believe it to be for and what did the loan application say it was for?
- Obtain on disclosure the correspondence between the lender and the solicitor/adviser to clarify who, and in relation to what, the solicitors were expected to advise about.

41.16   Armed with this information, advisers will be able to make a clearer judgment as to the strengths of the potential defence. It should be remembered that it is be open to the disadvantaged surety to take the initiative and, as a claimant, to seek a declaration that the mortgage was voidable as against him or her. There is no need to wait for the lender to seek possession.

CHAPTER 42

Sale of the security

Introduction

42.1   For the vast majority of borrowers in difficulty with their mortgage, the aim will be to try to preserve their occupation of the home. In possession proceedings, the lender will usually be looking to force the borrower into making increased payments to pay off arrears with the sanction that eviction will follow if sufficient payments are not made. Very often this threat will be backed by an order for possession postponed for as long as the relevant payments are made.

42.2   However, where it is clear that dispossession is inevitable then a borrower may seek the opportunity of selling the security, ie, the property mortgaged to the lender. Alternatively, where the borrower has given up possession either voluntarily in the face of possession proceedings or following eviction after proceedings, the borrower will be concerned as to the sale of the security by the lender. This would be either because there may be a surplus due to the borrower after the mortgage has been redeemed or because of the fact that the lender will wish to recover the amount of any shortfall if the sale proceeds were not sufficient to discharge the mortgage debt in total. Occupiers of a mortgaged property may also face a claim by the lender for a specific order from the court for the property to be sold. This may arise where the lender is unable to rely on the mortgage in order to obtain possession with a view to sale as mortgagee in possession. This may occur where, for instance, the lender is faced with an occupier who has successfully raised a *Barclays Bank v O'Brien* defence (for which see para 40.7) or where a joint owner has forged the signature of the other joint owner. In such a case the lender will be seeking an order for sale and possession under the Trusts of Land and Appointment of Trustees Act 1996. Such an order may be sought, as an alternative, in possession proceedings.

Sale by the borrower

42.3   As the owner of the mortgaged property, the borrower is at liberty to sell the property at any time. The lender's consent is not required. However, the purchaser will not normally complete the purchase until the seller's solicitors give a formal undertaking that they will provide either the receipted legal charge in the case of unregistered land, or, where the title is registered, a Form DS1 duly receipted by the lender. In turn, the seller's solicitors will not give such an undertaking, for which the partners of the solicitor's firm in question would be personally liable, until they are satisfied that the sale proceeds will be sufficient to redeem the mortgage or, if there is more than one, all the mortgages secured against the property. Where the seller is acting in person the buyer will want to ensure that some other arrangement is in place to ensure that any mortgage debt is paid off on completion.

42.4　　It is usually in both the lender's and the borrower's interests for the borrower to remain in occupation until the property is sold. In this way it is likely that the sale price will be higher than would be obtained by the lender if the security is empty following the borrower leaving. Additionally, any income support payable on account of mortgage interest will continue to be paid direct to the lender, while the borrower is in occupation, reducing the ultimate mortgage debt.

Where the mortgage debt can be paid off from the sale proceeds

42.5　　Where the sale proceeds are sufficient to pay off the whole mortgage debt, it is open to the borrower to argue that the arrears would be paid off out of the sale proceeds and that therefore Administration of Justice Act 1970 s36(1) would be available to assist the borrower providing that the court is satisfied that the sale would take place within a reasonable period. It is a question of fact for the court in each case whether the borrower will be able to sell within a reasonable period.[1] However, it is important to produce some evidence to support the assertion that a sale is likely within the proposed period.[2] Certainly, in the initial stages of the sale process a simple letter from an estate agent as to the likely time-scale should be sufficient. There is no reason why the reasonable period should not be six or nine or even twelve months, but in one case the Court of Appeal postponed a possession order for only three months to enable the borrowers to try to sell.[3]

42.6　　The length of time which the borrower might expect to be given by the court will obviously depend on the particular circumstances. However, the Court of Appeal has given some general guidance.[4] Where the property was already on the market and there was some

---

1　*National and Provincial Building Society v Lloyd* [1996] 1 All ER 630, CA. See generally M P Thompson, 'When Mortgaged Property should be Sold' [1998] Conv 125.

2　*Bristol & West Building Society v Ellis* (1997) 29 HLR 282; (1997) 73 P & CR 158, CA.

3　*Target Home Loans v Clothier* [1994] 1 All ER 439; (1993) 25 HLR 48, CA.

4　*Bristol & West Building Society v Ellis* (1997) 29 HLR 282; (1997) 73 P & CR 158, CA.

indication of delay on the part of the borrower, it might be that a short period of postponement of only a few months would be reasonable. Where there was likely to be considerable delay in selling the property and/or its value was close to the total of the mortgage debt and arrears (so that the lender was at risk as to the adequacy of the security), immediate possession or only a short period of postponement might be reasonable. Where there had already been considerable delay in realising a sale and/or the likely sale proceeds were unlikely to cover the mortgage debt and arrears, or there was simply no sufficient evidence as to the sale value, the normal order would be for immediate possession. It can be seen from these observations that the level of equity is of considerable significance.

42.7   It remains unclear as to whether section 36 can be relied upon in order to stay enforcement in relation to part of the security.[5]

Where the whole mortgage debt cannot be paid from the sale proceeds

42.8   Where the sale price is likely to be insufficient to discharge the mortgage debt in total then, in practice, the lender can prevent a sale by the borrower from proceeding. This is because the seller will be unable to redeem the legal charge on completion. In such circumstances it is open to the borrower to apply to the court for an order directing, at the court's instigation, the sale of the property under Law of Property Act 1925 s91.[6] Section 91(2) provides:

> In any action, whether for foreclosure, or for redemption, or for sale, or for the raising and payment in any manner of mortgage money, the court, on the request of the mortgagee, or of any person interested either in the mortgage money or in the right of redemption, and, notwithstanding that –
> (a) any other person dissents; or
> (b) the mortgagee or any person so interested does not appear in the action;
> and without allowing any time for redemption or for payment of any mortgage money, may direct a sale of the mortgaged property, on such terms as it thinks fit, including the deposit in court of a reasonable sum fixed by the court to meet the expenses of sale and to secure performance of the terms.

5   *Barclays Bank plc v Alcorn* [2002] EWHC 498; [2002] P & CR (D) 10; October 2002 *Legal Action* 29, ChD.
6   *Palk v Mortgage Services Funding plc* (1992) 25 HLR 56; [1993] Ch 330; [1993] 2 WLR 415; [1993] 2 All ER 481; (1993) 25 HLR 56, CA. See also *Polonski v Lloyds Bank Mortgages Ltd* [1998] 1 FLR 896; (1999) 31 HLR 721, ChD.

42.9 The court is given wide discretion as to whether to direct a sale and, if so, on what terms. Under Law of Property Act 1925 s91 the court has the discretion to order sale and to allow the borrower to remain in occupation pending sale, even where there is a negative equity.[7] However, where the sale proceeds would fall substantially below the amount of the mortgage debt, an order for sale will not be made save in exceptional circumstances.[8] The court is not limited to considering purely financial matters when exercising its discretion and is fully entitled to take into account the pressing social needs of the borrower.[9] In cases where the lender is pressing for possession with a view to sale, the county court has no discretion to suspend a warrant for possession to enable an application to be made in the High Court for an order for sale under Law of Property Act 1925 s91 except where there are funds available to the borrower to make up the shortfall on sale.[10] A borrower wishing to seek an order for sale must ensure that the application is determined before the lender seeks to enforce a possession order. The county court does nevertheless have residual discretion, in appropriate cases, to give conduct of the sale to the lender while postponing the execution of a warrant for possession and so allowing the borrower to remain in possession pending sale, even where there is little (if any) equity in the property.[11] This can be done where the court is satisfied:

- that possession would not be required by the lender pending completion of the sale but only by the purchasers on completion;
- that the presence of the borrowers pending completion would enhance, or at least not depress, the sale price;
- that the borrowers would co-operate in the sale; and
- that they would give possession to the purchasers on completion.

Both those claiming to have a beneficial interest in the security[12] and

---

7 *Barrett v Halifax Building Society* (1996) 28 HLR 634, ChD.

8 See *Palk v Mortgage Services Funding plc* (1992) 25 HLR 56; [1993] Ch 330; [1993] 2 WLR 415; [1993] 2 All ER 481; (1993) 25 HLR 56, CA and *Pearn v Mortgage Business plc* (1998) LSG 4 February, ChD.

9 *Polonski v Lloyds Bank Mortgages Ltd* [1998] 1 FLR 896; (1999) 31 HLR 721, ChD.

10 *Cheltenham & Gloucester plc v Krausz* [1996] 1 WLR 1558; [1997] 1 All ER 21, CA. See A Kenny, 'No Postponement of Evil Day' [1998] Conv 223 and M Dixon, 'Combating the mortgagee's right to possession: new hope for the mortgagor in chains?' [1998] *Legal Studies* 279.

11 *Cheltenham & Gloucester plc v Booker* (1997) 73 P & CR 412; (1997) 29 HLR 634, CA.

12 *Halifax Building Society v Stansfield* [1993] EGCS 147, CA.

tenants[13] have been held to have the right to apply for an order for sale under Law of Property Act 1925 s91.

42.10   Where the amount owing under the mortgage is in excess of £30,000 the county court has no jurisdiction to consider an application under Law of Property Act 1925 s91 and the application must be made in the High Court.[14] However, the High Court is likely to transfer the case to the county court for trial.

42.11   In the case of regulated mortgage contracts (see para 35.87) lenders are obliged to give 'consideration, where no reasonable payment arrangement can be made, to the [borrower] being allowed to remain in possession to effect a sale'.[15] Failure to give such consideration may be relied on as tending to show contravention of the lender's obligation to deal fairly with the borrower[16] and as such form the basis of a complaint to the Financial Ombudsman Service (see para 35.116).

Sale by the lender

42.12   Borrowers will be concerned about a sale by the lender in two circumstances. The first is where the lender has taken possession and is seeking (as mortgagee in possession) to sell and to recoup the outstanding mortgage debt from the sale proceeds. The second is where the lender is otherwise prevented from obtaining possession because an occupier has raised a defence which prevents the lender from obtaining an order for possession. In such circumstances, the lender has the option of applying to the court for an order for sale.

Lender selling as mortgagee in possession

42.13   In the context of residential mortgages, the lender will be seeking possession of the borrower's home with a view to evicting the borrower and selling with vacant possession. As a disincentive to the taking of possession, the common law imposes some fairly ill-defined obligations on the lender after possession has been taken. In practice, particularly in a depressed property market, disputes between the lender and the borrower tend to arise over, first, the timing of the sale and, second, the sale price.

---

13   *National Westminster Home Loans v Riches* [1995] CLW 43/95.
14   High Court and County Courts Jurisdiction Order 1991 SI No 724 article 2(4).
15   Mortgage: Conduct of Business sourcebook (MCOB) para 13.3.2 E (1) (e).
16   MCOB para 13.3.2 E (2).

42.14   As mortgagee in possession, the common law imposes an obligation on the lender to 'take reasonable precautions to obtain the true market value of the mortgaged property at the date on which he decides to sell'.[17] However, it is clear that while there is an obligation to obtain the best price at the date of sale, the timing of that sale is left to the judgment of the lender. In *Bank of Cyprus Ltd v Gill*[18] Lloyd J said: 'the law as I understand it, is that a mortgagee in possession is entitled to sell at any time. He is not obliged to wait on a rising market or for a market to recover.' In *Tse Kwong Lam v Wong Chit Sen*[19] Lord Templeman put it this way: 'The mortgagee is not, however, bound to postpone the sale in the hope of obtaining a better price.' However, in *Standard Chartered Bank Ltd v Walker*[20] Lord Denning commented, obiter, '[t]here are several dicta to the effect that the mortgagee can choose his own time for sale, but I do not think that this means that he can sell at the worst possible time. It is at least arguable that, in choosing the time, he must exercise a reasonable degree of care'.

42.15   This obligation on the lender in possession appears to protect the borrower against an unreasonable sale in the sense of the sale not resulting in the bona fide proper price. In *Predeth v Castle Phillips Finance Co Ltd*[21] Ralph Gibson LJ said that 'the law allowed [the lender] to sell at the time which suited its convenience, provided, of course, the property was fairly and properly exposed to the market or sold at a price which was based upon such exposure'. This duty is owed both to the borrower and any guarantor[22] although it does not extend to people claiming as beneficiaries under constructive, resulting or other trusts.[23] The borrower may bring an action for breach of duty against the lender, but a separate action in negligence may lie

---

17 *Cuckmere Brick Co Ltd v Mutual Finance Ltd* [1971] Ch 949 at 968H, CA.

18 [1979] 2 Lloyd's Rep 508 at 511, CA.

19 [1983] 1 WLR 1349 at 1355, PC.

20 [1982] 1 WLR 1410 at 1415, CA.

21 (1986) 279 EG 1355, CA. See generally P Devonshire, 'The Mortgagee's Power of Sale: a Case for the Equitable Standard of Good Faith' (1995) 46 NILQ 182, L Bentley, 'Mortgagee's duties on sale – No place for tort?' [1990] Conv 431, J Marriott, 'Sell and be sued? The mortgagee's duty on sale' LS Gaz 30 September 1987 p2756, H Wilkinson, 'The mortgagee's duty to mortgagors and guarantors' [1982] NLJ 883 and *Meftah v Lloyds TSB Bank plc (No 2)* [2001] 2 All ER (Comm) 741, ChD.

22 *Standard Chartered Bank v Walker* [1982] 1 WLR 1410, CA and *American Express International Banking Corp v Hurley* [1985] 3 All ER 564. See also *Skipton Building Society v Stott* [2000] 3 WLR 1031; [2001] QB 261, CA.

23 *Parker-Tweedale v Dunbar Bank plc (No 1)* [1991] Ch 26; [1990] 3 WLR 780; [1990] 2 All ER 588, CA.

also against the lender's selling agents.[24] The lender cannot discharge the duty of care by merely putting the sale in the hands of apparently competent estate agents and the lender will be liable for the negligence of the agents even if the lender may be able to recover damages payable to the borrower from the agents.[25] Provisions in a legal charge purporting to exclude the lender's duty to take reasonable care do not exempt the lender if loss arises from the lender's failure to take such reasonable care.[26]

42.16   In the case of a 'regulated mortgage contract' (see para 35.87) where a property is repossessed (either voluntarily or through legal action) a lender must take steps to market the property for sale as soon as possible and obtain the best price that might reasonably be paid, taking account of factors such as market conditions as well as the continuing increase in the amount owed by the borrower to the lender.[27]

42.17   Where a lender chooses to sell by auction, it is under a duty to ensure that the auction is preceded by appropriate advertisement.[28]

42.18   Where the lender has sold at an undervalue then the borrower's usual remedy will be a claim for damages based on the estimated undervalue.[29] However, in most cases the remedy will be by way of a set-off or counterclaim in an action by the lender for a money judgment against the borrower for the shortfall on sale.[30] It would be possible in the alternative, where the property has still to be sold, to seek an injunction to prevent the sale. It is open to a borrower to seek such an injunction even after exchange of contracts but before completion.[31]

42.19   Borrowers concerned about the possibility of a sale at an undervalue will wish to consider a number of issues[32] including:

- Was the property sold at auction? Sale at an auction is legitimate but the property must be properly described in adverts and in sale

---

24 See *Garland v Ralph Pay and Ransom* (1984) 271 EG 106 and *Minah v Bank of Ireland* [1995] EGCS 144.

25 *Tomlin v Luce* (1890) 43 ChD 191, CA.

26 See *Bishop v Bonham* [1988] 1 WLR 742, CA.

27 MCOB para 13.6.1 R.

28 *Pendlebury v Colonial Mutual Life Assurance Society Ltd* (1912) 13 CLR 676.

29 Law of Property Act 1925 s104(2). See *Michael v Miller* [2004] EWCA Civ 282; [2004] 2 EGLR 151, CA and *Mortgage Express v Mardner* [2004] EWCA Civ 1859. M P Thompson, 'Irregular Sales of Mortgaged Property' [2004] Conv 49.

30 *Platts v TSB Bank plc* [1998] 2 BCLC 1.

31 *Shercliff v Engadine Acceptance Corporation Pty Ltd* [1978] 1 NSWLR 729.

32 On the topic generally see National Association of Estate Agents, 'The Efficient and Effective Sale of Repossessed Residential Property' November 1994.

particulars, sufficient notice of the auction should be given and the reserve price should not be unusually low.

- How does the sale price compare with earlier valuations? What can the borrower say about other similar properties being sold in the area?
- Where was the sale advertised? Was this adequate exposure?
- Who was the buyer and was the property then resold soon afterwards?
- Did the sale price just cover the mortgage debt?
- Did the lender sell following one or more competent surveyor's recommendations?
- In the case of a specialised property was expert advice taken as to how and where to market the property?

It will, in any case where litigation is contemplated, be essential to obtain an expert's report on the value of the property. This should be done as soon as possible. Whether there is the possibility of successful litigation against the lender will ultimately depend on the strength of the expert evidence available.

42.20 On completion of the sale the borrower will be entitled to be paid the balance of the purchase monies after the mortgage(s) has been redeemed. For that reason the borrower should notify the lender of his or her whereabouts so that any balance can be forwarded to him or her where there are surplus proceeds of sale.

42.21 In the case of a 'regulated mortgage contract' a lender is obliged to take reasonable steps (as soon as possible after the sale) to inform the borrower of the surplus and subject to the rights of any other secured lender to pay it to the borrower.[33]

42.22 However, where the sale proceeds are insufficient to pay off the mortgage in full, there is nothing to prevent the lender suing the borrower for the shortfall on the personal covenant in the mortgage deed.[34] If this is likely, it is important to try to identify whether a mortgage indemnity guarantee policy was taken out at the time of the initial mortgage advance. A mortgage indemnity guarantee policy is simply an insurance policy taken out by the lender (although paid for by the borrower) to protect itself in part from any financial loss suffered when a mortgaged property is repossessed and sold. Such policies are commonly taken out when the mortgage advance is anything over (usually) 75 per cent of the value of the property which is the security for the loan. The policy is taken out for the benefit

---

33 MCOB para 13.6.6 R.
34 *Gordon Grant and Co Ltd v Boos* [1926] AC 781, PC.

of the lender and not the borrower.[35] Many borrowers are unaware of whether such a policy has been taken out because the cost of the insurance premium may well have not been paid for by the borrower at the outset of the loan but merely debited to the mortgage account. It is, however, important that the borrower is aware that the insurance company with whom the policy was taken out is, in law, entitled to seek to recover from the borrower any payment made by it. This is not, however, common in practice.[36]

42.23　The relevant limitation period for the recovery of the principal of the debt is 12 years (and 6 years for the interest) from the date of the accrual of the lender's right to the debt.[37] It is essential to consider the terms of the legal charge in question to assess when the right arose.[38] In the case of a 'regulated mortgage contract' (see para 35.87) a lender is obliged, as soon as possible, after the sale of the repossessed property to inform the borrower of the amount of the shortfall, and (where relevant) that the debt may be pursued by another company (for example, a mortgage indemnitty insurer).[39] Any decision to recover the mortgage shortfall must be notified to the borrower within six years.[40] Additionally members of the Council of Mortgage Lenders have agreed that (with effect from 11 February 2000) no enforcement action will be taken unless within six years from the sale of a property at a shortfall a borrower has been contacted about recovery of the outstanding debt.[41]

42.24　It is worth noting that there is no need to obtain an order from the court authorising sale of the property after possession is obtained. The lender's right to sell the property will have arisen either under the terms of the mortgage deed or under the Law of Property Act 1925.

35　See *Woolwich Building Society v Brown* [1996] CLC 625. See R Del Tufo, 'Mortgage Indemnity Guarantees: the Litigation Implications' [1996] SJ 612, D Ohrenstein, 'MIGS come under fire' LS Gaz 15 May 1996. See also D Falkowski, 'Mortgage Indemnity Insurance: are the Terms Unfair?' [1996] SJ 1080 for an interesting discussion of whether lenders could face a challenge to this orthodoxy under the Unfair Terms in Consumer Contracts Regulations 1994 SI No 3159 and 1999 SI No 2083.

36　See P Madge, 'A False Security' (1991) *Adviser* May 1991 p28.

37　*Bristol & West plc v Bartlett* [2002] EWCA Civ 1181; [2002] 4 All ER 544, CA.

38　*West Bromwich Building Society v Wilkinson* [2005] UKHL 44; [2005] 1 WLR 2303, HL.

39　MCOB para 13.6.3 R.

40　MCOB para 13.6.4 R.

41　See Consumer Guide, 'Debt Following Mortgage Possession' March 2002 at www.cml.org.uk/cml/consumers/guides/debt.

Lender seeking order for sale

42.25 Where land is held on trust, the Trusts of Land and Appointment of Trustees Act 1996 enables the court, among other things, to order its sale and the eviction of any occupiers. 'Trust of land' is widely defined and comprises 'any trust of property which consists of or includes land' irrespective of the date of creation or origin of that trust.[42] This will include express, implied, resulting or constructive trusts.

42.26 Trusts of Land and Appointment of Trustees Act 1996 s14(1)–(2) gives the court jurisdiction to make such order as it 'thinks fit' in resolution of any dispute as to whether trust land should be sold or retained for occupation by the trust beneficiaries. The county court is the relevant court irrespective of the value of the property the subject of the application for sale.[43] A mortgage lender, having an interest in the trust property, is able to apply to the court for an order for sale. The matters to which the court is expressly to have regard when determining whether to make an order for sale include:

- the intention of the person(s) who created the trust;
- the purposes for which the trust property is held;
- the welfare of any minor who occupies or might reasonably be expected to occupy the trust property as a home; and
- the interests of any secured creditor of any beneficiary.[44]

42.27 The initial case-law was unsympathetic to occupiers notwithstanding the clear policy change introduced by the 1996 Act's abolition of the statutory 'trust for sale'. A lender in possession proceedings faced with a binding overriding interest was able to apply successfully for an order for sale.[45] However, in *Mortgage Corporation Ltd v Shaire*[46] the court observed that the presumption of sale contained within the concept of the trust for sale had been abolished by the 1996 Act. Section 15(1) contains four factors to be taken into account with the interests of the secured lender being but one. There is no suggestion that those interests should be given any greater weight than the interests of children residing in the house. The court concluded that parliament had intended to relax the law so as to enable the courts

42 Trusts of Land and Appointment of Trustees Act 1996 s1(2).
43 High Court and County Courts Jurisdiction Order 1991 SI No 724, para 2(1)p.
44 Trusts of Land and Appointment of Trustees Act 1996 s15(1).
45 *Bank of Baroda v Dhillon* [1998] 1 FLR 524, CA.
46 [2001] Ch 743; [2001] 4 All ER 364; [2000] 1 FLR 973, ChD. See also S Pascoe, 'Section 15 of the Trusts of Land and Appointment of Trustees Act 1996 – A Change in the Law?' [2000] Conv 315 and M P Thompson, 'Secured Creditors and Sales' [2000] Conv 329.

to have more discretion in favour of families and against banks and other chargees. On the facts of the case an order for sale was made but was suspended on Ms Shaire paying interest on the sum effectively charged on the property in favour of the claimant. Whilst her signature had been forged on the legal charge, the claimant had a valid charge on the other joint owner's interest in the property. Providing the claimant was compensated in interest, the family's occupation of the home could be preserved and the lender was adequately compensated pending the eventual sale of the property. Whether, in any particular case, an order for sale will be postponed depends to what extent a secured creditor is at risk and if it can be compensated financially pending sale of the property[47] and repayment of the monies secured at that time. Issues such as ill health may be relevant when considering the duration of any period of postponement of sale but may be irrelevant in the absence of any compensatory payments to the lender when considering whether to reject a lender's application for sale.

---

47 *Bank of Ireland Home Mortgages Ltd v Bell* [2000] EWCA Civ 426; [2001] 2 All ER (Comm) 920, *Edwards v Lloyds TSB Bank plc* [2004] EWHC 1745; [2005] 1 FCR 139, ChD and *First National Bank plc v Achampong* [2003] EWCA Civ 487; [2005] 1 FCR 18. See R Probert, 'Creditors and Section 15 of the Trusts of Land and Appointment of Trustees Act 1996: First Among Equals?' [2002] Conv 61 and M P Thompson, 'Undue Influence before Etridge' [2003] Conv 314.

Possession claims by unsecured creditors

Introduction

43.1   Owner-occupiers are, in certain circumstances, at risk of possession claims by creditors who were, at least initially, unsecured creditors. Advisers should be alert to these possible actions when advising owner-occupiers in relation to their debts. The two ways in which owners can be evicted are by way of a successful application for sale (1) following a creditor obtaining a charging order, and (2) on application by the owner's trustee in bankruptcy. The two possibilities need to be looked at separately.[1]

Charging orders

43.2   Under the Charging Orders Act 1979 a creditor may, after obtaining a money judgment against a debtor, apply to the court for a charging order and then register a charge in relation to property owned legally or beneficially by a judgment debtor, whether alone or jointly with others. The procedure is regulated by Civil Procedure Rules (CPR) Part 73.

43.3   The relevant court to which to make application for a charging order is the county court except where the judgment debt is a High Court judgment in excess of £5,000,[2] in which case the judgment creditor has the option of using either the High Court or county court.

43.4   Following judgment, application is made without notice to the court for an interim charging order (previously known as a charging order nisi), and, once granted, a notice or caution can be registered at HM Land Registry in the case of registered land or as a pending land action in the case of unregistered land. The debtor is then served with notice of the hearing of the application for the charging order to be made absolute. The onus is on the debtor to show cause why the order should not be made absolute.[3] The court has discretion whether to grant the charging order and is required to take into account 'all the circumstances of the case and, in particular, ... (a) the personal circumstances of the debtor, and (b) whether any other creditor of the debtor would be likely to be unduly prejudiced by the making of the

---

1   See generally W Boyce and J Middleton, *Debt and Insolvency on Family Breakdown*, 2nd edn, Family Law, 2001.

2   Charging Orders Act 1979 s1(2) and County Courts Jurisdiction Order 1981 SI No 1123.

3   *Roberts Petroleum Ltd v Bernard Kenny Ltd* [1983] 2 AC 192, HL; [1982] 1 WLR 305 and *United Overseas Bank Ltd v Iwuanyanwu* (2001) 5 March, unreported, CA.

order'.[4] The court should not grant the charging order where the size of the debt is small compared with the value of the property,[5] or where a county court judgment has been ordered to be paid by instalments (unless and until the debtor has defaulted in payments).[6] The court imposed charge becomes enforceable 'in the same manner as an equitable charge created by the debtor by writing under his hand'.[7] In practice, however, it is not difficult for a creditor to obtain the charging order absolute. Variation or discharge of a charging order is possible on application by 'any person interested in any property to which the order relates'.[8]

43.5   Proceedings to enforce a charging order by sale of the legal interest are regulated by CPR 73.10 and PD 73. However, since a charging order can be granted against the beneficial interest of a judgment debtor owned subject to a trust with others,[9] a judgment creditor with a charging order in relation to that debtor's beneficial interest under such a trust, as a 'person interested', is also entitled to apply under the Trusts of Land and Appointment of Trustees Act 1996 for an order for sale. For an analysis of the law in this area see para 42.27.

43.6   Under CPR 73.10 the creditor can apply for an order for sale and for an order for possession by Part 8 claim form with supporting witness statement, setting out the charging order which it is sought to enforce, the amount still outstanding to the creditor, details of prior mortgagees and the sums outstanding and the estimated sale price. It has to be made by issuing a new claim. It cannot be made in existing proceedings. An application for an order for sale based on a charging order is an application to enforce an equitable charge. The county court has jurisdiction where the sum owing is under £30,000.[10] Otherwise

---

4   Charging Orders Act 1979 s1(5), *Harman v Glencross* [1985] Fam 49; [1986] 1 All ER 545, CA and *Roberts Petroleum Ltd v Bernard Kenny Ltd* [1983] AC 192, HL. For the exercise of the court's powers in the context of simultaneous divorce proceedings see also *Harman v Glencross* ibid, *Austin-Fell v Austin-Fell and Midland Bank plc* [1990] Fam 172; [1990] 3 WLR 33; [1990] 2 All ER 455 and J Warburton 'Victory for the Sprinter' [1986] Conv 218. See generally M P Thompson, *Co-ownership*, Sweet & Maxwell, 1988, p98 and P Madge and R Leszczyszyn 'Charging Orders' (1992) Jan/Feb *Adviser* p31.

5   *Robinson v Bailey* [1942] 1 All ER 498.

6   *Mercantile Credit Co Ltd v Ellis* [1987] CLY 2917; (1987) *Times* 2 April, CA.

7   Charging Orders Act 1979 s3(4).

8   Charging Orders Act 1979 s3(5).

9   Charging Orders Act 1979 s2. See also *National Westminster Bank plc v Stockman* [1981] 1 WLR 67.

10 County Courts Act 1984 s23 and High Court and County Courts Jurisdiction Order 1991 SI No 724.

the application must be in the High Court. The application is heard in the county court by the district judge. In practice, district judges are often unwilling to grant the creditor's application for sale and possession considering that the security of the charging order is adequate protection for a creditor who was originally unsecured.

43.7   When seeking to contest the application for sale, it is important to emphasise the fact that the creditor is already well protected and to point out the detriment which will result to innocent members of the family if the sale is allowed to proceed.[11] If the debtor is able to offer alternative ways of discharging the judgment debt, these should be put forward.[12]

43.8   When a judgment creditor obtains a charge on a property as security for a judgment debt, the creditor's security extends also to interest on the debt even if interest is not expressly mentioned in the order. In equity, the creditor is also entitled to add the costs of enforcing the charge to the security. The amount of interest recoverable under the charging order is not restricted by the Limitation Act 1980.[13] Similarly the judgment creditor is entitled to the costs of enforcing the charging order including the costs of fending-off claims by third parties that they had beneficial interests in the proceeds of sale of the property subject to the charging order.[14]

Trustees in bankruptcy

43.9   When a person becomes bankrupt his or her property vests in the trustee in bankruptcy as soon as that person is appointed. The property is vested in the trustee without the necessity of any deed of transfer.[15] The trustee's duty is then 'to get in, realise and distribute'[16] the

---

11   See generally *Harman v Glencross* [1985] Fam 49; [1984] 2 All ER 577, CA.
12   See generally M Sullivan 'Charging Orders and their enforcement in the county courts' (1999) 52 *Quarterly Account* p4, and P Madge 'Charging interest' (1999) 76 *Adviser* p32.
13   *Ezekiel v Orakpo* [1997] 1 WLR 340, CA.
14   *Holder v Supperstone* [2000] 1 All ER 457, ChD.
15   Insolvency Act 1986 s306(1) and (2). See generally Thompson, footnote 4, p103; E Bailey and C Berry 'The Matrimonial Home in Bankruptcy' (1987) 137 NLJ 310, E Bailey and C Berry 'Applications by the Trustee for Possession and Sale' (1987) 137 NLJ 347, M Cohen 'Homes and other assets in bankruptcy' (1996) *Money Advice* 28 and W Boyce and J Middleton, *Debt and Insolvency on Family Breakdown*, 2nd edn, Family Law, 2001.
16   Insolvency Act 1986 s305(2).

bankrupt's assets and to distribute the estate in accordance with the Insolvency Act 1986.

43.10   Where the legal and beneficial estate is in the sole name of the bankrupt, then the trustee is at liberty to dispose of that asset without the need to consider the position of others. However, where the legal estate is in the joint names of the bankrupt and a third party, or where the bankrupt and a third party have beneficial interests, then the trustee is a 'person interested' who can apply under Trusts of Land and Appointment of Trustees Act 1996 s14 for an order for sale. The bankruptcy of a 'beneficial joint tenant' operates as an act of severance, resulting in the property being held by the owners as a 'tenancy in common'.[17] Where there is a spouse or civil partner in occupation (but not a mere cohabitant) who has no legal or beneficial interest, then he or she will have to rely on any rights of occupation under Family Law Act 1996. A cohabitant who has neither a legal nor beneficial interest in the property will not be able to resist an application for an order for possession in advance of sale.

43.11   Insolvency Act 1986 s335A[18] provides that, when considering applications for sale and possession of property by the trustee under Trusts of Land and Appointment of Trustees Act 1996 s14, the court shall make such order as it thinks just and reasonable having regard to:

(a) the interests of the bankrupt's creditors;
(b) where the application is made in respect of land which includes a dwelling house which is or has been the home of the bankrupt or the bankrupt's spouse or civil partner or former spouse or former civil partner –
  (i)   the conduct of the spouse, civil partner, former spouse or former civil partner, so far as contributing to the bankruptcy,
  (ii) the needs and financial resources of the spouse, civil partner, former spouse or former civil partner, and
  (iii) the needs of any children; and
(c) all the circumstances of the case other than the needs of the bankrupt.[19]

The usual criteria by which the court assesses an application for sale under the Trusts of Land and Appointment of Trustees Act

---

17 *Re Gorman* [1990] 1 WLR 616; [1990] 1 All ER 717.
18 Inserted by Trusts of Land and Appointment of Trustees Act 1996 s25(1) and Sch 3 para 23.
19 Insolvency Act 1986 s335A(2). See generally G Miller 'Applications by a trustee in bankruptcy for sale of the family home' (1999) 15(6) IL & P 76.

1996 are expressly excluded where the trustee in bankruptcy is the claimant.[20]

43.12   The Insolvency Act 1996 provides for a statutory presumption in favour of the creditors *after* a 12-month period:

> ... after the end of the period of one year beginning with the first vesting ... of the bankrupt's estate in a trustee, the court shall assume, unless the circumstances of the case are exceptional, that the interests of the bankrupt's creditors outweigh all other considerations.[21]

43.13   While this statutory presumption would seem to favour the creditors 12 months after the bankruptcy, it does not prevent an application for sale/possession by the trustee during that period. However, faced with a defended application during the initial period, many trustees will prefer to wait for this statutory period to elapse before making the application. It is, however, arguable that this statutory presumption that the property is to be sold after the end of the 12 months infringes article 8 (and article 1 of the First Protocol) to the European Convention on Human Rights.[22]

43.14   The Insolvency Act 1986, therefore, allows for the enforcement of the interests of creditors to be delayed, but not indefinitely. The statutory period of 12 months will, in most cases, allow a breathing space for the third party to seek alternative accommodation. However, the Insolvency Act 1986, in effect, does allow this period to be exceeded where there are 'exceptional circumstances'. The fact that innocent third parties will be made homeless is not such an 'exceptional circumstance' as to prevent a sale being ordered.[23] In *Re Citro*[24] it was held, by a majority, that the interests of the creditors will usually prevail over the interests of a spouse and children, and that more than the ordinary consequences of debt and improvidence would be necessary before the court would be able to postpone sale for a substantial period. Where relevant, it is important to emphasise the personal circumstances of the debtor's family, including, for example, the effect on the children's education, particularly if they are shortly to take examinations. If this is the case, it may be possible to have the order

20 Trusts of Land and Appointment of Trustees Act 1996 s15(4).
21 Insolvency Act 1986 s335A(3).
22 *Jackson v Bell* [2001] EWCA Civ 387; [2001] BPIR 612 and *Barca v Mears* [2004] EWHC 2170; [2005] 2 FLR 1. See also 'Trusts of Land, Bankruptcy and Human Rights' [2005] Conv 161.
23 *Re Lowrie* [1981] 3 All ER 353.
24 [1991] Ch 142; [1990] 3 WLR 880, CA. Cf, *Re Holliday* [1981] Ch 405; [1981] 2 WLR 996.

for possession postponed until after the examination date.[25] In cases where there is severe ill health it may be possible to argue that this is an exceptional circumstance such as to enable the court to delay sale of the property until either death of the family member or his or her departure from the home.[26]

43.15　It follows that advisers are often left with little scope for manoeuvre when advising the bankrupt or other occupiers affected by the bankruptcy. It is, however, worth arguing that it is open to the trustee to apply under Insolvency Act 1986 s313 for a charging order over property in favour of the bankrupt's estate. If made, then such a charging order becomes subject to Charging Orders Act 1979 s3, and the court will have the power to impose conditions as to when the charge becomes enforceable. Additionally, the bankrupt may be allowed to remain living in the property notwithstanding the bankruptcy, conditionally on him or her making payments towards the mortgage and the other outgoings. The bankrupt would not, however, by virtue of this acquire any interest in the property.[27]

43.16　A joint owner who remains in the property following the date of the other owner's bankruptcy is entitled to be repaid (out of the bankrupt's share) for half of the mortgage payments made by him or her but this sum must be set off against an 'occupation rent' in favour of the bankrupt's trustee.[28]

43.17　With effect from 1 April 2004, where the property which vests in the trustee was the home of the bankrupt or his or her spouse or previous spouse, the trustee has three years from the date of bankruptcy to start action to realise the interest by sale or the property automatically revests in the bankrupt.[29] During that period the trustee must, most commonly, either realise the interest or apply for an order for sale or possession to avoid the revesting in the bankrupt. These provisions apply to pre-commencement bankruptcies resulting in automatic revesting of the bankrupt's interest in the bankrupt unless the trustee takes one of the steps mentioned above to avoid revesting by

25　See generally D Brown 'Insolvency and the Matrimonial Home – The Sins of the Fathers: *In re Citro (A Bankrupt)*' (1992) 55 MLR 284.

26　See *Re Bremner (A Bankrupt)* [1999] 1 FLR 912, ChD and *Claughton v Charalambous* [1999] 1 FLR 740; [1998] BPIR 558, ChD.

27　Insolvency Act 1986 s338.

28　*Re Byford; Byford v Butler* [2003] EWHC 1267 (Ch); [2004] 1 FLR 56. See also H Conway 'Co-Ownership, Equitable Accounting and the Trustee in Bankruptcy' [2003] Conv 533.

29　Insolvency Act 1986 s283A inserted by Enterprise Act 2004 s261(1) and Enterprise Act 2004 (Commencement No 4 and Transitional Provisions & Savings) Order 2003 SI No 2093.

1 April 2007.[30] The court must also dismiss a trustee's application for sale or possession where the net value of the bankrupt's interest in the property is below an amount prescribed in secondary legislation,[31] currently £1,000.[32] The value of the bankrupt's interest is calculated after deducting the value of any loans secured by mortgage or any other third party interests and the reasonable costs of sale.[33]

43.18   The procedure for applying for an order for sale is as set out above dealing with charging orders in the text (see para 43.5).

43.19   When ordering sale, the court does have the power to impose conditions on the sale, including a requirement to reimburse the joint beneficial owner who has paid the instalments to a mortgage lender (so preventing eviction and the sale of the property) to recompense him or her for the increase in the house value during the period he or she has repaid the loan.[34]

---

30 Enterprise Act 2004 s261(8). See also M P Thompson 'A Bankrupt Home for a Spouse' [2004] Conv 255.

31 Insolvency Act 1986 s313A inserted by Enterprise Act 2004 s261 and Enterprise Act 2004 (Commencement No 4 and Transitional Provisions and Savings) Order 2003 SI No 2093.

32 Insolvency Proceedings (Monetary Limits) (Amendment) Order 2004 SI No 547 article 2.

33 2004 SI No 547 article 3.

34 *McMahon's Trustee v McMahon* 1997 SLT 1090, CtS.

APPENDICES

Statutory notices and forms[1]

This section contains the following notices and forms

1 Notice of seeking possession of a secure tenancy
2 Notice requiring possession of a property let on a periodic assured shorthold tenancy
3 Notice seeking possession of a property let on an assured tenancy
4 Notice to quit

---

1 The forms reproduced in appendix A are for illustrative purposes only by kind permission of The Solicitors' Law Stationery Society Limited. Forms can be obtained from www.oyezformslink.co.uk.

1 Notice of seeking possession of a secure tenancy

Secure Tenancies (Notices) Regulations 1987,
Schedule, Part I as amended.

This Notice is the first step towards requiring you to give up possession of your dwelling. You should read it very carefully.

HOUSING ACT 1985

Section 83

Notice of Seeking Possession

(1) Name(s) of
Secure Tenant(s).

1. To (¹)

If you need advice about this Notice, and what you should do about it, take it as quickly as possible to a Citizens' Advice Bureau, a Housing Aid Centre, or a Law Centre, or to a Solicitor. You may be able to receive Legal Aid but this will depend on your personal circumstances.

(2) Insert name.

2. The landlord (²) intends to apply to the Court for an Order requiring you to give up possession of:

(3) Address of property.

(³)

If you are a secure tenant under the Housing Act 1985, you can only be required to leave your dwelling if your landlord obtains an order for possession from the Court. The order must be based on one of the Grounds which are set out in the 1985 Act (see paragraphs 3 and 4 below).

If you are willing to give up possession without a Court order, you should notify the person who signed this Notice as soon as possible and say when you would leave.

(4) Give the text in full of each Ground which is being relied on.

3. Possession will be sought on Ground(s) of Schedule 2 to the Housing Act 1985 which read(s) (⁴):

Whatever Grounds for possession are set out in paragraph 3 of this Notice, the Court may allow any of the other Grounds to be added at a later stage. If this is done, you will be told about it so you can argue at the hearing in Court about the new Ground, as well as the Grounds set out in paragraph 3, if you want to.

[P.T.O.

HA1/1

(5) Give a full explanation of why each Ground is being relied upon.

4. Particulars of each Ground are as follows (⁵):

Before the Court will grant an order on any of the Grounds 1 to 8 or 12 to 16, it must be satisfied that it is reasonable to require you to leave. This means that, if one of these Grounds is set out in paragraph 3 of this Notice, you will be able to argue at the hearing in Court that it is not reasonable that you should have to leave, even if you accept that the Ground applies.

Before the Court grants an order on any of the Grounds 9 to 16, it must be satisfied that there will be suitable alternative accommodation for you when you have to leave. This means that the Court will have to decide that, in its opinion, there will be other accommodation which is reasonably suitable for the needs of you and your family, taking into particular account various factors such as the nearness of your place of work, and the sort of housing that other people with similar needs are offered. Your new home will have to be let to you on another secure tenancy or a private tenancy under the Rent Act of a kind that will give you similar security. **There is no requirement for suitable alternative accommodation where Grounds 1 to 8 apply.**

If your landlord is not a local authority, and the local authority gives a certificate that it will provide you with suitable accommodation, the Court has to accept the certificate.

One of the requirements of Ground 10A is that the landlord must have approval for the redevelopment scheme from the Secretary of State (or, in the case of a housing association landlord, the Housing Corporation). The landlord must have consulted all secure tenants affected by the proposed redevelopment scheme.

[P.T.O.

HA1/2

(6) Cross out this paragraph if possession is being sought on Ground 2 of Schedule 2 to the Housing Act 1985 (whether or not possession is also sought on another Ground)

(7) Give the date after which Court proceedings can be brought.

5. (⁶) The court proceedings for possession will not be begun until after (⁷)

• Court proceedings cannot be begun until after this date, which cannot be earlier than the date when your tenancy or licence could have been brought to an end. This means that if you have a weekly or fortnightly tenancy, there should be at least 4 weeks between the date this Notice is given and the date in this paragraph.

• After this date, Court proceedings may be begun at once or at any time during the following twelve months. Once the twelve months are up this Notice will lapse and a new Notice must be served before possession can be sought.

(8) Cross out this paragraph if possession is not being sought on Ground 2 of Schedule 2 to the Housing Act 1985

(9) Give the date by which the tenant is to give up possession of the dwelling-house.

5. (⁸) Court proceedings for possession of the dwelling-house can be begun immediately. The date by which the tenant is to give up possession of the dwelling-house is (⁹)

• Court proceedings may be begun at once or at any time during the following twelve months. Once the twelve months are up this Notice will lapse and a new Notice must be served before possession can be sought.

• Possession of your dwelling-house cannot be obtained until after this date, which cannot be earlier than the date when your tenancy or licence could have been brought to an end. This means that if you have a weekly or fortnightly tenancy, there should be at least 4 weeks between the date this Notice is given and the date possession is ordered.

Signed

On behalf of

Address

Tel No.

Date

2 Notice requiring possession of a property let on a periodic assured shorthold tenancy

HOUSING ACT 1988
Section 21(4)(a)

Assured Shorthold Tenancy : Notice Requiring Possession: Periodic Tenancy
(Note 1)

(1) Name and address of tenant.

To(¹)

of

(2) Name and address of landlord (Note 2 overleaf).

From(²)

of

(3) Address of dwelling.

I give you notice that I require possession of the dwelling house known as(³)

(4) Date of expiry (Note 3 overleaf).

after(⁴)

(5) Note 3 overleaf.

Dated(⁵)

Landlord

(6) Name and address.

[Landlord's agent](⁶)

[P.T.O.

© 1999 Oyez 7 Spa Road, London SE16 3QQ.

5.1999 MM

HA 21A

HA21A/1

NOTES

1.   Where an assured shorthold tenancy has become a periodic tenancy, a court must make an order for possession if the landlord has given proper notice in this form.

2.   Where there are joint landlords, at least one of them must give this notice.

3.   The date specified must be:
     (a) the last day of a period of the tenancy.
     (b) at least two months after this notice is given; and
     (c) no sooner than the earliest day on which the tenancy could ordinarily be brought to an end by a notice to quit.

HA21A/2

Note: this is an *example* of a notice under Housing Act 1988 s21, the above notes on the form are not obligatory and there is no prescribed form which must be used.

3 Notice seeking possession of a property let on an assured tenancy

OYEZ Form No. 3 of the Assured Tenancies and Agricultural Occupancies (Forms) Regulations 1997

HOUSING ACT 1988

Section 8 as amended by Section 151 of the Housing Act 1996

Notice Seeking Possession of a Property Let on an Assured Tenancy or an Assured Agricultural Occupancy

- Please write clearly in black ink.
- Please tick boxes where appropriate and cross out text marked with an asterisk (*) that does not apply.
- This form should be used where possession of accommodation let under an assured tenancy, an assured agricultural occupancy or an assured shorthold tenancy is sought on one of the grounds in Schedule 2 to the Housing Act 1988.
- Do not use this form if possession is sought on the "shorthold" ground under section 21 of the Housing Act 1988 from an assured shorthold tenant where the fixed term has come to an end or, for assured shorthold tenancies with no fixed term which started on or after 28th February 1997, after six months has elapsed. There is no prescribed form for these cases, but you must give notice in writing.

(1) Name(s) of tenant(s)/ licensee(s).

1. To (¹):

(2) Address of premises.

2. Your landlord/licensor* intends to apply to the court for an order requiring you to give up possession of (²):

(3) Give the full text (as set out in the Housing Act 1988 as amended by the Housing Act 1996) of each ground which is being relied on. Continue on a separate sheet if necessary.

3. Your landlord/licensor* intends to seek possession on ground(s) in Schedule 2 to the Housing Act 1988, as amended by the Housing Act 1996, which read(s) (³):

(4) Continue on a separate sheet if necessary.

4. Give a full explanation of why each ground is being relied on (⁴):

Notes on the grounds for possession:

- If the court is satisfied that any of grounds 1 to 8 is established, it must make an order (but see below in respect of fixed term tenancies).
- Before the court will grant an order on any of grounds 9 to 17, it must be satisfied that it is reasonable to require you to leave. This means that, if one of these grounds is set out in section 3, you will be able to suggest to the court that it is not reasonable that you should have to leave, even if you accept that the ground applies.
- The court will not make an order under grounds 1, 3 to 7, 9 or 16, to take effect during the fixed term of the tenancy (if there is one) and it will only make an order during the fixed term on grounds 2, 8, 10 to 15 or 17 if the terms of the tenancy make provision for it to be brought to an end on any of these grounds.
- Where the court makes an order for possession solely on ground 6 or 9, the landlord must pay your reasonable removal expenses.

[P.T.O.
HA 32/1

(5) Give the earliest date on which court proceedings can be brought.

5.   The court proceedings will not begin until after(⁵):

- Where the landlord is seeking possession on grounds 1, 2, 5 to 7, 9 or 16, court proceedings cannot begin earlier than 2 months from the date this notice is served on you (even where one of the grounds 3, 4, 8, 10 to 13, 14A, 15 or 17 is specified) and not before the date on which the tenancy (had it not been assured) could have been brought to an end by a notice to quit served at the same time as this notice.

- Where the landlord is seeking possession on grounds 3, 4, 8, 10 to 13, 14A, 15, or 17, court proceedings cannot begin earlier than 2 weeks from the date this notice is served (unless one of grounds 1, 2, 5 to 7, 9 or 16 is also specified in which case they cannot begin earlier than two months from the date this notice is served).

- Where the landlord is seeking possession on ground 14 (with or without other grounds), court proceedings cannot begin before the date this notice is served.

- Where the landlord is seeking possession on ground 14A, court proceedings cannot begin unless the landlord has served, or has taken all reasonable steps to serve, a copy of this notice on the partner who has left the property.

- After the date shown in section 5, court proceedings may be begun at once but not later than 12 months from the date on which this notice is served. After this time the notice will lapse and a new notice must be served before possession can be sought.

6.   Name and address of landlord/licensor*.

To be signed and dated by the landlord or licensor or his agent (someone acting for him). If there are joint landlords each landlord or the agent must sign unless one signs on behalf of the rest with their agreement.

Signed: Date:

Please specify whether: landlord ☐   licensor ☐   joint landlords ☐   landlord's agent ☐
Name(s): (BLOCK CAPITALS)

Address

Telephone: Daytime: Evening:

What to do if this notice is served on you.

- This notice is the first step requiring you to give up possession of your home. You should read it very carefully.

- Your landlord cannot make you leave your home without an order for possession issued by a court. By issuing this notice your landlord is informing you that he intends to seek such an order. If you are willing to give up possession without a court order, you should tell the person who signed this notice as soon as possible and say when you are prepared to leave.

- Whichever grounds are set out in section 3 of this form the court may allow any of the other grounds to be added at a later date. If this is done, you will be told about it so you can discuss the additional grounds at the court hearing as well as the grounds set out in section 3.

- If you want advice about this notice, and what you should do about it, take it immediately to a citizens' advice bureau, a housing advice centre, a law centre or a solicitor.

HA 32

HA 32/2

4 Notice to quit

NOTICE TO QUIT

(BY LANDLORD OF PREMISES LET AS A DWELLING)

Name and
Address of
Tenant.

To

of

Name and
Address of
Landlord.

[I] [We] [as] [on behalf of] your landlord[s],

of

*Me/them or as
appropriate.

give you **NOTICE TO QUIT** and deliver up possession to*

† Address of
premises.

of†

‡ Date for
possession.

on‡   , or the day on which a complete period of your

tenancy expires next after the end of four weeks from the service of this notice.

Date of notice.

Dated

Signed

Name and
Address of
Agent if Agent
serves notice.

INFORMATION FOR TENANT
(See Note 2 overleaf)

1. If the tenant or licensee does not leave the dwelling, the landlord or licensor must get an order for possession from the court before the tenant or licensee can lawfully be evicted. The landlord or licensor cannot apply for such an order before the notice to quit or notice to determine has run out.

2. A tenant or licensee who does not know if he has any right to remain in possession after a notice to quit or a notice to determine runs out can obtain advice from a solicitor. Help with all or part of the cost of legal advice and assistance may be available under the Legal Aid Scheme. He should also be able to obtain information from a Citizens' Advice Bureau, a Housing Aid Centre or a Rent Officer.

[P.T.O.

Oyez   7 Spa Road, London SE16 3QQ   © Crown copyright.   5.1999 MM   L&T61/1

Landlord and Tenant 61

NOTES

1. Notice to quit premises let as a dwelling must be given at least four weeks before it takes effect, and it must be in writing (Protection from Eviction Act 1977, s. 5 as amended).

2. Where a notice to quit is given by a landlord to determine a tenancy of any premises let as a dwelling, the notice must contain this information (The Notices to Quit etc. (Prescribed Information) Regulations 1988).

3. Some tenancies are excluded from this protection: see Protection from Eviction Act 1977, ss. 3A and 5(1B).

L&T61/2

Statements of case and applications

This section contains the following statements of case and application

1 Claim form for possession of property (Form N5)

2 Particulars of Claim for rented residential premises (Form N119)

3 Defence form for rented residential premises (Form N11R) with Additional Defence form

4 Particulars of Claim for mortgaged residential premises (Form N120)

5 Defence form for mortgaged residential premises (Form N11M) with Additional Defence form

6 Application notice (Form N244) to set judgment aside

7 Witness statement in support of application to set judgment aside

8 Application notice (Form N244) to suspend warrant for possession and to postpone date for possession

9 Witness statement in support of application to suspend warrant and to postpone date for possession

10 Order for possession with no date fixed (Form N28A)

11 Order adjourning on terms

1   Claim form for possession of property (Form N5)

Claim form for possession of property	In the *ANYTOWN COUNTY COURT*
	Claim No. *AN6 09601*

SEAL

Claimant
(name(s) and address(es))

RAINBOW DISTRICT COUNCIL
TOWN HALL
ANYTOWN

Defendant(s)
(name(s) and address(es))

WAYNE ROSS
32 SMALL STREET
ANYTOWN, AN1 7DG

The claimant is claiming possession of :

32 SMALL STREET, ANYTOWN, AN1 7DG

which (includes) (does not include) residential property. Full particulars of the claim are attached.
(The claimant is also making a claim for money).

This claim will be heard on: *21 JULY*   20 *06* at *10.00*   am/pm

at *ANYTOWN COUNTY COURT, CASTLE STREET, ANYTOWN*

At the hearing
• The court will consider whether or not you must leave the property and, if so, when.
• It will take into account information the claimant provides and any you provide.

What you should do
• Get help and advice immediately from a solicitor or an advice agency.
• Help yourself and the court by **filling in the defence form** and **coming to the hearing** to make sure the court knows all the facts.

Defendant's name and address for service

WAYNE ROSS
32 SMALL STREET
ANYTOWN, AN1 7DG

Court fee	£
Solicitor's costs	£
Total amount	£

Issue date	*12 JUNE 2006*

Claim No. **AN6 09601**

Grounds for possession

The claim for possession is made on the following ground(s):

- ☑ rent arrears
- ☐ other breach of tenancy
- ☐ forfeiture of the lease
- ☐ mortgage arrears
- ☐ other breach of the mortgage
- ☐ trespass
- ☐ other *(please specify)* _____

Anti-social behaviour

The claimant is alleging:

- ☐ actual or threatened assault
- ☐ actual or threatened serious damage to the property

See full details in the attached particulars of claim

Does, or will, the claim include any issues under the Human Rights Act 1998? ☐ Yes ☑ No

Statement of Truth

*(I believe)(The claimant believes) that the facts stated in this claim form are true.
* I am duly authorised by the claimant to sign this statement.

signed *John Smith* date *6 June 2006*

*(Claimant)(Litigation friend *(where the claimant is a child or a patient)*)(Claimant's solicitor)
*delete as appropriate

Full name *JOHN SMITH*

Name of claimant's solicitor's firm *LEGAL SERVICES, RAINBOW DISTRICT COUNCIL*

position or office held *HEAD OF LEGAL SERVICES*
(if signing on behalf of firm or company)

Claimant's or claimant's solicitor's address to which documents or payments should be sent if different from overleaf.

*JOHN SMITH
LEGAL SERVICES
RAINBOW DISTRICT COUNCIL
TOWN HALL
ANYTOWN* Postcode

	if applicable
Ref. no.	
fax no.	
DX no.	
e-mail	
Tel. no.	

2 Particulars of Claim for rented residential premises (Form N119)

**Particulars of claim
for possession**
(rented residential premises)

In the *ANYTOWN COUNTY COURT* Claim No. *AN6   09601*

RAINBOW DISTRICT COUNCIL   Claimant

WAYNE ROSS   Defendant

1. The claimant has a right to possession of:

    32 SMALL STREET, ANYTOWN

2. To the best of the claimant's knowledge the following persons are in possession of the property:

    THE DEFENDANT, HIS WIFE ANN ROSS AND THEIR CHILDREN

About the tenancy

3. (a) The premises are let to the defendant(s) under a(n) *SECURE*   tenancy
    which began on *7 JULY 2003*

    (b) The current rent is £ *98.00*   and is payable each (week) (fortnight) (month).
    (other———————————)

    (c) Any unpaid rent or charge for use and occupation should be calculated at £ *13.96*   per day.

4. The reason the claimant is asking for possession is:
    (a) because the defendant has not paid the rent due under the terms of the tenancy agreement.
    (Details are set out below)(Details are shown on the attached rent statement)

    RENT ARREARS AT 7 NOVEMBER 2005 – £912.62
    RENT ARREARS AT 6 MARCH 2006 – £1103.16

    (b) because the defendant has failed to comply with other terms of the tenancy.
    Details are set out below.

    (c) because: (including any (other) statutory grounds)

N119 Particulars of claim for possession (rented residential premises) (10.01)   *Printed on behalf of The Court Service*

5. The following steps have already been taken to recover any arrears:

REPEAT CORRESPONDENCE WITH DEFENDANT.

HOME VISIT.

6. The appropriate (~~notice to quit~~) (~~notice of breach of lease~~) (notice seeking possession)
   (*other*   ) was served on the defendant on *8 NOVEMBER* 20*05* .

About the defendant

7. The following information is known about the defendant's circumstances:

THE DEFENDANT IS BELIEVED TO BE WORKING AND IN RECEIPT OF
WORKING TAX CREDIT

About the claimant

8. The claimant is asking the court to take the following financial or other information into account when making its decision whether or not to grant an order for possession:

THE CLAIMANT IS A LOCAL AUTHORITY RESPONSIBLE FOR MANAGEMENT OF ITS
HOUSING STOCK UPON WHICH THERE ARE CONSIDERABLE DEMANDS. THERE
ARE 11,500 FAMILIES AWAITING ACCOMMODATION IDENTIFIED AS LIVING IN
HOUSING NEED

Forfeiture

~~9.   (a) There is no underlessee or mortgagee entitled to claim relief against forfeiture.~~

~~or   (b)   of~~

~~is entitled to claim relief against forfeiture as underlessee or mortgagee.~~

What the court is being asked to do:

10. The claimant asks the court to order that the defendant(s):

   (a) give the claimant possession of the premises;

   (b) pay the unpaid rent and any charge for use and occupation up to the date an order is made;

   (c) pay rent and any charge for use and occupation from the date of the order until the claimant recovers possession of the property;

   (d) pay the claimant's costs of making this claim.

Statement of Truth

*(I believe)(The claimant believes) that the facts stated in these particulars of claim are true.
* I am duly authorised by the claimant to sign this statement.

signed _John Smith_   date _9 JUNE 2006_

(Claimant)(Litigation friend(where claimant is a child or a patient)*)(Claimant's solicitor)
delete as appropriate

Full name _JOHN SMITH_

Name of claimant's solicitor's firm _LEGAL SERVICES, RAINBOW DISTRICT COUNCIL_

position or office held _HEAD OF LEGAL SERVICES_
(if signing on behalf of firm or company)

3 Defence form for rented residential premises (Form N11R) with Additional Defence form

Defence form
(rented residential
premises)

In the *ANYTOWN COUNTY COURT*   Claim No. *AN6*   *09601*

RAINBOW DISTRICT COUNCIL   Claimant

WAYNE ROSS   Defendant(s)

Date of hearing   *16 JULY 2006*

Personal details

1. Please give your:

Forename(s)   *WAYNE*

Surname   *ROSS*

Address *(if different from the address on the claim form)*

post code

Disputing the claim

2. Do you agree with what is said about the premises and the tenancy agreement?   ☑Yes   ☐No

If No, set out your reasons below:

3. Did you receive the notice from the claimant referred to at paragraph 5 of the particulars of claim?   ☐Yes   ☑No

SEE ATTACHED ADDITIONAL DEFENCE FORM

If Yes, when: _____

N11R Defence form (rented residential premises) (10.01)   *Printed on behalf of The Court Service*

4.	Do you agree that there are arrears of rent as stated in the particulars of claim?	☐ Yes	☑ No

If No, state how much the arrears are: £ *N/K*   ☐ None

SEE ATTACHED ADDITIONAL DEFENCE FORM

5.	If the particulars of claim give any reasons for possession other than rent arrears, do you agree with what is said?	☐ Yes	☐ No

If No, give details below:

6.	Do you have a money or other claim (a counterclaim) against your landlord?	☑ Yes	☐ No

If Yes, give details:

SEE ATTACHED ADDITIONAL DEFENCE FORM

Arrears

7.	Have you paid any money to your landlord since the claim was issued?	☐ Yes	☑ No

If Yes, state how much you have paid and when: £ _____   date _____

8.	Have you come to any agreement with your landlord about repaying the arrears since the claim was issued?	☐ Yes	☐ No

I have agreed to pay £_____ each (week)(month)

9.	If you have not reached an agreement with your landlord, do you want the court to consider allowing you to pay the arrears by instalments?	☑ Yes	☐ No

10.	How much can you afford to pay in addition to the current rent?	£ *2.90* ____ per (week)~~(month)~~

About yourself

State benefits

11. Are you receiving Income Support? ☑Yes ☐No

12. Have you applied for Income Support? ☐Yes ☑No

    If Yes, when did you apply? _____

13. Are you receiving housing benefit? ☐Yes ☑No

    If Yes, how much are you receiving? £_____ per (week)(month)

14. Have you applied for housing benefit? ☑Yes ☐No

    If Yes, when did you apply? *8 WEEKS AGO*

15. Is the housing benefit paid ☐to you ☐to your landlord

Dependants *(people you look after financially)*

16. Have you any dependant children? ☑Yes ☐No

    If Yes, give the number in each age group below:

    [2] under 11 [ ] 11-15 [ ] 16-17 [ ] 18 and over

Other dependants

17. Give details of any other dependants for whom you are financially responsible:

    SHARON ROSS

Other residents

18. Give details of any other people living at the premises for whom you are not financially responsible:

		Weekly	Monthly
Money you receive			
19. Usual take-home pay or income if self-employed *including overtime, commission, bonuses*	£_____	☐	☐
Job Seekers allowance	£_____	☐	☐
Pension	£_____	☐	☐
Child benefit	£ *29,15*	☑	☐
Other benefits and allowances	£_____	☐	☐
Others living in my home give me	£_____	☐	☐
I am paid maintenance for myself (or children) of	£_____	☐	☐
Other income	£_____	☐	☐
Total income	£ *29,15*	☑	☐

Bank accounts and savings

20. Do you have a current bank or building society account?   ☐ Yes   ☑ No

If Yes, is it

☐ in credit? If so, by how much?   £_____

☐ overdrawn? If so, by how much? £_____   ✓

21. Do you have a savings or deposit account?   ☐ Yes   ☐ No

If Yes, what is the balance?   £_____

Money you pay out

22. Do you have to pay any court orders or fines?

Court	Claim/Case number	Balance owing	Instalments paid
ANYTOWN MAGISTRATES	*ATN 0162B*	*£120.00*	*£20.00*
	Total Instalments paid £ *20.00*		per month

23. Give details if you are in arrears with any of the court payments or fines:

NOT APPLICABLE

24. Do you have any loan or credit debts?   ☐ Yes   ☑ No

Loan/credit from	Balance owing	Instalments paid

Total Instalments £ _____ per month

25. Give details if you are in arrears with any loan / credit repayments:

Regular expenses

(Do not include any payments made by other members of the household out of their own income)

26. What regular expenses do you have?
(List below)

		Weekly	Monthly
Council tax	£ *10.00*	☑	☐
Gas	£ _____	☐	☐
Electricity	£ *20.00*	☑	☐
Water charges	£ *10.00*	☑	☐
TV rental & licence	£ *12.00*	☑	☐
Telephone	£ _____	☐	☐
Credit repayments	£ _____	☐	☐
Mail order	£ _____	☐	☐
Housekeeping, food, school meals	£ *50.00*	☑	☐
Travelling expenses	£ _____	☐	☐
Clothing	£ *5.00*	☑	☐
Maintenance payments	£ _____	☐	☐
Other	£ _____	☐	☐
Total expenses	£ *107.00*	☑	☐

Priority debts

27. This section is for **arrears** only. **Do not** include regular expenses listed at Question 26.

		Weekly	Monthly
Council tax arrears	£_____	☐	☐
Water charges arrears	£_____	☐	☐
Gas account	£_____	☐	☐
Electricity account	£_____	☐	☐
Maintenance arrears	£_____	☐	☐

Others *(give details below)*

Magistrates' Court fine	£ 20	☐	☑
	£_____	☐	☐
	£_____	☐	☐

28. If an order for possession were to be made, would you have somewhere else to live?   ☐ Yes   ☑ No

If Yes, say when you would be able to move in: _____

29. Give details of any events or circumstances which have led to your being in arrears of rent *(for example divorce, separation, redundancy, bereavement, illness, bankruptcy)* or any other particular circumstances affecting your case. If there are any reasons why the date any possession order takes effect should be delayed, give them here. If you believe you would suffer exceptional hardship by being ordered to leave the property immediately, say why.

SEE ATTACHED ADDITIONAL DEFENCE FORM

Statement of Truth

*(I believe)(~~The defendant(s) believe(s)~~) that the facts stated in this defence form are true.
*~~I am duly authorised by the defendant(s) to sign this statement.~~

signed ___*Wayne Ross*___   date ___*18 July 2006*___
*(Defendant)(~~Litigation friend(where defendant is a child or a patient)~~)(~~Defendant's solicitor~~)
*delete as appropriate

Full name ___*WAYNE ROSS*___

Name of defendant's solicitor's firm ___*RAINBOW LAW CENTRE*___

position or office held _____
                  (if signing on behalf of firm or company)

IN THE ANYTOWN COUNTY COURT   CASE NO: AN6 09601

BETWEEN

RAINBOW DISTRICT COUNCIL   <u>Claimant</u>

and

WAYNE ROSS   <u>Defendant</u>

ADDITIONAL DEFENCE FORM

1. This Additional Defence Form is filed to supplement the Defence Form filed in this action by the Defendant.
2. The Defendant admits that he occupies 32 Small Street Anytown ('the property') with his family under a secure tenancy within the meaning of the Housing Act 1985. The Defendant denies that the Claimant is entitled to termination of that tenancy and possession of the property as claimed.
3. The Defendant denies being served with the Notice Seeking Possession referred to at paragraph 6 of the Particulars of Claim.
4. The Defendant admits that he has failed to make some rent payments as they have fallen due but is not able to comment on the level of underpayment. The Claimant is put to strict proof as to the level of any rent underpayments. The Defendant asserts that in any event he is entitled to set off against any rent otherwise due the sums Counterclaimed as set out below.
5. In the alternative the Defendant claims the protection of Housing Act 1985 Section 84 and denies that in all the circumstances it would be reasonable for an Order for Possession to be made.

COUNTERCLAIM

6. The Defendant repeats paragraphs 1 to 5 above.
7. The Defendant is entitled to the benefit of the repairing covenant implied by Landlord and Tenant Act 1985 Section 11 in respect of which the Claimant is in breach. Further and in the alternative the Claimant is in breach of the express repairing obligations set out in paragraph 5 of the Tenancy Agreement.
8. In breach of these covenants the Claimant has since in or about January 2003 failed to keep the property in repair.

PARTICULARS OF DISREPAIR

(i) Roof leak to main roof

(ii) Rot to kitchen windowsill

(iii) Defective pointing to front wall

[........ *Set out the detail of the other defects complained about*]

9. The Claimant has had notice of these defects by reason of numerous verbal complaints to its employees since January 2003, a complaint made to the Local Government Ombudsman by the Defendant in October 2004 and by visits by various employees of the Claimant on various dates.

10. Because of the breaches of covenant the Defendant has suffered loss, damage, injury and inconvenience.

PARTICULARS

(i)   Due to damp penetration the Defendant has been unable to use the first floor rear bedroom since March 2003.

(ii) Decorationshave been ruined in the front first floor bedroom because of damp penetration with the result that the Defendant has spent £750 on decorating materials.

(iii) By reason of the dampness the Defendant spent additional sums on heating which he estimates at £500 for each Winter quarter.

(iv) The Defendant's wife has been depressed and a strain has been placed on their marriage.

[*Set out the detail of other consequences of the defects complained about*]

11. Further and in the alternative the Claimant is in breach of the Defective Premises Act 1972 Section4.

PARTICULARS OF BREACH OF DUTY

12. The Defendant repeats the Particulars set out in paragraph 10 above.

13. The Defendant claims interest pursuant to County Courts Act 1984 Section 69 at such rate and for such period as the Court will allow.

14. The Defendant Counterclaims for:

(1) Damages limited to £5000.

(2) A Mandatory Order or Order for specific performance to remedy such of the defects mentioned above as are outstanding at the date of the trial.

(3) Interest pursuant to County Courts Act 1984 Section 69.

(4) Costs.

Dated   18 July 2006

STATEMENT OF TRUTH

I believe that the facts stated in this Defence and Part 20 Counterclaim are true.

....
WAYNE ROSS
c/o Jenny Brown, Rainbow Law Centre, 1 Lavender Close, Anytown

To the Court Manager
And to the Claimant

4 Particulars of Claim for mortgaged residential premises (Form N120)

Particulars of claim for possession
(mortgaged residential premises)

In the *ANYTOWN COUNTY COURT* Claim No. *AN6   09615*

EQUITABLE SECURED HOME LOAN COMPANY LTD   Claimant

STEPHEN AND JOSIE NEILL   Defendant

1. The claimant has a right to possession of:

    1 CEDAR STREET, ANYTOWN

About the mortgage

2. On *19 FEBRUARY 2004* the claimant(s) and the defendant(s) entered into a mortgage of the above premises.

3. To the best of the claimant's knowledge the following persons are in possession of the property:

    THE DEFENDANTS

[Delete (a) or (b) as appropriate]

4 (a) The agreement for the loan secured by the mortgage (or at least one of them) is a regulated consumer credit agreement. Notice of default was given to the defendant(s) on *9 DECEMBER* 20*05*

    (b) ~~The agreement for the loan secured by the mortgage is not (or none of them is) a regulated consumer credit agreement.~~

5. The claimant is asking for possession on the following ground(s):

    (a) the defendant(s) ~~(has)~~(have) not paid the agreed repayments of the loan and interest. *Give details:*

    THE ARREARS AMOUNT TO £2100.06

N120 Particulars of claim for possession (mortgaged residential premises)(10.01)   *Printed on behalf of The Court Service*

(b) because:

(a) The amount loaned was £ *18,000*

(b) The current terms of repayment are: *(include any current periodic repayment and any current payment of interest)*

£450 ON 8TH OF EACH MONTH FOR 75 MONTHS

(c) The total amount required to pay the mortgage in full as at *19 JUNE*   20*06* (not more than 14 days after the claim was issued) would be £ *21,080.10*   taking into account any adjustment for early settlement. This includes £ *750.00*   payable for solicitor's costs and administration charges.

(d) The following additional payments are also required under the terms of the mortgage:

£	for	[not] included in 6(c)
£	for	[not] included in 6(c)
£	for	[not] included in 6(c)

(e) Of the payments in paragraph 6(d), the following are in arrears:

arrears of £

arrears of £

arrears of £

[(f) The total amount outstanding under the regulated loan agreement secured by the mortgage is £   ]

(g) Interest rates which have been applied to the mortgage:

(i) at the start of the mortgage   *14.5* % p.a.

(ii) immediately before any arrears were accrued   *14.5* % p.a.

(iii) at the start of the claim   *18.05* % p.a.

7. The following steps have already been taken to recover the money secured by the mortgage:

CORRESPONDENCE SENT TO DEFENDANTS.
HOME VISIT BY DEBT COUNSELLOR.

About the defendant(s)

8. The following information is known about the defendant's circumstances:
    (*in particular say whether the defendant(s) (is)(are) in receipt of social security benefits and whether any payments are made directly to the claimant*)
    THE DEFENDANTS ARE BELIEVED TO BE IN EMPLOYMENT

[Delete either (a) or (b) as appropriate]
9. (a) There is no one who should be given notice of these proceedings because of a registered interest in the property under section 31(10) of the Family Law Act 1996 or section 2(8) or 8(3) of the Matrimonial Homes Act 1983 or section 2(7) of the Matrimonial Homes Act 1967.

    ~~(b) Notice of these proceedings will be given to~~ ~~who has a registered interest in the property.~~

Tenancy

[Delete if inappropriate]
10. ~~A tenancy was entered into between the mortgagor and the mortgagee on~~
    ~~A notice was served on~~

What the court is being asked to do

11. The claimant asks the court to order that the defendant(s):

    (a) give the claimant possession of the premises;

    (b) pay to the claimant the total amount outstanding under the mortgage.

Statement of Truth

*(I believe)(The claimant believes) that the facts stated in these particulars of claim are true.
* I am duly authorised by the claimant to sign this statement.

signed *Jayne Osbourne* _____ date *16 JUNE 2006*

*(Claimant)(Litigation friend *(where claimant is a child or a patient)*)(Claimant's solicitor)
delete as appropriate

Full name ___*JAYNE OSBOURNE*_____

Name of claimant's solicitor's firm ___*MAMMON & CO*_____

position or office held _*SOLICITOR*_____
                        (if signing on behalf of firm or company)

5 Defence form for mortgaged residential premises (Form N11M) with Additional Defence form

Defence form
(mortgaged residential
premises)

In the *ANYTOWN COUNTY COURT*   Claim No. *AN6   09615*

EQUITABLE SECURED HOME LOAN COMPANY LTD   Claimant

STEPHEN AND JOSIE NEILL   Defendant(s)

Date of hearing *21 JULY 2006*

Personal details

1. Please give your:

   Forename(s) *STEPHEN AND JOSIE*

   Surname   *NEILL*

   Address *(if different from the address on the claim form)*

   post code

Disputing the claim

2. Do you agree with what is said about the property and the
   mortgage agreement in the particulars of claim?   ☑Yes   ☐No

   If No, set out your reasons below:

3. Do you agree that there are arrears of mortgage repayments as
   stated in the particulars of claim?   ☑Yes   ☐No

   If No, state how much the arrears are: £_____   ☐None

N11M Defence form (mortgaged residential premises) (10.01)   *Printed on behalf of The Court Service*

4. If the particulars of claim give any reasons for possession other than arrears of mortgage repayments, do you agree with what is said?   ☐ Yes   ☐ No

    If No, give details below:

    (Only answer these questions if the loan secured by the mortgage (or part of it) is a regulated consumer credit agreement)

5. Do you want the court to consider whether or not the terms of your original loan agreement are fair?   ☑ Yes   ☐ No

6. Do you intend to apply to the court for an order changing the terms of your loan agreement (a time order)?   ☑ Yes   ☐ No

    SEE ATTACHED ADDITIONAL DEFENCE FORM

Arrears

7. Have you paid any money to your mortgage lender since the claim was issued?   ☑ Yes   ☐ No

    If Yes, state how much you have paid and when: £ *150.00*   date *2.06.06*

8. Have you come to any agreement with your mortgage lender about repaying the arrears since the claim was issued?   ☐ Yes   ☑ No

    I have agreed to pay £ _____ each (week)(month).

9. If you have not reached an agreement with your mortgage lender, do you want the court to consider allowing you to pay the arrears by instalments?   ☑ Yes   ☐ No

10. How much can you afford to pay in addition to the current instalments?   £ *NIL*   per (week)(month)

About yourself

State benefits

11. Are you receiving Income Support?   ☐ Yes   ☑ No

12. Have you applied for Income Support?   ☐ Yes   ☑ No

If Yes, when did you apply?   _____

13. Does the Department of Social Security pay your mortgage interest?   ☐ Yes   ☑ No

Dependants *(people you look after financially)*

14. Have you any dependant children?   ☑ Yes   ☐ No

If Yes, give the number in each age group below:

| 1 | under 11 | | 1 | 11-15 | | | 16-17 | | | 18 and over |

Other dependants

15. Give details of any other dependants for whom you are financially responsible:

Other residents

16. Give details of any other people living at the premises for whom you are not financially responsible:

Money you receive		Weekly	Monthly
17. Usual take-home pay or income if self-employed *including overtime, commission, bonuses*	£ *1100.00*	☐	☑
Job Seekers allowance	£_____	☐	☐
Pension	£_____	☐	☐
Child benefit	£*115.40*	☐	☑
Other benefits and allowances	£_____	☐	☐
Others living in my home give me	£_____	☐	☐
I am paid maintenance for myself (or children) of	£_____	☐	☐
Other income	£_____	☐	☐
Total income	£*1215.40*	☐	☑

Bank accounts and savings

18. Do you have a current bank or building society account? ☑Yes ☐No

   If Yes, is it

     ☐ in credit? If so, by how much? £_____

     ☑ overdrawn? If so, by how much? £ *800*_____

19. Do you have a savings or deposit account? ☐Yes ☑No

   If Yes, what is the balance? £_____

Money you pay out

20. Do you have to pay any court orders or fines? ☐Yes ☐No

Court	Claim/Case number	Balance owing	Instalments paid
ANYTOWN MAGISTRATES	*ATN 6410C*	*£1200*	*£80*

Total instalments paid £ *80* per month

21. Give details if you are in arrears with any of the court payments or fines:

22. Do you have any loan or credit debts? ☑Yes ☐No

Loan/credit from	Balance owing	Instalments paid
BETTER FURNISHINGS PLC	*£500*	*£60*

Total instalments paid £ *60* per month

23. Give details if you are in arrears with any loan / credit repayments:

Regular expenses
(Do not include any payments made by other members of the household out of their own income)

24. What regular expenses do you have?
(List below)

		Weekly	Monthly
Council tax	£ *100*	☐	☑
Gas	£ *80*	☐	☑
Electricity	£ *60*	☐	☑
Water charges	£ *50*	☐	☑
TV rental & licence	£ *60*	☐	☑
Telephone	£ *80*	☐	☑
Credit repayments	£ *60*	☐	☑
Mail order	£	☐	☐
Housekeeping, food, school meals	£ *300*	☐	☑
Travelling expenses	£ *90*	☐	☑
Clothing	£ *60*	☐	☑
Maintenance payments	£	☐	☐
Other mortgages	£	☐	☐
Other	£	☐	☐
Total expenses	£ *940*	☐	☑

Priority debts

25. This section is for **arrears** only. **Do not** include regular expenses listed at Question 24.

		Weekly	Monthly
Council tax arrears	£ *80*	☐	☑
Water charges arrears	£	☐	☐
Gas account	£	☐	☐
Electricity account	£	☐	☐
Maintenance arrears	£	☐	☐

Others *(give details below)*

		Weekly	Monthly
	£	☐	☐
	£	☐	☐
	£	☐	☐

26. If an order for possession were to be made, would you have somewhere else to live? ☐ Yes ☑ No

    If Yes, say when you would be able to move in: _____

27. Give details of any events or circumstances which have led to your being in arrears with your mortgage *(for example divorce, separation, redundancy, bereavement, illness, bankruptcy)*. If you believe you would suffer exceptional hardship by being ordered to leave the property immediately, say why.

    SEE ATTACHED ADDITIONAL DEFENCE FORM

Statement of Truth

*(I believe)~~(The defendant believes)~~ that the facts stated in this defence form are true.
*~~I am duly authorised by the defendant to sign this statement.~~

signed   *Stephen Neill*   date *18 JULY 2006*

*(Defendant)~~(Litigation friend(where defendant is a child or a patient))(Defendant's solicitor)~~
delete as appropriate

Full name   *STEPHEN & JOSIE NEILL*

Name of defendant's solicitor's firm   *RAINBOW LAW CENTRE*

position or office held   _____
        (if signing on behalf of firm or company)

IN THE ANYTOWN COUNTY COURT

CASE NO: AN1 09615

BETWEEN

EQUITABLE SECURED HOME LOAN COMPANY LIMITED

<u>Claimant</u>

and

STEPHEN and JOSIE NEILL

<u>Defendant</u>

ADDITIONAL DEFENCE FORM

---

1. This Additional Defence Form is filed to supplement the Defence Form filed in this action by the Defendants.
2. The Defendants admit that the agreement for the loan secured by the mortgage in favour of the Claimant is one regulated by the Consumer Credit Act 1974. The Defendants claim the protection of the provisions of that Act and in particular the provisions relating to Time Orders contained in Consumer Credit Act 1974 Sections 129–136.
3. The Defendants do not dispute the information provided in the Particulars of Claim relating to the mortgage and to the Defendants.

COUNTERCLAIM

---

4. The Defendants repeat their Defence set out above.
5. In November 2005 the Defendant Josie Neill was dismissed from her employment because of ill health. Because of the loss of her salary the Defendants were unable to meet the payments under the agreement with the Claimant. The Defendants expect Josie Neill to return to work in October 2006. Attached to this Defence Form is a letter from the employer confirming that as soon as she is fit to resume work she will be re-employed on the same terms as previously. At that time the Defendants would then be able to resume payments in accordance with the terms of the agreement with the Claimant.
6. The Defendants ask that the Court make a 'Time Order' providing for the monthly instalments due under the agreement to be reduced to £140 with effect August 2006 until November 2006 and that pursuant to that Time Order the interest rate provided for in the agreement to be reduced to an annual rate of 8%.
7. The Defendants Counterclaim for:

    (1) Relief pursuant to Consumer Credit Act 1974 Sections 129–136.

    (2) Further or other relief.

Dated   18 July 2006

STATEMENT OF TRUTH

We believe that the facts stated in this Defence and Part 20 Counterclaim are true.

....

STEPHEN & JOSIE NEILL

c/o Rainbow Law Centre, 1 Lavender Close, Anytown

To the Court Manager
And to the Claimant

6 Application notice (Form N244) to set judgment aside

Application Notice

- You must complete Parts A **and** B, **and** Part C if applicable
- Send any relevant fee and the completed application to the court with any draft order, witness statement or other evidence; and sufficient copies of these for service on each respondent

In the	
ANYTOWN COUNTY COURT	
Claim no.	*AN6 09601*
Warrant no. (If applicable)	
Claimant (including ref.)	*RAINBOW DISTRICT COUNCIL*
Defendant(s) (including ref.)	*WAYNE ROSS*
Date	*3 AUGUST 2006*

You should provide this information for listing the application

1. Do you wish to have your application dealt with at a hearing?

   Yes ☑   No ☐   If Yes, please complete 2

2. Time estimate _*0*_ (hours) _*15*_ (mins)

   Is this agreed by all parties? ☐ Yes ☑ No

   Level of judge _*DISTRICT JUDGE*_

3. Parties to be served: _*CLAIMANT*_

Part A

1. Enter your full name, or name of solicitor

I (We) *WAYNE ROSS*   ~~(on behalf of)(the claimant)~~ (the defendant)

2. State clearly what order you are seeking and if possible attach a draft

intend to apply for an order ~~(a draft of which is attached)~~ that[2]

THE ORDER FOR POSSESSION DATED 21 JULY 2006 BE SET ASIDE AS because[3]

3. Briefly set out why you are seeking the order. Include the material facts on which you rely, identifying any rule or statutory provision

IT WAS OBTAINED IN MY ABSENCE, THERE IS A GOOD DEFENCE TO THE CLAIM AND I HAVE ACTED PROMPTLY IN MAKING THIS APPLICATION

Part B

I (We) wish to rely on: *tick one box*

the attached (witness statement)~~(affidavit)~~ ☑   my statement of case ☐

evidence in Part C in support of my application ☐

4. If you are not already a party to the proceedings, you must provide an address for service of documents

Signed *Wayne Ross*

(Applicant)~~('s solicitor)('s litigation friend)~~

Position or office held (if signing on behalf of firm or company)

Address to which documents about this claim should be sent (including reference if appropriate)[4]

RAINBOW LAW CENTRE
1 LAVENDER CLOSE
ANYTOWN

Tel. no. _____   Postcode *AN1 3DS*

if applicable

fax no.

DX no.

e-mail

The court office at

is open from 10am to 4pm Monday to Friday. When corresponding with the court please address forms or letters to the Court Manager and quote the claim number.

N244 Application Notice (4.99)   *Printed on behalf of The Court Service*

Part C   Claim No. *AN6   09601*

I (We) wish to rely on the following evidence in support of this application:

SEE ATTACHED WITNESS STATEMENT.

Statement of Truth

*(I believe)(The applicant believes) that the facts stated in this application are true

Signed

Wayne Ross

(Applicant)(~~'s solicitor~~)(~~'s litigation friend~~)

Position or
office held
(if signing on
behalf of firm or
company)

Date   *3 AUGUST 2006*

*delete as appropriate

7 Witness statement in support of application to set judgment aside

Defendant;
W Ross
First

3 August 2006

IN THE ANYTOWN COUNTY COURT

CASE NO: AN6 09601

BETWEEN

RAINBOW DISTRICT COUNCIL

<u>Claimant</u>

and

WAYNE ROSS

<u>Defendant</u>

WITNESS STATEMENT OF WAYNE ROSS

I Wayne Ross of 32 Small Street Anytown, currently unemployed, will say as follows:

1. I am the Defendant in this case and make this statement in support of my application to have the Order for Possession dated 21 July 2006 set aside having been obtained in my absence. The facts set out in this statement are within my own knowledge or are based on information provided to me by my Solicitors and which I believe to be true.

2. I am the tenant of 32 Small Street Anytown which I rent from the Claimant.

3. On 31 July 2006 I received a copy of the Order for Possession that had been granted to the Claimant on 21 July 2006. This was the first that I had heard about the proceedings that had been brought against me. At no stage have I received any Claim for Possession from the Court nor have I been told by anyone on the Claimant's behalf that proceedings had been started. I should add that I have experienced other problems with postal deliveries. In October 2005 a Giro cheque posted to me by the Department for Work and Pensions went missing and in due course they agreed to replace it.

4. I can only assume that if the Claim for Possession was posted by the Court (which I understand from my Solicitor is the usual practice) and that the envelope has gone missing somewhere in the postal system.

5. I wish to defend the proceedings brought against me and to Counterclaim against the Claimant for damages for breach of repairing obligation and for a Mandatory Order to require the Claimant to undertake repairs for which it is responsible. I refer to the draft Defence and Counterclaim marked WR 1 which is attached to this statement which I serve in these proceedings.

[Alternatively, a brief synopsis of the Grounds for Possession and Counterclaim should be set out]

6. I would respectfully suggest that I have shown that I had a good reason for not attending the hearing, that I have acted promptly in the making of this application and that I have a good defence to the claim brought against me by the Claimant. I would ask that the Possession Order dated 21 July 2006 be set aside and that the Court give Case Management Directions for the service of my Statement of Case and consequential Directions for the disposal of this claim.

7. I believe the facts stated in this Witness Statement are true.

W. Ross
....   Date...*3 August 2006*...............
WAYNE ROSS

To the Court Manager
And to The Claimant

8 Application notice (Form N244) to suspend warrant for possession and to postpone date for possession

Application Notice		In the
• You must complete Parts A **and** B, **and** Part C if applicable • Send any relevant fee and the completed application to the court with any draft order, witness statement or other evidence; and sufficient copies of these for service on each respondent		*ANYTOWN COUNTY COURT*

Application Notice

- You must complete Parts A **and** B, **and** Part C if applicable
- Send any relevant fee and the completed application to the court with any draft order, witness statement or other evidence; and sufficient copies of these for service on each respondent

You should provide this information for listing the application

1. Do you wish to have your application dealt with at a hearing?

   Yes ✓   No ☐   If Yes, please complete 2

2. Time estimate ___0___ (hours) _15_ (mins)

   Is this agreed by all parties? ☐ Yes ✓ No

   Level of judge *DISTRICT JUDGE*

3. Parties to be served: *CLAIMANT*

In the	*ANYTOWN COUNTY COURT*
Claim no.	*AN6 09601*
Warrant no. (if applicable)	
Claimant (including ref.)	*RAINBOW DISTRICT COUNCIL*
Defendant(s) (including ref.)	*WAYNE ROSS*
Date	*17 OCTOBER 2006*

Part A

1. Enter your full name, or name of solicitor

   I (We) *WAYNE ROSS*   (on behalf of)(the claimant)(the defendant)

2. State clearly what order you are seeking and if possible attach a draft

   intend to apply for an order (a draft of which is attached)|that

   THE WARRANT FOR POSSESSION BE SUSPENDED ON TERMS AND THE DATE FOR DELIVERY OF POSSESSION BE POSTPONED

3. Briefly set out why you are seeking the order. Include the material facts on which you rely, identifying any rule or statutory provision

   because

   I CAN PAY OFF THE ARREARS OVER A PERIOD OF TIME

Part B

I (We) wish to rely on: *tick one box*

the attached (witness statement)(affidavit) ✓   my statement of case ☐

4. If you are not already a party to the proceedings, you must provide an address for service of documents

evidence in Part C in support of my application ☐

Signed *Wayne Ross*   **Position or office held** (if signing on behalf of firm or company)

(Applicant)('s solicitor)('s litigation friend)

Address to which documents about this claim should be sent (including reference if appropriate)

RAINBOW LAW CENTRE
1 LAVENDER CLOSE
ANYTOWN

Tel. no. _____   Postcode *AN1 3DS*

	if applicable
fax no.	
DX no.	
e-mail	

The court office at

is open from 10am to 4pm Monday to Friday. When corresponding with the court please address forms or letters to the Court Manager and quote the claim number.

N244 Application Notice (4.99)   *Printed on behalf of The Court Service*

Part C   Claim No. *AN6   09601*

I (We) wish to rely on the following evidence in support of this application:

SEE ATTACHED WITNESS STATEMENT.

Statement of Truth

*(I believe)(~~The applicant believes~~) that the facts stated in this application are true

Signed		Position or office held	
	Wayne Ross	(if signing on behalf of firm or company)	
	(Applicant)('s ~~solicitor~~)('s ~~litigation friend~~)		
		Date	*17 October 2006*

*delete as appropriate

9 Witness statement in support of application to suspend warrant and to postpone date for possession

IN THE ANYTOWN COUNTY COURT   Claim No: AN1 09601

BETWEEN

RAINBOW DISTRICT COUNCIL   <u>Claimant</u>

and

WAYNE ROSS   <u>Defendant</u>

APPLICATION NOTICE (in From N244)

TAKE NOTICE that the Defendant intends to apply to the Court at

on   day the   day of   2005

for an order:

1. That the warrant for possession issued in this matter be suspended on such terms as the Court thinks fit;

2. That the order for possession dated 25th March 2005 be varied so as to postpone the date for possession on compliance with the terms in paragraph 1 and otherwise on such terms as the Court thinks fit; and

3. That the costs of this application may be provided for.

Dated, etc,

IN THE ANYTOWN COUNTY COURT   Claim No: AN6 09601

BETWEEN

RAINBOW DISTRICT COUNCIL   <u>Claimant</u>

and

WAYNE ROSS   <u>Defendant</u>

WITNESS STATEMENT

I, WAYNE ROSS, of 32 Small Street Anytown will say as follows:

1. I am the Defendant in this matter. I make this Witness Statement in support of my application for a suspension of the warrant and for a variation of the suspended possession order granted to the Claimant by this Court on 21 July 2006.

2. Under that order, the Court granted possession of 32 Small Street Anytown to the Claimant on 18 August 2006, but suspended enforcement of the order on terms that I should pay the current weekly rent plus the sum of £2.90 per week towards the arrears, which at that date stood at £1,599.93. I am advised that the form of that order had the effect of terminating my tenancy on the date specified, whereas the Court's intention had been to suspend the date for possession subject to my complying with the terms of the order

2. Following the order of 21 July 2006, I requested the Department of Work and Pensions to deduct the sum of £2.90 from my weekly income support entitlement and to make these payments directly to the Claimant. I understood that this arrangement would come into effect immediately, but I realised that this was not the case when my housing officer wrote to me informing me that no payments had been received. I contacted the social security office, and was informed that they had no record of the arrangement. I therefore had to complete another form of request. I understand that direct deductions came into operation several weeks later, and that they have continued to be paid at four weekly intervals in arrear.

3. At all times since the order was made, I have been in receipt of income support. I have also claimed housing benefit throughout, but my contributions towards the rent have changed frequently. At first, my full rent was covered by housing benefit, apart from the sum of £6.50 in respect of water rates and service charges. I have paid at least this sum every week, with the exception of six weeks in August/September 2006. I missed those payments because I was under extreme financial pressure at the time. The electricity company were threatening to cut off my supply because of an outstanding bill of £224. I incurred other debts to friends and family in borrowing the money to pay off that account.

4. Difficulties have also arisen because my son James Ross, who is aged 20 and who now lives with me, started employment in August 2006, and has had three different jobs in the last two months. This has led to a non-dependant deduction being applied to my housing benefit entitlement, resulting in my

weekly contribution to the rent increasing at intervals. I did not realise at first that James's wages would affect my housing benefit, so I did not understand the need to provide evidence of his income to the Claimant's housing benefit office. This resulted in an overpayment of benefit of £324, and this is being recovered from me by deductions of £8.00 each week from my ongoing benefit.

5. James has been in and out of work during this period. On each occasion that he has started work again, I have declared his income to the housing benefit office, but it has taken several weeks for them to inform me how much I should be paying towards the rent because of the non-dependant deduction.

6. I am currently paying a total of £29.30 towards my weekly rent, together with the weekly instalments of £2.90 off the arrears which are paid by direct deduction.

7. I have not always understood the correspondence which I have received from the housing benefit office, and in particular I did not understand at first that a deduction was being made from my housing benefit because of James's employment.

8. I was informed by my housing officer that unless I made up the shortfall in my payments under the order, a warrant for possession of my flat would be issued. I could not afford to make up these payments in a lump sum.

9. My household now consists of myself, together with James, my other son Jon, who is aged 9, and my daughter Kate, who is aged 10. I suffer from agoraphobia and depression and I am unable to work. I have done my best to comply with the terms of the court order

10. In the circumstances, I respectfully ask the Court to suspend the warrant of possession on terms that I will continue to pay the current rent plus the sum of £2.90 off the arrears. I also ask the Court to vary the order for possession so as to postpone the possession date, in order that my tenancy may be revived.

I believe that the facts set out in this Statement are true.

Dated: *17 October 2006*

Signed .... *W. Ross* ....

       Wayne Ross

       Defendant

To the Court and to the Claimant

10 Order for possession with no date fixed (Form N28A)

IN THE ANYTOWN COUNTY COURT   CASE NO: AN6 09601

BETWEEN

RAINBOW DISTRICT COUNCIL   <u>Claimant</u>

and

WAYNE ROSS   <u>Defendant</u>

ORDER

---

1. The defendant is to give up possession of 32 Small Street Anytown to the claimant.

2. The date on which the defendant is to give up possession of the property to the claimant is postponed to a date to be fixed by the court on an application by the claimant. The defendant's tenancy of the property will continue until that date.

3. The defendant must pay the claimant £1,599.93 for rent arrears and £150 for costs. The total judgment debt is £ 1,749.99 to be paid by instalments as specified in paragraph 4 below.

4. The claimant shall not be entitled to make an application for a date to be fixed for the giving up of possession and the termination of the defendant's tenancy so long as the defendant pays the claimant the current rent together with instalments of £2.90 per week towards the judgment debt.

5. The first payment of the current rent and the first instalment must be made on or before 31 July 2006.

6. Any application to fix the date on which the defendant is to give up possession may be determined on the papers without a hearing (unless the district judge considers that such a hearing is necessary).

7. This order shall cease to be enforceable when the total judgment debt is satisfied.

Dated   21 July 2006

DISTRICT JUDGE

To the defendant

The court has ordered that **unless you pay the arrears** and costs at the rate set out above **in addition to your current rent**, you must leave the premises.

Payments should be made to the claimant, not to the court. If you need more information about making payments, you should contact the claimant.

If you do not make the payments or leave the premises, the claimant can ask the court, **without a further hearing**, to fix a date for you to leave the premises and if you do not do so, to authorise a bailiff or High Court Enforcement Officer to evict you. (You can apply to the court to stay the eviction; a judge will decide if there are grounds for doing so.)

(If there is an order to pay money)

If you do not pay the money owed when it is due and the claimant takes steps to enforce payment, the order will be registered in the Register of Judgments, Orders and Fines. This may make it difficult for you to get credit. Further information about registration is available in a leaflet which you can get from any court office.

11   Order adjourning on terms

IN THE GREENFIELD COUNTY COURT   CASE NO: GF6 06111
BETWEEN

GREENFIELD DISTRICT COUNCIL   <u>Claimant</u>

and

CHRIS URBAN   <u>Defendant</u>

ORDER

Upon hearing the Solicitors for the Claimant and Defendant

It is Ordered that:

1. The Claimant's claim for possession be adjourned generally with liberty to restore on terms that the Defendant do pay the current rent plus £2.90 each week off the arrears of £1599.93 with the first payment towards the arrears to be made by 4 pm on 7 August 2006.

2. The Claimant have permission on written request to the Court to restore this action if the Defendant fails to comply with the terms set out in paragraph 1 above.

3. There be no order as to costs other than detailed assessment of the Defendant's costs pursuant to the Community Legal Service (Costs) Regulations 2000.

Dated   28 July 2006

DISTRICT JUDGE

Instructions checklist

Social and private sector occupiers
Occupiers
Full name, address, dates of birth, phone number, occupation, income and savings, relationships between.

Name of tenant(s)
Name and address and relationship to occupier.

Status
Protected/statutory/secure/assured tenant/assured shorthold/demoted/introductory/unprotected/successor tenant/assignee.

Details of accommodation
Room/flat/house, shared facilities, location in house.

Landlord/ agent/ solicitor
Name, address, telephone number, DX, e-mail, reference number.

Rent
Amount (inclusive/exclusive of services), rent registration, any irrecoverable rent, arrears, agreement as to level of arrears, is landlord accepting rent, method of payment.

Documents
Tenancy agreement, rent receipts, rent book.

Pre-tenancy notices
Type of notice, date and method of service.
Occupation prior to service.

Date of commencement of tenancy

Date of commencement of occupancy

Housing benefit
Amount received/date of claim/possible backdated claim/paid to tenant or landlord/housing benefit shortfall.

Notice to quit/ notice of intention to seek possession
Date received/method of service.

Court proceedings
Previous proceedings, current proceedings, hearing date, date of receipt of claim form.

Causes of action against landlord or other
Set off for disrepair and proof of notice of disrepair, third party action against local authority over housing benefit.

Correspondence

Details of any previous arrangements to remedy default

Proposals to pay off arrears
Amount/method of payment.

Regular financial commitments
Maintenance, court orders, credit agreement, etc.

Rehousing obligations
Children, pregnancy, vulnerability, community care issues.

Mortgage borrowers
Occupiers
Full name, address, dates of birth, phone number, occupations, income and savings, relationships between, date of commencement of occupation.

Legal owner
Name and address, relationship to occupier.

Mortgagee/solicitors
Name, address, telephone and reference numbers, priority (first, second, etc).

Type of mortgage
Repayment/endowment/pension/other.

Date of mortgage

Legal title
Freehold/leasehold, registered/unregistered land.
Joint owner/sole/trustee.

Payments
Monthly instalments (interest and capital/endowment), arrears, date of last payment.

Date of commencement of occupancy

Equitable owners
Previous properties occupied as such, details of contribution to purchase or mortgage payments, financial/other detriment.

Correspondence

Court proceedings
Previous/current proceedings, hearing dates, date of receipt of summons.

Details of any previous arrangements to remedy default

Amount required to redeem mortgage

Value of property with vacant possession

Insurance cover
Mortgage indemnity policy, mortgage protection policy.

Regular financial commitments
Maintenance, court orders, credit agreement etc.

Rehousing obligations
Children, pregnancy, vulnerability, community care issues.

Causes of action against lender or other
Misrepresentation, negligence against surveyor/solicitor.
Undue influence.

Protocol for Possession Claims based on Rent Arrears

Aims and scope of the protocol

This protocol applies to residential possession claims by social landlords (such as local authorities, Registered Social Landlords and Housing Action Trusts) which are based solely on claims for rent arrears. The protocol does not apply to claims in respect of long leases or to claims for possession where there is no security of tenure.

The protocol reflects the guidance on good practice given to social landlords in the collection of rent arrears. It recognises that it is in the interests of both landlords and tenants to ensure that rent is paid promptly and to ensure that difficulties are resolved wherever possible without court proceedings.

Its aim is to encourage more pre-action contact between landlords and tenants and to enable court time to be used more effectively.

Courts should take into account whether this protocol has been followed when considering what orders to make. Registered Social Landlords and local authorities should also comply with guidance issued from time to time by the Housing Corporation and the Department for Communities and Local Government.

Initial contact

1 The landlord should contact the tenant as soon as reasonably possible if the tenant falls into arrears to discuss the cause of the arrears, the tenant's financial circumstances, the tenant's entitlement to benefits and repayment of the arrears. Where contact is by letter, the landlord should write separately to each named tenant.

2 The landlord and tenant should try to agree affordable sums for the tenant to pay towards arrears, based upon the tenant's income and expenditure (where such information has been supplied in response to the landlord's enquiries). The landlord should clearly set out in pre-action correspondence any time limits with which the tenant should comply.

3 The landlord should provide, on a quarterly basis, rent statements in a comprehensible format showing rent due and sums received for the past 13 weeks. The landlord should, upon request, provide the tenant with copies of rent statements in a comprehensible format from the date when arrears first arose showing all amounts of rent due, the dates and amounts of all payments made, whether through housing benefit or by the tenant, and a running total of the arrears.

4 (a) If the landlord is aware that the tenant has difficulty in reading or understanding information given, the landlord should take reasonable steps to
ensure that the tenant understands any information given. The landlord
should be able to demonstrate that reasonable steps have been taken to
ensure that the information has been appropriately communicated in
ways that the tenant can understand.

(b) If the landlord is aware that the tenant is under 18 or is particularly vulnerable, the landlord should consider at an early stage:

(i)   whether or not the tenant has the mental capacity to defend possession proceedings and, if not, make an application for the appointment of a litigation friend in accordance with CPR 21;

(ii) whether or not any issues arise under Disability Discrimination Act
1995; and

(iii) in the case of a local authority landlord, whether or not there is a
need for a community care assessment in accordance with National
Health Service and Community Care Act 1990.

5 If the tenant meets the appropriate criteria, the landlord should arrange for
arrears to be paid by the Department for Work and Pensions from the tenant's benefit.

6 The landlord should offer to assist the tenant in any claim the tenant may
have for housing benefit.

7 Possession proceedings for rent arrears should not be started against a tenant
who can demonstrate that he has-

(a) provided the local authority with all the evidence required to process a
housing benefit claim;

(b) a reasonable expectation of eligibility for housing benefit; and

(c) paid other sums due not covered by housing benefit.

The landlord should make every effort to establish effective ongoing liaison with housing benefit departments and, with the tenant's consent, make
direct contact with the relevant housing benefit department before taking
enforcement action. The landlord and tenant should work together to resolve
any housing benefit problems.

8 Bearing in mind that rent arrears may be part of a general debt problem, the
landlord should advise the tenant to seek assistance from CAB, debt advice
agencies or other appropriate agencies as soon as possible.

After service of statutory notices

9 After service of a statutory notice but before the issue of proceedings, the
landlord should make reasonable attempts to contact the tenant, to discuss
the amount of the arrears, the cause of the arrears, repayment of the arrears
and the housing benefit position.

10 If the tenant complies with an agreement to pay the current rent and a reasonable amount towards arrears, the landlord should agree to postpone court
proceedings so long as the tenant keeps to such agreement. If the tenant
ceases to comply with such agreement, the landlord should warn the tenant
of the intention to bring proceedings and give the tenant clear time limits
within which to comply.

Alternative dispute resolution

11 The parties should consider whether it is possible to resolve the issues between them by discussion and negotiation without recourse to litigation. The parties may be required by the court to provide evidence that alternative means of resolving the dispute were considered. Courts take the view that litigation should be a last resort, and that claims should not be issued prematurely when a settlement is still actively being explored.

The Legal Services Commission has published a booklet on 'Alternatives to Court', CLS Direct Information Leaflet 23 (www.clsdirect.org.uk/legal-help/leaflet23.jsp), which lists a number of organisations that provide alternative dispute resolution services.

Court proceedings

12 Not later than ten days before the date set for the hearing, the landlord should:

(a) provide the tenant with up to date rent statements;

(b) disclose what knowledge he possesses of the tenant's housing benefit position to the tenant.

13 (a) The landlord should inform the tenant of the date and time of any court hearing and the order applied for. The landlord should advise the tenant to attend the hearing as the tenant's home is at risk. Records of such advice should be kept.

(b) If the tenant complies with an agreement made after the issue of proceedings to pay the current rent and a reasonable amount towards arrears, the landlord should agree to postpone court proceedings so long as the tenant keeps to such agreement.

(c) If the tenant ceases to comply with such agreement, the landlord should warn the tenant of the intention to restore the proceedings and give the tenant clear time limits within which to comply.

14 If the landlord unreasonably fails to comply with the terms of the protocol, the court may impose one or more of the following sanctions:

(a) an order for costs;

(b) in cases other than those brought solely on mandatory grounds, adjourn, strike out or dismiss claims.

15 If the tenant unreasonably fails to comply with the terms of the protocol, the court may take such failure into account when considering whether it is reasonable to make possession orders.

CPR Part 55 and Practice Directions

CPR Part 55: Possession claims

Practice Direction: Possession claims

Part 55B Practice Direction: Possession claims online

CPR Part 55: Possession claims

55.1 Interpretation

In this Part –

(a) 'a possession claim' means a claim for the recovery of possession of land (including buildings or parts of buildings);

(b) 'a possession claim against trespassers' means a claim for the recovery of land which the claimant alleges is occupied only by a person or persons who entered or remained on the land without the consent of a person entitled to possession of that land but does not include a claim against a tenant or sub-tenant whether his tenancy has been terminated or not;

(c) 'mortgage' includes a legal or equitable mortgage and a legal or equitable charge and 'mortgagee' is to be interpreted accordingly;

(d) 'the 1985 Act' means the Housing Act 1985[1];

(e) 'the 1988 Act' means the Housing Act 1988[2];

(f) 'a demotion claim' means a claim made by a landlord for an order under section 82A of the 1985 Act or section 6A of the 1988 Act ('a demotion order');

(g) 'a demoted tenancy' means a tenancy created by virtue of a demotion order; and

(h) 'a suspension claim' means a claim made by a landlord for an order under section 121A of the 1985 Act.

I   General rules

55.2 Scope

(1) The procedure set out in this Section of this Part must be used where the claim includes –

(a) a possession claim brought by a –

(i)   landlord (or former landlord);

(ii) mortgagee; or

(iii) licensor (or former licensor);

(b) a possession claim against trespassers; or

(c) a claim by a tenant seeking relief from forfeiture.

(Where a demotion claim or a suspension claim (or both) is made in the same claim form in which a possession claim is started, this Section of this Part applies as modified by rule 65.12. Where the claim is a demotion claim or a suspension claim only, or a suspension claim made in addition to a demotion claim, Section III of Part 65 applies).

(2) This Section of this Part

(a) is subject to any enactment or practice direction which sets out special provisions with regard to any particular category of claim;

(b) does not apply where the claimant uses the procedure set out in Section II of this Part; and

(c) does not apply where the claimant seeks an interim possession order under Section III of this Part except where the court orders otherwise or that Section so provides.

55.3 Starting the claim

(1) The claim must be started in the county court for the district in which the land is situated unless paragraph (2) applies or an enactment provides otherwise.

(2) The claim may be started in the High Court if the claimant files with his claim form a certificate stating the reasons for bringing the claim in that court verified by a statement of truth in accordance with rule 22.1(1).

(3) The practice direction refers to circumstances which may justify starting the claim in the High Court.

(4) Where, in a possession claim against trespassers, the claimant does not know the name of a person in occupation or possession of the land, the claim must be brought against 'persons unknown' in addition to any named defendants.

(5) The claim form and form of defence sent with it must be in the forms set out in the relevant practice direction.

55.4 Particulars of claim

The particulars of claim must be filed and served with the claim form.

(The relevant practice direction and Part 16 provide details about the contents of the particulars of claim)

55.5 Hearing date

(1) The court will fix a date for the hearing when it issues the claim form.

(2) In a possession claim against trespassers the defendant must be served with the claim form, particulars of claim and any witness statements –

    (a) in the case of residential property, not less than 5 days; and

    (b) in the case of other land, not less than 2 days,

before the hearing date.

(3) In all other possession claims –

    (a) the hearing date will be not less than 28 days from the date of issue of the claim form;

    (b) the standard period between the issue of the claim form and the hearing will be not more than 8 weeks; and

    (c) the defendant must be served with the claim form and particulars of claim not less than 21 days before the hearing date.

(Rule 3.1(2)(a) provides that the court may extend or shorten the time for compliance with any rule)

55.6 Service of claims against trespassers

Where, in a possession claim against trespassers, the claim has been issued against 'persons unknown', the claim form, particulars of claim and any witness statements must be served on those persons by –

    (a) (i) attaching copies of the claim form, particulars of claim and any witness statements to the main door or some other part of the land so that they are clearly visible; and

(ii) if practicable, inserting copies of those documents in a sealed transparent envelope addressed to 'the occupiers' through the letter box; or
(b) placing stakes in the land in places where they are clearly visible and
attaching to each stake copies of the claim form, particulars of claim and
any witness statements in a sealed transparent envelope addressed to 'the
occupiers'.

55.7 Defendant's response

(1) An acknowledgment of service is not required and Part 10 does not apply.

(2) In a possession claim against trespassers rule 15.2 does not apply and the
defendant need not file a defence.

(3) Where, in any other possession claim, the defendant does not file a defence
within the time specified in rule 15.4, he may take part in any hearing but the
court may take his failure to do so into account when deciding what order to
make about costs.

(4) Part 12 (default judgment) does not apply in a claim to which this Part
applies.

55.8 The hearing

(1) At the hearing fixed in accordance with rule 55.5(1) or at any adjournment of
that hearing, the court may –
(a) decide the claim; or
(b) give case management directions.

(2) Where the claim is genuinely disputed on grounds which appear to be substantial, case management directions given under paragraph (1)(b) will
include the allocation of the claim to a track or directions to enable it to be
allocated.

(3) Except where –
(a) the claim is allocated to the fast track or the multi-track; or
(b) the court orders otherwise,
any fact that needs to be proved by the evidence of witnesses at a hearing
referred to in paragraph (1) may be proved by evidence in writing.
(Rule 32.2(1) sets out the general rule about evidence. Rule 32.2(2) provides
that rule 32.2(1) is subject to any provision to the contrary)

(4) Subject to paragraph (5), all witness statements must be filed and served at
least 2 days before the hearing.

(5) In a possession claim against trespassers all witness statements on which the
claimant intends to rely must be filed and served with the claim form.

(6) Where the claimant serves the claim form and particulars of claim, he must
produce at the hearing a certificate of service of those documents and rule
6.14(2)(a) does not apply.

55.9 Allocation

(1) When the court decides the track for a possession claim, the matters to which
it shall have regard include –
(a) the matters set out in rule 26.8 as modified by the relevant practice
direction;

(b) the amount of any arrears of rent or mortgage instalments;

(c) the importance to the defendant of retaining possession of the land;

(d) the importance of vacant possession to the claimant; and

(e) if applicable, the alleged conduct of the defendant

(2) The court will only allocate possession claims to the small claims track if all the parties agree.

(3) Where a possession claim has been allocated to the small claims track the claim shall be treated, for the purposes of costs, as if it were proceeding on the fast track except that trial costs shall be in the discretion of the court and shall not exceed the amount that would be recoverable under rule 46.2 (amount of fast track costs) if the value of the claim were up to £3,000.

(4) Where all the parties agree the court may, when it allocates the claim, order that rule 27.14 (costs on the small claims track) applies and, where it does so, paragraph (3) does not apply.

55.10 Possession claims relating to mortgaged residential property

(1) This rule applies where a mortgagee seeks possession of land which consists of or includes residential property.

(2) Not less than 14 days before the hearing the claimant must send a notice to the property addressed to 'the occupiers'.

(3) The notice referred to in paragraph (2) must –

(a) state that a possession claim for the property has started;

(b) show the name and address of the claimant, the defendant and the court which issued the claim form; and

(c) give details of the hearing.

(4) The claimant must produce at the hearing –

(a) a copy of the notice; and

(b) evidence that he has served it.

55.10A Electronic issue of certain possession claims

(1) A practice direction may make provision for a claimant to start certain types of possession claim in certain courts by requesting the issue of a claim form electronically.

(2) The practice direction may, in particular –

(a) provide that only particular provisions apply in specific courts;

(b) specify –

(i) the type of possession claim which may be issued electronically;

(ii) the conditions that a claim must meet before it may be issued electronically;

(c) specify the court where the claim may be issued;

(d) enable the parties to make certain applications or take further steps in relation to the claim electronically;

(e) specify the requirements that must be fulfilled in relation to such applications or steps;

(f) enable the parties to correspond electronically with the court about the claim;

(g) specify the requirements that must be fulfilled in relation to electronic correspondence;

(h) provide how any fee payable on the filing of any document is to be paid where the document is filed electronically.

(3) The Practice Direction may disapply or modify these Rules as appropriate in relation to possession claims started electronically.

II　Accelerated possession claims of property let on an assured shorthold tenancy

55.11　When this section may be used

(1) The claimant may bring a possession claim under this Section of this Part where –

(a) the claim is brought under section 21 of the 1988 Act1 to recover possession of residential property let under an assured shorthold tenancy; and

(b) subject to rule 55.12(2), all the conditions listed in rule 55.12(1) are satisfied.

(2) The claim must be started in the county court for the district in which the property is situated.

(3) In this Section of this Part, a 'demoted assured shorthold tenancy' means a demoted tenancy where the landlord is a registered social landlord.

(By virtue of section 20B of the 1988 Act, a demoted assured shorthold tenancy is an assured shorthold tenancy)

55.12　Conditions

(1) The conditions referred to in rule 55.11(1)(b) are that –

(a) the tenancy and any agreement for the tenancy were entered into on or after 15 January 1989;

(b) the only purpose of the claim is to recover possession of the property and no other claim is made;

(c) the tenancy did not immediately follow an assured tenancy which was not an assured shorthold tenancy;

(d) the tenancy fulfilled the conditions provided by section 19A or 20(1)(a) to (c) of the 1988 Act2;

(e) the tenancy –

(i)　was the subject of a written agreement;

(ii)　arises by virtue of section 5 of the 1988 Act but follows a tenancy that was the subject of a written agreement; or

(iii)　relates to the same or substantially the same property let to the same tenant and on the same terms (though not necessarily as to rent or duration) as a tenancy which was the subject of a written agreement; and

(f) a notice in accordance with sections 21(1) or 21(4) of the 1988 Act3 was given to the tenant in writing.

(2) If the tenancy is a demoted assured shorthold tenancy, only the conditions in paragraph (1)(b) and (f) need be satisfied.

55.13 Claim form

(1) The claim form must –

    (a) be in the form set out in the relevant practice direction; and

    (b) (i) contain such information; and

        (ii) be accompanied by such documents,

    as are required by that form.

(2) All relevant sections of the form must be completed.

(3) The court will serve the claim form by first class post (or an alternative service which provides for delivery on the next working day).

55.14 Defence

(1) A defendant who wishes to –

    (a) oppose the claim; or

    (b) seek a postponement of possession in accordance with rule 55.18,

    must file his defence within 14 days after service of the claim form.

(2) The defence should be in the form set out in the relevant practice direction.

55.15 Claim referred to judge

(1) On receipt of the defence the court will –

    (a) send a copy to the claimant; and

    (b) refer the claim and defence to a judge.

(2) Where the period set out in rule 55.14 has expired without the defendant filing a defence –

    (a) the claimant may file a written request for an order for possession; and

    (b) the court will refer that request to a judge.

(3) Where the defence is received after the period set out in rule 55.14 has expired but before a request is filed in accordance with paragraph (2), paragraph (1) will still apply.

(4) Where –

    (a) the period set out in rule 55.14 has expired without the defendant filing a defence; and

    (b) the claimant has not made a request for an order for possession under paragraph (2) within 3 months after the expiry of the period set out in rule 55.14,

    the claim will be stayed.

55.16 Consideration of the claim

(1) After considering the claim and any defence, the judge will –

    (a) make an order for possession under rule 55.17;

    (b) where he is not satisfied as to any of the matters set out in paragraph (2) –

        (i) direct that a date be fixed for a hearing; and

        (ii) give any appropriate case management directions; or

    (c) strike out the claim if the claim form discloses no reasonable grounds for bringing the claim.

(2) The matters referred to in paragraph (1)(b) are that –
  (a) the claim form was served; and
  (b) the claimant has established that he is entitled to recover possession under section 21 of the1988 Act against the defendant.
(3) The court will give all parties not less than 14 days' notice of a hearing fixed under paragraph (1)(b)(i).
(4) Where a claim is struck out under paragraph (1)(c) –
  (a) the court will serve its reasons for striking out the claim with the order; and
  (b) the claimant may apply to restore the claim within 28 days after the date the order was served on him

55.17 Possession order

Except where rules 55.16(1)(b) or (c) apply, the judge will make an order for possession without requiring the attendance of the parties.

55.18 Postponement of possession

(1) Where the defendant seeks postponement of possession on the ground of exceptional hardship under section 89 of the Housing Act 19801, the judge may direct a hearing of that issue.
(2) Where the judge directs a hearing under paragraph (1) –
  (a) the hearing must be held before the date on which possession is to be given up; and
  (b) the judge will direct how many days' notice the parties must be given of that hearing.
(3) Where the judge is satisfied, on a hearing directed under paragraph (1), that exceptional hardship would be caused by requiring possession to be given up by the date in the order of possession, he may vary the date on which possession must be given up.

55.19 Application to set aside or vary

The court may
  (a) on application by a party within 14 days of service of the order; or
  (b) of its own initiative,
set aside or vary any order made under rule 55.17.

III   Interim possession orders

55.20 When this section may be used

(1) This Section of this Part applies where the claimant seeks an Interim Possession Order.
(2) In this section –
  (a) 'IPO' means Interim Possession Order; and
  (b) 'premises' has the same meaning as in section 12 of the Criminal Law Act 1972.
(3) Where this Section requires an act to be done within a specified number of hours, rule 2.8(4) does not apply.

55.21 Conditions for IPO application

(1) An application for an IPO may be made where the following conditions are satisfied –

    (a) the only claim made is a possession claim against trespassers for the recovery of premises;

    (b) the claimant –

        (i) has an immediate right to possession of the premises; and

        (ii) has had such a right throughout the period of alleged unlawful occupation; and

    (c) the claim is made within 28 days of the date on which the claimant first knew, or ought reasonably to have known, that the defendant (or any of the defendants), was in occupation.

(2) An application for an IPO may not be made against a defendant who entered or remained on the premises with the consent of a person who, at the time consent was given, had an immediate right to possession of the premises.

55.22 The application

(1) Rules 55.3(1) and (4) apply to the claim.

(2) The claim form and the defendant's form of witness statement must be in the form set out in the relevant practice direction.

(3) When he files his claim form, the claimant must also file –

    (a) an application notice in the form set out in the relevant practice direction; and

    (b) written evidence.

(4) The written evidence must be given –

    (a) by the claimant personally; or

    (b) where the claimant is a body corporate, by a duly authorised officer.

    (Rule 22.1(6)(b) provides that the statement of truth must be signed by the maker of the witness statement)

(5) The court will –

    (a) issue –

        (i) the claim form; and

        (ii) the application for the IPO; and

    (b) set a date for the hearing of the application.

(6) The hearing of the application will be as soon as practicable but not less than 3 days after the date of issue.

55.23 Service

(1) Within 24 hours of the issue of the application, the claimant must serve on the defendant –

    (a) the claim form;

    (b) the application notice together with the written evidence in support; and

    (c) a blank form for the defendant's witness statement (as set out in the relevant practice direction) which must be attached to the application notice.

(2) The claimant must serve the documents listed in paragraph (1) in accordance with rule 55.6(a).

(3) At or before the hearing the claimant must file a certificate of service in relation to the documents listed in paragraph (1) and rule 6.14(2)(a) does not apply.

55.24 Defendant's response

(1) At any time before the hearing the defendant may file a witness statement in response to the application.

(2) The witness statement should be in the form set out in the relevant practice direction.

55.25 Hearing of the application

(1) In deciding whether to grant an IPO, the court will have regard to whether the claimant has given, or is prepared to give, the following undertakings in support of his application –

(a) if, after an IPO is made, the court decides that the claimant was not entitled to the order to –

(i) reinstate the defendant if so ordered by the court; and

(ii) pay such damages as the court may order; and

(b) before the claim for possession is finally decided, not to –

(i) damage the premises;

(ii) grant a right of occupation to any other person; and

(iii) damage or dispose of any of the defendant's property.

(2) The court will make an IPO if –

(a) the claimant has –

(i) filed a certificate of service of the documents referred to in rule 55.23(1); or

(ii) proved service of those documents to the satisfaction of the court; and

(b) the court considers that –

(i) the conditions set out in rule 55.21(1) are satisfied; and

(ii) any undertakings given by the claimant as a condition of making the order are adequate.

(3) An IPO will be in the form set out in the relevant practice direction and will require the defendant to vacate the premises specified in the claim form within 24 hours of the service of the order.

(4) On making an IPO the court will set a date for the hearing of the claim for possession which will be not less than 7 days after the date on which the IPO is made.

(5) Where the court does not make an IPO –

(a) the court will set a date for the hearing of the claim;

(b) the court may give directions for the future conduct of the claim; and

(c) subject to such directions, the claim shall proceed in accordance with Section I of this Part.

55.26 Service and enforcement of the IPO

(1) An IPO must be served within 48 hours after it is sealed.

(2) The claimant must serve the IPO on the defendant together with copies of
  (a) the claim form; and
  (b) the written evidence in support, in accordance with rule 55.6(a).
(3) CCR Order 26, rule 17 does not apply to the enforcement of an IPO.
(4) If an IPO is not served within the time limit specified by this rule, the claimant may apply to the court for directions for the claim for possession to continue under Section I of this Part.

55.27 After IPO made

(1) Before the date for the hearing of the claim, the claimant must file a certificate of service in relation to the documents specified in rule 55.26(2).
(2) The IPO will expire on the date of the hearing of the claim.
(3) At the hearing the court may make any order it considers appropriate and may, in particular –
  (a) make a final order for possession;
  (b) dismiss the claim for possession;
  (c) give directions for the claim for possession to continue under Section I of this Part; or
  (d) enforce any of the claimant's undertakings.
(4) Unless the court directs otherwise, the claimant must serve any order or directions in accordance with rule 55.6(a).
(5) CCR Order 24, rule 6 applies to the enforcement of a final order for possession.

55.28 Application to set aside IPO

(1) If the defendant has left the premises, he may apply on grounds of urgency for the IPO to be set aside before the date of the hearing of the claim.
(2) An application under paragraph (1) must be supported by a witness statement.
(3) On receipt of the application, the court will give directions as to –
  (a) the date for the hearing; and
  (b) the period of notice, if any, to be given to the claimant and the method of service of any such notice.
(4) No application to set aside an IPO may be made under rule 39.3.
(5) Where no notice is required under paragraph (3)(b), the only matters to be dealt with at the hearing of the application to set aside are whether –
  (a) the IPO should be set aside; and
  (b) any undertaking to re-instate the defendant should be enforced, and all other matters will be dealt with at the hearing of the claim.
(6) The court will serve on all the parties –
  (a) a copy of the order made under paragraph (5); and
  (b) where no notice was required under paragraph (3)(b), a copy of the defendant's application to set aside and the witness statement in support.
(7) Where notice is required under paragraph (3)(b), the court may treat the hearing of the application to set aside as the hearing of the claim.

Practice Direction: Possession claims

This Practice Direction supplements Part 55

Section I – General rules

55.3 Starting the claim

1.1 Except where the county court does not have jurisdiction, possession claims should normally be brought in the county court. Only exceptional circumstances justify starting a claim in the High Court.

1.2 If a claimant starts a claim in the High Court and the court decides that it should have been started in the county court, the court will normally either strike the claim out or transfer it to the county court on its own initiative. This is likely to result in delay and the court will normally disallow the costs of starting the claim in the High Court and of any transfer.

1.3 Circumstances which may, in an appropriate case, justify starting a claim in the High Court are if –

(1) there are complicated disputes of fact;

(2) there are points of law of general importance; or

(3) the claim is against trespassers and there is a substantial risk of public disturbance or of serious harm to persons or property which properly require immediate determination.

1.4 The value of the property and the amount of any financial claim may be relevant circumstances, but these factors alone will not normally justify starting the claim in the High Court.

1.5 The claimant must use the appropriate claim form and particulars of claim form set out in Table 1 to Part 4 Practice Direction. The defence must be in form N11, N11B, N11M or N11R, as appropriate.

1.6 High Court claims for the possession of land subject to a mortgage will be assigned to the Chancery Division.

1.7 A claim which is not a possession claim may be brought under the procedure set out in Section I of Part 55 if it is started in the same claim form as a possession claim which, by virtue of rule 55.2(1) must be brought in accordance with that Section. (Rule 7.3 provides that a claimant may use a single claim form to start all claims which can be conveniently disposed of in the same proceedings)

1.8 For example a claim under paragraphs 4, 5 or 6 of Part I of Schedule 1 to the Mobile Homes Act 1983 may be brought using the procedure set out in Section I of Part 55 if the claim is started in the same claim form as a claim enforcing the rights referred to in section 3(1)(b) of the Caravan Sites Act 1968 (which, by virtue of rule 55.2(1) must be brought under Section I of Part 55).

1.9 Where the claim form includes a demotion claim, the claim must be started in the county court for the district in which the land is situated.

55.4 Particulars of claim

2.1 In a possession claim the particulars of claim must:

(1) identify the land to which the claim relates;

(2) state whether the claim relates to residential property;

(3) state the ground on which possession is claimed;

(4) give full details about any mortgage or tenancy agreement; and

(5) give details of every person who, to the best of the claimant's knowledge, is in possession of the property.

Residential property let on a tenancy

2.2 Paragraphs 2.3. 2.4 and 2.4A apply if the claim relates to residential property let on a tenancy.

2.3 If the claim includes a claim for non-payment of rent the particulars of claim must set out:

(1) the amount due at the start of the proceedings;

(2) in schedule form, the dates and amounts of all payments due and payments made under the tenancy agreement for a period of two years immediately preceding the date of issue, or if the first date of default occurred less than two years before the date of issue from the first date of default and a running total of the arrears;

(3) the daily rate of any rent and interest;

(4) any previous steps taken to recover the arrears of rent with full details of any court proceedings; and

(5) any relevant information about the defendant's circumstances, in particular:

(a) whether the defendant is in receipt of social security benefits; and

(b) whether any payments are made on his behalf directly to the claimant under the Social Security Contributions and Benefits Act 1992

2.3A If the claimant wishes to rely on a history of arrears which is longer than two years, he should state this in his particulars and exhibit a full (or longer) schedule to a witness statement.

2.4 If the claimant knows of any person (including a mortgagee) entitled to claim relief against forfeiture as underlessee under section 146(4) of the Law of Property Act 1925 (or in accordance with section 38 of the Supreme Court Act 1981, or section 138(9C) of the County Courts Act 1984):

(1) the particulars of claim must state the name and address of that person; and

(2) the claimant must file a copy of the particulars of claim for service on him.

2.4A If the claim for possession relates to the conduct of the tenant, the particulars of claim must state details of the conduct alleged.

Land subject to a mortgage

2.5 If the claim is a possession claim by a mortgagee, the particulars of claim must also set out:

(1) if the claim relates to residential property whether:

(a) a land charge of Class F has been registered under section 2(7) of the Matrimonial Homes Act 1967;

(b) a notice registered under section 2(8) or 8(3) of the Matrimonial Homes Act 1983 has been entered and on whose behalf; or

(c) a notice under section 31(10) of the Family Law Act 1996 has been registered and on whose behalf; and if so, that the claimant will serve notice of the claim on the persons on whose behalf the land charge is registered or the notice or caution entered.

(2) the state of the mortgage account by including:

(a) the amount of:

(i) the advance;

(ii) any periodic repayment; and

(iii) any payment of interest required to be made;

(b) the amount which would have to be paid (after taking into account any adjustment for early settlement) in order to redeem the mortgage at a stated date not more than 14 days after the claim started specifying the amount of solicitor's costs and administration charges which would be payable;

(c) if the loan which is secured by the mortgage is a regulated consumer credit agreement, the total amount outstanding under the terms of the mortgage; and

(d) the rate of interest payable:

(i) at the commencement of the mortgage;

(ii) immediately before any arrears referred to in paragraph (3) accrued;

(iii) at the commencement of the proceedings.

(3) if the claim is brought because of failure to pay the periodic payments when due:

(a) in schedule form, the dates and amounts of all payments due and payments made under the mortgage agreement or mortgage deed for a period of two years immediately preceding the date of issue, or if the first date of default occurred less than two years before the date of issue from the first date of default and a running total of the arrears;

(b) give details of:

(i) any other payments required to be made as a term of the mortgage (such as for insurance premiums, legal costs, default interest, penalties, administrative or other charges);

(ii) any other sums claimed and stating the nature and amount of each such charge; and

(iii) whether any of these payments is in arrears and whether or not it is included in the amount of any periodic payment.

(4) whether or not the loan which is secured by the mortgage is a regulated consumer credit agreement and, if so, specify the date on which any notice required by sections 76 or 87 of the Consumer Credit Act 1974 was given;

(5) if appropriate details that show the property is not one to which section 141 of the Consumer Credit Act 1974 applies;

(6) any relevant information about the defendant's circumstances, in particular:

    (a) whether the defendant is in receipt of social security benefits; and

    (b) whether any payments are made on his behalf directly to the claimant under the Social Security Contributions and Benefits Act 1992;

(7) give details of any tenancy entered into between the mortgagor and mortgagee (including any notices served); and

(8) state any previous steps which the claimant has taken to recover the money secured by the mortgage or the mortgaged property and, in the case of court proceedings, state:

    (a) the dates when the claim started and concluded; and

    (b) the dates and terms of any orders made.

2.5A If the claimant wishes to rely on a history of arrears which is longer than two years, he should state this in his particulars and exhibit a full (or longer) schedule to a witness statement.

Possession claim against trespassers

2.6 If the claim is a possession claim against trespassers, the particulars of claim must state the claimant's interest in the land or the basis of his right to claim possession and the circumstances in which it has been occupied without licence or consent.

Possession claim in relation to a demoted tenancy by a housing action trust or a local housing authority

2.7 If the claim is a possession claim under section 143D of the Housing Act 1996 (possession claim in relation to a demoted tenancy where the landlord is a housing action trust or a local housing authority), the particulars of claim must have attached to them a copy of the notice to the tenant served under section 143E of the 1996 Act.

55.5 Hearing date

3.1 The court may exercise its powers under rules 3.1(2)(a) and (b) to shorten the time periods set out in rules 55.5(2) and (3).

3.2 Particular consideration should be given to the exercise of this power if:

(1) the defendant, or a person for whom the defendant is responsible, has assaulted or threatened to assault:

    (a) the claimant;

    (b) a member of the claimant's staff; or

    (c) another resident in the locality;

(2) there are reasonable grounds for fearing such an assault; or

(3) the defendant, or a person for whom the defendant is responsible, has caused serious damage or threatened to cause serious damage to the property or to the home or property of another resident in the locality.

3.3 Where paragraph 3.2 applies but the case cannot be determined at the first hearing fixed under rule 55.5, the court will consider what steps are needed to finally determine the case as quickly as reasonably practicable.

55.6 Service in claims against trespassers

4.1 If the claim form is to be served by the court and in accordance with rule 55.6(b) the claimant must provide sufficient stakes and transparent envelopes.

55.8 The hearing

5.1 Attention is drawn to rule 55.8(3). Each party should wherever possible include all the evidence he wishes to present in his statement of case, verified by a statement of truth.

5.2 If relevant the claimant's evidence should include the amount of any rent or mortgage arrears and interest on those arrears. These amounts should, if possible, be up to date to the date of the hearing (if necessary by specifying a daily rate of arrears and interest). However, rule 55.8(4) does not prevent such evidence being brought up to date orally or in writing on the day of the hearing if necessary.

5.3 If relevant the defendant should give evidence of:

(1) the amount of any outstanding social security or housing benefit payments relevant to rent or mortgage arrears; and

(2) the status of:

(a) any claims for social security or housing benefit about which a decision has not yet been made; and

(b) any applications to appeal or review a social security or housing benefit decision where that appeal or review has not yet concluded.

5.4 If:

(1) the maker of a witness statement does not attend a hearing; and

(2) the other party disputes material evidence contained in his statement,

the court will normally adjourn the hearing so that oral evidence can be given.

Consumer Credit Act claims relating to the recovery of land

7.1 Any application by the defendant for a time order under section 129 of the Consumer Credit Act 1974 may be made:

(1) in his defence; or

(2) by application notice in the proceedings.

Enforcement of charging order by sale

7.2 A party seeking to enforce a charging order by sale should follow the procedure set out in rule 73.10 and the Part 55 procedure should not be used.

Section II – Accelerated possession claims of property let on an assured shorthold tenancy

55.18 Postponement of possession

8.1 If the judge is satisfied as to the matters set out in rule 55.16(2), he will make an order for possession in accordance with rule 55.17, whether or not the defendant seeks a postponement of possession on the ground of exceptional hardship under section 89 of the Housing Act 1980.

8.2 In a claim in which the judge is satisfied that the defendant has shown exceptional hardship, he will only postpone possession without directing a hearing under rule 55.18(1) if –

(1) he considers that possession should be given up 6 weeks after the date of the order or, if the defendant has requested postponement to an earlier date, on that date; and

(2) the claimant indicated on his claim form that he would be content for the court to make such an order without a hearing.

8.3 In all other cases if the defendant seeks a postponement of possession under section 89 of the Housing Act 1980, the judge will direct a hearing under rule 55.18(1).

8.4 If, at that hearing, the judge is satisfied that exceptional hardship would be caused by requiring possession to be given up by the date in the order of possession, he may vary that order under rule 55.18(3) so that possession is to be given up at a later date. That later date may be no later than 6 weeks after the making of the order for possession on the papers (see section 89 of the Housing Act 1980).

Section III – Interim possession orders

9.1 The claim form must be in form N5, the application notice seeking the interim possession order must be in form N130 and the defendant's witness statement must be in form N133.

9.2 The IPO will be in form N134 (annexed to this practice direction).

Section IV – Orders fixing a date for possession

10.1 This paragraph applies where the court has made an order postponing the date for possession under section 85(2)(b) of the Housing Act 1985 (secure tenancies).

10.2 If the defendant fails to comply with any of the terms of the order which relate to payment, the claimant, after following the procedure set out in paragraph 10.3, may apply for an order fixing the date upon which the defendant has to give up possession of the property. Unless the court further postpones the date for possession, the defendant will be required to give up possession on that date.

10.3 At least 14 days and not more than 3 months before applying for an order under paragraph 10.2, the claimant must give written notice to the defendant in accordance with paragraph 10.4.

10.4 The notice referred to in paragraph 10.3 must:

(1) state that the claimant intends to apply for an order fixing the date upon which the defendant is to give up possession of the property;

(2) record the current arrears and state how the defendant has failed to comply with the order referred to in paragraph 10.1 (by reference to a statement of the rent account enclosed with the notice);

(3) request that the defendant reply to the claimant within 7 days, agreeing or disputing the stated arrears; and

(4) inform the defendant of his right to apply to the court :

(a) for a further postponement of the date for possession; or

(b) to stay or suspend enforcement.

10.5 In his reply to the notice, the defendant must:

(1) where he disputes the stated arrears, provide details of payments or credits made;

(2) where he agrees the stated arrears, explain why payments have not been made.

10.6 An application for an order under paragraph 10.2 must be made by filing an application notice in accordance with Part 23. The application notice must state whether or not there is any outstanding claim by the defendant for housing benefit.

10.7 The claimant must file the following documents with the application notice:

(1) a copy of the notice referred to in paragraph 10.3;

(2) a copy of the defendant's reply, if any, to the notice and any relevant subsequent correspondence between the claimant and the defendant;

(3) a statement of the rent account showing:

(a) the arrears that have accrued since the first failure to pay in accordance with the order referred to in paragraph 10.2; or

(b) the arrears that have accrued during the period of two years immediately preceding the date of the application notice, where the first such failure to pay occurs more than two years before that date.

10.8 Rules 23.2.3, 23.2.4 and 23.2.5 (dealing with applications without a hearing), 23.7 (service of a copy of an application notice), and 23.10 (right to set aside or vary an order made without service of the application notice) do not apply to an application under this section.

10.9 On being filed, the application will be referred to the District Judge who:

(1) will normally determine the application without a hearing by fixing the date for possession as the next working day; but

(2) if he considers that a hearing is necessary:

(a) will fix a date for the application to be heard; and

(b) direct service of the application notice and supporting evidence on the defendant.

10.10 The court does not have jurisdiction to review a decision that it was reasonable to make an order for possession.

Part 55B Practice Direction: Possession claims online

This Practice Direction supplements CPR rule 55.10A.

Scope of this practice direction

1.1 This practice direction provides for a scheme ('Possession Claims Online') to operate in specified county courts –

(1) enabling claimants and their representatives to start certain possession claims under CPR Part 55 by requesting the issue of a claim form electronically via the PCOL website; and

(2) where a claim has been started electronically, enabling the claimant or defendant and their representatives to take further steps in the claim electronically as specified below.

1.2 In this practice direction –

(1) 'PCOL website' means the website www.possessionclaim.gov.uk which may be accessed via Her Majesty's Courts Service website (www.hmcourts-service.gov.uk) and through which Possession Claims Online will operate; and

(2) 'specified court' means a county court specified on the PCOL website as one in which Possession Claims Online is available.

Information on the PCOL website

2.1 The PCOL website contains further details and guidance about the operation of Possession Claims Online.

2.2 In particular the PCOL website sets out –

(1) the specified courts; and

(2) the dates from which Possession Claims Online will be available in each specified court.

2.3 The operation of Possession Claims Online in any specified court may be restricted to taking certain of the steps specified in this practice direction, and in such cases the PCOL website will set out the steps which may be taken using Possession Claims Online in that specified court.

Security

3.1 Her Majesty's Courts Service will take such measures as it thinks fit to ensure the security of steps taken or information stored electronically. These may include requiring users of Possession Claims Online –

(1) to enter a customer identification number or password;

(2) to provide personal information for identification purposes; and

(3) to comply with any other security measures,

before taking any step online.

Fees

4.1 A step may only be taken using Possession Claims Online on payment of the prescribed fee where a fee is payable. Where this practice direction provides for a fee to be paid electronically, it may be paid by –

(1) credit card;

(2) debit card; or

(3) any other method which Her Majesty's Courts Service may permit.

4.2 A defendant who wishes to claim exemption from payment of fees must do so through an organisation approved by Her Majesty's Courts Service before taking any step using PCOL which attracts a fee. If satisfied that the defendant is entitled to fee exemption, the organisation will submit the fee exemption form through the PCOL website to Her Majesty's Courts Service. The defendant may then use PCOL to take such a step.

(Her Majesty's Courts Service website contains guidance as to when the entitlement to claim an exemption from payment of fees arises. The PCOL website will contain a list of organisations through which the defendant may claim an exemption from fees).

Claims which may be started using possession claims online

5.1 A claim may be started online if –

(1) it is brought under Section I of Part 55;

(2) it includes a possession claim for residential property by –

    (a) a landlord against a tenant, solely on the ground of arrears of rent (but not a claim for forfeiture of a lease); or

    (b) a mortgagee against a mortgagor, solely on the ground of default in the payment of sums due under a mortgage, relating to land within the district of a specified court;

(3) it does not include a claim for any other remedy except for payment of arrears of rent or money due under a mortgage, interest and costs;

(4) the defendant has an address for service in England and Wales; and

(5) the claimant is able to provide a postcode for the property.

5.2 A claim must not be started online if a defendant is known to be a child or patient.

Starting a claim

6.1 A claimant may request the issue of a claim form by –

(1) completing an online claim form at the PCOL website;

(2) paying the appropriate issue fee electronically at the PCOL website or by some other means approved by Her Majesty's Courts Service.

6.2 The particulars of claim must be included in the online claim form and may not be filed separately. It is not necessary to file a copy of the tenancy agreement, mortgage deed or mortgage agreement with the particulars of claim.

6.3 The particulars of claim must include a history of the rent or mortgage account, in schedule form setting out –

(1) the dates and amounts of all payments due and payments made under the tenancy agreement, mortgage deed or mortgage agreement either from the first date of default if that date occurred less than two years before the date of issue or for a period of two years immediately preceding the date of issue; and

(2) a running total of the arrears.

6.4 If the claimant wishes to rely on a history of arrears which is longer than two years, he should state this in his particulars and exhibit a full (or longer) schedule to a witness statement.

6.5 When an online claim form is received, an acknowledgment of receipt will automatically be sent to the claimant. The acknowledgment does not constitute notice that the claim form has been issued or served.

6.6 When the court issues a claim form following the submission of an online claim form, the claim is 'brought' for the purposes of the Limitation Act 1980 and any other enactment on the date on which the online claim form is received by the court's computer system. The court will keep a record, by electronic or other means, of when online claim forms are received.

6.7 When the court issues a claim form it will –

(1) serve a printed version of the claim form and a defence form on the defendant; and

(2) send the claimant notice of issue by post or, where the claimant has supplied an e-mail address, by electronic means.

6.8 The claim shall be deemed to be served on the fifth day after the claim was issued irrespective of whether that day is a business day or not.

6.9 Where the period of time within which a defence must be filed ends on a day when the court is closed, the defendant may file his defence on the next day that the court is open.

6.10 The claim form shall have printed on it a unique customer identification number or a password by which the defendant may access the claim on the PCOL website.

6.11 PCOL will issue the proceedings in the appropriate county court by reference to the post code provided by the claimant and that court shall have jurisdiction to hear and determine the claim and to carry out enforcement of any judgment irrespective of whether the property is within or outside the jurisdiction of that court.

(CPR 30.2(1) authorises proceedings to be transferred from one county court to another.)

Defence

7.1 A defendant wishing to file –

(1) a defence; or

(2) a counterclaim (to be filed together with a defence) to a claim which has been issued through the PCOL system, may, instead of filing a written form, do so by –

(a) completing the relevant online form at the PCOL website; and

(b) if the defendant is making a counterclaim, paying the appropriate fee electronically at the PCOL website or by some other means approved by Her Majesty's Courts Service.

7.2 Where a defendant files a defence by completing the relevant online form, he must not send the court a hard copy.

7.3 When an online defence form is received, an acknowledgment of receipt will automatically be sent to the defendant. The acknowledgment does not constitute notice that the defence has been served.

7.4 The online defence form will be treated as being filed –

(1) on the day the court receives it, if it receives it before 4 p.m. on a working day; and

(2) otherwise, on the next working day after the court receives the online defence form.

7.5 A defence is filed when the online defence form is received by the court's computer system. The court will keep a record, by electronic or other means, of when online defence forms are received.

Statement of truth

8.1 CPR Part 22 requires any statement of case to be verified by a statement of truth. This applies to any online claims and defences and application notices.

8.2 CPR Part 22 also requires that if an applicant wishes to rely on matters set out in his application notice as evidence, the application notice must be verified by a statement of truth. This applies to any application notice completed online that contains matters on which the applicant wishes to rely as evidence.

8.3 Attention is drawn to –

(1) paragraph 2 of the practice direction supplementing CPR Part 22, which stipulates the form of the statement of truth; and

(2) paragraph 3 of the practice direction supplementing CPR Part 22, which provides who may sign a statement of truth; and

(3) CPR 32.14, which sets out the consequences of making, or causing to be made, a false statement in a document verified by a statement of truth, without an honest belief in its truth.

Signature

9.1 Any provision of the CPR which requires a document to be signed by any person is satisfied by that person entering his name on an online form.

Communication with the court electronically by the messaging service

10.1 If the PCOL website specifies that a court accepts electronic communications relating to claims brought using Possession Claims Online the parties may communicate with the court using the messaging service facility, available on the PCOL website ('the messaging service').

10.2 The messaging service is for brief and straightforward communications only. The PCOL website contains a list of examples of when it will not be appropriate to use the messaging service.

10.3 Parties must not send to the court forms or attachments via the messaging service.

10.4 The court shall treat any forms or attachments sent via the messaging service as not having been filed or received.

10.5 The court will normally reply via the messaging service where –

(1) the response is to a message transmitted via the messaging service; and

(2) the sender has provided an e-mail address.

Electronic applications

11.1 Certain applications in relation to a possession claim started online may be made electronically ('online applications'). An online application may be made if a form for that application is published on the PCOL website ('online application form') and the application is made at least five clear days before the hearing.

11.2 If a claim for possession has been started online and a party wishes to make an online application, he may do so by –

(1) completing the appropriate online application form at the PCOL website; and

(2) paying the appropriate fee electronically at the PCOL website or by some other means approved by Her Majesty's Courts Service.

11.3 When an online application form is received, an acknowledgment of receipt will automatically be sent to the applicant. The acknowledgment does not constitute a notice that the online application form has been issued or served.

11.4 Where an application must be made within a specified time, it is so made if the online application form is received by the court's computer system within that time. The court will keep a record, by electronic or other means, of when online application forms are received.

11.5 When the court receives an online application form it shall –

(1) serve a copy of the online application endorsed with the date of the hearing by post on the claimant at least two clear days before the hearing; and

(2) send the defendant notice of service and confirmation of the date of the hearing by post; provided that

(3) where either party has provided the court with an e-mail address for service, service of the application and/or the notice of service and confirmation of the hearing date may be effected by electronic means.

Request for issue of warrant

12.1 Where –

(1) the court has made an order for possession in a claim started online; and

(2) the claimant is entitled to the issue of a warrant of possession without requiring the permission of the court

the claimant may request the issue of a warrant by completing an online request form at the PCOL website and paying the appropriate fee electronically at the PCOL website or by some other means approved by Her Majesty's Courts Service.

12.2 A request under paragraph 12.1 will be treated as being filed –

(1) on the day the court receives the request, if it receives it before 4 p.m. on a working day; and

(2) otherwise, on the next working day after the court receives the request.

(CCR Order 26 rule 5 sets out certain circumstances in which a warrant of execution may not be issued without the permission of the court. CCR Order 26 rule 17(6) applies rule 5 of that Order with necessary modifications to a warrant of possession.)

Application to suspend warrant of possession

13.1 Where the court has issued a warrant of possession, the defendant may apply electronically for the suspension of the warrant, provided that:

(1) the application is made at least five clear days before the appointment for possession; and

(2) the defendant is not prevented from making such an application without the permission of the court.

13.2 The defendant may apply electronically for the suspension of the warrant, by –

(1) completing an online application for suspension at the PCOL website; and

(2) paying the appropriate fee electronically at the PCOL website or by some other means approved by Her Majesty's Courts Service.

13.3 When an online application for suspension is received, an acknowledgment of receipt will automatically be sent to the defendant. The acknowledgment does not constitute a notice that the online application for suspension has been served.

13.4 Where an application must be made within a specified time, it is so made if the online application for suspension is received by the court's computer system within that time. The court will keep a record, by electronic or other means, of when online applications for suspension are received.

13.5 When the court receives an online application for suspension it shall –

(1) serve a copy of the online application for suspension endorsed with the date of the hearing by post on the claimant at least two clear days before the hearing; and

(2) send the defendant notice of service and confirmation of the date of the hearing by post; provided that

(3) where either party has provided the court with an e-mail address for service, service of the application and/or the notice of service and confirmation of the hearing date may be effected by electronic means.

Viewing the case record

14.1 A facility will be provided on the PCOL website for parties or their representatives to view –

(1) an electronic record of the status of claims started online, which will be reviewed and, if necessary, updated at least once each day; and

(2) all information relating to the case that has been filed by the parties electronically.

14.2 In addition, where the PCOL website specifies that the court has the facility to provide viewing of such information by electronic means, the parties or their representatives may view the following information electronically –

(1) court orders made in relation to the case; and

(2) details of progress on enforcement and subsequent orders made.

Index